WITH THEIR BARE HANDS

OSPREY
PUBLISHING

WITH THEIR BARE HANDS

GENERAL PERSHING, THE 79TH DIVISION, AND THE BATTLE FOR MONTFAUCON

GENE FAX

Dedicated to the memory of
Sergeant Oscar Lubchansky (later, Lobe)
1896–1958
Company G, 313th Infantry Regiment, 79th Division,
American Expeditionary Forces

It seems to me proven that the Infantry of the 79th Division attacked the strong German machine gun positions with very little artillery support, and to this fact is due its disorganization and failure to take its objectives. . . . To recapitulate, the infantry of the 79th Division attempted to capture the German positions with their bare hands.

Colonel C.F. Crain, 79th Division Field Notes, May 16, 1919

First published in Great Britain in 2017 by Osprey Publishing,
PO Box 883, Oxford, OX1 9PL, UK
1385 Broadway, 5th Floor, New York, NY 10018, USA

E-mail: info@ospreypublishing.com

Osprey Publishing, part of Bloomsbury Publishing Plc

OSPREY is a trademark of Osprey Publishing, a division of Bloomsbury Publishing Plc

ISBN: 9781472819239
PDF e-book ISBN: 9781472819246
ePub e-book ISBN: 9781472819253

Index by Zoe Ross
Typeset in Garamond Premier Pro and Adobe Garamond Pro
Maps drawn by Dan Mooney, Harwich Port, MA, based on originals from the American Battlefield
Monuments Commission.
Quoted materials from Donald Smythe, *Pershing: General of the Armies* (Indiana University Press,
1986) reprinted with permission of Indiana University Press.
Originated by PDQ Media, Bungay, UK
Printed in China through World Print Ltd.
17 18 19 20 21   10 9 8 7 6 5 4 3 2 1

Osprey Publishing supports the Woodland Trust, the UK's leading woodland conservation charity.
Between 2014 and 2018 our donations are being spent on their Centenary Woods project in the UK.

To find out more about our authors and books visit **www.ospreypublishing.com**. Here you will find
extracts, author interviews, details of forthcoming events and the option to sign up for our newsletter.

Front Cover: Company G, 313th Infantry, in the Troyon sector. (AHEC)
Author photograph: Photographer: MKarmel, photobymmk.com
Translation of Hebrew verse on final page: This book is complete and done, Praise to God the
Eternal Lord. And with gratitude to my parents, my teachers and my wife; I am Elyakim Getzel
ben David Tzvi.

The following will help in converting measurements:

1 mile=1.61km	1 inch=2.54cm
1 yard=0.91m	1 US ton=0.91 metric tonnes
1 foot=30.48cm	1lb=0.45kg

Contents

ACKNOWLEDGEMENTS

Friends, family, historians, librarians, and archivists have been unfailingly helpful and encouraging throughout the twenty-year process of writing this book. Christina Holstein, Shreedhar Kanetkar, Neil Grauer, John Claussen, Teo Dagi, David Diamond, Philip Fishman, and my brother Chuck read all or portions of the book and offered valuable comments and criticism. Chuck, Ingrid Ferrand, and Rob de Soete walked the battlefield with me. Robert Ferrell, professor of history emeritus at Indiana University; Douglas V. Johnson II, formerly of the US Army War College; and Jonathan Sarna, professor of history at Brandeis University gave of their knowledge and enthusiasm. I owe a special debt to Brigadier General (ret.) Robert A. Doughty, formerly of the US Military Academy, who introduced me to then-Lieutenant Colonel Frédéric Guelton of the Service Historique de l'Armée de Terre (now the Service Historique de la Défense). Colonel Guelton in turn gave me access to the files of that formidable institution. Other archivists who helped me unstintingly were Richard J. Sommers and David Keogh of the Military History Institute (now the US Army Heritage and Education Center); Susan Lintelmann of the US Military Academy; Tim Nenninger and Mitchell Yockelson of the National Archives and Records Administration at College Park; and the indefatigable staff of the NARA reading room. Mitch, Robert Doughty, and Dennis Showalter, professor of history at Colorado College read the manuscript, for which much thanks. Emmanuel Dumas obtained from the Bibliothèque de Documentation Internationale Contemporaine relevant portions of the histories of over twenty German regiments; Julie Allen and Neil Berkowitz translated the blackletter text into English. The research staff of the Newton (Massachusetts) Free Library never failed to locate a document I requested, however obscure. Others who supplied me with materials were the late

Hannah Zeidlik, who told me the whereabouts of General Kuhn's papers, and Betty K. Boothe, who sent me materials on Tenney Ross, her great-great-uncle. Therry Schwartz, the late Len Shurtleff of the Western Front Association, and the late Sydney Wise of Carleton University inspired me early in the process. The book has benefited immensely from the scrutiny of my agent, Leila Campoli of Stonesong, and of Kate Moore and Laura Callaghan of Osprey Publishing. Errors of fact or judgment are my own. My great appreciation goes as well to the 3M Company, inventors of Post-It® Notes; how were books written before they existed?

Finally, I cannot thank enough my wife Ruth, who inspired me to undertake this project in the first place, who read several versions of the manuscript, and whose love and patience—and occasional impatience—were crucial to its completion.

MAPS

Map Key

Unit symbol

Regiment no.   Division no.

Commander

Unit symbols:

xx - Division
x - Brigade
III - Regiment

Boundary symbols:

———xxx——— Corps
———xx——— Division
——— x ——— Brigade

Notes:

Front line shown as of midnight
  on the indicated day
Positions of German units approximate
Regiments shown for U.S. 79th Division only
Artillery brigades and machine gun
  battalions not shown
Commanders shown for U.S. units only

NOTES FROM THE AUTHOR

Times

From September 16, 1918, through October 5, French and German clocks showed the same time. From October 6 through November 11, German clocks were ahead by one hour; i.e., when French clocks showed noon, German clocks showed 1:00 p.m.[1] Times herein have been adjusted where necessary to conform to French clocks.

In World War I the United States Army had not yet standardized its notation for clock time. A given time might be recorded in war diaries, field messages, and operations reports as 6:15 p.m., 18 H 15, 18:15, or variations on all of them. To accommodate the lay reader, this work expresses times (except in direct quotations) using the conventional 12-hour clock.

Distances

The AEF used both English and metric units in designating distances. I use English units (yards, miles) for distances over the ground, such as the width of a front or the depth of an advance. I use metric units (meters, kilometers) for distances that are specified in orders, such as artillery firing ranges or intervals between units, or that are contained in direct quotes.

Spelling and Grammar in Quoted Materials

While most American soldiers were literate, many used idiosyncratic spelling and grammar in their letters and diaries. I have left such "errors" uncorrected in order to preserve the unique character of each person's writings.

Army Organization

The largest permanent organization in most armies in World War I was the division. The division's subordinate units, from largest to smallest, were the brigade, the regiment, the battalion, the company, the platoon, and finally the squad or section. (For more detail on the organization of an AEF division, see Appendix A.) This hierarchy was followed by more or less all of the belligerents in World War I. The number of men in each unit and the number of subordinate units assigned to each superior formation varied by country and, within each country, over time. By 1917 the French and German infantry divisions, being roughly half as large as the American ones, did not have brigades; the British had brigades but not regiments. Divisions were typically grouped into corps and corps into armies depending on the anticipated operational requirements. Similarly, divisions were often augmented temporarily by adding regiments, battalions, or companies of specialized arms such as artillery, machine guns, and tanks.

PROLOGUE

Private James M. Cain was lost. Hours before – his fogged brain could not recall how many – Major General Kuhn, commander of the 79th Division, had ordered him to find Brigadier General Nicholson. Nicholson was in charge of the 157th Brigade, comprising one-half of the division's infantry strength. Cain was to deliver a message ordering a renewal of yesterday's attack on a hill called Montfaucon. But the division staff had no idea where Nicholson was, so Cain had been sent to find him. And now he himself was lost.

Not often did a major general give a direct order to a private, and the reason it had happened now did not reassure Cain. Kuhn had given him the mission because he, of all the 27,000 men in the division, was probably the only one who had a chance of finding Nicholson in time for the order to have its effect.

In fact, he had found Nicholson once already. Around six o'clock the previous evening, 12 hours or so into the attack, Captain Madeira, commander of the Headquarters Troop, had told him to locate Nicholson's command post, then about a thousand yards west of division headquarters, and report back its exact position. The trenches ran east–west, so Cain and another private had followed the main trench westward. In ten minutes they had found the command post (called, in the French style, a PC) and had identified themselves to General Nicholson. It remained only to get back to Captain Madeira and report.

But Nicholson and his staff were about to go forward and set up a new PC closer to the fighting. "What the hell good is it," Cain asked his companion, "for us to go back and tell them we found this PC, when in a couple of minutes there ain't going to be nobody in it?" The other man protested that they had done what they were told and it was time to get out of there. After a minute's argument they agreed to join Nicholson until he established his new command post and to report back to the division afterward.

By then night had fallen. Cain and his companion set off in the dark after Nicholson and his aides. Their route took them over No-Man's Land, in and out of trenches, around, and often into, shell holes. Barbed wire slashed at their legs and invisible debris pitched them into the mud. Dead horses littered the field, giving no sign of their presence until the men were wading among their innards. Cain stumbled into a soldier leaning against the side of a trench in firing position. He started to murmur an apology and then saw that the man was dead.

Eventually they reached the new brigade PC, marked only by a piece of corrugated iron by the side of a road. It was time to return to the division and report. Not relishing the thought of blundering back across No-Man's Land in the dark, Cain had an idea. From the maps at headquarters he knew how the roads ran. He could follow this one toward the American rear. Once he saw where it came out, he would know how to reach General Kuhn. An engineer repairing the road thought it led to Avocourt, which sounded all right to Cain; from there he could take another road east to Esnes, where Kuhn's PC was.

The two men started back and soon were at Avocourt. The moon rose, showing them the way east. A few miles along they reached Esnes; a left turn and a short walk took them to General Kuhn's dugout. In a moment they could report and turn in. But before Cain had a chance to ask for Captain Madeira, men started yelling into the dugout that they had arrived. The captain came running. "Thank God you've come," he said.

This was not how captains traditionally greeted privates. "What's the matter?" Cain asked. Surely the brass hats were not worried sick over a couple of enlisted men.

"General Nicholson has broken liaison," said Captain Madeira, "and we've got not a way on earth to reach him unless you fellows can do it." There was more. General Kuhn himself wanted to see Cain. The private followed the captain into the dugout.

Kuhn was normally a trim figure, square of jaw and steady of gaze. Tonight he looked a wreck. Hollow eyes stared from an unshaven face. His division was supposed to have taken Montfaucon the previous day. It hadn't. The divisions to its left and right had advanced, but the 79th was stuck below the hill. The resulting cavity in the American front line glared from the situation map like an abscess. V Corps was angry. First Army was angry. General Pershing was angry. Madeira announced Cain's arrival.

"Do you know where General Nicholson is?" Kuhn asked.

"Yes sir," said Cain, "but I don't think *he* does."

Kuhn muttered something Cain took to be agreement; then, "I want you to take a message to him." He wrote out the message and read it to Cain, in case the note got lost. It said, "Imperative orders from Commander-in-Chief require that the 79th Division advance at once to come in line with neighboring Division. Owing to your having broken liaison, it was necessary to place Gen'l Noble in charge of the 315th and 314th Regiments to make an immediate advance. You are directed to take command of the 313th and 316th Regiments and to push on with all possible speed. Location of these Regiments not definitely known."[1] After telling the captain to give Cain a good horse, Kuhn said, "I'm moving my PC to Malancourt in the next hour. Do you know where that is?" Cain did; it was three miles north of Esnes. "Then report to me in Malancourt," said the general. Cain and the captain saluted and left.

Cain, on horseback, retraced his steps to Avocourt; a right turn would put him on the road to Nicholson's PC. But in the early light he noticed something he had missed on his previous trip. Not one but two roads went off to the right, one heading north and one northeast. Which was the route he had earlier come down? He closed his eyes to recall how the crossroads had looked in the moonlight, remembering the pattern of the shell holes he had passed. It was no use; the engineers had since filled the holes and spread gravel over the surface.

There was nothing to do but guess. Cain picked the right-hand road and followed it for a while until he reached a track heading to the left. This didn't look right; he couldn't remember passing an intersection on his earlier journey. He must have taken the wrong road out of Avocourt. But this new, westward path would set him straight. In a few minutes he reached the road north and turned toward the front. Shaking off sleep, he spurred the horse into a run. "Thank God I'll be in time," he thought.

Soon he saw some infantrymen by the road. "Which way to the 157th Brigade PC?" he shouted. Never heard of it, they said. Farther on he came upon a column of doughboys going into the line. He repeated his question; no one bothered to answer. With the next group he tried a different tack.

"What outfit, buddy?" he called.

This time he got a volley of answers. "AEF," one fellow yelled. "YMCA," said another. "Company B," offered a third.

Were these guys crazy? Then he realized what was going on. Since they had arrived in France the men had been warned: if someone at the front asks you your unit, don't tell him; he might be a spy. For the same reason, road signs were forbidden and PCs were unmarked. Cain doubted the soldiers had thought him a spy. It was probably worse; they thought he was an MP testing their obedience to the rule. He would get nowhere asking for help. Kuhn's order was starting to weigh heavily in his pocket.

Spotting a captain and a lieutenant by the side of the road, Cain reined in and, in a tone used more often at him than by him, barked, "Which way is General Nicholson's PC?" The officers saluted. That he wore no insignia didn't bother them; lots of officers took theirs off at the front.

"General Nicholson?" the captain asked. "Not around here, I'm pretty sure, sir."

"Hundred and Fifty-Seventh Brigade?" Cain asked curtly.

"Oh no, that wouldn't be in this division. This is all 37th."

This was terrible news. The 37th Division was to the left of the 79th. Cain should have stuck to the original road northeast out of Avocourt. Instead he had wandered completely out of his division's sector. Without Kuhn's order Nicholson would not attack and the assault of the division, possibly of the whole First Army, would fail.

After that Cain's memory became hazy. He knew he had left the road and struck cross-country heading east, hoping to find Nicholson somehow. But clouds obscured the morning sun and trenches and shell holes made riding a straight course impossible. He must have wandered up to the front line because a doughboy had shouted to watch out for snipers. At the edge of an immense crater his horse finally quit. Frantic, Cain dropped to the ground and began to beat the animal. Then, overwhelmed by the futility of his situation, he wept.

He would lead the 79th straight to Berlin, General Kuhn had told the newspapers back in the States; he had already picked out the hotel where he would set up his headquarters.[2] But it wasn't working out that way. It wasn't working out that way at all.[*]

---

[*] This anecdote is based mostly on James M. Cain, III, "The Taking of Montfaucon," in *Americans vs. Germans: The First AEF in Action*, ed. Editors of The Infantry Journal (Washington: Penguin Books and The Infantry Journal, Inc., 1942), pp. 67–82. For this piece Cain—after the war, a celebrated novelist—adopted the colloquial, Lardnerian style he used in some of his short stories. The details are nonetheless accurate; see Roy Hoopes, *Cain: The Biography of James M. Cain* (New York: Holt, Rinehart and Winston, 1982), pp. 66–67.

INTRODUCTION

I have often been asked the purpose of this book. It is a legitimate question, as there are already many excellent studies of the American participation in World War I. Its purpose, first and foremost, is to tell a good story that has never been told—how an American division transformed itself from essentially an untrained mob into a competent fighting force in only seven weeks. The centerpiece of the narrative is the fight of the American 79th Division at Montfaucon, a battle that is now largely forgotten. Yet it was not always that way. When the family of Major John Baird Atwood, who died at the Bois de Beuge, erected a memorial arch at Princeton University they had it inscribed in large letters, "Killed in Action Near Montfaucon, Argonne." For years graduates of the Military Academy had themselves and their families photographed in front of the Montfaucon periscope, captured from the Germans and exhibited on a wall at West Point as the prime trophy of the war. And when General Pershing designed the memorial to the Meuse–Argonne offensive, the massive American attack that helped end the conflict, he chose the summit of Montfaucon on which to place a 180-foot shaft.

Apart from the battle itself, the book tries to explain how the division got there, why it fought as it did, how it gained (or failed to gain) its objectives, and how it changed over time. It attempts to show how decisions made at the political and command levels affected the fate of the men in their trenches and shell holes. To do all that, the narrative must first explain the nature of the battleground, the origins of the division in the 1917 draft, its training, and its organization. These make sense only in the context of the creation, doctrine, development, and operations of the American Expeditionary Forces of which the division was a part. The history of the 79th therefore serves as a window on the nature and performance of the AEF as a whole.

The book treats World War I and the American participation in it neither as tragedy nor as triumph. Rather, it considers the war (and war in general) as a human endeavor susceptible to critical analysis. More than most human endeavors, of course, war abounds in tragedies, triumphs (for some), ironies, and absurdities, and these the book tries to capture where they impinge on the narrative. To do this, it tells the story not only of the division and its subordinate units but of individual men as they are drafted, trained, sent into battle, and—some of them—wounded or killed.

Until the 1980s, historians of the American participation in World War I dwelt on topics such as the Marines at Belleau Wood, the siege of the "Lost Battalion" (the quotation marks are in deference to the frequent observation that it was neither lost nor a battalion), and the exploits of Sergeant Alvin York—stirring episodes in a war notably lacking in stirring episodes. Almost nothing was written that analyzed the organization of the army or the doctrines and tactics that determined the outcome of the battles and, hence, the outcome of the war. In large part that was because the AEF's strategies were uninspired, its tactics mistaken or poorly applied, and its battles inconclusive—as was, indeed, the war itself.

About 30 years ago historians such as James Rainey, Donald Smythe, and Timothy Nenninger began to question the conventional narratives, particularly by applying critical intelligence to General Pershing's doctrine of open warfare and how he used it on the Western Front. Even so, little has been written on how the operations of the American Expeditionary Forces were affected in their details by the doctrines of Pershing and his staff. Not until 1983 was a critical history published on the great Meuse–Argonne offensive, the largest American battle until the Normandy invasion, and only five more have appeared as of this writing.

Like the Meuse–Argonne offensive of which it was a part, the battle for Montfaucon was beset by errors at all levels: the training of the troops, the arms and equipment they were issued, the plan of attack, the staff work, and the command decisions made during the action. Moreover, neither Montfaucon nor the Meuse–Argonne offensive as a whole fulfilled the commanders' inflated expectations. Progress was unnecessarily slow, casualties needlessly high. It may seem perverse to concentrate on failure. But more is learned from failure than from success, and by the end of the war the AEF—and the 79th with it—had become an effective fighting force, capable of doing its job on the battlefield. Further, the lessons learned from the American performance in the Meuse–Argonne served the United States well in its next war.

And on its own terms the AEF did not fail, either at Montfaucon or in the larger Meuse–Argonne campaign. It took its objectives. It forced the German Army to retreat over 30 miles in seven weeks. It took 26,000 prisoners, inflicted about 100,000 casualties, and captured 874 guns and over 3,000 machine guns. Nor did the AEF fail relative to the performance of its allies. It is generally forgotten that the Americans fought *as an army* for only the last nine weeks of the war. Until the formation of First Army on August 10, 1918, US divisions were parceled out to the British and French. Not until September 12, at St Mihiel, did the vast bulk of the American forces advance together under their own commander-in-chief. Additionally, the experience of the AEF was qualitatively different from that of its allies on the Western Front. Neither the British nor the French achieved a meaningful advance during the first three and a half years of the war; the many bloody attempts to produce one generally led to a few thousand yards gained, a German counterattack, and the Allies ending up in the trenches from which they had started. The Americans, once they left their trenches, never returned. The French and British criticized the Americans bitterly for their mistakes. In fact, as I try to show, the AEF's learning experience recapitulated almost point for point that of the French and British, in a much shorter time. In those last nine weeks the AEF learned as much about modern warfare as their allies and enemies had learned in four years. This also is the story the book intends to tell.

To accomplish this, I have relied on primary sources wherever possible. These include plans, orders, field messages, unit histories (which were generally written by the officers), contemporary reports and analyses, memoirs, diaries, and letters. Their virtue is that they describe events as the participants saw them (or thought they saw them), unfiltered by others' judgments as to which facts are important and which are not.* But

---

* I do not include here the memoirs published by high-ranking officers after the war. Researched and edited as they were, they hardly qualify as primary sources. They often give pertinent facts, but just as often suffer from myopia and self-justification. Pershing himself, for example, was perfectly willing to manipulate the record to his own and the AEF's advantage, as has been documented by several historians. In his memoir, John J. Pershing, *My Experiences in the World War*, 2 vols (New York: Frederick A. Stokes Co., 1931), he retroactively changed the purpose of the Meuse–Argonne offensive from a breakthrough to a diversion (David F. Trask, *The AEF and Coalition Warmaking, 1917–1918*

they have their own problems, and must be used carefully. It is well known, for example, that individual soldiers' accounts of their experiences are unreliable, not because the witnesses themselves misunderstood what they saw (although that certainly happened) but because each soldier could see only the small piece of the field in front of him and the events that impinged on him personally. Thus, soldiers in the same action separated by only a few hundred yards could describe two vastly different battles, one placid and uneventful and the other terrifying and deadly. Even generals, who presumably had the big picture, were often unaware of important events on the battlefield or in the War Department that caused the outcomes they describe. Most of the diaries, letters, and memoirs left by the officers and men of the AEF, therefore, are not particularly valuable for facts. But they give a vivid picture of the texture of life at the front: the wretched living conditions, the small amusements, the amazing sights, the rumors, the loneliness, the boredom, the anxiety for those at home, the fear of injury or death, and the vast range of emotions that attend military service.[*] I have used them for that purpose.

Plans and orders are the bedrock of military documentation because they show how the generals intended to impose their will on the adversary. Moltke's observation that no battle plan survives first contact with the enemy has become a cliché, but it expresses a truth useful for our purpose:

(Lawrence, KS: University Press of Kansas, 1993), p. 211.); moved a German rail line the better to justify his plan to capture Metz (Allan R. Millett, "Over Where? The AEF and the American Strategy for Victory, 1917–1918," in *Against All Enemies: Interpretations of American Military History from Colonial Times to the Present*, ed. Kenneth Hagan and William R. Roberts, Contributions in Military Studies (New York, Westport, CT, and London: Greenwood, 1986), p. 252); and wholly invented a picture of the AEF's efficiency and skill (Mark E. Grotelueschen, *Doctrine under Trial: American Artillery Employment in World War I*, Contributions in Military Studies (Westport, CT, and London: Greenwood, 2001), p. 140; Trask, *AEF and Coalition Warmaking*, pp. 207–08). He also took credit for inspiring the French to adopt open warfare principles, whereas Marshal Foch had ordered such tactics three months before Pershing brought the subject up with him. (Hubert C. Johnson, *Breakthrough! Tactics, Technology, and the Search for Victory on the Western Front in World War I* (Novato, CA: Presidio Press, 1994), p. 256; Douglas Valentine Johnson, II, "A Few 'Squads Left' and Off to France: Training the American Army in the United States for World War I" (Ph.D. thesis, Temple University, 1992), p. 188.)

[*] Enlisted men's letters from France rarely gave details of actual battles. This was not because of censorship; the letters I reviewed hardly ever showed signs of the censor's razor blade. More likely, it is because the private soldier's motive in writing was to reassure the folks at home that he was all right even when, as sometimes happened, he was in a hospital bed, dying.

plans and orders tell what was supposed to have happened, not what actually happened. Their chief merit, besides being statements of intent, is as benchmarks against which to judge success or failure. In the case of the AEF, such documents have a particular shortcoming. The plans and the orders are in the archives, sometimes in several drafts. But there are almost no records of how they came to be written. The debates among the commanders and their staffs, the actions considered and rejected, who advocated which alternatives and who opposed them, and how the final results came about are all missing. Perhaps proper minutes were never taken, or perhaps they were discarded as unimportant; whatever the case, how certain critical decisions were made remains a mystery.

Field messages and operations reports written in the course of battle would seem to be reliable; after all, lives depended on clear communication. Unfortunately, clarity was not always a military virtue, at least by the evidence in the archives. Field messages, often scribbled by officers in shell holes under fire, frequently lacked the times, dates, coordinates, or unit designations that one needed to make sense of them. (And indeed, lives were lost as a direct result.) Nowadays, reading a message as sent from the field, one often cannot tell when, or whether, it was received. Conversely, reading the version that was typed up back in headquarters, one often cannot tell when it was sent. Even when the original message was reasonably complete, typists (or their officers) frequently omitted, sometimes distorted, and occasionally inserted information. Add to this the poor handling of AEF records after the war and inadvertent mis-filings by generations of archivists and researchers, and it becomes almost impossible to get a coherent picture of a battle from this source alone.[1] But little transmits the immediacy of combat more than a penciled note in a shaky hand that says, "We have been under artillery fire all night … The men are getting so weak on account of getting no food there is not much driving power left. We are going to do the best we can but I am afraid the losses will be very heavy."[2]

Units at all levels wrote reports of their operations during the campaign, sometimes daily. Dry and factual, these record the organizations' movements and actions, locations of command posts, distances advanced (or sometimes withdrawn), casualties suffered, prisoners taken, machine guns and artillery pieces captured, and similar details. They describe any problems the unit encountered that were not its own fault. They omit, however, anything that would reflect adversely on the unit itself and especially on its officers and men. Also, they are wholly without context, mostly ignoring events to their left and right. Except to clarify details of placement and movement, such reports are rarely useful.

Unit histories have different merits and drawbacks. Almost all were written by officers or former officers of the regiment, company, or other organization, themselves participants in the actions they describe. Such "histories" are therefore reliable as to the unit's movements, combat actions, and other activities. But they were written for a special audience: the veterans of the unit itself or their survivors. Their purpose was to memorialize the events of the war for those who participated in it, and especially to honor the dead. Equally, it was to recall the times of victory, defeat, or just plain survival in terms that gave them meaning and importance. Thus, all officers were wise and brave and all soldiers were dedicated to their duty. All were inspired by loyalty to country and comrades. Victory resulted from courage and sacrifice; defeat from the overwhelming odds the men faced, despite their courage and sacrifice. (No regimental historian ever wrote, "We lost because the enemy was smarter and braver than we were.")

The histories of German regiments pose a special problem in this regard. As the losers, the Germans had a harder time assuring themselves that their wartime experiences had meaning. This difficulty was compounded by the widespread conviction that the German Army had not lost at all, it had been "stabbed in the back" by Jews and Socialists. Many of the earlier histories are therefore dedicated to German youth, to show them the heroism and stoicism of their elders and to prepare them for future sacrifices. As the publication dates advance into the 1930s this message becomes more explicit, and the mind's ear starts to hear the ruffle of drums, the cheers of the crowd, and a strident, high-pitched voice. I have used these histories for their factual material and for anecdotes, but have avoided relying on them for insights into morale or motivation.

Some of the sources I have used have not, to my knowledge, ever been referred to before. These include the histories of the German regiments that opposed the 79th and its adjacent divisions, written by their officers; the combat reports of the French advisers and tank commanders attached to the 79th; and the letters of the commander of the 79th, Major General Joseph E. Kuhn, to his wife. In all cases they have shed unexpected (by me, at least) sidelights on the standard versions of the narrative. Of course, a pitfall in using multiple primary sources to describe the same events is the inevitability of inconsistencies and contradictions. In particular, the portrayals of combat often depict situations and actions that cannot be reconciled among the accounts of the American, French, and German witnesses. In such cases I have used in the text the version of events that I believe to be supported by the weight of evidence, while acknowledging other narratives in the footnotes.

The story of the 79th contains no heroes in the mold of Sergeant York or Major Charles Whittlesey, the commander of the Lost Battalion. The heroes are the men who, plucked from civilian life, endured and—if they were not killed or wounded—ultimately prevailed in circumstances unimaginable to them before the war or to us now. The soldier of the 79th to whose memory this book is dedicated, Sergeant Oscar Lubchansky, my maternal grandfather, serves as their representative.

CHAPTER 1

SETTING THE STAGE

*In constructing a narrative, in charting the movement of
armies, the facts of geography stand first.*

—John Keegan[1]

Two hundred and fifty million years ago the ground on which the American
Expeditionary Forces would fight lay under a shallow sea. For 185 million
years erosion from nearby highlands deposited layers of shale and sandstone;
these alternated with limestone formed by calcareous organisms precipitating
out of the water. Eventually the land emerged from the sea; the part of the
region that would one day underlie Paris subsided, while the eastern parts,
the future provinces of Champagne and Lorraine, rose. In these uplifted
areas to the east, erosion produced a series of plateaus wherever hard
limestone or shale was exposed, alternating with valleys where the surface
was soft sandstone.

The plateaus and the valleys run roughly north–south. As one travels east
from Paris one comes in turn upon the Dry Champagne plateau, then the
valley of the Aire River, the Argonne plateau with its forest, a broad lowland
leading to the Meuse River, the Heights of the Meuse, the Woëvre plain,
and the Moselle plateau. The western slopes of the plateaus tend to rise
gently and smoothly; their eastern faces are often rocky cliffs. The topmost
slopes of the plateaus are generally wooded and the lowlands are cleared, so
that alternating bands of forest and farmland also run north–south.

Midway across the valley between the Argonne Forest and the Meuse

THE ALLIED LINE IN LORRAINE, FRANCE, MARCH 20, 1918

River is a narrow, deeply gullied north–south ridge that geologists call the Barrois plateau, which divides the valley into two parallel north–south corridors. As you look to the north the left corridor, bounded by the Argonne Forest on the west and the Barrois on the east, is obstructed at its southern end by the hill of Vauquois. The southern end of the right most corridor is bounded by the swampy stream of Forges Brook that lies just beyond the transverse ridges of Hill 304 and the Mort Homme, the Dead Man.[*] The names of these hills still send shudders up French spines, for reasons that we shall shortly see.

The sides of the Barrois itself are cut by streams that flow respectively east and west, yielding a series of transverse ridges with smooth slopes and uplands. The resulting landscape, viewed from the south, resembles the supine skeleton of a gigantic fish seen from the tail: the crest of the Barrois is the spine, rising smoothly toward the north; the east–west ridges on either

---

[*] Unnamed hills and woods were designated by their height in meters above sea level.

side are the ribs. Perched on top of the Barrois, visible for 30 miles or more in every direction, is the conical hill of Montfaucon—Falcon Mountain.[*]

Two other features of the landscape deserve mention, because they affected every modern army that operated there back to 1870. First, the Mesozoic limestones and shales that eroded out of the uplands and into the valleys form a deep, dense, gray-orange mud that clings to itself and everything else, quickly turning boots into leaden weights and carriage wheels into millstones. In the fall rainy season, all traffic was forced to use the roads. But the roads in Lorraine in the early 1900s were no bargain. The few well-constructed highways in the region had been designed to carry armies to the borders and taxes to the royal treasury; they had no relationship to centers of production or to markets, which were situated in the towns and villages. Instead, "Trails, paths, tracks, lanes, and causeways covered the countryside: rough roads where, as the peasants put it, the Good Lord did not often pass."[2] These led to and from the farms and villages of the peasants, or followed the traditional routes of pilgrims and processionals. Certain tradesmen, such as glassmakers, salt sellers, and potters, had their own trails; other dedicated paths served mines, forges, and quarries. By 1914, some of the roads had been paved, but most were still farm tracks unsuitable for vehicles; at the turn of the twentieth century, there were still people alive who could remember when the first cart, carriage, or wagon came to their village. In the 20-mile expanse between the Argonne Forest and the Meuse River, only three paved roads ran north–south, and they were built to handle farm wagons, not tanks and artillery.

The east-facing cliffs and the wooded plateaus form a natural fortress facing east. The invader from that direction must traverse a series of barriers, each consisting of "muddy and marshy lowlands, precipitous scarps, rugged zones of dissected plateau, belts of forest, and deep river trenches."[3] In the rainy season the muddy soil of the lowlands forced all movement to the roads, which were easily viewed by artillery observers on the heights of the next plateau to the west. The roads themselves were rendered almost impassable by the slow drainage. Even in dry weather the roads channeled all traffic into a small number of natural declivities carved in the escarpments.

---

[*] The commanding aspect of the hill, still impressive today, was even more so before the war. A large church, dating in part from the fifteenth century, crowned its peak; the steeple towered another 170 feet above ground level.

These gateways, easy to defend from above, had to be conquered by the attacker before heavy guns and supplies could be brought forward. The most prominent examples are the Nancy gateway through the Moselle uplands, the Toul valley through the Meuse plateau, and the Grandpré gap through the Argonne.

Although formidable, the highlands of the Meuse and its environs are not a continuous barrier. The Romans took advantage of a gap at Clermont to build a road from Paris eastward through Reims to Metz. At the place where this highway crossed the north-flowing Meuse they built a town they named Viriodunum; as time passed, the fortified cities that succeeded it came to be called Verdun.

As a major continental crossroads, Lorraine—including the region between the Meuse River and the Argonne Forest—was both a highway and a barrier to armies. In 886, a Viking horde that had been besieging Paris fled eastward from Odo, King of the West Franks; they hoped to reach the Meuse, the nearest river that would carry them to the North Sea and safety. They didn't make it. Taking refuge on Montfaucon hill, they were slaughtered by Odo's army. In 1544 the forces of Holy Roman Emperor Charles V, seeking to bypass the Argonne in the south, got from Metz past Commercy, over the Barrois and down the Marne but were defeated by the resistance of the town of St Dizier. During the Wars of Religion in the late 1500s, German troops marched through Lorraine on their way to aid the Huguenots, burning the town of Montfaucon as they passed. In the Thirty Years' War, French, Spanish, Austrian, and Swedish armies used the province as a thoroughfare; again Montfaucon was destroyed, only one house being left standing. In 1637 the Marshal de Châtillon, at the command of Louis XIII, demolished the Spanish Hapsburg garrisons along the Meuse. Twenty years later, the rebellious Duke of Lorraine held the heavily fortified town of Montmédy against Louis XIV; the Marquis de Vauban took it after what he called one of the most difficult sieges of his career.[4]

The European coalitions that opposed the French Revolution and Napoleon's Empire most frequently used the direct route to Paris from the east. In 1792 the Prussians were beaten at Valmy on the eastern face of the second escarpment of the Dry Champagne plateau. Afterward, the victorious General Dumouriez called the defiles of the Argonne "the Thermopylae of France." In 1813–14 the Allies pushed Generals Ney and Mortier back from the Champagne defenses and advanced along the Marne valley and parallel to the Petit Morin further south. This offensive was defeated by Napoleon, but the Allies recovered and attacked successfully along the Petit and Grand Morins.

In 1870 Marshal François Bazaine allowed the Prussians to bottle his army up in the fortress of Metz, offering General (later Count) Helmuth von Moltke an open highway through Lorraine. When the French sent out an army to relieve Metz Moltke outmaneuvered it, pursuing it north to its eventual doom at Sedan. But the army of Emperor Louis Napoleon was almost saved by the muddy roads of the Meuse–Argonne. Moltke's otherwise efficient columns, with 150,000 men accompanied by artillery and supply wagons, churned the few northward paths into an almost impassable soup. "Marches were prolonged, routes overlapped, supply-columns went astray, and many German units were tried almost beyond their strength."[5]

Northeastern France was quiet until the outbreak of World War I. Then, in 1914, the famed Schlieffen Plan dictated that the Germans take the northern route to Paris through Belgium and Flanders, outflanking the natural barriers of Lorraine and Champagne. Six armies abreast, the Germans swung west, then south, like a giant door with its hinge in the Vosges Mountains, 80 miles southeast of Verdun. As the enemy passed through the Ardennes Forest the thought struck Marshal Joffre, the French commander-in-chief, that the fortress of Verdun looked too much like Metz in 1870 and he ordered it abandoned. But the commander of the fortress ignored the order and withstood several German assaults. This put a kink in the German line but did not halt its progress south. Several times the retreating French stood and held their ground: at the scarp of the overlapping Meuse and Argonne plateaus, 13 miles southwest of Mézières; on an east–west line from Attigny to Grandpré; and at Montfaucon. But the German advance continued, now with Verdun as its hinge. At the end the German Fifth Army was facing almost due east, nearly cutting Verdun off completely. However, the defeat on the Marne on September 9, 1914, made a general retreat inevitable. Withdrawing northward, the Germans stabilized their front on an east–west line from south of Grandpré in the Argonne, running south of Montfaucon, to the defenses of Verdun on the east.

Although the Germans had been checked, they did not stop trying to encircle Verdun. On September 20 they attacked west of the Meuse, capturing the town of Varennes, a large part of the Argonne Forest, the hill of Vauquois, and several other eminences before being stopped. Their line now ran parallel to, and within artillery range of, the main access line to Verdun from the west, the road from Reims (nowadays the N3) and the railroad. On the right bank of the Meuse, the Germans captured the town of St Mihiel and its environs, blocking river access to Verdun from the south. Only a narrow-gauge railroad from Bar-le-Duc and a country road parallel to it still led to Verdun.

The Germans, having fortified Vauquois and Montfaucon, seemed to hold an impregnable position on the Barrois plateau. The French attacked Montfaucon unsuccessfully in 1914 and 1915. Their Third Army failed to capture Vauquois in the middle of February but ten days later, after a fierce artillery preparation, took the hill.* After that, a temporary stalemate took hold. The French controlled the spurs of the Argonne and the south side of Vauquois hill, Forges Brook and the Mort Homme, preventing the Germans from completing their encirclement of Verdun from the west. But the Germans dominated the main routes into the city, thus neutralizing it as a strategic position.

The stalemate ended in February 1916, when Erich von Falkenhayn, Chief of the German General Staff, opened at Verdun a battle of attrition designed to weaken fatally the French Army. Before the war, exercises had shown that an attack on both banks of the Meuse River would be necessary to avoid flanking artillery fire. But Falkenhayn's plan did not include the western bank, and the attack of the Fifth Army, commanded by Crown Prince William, faltered as a result. Despite their dramatic advance east of the Meuse, the Germans suffered heavy losses to French artillery, massed on the unassaulted left bank, which had a panoramic view of their targets.

To rid themselves of this torment, on March 6 the Germans launched a powerful attack on the Mort Homme, a ridge that dominated the hills on which the French had sited their artillery. The French, knowing their defense of Verdun depended critically on those guns, resisted just as fiercely. By the end of the month, 81,600 Germans and 89,000 French had died in the battle for the hill.[6] But the French set up more guns on a rise further to the

---

* But not all of it; the north slope remained in German hands. From September 1914, to the American campaign in September 1918, the two sides fought each other by tunneling into the hill from opposite sides, alternately blowing each other up. This four-year subterranean battle, isolated from the rest of the war, left the hill honeycombed with tunnels, shafts, and galleries that can be visited today. The crest of the hill, where the village of Vauquois once stood, is now a wilderness of craters, some of them hundreds of feet wide.

west called Hill 304. The German attack then ran into the same problem as had their original assault on Verdun: artillery fire pounding their lines from the right flank. As the German attacks on the Mort Homme ended with bloody losses, the Germans redirected their efforts to Hill 304.

To outflank Hill 304 from the west, the Germans attacked in the Bois de Malancourt, between the villages of Malancourt and Avocourt. The position was heavily fortified but the French unit defending it was the exhausted 29th Division, deserters from which told the Germans the routes through the wire. The position fell within four hours, with the surrender of a whole French brigade. The Germans tried to follow up this success with an assault on Hill 304 itself. The attack was stymied by well-sited French machine guns firing from three sides, abetted by a ferocious rainstorm that flooded the battlefield, preventing the Germans from bringing up their heavy mortars. The Germans lost 2,400 men that day. The French counterattacked on March 29, to no avail.

Despite the Germans' exhaustion, their advance toward Hill 304 continued to make progress. Malancourt fell on March 31, Haucourt on April 5, Béthincourt on April 8. On April 9, Falkenhayn ordered a general attack on both sides of the Meuse. German infantry, after staggering losses, secured the north slope of the Mort Homme but not the crest; French counterattacks later in April took it back. On May 3, the Germans opened up on Hill 304 with 500 guns. The bombardment lasted two days; entire battalions disappeared in the chaos, many of their men buried alive. One officer reported having been buried by shell fire three times; each time his men dug him out. As the shelling abated, German infantry advanced, but it took them three more days to secure the hill. By the end of the month they had taken the Mort Homme as well.

That was as far as they got. By the end of August, when the German push clearly had failed, Falkenhayn resigned; on September 2, Field Marshal Paul von Hindenburg, the new Chief of Staff, called off offensive operations at Verdun. The French counterattacked on the right bank and within four months regained much of what they had lost; but not until August of 1917 did they attempt to reconquer the ground they had given up on the left bank of the Meuse.

At that time, Marshal Philippe Pétain ordered the Second Army forward to take pressure off the British who were fighting at Passchendaele. Hill 304 and the Mort Homme were among its objectives. The plan was to economize on infantry by emphasizing artillery preparation. Three thousand guns fired three million shells between August 11 and August 20, after which the infantry moved forward. The French took all of their objectives on the first day except for Hill 304, which they finally captured on August 24 along with 10,000 prisoners and hundreds of field guns and machine guns. Then Pétain, to the amazement and delight of his troops, halted the attack.

And there, until 5:30 a.m. on September 26, 1918, the front line rested.

CHAPTER 2

WAR COMES TO BALTIMORE

One thing was certain in January of 1917: the United States would not go to war in Europe. Two months earlier Woodrow Wilson had been re-elected President on that promise, and he had spent the previous three years defending American neutrality against Great Britain's high-handed maritime demands and the outrages of the Kaiser's armed forces. Yet on April 2, Wilson delivered a ringing speech to Congress asking it to declare war on Germany and on April 6 Congress, with overwhelming majorities in both houses, obliged. On June 5, young men who a few months earlier had had no thoughts of war willingly lined up to register for the draft. How a neutral power turned into an enthusiastic belligerent seemingly overnight is worth examining, as it illuminates the character of the American Expeditionary Forces and, particularly, the regiment that Baltimore sent to France.

It is often assumed that the United States identified with France and, especially, Britain from the start of the war, and that only an atavistic attachment to George Washington's principle of avoiding "foreign entanglements" plus Wilson's personal pacifism prevented the nation from joining the Allies earlier. The situation was more complex. England, not Germany, was America's hereditary enemy. Besides the Revolution and the War of 1812, the two countries had almost come to blows several times. The British recognized the Confederacy as a belligerent power in 1861 and almost joined it as an ally. In 1895 Lord Salisbury, the Foreign Secretary, denounced the Monroe Doctrine and asserted the British right to intervene in a South American boundary dispute. In response, President Cleveland asked Congress to appoint a commission to adjudicate the dispute and to enforce its conclusions by "every means."[1] The bill passed unanimously, while much of the press agitated for war. As recently as 1910, when the Army War College was developing strategic plans for defending the United States, the power to be defended against was assumed to be Great Britain. As the war progressed, the British did themselves no good with the American public by brutally repressing the Easter Rebellion in Ireland, proposing postwar retaliatory trade measures against neutrals, including the United States, and threatening to blacklist American companies suspected of trading with Germany.

Many segments of the American populace either admired Germany and Austria or distrusted the British or both. German-Americans were the largest population group by descent in the country, having long passed the British and Irish. In the nineteenth century five million Germans emigrated to the United States[2] and a further million or so arrived in the decade and a half before World War I; they and their descendants dominated a large swath of America from Pennsylvania and Maryland through the Midwest to Northern California and the Pacific Northwest. By 1910 more than ten million Americans came from Germany or Austria-Hungary.[3] German was commonly heard on the streets of Baltimore, Cincinnati, St Louis, Milwaukee, and many farm towns. Americans saw Germany as a world leader in science, mathematics, industry, and culture, and as a model for the United States in those fields. Wilson's support among antiwar German-Americans likely accounted for the slim majority by which he was re-elected.

In the teeming cities of the East Coast, where European immigrants and their children were a large part of the population, attitudes toward Britain and to the Allies in general were often less than favorable. Many Irish-Americans alive at the start of the war would have heard their parents' or grandparents' tales of suffering in the Potato Famine of 1845, which was caused by the predatory practices of English landlords and made worse by the refusal of Lord Russell, the relief administrator, to provide any actual relief, on the grounds that the famine was God's judgment on the Irish. As the war in Europe progressed, America's increasing support for Britain posed conflicts for them. Some formed Irish–German societies to combat British propaganda and promote Irish freedom, while others tied themselves to Irish radicals and secret revolutionary societies. Jews, both immigrants and those long settled, admired Germany for its high culture and for granting their co-religionists full civil rights in 1871. They also revered the Austro-Hungarian Kaiser Franz Joseph for his enlightened policies toward the Jews of his empire. But Russia, now allied to France and Britain, was the nemesis. Centuries of popular and official anti-Semitism had culminated in more than 250 government-tolerated (and often government-sponsored) pogroms between 1903 and 1906 in which more than a thousand were murdered and many thousands more injured or expelled from their homes. Impelled by such atrocities, as well as by a desire for economic opportunity (denied them by law in Russia) and to avoid conscription into the Czar's brutal army, more than two million Jews emigrated from eastern Europe to the United States between 1880 and 1914.[4] The last thing they wanted was to send their sons to war on the side of Russia. Italian-Americans, on the other hand, were happy to support anyone who would fight the Austro-Hungarian Empire, captor (as they saw it) of the Italian-speaking cities of Trieste and Trento.

Yet there were financial and strategic reasons why America as a whole would naturally side with the Allies, particularly Britain. Because of the British blockade of Germany, American trade was almost entirely with the Allies. By early 1917 40 percent of British outlays for the war were being spent in the United States, which furnished a vast array of munitions, food, and other supplies. The financing of British trade with the US as well as the purchasing itself were monopolized by the New York firm of J.P. Morgan. Finally, American strategic interests aligned with those of Great Britain in one major respect: For a land power in Europe or Asia to achieve dominance would endanger the security of both countries and would threaten the democratic civilization that America believed it was destined to spread throughout the world.

It was crucial for the Germans to avoid war with the United States, but they could not seem to refrain from antagonizing it. Americans had been shocked in 1914 by the violation of Belgian neutrality, compounded by the burning of the medieval library of Louvain, the shooting of civilian hostages, and the execution of British nurse Edith Cavell for helping prisoners of war escape. Most revolting was the deportation of (eventually) 300,000 Belgians to serve as forced laborers.[5] British propaganda magnified German crimes a hundred-fold with tales of soldiers bayoneting babies and cutting off children's hands. But although horrific, those real and invented episodes did not impinge on the United States. More disturbing was a string of German attacks on American ships (the *Cushing*, April 28; the *Gulflight*, May 1) culminating in the sinking of the Cunard passenger liner *Lusitania* by a submerged German U-boat on May 7, 1915, with the loss of 1,198 civilian lives, 128 of them American. The German government pointed out in its defense that before the ship sailed from New York the embassy had warned passengers that it might be attacked; this merely convinced the public that the sinking was a case of deliberate murder. Wilson issued several protests, but three months later a U-boat sank the liner *Arabic*; 44 passengers and crew died, among them two Americans. On August 28 the German Chancellor, realizing the danger of drawing America into the war, announced the cessation of submerged attacks on merchant vessels; but the fuse had been lit that would eventually bring the explosion the Germans feared.

Even with unrestricted submarine warfare supposedly out of the way, the Germans could not keep themselves from blundering into America's bad graces. On July 30, 1916, saboteurs blew up a huge munitions depot on Black Tom Island in New York harbor; the noise was heard as far away as Maryland and Connecticut. The culprits, quickly caught, proved to be German agents. On January 19, 1917, Dr Alfred von Zimmermann, the new German Foreign Minister, wired to the German Minister in Mexico City a harebrained scheme to support Mexican re-conquest of Texas, New Mexico, and Arizona in case the United States entered the war. The telegram was soon deciphered by British intelligence, which forwarded it to the US but did not immediately make it public. Not knowing the skills of British cryptographers, Count Johann von Bernstorff, the German Ambassador to the United States, requested on January 23 that Berlin send $50,000 to bribe American congressmen to support neutrality; this message also was intercepted.[6]

By late 1916 the Germans, concluding that the Americans were *de facto* belligerents despite their formal neutrality, figured they had a lot to gain and nothing to lose by resuming unrestricted submarine attacks, the only means they had of cutting off Britain's maritime lifeline. At a meeting of the Crown Council on January 9, 1917, the Kaiser asked Admiral Henning von Holtzendorff, the Chief of the German Naval Staff, about America's reaction. Holtzendorff replied that it would likely enter the war but added, "I will give Your Majesty my word as an officer that not one American will land on the Continent."[7] Desperate to stanch the flow of supplies to the enemy on the Western Front, Hindenburg seconded the idea. The Kaiser approved the measure, aimed at all shipping regardless of cargo or nationality, beginning

February 1. Ambassador Count von Bernstorff so informed the American government on January 31.

One of the first German acts upon resuming submarine warfare was to sink the *Housatonic*, an American cargo ship, off the Scilly Isles on February 3. That same evening, Zimmerman expressed to US Ambassador James W. Gerard his belief that America would stay neutral because Wilson desired peace above all else. At almost that very moment, Wilson told Congress he was breaking off diplomatic relations with Germany.

Wilson personally hated Germany. He told his acquaintances and advisers, in private, that his sympathies were all with the Allies; but he refused to impose his personal opinion on the country, large sections of which he knew disagreed with him. He believed passionately that America's destiny was to transform the decadent political cultures of Europe. But his proposals for "peace without victors or vanquished" were an embarrassment to the Allies as well as the Central Powers, all of whom had territorial ambitions that they did not wish to reveal. The President took their indifference personally, and let his desire to impose his own form of peace overcome his innate pacifism, leading to his willingness to intervene.[8]

By early 1916 Wilson realized that his inability to compel the belligerents to accept mediation stemmed from the military impotence of the United States. Up to then he had rigorously suppressed any federal efforts to prepare for war, stamping out preparedness campaigns in 1914 and 1915 and flying into a rage when the *Baltimore Sun* reported that the General Staff was developing plans in case of war with Germany. Now he became an advocate of preparedness, declaring himself in favor of building "the greatest navy in the world" and urging that civilians receive military training so that the country would not be in the position of "putting raw levies of inexperienced men onto the modern field of battle."[9]

But preparedness for what? Already in 1915 Wilson, in response to the sinking of the *Lusitania*, had introduced a bill that became the National Defense Act, passed by Congress on June 3, 1916. The Act more than doubled the size of the Army, in five annual installments, to roughly 11,450 officers and 223,580 men. The National Guard was authorized to reach a full strength of 17,000 officers and 440,000 men and was obligated to serve under federal control when called up by the President. At the same time, in deference to those who opposed a powerful army, the Act crippled the Army's ability to plan and command by setting the number of officers assigned to the General

Staff at 54, strictly limiting the number who could be assigned to Washington at any one time, and leaving the all-powerful bureaus independent.[*] Additionally, the Act was divorced from considerations of strategy: although the obvious danger to any American participation in the war would be from submarines, it authorized 16 useless battleships but only 50 destroyers.

The popular Preparedness movement that developed after the sinking of the *Lusitania* did not want intervention in the European war. It wanted the military to prepare to defend the US against whoever the victor in Europe might be. This justification, had it been supported by Congress, would have given the Army the opportunity to modernize, rearm, and expand while adhering to the neutral stance mandated by the President. Furthermore, universal military training (UMT) had been advocated in many parts of American society since 1914. The military saw it as a way to build up its strength in peacetime against possible necessity in war. Social reformers saw other benefits: it would assimilate immigrants into American society, build idealism and patriotism, inculcate efficient habits of behavior, and reconcile social classes. But others saw the draft as a conspiracy to Prussianize society by imposing on the working (enlisted) classes subservience to the wealthy (officer) class; or (like the Progressive Amos Pinchot) as a policy of industrialists to militarize and thus tame the unruly workforce. So Congress failed to approve either a national reserve or conscription.

Wilson could not react to German provocations, some of which had been abetted by Americans of German ancestry, without violating his stance of neutrality. Instead, tapping a deep-rooted strain of nativism in the American psyche, he launched a campaign against disloyal immigrants, which in the popular mind quickly came dangerously close to meaning all immigrants. "There are citizens of the United States, I blush to admit," he said in his third annual message to Congress, "born under other flags but welcomed under our generous naturalization laws to the full freedom and opportunity of America, who have poured the poison of disloyalty into the very arteries of our national life ... Such creatures of passion, disloyalty, and anarchy must be crushed out." This phrase received the most applause of the entire speech.[10] Clearly, the effect of a tidal wave of immigrants on American

---

[*] This compared with 232 for the British, 644 for the French, and 650 for the Germans as they entered the war in 1914. (Gary Mead, *The Doughboys: America and the First World War* (Woodstock and New York: Overlook Press, 2000), p. 69.)

life was a real issue; but to assert that as a group they were subverting American democracy was simply to display ignorance, bigotry, and paranoia when sober policy was called for.

As Wilson's new term began, he told his friend and adviser Colonel Edward M. House, "There will be no war. This country does not intend to become involved in war. It would be a crime against civilization for us to go into it."[11] But the edifice of neutrality began to crack on February 25, 1917 when a U-boat sank the Cunard liner *Laconia*, en route from New York to Liverpool, off the Irish coast. The *Houstonic* had at least been warned according to the rules of war so that it could be abandoned before it was sunk; the *Laconia* was not. Of 73 passengers, six were American; two of the latter, a woman and her daughter, died. The following day, Wilson asked Congress to authorize the arming of merchant ships. At this critical juncture the Wilson administration, now convinced that the Zimmerman telegram was authentic, released it to the press, which published it on March 1. The same day, the House voted 403 to 13 in favor of Wilson's "armed neutrality" bill; three days later the Senate's Republican minority, led by Midwestern antiwar senators, killed the measure by filibuster.

The torpedoing of the *Laconia* was soon followed by sinkings of more American merchantmen: *Algonquin*, March 12; *Vigilancia*, March 16; *City of Memphis*, March 17; *Illinois*, March 18; *Healdton*, March 21; *Aztec*, April 1. The drumbeat of headlines was inescapable, the result inevitable. At a meeting of Wilson's cabinet on March 20, every member declared himself, however reluctantly, in favor of war with Germany. On the evening of April 2, Wilson asked a special joint session of Congress, with the Supreme Court, cabinet, and diplomatic corps in attendance, to declare war. The resolution passed the Senate by 82 to 6 on April 4, the House by 373 to 50 on April 6. Wilson signed it the same day; the United States had joined the World War.

The effect of the declaration of war on what was now the home front was far from electric. Public band and orchestra concerts, then major forms of public entertainment, broke into the National Anthem, accompanied by cheers and singing. Flags were prominently displayed. Recruitment offices had long lines. But many parts of America were still against the war. Farmers in the South and

Midwest were against it. Immigrants from Russia and Scandinavia had come to the US to avoid war and conscription. Those from Austria and Germany didn't want to fight their cousins. The Irish hated England. Progressives feared that their domestic program would suffer. Those on the left were happy to leave the capitalists and imperialists of Europe to fight one another to the death. As late as two months into America's war, British intelligence was reporting that the national mood was one of reluctance and inevitability rather than enthusiasm. Joe Tumulty, Wilson's press secretary, told Colonel House that "the people's 'righteous wrath' seems not to have been aroused."[12]

To instill in Americans the proper patriotic attitude, Wilson on April 13 established the Committee on Public Information and allotted it a budget of several million dollars. He appointed as its head George Creel, a Progressive journalist and reformer who had become one of Wilson's most vocal supporters. The CPI mounted a federal publicity campaign unparalleled up to that time, and hardly ever since. Newspapers and magazines were deluged with prowar advertisements. Posters, billboards, cartoons, parades, and movies took the message to those Americans who didn't read the papers. Mock battles using real troops lent excitement and authenticity. Front organizations were set up to co-opt the more reluctant parts of society: the American Alliance for Labor and Democracy for workers, the Friends of German Democracy for German-Americans. Creel's biggest innovation was to recruit 75,000 mostly amateur speakers to deliver short pro-war messages in movie theaters, fraternal organizations, concert halls—wherever the public assembled.[*] Thirty-three million pamphlets were printed covering more than 30 topics, tons of which were sent to school teachers. Nor did the public see this propaganda as heavy-handed or unwelcome. On the contrary, the country got into the spirit of the thing, decorating streets and automobiles with flags and plastering bond drive posters on every available surface.

One aspect of war fever needed no encouragement: the traditional suspicion of immigrants, which now spilled over into ugly action. The anti-immigrant movement known as "100 percent Americanism" was aimed at all immigrants, but most virulently at German-Americans, who previously had been among the ethnic groups most admired for embodying the American ethic of hard work and community spirit. German words like

---

[*] At war's end Creel claimed his men had given more than seven and a half million speeches to almost 315 million people.

"hamburger" and "sauerkraut" were excised from the language, the speaking of German was banned in some localities, and otherwise inoffensive people of German birth were assaulted in public places. Orchestra conductors of German or Austrian descent were removed from the podium—Fritz Kreisler was banned in Pittsburgh, while Carl Muck was arrested in Boston and Ernst Kunwald in Philadelphia. In many cities and towns German-speakers were beaten on the street. A young German-born American named Robert Prager was lynched by a mob of 500 in a town near St Louis in April. It took a jury 25 minutes to acquit the ringleaders, after which one juryman exclaimed, "Well, I guess nobody can say we aren't loyal now." The *Washington Post* opined that while lynchings were regrettable, the anti-German agitation was "a healthful and wholesome awakening."[13]

Nor was the traitor hunt limited to immigrants. As the country was officially at war, union organizers and pacifists who opposed it were now "disloyal." In April 1917 an organizer for the International Workers of the World was dragged behind a car and hanged from a bridge in Butte, Montana. The *New York Times*, while opposing the lynching, wrote that "the IWW agitators are in effect, and perhaps in fact, agents of Germany. The Federal authorities should make short work of these treasonable conspirators against the United States." Columbia University expelled professors whom it deemed subversive: one for supporting several peace organizations and another for petitioning Congress against sending troops to Europe. The *Times* applauded the action.[14]

Even more corrosive of American society were the official efforts to stir up enthusiasm for the war and to root out disloyalty. The Espionage Act of 1917 instituted heavy fines and prison terms for those interfering with military operations in wartime or using the mails in violation of the Act. Postmaster General Albert Burleson immediately set about using the authority of the Act to suppress the activities of groups he deemed seditious. Immigrants' societies, left-wing labor unions, and minority political parties, most prominently the Socialists, found their mailing privileges terminated and their membership depleted. Congress granted him yet more powers in its renewal of the Act in October 1917. Foreign-language newspapers now had to obtain advance approval from the Post Office Department to publish any articles that referred to the government, to the belligerents, or to the war itself. English translations had to be submitted to the Post Office in advance, a requirement that increased costs and prevented timely publication even if an article was ultimately approved. Questioning the virtuousness of the Allies' actions and motives was banned, even regarding their imperialist policies, which were portrayed as liberal and even selfless, in contrast to the rapacious behavior of the Germans. Local and national self-proclaimed patriotic groups, under the sponsorship of US Attorney General Thomas W. Gregory, took action against suspicious-looking people in their neighborhoods and workplaces: opening personal mail and telegrams, burglarizing homes, slandering the innocent, committing illegal arrests, and conducting private raids against "slackers" who, they believed, were avoiding the draft.

Pacifists, labor organizers, and German-Americans had little alternative but to keep their heads down. The Progressives dropped their pacifism and adopted the view that the war abroad presented possibilities for reform at home in areas such as child labor, women's rights, land reclamation, and a fairer income tax. The German community in particular fell prey to the rampant anti-immigrant and specifically anti-German mood of the time. The National German-American Alliance, a society set up in 1907 to further German culture, literature, and language, had two million members in 1914. In 1918, as membership plummeted and Congress investigated it, the organization disbanded. Americans of other ethnicities were intimidated as well. Foreign-language newspapers in general, eager to avoid charges of disloyalty, often supported press censorship.[15]

Yet the ethnic communities' acceptance of American participation in the war was not all the result of coercion. Some saw it as a blow for their native lands' freedom from imperial domination—in particular, Czechs and Slovaks from the Austro-Hungarian Empire and Poles from Russia. Many Jews saw a heightened opportunity to establish a homeland in Palestine. All four groups raised volunteer "foreign legions" to fight with the Allies in Europe and the Middle East. Most Americans of Italian descent had not identified with their home country's role in the war before October 1917. But on October 24, the Germans overwhelmed the Italian Army at Caporetto, advancing more than 60 miles in three weeks, killing 40,000, and capturing 280,000. Now the war became a sacred struggle for Italy's survival. Relief societies sprang up, their fund-raising bolstered by mass public meetings. Native-born Americans expressed new sympathy for Italians; even the students at Yale University took up a collection for Italian refugees.

Ethnic communities saw Army service as a good way to Americanize and to raise their people's status among "native" Americans. Many of their leaders exhorted their young men, either directly or through their social and political societies, to enlist, to register for the draft, and, if drafted, to report for service. The cohesion of immigrant communities—they tended to live together, speak their own languages, eat their own foods, and congregate in their own churches and social, political, and nationalistic organizations— lent a particular flavor to their new Americanism. They took pains to show their loyalty, but in their own fashion, holding flag-waving patriotic marches in their native costumes and staging rallies at ethnic social halls and in their own languages. Thus they co-opted much of the rant of the "100 percent Americans" to advance their own purposes.

American blacks took little notice of the war at first. As American involvement grew more likely, however, their support grew as well, and for much the same reason as the European immigrants: Here, they thought, was a way to elevate their status in the broader society. This sentiment grew slowly; but by 1917, in meetings, proclamations, and newspaper editorials they urged other blacks to show their patriotism by buying war bonds and registering for the draft. One major theme emerged: the demand that blacks be allowed to serve in the armed forces. A typical sentiment was voiced by the supervisor of a large manufacturing firm in Kingston, North Carolina, who said that a million "colored" men awaited national service: "Call us, arm us, give us a place at the front, and we will make America feel proud of her colored citizens or report to God the reason why." As we shall see later, they would get their wish; but they may have regretted what they wished for.[16]

Nowhere were the cross-currents of American patriotism, ethnic identification, and racial and economic status more evident than in Baltimore, the city that would furnish most of the men for the 313th Infantry Regiment, one of the four infantry regiments in the 79th Division. Baltimore was the most heavily used port of entry after New York and its population showed it. Of the 470,000 white residents of the city in 1910, more than one-third either were foreign-born or had two foreign-born parents.* Of these, 43 percent were of German

---

* The roughly 16 percent of the population who were black were excluded from most of the Census tabulations.

extraction, more than one-tenth were Irish, and about one-quarter were Russians, the vast majority of them Jews.[17] German financial and cultural influence was particularly prominent; toward the end of the century German-Americans had achieved leading positions in commerce, education, banking, and the performing and fine arts. They clung tightly to their language and culture; in 1900, more than 30 Baltimore churches held their main services in German. With the outbreak of war in 1914, the German community was enthusiastic in its support of the homeland. By 1917 they had collected almost a million dollars for widows and orphans of German and Austrian soldiers. In the parish house of the Zion Lutheran Church, a nail was driven into a large German eagle for each contribution.[18]

Almost as prominent in business and academia were the Jews of German descent. In the mid-1800s the German Jews of Baltimore allied themselves with the general German-American community and apparently were accepted. Jews participated in German gymnastic, literary, and cultural associations, singing societies, and fraternal organizations. By the first decade of the twentieth century, Baltimore's German Jews were prominent in charities and other civic organizations, academia, and politics, while remaining leaders in their synagogues. A German Jew was even chosen as president of the Maryland Historical Society, a bastion of old-line Baltimore aristocracy. To this group, Germany and Austria were centers of culture, science, and the arts; for the time being, therefore, they continued to identify with the broader Baltimore German community. Far different were the masses of Jews who emigrated from Russia and eastern Europe in the decades from 1880 to 1914. Low wages and poor working conditions led many of them to affiliate with the labor movement or to adopt socialist ideals. Like many immigrants, they saw no reason to support the empires of Britain, France, and especially Russia, from which many had fled at the risk of their lives.

Baltimore's Irish followed their cousins in other cities by denouncing Britain and all it stood for, especially after the repression of the Easter Rebellion in 1916. One of many mass meetings took place at Ford's Opera House in June of that year. Justice John Jerome Rooney of the New York Supreme Court and Joseph D. McLaughlin, national president of the Ancient Order of Hibernians, denounced the "English" as "liars, hypocrites, and slanderers." "Men in the audience stood up and shouted and waved their hats," reported the *Baltimore Sun*.[19] Nevertheless, against the eventuality that America might join the war, the Irish hastened to assure each other and the outside world that they would do whatever their adopted country required of them. Reverend P.J. Kenny of St Peter's Catholic Church addressed a banquet of the Hibernians' Ladies' Auxiliary in February 1916, saying that if the United States should go to war, Irish-Americans would fight for their country. "The Irishmen of the United States are working hard to promote the interests of their country in time of peace. They will fight just as hard to preserve her dignity in time of war," he intoned.[20]

Before 1917, the blacks of Baltimore had more pressing things to worry about than foreign wars. They had escaped slavery but they had not escaped Jim Crow, the system of legal and extra-legal restrictions that kept them socially, politically, and economically repressed. Their white neighbors saw them mostly as domestic servants, criminals, or threats to jobs and property values. Black public leaders gave most of their attention to exposing prejudice in housing and employment, protesting assaults and lynchings and, especially, fighting the segregationist policies of the Wilson administration and the Southern Democrats in Congress.* At the same time, the city's black newspapers were eager to publicize their community's accomplishments in education, religion, the arts, and business. Only as war was imminent did they turn their attention to the role blacks might play in a future conflict.

During the first two years of the European war, Baltimore's mainstream press followed Wilson's injunction to be "impartial in thought as well as action."[21] The *Sun* maintained a studied neutrality. In a 1916 tribute to a young Baltimorean wounded in action with the Royal Flying Corps, the paper rhapsodized:

> Should we not envy young Marburg and all like him, whether British, French, German, Austrian or Russian, who have received the patent of a great nobility, who have been caught up in the spirit and had such visions of human duty and service as come to few of us, who have been admitted to the very presence of the King?[22]

Speeches by pacifists were reported dispassionately and printed at length. In endorsing the "preparedness parades" that broke out in 1916, the paper

---

* Wilson supported Postmaster General Albert Burleson's efforts to increase segregation among federal employees, rudely dismissed a delegation of black leaders who visited him to protest Burleson's policies, and praised the pro-Klu Klux Klan interpretation of post-Civil War history expressed in the film *Birth of a Nation*. (David M. Kennedy, *Over Here: The First World War in American Society* (Oxford, New York, Toronto, Melbourne: Oxford UP, 1980), p. 281.)

even held Germany up as a model for the United States: "We have got to get together and work together like on a great team. It is the German teamwork that has told in peace as well as in this war. Each German has been for the nation, and the nation has been for every German."[23]

Cracks in the facade started to appear, however, as the Germans continued to outrage American sensibilities. When the *Lusitania* was sunk, the *Sun*, although not ready itself to take sides against Germany, had no qualms about reprinting an editorial from the *New York World*:

> The size, speed and renown of the vessel, the general interest in her movements and fate, the elaborately advertised warning published a week ago by the German Embassy coincidentally with the *Lusitania*'s last departure from the port of which she was the pride and favorite, combine to intensify the horror with which American opinion regards this German innovation on accepted methods of warfare at sea. That it was premeditated we know; that it was reckless of innocent noncombatant lives we are sure; and "dastardly!" is the word on millions of American lips this morning.[24]

By the time Germany resumed unrestricted submarine warfare in 1917, Maryland newspapers were anticipating the inevitable. The Hagerstown *Morning Herald* seemed almost disappointed when the Germans sank the *Housatonic* and the *Philadelphia* "with full regard for American rights and international law ... The United States tonight settled down to wait for an overt action by the German naval forces in violation of the German government's submarine pledges."[25] The *Baltimore American* reported with glee how, when a pacifist spokesman ("born in Switzerland of Swiss-German parents") called on Senator Henry Cabot Lodge of Massachusetts in his office, the senator punched him in the face.*[26] The *Sun* full-throatedly endorsed Wilson's justification for entering the war, as delivered to Congress on April 2:

> No one else has made it quite so plain as the President did last night that Germany as it is now constituted, ruled "by little groups of men who are

---

* Violence was not confined to the halls of Congress. The Emergency Peace Federation asked its leading spokesman, David Starr Jordan, a past president of Stanford University, to address an antiwar assembly in Baltimore. The building was invaded by almost a thousand enraged citizens who headed directly for Jordan, who was on the podium. Some quick wits in the audience began to sing the *Star Spangled Banner* and the "patriots," forced to stand to attention, had to let Jordan escape. Gangs searched for him all night but he got away. (Kennedy, *Over Here*, p. 16.)

accustomed to use their fellow-men as pawns and tools," can never be a fit member of the society of nations; that no other nation can be secure while it is so constituted.[*27]

The deeper into the war the US got, the more the patriotism of Baltimoreans became a campaign against all people and things German. The president of Johns Hopkins University suggested that "all teachers of German birth or antecedents, or even of German extraction, should be regarded with suspicion," and the headmaster of a prestigious private school added his remarks:

> If ... the utterly debauched philosophy of life of the present Germany, with its dreadful menace of efficient treachery, scientific cruelty and arrogant tyranny, is at all likely to survive this war, and if the study of German anywhere, under any circumstances, will serve to spread that philosophy of life, then no consideration warrants our continuance of the study of German. The sooner the mouth out of which that black heart speaketh is closed, the better.[28]

Although German was the most common language of engineering and mathematics texts and was mandatory for all students, the school board voted to eliminate it from the curriculum of the Baltimore Polytechnic Institute and to substitute French. The *Sun* helpfully ran a feature educating its readers on how to identify "pro-Germans":[†]

---

[*] For a while, the *Sun* was not above using a measure of irony in its reporting. Two weeks after the sinking of the *Housatonic*, in a story entitled, "School Board Pro-U.S.," it led with, "Patriots strove to out-patriot each other at the meeting of the School Board yesterday afternoon. Not only the living but the dead were called upon to witness the loyalty of the members of the board to the colors of the United States of America. Commissioner Biggs declared, in a voice that trembled with feeling, that he had nine relatives in soldiers' graves, to whose memory he was striving to be true. Commissioner Dugan just as heatedly stated that he had as many dead soldiers among his relatives as Mr. Biggs." ("School Board Pro-U.S.," *Baltimore Sun*, February 15, 1917, p. 6.)

[†] Ironically, what Baltimoreans did not know was that there were indeed German-Americans in the city who were plotting against the Allies. The Black Tom explosion of 1916 was coordinated by Paul Hilken, a member of a prominent Baltimore German family and manager of the local operations of the North German Lloyd Steamship Company. In his office on the corner of Charles and Redwood (formerly German) Streets, Hilken received orders and money from Franz von Papen, a military attaché to the German embassy (and later, briefly, Hitler's Vice-Chancellor), and paid the conspirators who set the charges. (Jacques Kelly, "A World War I-Era Terror Plot Hatched Downtown," *Baltimore Sun*, January 30, 2010, www.baltimoresun.com/news/maryland/bal.-md.kelly30jan30,0,0,165669. column, p. 1, accessed January 30, 2010.)

A Pro-German is a man who, by private or public utterances, stands in the way of a whole-hearted prosecution of this war and the defeat of the German will to conquer ... He may do it by finding fault with the conduct of the war. He may do it by impracticable peace arguments. He may do it through a mistaken policy. He may do it because he is in the pay of the German Government ... Do not let these pro-Germans poison the atmosphere in your locality by slandering our allies without challenge.[29]

Although large parts of the American population were slow to embrace the war, Baltimoreans quickly got the message: show your loyalty. Local business organizations with international ties hastily met to pledge their allegiance to the United States. The German-American Bank became the American Bank. Ethnic minorities caught on early; on March 5, a month before the declaration of war, many hundreds of foreign-born Baltimoreans accompanied the Maryland National Guard and various Regular Army units in a preparedness parade in Washington before 200,000 cheering citizens. Among them were a thousand members of "Baltimore Polish military organizations" and 200 Italians in flamboyant uniforms.[30] Once war was declared, the demonstrations of loyalty accelerated. Foreign-born citizens, even those of German descent, subscribed conspicuously to bond drives. In a massive Fourth of July parade in Baltimore, participants marched by nationality, many in the costumes of their homelands: Bohemians, the Slovak League, the Scandinavian League, various British and French societies, Greeks, and Poles. The hits of the parade, as always, were the Italians, the largest contingent (although one of the smaller minorities in Baltimore), all of whom were decked out in their national colors. The press remarked on their ebullience, and attributed it to the fact that Italy had just thrown the Austrian-German armies back over the Piave River. (The press also remarked pointedly that the Irish, while present as individuals, were not represented by an organization and did not fly a flag.) At the end of the procession were "200 negro members of the Stevedores' Union. Just how or why they got in a parade of the foreign-born was hard to fathom, but they enjoyed themselves and got no little applause along the line."[31] The upsurge of patriotic unity at these parades spread to the crowd: at one, the *Sun* reported:

On the roof of a one-story garage on McCulloh Street stood seven fine specimens of America's future manhood, each shouting at the passing troops at the capacity of his lungs. Segregated, and at the extreme end of the roof, was a little colored girl waving a small and bedraggled flag, almost drowning the shouts of the boys with her screams of enthusiasm. Acknowledging defeat in their competition the boys commissioned her to join their forces. Another incident of democracy.[32]

Jews, having no national homeland, flag, or costume, were not particularly visible in the patriotic marches and demonstrations. Suspected by many as either Germans (the old families) or socialists (the immigrants), they took every occasion to pronounce their patriotism in their synagogues, social organizations, and charity drives.[*] Children of the Hebrew Orphan Asylum gave their scant savings to buy war stamps which, in the words of the *Sun*, "should be an inspiration to others so situated."[33] Many Baltimore Jews saw the war as portending the fulfillment of Jewish national aspirations. They filled the Hippodrome and Palace Theaters to hear speakers acclaim the British government, in English and Yiddish, for its declaration in favor of a Jewish homeland in Palestine. Professor Felix Frankfurter, then an assistant to the Secretary of War, said at a dinner at the Hotel Emerson that Zionism "is one of the issues of the war and one of the war's necessary conclusions."[34]

The blacks of Baltimore did not feel compelled to prove their loyalty— what other country could they be loyal to? Except for a few radicals, they were not subject to the suspicions inflicted on immigrants and those of German descent. Their chief interest lay in using the war to overcome stereotypes and to advance their social and economic status. Visible participation in the military could accomplish both of these goals. The Baltimore *Afro-American* proudly reported in March 1917 that the Army was mustering the 1st Separate Colored Battalion of the National Guard into federal service with the mission of guarding government and railroad facilities in Washington. Particularly gratifying was that the Army had made special arrangements for the men to eat in three restaurants near their posts so that they would not have to go back to their quarters for meals three times a day.[35] The Plattsburg movement, which trained white, largely middle-class men to be officers, posed a special challenge: whether to establish similar training camps for blacks. The *Afro-American* editorialized

---

[*] It may also have occurred to some that an angry mob might not make the fine distinction between a person on the street speaking German and one speaking Yiddish.

that "many colored educated men ... would like to attend the summer camps for the discipline and the contacts they afford. But to go to a Jimcrow Plattsburg to learn how to lead Jimcrow regiments is too much." Other black leaders believed that, despite the evil of segregation, the opportunity for officer training in any form was too good to pass up, as it would yield a group of black leaders who could work for integration more effectively in the future.[36]

The true test of Baltimoreans' patriotism came on May 18, 1917, when President Wilson signed the Selective Service Act and set June 5 as the beginning of registration. The history of conscription in the US was bloody. During the Civil War, the attempt to draft Irish immigrants into the Union Army resulted in a five-day riot in New York City in which 50 buildings were destroyed by fire and more than a hundred people killed, including 11 blacks who were lynched. In 1917 many considered America's ethnic minorities so unreliable that national publications from the *New Republic* to the Hearst papers, not to mention many Congressional Democrats, favored two armies, a volunteer force to be sent overseas and a draft army to be held at home. How would Baltimore's ethnic communities react on June 5—the Irish who despised Britain, the Jews who detested Russia, the blacks who hated Jim Crow, the Germans who revered their culture and their native land?

The citizens of Baltimore need not have worried. With a journalistic sigh of relief the *Sun* reported that the first day's draft registration was heavier than expected, no public incidents occurred, and extra registration cards had to be sent for. The paper was especially impressed that 200 "negroes," newly arrived to work for the Pennsylvania Railroad, expressed their intent to live in Baltimore for a while and asked to be registered, which they were.[37] It stressed that participation in the registration drive was heaviest in the districts populated by "foreigners." Wards with heavily immigrant populations had registration rates ranging from 57 to 95 percent. The Fifth Ward required interpreters in "German, Italian, Spanish, Yiddish, Slavonic, and a variety of Russian Dialects." These figures contrasted with the "uptown" wards, predominantly native-born, which yielded only around 41 percent. The paper was pleased to report that in the mostly black 17th Ward, registration was "very heavy, 10,087 negroes [*sic*] having registered."[38]

Six months earlier, for the young men of Baltimore, war had been an impossibility. Now, for most of them, it was their patriotic duty.

CHAPTER 3

CREATING AN ARMY

In April 1917, the American people were ready to fight. The Army, however, was not. The largest force it had mustered since the end of the Civil War was the Cuban expedition of 1898, which numbered 17,000 men along with six artillery batteries and one company of Gatling guns.[1]* The National Defense Act of 1916 was intended ultimately to expand the Army to about 250,000 officers and men; but by the time of America's entry into the war only about 120,000 men and 5,000 officers were in uniform, few of whom had ever seen action. The National Guard contained about another 80,000 soldiers, but was not a professional force.[2]

Numbers were not the only weakness. With the exception of the Civil War, the American Army had historically pursued only two purposes: to protect the coasts, especially strategic harbors, from attack and invasion; and to subdue fractious Indian tribes. Two almost unrelated armies had therefore developed. The Coastal Artillery occupied heavy fortifications equipped with the latest long-range guns and was led by engineering officers, the top graduates of West Point, who were typically promoted every two or three years. The field army spent its time as a constabulary force, spread over the landscape in detachments of one to three companies or an occasional battalion, policing the southern border and chasing, though rarely fighting,

---

* The force sent to suppress the Philippine Insurrection (1899–1902) eventually numbered around 70,000, but it was distributed in relatively small detachments across the islands. (Charles Reginald Shrader, ed., *Reference Guide to United States Military History, 1865–1919* (New York: Facts on File, Inc., 1993), p. 68.)

Indians. Such combat as took place was closer to guerrilla warfare than to pitched battles in the European style. Unlike the engineers, officers in the infantry, cavalry, and field artillery were promoted only every six or seven years, if that. As a result, at the end of the nineteenth century, almost the entire Army hierarchy was in the hands of Civil War veterans, including the immediate superiors of the junior officers who would be top commanders in World War I. Lieutenant Peyton March, later Wilson's wartime Chief of Staff, found on joining the Third Artillery in 1888 that his regimental commander was a veteran of the Mexican War. Up to 1900, all regimental commanders in all three arms were Civil War veterans, and many officers of lower formations were too. In the words of historian Robert Ferrell, "The Army in April 1917 was a home for old soldiers, a quiet, sleepy place where they killed time until they began drawing their pensions."[3]

Important changes had been made at the top, but they had not yet resulted in anything like a modern army. In 1903 President McKinley's Secretary of War, Elihu Root, had streamlined management by combining authority for administration, training, and operations in a single person, the Chief of Staff, who reported to the President through the Secretary. He established the first full-time, long-range planning body, the General Staff, an innovation that the Germans had adopted in the 1860s. His reforms led to the creation, between 1901 and 1913, of the General Staff and Service colleges at Fort Leavenworth; the Army War College; and a galaxy of other specialized schools to re-educate the officer corps in modern warfare and military administration. The War College quickly became the *de facto* planning arm of the General Staff. But the General Staff was hobbled in its authority by the jealousy of the old bureaus that controlled procurement and administration. As a result, these reforms made the Army fit to control the island empire won in 1898 but not to take on the large, professional armies of Europe.

For decades, Congress systematically denied the Army the funds to equip itself. Every year from 1909 through 1916 the Quartermaster General asked for an allocation to build up a reserve supply of clothing; every year Congress cut his requests by two-thirds. Nor did the National Defense Act of 1916 help much. In that year General William Crozier, the Chief of Ordnance, pointed out that 18 months' notice would be necessary to put factories on a war footing for arms production, and asked for funds to produce enough weapons in three years to equip a million-man army. In committee, Congress cut the proposed amount by 35 percent. One thing the Act did do, however, was to add positions for four major generals and 19 brigadier generals to the Army establishment. The 1916–17 promotions to brigadier general were based, as of old, on seniority rather than on fitness for command. There was, however, one exception: Joseph E. Kuhn, an engineer and the top graduate of the West Point Class of 1885. He was one of the General Staff's experts on the German Army; in March 1917 he was appointed chief of the Army War College. We shall hear more of General Kuhn.

The war being fought in Europe was based on industrial technology and the United States was an industrial power, but one would never have guessed either fact by observing how the US Army waged war. The Army's innocence of the effects of technology on warfare is well illustrated by its response to the machine gun. Until 1900 its experience with rapid-fire weapons was limited to the Gatling gun, hand-cranked with multiple rotating barrels, which could not be traversed horizontally and which was usually classified and used as artillery. By the start of the war, American inventors had created four highly efficient designs—the Maxim gun (for heavy use), the Browning medium machine gun, the Lewis gun (a light, company-level weapon) and the Browning Automatic Rifle (which became the famed BAR of World War II). Although the European powers had adopted the Maxim gun as early as the 1880s and the British had taken up the Lewis gun at the outbreak of the war, the American Ordnance Department tested and rejected all four weapons and thereafter virtually ignored modern automatic weaponry until 1917. As a result, when it entered the war, the Army possessed a grab-bag collection of only 1,453 automatic weapons, most of them of inefficient design.[4]*

Modern artillery fared little better in the hands of the prewar Army. American military doctrine was based on mobility and quick, fierce offensives aimed at shattering the enemy's formations by a combination of

---

* The American lack of respect for machine guns as defensive weapons is surprising. Pershing himself had seen them used in support of fortified positions, as an observer in the Russo-Japanese War and at Japanese Army maneuvers in 1907. From 1907 to 1914 he directed a number of training exercises that used machine guns, and he used them in the Mexican Punitive Expedition of 1916. In the latter, an American cavalry charge was turned back by a single Mexican machine gun; but Pershing only exulted that American rifles had still killed 30 Mexicans and wounded 40. Although intellectually aware of the power of the machine gun and the difficulty of attacking modern fortifications, Pershing was unable to shake off the effects of military tradition and training. (James W. Rainey, "Ambivalent Warfare: The Tactical Doctrine of the AEF in World War I," *Parameters* 13, September (1983), pp. 36–37.)

maneuver and firepower. Based on experience in the Civil War and against the Indians, it relegated artillery to a strictly supporting arm. The Army *Field Service Regulations* said, "The artillery is the close supporting arm of the infantry and its duties are inseparably connected with those of the infantry. Its targets are those units of the enemy which ... are most dangerous to the infantry or that hinder infantry success."[5] Conservation of ammunition was a major principle of artillery operations.

These principles took no account of the development of artillery since the end of the previous century. Formerly, the barrel of a gun was hard-mounted on the carriage so that the entire assembly leaped backward when the gun was fired. The whole gun then had to be re-aimed before it could be fired again. The propellant was black gunpowder, which caused the gunners' view to be blocked by a dense white cloud of smoke after the first shot and instantly revealed their position to the enemy. In 1897 the French Army adopted a 75mm gun fitted with an oil-compression-based shock absorber that contained the barrel's recoil, left the gun carriage relatively motionless, and automatically repositioned the barrel for the next shot. It had three effects. The rate of fire, previously five rounds per minute, quadrupled, because the crew could reload and fire repeatedly without having to re-aim the gun. Fire became much more accurate, because it was now possible to correct the gun's aim based on the fall of the previous shot. Sighting, ranging, and fuze-setting mechanisms added to accuracy; smokeless powder gave a clear view and made it harder for the enemy to locate one's own guns and suppress them with counterbattery fire. Most important was the development of indirect fire. The Russo-Japanese War of 1904–05 demonstrated that the old artillery doctrine, where the opposing batteries could see their targets, was obsolete. To protect their guns from counterbattery bombardment, the Japanese put them on the rearward slopes of ridges, out of the enemy's view. Although the Russian guns were superior weapons, they could not find the Japanese batteries, while the Japanese readily destroyed the Russian pieces, which were placed in the open. The Russians eventually adopted the new methods, as did all European powers soon afterward. Relying on forward observers linked to concealed batteries by telephone or signal flags, artillery was no longer limited to firing at targets within view.

If the experience of the war from 1914 to 1917 taught anything, it was that artillery ruled the battlefield. But American gunnery lagged Europe's by several decades almost until the moment of its entry into the war. American officers in the early 1900s only grudgingly acknowledged that modern artillery would dominate the infantry in modern warfare. Many still held that too much artillery was a liability because it hindered movement. Some officers came to the realization, with the Europeans, that Japanese fire superiority over the Russians in 1905 had resulted from better organization and use of their guns, rather than the quality of the weapons themselves. Senior artillerists began pressing for a new doctrine that emphasized indirect fire. This was partially achieved in the *Drill Regulations* of 1907, which said, "By rendering the guns inconspicuous, or entirely concealing them, their sustained service may be counted upon, while the difficulties of the enemy in locating his targets and adjusting his firing are increased."6 Additionally, some artillery officers were aware of tactical developments in Europe and particularly of the dominating role of artillery. But this perception conflicted with the prevailing US doctrine, which stressed light artillery in support of mobile offensives, and such insights were limited to the few artillery officers who studied their profession. The reports of the US military observers in Europe, which could have revolutionized American gunnery, contained almost no useful information. In any event, they were sent to the War College, filed, and forgotten.7

American weaponry also lagged behind. At the end of the nineteenth century, the standard American field gun lacked a recoil-absorption system. The powder charge and the shell had to be loaded separately, a slow process. The propellant and the bursting charge were black powder, which proved an almost fatal failing in Cuba in 1898, where modern Spanish artillery was able several times to silence or disperse the American batteries by firing at their white smoke cloud. Attempts at modernization began soon afterward. A series of unsuccessful experimental designs eventually led to the development of the Model 1902 3-inch field gun, the first true rapid-fire artillery piece to be used by the US Army. But field trials showed that the shells of the Model 1902, whether conventional or high explosive, were ineffective against fortifications, so guns and howitzers of heavier caliber were developed. The guns fired "fixed" ammunition, but the howitzer designs still separated the powder charge from the shell.*

---

* Guns fire their shells in a relatively flat trajectory and are effective against troops and equipment in the open. Howitzers shoot at a high angle, producing a plunging fire that can reach into entrenchments and fortifications. Field guns (as opposed to fixed guns, such as coastal artillery) are generally lighter and more mobile than howitzers.

For these innovations to have any effect, the gunners would have to be trained in their use, and therein lay failure. The existing training establishment still clung to the old direct fire methods; it was not until 1911 that the School of Fire for Field Artillery was established at Fort Sill, Oklahoma to give both practical and theoretical instruction. Moreover, the development of an effective artillery arm was throttled by the parsimony of Congress and the War Department. Training was mostly in the classroom; budget constraints limited ammunition, which curtailed the amount of range practice. Firing in bad weather or at night was prohibited, as if gunners need not worry about such conditions. The commandant of the School of Fire protested almost as soon as he was appointed that failure to allot adequate funds for training would cause the horse and foot soldiers to pay "in blood for the mistakes made by our [artillery] arm, through the lack of [training] opportunity given to its officers. A field artillery captain who cannot direct the fire of his battery is useless ... to any army."[8] His words were prophetic.

The Army didn't catch up until after its divisions had reached Europe. Colonel Conrad Lanza, a senior artillery officer in the AEF, wrote after the war that, upon arriving in France, US field artillery officers expected to find the enemy guns arrayed on opposing ridgelines as in the Civil War, and that fire would be "for effect"—that is, the gunners would be able to watch their targets explode as they were hit. Their French hosts had to point out that enemy guns were generally invisible, even from forward observation posts. [9]

The situation was no better with regard to the weapons themselves. General Crozier had long maintained that supplying artillery for a large army would take two years. But he compounded the problem by relegating the successful Model 1902 3-incher to the training camps in favor of a new, experimental 75mm gun, the design of which had some advantages over the French model of the same caliber. This gun, the Model 1916, turned out to be inaccurate, unreliable, and difficult to manufacture. The only option in the end was to buy guns directly from the French and British once the Army arrived in France. No gun made in the States ever reached the battlefield.

The very latest development in European artillery was gas.[*] Several types were used, depending on whether the commander using it wanted an immediate but short-lived effect on enemy troops or persistent contamination

---

[*] Although repugnant to modern sensibilities (and to many at the time), poison gas was a fact of warfare in 1915–18, and a historical discussion must deal with it as such.

of fortifications and gun positions. Major General William Gorgas, the US Surgeon General, sent medical officers to the British and French to observe gas warfare. They reported on the medical aspects, including diagnosis and treatment, beginning in 1916. But neither General Gorgas nor the Adjutant General, Major General Henry P. McCain, took any steps to develop protective devices. In February 1917 the Quartermaster General, Major General Henry G. Sharpe, finally took notice of reports of poison gas, and asked the Adjutant General which bureau was responsible for supplying gas masks. No one knew. As the country entered the war, the Adjutant General, the Chief of Ordnance, the Quartermaster General, and the Surgeon General were still discussing the problem.[10]

The Army's late start at developing modern guns and fire doctrine, compounded by the prewar lack of funds to train gunners and manufacture weapons, meant that the rapid expansion of the Army for service in Europe was doomed to chaos, at least as far as the artillery was concerned. In 1914 the US Army had six regiments of field artillery comprising 266 officers and 4,992 enlisted men. In response to the National Defense Act of 1916, this establishment was increased to nine regiments by April 1917. With an additional 16 regiments of National Guard field artillery, the total complement was 1,130 officers and 21,874 men at various levels of training, mostly low.[11] On their shoulders would fall the initial burden of instructing the roughly 150 brand-new artillery regiments that would be part of the two million-man army being sent to France.

Aviation, which the Americans had invented, was in an equally parlous state. In 1908 Orville Wright crashed a plane during a demonstration flight, killing an Army Signal Corps lieutenant who was a passenger, the first air fatality ever. That event, coupled with preoccupation over Army reforms and the purchase of traditional but necessary weapons, was the likely reason Congress failed to appropriate any funds in 1909 or 1910. By late 1909 the air arm consisted of one Wright biplane and one pilot, Lieutenant Benjamin D. Foulois (who later was to command Pershing's Air Service). His budget, obtained from the Signal Corps, was $150. Between 1908 and 1913 France and Germany each spent $22 million on military and naval aviation; Russia spent $12 million and even Belgium spent $2 million. The United States spent $430,000. An aviation section of the Signal Corps was not authorized until 1914. On declaring war, the Army had only 65 officers, of whom 26 were actual pilots, and 1,100 enlisted and civilian personnel. The Signal

Corps prior to 1917 had bought only 142 aircraft.[12] Eventually, of the 6,624 combat aircraft operated by the US Air Service, the French supplied 4,879, 1,440 came from the US (all of them DH-4 bombing and observation craft based on a British design), and 291 were from the British and Italians.[*][13]

Small arms was virtually the only category of weapon in which the US Army made a respectable showing in April 1917. In 1911 the .45-caliber Colt automatic pistol replaced the .38-caliber revolver, which had failed to stop charging Moro tribesmen in the Philippines; it was to remain the standard service pistol for over 80 years. The war with Spain had revealed the need for a rifle that could compete with the German-made Mauser, so in 1903 the Army introduced the modern Springfield, a bolt-action weapon (as were all service rifles of the time) that fired a five-round clip with high accuracy. On the eve of war, the Army had 890,000 of the excellent .30-06 Model 1903 in inventory.[14]

But a large collection of modern rifles did not make an army. An article published by a German officer in 1911 concluded that, if judged by the standards of Europe and Japan, the American Army did not exist. It was "deficient in training and in everything else that is necessary for the constitution of an armed force." It is more than likely that this perspective encouraged the German High Command to ignore the possibility of a significant American military contribution when it considered resuming unrestricted submarine warfare in the winter of 1916–17.[15] Admiral von Holtzendorff's statement to the Kaiser on January 9, 1917 that "not one American will land on the Continent" was not vainglory; it was a sober assessment of the situation.

At the beginning, it was not clear that America would need much of an army at all. Many thought that aid to the Allies would be limited to loans, ships, weapons, and food. The New York *Morning Telegraph* said, "They don't need more warriors, they want money and food, and munitions of

---

* Much of the American-made equipment was faulty. The airframe of the DH-4 was not strong enough to survive the engine vibrations at full throttle. DH-4s had pressure-fed fuel lines but no self-sealing gas tanks, which meant that a single hit could engulf the whole plane in flames. They were nicknamed "flaming coffins." (John H. Morrow, Jr., *The Great War in the Air: Military Aviation from 1909 to 1921* (Washington: Smithsonian Institution Press, 1993), p. 338.)

war."[16] Many officers thought that the prevailing shortage of transport would prevent sending more than a token force. The British and French at first insisted they did not want an American army, they wanted only to recruit several hundred thousand Americans into their units. Congress certainly did not understand what it had gotten into when it declared war; a few days later the chairman of the Senate Appropriations Committee stated, "Congress will not permit American soldiers to be sent to Europe."[17] It took two months, until June 5, to authorize $3 billion to purchase the first installment of weapons for a million men; another $3.7 billion for the second million men did not pass until early October.

The decision to send a sizeable American force to France was made gradually and in spite of President Wilson's resistance. In mid-April, British and French military missions met with Newton D. Baker, the Secretary of War, and a board consisting of Major General Hugh L. Scott, the Army Chief of Staff, Major General Tasker H. Bliss, the Assistant Chief of Staff, and General Kuhn to coordinate the American assistance. Marshal Joseph Joffre, the French former commander-in-chief, hero of the battle of the Marne and leader of the French mission, was the first to realize that the Americans would never consent to have their soldiers absorbed into French and British units. His request to the General Staff board was to send one division to France as soon as possible, to raise morale by showing the Stars and Stripes on the Continent. This should be followed quickly by technical troops, such as transportation units, for the Allies' immediate use. He advised the Americans to create and train a large army, to be kept independent. Although the British privately insisted that they mostly needed money and ships, officially they seconded Joffre's recommendation. On May 2 Joffre met with Wilson and urged sending a division within a month; Wilson agreed. But by May 24 or 25 Baker understood that sending a token American force to France, while other units trained for a year or more at home, would not suffice. On May 27 he wrote Wilson urging that the public would not support a drawn-out training program at home justified by only a vague plan of future combat. In addition, waiting increased the risk that France or Russia would collapse before American troops could appear in combat. Even so, the President continued to toy with other solutions. Baker tolerated Wilson's distractions until November, when he put his foot down and insisted that the administration honor its pledge to support the British and French on the Western Front. Wilson finally acquiesced.

The Army's chief problem, even more than the lack of munitions, was its lack of men and officers. It was clear that many new soldiers would be needed—but how many, and how would they be recruited? General Joseph E. Kuhn's War College Division at first recommended a relatively small army of one and a half million, figuring that anything larger would impede the vital effort to send money, food, and munitions to the Allies. The Regular Army and the National Guard would stay home, so they could train the new divisions. General Pershing, as he sailed to France with his staff in early June, figured that one million men should be sent to France as soon as possible, with further numbers to be determined after his arrival.[18] For 50 years the US had not mustered an army close to this size.

When it came to finding these men, two alternatives presented themselves: volunteerism and conscription. With the partial exception of the Union Army during the later years of the Civil War, all of the United States' fighting forces had been made up of volunteers, and many assumed that the same course would prevail in this war. Prominent old-stock Americans such as Theodore Roosevelt, Oliver Wendell Holmes, and Wilson himself perpetuated the image of war as romantic and liberating. Princeton president John Grier Hibben rhapsodized over the "chastening and purifying effect of armed conflict." This ethos was disseminated in many popular movies and books, which portrayed war in terms of the medieval chivalry familiar to American minds from the novels of Sir Walter Scott. The pictures they painted of willing sacrifice among heroic comrades neutralized the factual accounts of slaughter at the Somme and Verdun. Within three months of the declaration of war, 301,000 men had volunteered for the Army and the National Guard and another 109,000 for the Navy.[19]

Not everyone welcomed the idea of a volunteer army. Regular Army officers, most of whom had led volunteers in the West, had a poor opinion of them, believing with some justification that they represented the dregs of society:

> *We had our choice of going to the army or the jail,*
> *Or it's up the Hudson River with a copper take a sail*[20]

ran the old soldiers' marching song, and their officers considered that men who would sign up to spend much of their adult lives at a succession of isolated, flyblown outposts with low pay and few prospects must be drunks, misfits, or criminals. Conscription, on the other hand, would summon the best of the nation's manhood—the strong, healthy field hands, the skilled factory workers, the educated professionals—who were used to getting the job done.

Wilson and Baker at first were against conscription. Wilson felt that the draft was a betrayal of the American ideal of individual freedom in favor of the European ethos of compulsion. In February 1917 Wilson and Baker refused to back proposals for conscription-based Universal Military Training. But that same month, soon after the United States and Germany had broken diplomatic relations, General Scott, the Chief of Staff, insisted to Baker that the draft be implemented immediately if the US should enter the fight. "If you do not secure conscription now," he wrote, "you will already have lost this war."[21] He cited the experience of the British, who waited until 1916 to institute a draft, while unrestrained volunteering drained the mines and factories of workers. Baker agreed and told Wilson. Once conscription was presented as a rational (i.e., "progressive") way of allocating labor rather than as coercive militarism, Wilson adopted it and ordered that a law to that effect be drafted so it would be ready to present to Congress if the need should arise. In his speech to Congress on April 2 asking for a declaration of war, Wilson specified that the manpower buildup would be based on "the principle of universal liability to service."[22]

Democrats in Congress, especially from the South and West, strongly opposed Wilson's draft law. The House Military Affairs Committee voted 13 to 8 in favor of a bill that supported expansion of the military through volunteers rather than the draft. And Wilson might have compromised with Congress but that former Rough Rider Teddy Roosevelt and former Chief of Staff General Leonard Wood launched a public campaign to raise a volunteer division with Roosevelt at its head. The scheme was militarily ludicrous. TR wanted most of the officers—if possible, most of the enlisted men—to be Ivy League graduates, and wanted to give staff positions to offspring of French nobility, in memory of Lafayette. The easiest way to prevent such distractions was to discourage volunteering in general. The Selective Service Act allowed the Regular Army, Navy, and National Guard to accept volunteers, but not the National Army, which would eventually provide 77 percent of the men. Wilson signed the draft bill on May 18. As he did so, he set June 5 as registration day. In his proclamation he called selective service "a selection from a nation which has volunteered in mass."[23]

But the draft as an institution was still unpopular in the country and in Congress, largely because of the bad experience in the Civil War. To overcome this antipathy, Baker instructed the head of the Selective Service System, General Enoch Crowder, to administer the draft through local civilian boards appointed by the state governors. This avoided the need to post conscription officers in communities or to turn government facilities such as post offices into draft centers. It worked; on June 5 over nine and a half million men between the ages of 21 and 30 signed up for the draft lottery. Eventually, roughly 24 million men registered at 4,648 local draft boards, which provided 2,758,542 men to the armed forces, almost all of whom went to the Army.[24] Crowder wrote after the war, "Conscription in America was not ... drafting of the unwilling. The citizens themselves had willingly come forward and pledged their service."[25]*

"Willingly" was a term open to interpretation. In Baltimore, soon to be the home city of the 313th Infantry Regiment, the *Sun* kept up a fusillade of headlines such as:

GO IN SERVICE AT ONCE
Slackers Must Step Up To Fill Places
Of Those Who Are Declared Exempt[26]

and

MANY SLACKERS REGISTER
More Than 100 Of Them Caught
In City-Wide Sweep[27]

Blacks, said the *Sun*, were under particular suspicion of being draft dodgers. They were often rounded up on the street and ordered to present their baptismal certificates to the US Marshal in order to establish their ages and identities.[28] No doubt such propaganda, coupled with more coercive measures such as slacker raids and the vigilant surveillance of "patriotic" neighbors, turned many civilians into "willing" conscripts. In the end, about 337,000 men subject to the draft, or about 12 percent, avoided conscription. As David M. Kennedy has written, "Thus rudely was the fiction abandoned that the government merely selected from a people who had 'volunteered in mass.'"[29]

---

* In the words of David M. Kennedy, "This insistence that the draft was in reality a voluntary affair should not be dismissed as willful buncombe, though the government was assuredly not above a little pious flummery to gain the confidence of a public whose acceptance of conscription was in considerable doubt." (Kennedy, *Over Here*, p. 153.)

Another stereotype shattered by the draft was the image of the American soldier as the classic White Anglo-Saxon Protestant. The vast immigration of the previous 30 years dictated that many recruits would have been born in foreign lands, mostly in southern and eastern Europe. In the event, over half a million conscripts were immigrants, making up 18 percent of the Army's manpower, and children of immigrants added many thousands more.[30] The Army was faced with two tasks regarding the huge influx of foreign-born soldiers, many of them European Jews and Catholics. Delighted to have access to this huge pool of manpower, the leadership knew it faced two problems before they could be turned into effective fighters. First, the Army had to build up the immigrants' morale as soldiers. Second, it had to impart values of loyalty, patriotism, and hard work. It took pains to maintain their morale, partly by accommodating their cultural and religious needs and partly by recruiting Progressive reformers, leaders in the ethnic communities, and social workers used to dealing with immigrants to acculturate the newcomers to American and Army life.

This effort was manifested at the top by the Foreign-Speaking Soldier Subsection (FSS) of Military Intelligence, created in January 1918 by the Secretary of War, Newton D. Baker. The FSS visited Army training camps and reported on the cultural, linguistic, and religious problems the immigrants faced. As a result of these investigations, it instituted "development battalions organized by native language and led by officers who were native speakers. The effect was dramatic; before the arrival of the FSS, virtually all of the foreign-language speakers refused to go overseas. Afterward, 85 percent (later, 92 percent) were eager to go to France.*[31] Over time the immigrants became accepted, if not as equals, then as legitimate soldiers. A private at Camp Oglethorpe, Georgia, wrote in his diary for March 28, 1918: "This is

---

* Training immigrants could have its lighter moments, at least as seen from a later time. At Camp Upton on Long Island, three Morris Cohens served in the same company. In another example, a drill sergeant, frustrated by foreign names he couldn't pronounce, finally blurted out, "Well, who in hell ever this is, answer here!" A captain in the 306th Infantry took over a company and put it through its drill. It did fine until he rearranged the men by height to achieve a more military appearance. At his first order, "Right by squads," some men obeyed but most went off in the wrong direction or milled about aimlessly. The officer inquired of the NCOs as to what was going on and discovered that the men had previously organized themselves into squads by language; when an order was given in English, the corporal in charge of the squad translated it into the appropriate tongue. (Christopher M. Sterba, "The Melting Pot Goes to War: Italian and Jewish Immigrants in America's Great Crusade, 1917–1919" (Ph.D. thesis, Brandeis University, 1999), pp. 230–31.)

Jewish Passover, and to celebrate we are eating roast pork and matzoth bread. Today, sausage; and tomorrow being Good Friday, we shall probably have hot cross buns, matzoth, roast beef, and ham."*[32]

Parallel to the search for men was the search for officers to lead them. In April 1917 the Regular Army and National Guard between them had only 18,000 officers; over 200,000 would be required. As part of the prewar Preparedness movement, General Leonard Wood had organized a camp at Plattsburg in upstate New York at which Regulars had given some elementary officer training to about 16,000 civilians. Another 16,000 could be obtained by promoting qualified enlisted men, and specialized services, such as the Medical Department, granted commissions to 70,000 civilians; the rest had to be trained from scratch, and quickly.

On May 15, 16 officer training camps based on the Plattsburg model went into service at 13 Army posts, with 30,000 candidates enrolled, most of them from the educated upper middle class—Ivy Leaguers, businessmen, and professionals. The course lasted three months and concentrated on basic soldiering skills. But the training hardly went beyond that of enlisted men, and suffered the same shortages of qualified trainers, equipment, and facilities. Leadership and tactics were given little attention; such tactics as were taught were based on the Army's recent experience fighting Indians and guerrillas. Eventually, almost half of the officers who served in the AEF were trained in this way. The rest came from officers' training programs in the divisional camps, which later gave way to eight consolidated officers' training schools. Despite their training's shortcomings, in the judgment of military historian Maurice Matloff, "these officers provided the Army with a leadership far surpassing that of the average new officer in any previous war."[33]

---

* This discussion may give the impression that the Regular Army was amenable to minorities and immigrants. It was not; anti-Semitism, racism, and xenophobia prevailed. The racial theories of eugenicist Charles Davenport, later adopted by the Nazis, were taught at the Army War College. Many officers, some of whom became major personalities of World War II such as George Patton, George van Horn Moseley, Sherman Miles, and Albert C. Wedemeyer, believed that white, Christian America was under attack from the greedy and devious Jews, the brutish and sex-crazed blacks, and the indolent, socialistic swarms of southern and eastern Europe. Many of those who did not hold such views, such as Dwight D. Eisenhower, tended to tolerate them in others. See Joseph W. Bendersky, *The "Jewish Threat": Anti-Semitic Politics of the U.S. Army* (New York: Basic Books, 2000); Arthur E. Barbeau and Florette Henri, *The Unknown Soldiers: African-American Troops in World War I* (Philadelphia: Temple University Press, 1974); and Jean Edward Smith, *Eisenhower in War and Peace* (New York: Random House, 2012), pp. 95–96.

As it turned out, the weakness in the officer corps of the AEF lay not in its junior officers, but in the higher commands and their staffs. The vast majority of the senior officers of 1917 had been trained at the US Military Academy at West Point. The Academy at the end of the nineteenth century was an intellectual backwater, caught in its memories of the Civil War and in reverence for its heroes. Traditions—including the traditional curriculum—"were as carefully preserved as the captured cannon on Trophy Point."[34] All ideas for curricular reform were rejected by the Academic Board, whose members were themselves Academy products. The Corps of Cadets looked down on any of its members who showed any military ambition. In fact, the institution was primarily an engineering school, and status accrued to those who did well in mathematics and the sciences and who stood high in their class. The only military skills the graduating cadets had besides riding and fencing were small-unit infantry and cavalry tactics, how to work guns large and small, and the technical details of equipment and weapons. The Board of Visitors of the House of Representatives was moved to ask, in its 1884 report, how the Academy could fulfill its purpose of turning out military leaders if it paid scant attention to matters such as leadership, supply, sanitation, and training of troops.[35]

Elihu Root had introduced an element of professionalism, but no more than an element, into the Regular Army officer corps. Between 1900 and 1902, he and his advisers instituted sweeping reforms in the education of officers. At the base of their system were schools at each major army post that taught junior lieutenants a standardized curriculum of tactical and administrative duties. Those who excelled went on to schools for the technical branches (signals, artillery, engineers) or to the School of the Line and the Staff College at Fort Leavenworth. At the top of the pile was the Army War College, which was to teach strategy, mobilization, training, and logistics. (Over time, the curricula of the War College and the Staff School converged until they were indistinguishable.) General Tasker H. Bliss, the first War College president, stated its educational policy: Officers must "learn things by doing things." These things included analyzing map problems involving large bodies of troops, augmented by tactical rides over the actual terrain. But the emphasis was on battles of maneuver such as Chancellorsville, Antietam, the Peninsula, and Gettysburg. The siege of Petersburg, closer to the future experience in France, was given little attention. Also, the emphasis on the Civil War, combined with the method of re-enacting the roles of commanders and staffs, paid little attention to the implications of vastly greater firepower for the modern battlefield. They would have done better to have studied the Russo-Japanese War.

As the Army itself was very small, no practical experience commanding large units could be had. The closest many graduates of the service schools came was the joint Army–National Guard exercises held intermittently in the decade before the war, some of which included as many as 125,000 troops. These were expensive and unrealistic from a tactical point of view, but they gave the regular officers assigned as instructors, observers, umpires, or assistant directors the opportunity to manage and observe large bodies of troops in the field. The men had to be fed, equipped, transported, and maneuvered on a scale not normally seen by junior (or even senior) officers. The maneuvers also supplied the human factor— fatigue, discomfort, miscommunication, frustration—that was missing in classroom exercises.

Many of the officers who would lead the divisions of the AEF had combat experience, only some of which would prove beneficial on the Western Front. All of the division commanders who got to France and about half of their chiefs of staff served during the Spanish-American War or the Philippine Insurrection, and a few fought in the Boxer Rebellion of 1900–01. Combat consisted of small-unit actions typified by marches through hostile country; short, sharp attacks against enemy strong points; and, in the Philippines and China, guerrilla warfare. More usefully, they learned to operate in hostile territory, control their fear, and make independent decisions; and they experienced the reality of war rather than the scholarly, literary, or official views of it. While their experience and training did not relate to the conditions of the Western Front of 1917, in the words of Edward Coffman:

> One could argue that graduates of Leavenworth and the War College and those who had seen combat in the Spanish War and the Philippine Insurrection were as professionally prepared, if not more so, than their French and British counterparts had been, on the basis of their schooling and colonial war experience, in 1914.[36]

So through improvisation, trial, and much error, the Army began to gird itself with materiel, men, and the officers to command both. But it still had to learn how to fight.

The 79th Division, authorized by the Selective Service Act of 1917, came into existence on August 25 of that year. Like almost all of the new American divisions, it comprised two infantry brigades (the 157th and 158th), an artillery brigade (the 154th), and a machine gun battalion (the 310th). Also assigned to the division were an engineer regiment (the 304th), a field signal battalion, a sanitary (i.e., medical and ambulance) train, and trains for ammunition, supplies, and military police. Each infantry brigade contained two infantry regiments (the 313th and 314th in the 157th Brigade, the 315th and 316th in the 158th Brigade). Additionally, each brigade had its own machine gun battalion. The artillery brigade contained three regiments of field artillery—two light (75mm guns) and one heavy (155mm guns) plus a battery of trench mortars. This organization would hold more or less throughout the war, except for a swap of artillery brigades upon reaching France and, later, a reshuffling of infantry brigade assignments under rather dramatic circumstances that we shall encounter. At first, of course, these units existed on paper only. They contained essentially nothing; officers, men, and materiel would have to be found, assigned, transported, housed, and organized.

On August 26, the 79th received its commander, newly promoted Major General Joseph E. Kuhn, and his staff, led by Lieutenant Colonel Tenney Ross. By some measures, they were the ideal pair to command a division. Kuhn, short and trim of build, meticulous of dress and bearing and sporting a silver brush mustache and a penetrating gaze, had accumulated in his 32 years of service a list of credentials that made him almost unique among American general officers. As a result of his experience, or perhaps because of his innate character, he radiated a confidence that inspired his men but often irritated his colleagues. First in his West Point Class of 1885—one year ahead of Pershing—he entered the Corps of Engineers and served with distinction in a number of posts around the country, eventually returning to the Military Academy to serve as head of the Department of Practical Military Engineering. When the Moros in the Philippines revolted, he commanded a battalion of engineers in the force sent to suppress them. During the Russo-Japanese War he was a military observer attached to the Japanese Army, where he witnessed the

THE 79TH DIVISION AS RAISED AT FORT MEADE, AUGUST 3, 1917

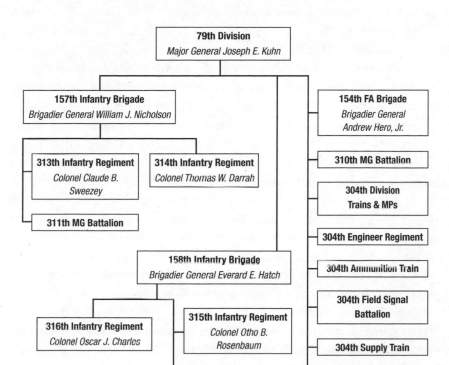

first employment of modern artillery, machine guns, fortifications, and assault tactics. In 1906 he was a US observer at the German Army's annual maneuvers, where he met with the Kaiser and discussed strategy and tactics. Among his assignments upon returning to the United States was a term as Director of Instruction at the US Army Command and General Staff College at Fort Leavenworth.

Kuhn's most important postings, from the point of view of an incipient division commander, were his appointments in December 1914 as leader of the US military mission to Germany and in March 1915 as military attaché to the American Embassy in Berlin. His arrival coincided with the end of the mobile phase of the war and the beginning of what Kuhn called "the siege of the middle powers"—trench warfare.[37] Soon after his appointment, news arrived in Berlin of the large loan from New York bankers to the French and British and of the placing of large Allied orders for munitions with American manufacturers. This was the first intimation to the Germans that America would be neutral only in the most formal sense. Thus began the Germans' public and private hostility to America that would plague Kuhn's mission during its lifetime.

At first the American mission under Kuhn was allowed extensive access to the German commanders and front-line positions. Kuhn inspected the German lines in the Vosges (where he came under French artillery fire), the Meuse, the Russian front in Poland, and even Louvain, the medieval city the Germans had destroyed in their August 1914 advance to the Marne. But mounting German hostility, including the refusal of some German officers to accommodate or even meet with the American mission, soon made clear to Kuhn and the rest that their effectiveness was almost at an end. James W. Gerard, the American ambassador, agreed, and arranged for their departure. But the War Department ordered Kuhn, much to his chagrin, to stay on to replace the departing US military attaché. As the attaché of a neutral country, Germany had to treat him with the courtesy due to all other neutral diplomats.

Kuhn's first field excursion as military attaché was to the Flanders front. Although the Germans had recently launched a successful gas attack to take the British and French positions opposing them, Kuhn's German guides did not mention the use of gas and he did not find out about it for another two months, and then from the foreign press. On the way to Ypres, he heard (from a German officer) the news of the sinking of the *Lusitania*, which led him to expect a quick break in diplomatic relations; the break did not come for two more years. While in the Ypres sector Kuhn visited the front-line position at St Julian Farm; he was to visit the farm again in January 1918 when it was back in British hands and America was in the war. When Warsaw fell in August 1916, Kuhn was in the headquarters of General Max von Gallwitz, whom he would face two years later in Lorraine. On subsequent trips to the Western Front he observed from up close the German "Big Berthas" using balloon-directed fire at British positions. In Poland he watched German engineers throw a bridge across the Vistula and three divisions cross it in rapid order.

But as the probability of America joining the Allies increased and anti-American feeling grew, Kuhn was progressively excluded from the groups of attachés sent to visit the front. Although this was against protocol, Kuhn registered no complaint until confronted with the situation by the Chief of

Intelligence of the German General Staff. "For once I lost my temper," he wrote after the war, "and I fear that my conversation transgressed the usual bounds of diplomatic usage."[38] His usefulness at an end, the War Department ordered Kuhn home. He left on December 5, 1916. Months after his departure Gerard praised Kuhn as "perhaps our greatest American expert in modern war," and said that, as president of the Army War College (Kuhn's next posting), "his teachings will prove of the greatest value to the armies of the United States."[39]

Something of a hero within the Army for having effectively been expelled from Germany, Kuhn continued to enjoy a flourishing career upon his return. When the National Defense Act of 1916 created four new positions for major generals and 19 for brigadier generals, all of the appointments were based on seniority rather than merit except for Kuhn's; it was clear he was being groomed for greater things. (At one point, rumors circulated that he was to be made Army Chief of Staff. Kuhn wrote to his wife, "I don't believe it and I hope not."[40]) The Presidency of the Army War College was indeed Kuhn's next post, where, as an ex-officio member of the General Staff, he was at the center of American war planning. One of his early tasks was to participate in an informal committee of four generals, including Major General Tasker Bliss, Assistant Chief of Staff, to appoint new generals. Meeting over three nights, the group made their selections from a list of colonels; their recommendations were approved by Secretary of War Baker and passed by Congress with no changes. One hundred and twenty freshly minted generals now owed their appointments, in part, to Joseph Kuhn.[41]

As war approached, the Army Chief of Staff, General Scott, had Kuhn write a detailed "Plan for a National Army" based on the idea of universal military training (see Chapter 2). It called for a five-year buildup culminating in a regular army of 310,000 supported by two and a half million trained citizen-reservists. But despite the approach of war, the administration in January 1917 would consider neither universal military training nor a draft, so the plan went nowhere. Once war was declared, Kuhn participated in the decision to create divisions that were double the size of the Allies', and conferred with French Field Marshal Joffre on whether and what kind of force to send to France. Along with Generals Bliss and Scott and General Enoch Crowder, the Provost Marshal, Kuhn prepared—at Secretary of War Baker's request—"a draft of legislation to provide an army of one million men to meet possible contingencies."[42] This became the Selective Service

Act of 1917. In short, the commander of the 79th Division had more exposure to the planning and practice of modern warfare than possibly any officer in the United States Army.

But Kuhn had significant weaknesses. For a start, being first in one's class at West Point was not the accomplishment in 1885 that it would later become. Ignoring military theory, leadership, strategy, and tactics (except for those of small units), the Academy taught engineering and its military applications, primarily weapons and fortifications. Kuhn inherited this mentality of single-minded attention to technical detail. His reports from Manchuria, although comprehensive and thorough, were pedantic and unimaginative. He noted the devastating effect of high explosive shells, the destruction wrought by machine guns, the importance of fixed fortifications, and the dominance of position warfare over mobile tactics; but he failed to draw any lessons that might have informed American doctrine as the country entered the era of modern war. He wrote:

> If there is one fact more than any other which has impressed itself on my mind it is that in its general features at least, the war was conducted by both sides along strictly orthodox lines. The formation of infantry for the attack, the massing of guns, and the concentration of their fire, the value and employment of field fortifications, the siege of permanently fortified localities and many other features, all savor strongly of the textbook. So far as I am able to judge, the recognized rules and principles for conducting warfare underwent no serious modification in their application.[43]

After all, despite their massive losses, the Japanese frontal attacks succeeded. So among the "rules and principles" that Kuhn, along with most western observers, derived from the experience was the continued dominance of the bayonet, even over fire superiority, as the essential element of tactics.

Kuhn's most critical deficiency was that he had never commanded a combat unit, not so much as a platoon. He therefore had no experience in either the tactical or the administrative aspects of field command. This might have been overcome in part by education (after all, few commanders of American combat units had seen action in their careers), but his formal training was not up to the standards of many American generals, even of the time. He attended neither the Leavenworth Schools nor the Army War College, although he taught at the former and was president of the latter. Thus he did not benefit from their curricula, which taught staff work, order writing, combined-arms operations, logistics, mobilization, and training of troops. Of equal importance, the schools taught a common way of approaching problems that led to a "harmonious style of thinking ... among their graduates."[44] Kuhn, the engineer, would not be a part of this fraternity.

Why was Kuhn picked for a field command at all? Apparently, no record of the selection process survives. Most likely the War Department, strapped for senior officers, saw him as available and fit to organize the division's training. No doubt Kuhn's earlier prestigious assignments made him appear a safe choice. But Pershing had his own criteria for division commanders, and as head of the AEF did not feel bound by the decisions of the War Department. Just because an officer was fit to organize and train a division in the United States did not mean Pershing wanted him to command it in the field. He insisted on young, vigorous subordinates who were loyal to him. A somewhat cryptic note in Pershing's files in the National Archives may shed some light. Headed "Confidential Memorandum for the Commander-in-Chief" and dated February 22, 1918, it was issued by the office of the AEF Chief of Staff but is not signed. Nevertheless, it almost certainly reflects the personal opinions if not the literal words of General James G. Harbord, Pershing's Chief of Staff and close personal confidant. It records the author's impressions of about a dozen major generals and their fitness for divisional command. With respect to General Kuhn it reads:

> One of the star men of the Engineers. 53 years of age, probably in the prime of his mental vigor. He is slight, not encumbered by superfluous flesh and should be physically active. I never knew him until last year at the War College. Great things were expected from him there but he was a disappointment ... General Kuhn has had perhaps better opportunity for observing war than any other officer of the army: in Manchuria and Germany. He impresses me as being an extremely conceited man. He should be given an opportunity to command a division.[45]

So Pershing allowed Kuhn to continue to lead the 79th in France because he was young and vigorous enough and had seen modern warfare, but in spite of his less-than-stellar performance at the War College, his irritating demeanor, and his lack of command experience. (The "star men of the Engineers" remark is almost certainly a slighting reference; field officers considered the engineers a separate species. Kuhn was the only one of 41 divisional commanders who came from the Corps of Engineers.)

Any gaps in Kuhn's background were more than filled by his chief of staff, Lieutenant Colonel Tenney Ross, a veteran of the frontier army. Tall and round-faced, with a wide mouth and wide-set eyes, Ross was an imposing figure. As a youth he had been appointed to West Point by President Grover Cleveland, but he acceded to his father's wishes by attending Georgetown Law College and going to work in a bank. When the Spanish-American War broke out, Ross took quick advantage of the government's call for volunteers and joined the 3rd Infantry Regiment in Cuba. When the regiment went back to its base at Fort Snelling, Minnesota he went with them as a Regular Army officer. Soon afterward, a group of Chippewa Indians on the Leech Lake, Minnesota, reservation, angered by the local Indian Agency's policy of seemingly arbitrary arrests and by exploitation at the hands of lumber companies, engaged with local law-enforcement officers in a scuffle that got out of hand. A group of soldiers commanded by Major Melville Wilkinson and Lieutenant Ross was sent to Leech Lake to help the civil authorities. Shooting broke out; Major Wilkinson was killed and Ross took over. By the next day the Chippewa—none of whom had been killed—had dispersed, but seven soldiers were dead. At first it was reported that Ross was the officer who had been killed; it took some time for his anguished family to learn that he had emerged unscathed, although the crown of his hat was graced by a neat bullet hole. For this action he was awarded a Silver Star for gallantry. This was the last engagement fought between Native Americans and the United States Army.[46]

Subsequently, Ross attended the Staff College and the Infantry–Cavalry School at Leavenworth, where he graduated with distinction. As a recent service school graduate he almost certainly would have attended one of the joint Army-National Guard maneuvers held in 1904 (with 25,000 guardsmen and 10,000 regulars), 1906 (when seven were held), or 1908 (with eight held during the year). From a tactical point of view they were useless; but as the only peacetime occasions when large numbers of troops marched, ate, and bivouacked as a body, they would have been invaluable training for a divisional chief of staff headed to France.

After seeing action in the Philippines against the Moros in 1906 Ross returned to Washington where, among other things, he served on the General Staff for two years until the declaration of war. Now a lieutenant colonel in the National Army, he was assigned to the 79th Division as General Kuhn's chief of staff. To his job he brought a background of leadership and combat experience, augmented by formal training in military operations and staff work, all attributes that Kuhn himself lacked.

Ross was liked by the other officers of the division, but as an Old Army type he expected them to show a military punctilio rarely found among the civilians they recently had been. One officer of the 315th Regiment wrote of an episode early in the division's training:

> About this time the Division Commander believed the officers should be jacked up, so Colonel Ross, his Chief of Staff, was given the job and he did it in a tough way. The method was to tell regimental officers how rotten they were, that they didn't even look like officers, and more to the same effect. To correct this, his program was to take us to a more or less secluded field and put us through close order drill, all serving in the ranks. This may or may not have helped us, but it made Ross feel a lot better.[47]

The first job Kuhn and Ross faced was to get the 79th Division settled in its new training ground. This was to be Camp Meade, set among the rolling hills of Ann Arundel County, Maryland, about midway between Washington and Baltimore and about a 45-minute ride from either city on the interurban railroad. Named after the Union general who repulsed Robert E. Lee at Gettysburg, the camp occupied 4,000 acres and was planned with a capacity of 40,000 men. Construction began on July 2, 1917. Kuhn got his first view of the camp a week before he was due to take command, and it was disheartening. The site was one of the last the Army acquired. Only one-third of the work had been completed, barely a week and a half before the recruits were scheduled to start arriving. Water supply, sanitary system, and roads were nonexistent. Although materials and men littered the landscape, all was in chaos. An officer in the 315th Infantry Regiment described the scene:

> At this time, great gangs of darkies were clearing sites and blasting stumps, hiding under any small brush nearby until after the explosion, frightened ashen-grey one moment and singing heart-high the next. Trucks from Truck Company 328, which had only recently arrived from Texas, roared up and down the sandy roads, carrying piles of lumber and pipes, as well as cots and blankets for the first few barracks that were up. On many occasions, these trucks sank hub-deep in the soft Maryland sand, and it was no uncommon sight to see a mixed crowd of soldiers and laborers digging one of the mired trucks out of its over-soft resting place. Day and night the

pile-drivers were at work and were followed in turn by gangs of carpenters, erecting the framework of barracks, laying floors and putting on roofs, so that the Camp seemed to spring up from a waste almost by magic.[48]

On September 1, Camp Meade was still woefully unprepared to receive the coming deluge of 40,000 trainees. Living quarters and lavatories were less than half completed; the water distribution system lacked pumps and storage tanks and the piping was unfinished, although most of the material was on site; and less than half of the electrical equipment had been installed.

As a result of these and other deficiencies the arrival date of the first draftees at Camp Meade—alone among the Army's 32 training camps—was pushed back two weeks to September 19 with the proviso that 15,000 men be accepted on that date. Still, the facilities were not completely in order, and Kuhn's anxiety did not let up. He wrote to his wife, "Have just finished, 10:30 P.M., a session with my people and have wired Washington not to send any more men on Oct. 3 as state of supplies too precarious. It will make some consternation but I know I am right. I will not have my men uncomfortable or suffering for the sake of calling them in a few weeks earlier."[49] Fortunately, good weather and improvisation of water supplies and other necessaries made life bearable until the construction could be completed.

When finally finished on November 30, Camp Meade was the second-largest city in Maryland. It comprised 120 barracks and other wooden buildings, grouped in an inverted "U" around a parade ground. A railroad line passed along the southern edge; along it ran a mile of warehouses. Fifty miles of water pipe supplied three million gallons of water a day; 52 miles of sewer pipe carried away the waste.[50]

The first cadre arrived on August 25, the same day as Kuhn and Ross. It consisted of Regular Army officers who would command the division and its brigades and regiments; 600 enlisted men from the Regular Army who would be the first non-commissioned officers; and 1,100 graduates of the Officers' Training Camp at Fort Niagara, New York. Their quality was highly uneven. Of the Regulars, only a few knew how to organize and train a body of recruits. The graduates of Fort Niagara Training Camp fell into two groups, one with experience as enlisted men, NCOs, or officers in the National Guard and one with no experience beyond the three months of training they had just completed. Still, they adapted quickly. Several of the captains had been promoted from sergeant in the Regulars. Besides being expert in Army ways, they were colorful characters. One of them, a "tough old bird," was fond of saying, "In the army it's what you get away wid, not what you do." Despite his gruffness, the men respected him for having "a big heart, a great fund of common sense, and an unlimited supply of army knowledge ... He could command the loyalty of men as could few others in the division."[51] The others learned fast. On one occasion the colonel of the 315th turned to a company commander and asked:

"Captain Patterson, how many pairs of serviceable shoes have you in your Company?" This was a tough one, but he never batted an eye, and with no hesitation replied; "One hundred ninety-seven, Sir!" Even the Colonel smiled at that one, but he went on to the others and everyone had an exact figure to report. After Officers' Call they all hurried off to their Company clerks to check up, and needless to say no one was even close.[52]

The division's NCOs were drawn from men of the Regular Army, but they had seen only brief service, as the more experienced ones had been assigned to the new Regular Army divisions. Furthermore, the training cadres sent to train the National Army were often the way for the Regular Army divisions to get rid of their dead wood; they were of little help.

The first conscripts, who arrived on September 19, were mainly from the District of Columbia, Maryland, and Pennsylvania. Later they were joined by draftees from New York, Ohio, Rhode Island, and West Virginia. From these meager beginnings the division would grow in 11 months to its ultimate strength of 27,000 men.* One observer described the new recruits as they arrived at camp:

---

* The authorized strength of the American division was 28,000 men, twice as large as those of the British, French, or Germans. The large division caused many problems. Training camps had to be expanded. The burden on commanders and their staffs was greatly increased. Mobility was impaired. Coordination of transport and supply with the smaller British and French divisions was made more difficult. And no US officer, including Pershing, had ever commanded a normal-sized division, let alone one of double strength. Although the number of men was twice that of the Allied divisions, the artillery allotment was the same, so that on a per-man basis the US division was in fact weaker. (Donald Smythe, *Pershing: General of the Armies* (Bloomington: Indiana UP, 1986), pp. 36–38.) In the end, the large size of the American divisions actually reduced their staying power. This was because not enough troops were assigned to support services such as supply, burial, and casualty evacuation. The infantry themselves, already strained under combat, had to do these things for themselves. Even units that were not in combat were always exhausted. (Timothy K. Nenninger, "American Military Effectiveness in the First World War," in *Military Effectiveness, Vol. 1: The First World War*, ed. Allan R. Millett and Williamson Murray, Series on Defense and Foreign Policy (Boston, London, Sydney, Wellington: Allen & Unwin, 1988), p. 151.)

Nervous groups of company officers were at the detraining point an hour before train time, and when it arrived there poured out as motley a collection of individuals in appearance as ever gathered together, with clothes and bags of every description, some in shirt sleeves, some with coats, some with hats and some without, some carrying suitcases or paper parcels, some with nothing but the clothes on their backs.[53]

As soon as they arrived, recruits were issued uniforms, shoes, and hats of random sizes. This did not help their appearance, and allowed the top sergeants to take immediate advantage of their odd demeanor to chew them out for being unmilitary.

The thousands of men who poured daily into Camp Meade beginning on September 19 had to be organized into brigades, regiments, battalions, and companies. In addition, they had to be categorized according to their trades or technical abilities, if any—cooks, drivers, horse handlers, mechanics, and hundreds of other job descriptions. No procedures existed; the officers did it all by improvisation. In Kuhn's recollection, among the thousands of draftees were individuals with all of the necessary trades and professions; they were quickly identified and organized according to their specialty.[54] More likely, the experience of William L. Hanson, a physician in the 304th Sanitary Train, was typical:

> Nearly all the enlisted men in my ambulance company were from Detroit, where they had worked for the automobile companies. They were excellent auto and truck mechanics. So where were they assigned? To the mule-drawn vehicles, of course. Men who had never seen an internal combustion engine were assigned to the motorized ambulances.[55]

What struck the officers and NCOs most forcibly about their new charges was their diversity. Sergeant Edward Davies of the 315th got his first look at the men he would be training when he met them at the railroad station in Philadelphia on the way to Camp Meade:

> What a motley looking crew they are, Italians, Jews, Poles and what not. Of the 22 of them one other boy and myself are the only English speaking Americans in the bunch. Before we reached Baltimore M.D. our gang was pretty much under the weather, most of them had plenty of liquor with them, and they used it freely. A fight started just before we reached Baltimore but the MPs who boarded the train there put an end to it before any damage was done.[56]

A survey of the 310th Field Artillery Regiment showed how various the troops were. Represented were 15 nationalities—American, Russian, Italian, Polish, Austrian, Jewish, Swiss, English, Lithuanian, Greek, Bohemian, French, Irish, Rumanian, "and even German"; and four religions—Roman Catholic, Protestant, Greek Catholic, and Jewish. Of the roughly 1,500 enlisted men in the regiment, only 50 had ever attended college and 114 had no education at all.[57] The Baltimore press loved to play up the division's polyglot composition. Reporting on the arrival of recruits from Baltimore city and some of the Maryland counties, the *Sun* observed "good humor and cheerfulness" with much whistling and singing. Some of the Baltimoreans were downright boisterous: The first group to detrain was from the Eighth Ward, many of them "Bohemians" (Czechs) who had practiced marching and physical skills in their gymnastics clubs. They were followed by the Irish Fusiliers from the Tenth Ward who marched to their anthem, "There'll Be a Hot Time in the Old Town Tonight." On they came, the Baltimoreans by ward and the others by county. As fast as they got onto the platform they were formed into groups of 500 to 600 men by their newly trained officers and marched off to barracks. The *Sun* reported that the camp contained English, Germans, French, Italians, Poles, Dutch, Bohemians, Irish, Swedes, Scots, Spanish, Mexicans, an East Indian, a Japanese, and a "Chinaman."[58] This was a new phenomenon in an American army. Minorities had served before—Germans and Swedes in the Revolution; Germans, blacks, and Irish in the Civil War—but not so many, not mixed up within units, and not all at the same time. The last word on the recruits' ethnic variety will be left to Lieutenant J.W. Kress of the Machine Gun Company of the 314th Regiment:

> Looking at the numerous Italians, Russians, Poles, Hungarians, Greeks, Serbs, Slavs, Roumanians, and even Austrians and Germans in this vast Army, one at first wondered where the real American was keeping himself. Slowly the realization came that this conglomeration of nationalities was the real body of American people—they were the real Americans.[59]

One minority, however, was not counted among the "real Americans": the blacks. The War Department, desperate for manpower, decided early to draft African-Americans into the ranks. Southern Congressmen, driven as much by fear as by prejudice, bitterly opposed the War Department's intentions. Said Representative Richard S. Whaley of South Carolina:

We of the South cannot stand for inclusion of Negroes in the universal service plan ... [It] would accomplish the very thing which the South has always fought against, the placing of arms in the hands of a large number of Negroes and the training of them to work together in organized units.[60]

To mitigate the possibility of racial violence and generally to maintain discipline, Secretary of War Baker adopted three policies. First, blacks would be organized and trained in their own separate divisions. (Thus, ironically, segregation was adopted in part to protect black soldiers; the whites couldn't abuse the blacks if they couldn't see them.) Second, the ratio of whites to blacks in any one training camp would be no less than two to one. This had the unintended adverse effect of ensuring that Southern blacks would be exported for training to Northern states, because to keep them at home would necessarily create dominant black populations in the Southern camps. Finally, the bulk of black soldiers would be assigned to labor battalions rather than be trained for service in the field. Secretary Baker promised the radical civil rights campaigner W.E.B. DuBois that more than one-third of blacks would become combat soldiers; in the event it was 20 percent.[61]

In October 1917, 5,000 "colored" draftees, comprising the 368th Colored Infantry Regiment, were assigned to Camp Meade. After the war, blacks remembered Camp Meade as a place where they were treated relatively well, especially as it was a "Southern" camp. In particular, they had more opportunity for drill and rifle practice than elsewhere. At other camps they were routinely degraded and abused; it was common practice, for example, to hire black recruits out to local contractors as laborers, with the white officers keeping the money. While this and other discriminatory practices were recorded at Camp Meade, they were apparently nowhere near as prevalent as at many other facilities.[62] Nonetheless, life could be grim for the black recruits, whose burden of discrimination fell on top of the soldier's normal loneliness.

To the men of the 79th, however, segregation made the black recruits virtually invisible. The division had now arrived at its training grounds. A question now became urgent: What would they be trained to do?

CHAPTER 4

WHAT PERSHING SHOULD HAVE KNOWN

When the US entered the war in April 1918, its military doctrine was embodied in the *Infantry Drill Regulations* of 1911 as amended to February, 1917. That manual, with few changes, would have made easy reading for Generals Grant and Sherman. It offered such dicta as:

> An attack is bound to succeed if fire superiority is gained and properly used. To gain this superiority generally requires that the attack employ more rifles than the defense; this in turn means a longer line, as both sides will probably hold a strong firing line ... If the attack can be so directed that, while the front is covered, another fraction of the command strikes a flank more or less obliquely (an enveloping attack) the advantages gained are a longer line and more rifles in action; also a converging fire opposed to the enemy's diverging fire ... To reap the full fruits of victory a vigorous pursuit must be made. The natural inclination to be satisfied with a successful charge must be overcome ..."[1]

Artillery was virtually ignored.[*] Tanks, only recently introduced on the Western Front, were not mentioned, but neither were aircraft, which had

---

[*] The artillery's own service regulations, in three volumes, had one sentence on its combat role: "The reason for the existence of Field Artillery is its ability to assist the other arms, especially the Infantry, upon the field of battle." (War Department, *Provisional Drill and Service Regulation for Field Artillery (Horse and Light), 1916, Corrected to April 15, 1917*, 3 vols, Document No. 538 (Washington, DC: GPO, 1917), p. 17.)

been in action since 1914. Machine guns were virtually dismissed as "... weapons of emergency. Their effectiveness combined with their mobility renders them of great value at critical, though infrequent, periods of an engagement."[2] Four brief paragraphs described attacks on fortified positions, giving such advice as:

> If the enemy is strongly fortified and time permits, it may be advisable to wait and approach the charging point under cover of darkness ... If the distance is short and other conditions are favorable, the charge may be made without fire preparation. If made, it should be launched with spirit and suddenness at the break of day.[3]

Such statements now seem quaint in light of the reality in Europe, where millions of soldiers, mired in continuous, elaborate, virtually static trench lines, were using the most modern machinery to kill each other with industrial efficiency. But to the Commander-in-Chief, the infantry attack with rifle and bayonet remained the *sine qua non* of warfare, particularly American warfare. Steeped in the mythology of the frontier; educated at West Point by Civil War veterans; and hardened by small-unit combat against Indians in the West, the Spanish in Cuba, the Moros in the Philippines, and Pancho Villa's revolutionaries in Mexico; Pershing believed that the American soldier had a natural affinity for marksmanship and individual initiative. It was this essential characteristic that, in Pershing's belief, distinguished the Americans from their allies. Only they had the morale, the numbers, and the proper offensive doctrine. For the duration of the war he bombarded the War Department with cables stressing this point; a typical one read:

> Close adherence is urged to the central idea that the essential principles of war have not changed: that the rifle and the bayonet remain the supreme weapons of the infantry soldier and that the ultimate success of the Army depends upon their proper use in open warfare.[4]

Pershing was not ignorant of the nature of warfare on the Western Front. On the contrary, he had concluded that the stalemate was the product of wrong doctrine and training, particularly the French and British emphasis on trench warfare. Trench warfare, in Pershing's view, was the antithesis of effective combat as practiced by Americans. A tactical manual written by his staff said:

Trench warfare is marked by uniform formations, the regulation of space and time by higher command down to the smallest details, absence of scouts preceding the first wave, fixed distances and intervals between units and individuals, voluminous orders, careful rehearsal, little initiative upon the part of the individual soldier. Open warfare is marked by scouts who precede the first wave, irregularity of formation, comparatively little regulation of space and time by the higher command, the greatest possible use of the infantry's own fire power to enable it to get forward ... and the greatest possible use of individual initiative by all troops engaged in the action. (AEF Document 1348, "Combat Instructions," September 5, 1918)[5]

Trench warfare drained troops of their aggressive instincts; it instilled in them a sense of dependency on their orders, on their superiors, on fortified positions, and especially on artillery support. Soldiers trained in this doctrine might capture a trench, even a portion of the enemy's main line, but they would not know how to exploit a breakthrough if it occurred. They would dig in, waiting for orders and artillery, while the enemy re-formed his defenses.

There are several ironies in Pershing's system of beliefs. First, as an observer in the Russo-Japanese War, he had seen for himself the effects of massed machine guns and artillery on attacking infantry. At Port Arthur almost all of the many Japanese assaults failed with heavy losses. By the time the city surrendered, the Japanese had lost 65,000 men killed and wounded. The Japanese eventually succeeded because the corruption and incompetence of the Russian Army's officers and the poor training of its men made a consistently effective defense impossible. But Pershing, along with most other observers, drew the conclusion that a sustained frontal assault by zealous infantry would, eventually, overcome the most intense machine gun and artillery fire, however heavy the casualties.

The second irony is that, at the time Pershing made his comments about the effects of trench warfare on infantry morale, he was right. A member of Pershing's staff, analyzing the British collapse in the face of the German attack on March 28, 1918, quoted British infantry officers as saying, "[The men] get out into the open and act as though they were suddenly thrust naked into the public view and didn't know what to do with themselves, as if something were radically wrong and that there ought to be another trench somewhere for them to get into."[6] During the German assault in April 1918 a "senior leader of the French Army," otherwise unidentified, wrote:

The only formations which the infantry is now acquainted with are those of a rigid nature in lines or waves. It has lost the idea of maneuver. On the other hand, it has become accustomed to getting a degree of support from the heavy and light artillery which it is impossible to furnish to it in open warfare; it seems to be no longer able nor willing to do without such support. It is ignorant of its greatest power, of which maneuver makes it capable.[7]

At around the same time another French officer complained, "An infantry which, when it comes under the fire of a hostile machine gun, lies down and waits, inert, for something (just what, it does not know) to happen which may keep it along, is abandoning the battle; it refuses to display any will power or intelligence."[8]

Pershing's belief that the Europeans were wedded to a failed doctrine of trench combat while Americans properly believed in open warfare was, in the words of Russell Weigley, "a false distinction based on a misconception."[9] Far from being committed to trench warfare, the British and French commanders despised it. The problem, unrecognized by any of the armies at first, was that firepower and engineering—machine guns, quick-firing artillery, barbed wire, concrete fortifications—had far outdistanced the ability of even the most ardent cavalry to penetrate defensive lines and the most determined infantry to conquer them. The military history of the Western Front is largely a chronicle of their failed attempts to force their opponents out of the trenches and defeat them in the open field. Eventually, faced with the same problems, the armies in France would evolve their own variations on the same solution. The history of that evolution is worth reviewing briefly because the AEF, in its doctrine, training, and combat performance, would recapitulate virtually all of the troubles that its allies had endured. Had Pershing and his generals taken this history seriously, it is likely that the American Army could have avoided many costly errors and accomplished more in the field than it did.

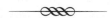

For much of the war French military doctrine corresponded closely to the principles that Pershing regarded as uniquely American. As early as 1912 the French Army's commander, General Joseph Joffre, issued a regulation that decreed, "The teachings of the past have borne their fruit. The French Army, reviving its old traditions, no longer admits for the conduct of operations any other law than that of the offensive."[10] As the Germans poured through Belgium and northeastern France, the French, in their offensive fervor, attacked eastward into Alsace and Lorraine. The infantry regulations of 1913 and 1914 had prescribed the bayonet as the "supreme weapon" of the infantry and relegated artillery to a supporting role. The infantry advanced accordingly, with fixed bayonets but without artillery preparation. A British observer wrote of these tactics, "They are very brave and advance time after time to the charge through appalling fire, but so far it has been of no avail. No one could live through the fire that is concentrated on them."[11] Within six weeks, the French incurred 385,000 casualties, of whom 100,000 were dead. These were, in essence, the tactics that Pershing would prescribe for the AEF; what happened to the French is what would have happened to the AEF had the literal sense of Pershing's doctrine prevailed.

Such losses were unsustainable, and the obvious advantages of defensive technology were such that, by November 1914, the front had solidified into a 450-mile-long line of trenches and fortifications from Switzerland to the North Sea. By late 1914, Joffre concluded that artillery preparation was essential and that slow, methodical attacks against successive enemy positions as advocated by General Ferdinand Foch would bring better results with fewer casualties.[*][12]

The doctrine of the continuous offensive was revived and modified by his successor, General Robert Nivelle, whose successful counterattacks at Verdun had catapulted him to leadership of the French Army. Nivelle, an artillery officer, concluded that firepower, coupled with a sustained infantry

---

* In fact, Foch's offensive tactics at the Somme used many of the advanced techniques later credited to the Germans. Foch did away with repeated frontal assaults by lines of infantry—the formation the British were to use in that battle. Instead, small groups of infantry supported by artillery would advance against strong points by fire and maneuver, bypassing them when possible so as to maintain the momentum of the attack. Second-wave troops would mop up bypassed positions and any remaining pockets of resistance. As a result, on the first day of the Somme battle, the French with six divisions gained two miles at a cost of 1,590 casualties; the 14 divisions of the British lost 19,240 men killed and 37,646 wounded and missing while mostly failing to reach the German first line. (William Philpott, *Three Armies on the Somme: The First Battle of the Twentieth Century*, Knopf paperback edition of Little, Brown hardcover edition (New York: Knopf, 2009), pp. 146, 202; Robert A. Doughty, *Pyrrhic Victory: French Strategy and Operations in the Great War* (Cambridge, MA and London: Belknap Press, 2005), p. 293.)

assault in a narrow sector, could break through the German line. Nivelle put his principles to work at an exposed German salient atop a ridge in Champagne named after a highway along its crest, the Chemin des Dames; the ensuing battle would in many respects foreshadow the experience of the AEF at the Meuse–Argonne. Nivelle's plan was to saturate the entire depth of the German line with an immense bombardment. The artillery would then lay down a rolling barrage that would allow the infantry to pass unopposed through the shattered trenches and stunned defenders into the rear areas.* Fresh divisions would pass through tired ones to keep up the momentum. Once the breakthrough had been achieved, open-field warfare would commence. Troops were trained in the long-abandoned techniques of mobile operations, which emphasized rifle fire over grenades and mortars. On January 29, 1917, Nivelle sent his orders to General Micheler, commanding the army group that would carry out the attack:

> I insist on the characteristics of *violence, brutality,* and *speed* that must permeate your offensive and, in particular, its first stage, the rupture, which must at the first blow conquer the enemy's positions and the entire zone occupied by his artillery ... To set objectives for the Army Corps that are distant enough ... without limit; (it is necessary to go as far as possible on J-Day). [Italics in the original.][13]

The order could have been written by Pershing himself.

In a six-day bombardment 5,350 guns fired more than 11 million shells on a 15-mile front. But the plan started to unravel as soon as the infantry moved forward on April 16. The troops, slowed by mud, rain, and the tortured ground surface, fell behind the barrage, which had been set to advance at the hopelessly fast rate of 30 meters per minute. German machine gun nests, many untouched by the bombardment, swept the French formations, keeping many attackers huddled in their jumpoff positions. The French reserves, as if on an unstoppable conveyor belt, were dumped into the forward trenches according to plan, congesting them still further. Rain gave way to snow and sleet. Visibility on the ground or

---

* The rolling barrage was a wall of exploding shells that advanced ahead of the attacking troops at a distance of 100 meters or less. Its purpose was to keep the defenders—particularly machine-gunners—in their dugouts and away from their weapons up to the moment the attacking infantry fell upon them.

from the air was nil. The artillery lost track of the infantry's positions. Some batteries, hearing wrongly that the troops were still in their trenches, started their rolling barrages all over again, drawing the line of exploding shells back and forth over their own men. When the tanks appeared in the afternoon, German artillery was ready for them; they and their accompanying infantry were almost wiped out. In the mid-afternoon the Germans counterattacked, pushing the French advanced units, already crowding the battlefield, back into the regiments coming up from the rear. The roads leading to the front became impassable, jammed with reserves waiting to move forward. Within a day it became apparent that the infantry could make only local gains; by April 22 the operation was reduced to limited offensives and on May 9 it was called off altogether. The French incurred roughly 130,000 killed, wounded, and missing, the vast majority in the first few days of the operation.[14]

General Philippe Pétain, who succeeded Nivelle in May, put an end to major offensives for the time being. Appalled at the losses suffered in the French offensives of 1914–15 and in the defense of Verdun, and obliged to suppress the mutinies that followed the Chemin des Dames, he advocated limited actions that would be heavy on artillery and light on infantry. Each local offensive would end with consolidation of the positions gained, and not be followed up until artillery support could again be brought into position. Yet Pétain's apparent conservatism was deceptive. He was the first to take tanks seriously as an element of offensive tactics and ordered many more into production, along with aircraft, heavy artillery, and smoke and gas shells. He emphasized the formation and training of combined-arms teams that integrated artillery, infantry, and tanks into highly capable units that would be supported by aircraft. Pétain's combined-arms tactics paid off in three limited offensives culminating in the battle of Malmaison, fought between October 21 and 25, 1917, which finally captured the Chemin des Dames position. The Sixth Army took almost 12,000 prisoners, 200 guns, and 720 machine guns while suffering 12,000 dead, wounded, and missing, relatively light casualties in proportion to the gains.[15] At that point, Pétain—in opposition to the British—refused to consider any more large offensives until attrition had so weakened the Germans that they could no longer defend their entire line.

It was Ferdinand Foch, appointed "General-in-Chief of the Allied Armies" in March 1918, who first recognized the opportunity for a full-scale campaign. The German Spring Offensives of March–June 1918 that had pushed back the French and British by now had run their course; the Germans were overextended, tired, and far from their strongly built defenses. From Verdun to Flanders their line formed a gigantic salient bulging westward into France. Foch reasoned that a series of limited attacks, delivered rapidly against different parts of the salient, would wear out the enemy, prevent him from concentrating his reserves, and eventually produce the conditions that could lead to a breakthrough. He therefore asked Pétain to write an order that would prepare the Army to resume the offensive. The result was Directive No. 5, issued on July 12. It said:

> Henceforth, the armies should envisage the resumption of the offensive. Commanders at all echelons will prepare for this; they will focus resolutely on using simple, audacious, and rapid procedures of attack. The soldier will be trained in the same sense and his offensive spirit developed to the maximum.[*][16]

The Directive went on to order that the soldiers' training instill a "spirit of maneuver and an aptitude for movement"; that operational security be practiced, including concealment of attacking units until the last moment; and that senior commanders issue clear, concise orders that left the details of execution to the individual unit commanders. The offensive principles were to be surprise, rapid execution, deep expansion, and thorough exploitation of initial success, both immediate and long-distance. As Robert Doughty has pointed out, "After four years in the trenches and a year of preparing only for the defense, the French Army required much coaching before it could conduct a large offensive operation."[17] At Soissons the French surprised the Germans with two armies, 750 tanks, and a two-to-one artillery advantage. Instead of a preparatory bombardment there was an intense rolling barrage that landed one heavy shell every 1.27 yards of ground and three field artillery shells per yard.[18] Objectives were unlimited. The operation was a complete success. Pershing kept insisting, long after the war, that the French and British had lost the offensive spirit and only the Americans were able to restore it; but Soissons showed this to be a gross misrepresentation.[†]

---

[*] Translation by the cited author.

[†] See, e.g., Pershing, *My Experiences*, vol. 1, p. 151 and vol. 2, p. 36.

The British Army entered the war in a very different state than that of the French or Germans. Heir to the colonial small-war tradition, it numbered only 250,000 regulars in 1914; Parliament had kept it small so as to devote funds to the naval buildup, to paying off the debt of the Boer War, and to remedying the defects in the Army's weapons and organization which that war had revealed. The expert Afrikaner gunners had taught the British to spread out in the advance, use terrain for cover, and suppress the enemy's guns with one's own. But those lessons were reversed by 1911, when a new infantry training manual stipulated that offensive tactics would be based on the massed bayonet assault supported only by direct artillery fire (that is, where the gunners themselves could see their targets). Machine guns, the proper use of which was not yet understood by any army, were relegated to local supporting roles. So far, Pershing would have said, so good.

The retreat from Belgium and subsequent battles in 1915 quickly showed that such tactics were obsolete. At Le Câteau (August 26, 1914), the exposed British guns were annihilated by German indirect fire. At Neuve Chapelle (March 10, 1915), two battalions totaling about 1,500 men were virtually eliminated by two German machine guns.[19] The new British commander, Sir Douglas Haig, concluded that the only way to break into the German lines was to saturate them with heavy indirect fire for several days and then launch waves of infantry, unencumbered by supporting weapons except for machine guns, against the presumably helpless enemy. Artillery units, which could not communicate with the troops once the latter had left their trenches, were to fire according to a strict timetable, the initial bombardment against stationary targets becoming a rolling barrage that would precede the troops at a fixed rate of advance. It was up to the infantry to keep up with the barrage; if they stayed close behind it, they should be able to overwhelm any surviving Germans before the latter could emerge from their dugouts and regain their firing positions. This appeared to be the only doctrine that the new, volunteer army could execute, without extensive training that time did not permit. It became the British offensive method from Loos (September 25, 1915) through the Somme (July–November 1916), during which period 170,000 of their men were killed and 510,000 wounded.[20] It never succeeded—the German dugouts were too strong and indirect fire was too inaccurate to eliminate the machine guns and the defending artillery—but, given the army they were working with, it was the only doctrine the British had.*

Pershing in his memoirs unjustly accused the British General Staff of wanting to "[win] the war by attrition, with isolated attacks on limited fronts."[21] On the contrary, all of the General Staff's efforts during the war were dedicated to achieving a breakthrough; in every one of his battles Haig had a mass of cavalry assigned to rush through the expected gap into the enemy's rear. Throughout the war, elements of the British command understood the need for breakthrough tactics and pursued their development. E.D. Swinton, a British officer and prewar tactical authority, upon returning from the first battles in France advocated the development of armed, armored vehicles based on the American-built Holt farm tractor, which ran on caterpillar treads. They were to attack with infantry in mutual support, with aircraft neutralizing enemy artillery positions that otherwise would threaten the armor. Swinton's recommendations could not be implemented for some time because of their unfamiliarity, the inability of the troops to execute such tactics, and the time it took to develop tanks that were even minimally effective in combat. His innovation was to recognize the need for mobile, armor-assisted tactics and then to develop them even before any tanks had been designed, let alone built.

The Somme itself was the cradle of many innovations that ultimately led to combined-arms warfare. Two weeks after the battle opened the staff of Fourth Army surveyed divisional commanders to elicit their wisdom as to how weapons and men were best to be used. Some topics were basic: the proper role of infantry weapons, how to overcome enemy strong points, how to mop up after an attack, how to assault obstacles such as woods, trenches, and villages. Other subjects required more advanced development: How to integrate artillery with the infantry assault, how to communicate

---

* Haig has long been castigated for repeatedly using attrition tactics at the Somme that resulted in immense casualties. Whether such tactics were the only ones available is hotly debated by historians; but what Haig could not do was stop fighting—the possibility of a French defeat at Verdun required him to keep as many German divisions occupied as possible. The judgment of historian Michael Howard on the commanders of a later world war would seem to apply here: "[T]he only 'lesson' that a historian would be justified in deriving from these events is that in war, in any war, this is the kind of thing that armed forces may find themselves having to do; not necessarily through the stupidity of their leaders, but because all other options seem to be foreclosed or appear demonstrably worse." (Michael Howard, *The Lessons of History* (New Haven, London: Yale UP, 1991), p. 10.)

effectively with the attacking units, and the proper role of the staff. Many of these themes were picked up later by General Ivor Maxse, whose division was the only one to penetrate the German positions at the Somme and inflict more casualties than it suffered. In early 1918 he was made Inspector General of Training for British forces in France. In a memorandum analyzing the failed Passchendaele offensive of the previous year he emphasized the importance of training in combined arms, particularly in the interaction of infantry, machine guns, artillery, tanks, and aircraft. With regard to enemy strong points, Maxse advocated using flexible combined-arms tactics to allow some soldiers, aided by tanks, to provide covering fire while others worked to the enemy's flanks and rear—the "fire and maneuver" method that has remained the bedrock of modern infantry tactics to this day.

The first full-scale use of tanks took place in the assault on Cambrai on November 20, 1917. Haig abandoned the usual days-long bombardment in favor of a 370-tank force supporting the infantry. The attackers were divided into teams consisting of three tanks supported by a small detachment of infantry advancing in open order. By the end of the first day, the British had advanced five miles on an eight-mile front. (Failure to consolidate their gains allowed the Germans to recapture most of the ground in a counterattack ten days later.) Pershing observed the attack and admired the tactics.

The culmination of British open-warfare tactics was General Sir Henry Rawlinson's August 1918 counterattack at Amiens to roll back the German gains from their Spring Offensives of earlier that year. Rawlinson's plan was based on principles developed by General Sir John Monash, commander of the Australian Army Corps. At the battle of Hamel the previous month, Monash had eliminated a German salient in two hours using surprise and close cooperation between infantry, artillery, aircraft, and armor—"a fully realized application of combined arms doctrine" in the words of David Trask. [22] Monash wrote, "The true role of infantry was not to expend itself upon heroic physical effort, not to wither away under merciless machine gun fire, not to impale itself on hostile bayonets, but on the contrary, to advance under the maximum possible protection of the maximum possible array of mechanical resources, in the form of guns, machine-guns, tanks, mortars, and aeroplanes."[23] Rawlinson assigned 2,070 guns, 800 aircraft, and 540 tanks to support 13 infantry and three cavalry divisions. On August 8 the attackers achieved their objectives by 1:00 p.m. But British casualties were still heavy, 189,000 men between August 8 and September 26.

The Australians and Canadians, the shock troops of the British Army, used combined-arms tactics to the end of the war; but the rest of the Army did not. Rawlinson, anxious for the War Office to keep sending men, insisted as early as August 29 that infantry was key to winning and that overinvestment in planes and tanks would be a waste of manpower. As a result, the BEF largely reverted to "semi-traditional" warfare when it reopened the offensive in late August. Artillery remained a major actor, firing immense bombardments; Lewis guns, trench mortars, and machine guns were used to deliver more fire than previously, and surprise and deception were employed. But the idea of combining infantry and artillery with tanks and planes was dropped.[24] Nevertheless, Pershing's judgment— reflected in a memorandum by his training chief, Colonel Fiske—that "the offensive spirit of the [British Army] has largely disappeared as a result of their severe losses" was greatly in error.[25]

By the time the United States entered the war, the Germans had mastered offensive techniques that could penetrate the trench lines and lead to open warfare. Historians differ as to the origins of the German offensive methods, which are variously referred to as stormtoop tactics, infiltration tactics, or Hutier tactics. In fact, they appear to have resulted from several developments, some infantry-based and some artillery-based, that started out independently but eventually coalesced. The first stage was an attempt in 1915 to find a way to move guns forward across heavily shelled No-Man's Land to support advancing infantry. It was assigned to Captain Willy Rohr, former commander of a company of the Garde-Schutzen-Bataillon, an independent, aggressive, mobile light infantry battalion equipped with its own machine gun company. Rohr's mission was to train his detachment in whatever tactics he thought appropriate. In addition to the light infantry Rohr was given a platoon each of machine guns, mortars, and flame throwers, to which he added a light, portable field gun. The effect was to create a multiple-weapon, flexibly organized battalion that operated as a set of interrelated weapons teams. Rohr found that the best protection for his assault troops was speed and violence in the attack. He therefore replaced the traditional extended skirmish lines with an attack by squad-sized units of stormtroops (*Stosstruppen*, *Sturmtruppen*), supported by some of his light weapons. After a few weeks' training Rohr's detachment was ordered to take a French position in the Vosges Mountains; it was completely successful. Within seven months of the formation of Sturmbataillon Rohr, Erich von Falkenhayn, Chief of the German General Staff, ordered the diffusion of its methods to all of the armies in the West. Each army was to send small detachments to be trained by Rohr; these would then train their own armies, which were to form assault groups in every unit down to the level of companies. Within six months, over 30 divisions and many other units from corps down to company had their own *Sturmabteilungen*.[26] Rohr codified his doctrine in a manual that was disseminated throughout the Army. At Verdun in the first half of 1916, Rohr and his *Sturmabteilung* spent most of their time to the rear of the lines, training the assault groups assigned to the infantry battalions. Infiltration tactics played an important role on the Verdun battlefield, particularly in countering the defense in depth that the French adopted to take advantage of the cut-up terrain.[27]

The second strand of German tactical innovation was in artillery. Lieutenant Colonel Georg Bruchmüller, a previously undistinguished artillerist called back from retirement in 1914, observed that an extensive preparatory bombardment gave away the element of surprise. He therefore developed the "predicted fire" technique in which guns were aimed on the basis of their targets' map coordinates (provided by aerial reconnaissance) rather than by using preliminary registration fire. To make this system effective, however, required that command of the artillery be taken away from the individual divisions, where it normally resided, and centralized at the army level. In April of 1916, at Lake Narocz, his system pulverized the Russian forces; Bruchmüller's division alone took 5,600 dazed and shattered prisoners. He soon repeated his success in various counterattacks against Russian offensives.[28]

Bruchmüller's doctrine developed as the war progressed but its central features remained the same. Before the attack, the artillery of the assaulting units was heavily reinforced. Control of the artillery was centralized at the army level, with close-support missions being delegated to divisional artillery commanders and far operations being assigned to the corps artillery. The preparatory bombardment was no longer intended to destroy the enemy defenses; it was to neutralize them long enough so they could not interfere with the infantry and to create gaps through which the infantry could advance.[29] Preparatory fire would last only a few hours instead of the usual days or weeks, making up for it in extreme intensity and surprise. High explosive shells would be supplemented by gas to incapacitate key enemy positions and to protect the flanks of the attacking infantry.

As the infantry started forward, the preparatory bombardment would give way to a rolling barrage that proceeded slightly ahead of the foot soldiers, who followed it at a distance of a few tens of yards. It would pause at a series of planned "phase lines" to allow the infantry to catch up and to mop up whatever defenders survived. Gas and the rolling barrage were not new; Bruchmüller's innovation was to integrate them with centralized artillery control and the short, intense preparatory bombardment. Also new was his attention to detail: assigning the mix of guns and ammunition that was perfectly suited (according to his own experiments) to the job at hand; personally explaining his artillery plan to the attacking troops; and conducting artillery drills to maximize the reliability of the rolling barrage so that, in the words of Bruce Gudmundsson, he could "convince the infantry that following fifty meters or less behind a curtain of exploding shells was a good idea."[30]

The two channels of tactical innovation, infantry and artillery, first came together in the German attack on Riga, the Baltic anchor of the Russian line, in September 1917. The 13 attack divisions of General Oskar von Hutier's Eighth Army trained for ten days 75 miles behind the front. Only on the night before the attack did they enter the forward trenches. At 4:00 a.m. on September 1 a five-hour bombardment dropped over 560,000 shells on top of the Russians, first concentrating on the artillery and then switching to the infantry positions. After crossing the Dvina River on boats, Hutier's infantry advanced behind a rolling barrage, the speed of which they could regulate by signaling to the rear. Riga was taken in two days; the Germans suffered only light casualties. Within three months Russia was out of the war. By that time, Hutier and Bruchmüller had been transferred to the Western Front to work their magic against the British and the French.

In early 1918 the Germans in the West faced a threat and an opportunity. The threat was the impending arrival of millions of fresh, well-armed, and well-supplied American troops on the battlefield. The opportunity was the availability of up to 45 veteran German and Austro-Hungarian divisions that were no longer needed in Russia.* General Erich Ludendorff, First Quartermaster General (in reality, *de facto* commander in chief) of the German Army, resolved to use the methods of Hutier and Bruchmüller to force the French and British to sue for peace in the spring, before enough trained American divisions had arrived to turn the tide. He commissioned a new tactical manual that married trench warfare techniques with those of open warfare to bring about a breakthrough. The German method combined two elements: tight central control in setting objectives and coordinating the activities of major units, and a high degree of local initiative and rapid exploitation of a break in the enemy's front.[31] Additionally, Ludendorff designated a portion of his divisions as "attack divisions" (*Angriffsdivisionen*); these received the highest-quality replacements, weapons, and training. The remaining divisions (called *Stellungsdivisionen*) were assigned to defense. This two-track system, as we shall see in Chapter 9, eventually caused more problems than it solved.

Ludendorff's plan of attack began with an artillery preparation à la Bruchmüller: A short, heavy bombardment to demoralize and isolate the defenders; random start-and-stop shelling to conceal the infantry's jumpoff time; training the junior artillery and infantry officers in the new technique; and assigning the best weapon to each kind of target. The rolling barrage would be laid down by howitzers at the corps level rather than by divisional field guns, because the howitzers were more accurate and thus safer for the advancing troops. Fire would concentrate on strategic points: observation posts, command posts, radio transmitters, phone exchanges, bridges, approach roads. Artillery officers and observers would go forward to adjust fire based on activities on the battlefield. The effect would be to cut off the enemy's communications, prevent reinforcement, and fragment the opposing units.

As the preparatory fire gave way to the rolling barrage, the storm battalions of each regiment would move forward. Supported by trench mortars, mobile artillery, flame throwers, combat engineers, and additional machine guns, the storm battalions would use infiltration tactics, moving in

---

* In the event, only 33 German divisions were actually sent west, not enough (compared to the approximately 200 already fighting there) to be decisive.

groups as small as sections[*] and bypassing strong points by advancing in ravines or between outposts. Bypassed positions would be mopped up by conventional infantry following the main attack. In the final phase, the infantry would attack the enemy's rear echelons, disrupting communication and command centers, overwhelming artillery batteries, causing enemy commanders to lose control of their troops, and precipitating the complete collapse of resistance.

On March 21 at 4:40 a.m., 6,000 guns opened up on the British Third and Fifth Armies ranged on either side of the Somme River. Seventy-one German divisions attacked 26 British, some of them under strength and recovering from combat. British units fragmented; headquarters lost control; Fifth Army virtually disappeared. By April 5 the British had lost 164,000 casualties, 90,000 prisoners, 200 tanks, 1,000 guns, 4,000 machine guns, and 70,000 tons of ammunition, and had a hole in their front 40 miles wide and 40 miles deep. But as the Germans expended their trained storm troops, command and control broke down and the intricate attack system fell apart; assaults were poorly prepared and troops tended to advance in waves.[32] Furthermore, the Germans were outrunning their supplies; exhausted troops stopped to loot captured towns and British supply dumps for food and wine. On April 6 the campaign was called off.

Ludendorff mounted four more offensives against the British and French in May, June, and July, all of them using the principles perfected by Hutier and Bruchmüller. Everywhere the Germans met with initial success; everywhere their advance bogged down as the troops outran their artillery and supplies and succumbed to hunger, exhaustion, and disorganization. Between March and July they incurred almost one million casualties, of whom 125,000 had been killed and 100,000 had gone missing. Morale suffered, as evidenced by looting of Allied supply dumps and increased desertions. These developments, as well as half a million cases of the flu, caused the German Second Army to report on August 1 that out of 13 divisions two were combat-ready, five were capable of defense only, three were of dubious quality even in defense, and three needed to be taken out of action.[33]

In fact, the German methods carried the seeds of their own failure, once the enemy declined to collapse at the first blow. Although they were ideally

---

[*] The German and British term for what Americans call squads, which typically had eight to ten men.

suited to gain a break*through*, Ludendorff's tactics could not achieve a break*out*. Having penetrated the defensive line, there was no guidance as to what the infantry should do next; they tended to dig in and wait. As a result his five offensives, rather than reinforcing each other, became a series of limited, diverging attacks. But even had they broken out they would have been self-constrained; as at Caporetto, the lack of roads and the poor condition of the terrain restricted the Army's mobility and made it hard to supply. Eventually, the assault would congeal into a new, static position. As it was, by leaving his assault divisions depleted, exhausted, and in hastily dug defenses, Ludendorff opened the door to an Allied victory.

Pershing was unreserved in his admiration of the German achievement, which, he believed, vindicated his faith in open warfare. But he persisted in drawing only the lessons he wanted to learn. In July he wrote:

> Two of the main characteristics of the successful German offensive were: The intelligent initiative of junior officers and superiority of fire. Americans have inherent qualities in both these respects far superior to those of the Germans ... All infantry officers must pay especial and constant attention to perfecting the instruction of the infantry soldier in the use of the rifle and to increase his reliance on that weapon as his only indispensable arm.[34]

He thus ignored the true reasons for German success, the same reasons that applied to the French victories at Malmaison and Soissons and those of the British at Cambrai and Amiens. These were: the use of massive, sophisticated, and flexible artillery support, both before and during the operation; a multitude of different types of infantry weapons at the squad and platoon levels; flexible teams, operating semi-independently, to penetrate weak spots and bypass strong points; close support by aircraft and (in the case of the Allies) tanks; and above all, intensive training in combined-arms tactics, especially infantry with artillery. Without that last element, the technical expertise and the crucial cooperation within infantry formations and between the infantry and the artillery would be absent. In his concentrated antipathy toward what he considered to be trench warfare—rolling barrages, phase lines, timed advances, limited objectives—Pershing neglected any means of getting through the trenches to the open country in which he wanted to fight.[35] Worse, by objecting to American troops being trained by French and British officers, he closed off access to a year or more of his allies' most recent experience.[*] Pershing's stubbornness in this regard would cause confusion and waste when it came to the training of American divisions. What problems his attitude would produce once the AEF actually reached the field of battle was yet to be seen.

---

[*] Pershing's disdain for French tactical thought is demonstrated in his note of July 12, 1918 on a memorandum by the Allied Commander-in-Chief, General Ferdinand Foch. Foch's memo gave a thorough and accurate analysis of Ludendorff's offensive methods and how to defend against them. Pershing transmitted it to his subordinates with a proforma endorsement that read in its entirety, "Commanders will show by their attitude that they give full, loyal and sympathetic support to the execution of the above instructions of the Commander-in-Chief of the Allied armies." (Department of the Army Historical Division, *USAWW*, 17 vols (Washington, DC: GPO, 1948), vol. 3, pp. 335–36.)

CHAPTER 5

TRAINING—THE ARMY AT WAR WITH ITSELF

President Wilson may have decided to field an autonomous American army, but his allies continued to have other ideas. The French failure at the Chemin des Dames in April 1917 and the subsequent mutinies made them desperate to put Americans into the line as quickly as possible; the fastest way to do that was to integrate them into the French command and logistical system. The British, having incurred immense losses at the Somme in 1916 and at Passchendaele in 1917, had the same desire. Neither the French nor the British believed that the US could train commanders or their staffs fast enough to organize an independent army that would be useful; nor did either believe that shipping would be available to bring over the necessary arms and equipment in addition to the men. Both subjected Pershing to repeated demands that he subordinate his army to theirs by shipping only riflemen and machine gunners, to be assigned by battalions to the French and British armies, an arrangement termed "amalgamation." Pershing resisted such contentions with arguments of his own: national pride would not allow his army to be parceled out to others; Irish-American soldiers would not serve with the British; American officers spoke little French, and vice versa; the United States would lose influence at the inevitable peace settlement; and there would be recriminations if Allied generals ran up large American casualties. Above all, he had his orders. The letter given to him by the General Staff and signed by Secretary of War Baker read, in part:

In military operations against the Imperial German Government you are directed to cooperate with the forces of the other countries employed against that enemy; but in so doing, the underlying idea must be kept in view that the forces of the United States are a separate and distinct component of the combined forces, the identity of which must be preserved. This fundamental rule is subject to such minor exceptions in particular circumstances as your judgment may approve.[1]

Orders or not, Pershing was devoted to the concept of a separate American army, fully staffed and equipped and capable of independent action. This attitude followed naturally from his belief in a unique American approach to war, emphasizing the initiative of the individual rifleman in the open field over the elaborate planning, strict timetables, limited objectives, and rigid conformity to orders that characterized trench warfare.[*] To subsume American units into Allied armies would not only rob them of their national pride, it would squander their real assets: aggressiveness, resourcefulness, and enterprise. In Pershing's view, even to have French and British officers train them ran the danger of destroying their offensive spirit. Yet three things were apparent to him and others by late 1917. First, his men would have to get through the trench zone somehow before they could apply their open warfare skills. Second, the Americans had no experience of modern war, whereas the British and French had ample. Third, the United States had to ship at least some entire divisions to France as early as possible to establish a presence; the Allies could not wait much longer for a meaningful American contingent to arrive.

Pershing resolved this dilemma by working out an agreement with the War Department.[†] To speed their arrival, the first four divisions to leave, the

---

[*] Pershing's dislike for trench warfare is sometimes attributed to his aversion to its wastefulness in lives. H.C. Johnson, for example, describes the general's reaction to the British and French proposals to absorb American battalions: "Pershing aptly and frankly described this effort as a search for cannon fodder to replace casualties lost in fruitless siegecraft." (Johnson, *Breakthrough!*, p. 243.) Pershing did not in fact express such a sentiment, certainly not in the pages of his memoir to which Johnson refers. Pershing disliked trench warfare not because it was expensive in men—as bad as that was—but because he believed it was ineffective in defeating the enemy.

[†] The relationship between Pershing and the War Department was another aspect of the dysfunctionality of the American war effort. The Chief of Staff, General Peyton March, believed that his office was the supreme military authority in the Army, subordinate to no one but the Secretary of War. Pershing's view was that, as Commander of the AEF, he reported directly to the President through the Secretary of War, and that the job of the Chief of Staff was to give him whatever support he needed. (Smythe,

1st, 2nd, 26th, and 42nd, would be trained entirely in France in both open and trench warfare. Those scheduled to go later would receive open warfare training at home and a brief indoctrination in trench operations once they got to France, where there were plenty of trenches. He reiterated the need to emphasize open warfare training at home in a series of cables to the War Department. Unfortunately, trying to influence the War Department from France was like pushing on a rope.

The lack of relevant training materials meant that the War Department would have to use foreign ones; since the Americans expected to serve mostly on the French front, they used French texts translated into English. Because there were no experienced trainers, British and French officers would be imported until Americans could take over.[*] Even Pershing recognized this need, although he tried to limit the use of foreigners to training in military specialties:

> Since we have practically no qualified instructors, these schools must at first be for the training of instructors who in turn must train others in schools within the organizations, until a fair amount of the training has been disseminated among the troops. To establish these first schools in the United States with the least practicable delay, the board [actually, an informal committee convened by Pershing] recommends the utilization of French and British officers and noncommissioned officers as advisors to our own officers, who will be the commandants and instructors in these schools. (July 11, 1917)[2]

Nevertheless, he had no hesitancy in trying to dictate the content of the

Pershing, p. 89.) To complicate matters, military policy was to be set jointly with the French and British through the Supreme War Council in London, to which General Tasker Bliss, a former Army Chief of Staff, was the War Department's delegate. Bliss and Pershing usually saw eye to eye, but Pershing could not resist offering opinions directly to the SWC on matters that were rightly the prerogative of the Wilson administration (see, e.g., Trask, *AEF and Coalition Warmaking*, p. 156).

[*] The cultural problems involved in having foreign officers, even ones who spoke the same language, train Americans can be glimpsed in a quote from a book by a Royal Artillery officer sent over to talk to the recruits. About the unfamiliar ritual of saluting he wrote, "In England the matter is simpler than it is in America, for over there a great deal that is not bad in the old feudal system still remains. A youth in a village generally touches his hat to the squire and the squire always returns the greeting. To do anything else never occurs to either. It is merely an exchange of courtesy." One can only imagine the reaction of the Philadelphia steamfitter or the Nebraska farm hand to such warm evocations of medieval customs. (Hector MacQuarrie, *How to Live at the Front* (Philadelphia and London: J.B. Lippincott, 1917), p. 59.)

stateside training. A typical Pershing cable to the War Department read:

> Recommend therefore following outline for training in United States: thorough instruction in marksmanship to include known distance firing for all men to 600 yards and in battle practice after methods school musketry. Production [*sic*] excellent close order drill to further high discipline. Thorough instruction both officers and men in open warfare. Small units should be thoroughly grounded in patrolling, in all forms of security, and in attack and defense of minor warfare.[3]

The fundamental disconnection between what Pershing wanted and what the War Department could provide can be traced through the training manuals issued by each. The texts that existed before the war were based largely on the Army's experience with Indian and guerilla warfare. The prewar *Infantry Drill Regulations* and *Field Service Regulations,* even into their 1918 editions, declared rifle-based firepower to be the dominating factor in the infantry charge, with artillery relegated to a supporting role and machine guns to emergency use only (see Chapter 4).[4] Pursuit of the fleeing enemy was stressed in both.

The War Department had first crack beginning in May 1917, issuing a series of instruction manuals intended to reflect its understanding of the Western Front. A typical one was Document No. 656, entitled *Infantry Training,* issued in August. Its very first paragraph read:

> In all the military training of a division, under existing conditions, training for trench warfare is of paramount importance. Without neglect of the fundamentals of individual recruit instruction, every effort should be devoted to making all units from the squad and platoon upwards proficient in this kind of training ... The responsibility for the instruction in trench warfare of field officers, staff officers, and higher commanders rests with special force upon the division commander.[5]

The subjects of instruction specified for squads, platoons, and companies all assumed a static front. Thus, musketry training included target designation, range-finding, distribution of fire, fire discipline, fire control, and communications. There was no mention of fire and movement. Offensive maneuvers were not included in the 16-week program.[6]

In October Pershing's headquarters put out the first training manual aimed at the AEF. Compiled by his Adjutant General, General Benjamin

Alvord, it prescribed a 16-week program for the 1st Division and asserted that:

> The general principles governing combat remain unchanged in their essence. This war has developed special features which involve special phases of training, but the fundamental ideas enunciated in our drill regulations, small arms firing manual, field service regulations and other service manuals remain the guide for both officers and soldiers and constitute the standard by which their efficiency is to be measured, except as modified in detail by instructions from these headquarters.[7]

"Special features which involve special phases of training" is as close as Alvord got to acknowledging the reality of the trenches. To hasten the entry of newly arrived divisions into the line, subsequent versions of the manual compressed the program down to four weeks.[*]

The War Department had told Pershing it acquiesced in his October 1917 training recommendations "with the exception that it is believed advisable to impart some specialty training for the purpose of sustaining interest of troops," as would be specified in Document No. 656.[8] Of course, Document No. 656 was only incidentally about specialty training; its subject was trench warfare. When he saw it, Pershing blew up.[†] On December 8 he sent Cable 348-S, which likely charred the paper it was typed on:

> Referring paragraph 6 your cablegram 352. War Dept. document 656 has been received and examined. In my opinion this pamphlet is not in harmony with [my] recommendations ... in regard to the training of divisions in United States. The first paragraph of War Department document announces that in all the military training of a division, under existing conditions, training for trench warfare is of paramount importance ... I invite attention to paragraph 16 my cablegram 228 and repeat my recommendations contained therein that intensive training in all the phases of open warfare be accepted as the principal mission of divisions before embarkation, trench

---

* The four-week version omitted exercises at the regiment, brigade, and division levels. Since those were the levels to which artillery was assigned, there would be no training in joint operations with the artillery. (Nenninger, "Effectiveness," p. 149.)

† In his memoirs Pershing wrote, "The responsibility for the failure at home to take positive action on my recommendations in such matters must fall upon the War Department General Staff." (Pershing, *My Experiences*, vol. 1, p. 154.)

warfare and the use of special arms being taught in connection with the assumption of the offensive from an entrenched position. It is urged that future programs of training for divisions in the United States be prepared accordingly.[9]

Pershing continued to ignore the War Department's documents and to lob cables of similar tone at the War Department.

Nevertheless, Pershing's own directives showed an evolution of his thought, or at least that of his staff. Manual No. 160, *Instructions on the Offensive Conduct of Small Units,* gave a realistic description of conditions on the Western Front, including German tactics of defense in depth and heavy use of machine guns in overlapping fields of fire. It described infantry attacking in waves behind a rolling barrage. But it concluded that the situation "demands no essential modification in our offensive tactics" and that German defenses "can be defeated by infantry, formed in depth ... advancing close behind the barrage."[10] This was the AEF's first acknowledgment of trench tactics.[*]

Eventually, Pershing lost patience with the War Department altogether. He had General Fiske write a *Program of Training for Divisions in the United States* and send it to General March. So that there should be no mistake at the receiving end, Fiske declared the purpose of the training to be "... to make of the division a handy, flexible team capable of rapid maneuvering to meet the varying situations of warfare in the open under current conditions in France." The 64-page plan was based on the original 16-week training schedule drawn up for the 1st Division in June, but with more detail. It included activities at the company, battalion, regiment, brigade, and division levels; divisional exercises included:

> A division attack, in a general engagement; gaining ground for several miles through hostile zones of defense, overcoming successive lines and centers of resistance, redoubts, etc.

---

[*] The hermaphrodite quality of Manual No. 160 is illustrated by a sentence early in the Introduction: "These [German defensive] tactics can be defeated by infantry, formed in depth, capable of rapid and flexible action, advancing close behind the barrage, and acting by surprise." (War Department, *Instructions on the Offensive Conduct of Small Units*, Document No. 583 (Washington, DC: GPO, 1917), p. 5.) Closely following the rolling barrage is the exact opposite of rapid, flexible action and acting by surprise.

An attack. Division in general engagement. To include assault hostile trenches, progress through intrenched [*sic*] zone, and pursuit.[11]

The descriptions of the exercises never expanded beyond this telegraphic style. How the training officers were to conduct them was not spelled out; no examples, problems, maps, or diagrams were provided. Training bulletins, manuals, and memoranda continued to flow from both Pershing's staff and the War Department for the rest of the war. They had little impact on actual training, either because they were hopelessly vague or unrealistically optimistic, or simply because they appeared too late in the war to be put into practice.[*]

If the reader finds this tale of manuals and countermanuals confusing, imagine the plight of the training officer who had to use them. A large part of the problem was that Pershing never actually defined "open warfare" in operational terms, nor did he indoctrinate his commanders in how to recognize and exploit opportunities for its use. The phrase was used by everyone, but how it was to be put into practice was never described. In fact, the phrase itself does not appear in the titles of any of the over 100 documents produced by Pershing's training staff. In April 1918 General Hunter Liggett, one of Pershing's corps commanders, wrote to General Headquarters:

> I am enclosing a copy of a memo which I have drawn up, and which it is believed will enable Division Commanders of the 1st Corps to train upon some practical line for open warfare, offensive and defensive. I can find nothing in the mass of literature I have received which teaches this, to me essential question.[12]

And the commander of the 343rd Infantry Regiment, Colonel C.R. Howland, wrote of the manuals he received, "The effect on the mind ... was more or less confusing, with the result that at the present time the infantryman does not exactly know what regulations in respect of drill are in force over him."[13]

Manuals, as it happens, were not the main problem. The efforts of Pershing's staff—as well as those of the War Department—to rationalize

---

[*] By the end of July 1918, all the divisions that would see combat had already arrived in France. (Leonard P. Ayres, *The War with Germany: A Statistical Summary* (Washington, DC: GPO, 1919), pp. 33, 102.)

troop training in the States came to naught because neither body had a realistic grasp of the situation in the training camps. By the end of 1917 it was becoming apparent that divisions training in the States were not up to the expected standard. On November 28, Acting Chief of Staff Major General John Biddle asked division commanders to report on their commands' training status relative to the requirements of War Department Document No. 656. Divisions from all around the country reported a lack of instruction in hand grenades, target practice, artillery, and other basics. The reasons ranged from shortages of weapons, equipment, and practice ranges to disease and late arrival of recruits.[*]

Beyond that, the Army's training doctrine itself was faulty. To promote unit cohesion and make it less obvious how many losses the War Department expected to incur, Secretary Baker and General Scott early on decided to form whole divisions and keep them intact from basic training through advanced training and combat service. This put the responsibility for training on the divisional officers, who were not prepared for the task. Worse, instead of forming divisions once men were available to fill them, the War Department chose to activate them as cadres of officers and NCOs drawn largely from the Regulars and the National Guard, and then to fill them up as recruits became available. The effect on divisional training was catastrophic; newly recruited men were continually joining divisions that were in the midst of training, so that either training had to restart continually or the division held men at many levels of proficiency, from expert to none. The situation was compounded when divisions were repeatedly stripped of their most highly trained men for assignment either to specialty schools or to divisions that were about to ship out. This state of affairs prevailed even as the divisions sailed for France.

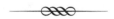

---

[*] At this time the flu had not yet made its appearance. When it first emerged in the training camps in late March 1918, it was not regarded as a major threat. Although the disease spread with alarming speed, cases mostly cured themselves in a few days, caused relatively few deaths, and largely petered out over the summer. The second wave, beginning in the late summer, was a different matter, as we shall see. (Carol R. Byerly, *Fever of War: The Influenza Epidemic in the U.S. Army During World War I* (New York and London: NY UP, 2005), p. 73.)

As the recruits of the 79th Division got their first view of their new quarters at Camp Meade, their reaction was one of dismay. "Sand, dust and a scorching sun welcomed us. Back of the lines of warehouses and shanties along the railroad siding that had been run up into the camp we could distinguish the row upon row of barracks," wrote Ernest L. Loomis, the chaplain of the 304th Ammunition Train (and author of its unit history). To his surprise, the barracks themselves lacked the comforts of home: "No sheets or pillowcases, no plaster or wallpaper, no pictures on the walls, and no rugs or carpets on the floors."[14] The "scorching sun" quickly became a fond memory as September turned to October. The recruits complained that the nights were freezing cold, they had only two thin blankets, and they were ordered to keep their windows open at night. General Kuhn himself had to beg Baltimore businessmen and the Red Cross to furnish sweaters and blankets. At drill, they were not allowed to wear coats, on the grounds that it was not really cold yet. William Schellberg, a machinist from Baltimore, wrote home, "I received the sweater and it feels good but I can't wear it at drill because they don't allow anything to hide the uniform. I look like a real soldier now but I ain't."[15] The food, at least was good—General Kuhn had insisted on that, and for once the men agreed, although the service was not what they were used to:

> Bread, but no butter. Roast beef and potatoes and tomatoes all together in the messpan. And a big K.P.– we learned afterward that K.P. stood for kitchen police ... who doused a spoonful of rice pudding on your messpan cover. Someone who knew tipped us off to the handle on our cup before we got to the coffee station. But the handle wasn't altogether reliable, as some of us discovered to our own chagrin and the amusement of others later when it unceremoniously dumped a good pint and a half of coffee all over the last remnant of civilian life.[16]

The men were quickly put to work making their quarters livable and building a trench warfare course. But proper equipment for training was lacking. None of the Pattern 17 Enfield rifles that the unit was to use had been issued, so they trained with 5,000 worn-out Krag-Jorgensens dating from the Spanish-American War. Those who got rifles considered themselves lucky, even though they had to go to the effort of keeping them clean; those who did not used wooden sticks. Only two old 5-inch guns and two obsolete 7-inch howitzers could be found for the entire artillery brigade; in place of artillery and machine guns, the men used wooden dummies. So instead of proper training, the men drilled: "Squads left, squads right, nine hours a day."[17] Real training did not start in earnest until November with the completion of the rifle ranges, trenches, and bayonet courses. At that point the division embarked on the 16-week regimen prescribed by War Department Document No. 656, which emphasized trench warfare (and to which Pershing had reacted with anger; see above). Small contingents of French and British officers and NCOs, specialists in various aspects of modern warfare, arrived to teach courses in riflery, grenades, automatic weapons, artillery, and gas defense, as well as in the support disciplines such as engineering, signaling, and first aid.

In January the Inspector General's office reviewed the training the division had undergone so far. The inspector, Colonel F.M. Caldwell, expressed satisfaction that the instruction had followed the schedule contained in Training Circular No. 5 (the same document as War Department Document No. 656). With regard to the infantry, "Instruction is thorough and the results good. Officers and men display, as a rule, snap, spirit, and interest in the work ... At present a good foundation for training is being laid." The 304th Engineers, although only at half strength, were well trained and their equipment was complete. Overall, the men were in fine physical condition. But all was not well. Caldwell summarized the deficiencies in his conclusion:

> This division is not fit for service abroad. It is over 10,000 men short of its authorized strength. It has had no target practice of any kind. It is short of equipment for training, especially artillery and machine guns. The supply trains are not sufficiently organized or trained, due to the lack of motor transportation, to perform their functions immediately upon arrival in France ... Men are constantly transferred from this division; this is especially true of men with special training in any line.[18]

Among his recommendations was the following:

> That this Division be filled up and left intact in order that it may be trained as a fighting unit for service abroad. Permanency of personnel is absolutely essential to efficient training ... The constant drain of men from the units of the Division is discouraging to officers and men alike, and has a detrimental effect upon the efficiency of their work.[19]

Had his prescription been followed, it would have greatly changed the fortunes of the 79th.

The men at Camp Meade did not lack for diversion. The YMCA, the YWCA, the Jewish Welfare Board, the Knights of Columbus, the American Red Cross, and many other service organizations set up offices and, in the case of some, entire buildings to provide entertainment, education, and (supervised) female companionship to the recruits. Days were filled with sports competitions among the units. Nightly events included boxing matches, singing contests, plays, and musicals (the YMCA built its own theater). The 79th even had an official singing officer, a Princeton graduate, who led the men in choruses of "Tipperary" and "Long, Long Trail." For the illiterate, there were reading classes and, for the foreign-born, English lessons.

Patriotism too was on the agenda. On October 11, General Kuhn addressed the men on behalf of the Second Liberty Loan Drive, this being the first time the division as a whole had been assembled. Following his speech, the combined divisional bands delivered what the historian of the 79th described as "a creditable performance." (One can only guess what that meant.) In the course of the bond campaign the men of the 79th raised $1.7 million, taking second place among all the camps and cantonments in the country.[20] At a Lincoln's Birthday celebration in the Jewish Welfare Building, reported the *Sun*, a group of Jewish soldiers, some of them recent immigrants from Russia, listened to Lincoln's Gettysburg Address. The Russians had to have the text read slowly, but it was explained to them that the words "dedicated to the great task remaining here before us" applied to their brothers who fell fighting German autocracy—a glorious death that the Bolsheviks were now trying to besmirch by making a "dishonorable" peace.[21]

Weekend leaves were common; trains took the men to spend time with their families or to visit the big-city attractions of Baltimore, Washington, or Philadelphia. Thanksgiving and Christmas were celebrated with lavish (by Army standards) meals. Citizens of Baltimore and Philadelphia, anxious for the welfare of their sons and husbands, swamped the delivery services with packages of food. It took them a while to understand what Army service meant for their men; for a time, Kuhn had to answer telephone calls from wives of recruits who assumed their husbands would have private rooms with their own phones. Visitors descended on the camp each weekend. "Every train into camp brought thousands. Automobiles carried thousands more. The crowded streets looked like Fifth Avenue on a balmy spring afternoon and, toward dusk, when the crowds began to besiege the station at the 'loop,' that terminal might have been Grand Central Station."[22] Wrote Lieutenant John W. Kress of the Machine Gun Company of the 314th Infantry, "I know the soldiers of Meade will never forget the untiring efforts of the people of Baltimore to entertain them. Troupe after troupe visited us from the city. Usually it was necessary only for a girl to show herself and those love-starved Camp Meade warriors literally 'raised the roof' with their applause."[23]

This led General Kuhn into a new and unexpected role—overseer of morals. Secretary Baker and Raymond Fosdick, chairman of the Commission on Training Camp Activities, reacting to President Wilson's concern about the troops' extracurricular activities, took an extremely hard line on sex. This was partly out of concern that manpower would be lost to venereal disease, but it also arose from the Progressives' belief that it was the government's responsibility to improve the moral character of the populace. The Selective Service Act mandated vice-free zones around training camps and prohibited the sale of liquor to servicemen. On occasion, the War Department took strong action: a camp intended for San Antonio was canceled because of concerns about local bars and prostitutes.[24] There is no record of such problems at Camp Meade—the surrounding countryside was farmland, after all—but General Kuhn was occasionally called on to exercise his judgment. According to the Baltimore *Sun*, "The general gave the once-over to the painting of a very pretty young girl who was dressed in a skirt and flimsy waist. The skirt was rather short—especially for a day like today, which was the coldest of the season." It was one of a group of posters that hung in the YMCA's main auditorium, and the rumor was that they were advertisements for a burlesque show. Taking the matter in hand, "He put on his eye-glasses, looked over the dame, who smiled back at him. The general decided that she was all right and could go back to the 'Y' ... The scantily clad young woman still smiles at the fellows all wrapped up in their big army overcoats."*[25]

---

* At one point Fosdick called Baker in a sweat—he had discovered that there were women at Camp Meade! Urgent inquiries were made and Kuhn was able to explain that these were telephone operators, housed in a separate building surrounded by barbed wire, guarded by a special sentry, and transported to and from their trolley station in a closed wagon. He heard no more of the matter. (Joseph E. Kuhn, "Allied Officers Arrive to Help Train Recruits," *Washington Post*, March 16, 1926, p. 5.)

The first public test of the men's training came on April 6, 1918, the anniversary of America's entry into the war. The division marched the 22 miles from Camp Meade to Baltimore to participate in a review by President Wilson. Waxing lyrical, the divisional historian wrote:

> It was a great day for the Division as rank after rank of those, who a few months before had been untrained civilians, passed through the streets, erect in carriage, keen eyed and bronzed by the outdoor training. With "eyes right," platoon after platoon passed the official reviewing stand whereon the President and his party showed their appreciation of the moulding [sic] of a greater American Army as typified by the Seventy-ninth Division.[26]

The march was especially meaningful to the men of the 313th, Baltimore's Own, who had not seen their home city since they were drafted and who were now marching under the eyes of their parents, children, wives, and sweethearts.

Upon their return to Camp Meade, marksmanship training was first on the agenda. Each regiment in turn camped out on the firing range for a week, doing target practice during the day. It was productive; the 314th Regiment received "highest honors" for rapid-fire riflery at 100, 200, and 300 yards. At the end of the week, the recruits' shoulders were so sore it took them a few days to regain the use of their right arms.[27] Next came training in open warfare, such as Kuhn and his officers understood it. The exercises included bayonet assaults, maneuvering large formations, capturing strong points, and surprise attacks on enemy encampments. Each day the separate units of the various regiments practiced "storming and conquering every hill and dale in the Meade vicinity, slaughtering imaginary Germans by the thousands."[28] There is no indication that the units practiced cooperating with artillery or handling problems of transportation, supply, and evacuation of the wounded. Afterward, in France, the men would laugh at how unrealistic their training had been. In mid-May the 79th received its first automatic weapons, the Browning .30-caliber machine gun and the Browning Automatic Rifle. It was the first division in the US Army to be issued these weapons, which were greatly superior to the Hotchkiss and Chauchat guns that other divisions received from the French.[29] The division became quite proficient at their use; at one point, officials from the War Department and other high-ranking Army officers arrived at Camp Meade to see the new .30-caliber machine guns in action. Under the supervision of their trainer, a British major, the machine gunners of the 79th demonstrated indirect and barrage firing. The Browning's reliability in this exhibition, according to the historian of the 79th, was a major impetus to its ultimate adoption as standard equipment.[30]

Between June 19 and 27 the division underwent a second inspection, this time to determine its readiness for shipment to France. It was almost at full complement: 985 officers and 24,713 enlisted men.[31] But the numbers were illusory; the regiment had been pillaged of many of its trained soldiers. In December a large contingent was sent to the 4th Division, a Regular Army unit (and destined to be the next-door neighbor of the 79th at Montfaucon). In April 1918 another group was shipped to the 28th Division, the Pennsylvania National Guard. In all, around 95,000 men were trained by the 79th, of whom only 27,000 actually served with the division. Of the men who served, about 15,000 were called up in the June 1918 draft and thus had virtually no training before embarking for France. In the words of the division's historian, "In the time allotted before sailing, it was impossible to give these men, representing fifty-eight percent of the Division, more than the mere rudiments of a military education. They secured overseas clothing, accoutrements and rifles along with the rest of the Division, learned the elements of movement by columns, had a brief lesson or two in the use of the gas mask and that was all."[32] The inspectors concluded:

> ... that all has been done that reasonably could be expected to place the Division in a state of training fit for war. That it is not so, is due to the large number of recruits which it has been necessary to assign to it to fill its enlisted personnel to war strength. Had it been possible to fill the division up at the outset of its organization and maintain that personnel, there is no doubt it would form today an efficient fighting unit, ready to put into the line as soon as the various units had become familiar with the routine of trench warfare. With the more than 50% of new men the division should have three months intensive training to make it a dependable and efficient fighting unit ... None of the new men of the Infantry regiments have had proper training in shooting, some of them have had none and all have been hurried to the range with practically no preliminary training. Opportunity should be afforded in Europe to correct this defect.[33]

The Inspector General's office sent its report to the War Department's training section on July 16 with a hand-written cover note: "In view of the Div. having sailed, recommend no further action."[34]

In June, the 79th (except for its artillery brigade) received orders to entrain for Hoboken, New Jersey, there to board ship for France. Its ultimate destination was kept secret from the men, who found it out from the Red Cross ladies who served coffee and doughnuts at the pier and from other civilians who showed up to wish them well.[35] General Kuhn left Hoboken on June 30 aboard the *Calamares*, a former liner of the United Fruit Company, and arrived at Brest, in Brittany, 12 days later. The division's constituent units were assigned to six ships of varying size and age. Largest and grandest was the *Leviathan*, displacing 54,282 tons and with a troop capacity of 12,000 men.[36] Formerly the *Vaterland*, flagship of the Hamburg–Amerika line and designed to carry 3,600 passengers in luxury, it was interned on the outbreak of war in 1914 along with other German ships that happened to be in US ports.[*]

The 157th Infantry Brigade, comprising the 313th and 314th Infantry Regiments, along with several divisional battalions, drew the prize; they boarded the *Leviathan* on July 7 and 8. On the afternoon of the 8th, the men noticed that the sailors were preparing the ship for sea. Around 6:00 p.m. they were called to a lifeboat drill just as the ship left the pier. As they headed out of the harbor, they got a sunset view of the Statue of Liberty and the skyline of New York; the roofs of the buildings were packed with people. The soldiers hurrahed, the onlookers cheered, whistles blew, and the regimental bands completed the ensemble. Submarines had been seen off the coast, so several cruisers accompanied the big ship out to sea; but after 12 hours the *Leviathan* left its escort and proceeded alone at its top speed of 22 knots.

Aboard ship, elaborate systems had been invented to allow the 10,500 troops and 1,800 crew members to eat, sleep, and relieve themselves. The logistics of food supply received the most attention. In New York, the ship

---

[*] Among the miscalculations of the German High Command was the number of troops the United States could ship to Europe. The Germans greatly underestimated the Americans' ability to convert freighters and passenger liners to high-capacity troopships. By the end of the war, 24 ex-German liners and 84 cargo ships carried half a million soldiers to France. (James A. Huston, *The Sinews of War: Army Logistics, 1775–1953* (Washington, DC: Office of the Chief of Military History, United States Army, 1966), p. 350.)

took on 260,000 pounds of fresh and canned meat, 25,000 pounds of fresh poultry, 360,000 eggs, 200,000 pounds of flour, and 595,000 pounds of fresh fruits and vegetables. At mealtime, officers sat in the First Class dining room and were served by waiters. Enlisted men, however, were subjected to a different system. They entered the dining room's lower level through the grand stairway, filed past 12 serving stations, ate as they shuffled through the huge hall, and cleaned their dishes and utensils at stations set up by the exits. This system allowed the staff to feed almost 11,000 men in one and a quarter hours.[37]

The men had to be in bed by 9:00 p.m. and had to sleep fully clothed, except for their shoes. Bunks were stacked one above another every two feet. Private Andrew Kachik of the 314th Regiment thought himself lucky to have a top bunk: "The poor guy below me didn't have much room to move around."[38] The combination of hot weather, the warm Gulf Stream, and the rocking of the ship made many seasick, especially on the odoriferous lower decks where the men slept. To get fresh air, companies had to take turns going on deck as there was not room for all of them. Some soldiers, befriending members of the crew, were shown routes by which they could avoid the sentries who guarded the decks from unauthorized visitors; these enterprising individuals spent the voyage lounging on deck chairs when not eating or asleep. The *Leviathan* reached Brest without incident on July 15.

The other ships were divided into two convoys. The first left Hoboken on July 9, with five ships carrying the two infantry regiments (the 315th and 316th) and the machine gun battalion of the 158th Infantry Brigade plus auxiliary units. Conditions could be primitive. Aboard the French transport *Lutetia*, Gerald Gilbert of the 316th Ambulance Company complained about the food: "We are being fed with French war bread which is black as a hat and hard as a rock. It is so hard we can hardly sink our teeth into it and when we do get a mouthful it tastes like sawdust. All the cooking is being done by French cooks and they give us the worst mess of grub a person can think of."[39] The convoy ran into trouble five nights out of New York when the large transport *America*, steaming without lights at 15 knots, rammed the British freighter *Instructor*.* The heavy ship cut the smaller one almost in two, sending it to the bottom in seven minutes. Samuel Fleming, an officer of the 315th aboard the *America*, described the scene:

---

* The *America*, formerly the *Amerika*, was another interned German passenger liner.

She was going down bow first, and as the stern lifted there was a great clattering and sliding of gear down her decks. As I thought about it later, it was remarkable that all these sounds were so clear. The reason was comparative quiet elsewhere, almost absolutely so on our transport; on the other vessel no sounds except the clattering of things sliding down the deck, and the appalling cries, not many and not loud, of men still on the sinking ship and in the water, some near us and some near the stricken vessel.[40]

Eleven of the *Instructor's* crew of 42 made it to a lifeboat and were saved; but the threat of submarine attack forced the convoy to proceed without lingering to rescue those in the water. Three days later, near Brest, a German submarine approached the convoy but French sub-chasers dropped depth charges and it disappeared. The ships reached port on July 18.[41]

The second convoy, carrying the 154th Artillery Brigade, the 304th Ammunition Train, and several divisional battalions, sailed on July 13 from Philadelphia. It comprised a motley collection of vessels: small liners, war-weary French and British troopships, and former horse and cattle transports. The ships reached Halifax, Nova Scotia, on July 17. Eight months earlier a collision between a French ammunition ship and a Norwegian freighter had caused a blast that leveled the city and killed 2,000 people; the men marveled at the destruction, which was still evident. Approaching Liverpool two weeks later, the slow convoy came under attack by at least two submarines. As the ships zigzagged as fast as they could, the soldiers watched from the decks while depth charges exploded and destroyers darted through the formation. The fight ended when a cruiser made a direct hit on one of the subs. "A vivid flame shot into the air with a loud explosion. Fragments of metal shot in all directions over the water and then the sea settled down."[42] By July 31 the Artillery Brigade and the 304th Ammunition Train had disembarked in Liverpool and several other British ports, from where they crossed to Le Havre and Cherbourg between August 5 and 8. The Artillery Brigade did not reunite with the main body of the 79th until the war was over. As they had never fired (or even received) their guns, Pershing's headquarters decided they needed a lot more practice than the rest of the division and sent them to a succession of training camps, where they spent the rest of the war.

Once arrived in Brest, the men were disappointed in their first contacts with the residents of the French port, thinking them a "very low class of people." But as they reached the small towns further inland, they became more enamored of the locals. Companies G and H of the 313th Infantry Regiment were billeted in the picturesque town of Larrey, complete with medieval cathedral; the Catholics among them lost no time making the acquaintance of the parish priest, who gave them a tour.* Ten or twelve men were assigned to every available barn and stable:

> Some of these billets were fairly comfortable and respectable, while in others there was a continual fight between the cows, chickens, and goats and the helpless Yanks ... Beside the entrance to each dwelling was a manure pile. In France, it was claimed, the size of this manure pile determined the wealth of the dweller, and the Frenchman was proud of this possession.[43]

The division did not stay long near Brest. On July 19 divisional headquarters, the 157th Infantry Brigade, and the 310th Machine Gun Battalion loaded themselves onto French trains—the famous boxcars with *Hommes 40, Chevaux 8* stenciled on their sides—for the ride eastward to their training grounds. The rickety cars held 40 men all right, but they couldn't all sit or lie down at the same time; they had to take turns standing and sleeping on the straw-lined floor. When it rained, the men had a choice of leaving the air hatches closed and choking with heat and stuffiness or opening them and getting soaked. The small, light cars bounced over the rails, giving an impression of speed that was wholly illusory. "Side-door Pullmans," the soldiers called them. They reminded the men of the toy railroads that circled the Christmas trees at home; the thin shrieks emanating from the engines sounded like the penny-whistles they had played with as boys. From the open car doors the men could see German prisoners of war working on the roads and women tending the fields. When they stopped in a town they noticed that no adult men were about, only the very young and the very old.[44] If time permitted, the men would crowd around the kitchen doors of the nearby farmhouses crying, "Oofs! Oofs!" The farm wives were alarmed at first, but soon realized that the Americans sought *des oeufs* and would pay for them; international understanding was quickly restored.[†45]

---

* In another town, the priest hit on an ingenious method for hearing confession from American soldiers who knew no French. He had a list printed up in English of all the sins he could think of; the soldier had only to point. (Andrew J. Kachik, untitled memoir, n.d., World War I Survey, Box: 79th Division; 157th and 158th Inf. Brigades; File: Kachik, Andrew, 314th Inf., AHEC, p. 13.)

† Although based on a personal reminiscence long after the war, this story is supported by the

After the usual Army confusion, a few false starts, and a certain amount of backtracking, the division assembled in the Tenth Training Area in the Champagne-Ardennes region, midway between Dijon and Langres. Kuhn expressed his frustration in a letter to his wife:

> After half of my men had been comfortably billeted and the other half were en route on trains, an order came changing the training area to another place 60 miles away. The troops on the trains were diverted and the work of transferring by trucks those who had arrived commenced at once. Some job I can tell you.[46]

Again the men were billeted in private homes. Relations with their hosts were not always cordial:

> In the large house living with us were the owners, father and mother, a son home on leave from the army, and two beautiful daughters, (fairly beautiful anyhow), one married to a man we believed was a Persian rug dealer working in Dijon, and home on weekends which he would spend scowling at several of our handsome officers who smiled too sweetly on his wife and sister-in-law. When he wasn't home to scowl, the old folks scowled for him and muttered what must have been uncomplimentary remarks about us. I can't blame the civilians too much for becoming fed up with the A.E.F.: we were not only better dressed, better fed and better paid than most of them in or out of the Army, but we occupied the best rooms in their houses, and bothered them considerably. However, we were there to help France, and we did pay them rent and damages for use and abuse of their property, so I suppose it evened up.[47]

Not all the natives were hostile. Sergeant Edward Davies of the 315th sought female companionship:

> Reid and I going to meet a couple of French Chicks tonight. Jack says they are some skirts.

But he was disappointed:

observations of Bruce Bairnsfather, the famous British war cartoonist. In his memoirs, he marveled at the Americans' appetite for fresh eggs. He was amazed to find that a plate with a dozen fried eggs was all for one man. (Bruce Bairnsfather, *From Mud to Mufti: With Old Bill on All Fronts* (London: G.P. Putnam's Sons, 1919), p. 178.) Eggs feature in many of the diaries and memoirs written by AEF veterans.

No more French chickens for me—they don't look good at all. Jack says he is going to take the next ones we meet down to the river for a bath, most of them look as tho' they need one bad. They sure are a queer bunch.[48]

The reactions of the "chickens" to the American soldiers is not recorded. Whatever the state of their physical and moral wellbeing, the men of the 79th were ready to learn what the AEF could teach them about war.

Even apart from the issue of open versus trench warfare, General Pershing was well aware of the deficiencies in the training the divisions had received in the States. In late April 1918 he wired the War Department:

Have learned from division commanders and staff officers recently arrived from the United States that large numbers of recruits have been assigned to divisions designated for service in Europe ... In view of the urgency of the situation here there is no time to drill raw recruits in France in elementary work. To send them into the trenches or into battle without requisite training would mean useless and unwarranted loss of life. Therefore urgently recommend that no men be sent over who have not had at least four months intensive training and who have not also had full and thorough instruction in target practice.[49]

He continued in that vein for much of the rest of the war. His original plan for training in France assumed that whole divisions would arrive on a systematic schedule. Each would undergo three one-month training courses before entering combat: one month in small-unit operations, emphasizing open warfare; one month in a quiet British or French sector of the line for seasoning under fire; and one month's maneuvers at the regiment, brigade, and division levels. The German offensives of spring 1918 knocked that idea into a cocked hat, as Pershing was forced to take divisions out of training to bolster the French line. In the event, only the first four divisions to arrive in France—the 1st, 26th, 42nd, and 2nd—followed this plan in its full detail. Later ones had more perfunctory indoctrination and six, including the 79th, had only the first phase before they were sent into battle.[50]

Such divisional training as there was suffered from the inefficiencies of the training grounds. To build self-contained bases for complete infantry divisions would have taken too much effort and material, so it was necessary to billet the men in private homes over a wide area, often over 20 square miles. Assembling the units for training by regiment, brigade, and division required much marching and bivouacking, which took time away from the training itself. During the growing season, land for maneuvering was limited, and because of the high population density, few places were available that could be used as target ranges. Training in anything resembling open warfare was out of the question.

Having had no access to actual weapons and often lacking horses, most of the artillery brigades were even further behind than the infantry. Pershing had laid out his requirements for artillery training in the States:

> Perfection of mounted instruction over difficult ground and at increased gaits, care of horses, accurate laying by frequent verification and computation, observation of fire with most stress on fundamentals and some advance and lateral observation ... rapid preparation and conduct of fire without maps, rapid reconnaissance and occupation of positions under tactical situation, changes of position by echelon, ammunition resupply, telephone.[51]

Little of this had happened. Yet the necessity of artillery support in the attack, demonstrated throughout the war, meant that infantry–artillery coordination would have to be extremely tight. Some artillery units would have to move forward behind the troops, to keep the German rear areas within range as the front receded, while others remained in place to support the current fighting; then their roles would have to reverse as the most rearward batteries leapfrogged their comrades to follow the troops yet again. Engineers would have to repair the roads almost instantly from the effects of German and American shell fire, as well as from the pounding of American trucks, wagons, and gun carriages. And the infantry and artillery would have to be in constant communication so that the latter could assist in any local situations the former might encounter.[52]

This kind of cooperation required intensive and specialized training, and few American divisions received it. Divisional training areas didn't usually provide enough space for firing ranges, so the artillery brigade would be sent to a French range, generally near the west coast, for equipment and practice. The plan was for field artillery to train in four phases: technical instruction, assignment to the front under British and French supervision, maneuvers with the infantry of their own division, and training for staff and senior officers. No artillery brigade completed this program. While most went through the first phase, fewer than half made it through the second and only two or three made it through the third. This meant that both artillery and infantry were ignorant of the key skill on the Western Front, combined operations.[53] Because it took longer to train competent artillery than infantry, the two parts of the same division were rarely reunited. Instead, an artillery brigade that had finished its training would be assigned to support an unfamiliar division. This meant that not only had the gunners and the foot soldiers not trained together, they didn't know each other. Such training as the artillery did receive was geared largely toward positional, not open, warfare—firing from map data, corrections for weather and barrel wear, precision adjustments, and massive bombardment of enemy defenses. Partly this was because of the same geographical constraints under which the infantry suffered. Mostly it was due to the Americans' complete dependence on French guns and instructors.[54]

Another deficiency Pershing knew he had to correct was the lack of officer training, both for staff and line duties. His first action was to create a General Staff College, which opened in November 1917 under the direction of Lieutenant Colonel Alfred W. Bjornstad, an experienced teacher and administrator.[*] At his instigation the College developed a curriculum based on map problems such as had been used at Leavenworth. This was a useful approach, but it neglected the training of chiefs of staff in their actual duties, which was to prepare the orders that supported the map problems. Additionally, aviation was given short shrift; gas and tank warfare and combined-arms operations in general were omitted entirely. In the end, the General Staff College did not contribute much to the AEF. Only 537 officers

---

[*] Bjornstad turned out to be a pompous and divisive figure who harbored delusions of grandeur. He believed that the purpose of the College was to train and advise divisional chiefs of staff, who would formulate plans and oversee their execution, while the commander's job would merely be to inspire and supervise his subordinates during action. This conception, of course, offended the commanders. He saw the General Staff College as a source of doctrine, not merely a teaching institution, equivalent to the Army War College in Maryland or the Staff College at Fort Leavenworth. (James J. Cooke, *Pershing and His Generals: Command and Staff in the AEF* (Westport, CT; London: Praeger, 1997), pp. 34–35, 41.) We shall meet Bjornstad again during the Meuse–Argonne offensive in his capacity as chief of staff for III Corps.

graduated (for a two million-man army!) and not all of them were qualified to serve on a divisional or corps staff.[55]

Pershing also ordered the creation of 13 Army schools to train officers at the divisional and corps levels and to train instructors at corps schools; and nine additional schools in each corps, which were to train unit commanders. Unfortunately, these schools undercut his own three-phase divisional training program by diverting officers to serve as instructors and to attend classes, leaving their units without leadership just as they were undergoing training. Several raw divisions, the 79th among them, lost many of their officers just before their participation in the Meuse–Argonne attack. This practice, carried out by the Training Section at AEF General Headquarters, damaged unit cohesion, morale, and performance. In the end, Pershing's school system failed to produce useful numbers of trained staff officers while it deprived units of talented leaders when they were sorely needed. The pace of events at the front simply did not allow Pershing the luxury of withholding American divisions from combat while they were being trained. Nevertheless, his intention was to create a self-sufficient American army, so the system continued to the end of the war and beyond.[56] A parallel program of corps-level schools worked well, and helped offset the deficiencies of the army school system.[57]

Because American instructors were lacking, especially in artillery and in staff work, the AEF continued to rely on foreign ones, particularly the French. But Pershing didn't like it. By January 1918 he was writing to Marshal Pétain:

> [R]eports have been made by several officers whose units have been most closely associated with French units, and, while appreciating the value of French assistance, the opinion is very generally expressed that beyond the details of trench tactics, our troops have made better progress under their own instructors and according to our own methods. ... The principal reasons cited for the above conclusions are differences in language and methods, and the difficulty found in giving direction to our training into channels most needed.[58]

The last sentence obviously refers to the French propensity to train in positional tactics to the exclusion of mobile warfare. Pershing and his training chief Colonel Fiske were convinced that the French were trying to subvert their open-warfare training program. This was confirmed, in their eyes, by a couple of secret memoranda from Marshal Pétain's headquarters to French division commanders that came to Fiske's attention. They complained that Pershing's training program was too limited and rigid and had little relation to the realities of the Western Front. Of American doctrine one (May 1, 1918) said, "Americans dream of operation in open country, after having broken through the front. This results in too much attention being devoted to this form of operations, which the Americans consider as superior." The Americans did not understand the "mass warfare" in which they were engaged, and did not appreciate the effects of automatic weapons and grenades.[59] Fiske commented on these memos to Major General James McAndrew, the AEF Chief of Staff:

> Neither the French nor the British believe in our ability to train men or in the value of the methods adopted by us. Both forget that in dealing with our officers and men they are dealing with men of different characteristics from those of their own people, and that methods which produce excellent results with the French or British officer or soldier may not be the best for the American ... I strongly recommend that the earliest practicable opportunity be taken to secure our emancipation from Allied supervision." (July 4, 1918)[60]

Pershing wrote in the margin of his copy:

> This is entirely my own view ... Col. Fiske should draw up a memorandum carefully worked out to our officers giving our ideas on the plan of training to be followed and contradicting all these heresies found in this memo of the French.[*][61]

Nor were these objections solely theoretical. American officers developed a high degree of antipathy to French methods of staff work and command. During the Aisne–Marne campaign of late July, French commanders

---

* In fact, Pétain's directive of May 1 did not oppose the Americans' preference for open warfare, it only pointed out that they did not understand what it involved. "Evolution, Orientation, Direction: These are details which should be especially carefully gone into. A knowledge of shifting of units on the field, study of maps, the use of the compass, orientation, direction, all forms of liaison, utilization of approaches, are things which are entirely new and difficult to realize for inexperienced officers ... They will be slow to grasp the idea of flanking movements. It is essential to instill this principle in our Allies, together with that of the counterattack, carefully planned and immediately launched." (Historical Division, *USAWW*, vol. 3, p. 294.)

three times caused heavy casualties in the 28th Division—on the Marne and Ourcq Rivers and at Fismette—by using faulty tactics, frequently changing orders, ignoring the situation on the ground, and failing to pay heed to logistical requirements. This made it particularly hard for the Americans to put up with the patronizing attitude of the French toward the training and capability of the AEF, and strengthened their belief in the superiority of American methods and in the necessity of an independent American force.[62]

Finally Pershing reached his limit. On July 28 he had McAndrew give the French a graceful shove out the door:

> I feel that the time has come when we are no longer warranted in imposing upon the generosity of the French and permitting the American forces to deprive the French army of so many of its highly trained officers and men. . . . I have therefore decided that I must dispense with the services of all French officers and soldiers on duty with American divisions and various army schools except the usual agents of tactical liaison with adjoining units in the actual line of battle ... I cannot, however, part with these officers and soldiers without expressing the great admiration that I have for their splendid efforts ... [63]

However the recently arrived divisions would be trained, it would not be with the help of the French.[*]

By July 30 it was possible to assemble the entire 79th Division (less the artillery brigade) in one place for training. But although the men could practice maneuvering and using their weapons, no proper firing ranges were

---

[*] After the war, Pershing maintained that the French admitted they were wrong and he was right regarding the primacy of open warfare: "The armies on the Western Front in the recent battles that I had witnessed had all but given up the use of the rifle. Machine guns, grenades, Stokes mortars, and one-pounders had become the main reliance of the average soldier ... Ultimately we had the satisfaction of hearing the French admit that we were right, both in emphasizing training for open warfare and insisting upon proficiency in the use of the rifle." (Pershing, My Experiences, vol. 1, p. 153.) But Pershing's own research assistant, Lieutenant Carlisle V. Allan, could find no support for the last statement. (Smythe, Pershing, p. 235.)

available, so they were reduced to shooting only at short distances, potting at empty kerosene cans and targets improvised out of newspaper. Nevertheless, through August and into early September useful work was done. "From dawn till dark, the fields and hillsides were alive with men, drilling, maneuvering, and practicing their weapons."[64] Platoons and companies maneuvered over the countryside. Sergeant Davies of Company B, 315th Infantry, wrote:

> We were instructed how to go in and out of trenches, how to detect and clean up machine gun nests, how to go "over the top" in the proper manner also how to use the gas masks in a gas attack ... The gas masks are the most uncomfortable things I have ever experienced. We also wore our steel helmets. They weigh a ton.[65]

But it was still a far cry from the real thing. Five "division terrain exercises" were held, but it appears from the records that these were map studies for divisional, brigade, and regimental commanders and their staffs and did not involve the men themselves.[66] Kuhn was keenly aware of his division's tactical weaknesses, and he predicted their outcome on the battlefield:

> It has been noted that in practicing battle formations troops advancing in small columns (platoon, half platoon or group) have been so disposed as to furnish excellent targets for hostile artillery and machine guns. Sometimes when these groups halt the men have closed up and knelt, with the result that a hostile machine gun well posted for fire effect might have annihilated the entire column with one burst of fire or a single H.E. [high explosive] shell might have effected disastrous results.[67]

He issued extensive and detailed orders on how infantry, machine guns, and artillery were to cooperate in the attack. His instructions were a comprehensive catalog of offensive methods: how to deploy infantry for an assault on an entrenched position; how to penetrate the wire; how the artillery barrage should be laid down and followed; how to deploy for further penetration; how to organize captured ground against counterattack; and the proper use of tanks, mortars, and machine guns. Most of his dicta were intelligent and based on the experience of other divisions, and would have greatly enhanced the effectiveness of the 79th. But they remained words on paper; there was no time to train the men.[68]

Pershing as well was aware of the under-trained condition of the 79th. In a memo to Foch's headquarters, McAndrew wrote:

> The Commander-in-Chief has directed that the instruction of the 79th and 91st Divisions be intensified so as to fit them for the battle. It has been found necessary to increase the northern group of attack and the Commander-in-Chief believes that both these divisions must be used in the attack with which the Allied Commander-in-Chief [i.e., Foch] has charged him.[69]

And in the midst of it all, First Army's chief of staff, Brigadier General Hugh Drum, continued to send over packages of training manuals on various topics: tanks, machine guns, even trench warfare. By this time, the staff of the AEF were fully aware of the need to use trench tactics to break into the German lines. Paragraph (b) of Drum's instructions read:

> The conquest of this [German forward] zone requires trench warfare methods, which means that the operation must be planned in great detail and carried out according to a fixed schedule. Any slurring over these preparations and instructions will be serious. The advance of the troops should be covered by a dense artillery barrage and facilitated where possible by tanks and by heavy neutralization fire on suspected strong points. All must move according to schedule and along carefully defined predetermined lines.[70]

Pershing himself would have had to approve the release of these instructions. But how anyone was supposed to benefit from this material in the short time left before combat Drum did not explain.

Amid the field maneuvers and range practice, the men found time to relax. Off-duty soldiers saw the local sights and sampled the wine in the nearby villages. The villages themselves appeared exotic to the men. Unlike American farmers who lived on their land, the French grouped their homes together along narrow streets that radiated from a village square, which itself was fronted by the local church. The fields lay around the village in medieval style; each farmer might own several small plots in various directions from his home. The dwellings themselves, made of stone and occasionally finished with stucco, had two halves, each with its own entry from the street. One half was the living quarters; the other was a combination barn and stable for the livestock and draft animals. (This arrangement still prevails in many villages in Lorraine, with a tractor taking the place of an ox team). Well configured for armed defense by virtue of their stone buildings, villages on the front lines would become important tactical objectives.

The men's evenings were filled with band concerts and baseball games. A few took French lessons—and perhaps other pleasures—from the local women. Harold Craig, a sergeant in the Headquarters Company, revealed in his diary what must have been a common reaction to American advances on French women: "French lesson 'ce savoir' with E.P. at Mlle. Merthe. The old man got fussy when we tried to help the girl on with her sweater. We will let him cool off before going back."[71] The first mail caught up with the division, most but not all of it from families and sweethearts. Colonel Claude B. Sweezey, commanding officer of the 313th Infantry, received letters from worried wives and mothers asking about their sons. Sweezey was a tough cavalryman who had served in the Philippines and on the Mexican border and who never appeared—even in combat—without a cigar screwed into his massive jaw.[72] But he knew how much the morale of his men depended on that of their relatives back home. A typical letter he received went like this:

Dear Sir

When you went from Camp Mead over Sea my boy J. Talbott Kelley 313th Inf. went with you and I have heard nothing from him since. It has been over two month since I have seen my boy. I can stand the strain of mind no longer. I must know if my boy is living or dead ... Tell him to be brave and true and ever keep a mothers and dear little sisters face in his mind and to fight for one thing—to come back to us and his dear old America again ... If my boy is dead please let me know. Thanking you for anything you can do for me I remain a mother pleading for news of her boy.

Mrs. J. Talbott Kelley[73]

Sweezey was quick to reassure her:

My Dear Mrs. Kelley:

In reply to your letter, concerning your son, which I just received, will state that I at once sent for your son who is a member of Company "B" of this regiment and talked with him. He is in the best of health, and you need have no worry as to his condition. He looks to be husky enough to stand most anything, and I think will go through the war with safety. He told me to tell you that he was well, happy, and getting along finely. Your letter to me was read to him, and he appreciated hearing it. He states to me that he is not able to read or write himself, but has had other men of his company write for him, and I suppose you have received these letters before this. I thank you for your good wishes, and I am sure that we are as anxious to have the war over as you are at home.[*][74]

Other letters were heartbreaking:

Dear Sir,

Will you kindly if possible do us a great favor their is a young Sargent in your unit Sargent Roland Harkum Co. M 313 Infantry whose mother passed away Friday 26, 1918 at quarter to eleven & we would like you to kindly to break the news to him as gently as possible tell him that she had a little Boy born to her at 10 oclock & died at quarter to eleven the Baby is also dead we certainly will thank you & also tell him Blanche was with his mother when she died she was only sick 2 hours we dont know who else to ask but you & he will have to know it as his letters coming to her from him remaining unanswered he won't know what to think, we think you are the most capable one to tell him break it gently & kindly let us hear from you what he has to say & tell him to bear up & trust in God. I remain a friend of the Sargent.

Mrs. Lillian Meyers[75]

When not drilling, playing ball, or reading mail, the men engaged in one of the oldest military pursuits—swapping rumors. The future historian of Company F, 316th Infantry, heard:

... that the 79th was to be a Shock Division, hurled only into critical gaps on the front; that the Allies were on German soil in three places; that Edison had invented a gas so potent it could poison every German; that Von Hindenburg committed suicide and the Crown Prince surrendered when they heard of the invention; that General Pershing had declared Company F would be in Heaven, Hell, or Hoboken by Christmas; and that the 79th

---

[*] Private Kelley does not appear in the "Roll of Honor" of the 79th Division, so it is likely he survived the war.

Division would confront the enemy within a few weeks. The last rumor was unique; it was true.[76]

Sure enough, on September 7 came orders from General Drum for the division to proceed by train the next morning to the Robert-Espagne area, there to report to the French Second Army "for tactical control and administration."[77] The Second Army held the front opposite the Argonne Forest, the Heights of the Meuse, and Montfaucon. Ready or not, the 79th would be going into the line.

CHAPTER 6

AMERICANS REACH THE BATTLEFIELD

By May 1917 the Allies' original strategy for the war had collapsed; its four main assumptions had proved false. First, the Royal Navy was supposed to keep the sea lanes open by destroying the German fleet so that supplies could flow to Britain and France indefinitely. But with rare exceptions the German Navy refused to engage the British fleet and instead resorted to submarine warfare against merchant shipping. Second, Britain would fund the Allies' war efforts. But in November 1916 the US government "advised" American banks to stop lending to the warring powers; since the British were borrowing from the US as much as they were lending to its Allies, they were caught short. Third, France and Russia would bear the burden of containing the German and Austro-Hungarian armies in Europe until early 1917, when—fourth—all armies would be exhausted and Kitchener's New Armies would step in to sway the balance against the Central Powers. But Russian enthusiasm for the war disappeared in the face of huge casualties and massive food shortages, and the revolutionary government of March 1917 told its Allies it was incapable of further offensives before the summer. French morale collapsed in the wake of Nivelle's April offensive, after the New Armies had already been chewed to pieces at the Somme. In July Winston Churchill, then British Minister of Munitions, advised Lloyd George to forgo any more offensives until American troops could provide numerical superiority. But Haig, indefatigable, insisted on launching a battle that turned into the catastrophe of Passchendaele, in which the British suffered 245,000 casualties, twice the German total. The Italian Army was crushed at Caporetto in October, losing 300,000 men of whom 275,000 surrendered. At the same time, the Bolsheviks seized power and sued for peace, freeing over 40 German and Austro-Hungarian divisions for use on the Western Front. The only strategy left to the Allies was to accumulate weapons, supplies, and men while waiting for the Americans to reach the battlefield.

The problem was shipping. Throughout 1917, Bliss and Pershing stressed to the War Department the need to find adequate tonnage not only to carry US troops and supplies to France, but to make up losses to submarines. By the end of 1917 there was still no effective agreement with the Allies and only four combat divisions and 177,000 soldiers had reached France.[1] Even by mid-November it was becoming clear to the British that Pershing would not come close to achieving his goal of one million men in France by the summer of 1918; a more realistic estimate was 525,000 by May. The lack of tonnage was not the only problem; inexperience was a factor—although many American ships were packed to the gunwales, some crossed the ocean less than half full.

In early January Sir William Robertson, Chief of the Imperial General Staff, suggested to Pershing that the 15 divisions scheduled to reach France in 1919 after they had finished training in the States be sent over earlier, broken up, and assigned to British units by battalions. British shipping would transport them. Pershing saw this as a typically self-serving British proposition: they would provide shipping only on condition that the troops brought over be assigned to their army. If shipping was available, Pershing maintained, it should be used to bring over whole divisions, and it should have been offered earlier. The British had to acquiesce, although they won agreement that the infantry and the divisional staffs would train with the British, the artillery with the French, and they would be reunited as complete divisions afterward.* The issue arose afresh almost every time Pershing met with his British and French opposite numbers.

As the year progressed the slowness of the American buildup became particularly galling as German strength on the Western Front increased due

---

* Although generally resolute in his rejection of such proposals, Pershing was willing to make an exception for black troops. The 93rd Division was broken up and its four regiments distributed among as many French divisions, where they served with distinction.

to the transfer of troops following the Russian collapse. German potential strength in the West was 217 divisions, compared with the Allies' 169, leaving aside the Americans.[2] The Supreme War Council increased pressure on the Americans to increase the rate of troop arrivals. Bliss's cables to the War Department grew increasingly desperate:

> French Minister of War, M. Clemenceau has asked for an interview with me on this subject at three o'clock tomorrow afternoon. Can you rush me a reply giving me any assurance to communicate to him? Can you assure me whether beginning with the month of March there will be a material increase in the rate of despatch of our troops and whether the increase in rate will give us fifteen combatant divisions by July 17?[3]

The War Department cabled back that it could do it, given certain adjustments in Allied shipping priorities.[4] And the War Department kept its word; two divisions arrived in April, nine in May, and eight in June. Gradually, American troop arrivals began to reverse the balance of manpower on the Western Front.

Of course it was not sufficient to get the troops across the Atlantic; they had to get to the front. But the Army had no modern experience at moving large numbers of men and massive amounts of materiel. Major General James E. Harbord, the eventual commander of the Services of Supply, described the situation in his memoirs:

> There was, of course, the knowledge that some new construction would be necessary at the ports and in the Zone of the Armies; but that improvements on a vast scale would be needed all the way from the seacoast to the firing line, and that the ports and railways would have to be equipped and operated in large part by American forces, acting jointly with those of the French, was not even a matter of conjecture.[5]

The need was acute; a single division with its equipment took 50–58 railroad trains to move and required 25 carloads of supplies a day.[6] Men, equipment, and supplies had to be moved 400–500 miles from the French ports in the west to the front in the east. To create the necessary facilities, Pershing in July 1917 created the Transportation Service.* By the fall, the Service had

---

* Pershing had little understanding of modern logistics. He blamed the War Department and the French for the supply problem, but he was responsible as well. Members of a committee from the US

undertaken major expansion projects in nine French ports as well as construction of nine large depots, 12 railroad lines, and associated railroad facilities; and it had ordered 1,000 railroad locomotives, both standard and narrow-gauge; 9,000 railroad cars; and assorted steam tugs, barges, floating derricks, cranes, and steam shovels.[7]

Another surprise awaited the Army as its divisions started to arrive. It found that the French had no organization dedicated to the feeding, housing, arming, and introduction into combat of the new arrivals. Although the French and British had faced the same supply problems for three years, it had never occurred to them to coordinate their purchasing efforts. Their competition with each other, as well as with the Americans, was pushing up prices and causing local shortages and surpluses. Pershing was unable get his allies to consolidate their purchasing, but he was at least able to keep the AEF from competing with itself. On August 20 he created a General Purchasing Board, despite the unanimous opinion of his advisers that it was illegal, with Colonel Charles G. Dawes in charge. Dawes' mission was to find European sources for as much of the American supply requirement as he could to free up transatlantic shipping capacity. The GPB coordinated requirements, stockpiles, and acquisitions across all Army purchasing departments as well as the Red Cross and the YMCA. By war's end, Dawes had bought ten million tons of supplies in a Europe supposedly stretched to the limit already, compared with seven million shipped by the War Department. This kept the shipping problem from becoming worse than it already was. Nevertheless, for a long time the lack of trained staff officers led to mammoth tie-ups that paralyzed ports and rail yards. Ships could not be unloaded fast enough to free up berths for new arrivals, and unloaded cargo could not be moved inland as fast as it hit the docks. Rail yards were packed solid. In the words of historians Douglas V. Johnson, II, and Rolfe Hillman, Jr., "What was in the cars no one knew; where they were supposed to be going, none could say; how they were to get from one point to another was beyond imagining. Scale had overwhelmed talent."[8]

visited his Chaumont headquarters to talk the subject over and found that he did not understand it. According to Brigadier General Mason M. Patrick, Chief Engineer Officer of the AEF and a West Point classmate of Pershing, "He handled the matter rather poorly and haltingly—asked a few questions about docks available. Said he was not satisfied with progress being made, thought fault *might* lie with the organization ... " [emphasis in original] Patrick definitely thought the fault was with the organization, and mainly at the top. (Smythe, *Pershing*, p. 82.)

The reaction of the French to the American troops was ecstatic. Upon first arriving in Paris, on his way to the Hotel de Crillon, Pershing and his cavalcade were assaulted by hysterical mobs with flowers, flags, and shouts of "Vive l'Amérique!" Many wept. The Americans' robustness amazed the French populace. They are, one French instructor exclaimed, "energetic and untiring. Yesterday we did 26 or 28 kilometers." The popularity of sports was a novelty, particularly baseball, which seemed to require considerable skill, and boxing, in which the Yanks showed perhaps too much enthusiasm. The French peasants' chief regret was that such physical virtuosity was not employed in more productive pursuits, such as agriculture. "In sum, the growing number of American soldiers in France, their contacts with French troops, their increasingly frequent participation in combat, the presence of officer-trainees in French regiments, were so many factors that contributed to raising French morale."*9

The Allies' fears that the Americans were not ready came true sooner than expected. On March 21, Ludendorff unleashed his first Spring Offensive, Operation *Michael*, against the British lines at Amiens. Seventy-one German divisions trained in infiltration and combined-arms tactics attacked 26 British divisions, 19 of them understrength and recovering from Passchendaele. Six thousand guns, the largest bombardment in history, opened up on the British Third and Fifth Armies. When 2,500 British guns fired in reply, hardly anyone noticed. The Third Army fell back, the Fifth virtually disintegrated. The offensive petered out on April 5 as the Germans outran their supplies and the stamina of their troops; but they had advanced 40 miles, sweeping over the old Somme battlefield almost to the critical British communication center of Amiens, and had occupied almost 1,200 square miles. The British had lost over 160,000 men, 90,000 of them prisoners. In this cataclysm, the American battle contribution was minor and inadvertent. To protect the British line east of Amiens, a scratch force of 3,000 men was improvised from stragglers and stray units, among them two companies of American railroad engineers who happened to be caught up in the fighting. Otherwise, the AEF did not assist in repelling *Michael*;

---

* Up to a point. Many American soldiers had experiences such as the one Captain Will Judy of the 33rd Division recorded in his diary: "The price of beer has been increased to twenty centimes or two cents for the large glass. The French soldiers curse us and their own countrymen for raising prices." (Will Judy, *A Soldier's Diary: A Day-to-Day Record in the World War* (Chicago: Judy Publishing Co., 1930), p. 124.)

the three divisions it had in the line were in sectors far from the fighting, its others scattered across 12 training areas behind the French front.

The shock of the German success had one salutary effect on the Allied front. To now there had been no unified Allied command; coordination between the British and French (and, at times, the Italians and Belgians also) was by agreement among their political and military leaders. Of course those leaders' priorities tended to change over time, so a deal reached with regard to a particular course of action might evaporate as the date for action approached. This had happened at the Somme in 1916, and it was happening now. Even with foreknowledge of a German attack, the Allies could not agree to appoint a joint commander in chief, wanting instead to preserve their national independence. The French wanted a Supreme Commander to be French, because they had the largest army and had the most to lose, while the British didn't want to allow the possibility that a foreign general could order their troops to their deaths. It became clear that the British priority was to protect their lines of communications to the Channel and the French imperative was to shield Paris—in other words, without a firm commitment otherwise, the armies would withdraw in different directions. At a conference at Doullens on March 26, Haig asked General Foch, then without command responsibility, for his advice. The meeting ended with Foch being appointed "to coordinate the action of the Allied Armies on the Western Front." But not until a further conference at Beauvais on April 3 was he given adequate power, and not until April 14 did Clemenceau and Lloyd George (now British Prime Minister), at his request, award him the title of General Commander-in-Chief of the Allied Armies in France.[*]

A second effect of Operation *Michael* was to make a dent in Pershing's aversion to amalgamation. General Tasker Bliss, the American representative on the Supreme War Council, got tired of Pershing's refusal to accommodate the Allies even in the emergency and drew up what became SWC Joint Note No. 18. It proposed to bring over only infantry and machine gun units,

---

[*] Pershing thought Foch was selected because he was available, "certainly not because of any particular military ability he had displayed up to that moment." (Smythe, *Pershing*, p. 100.) But Foch was the right choice. In charge of the French forces at the Somme, he had gradually assumed a *de facto* role coordinating the action across the entire front. As Philpott has pointed out, managing three forces in semi-independent sectors—the French straddling the river and the British armies to the north of the French—gave him the experience he would need to direct three armies in 1918. (Philpott, *Three Armies*, p. 213.)

which would serve as reinforcements; later they would be re-integrated into the American Army. At a meeting on March 28 with Bliss and Secretary Baker, who was in France, Pershing railed at Bliss for acceding to the Allies' demands, saying that it would prevent forming an American army any time soon. But Baker backed up Bliss, and Pershing got the point. That very afternoon he drove over to Foch's headquarters at Clermont-sur-Oise and declared his full cooperation with the French general. Foch had been meeting with Pétain, Premier Clemenceau, and Louis Loucheur, the Minister of Munitions. He grabbed Pershing by the arm, dragged him into the garden, and made him repeat what Pershing had just told him to these dignitaries. In better French than he knew he could speak, Pershing said:

> I have come to tell you that the American people would consider it a great honor for our troops to be engaged in the present battle. I ask for this in their name and my own. At this moment there are no questions but of fighting. Infantry, artillery, aviation, all that we have are yours; use them as you wish. More will come, in numbers equal to the requirements. I have come especially to tell you that the American people will be proud to take part in the greatest battle of history.[10]

Foch and Clemenceau were filled with gratitude and admiration. As it happened, Operation *Michael* had already started to subside, and it is doubtful that Pershing ever intended to comply with Note #18 to the extent of breaking up US divisions as they arrived in France. But the principle was clear: the United States would support the Allies in the current crisis, even if it meant postponing the formation of an American army.

The next German blow, Operation *Georgette* on April 9, struck further north on the Lys River, where the British First and Second Armies were defending Hazebrouck, another British command center. It too gained surprise and territory, but not the breakthrough experienced before Amiens. Again the Americans, who were deployed considerably to the south, were absent from the defense. While the operation was in progress, however, they participated in an incident that worried their Allies even more than their minuscule presence in the line. The 26th Division, raised from the National Guards of six New England states (hence its nickname, the "Yankee Division"), was attached to a French corps in a quiet sector near St Mihiel, south of Verdun. On April 20 its position in the village of Seicheprey was attacked by 2,800 troops of the German 78th Reserve Division. The 26th held the position but lost 81 dead, 401 wounded (including 214 by gas), and 187 taken prisoner or gone missing. The German report on the action praised the fighting qualities of the American troops, but criticized their commanders for not controlling the infantry or artillery and failing to assign forces for a counterattack.[11] Pershing wanted to fire several senior officers, but the French corps commander, General Passaga, awarded them the Croix de Guerre as a morale-boosting measure. The British and French High Commands were not fooled, and looked on American prospects with foreboding. Lloyd George, Foch, and Clemenceau used the *Georgette* incident as the occasion to insist that Pershing implement the terms of SWC Joint Note No. 18; they continued to insist well into July, by which time the formation of an American army was a *fait accompli*.[12]

After *Michael*, the French Third Army had replaced the destroyed British Fifth Army south of Amiens; General Humbert, its commander, placed the American 1st Division in the Montdidier sector, where Operation *Michael* had penetrated the furthest. With the waning of the *Georgette* offensive on the Lys, the French decided that the Americans could be entrusted with a minor attack; they selected the village of Cantigny, situated on a low rise that gave the Germans a good view of the American lines, as the target. Major General Robert L. Bullard, the division commander, assigned the 28th Infantry Regiment, commanded by Colonel Hanson Ely, to make the assault. Preparations were meticulous. Bullard reinforced the 28th with divisional machine guns and artillery, machine gun and rifle companies from two other regiments, and a company of engineers. French tanks and artillery, flame throwers, and aircraft were added to the lineup. Detailed plans were issued and the infantry, tanks, and airplanes practiced on a model of the village.

The attack went off without a hitch. On May 28, at 5:45 a.m., the artillery opened up on the target. After an hour it switched to a rolling barrage and the infantry moved out behind it. By the end of another hour the 28th had secured the position with a loss of only 50 men and was digging in. But the Americans' luck was not to hold. Small groups of Germans, hidden in cellars and overlooked by the mopping-up teams, attacked from the rear. Worse, a day earlier and 40 miles to the south, the Germans began Operation *Blücher*, launched over the old Chemin des Dames battlefield and aimed directly at Paris, and their rapid advance forced the French to withdraw their heavy artillery and machine guns from the

Cantigny sector. German counterattacks began almost as soon as the 28th had taken the village and continued for three days, opposed only by the rifles and the 75mm field guns of the Americans. The latter, although able to break up counterattacks at close range, did not have the reach to hit the Germans' heavy guns, which continued to pound the defenders. By the third day, the 28th had lost almost one-third of its men and the remainder were staggering wrecks; had the German infantry and artillery coordinated their counterattacks properly, the regiment might well have lost the town. Ely asked Bullard to relieve it and send in one of the other regiments that had been sitting out the battle. The 18th Infantry replaced them, taking shell fire but no counterattacks until the Germans abandoned the fight.[13]

Although the 28th had been badly chewed up, Pershing was elated. The superiority of the American fighting man and the virtue of his own training doctrine in particular had been vindicated. Cabling the War Department, he reported:

> Our infantry reached its objective in scheduled time and immediately organized its new position ... Five strong counterattacks were made by the Germans all of which were dissipated, leaving prisoners in our hands. Our staff work was excellent and the liaison perfect. Twenty minutes after the new position was reached the information was at divisional head-quarters: soon thereafter telephone communication was established and maintained. The Allies are high in praise of our troops.[14]

When André Tardieu, recently French High Commissioner in the United States, spoke critically of American commanders and their staffs, Pershing told him he was tired of being patronized and would stand for no more such nonsense.[15]

One month after *Georgette* ended Ludendorff struck for the third time, this time at the Chemin des Dames. The AEF's intelligence staff anticipated German intentions and warned, but to no avail; clever concealment by the Germans and a lack of French air reconnaissance led General Denis Duchêne to believe he was in no danger. Opposite the French Sixth Army, commanded by Duchêne, the Germans had placed 30 divisions, 6,000 guns—the largest concentration yet of artillery—and two million shells. At 1:00 a.m. on May 27, the Germans opened Operation *Blücher* with a massive bombardment; all two million shells were expended in slightly over four hours. The French were unfamiliar with infiltration tactics. Duchêne refused to deploy a defense in depth, placing his men in the front trenches where they would bear the full weight of the artillery. His line buckled on contact. Within three days the Germans had advanced 30 miles, taken Soissons, captured 60,000 prisoners and 650 guns, and were sitting on the north bank of the Marne, 56 miles from Paris, showing no signs of stopping.[16]

As the Germans approached the Marne, the French became increasingly desperate. Clemenceau's government started packing to evacuate Paris and began to plan extreme measures such as abandoning northern or northeastern France entirely and regrouping the French divisions behind the Somme or south of Reims. This extremity placed even more pressure on Pershing to amalgamate his 650,000 troops into the French and British armies. But few of them were trained and most of those who were were not in position to repel the immediate attack. On May 30, after dining with Foch, Pershing agreed to move his five available divisions to the Marne front. But it had already started to happen. On the afternoon of the previous day General Ragueneau of the French Military Mission burst in on Fox Conner, Pershing's Chief of Operations, exclaiming, *"C'est terrible! C'est affreux! Les Boches sont arrivés au Marne. Au secours!"* Conner consulted a map, then offered the 2nd Division. Ragueneau protested it wasn't nearly enough. Thereupon Conner got on the phone to the 3rd Division, only three weeks in France and untrained in trench warfare, and ordered it into the line.[*][17]

The 3rd Division was the first to see action. Near dusk on May 31, two companies of its 2nd Machine Gun Battalion reached the south bank of the Marne opposite the town of Château Thierry. Expecting a full German assault, they emplaced their guns and proceeded to fire into the enemy formations on the other side. The division's 17,000 infantrymen arrived the next day, its artillery still far behind. For the next two weeks the regiment defended the south bank, repelling several crossing attempts and mopping up the small contingents of Germans who had made it to the south side. Major General Mondésir, the French corps commander, shuffled the regiments and battalions of the 3rd to wherever he thought they were needed. Only in mid-June, once joined by its artillery, did the division get its own sector. In truth, the action of the 3rd Division at Château Thierry

---

[*] It is highly improbable that Conner would have taken such action without Pershing's knowledge. Most likely Pershing had already told Conner of his intentions.

on May 31 was of more psychological than material benefit to the Allies; the German attack had almost run its course for the same reasons that previous offensives had failed: fatigue and lack of supplies. Nonetheless, the Americans' stand, in which they not only held the line but were able to advance in places, gave a great lift to French spirits. Jean de Pierrefeu, on Pétain's staff, wrote, "We all had the impression that we were about to see a wonderful transfusion of blood. Life was coming in floods to reanimate the dying body of France."[18]

Five miles northwest of Château Thierry, also at the limit of the German advance, lay a patch of woodland known as the Bois de Belleau. On June 1 through 3 the 2nd Division, newly arrived from its training grounds in Normandy and Picardy, took up positions just south of the wood as part of the French XXI Corps under Major General Jean Degoutte. En route, they had marched against a tide of humanity fleeing the Germans: peasants pulling carts piled high with belongings, mothers pushing baby carriages, farmers driving goats and sheep. French soldiers were heading south too, "the motley array which characterizes the rear of a beaten Army," in the words of General Harbord, now commanding the Fourth "Marine" Brigade of the 2nd Division.[*][19] Approaching the area to which they had been assigned, Harbord expected to find French staff officers awaiting him with maps and orders. Instead he found chaos—no one could tell him where his brigade was to go, or even where the front was. Around 6:00 a.m., directed by a villager, he found General Degoutte, who told him to have his men—who had been traveling, almost sleepless, for three days—ready to go into the line in five hours. He got an extra hour; at noon, the division commander, Major General Omar Bundy, ordered him to put his two regiments, the Fifth and Sixth Marines, into line on either side of the Paris–Metz highway, and passed along Degoutte's order to dig in several hundred yards behind their position "just in case." Harbord replied, "We will dig no trenches to fall back to. The Marines will hold where they stand."[20]

As it happened, holding wasn't necessary. Except for harassing fire from German guns and a few exploratory skirmishes, the 2nd Division did not come under attack. But Belleau Wood was an excellent place for the Germans to hide infantry and artillery, and Degoutte had ordered that

---

[*] The French soldiers shouted to the Americans, "*La guerre est finie!*" The Americans yelled back, "*Pas finie!*" The area became known as the Pas Fini Sector.

ground lost was to be recovered wherever possible, so Harbord determined to take it. Unknown was just how difficult an objective the Wood would prove. Rugged, boulder-strewn topography and dense woods had been improved for defense by a system of echeloned trenches reinforced with barbed wire and studded with machine guns. None of this was shown on maps; the French thought the wood to be largely unoccupied, and the Americans were too inexperienced to do their own reconnaissance. On June 6, after a good start in the early morning, two Marine battalions attacked the woods across a wheat field, walking shoulder to shoulder as if on parade, just as Longstreet's Confederates had done in the Wheatfield at Gettysburg. Following Pershing's doctrine of the self-reliant rifleman, artillery support was negligible. The German machine guns cut the Marines to pieces; 1,097 men became casualties that day. Similar attacks occurred on succeeding days, with similar results. After the war Major General John Lejeune, the eventual commander of the 2nd Division, wrote that in each attack, "little progress was made and it became apparent that the reckless courage of the foot soldier with his rifle and bayonet could not overcome machine guns, well-protected in rocky nests."[21]

On the 8th, Brigadier General William Chamberlaine, commander of the 2nd Division's artillery brigade, suggested a different approach. Light and heavy guns would shell known strong points in the woods as well as important locations in the rear. The 75mm guns would provide a rolling barrage ahead of the infantry advance. Twelve machine guns to the east of the woods would fire on retreating Germans. Two days later, using this plan, the Marines took the southern half of the wood losing eight dead and 24 wounded. With continued artillery support they made further progress on the next two days, but bogged down as the Germans reinforced. Despite the success his division had had when supported by artillery, Harbord then ordered several more days of infantry-only assaults, with predictable results. Only on June 25 did he withdraw his riflemen and have all of the division's guns plaster the remaining German positions. That did the trick; the next day his leading battalion commander signaled, "Wood now US Marine Corps entirely."[22] Five days later the division attacked the nearby town of Vaux after detailed reconnaissance and a meticulously planned artillery bombardment assisted by aerial observation.

It captured the town in 90 minutes and secured it the same day.[*] The Germans were impressed:

> The various attacks of both regiments on Belleau Woods were carried out with dash and recklessness. The moral effect of our fire-arms did not materially check the advance of the infantry; the nerves of the Americans are still unshaken ... The individual soldiers are very good. They are healthy, vigorous and physically well developed ... The troops are fresh and full of straightforward confidence. A remark of one of the prisoners is indicative of their spirit: "We kill or get killed."[23]

Ludendorff was not finished. On June 8 two armies attacked the French between Montdidier and Noyon, attempting to fill in the gap between the salients at Amiens and Château Thierry. Despite the French having gotten advance warning by deciphering the German orders, the Germans advanced more than five miles, taking 8,000 prisoners. On June 9 they continued for another two miles. But the French Third Army, along with the American 1st Division dug in at Cantigny, held fast, and by June 11 the operation was canceled. Still determined to divert Allied reserves away from Flanders, Ludendorff on July 15 launched an attack east of Château Thierry on either side of Reims. This time the French used advance intelligence to good effect, bombarding the German troops as they were forming up for the assault and getting them off to a rocky start. East of Reims, the French defense in depth— held in part by the 42nd Division—worked well; the attackers were stopped by 11:00 that morning. But to the west, on the southern flank of the salient from June's Operation *Blücher*, a forward defense was in place; the Germans were able to cross the Marne and advance for five miles, but no farther. Once again the 3rd Division stood firm against the advance, although attacked on three sides. On the 17th Ludendorff halted the offensive.

The Germans were stunned by the ferocity of the defense on the Marne and the magnitude of their casualties. A German lieutenant wrote:

---

[*] Historian Russell Weigley suggests that Pershing's infantry-heavy doctrine was overly conservative given technological advances since the Civil War. Nevertheless, he opines, "His insistence upon the rifle and bayonet training appropriate to warfare outside the trenches paid off when his men threaded their way through Belleau Wood and the Argonne Forest." (Russell F. Weigley, *History of the United States Army*, ed. Louis Morton, The Wars of the United States (New York, London: Macmillan, 1967), p. 390.) But the officers of the 2nd Division attributed their success at Belleau Wood to artillery, not rifle and bayonet.

> Never had I seen so many dead, never contemplated a spectacle of war so frightful as on the northern slopes of the Marne. On the southern side the Americans in a hand-to-hand fight had completely wiped out two of our companies. Hidden in the wheat in a semicircle, they had let our men advance, then had annihilated them with a fire at thirty or forty feet away. This enemy has coolness, one must acknowledge, but he also gave proof that day of a bestial brutality.[24]

As the German offensives became progressively weaker, Foch sensed opportunity. American troop arrivals had altered the balance of manpower on the Western Front. On June 1, the Allies could muster 1,496,000 bayonets (infantry actually serving in the trenches), the Germans 1,639,000. By July 1, the edge had reversed: 1,556,000 to 1,412,000. In the words of French historian André Kaspi, "It was this growing superiority that permitted Foch to launch his July counteroffensive."[25] Foch already had four armies positioned opposite the bulge made by the Germans' advance to the Marne. As early as July 7 he began concentrating them, under great secrecy, for an assault on the salient, in which Soissons was the major city. On the 18th, the day after the fifth German offensive ended, he counterattacked. Because the Germans had not had time to fortify their positions on the south side of the Marne, Foch could maintain surprise by dispensing with the preliminary bombardment. Two of his armies made rapid advances against the west side of the salient; two others on the south side did not. Thereafter the German resistance stiffened, but it didn't matter; seeing that their position was weak and his men exhausted, on July 22 Ludendorff ordered the complete evacuation of the Marne salient. Two days earlier he had canceled Operation *Hagen,* his cherished and long-planned attack against the British in Flanders, for which his Spring Offensives had been mere diversions—and in which his army had lost one million men killed, wounded, captured, or missing.[*][26]

Supporting the French were five American divisions. The 1st and 2nd, separated by the French First Moroccan Division—one of the best in the French

---

[*] Additionally, in June and July the Germans incurred half a million cases of flu in the second, more deadly wave of the disease. As a result of these developments, as we have seen, the divisions of the German Second Army were gutted. Battalions were down to 200 rifles and 15–20 light machine guns. NCOs and officers were in short supply. British historian Tim Travers has written, "It can be argued, therefore, that the German army on the western front really lost the war between March and July through the costly failure of its own offensives." (Tim Travers, "The Allied Victories, 1918," in *World War I: A History*, ed. Hew Strachan (Oxford, New York: Oxford UP, 1998), p. 208.)

Army—attacked the western side of the German salient. The 4th, in France for only six weeks and with its two brigades split between two French corps, also advanced from the west a few miles south of the 2nd. The 26th, at the southwest extremity of the bulge, and the 3rd, to its right at Château Thierry, joined the advance as the Germans evacuated their position on July 22. Eventually the 26th was relieved by the 42nd and the 3rd by the 32nd. By August 6 the salient had been completely eliminated, at a cost of about 7,000 casualties—a relatively modest number.[27] French and American divisions sat on the south bank of the Vesle River, from which Ludendorff had launched Operation *Blücher* 18 weeks earlier. Pershing was jubilant. But the end result obscured many problems that attended the Americans' performance, problems that were to dog the AEF almost until the end of the war. Command posts were too far to the rear, and communications with the front lines were throttled by congestion on the roads. The French provided tank support but none of the divisions had trained with tanks, so there was little cooperation. American commanders complained afterward that German aircraft dominated the skies, but none of them thought to ask for antiaircraft support at the time. Men bunched up on the attack, increasing the frequency of casualties. Auxiliary infantry weapons were not effectively used, especially the 37mm guns that had been provided to suppress enemy machine gun positions. A major error in the operation was the Americans' indifference to artillery support. Although the French provided heavy artillery in plenty, there is only one record of a commander requesting fire support on a difficult position. In the words of Johnson and Hillman, "[T]he artillery did not get forward soon enough, moved its rolling barrages too fast for the infantry to follow, fired only upon prearranged targets rather than attacking 'targets of opportunity,' had far too few observers, and failed to employ smoke or offensive gas."[28] Largely because of this, the 1st and 2nd Divisions between them took 11,000 casualties and the 26th and 42nd suffered a similar number. The 3rd Division alone incurred 8,000 dead and wounded.[29]

French observers had their own criticisms. In the attack the Americans were impulsive and careless. They dropped all inconvenient equipment, including packs, ammunition, even excess clothing. As a result, they were often lacking important items and supplies. They made no attempt to dig in or to conceal themselves, which resulted in heavy casualties. They were hard to manage on the march, not for lack of endurance but because they had no regard for road discipline, varying their speed unpredictably and leaving the column for no good reason. They ate their rations all at once, not saving any reserves. Food was simultaneously abundant and wasted; cooks, supplied with 500 grams of meat per man, could not provide a single meat meal per day. These problems were for the most part ascribed to the inexperience of the line officers and the staffs.[30] But Teilhard de Chardin, then a stretcher-bearer in the 1st Moroccan Division, added: "The only complaint one would make about [the Americans] is that they don't take sufficient care; they're too apt to get themselves killed. When they're wounded, they make their way back holding themselves upright, almost stiff, impassive, and uncomplaining. I don't think I've ever seen such pride and dignity in suffering."[31]

Despite repeated demonstrations that artillery support was crucial, Pershing and his staff concluded that the lesson of the fighting in July vindicated the doctrine of self-reliant infantry. They wrote, "The rifle again proved to be the chief weapon of the infantry soldier." And, although mobile artillery was not a factor as the Soissons attack proceeded, leading to heavy losses as the offensive ended, they concluded, "The regulation methods of handling artillery in open warfare were found to be sound and capable of execution."[32]

To counter the deleterious effects of serving with the French and British during the German Spring Offensives, Pershing ordered his training chief, McAndrew, to devise a training program for divisions sent into reserve after combat. Issued on August 8, it was a strange memorandum. It mandated two days of rest and refit before resuming training behind the lines; this was too little to rest from combat, or to assimilate replacement men and equipment. It emphasized training for open warfare "such as encountered by our forces in the operations of the last few months;" but the Allied counteroffensive had been a series of trench-warfare set pieces. The tactics were to include use of scouts to locate the enemy, and outflanking maneuvers by the main body once the enemy had revealed himself; but the Germans never made themselves hard to locate, and there were no flanks. It said that "intelligent use of fire to cover movement enables ground to be gained at relatively small cost;" but attacks, even with heavy artillery support, were never cheap on the Western Front. As historian James W. Rainey comments, "The Germans were not going to behave like Plains Indians or Moros, however much Pershing wished they might. But Pershing was so much the captive of his experiences that he could not publicly renounce his heritage and admit to a new form of warfare."[33]

The July counteroffensive had a devastating effect on the German Army beyond the loss of their salient on the Marne. Crown Prince Rupprecht, commanding the army group that held that part of the German line, reported to OHL[*] on the deterioration of morale, particularly among the troops, many of them elderly, who had arrived from Russia in late 1917. Twenty-percent rates of absence from duty were common; desertion surged; troops refused to obey orders or fired their rifles from trains; and many gave up to the Allies at the first opportunity. OHL had lost the capacity for effective decision-making. General Fritz von Lossberg, chief of staff of the German Fourth Army, pleaded with Ludendorff to retreat to the Hindenburg Line as Mangin's Tenth Army and Degoutte's Sixth pierced the German front; but Ludendorff, paralyzed, insisted that the Army was unimpaired. In retrospect, the reduction of the Marne salient was the beginning of the end. In the words of Martin Gilbert, "The Germans had not been pushed back like this before. On July 15 they had still expected to be receiving Allied peace proposals within two months, with Paris at their mercy. 'That was on the 15th,' the German Chancellor, Georg von Hertling, later wrote. 'On the 18th even the most optimistic among us knew that all was lost. The history of the world was played out in three days.'"[34]

Two days after the close of the French counteroffensive on the Marne, the German command's paralysis turned to despair as the British Fourth Army attacked the Amiens salient. The combined-arms assault comprised 17 infantry divisions, 530 tanks, 2,000 guns, and 800 airplanes, along with an elaborate program of deception and surprise. It was supported by the French First Army to the south with 15 divisions and 1,600 guns. Between August 8 and 12 the attack gained 12 miles. By September 4 the Germans had retreated 40 miles, back across the Somme into the same Hindenburg Line that they had occupied before Operation *Michael* on March 21. Ludendorff told Chancellor Hertling that military means could no longer force the Allies to seek peace, so a diplomatic solution should be sought. Kaiser Wilhelm then authorized Admiral Paul von Hintze, the newly appointed Foreign Minister, to start peace negotiations, possibly through a neutral country. Even so, Ludendorff could not bring himself to reveal the full extent of the impending catastrophe. His failure let the government think it should wait for a favorable military development before starting talks—but that development never came, and Germany wasted its last chance to negotiate a tolerable peace.

---

[*] *Oberheeresleitung*, the German High Command.

CHAPTER 7

FIRST ARMY TAKES
THE FIELD

The events of spring 1918 changed the Allies' strategic thinking. Until Foch took over as commander-in-chief, strategy was left to the commanders of the individual armies—in the case of the French, Pétain. Having held the line at Verdun and brought the Army back from mutiny after the failure of the Nivelle campaign, Pétain adopted a strategy of strictly limited offensives while waiting for the Americans to arrive in force. Foch, finally invested with overall command, replaced the Army's defensive strategy with an offensive one, after concluding that Pétain's incremental methods could not end the war any time soon.[*] Once the Spring Offensives had been contained, Foch recognized that the Germans had made themselves vulnerable by abandoning their former defensive positions and supply depots and distributing their forces over a broad front; it was time to attack. At first Pétain resisted Foch's direction, but Clemenceau intervened and made it clear who would be in charge. Pétain thereupon acceded and on July 12

---

[*] As early as January 1, 1918 Foch had written to General Maxime Weygand, his chief of staff: "We must respond [to an enemy offensive] ... with an attitude that will comprise, for the armies of the Entente, the resolve to seize every occasion to impose their will on the adversary by retaking, as soon as possible, the offensive, the only means that leads to victory ... In case of an enemy attack, [the Allied armies must] not just stop him and counter-attack on the same ground as his attacks, but, more, must undertake powerful counter-offensives of disengagement on terrain chosen and prepared in advance, executed as rapidly as possible." (Ministère de la Guerre, Service Historique, *AFGG*, Tome Vi, 1er Volume, Annexes – 1er Volume (Paris: Imprimerie Nationale, 1920–38), p. 410.)

issued Directive No. 5: "Henceforth the armies should envisage the resumption of the offensive ... They will focus resolutely on using simple, audacious, and rapid procedures of attack. The soldier will be trained in the same sense and his offensive spirit developed to the maximum," so that he would be suited for rapid advance in open country. Pétain prescribed training so as to instill a "spirit of maneuver and an aptitude for movement;" clear, concise orders that left the details of execution to the individual unit commander; surprise; rapid execution and deep expansion of the attack; and exploitation, both immediate and long-distance.[1] If this wasn't open warfare, nothing was.

A second development finally gave Pershing what he wanted—an American army. Foch had agreed to this in principle in late April, but it was a minor concession at the time; Pershing had already consented to lend his divisions to the French and British to repel the German offensives. In mid-June Pershing thought the time had come to consolidate his forces, but Foch proposed instead that he assign some of the best trained US regiments to depleted French divisions, to be returned in early August. Pershing refused. At a conference at Bombon on July 9 Pershing brought up the issue again. Now Foch agreed the time was right. From the Americans' minutes of the meeting:

> General Foch says he wishes to express his satisfaction about the fact that General Pershing's views on the situation are so much like his. He is going to be still more American than the Americans. It is, in his opinion, absolutely necessary to organize the American troops in American army corps and armies, with a view to operate them in an American sector on an American battlefield ... One million Americans are now in France. It is the absolute right of the American army to play, as an army, a role corresponding to the above figure.[2]

Foch proposed to put American divisions still lacking their artillery into quiet sectors or training areas, and Pershing agreed. On July 24 Pershing ordered the formation of the American First Army on August 10.

The next question was where First Army would serve. Pershing had addressed this soon after arriving in France, his main consideration being that the location should accommodate a force of several million men comprising a unified American army. The left wing of the line was unsuitable because the British needed to protect their supply lines through the Channel ports. The French had to occupy the center of the line, because they needed to defend Paris. The right portion of the front, located in Lorraine, offered opportunities. It was generally quiet and uncongested with troops and offered areas for billeting and training. It gave potential access to ports on the Atlantic and the Mediterranean, so that the Americans' supply lines would not conflict with those of the British. Furthermore, those lines would run south of Paris and would be less vulnerable to a German advance, an important consideration if the Americans were to take over a greater load from a depleted French army. And there were attractive strategic objectives. The sector included the St Mihiel salient, a wedge that protruded into the Allied lines for 15 miles and obstructed the Paris–Nancy rail line. Just north of the front lay the Longwy–Briey iron mines, the Saar coal beds, and the critical rail hub of Metz. From Lorraine the US could deliver a decisive attack that would disrupt the enemy's logistics along the entire front, forcing them to retreat to the German border or even the Rhine.[3]

Historians have criticized the strategic basis for placing the AEF in Lorraine. The resources of Longwy–Briey and the Saar basin were not critical to the German war effort; they provided only about 10 percent of its raw materials. The critical railroads that supplied the German divisions ran not through Metz but through Thionville, some 18 miles further north, requiring a much more ambitious offensive to disrupt.[*] The Germans had held Metz since 1870 and had spent the time installing elaborate fortifications around the city itself and in the surrounding countryside. The Woëvre plain, which the Americans would have to cross to get to Metz, was filled with impediments to the free movement of troops: poorly drained, clayey soils laced with small streams and ponds, and surrounding heights that allowed the Germans to overlook the entire region. Perhaps a reason Foch readily agreed to put the AEF in Lorraine was one that would have been obvious to any French officer who looked at a map: there were no important strategic objectives *behind* the American lines to tempt Ludendorff into a full-scale assault against Pershing's inexperienced and half-trained army.[†]

---

[*] Alan Millett points out that the German rail network is shown correctly in Vincent J. Esposito, ed., *The West Point Atlas of American Wars, Volume II: 1900–1918*, vol. 2 (New York: Henry Holt, 1959, reprinted 1997), map 68; Historical Division, *USAWW*, vol. 1, p. 26; and in several German sources. The maps in Pershing, *My Experiences*, show the main lateral line running from Metz to Sedan, which is wrong. (Millett, "Over Where?" p. 252.)

[†] The Paris–Avricourt rail line, which ran behind the American position, was already cut by the Germans at Château Thierry and was within range of their artillery at St Mihiel.

The issue of where the Americans would fight arose again with a vengeance in mid-August, just as Pershing had taken command of First Army. So far, Allied counterattacks had been local, aimed at reversing the German salients gained in the Spring Offensives. Around August 16, Haig convinced Foch to switch from local attacks to a general offensive against the entire German line from Verdun to the sea—itself one huge, westward-bulging salient. He proposed that the British continue their action at Amiens by attacking eastward toward Cambrai, to sever the German lateral rail supply line near Maubeuge. The French and Americans would mount a converging attack on the south face of the German position west of the Meuse, also cutting the railroad that supplied the German armies and interfering with Ludendorff's ability to move reserves to meet the British. This would force Ludendorff into a general withdrawal from the Hindenburg Line, the great, 200-mile-long trench system that had anchored the German position in northeast France since early 1917. In the context of such an operation, a sustained assault beyond St Mihiel toward Metz made no sense; instead of converging, it would deviate from the axis of the British and French advances. Haig's plan therefore reduced to eight divisions the American forces for attacking St Mihiel, making an advance on Metz impossible.

From the beginning of his tenure as commander-in-chief, Foch envisioned a joint attack by the French and the Americans. In his notes from the Bombon meeting on July 10, Fox Conner, Pershing's Assistant Chief of Operations, reported that the French command insisted that, "[t]o bring about a certain spirit of emulation, considered (by Foch and Weygand) as essential in securing the necessary coordination, the attacks must be launched in the same general region with interdependent objectives ... The vital spark of emulation would misfire should the plan be an attack by the Americans in Lorraine while the French and British attack in the north (Weygand)."[4] Foch clearly wanted the Americans to emulate the French, not trusting the newcomers to know their business. Pershing, either naïvely or (more likely) deliberately, neatly turned this back on Foch:

[T]he most valid of the reasons advanced by General Foch and General Weygand in support of the practically continuous front of attack is to be found in the idea of securing emulation between the several armies. The very distinct impression left on my mind by the conversation of both General Foch and General Weygand was a *doubt on their part of the ability of both the*

French and British [to] attack unless carried along by the enthusiasm of Americans acting in the same region against common objectives. If such were the fact it would perhaps be sufficient reason for adopting the proposed plan. [Emphasis added.][5]

Thus Foch and Pershing reached agreement in fact while diverging by 180 degrees in principle.

On August 30 Foch met with Pershing at Ligny-en-Barrois (First Army headquarters since August 29) to present his version of Haig's plan. Foch wanted the French Second Army to attack northward between the Meuse and the Argonne; the American First Army between the Argonne and a line west of the Aisne; and the French Fourth Army west of that. He wanted four to six American divisions to reinforce the French Second Army. This would have broken the American forces into three groups: a small one to attack the southern flank of the St Mihiel salient; one with the French Second Army; and the main body operating up the Aisne. Each American force would be separated from its fellows by French units. Pershing reacted negatively: "This virtually destroys the American Army that we have been trying so long to form."[6] This was an exaggeration, but the plan did move the Americans westward away from their supply lines, hospitals, training centers, and other support facilities. The discussion became intense. At one point Foch asked, "Do you wish to take part in the battle?" "Most assuredly," replied Pershing, "but as an American Army."[7] Two days later Foch proposed that First Army execute a limited operation to reduce the St Mihiel salient, then redirect itself northward to a sector between the Meuse River (on the east) and the Argonne Forest (to the west) to participate with the French in the main assault. The St Mihiel attack would start on September 10 using eight to ten divisions; the Meuse–Argonne offensive would begin sometime between September 20 and 25 and would occupy 12–14 divisions. Pershing agreed; he would not get his attack on Metz, at least not soon, but he retained control of a unified American army.

Pershing's acceptance of Foch's counterproposal for St Mihiel overcommitted the Army. In the words of Donald Smythe, Pershing's biographer:

> An American Army, untested and in many ways untrained, was to engage in a great battle, disengage itself, and move to another great battle some sixty miles away, all within the space of about two weeks, under a First Army staff

that Pershing admitted was not perfect and, as of this date, had no inkling that an operation west of the Meuse was even contemplated. Army staffs normally required two to three months to form a fully articulated battle plan with all its technical annexes; this staff—and, again, it must be emphasized that it was new, inexperienced, and untested—would have about three weeks. It was a formidable commitment, not to say impossible, and it is not clear that Pershing should have made it.[8]

But the alternative was to attack north with the St Mihiel salient remaining to threaten the American rear. Nevertheless, the Army suffered consequences from this decision for the rest of the war, particularly as it prevented most of the best divisions from participating early in the Meuse–Argonne offensive.

Having won his chance at a purely American offensive, Pershing now had to deliver. The V-shaped St Mihiel salient, about 15 miles deep, protruded southwestward into the American lines. Pershing's plan called for three divisions, comprising IV Corps, to attack the south face with a further four divisions in support, while the three divisions of V Corps attacked the west face with three divisions in reserve. His force included his five most experienced divisions—the 1st, 2nd, 4th, 26th, and 42nd—some of which would therefore be unavailable for the opening of the Meuse–Argonne offensive. In all, the attacking forces numbered 550,000 American and 110,000 French troops, opposed by 23,000 Germans and Austrians, representing seven vastly understrength divisions.[9] The attackers were supported by 3,000 guns, 267 tanks, and 1,400 airplanes, all of them borrowed from the French.[*][10]

Pershing's preparations included a generous helping of deception. Registration fire was prohibited; the artillery was to use mass of fire and aiming by use of map coordinates to suppress enemy guns.[†] In early September, three officers from each of six divisions—the 79th among them—were dispatched to Belfort, 100 miles south in Alsace, to conduct

---

[*] First Amy's lack of artillery, transport, and aircraft arose directly from Pershing's agreement, at the frantic behest of his allies, to ship only infantry and machine gun units during the Spring Offensives. In the words of David Trask, "Pershing never came close to completing his design for a completely independent army. He depended heavily on the Allies for support in deficient categories until the end of the war." (Trask, *AEF and Coalition Warmaking*, p. 101.)

[†] Registration was the practice of firing a few shells in advance of the real bombardment, having air reconnaissance report where they fell, and correcting aim accordingly. It generally tipped off the enemy that an attack was coming.

"reconnaissance" and thereby to convince the Germans that the true attack would fall there. (Pershing's staff were probably hoping they would be captured. They weren't, and the Germans weren't fooled, although Kuhn and several other American generals assumed that was where their divisions were to be sent.[11]) And the general made sure to exhort his commanders to observe the principles of open warfare, despite the fact that this was to be essentially a set-piece attack. His Field Order No. 49 directed that "penetration will be sought by utilizing lanes of least resistance in order to cause the fall of strong points by out-flanking." Any "success" in the attack was to be "vigorously exploited," although just how this was to be done was not described.[12]

The attack jumped off on September 12, the first day that American forces fought as a unified army. It was a walkover. Unknown to the Americans, the Germans had ordered that the salient be evacuated beginning on September 10. As a result, few German guns were in place, and those that were lacked ammunition. The remaining German troops were more interested in getting away than resisting, which kept American casualties to only 7,000. Four hundred and fifty guns and 16,000 prisoners were taken. Achieving all of its objectives in four days, the attack liberated 200 square miles of French land, opened the Paris–Nancy railroad, protected the right flank of the future Meuse–Argonne assault, and provided a staging area for possible attacks on Metz, the Longwy–Briey industrial region, and the railroad supplying the German Army to the northwest. It also demonstrated that the American Army was capable of full-scale operations.[13]

Although the Germans officially pooh-poohed the American victory, pointing out that they were abandoning the salient anyway and that the withdrawal had been orderly, the German High Command was in fact upset. General Max von Gallwitz, commander of the army group defending St Mihiel, wrote, "I have experienced a good many things in the five years of war and have not been poor in successes, but I must count the 12th of September among my few black days."[14] Pershing was ecstatic, seeing the victory as confirmation of his doctrine: "For the first time wire entanglements ceased to be regarded as impassable barriers and open-warfare training, which had been so urgently insisted upon, proved to be the correct doctrine."[15] Even his allies were impressed. The salient had been held by the Germans for four years and the French had failed twice to take it. French officials, including President Raymond Poincaré, rushed to visit Pershing and congratulate him. Premier Georges Clemenceau had less luck; Pershing allowed him to advance only as far as Thiaucourt, 25 miles behind the lines, but could not prevent him from seeing the congestion on the roads.[16]

That congestion was a symptom of three problems that foreshadowed greater troubles to come. The first was transportation and supply. No measures had been taken to ensure smooth operation of the transportation system. The staff had failed to determine correctly the capacity of the roads and the drivers, particularly the French ones, had failed to maintain road discipline. The engineers had poorly organized the supply of laborers to repair the shell-shattered tracks. As a result, traffic jams lasted for days. Major General Ernest Hinds, chief of the AEF's artillery, wrote in a memorandum to Hugh Drum, Pershing's Chief of Staff:

> There was ignorance and lack of discipline shown in the management of our traffic. The regulations are not understood by drivers and traffic police and are not carried out with sufficient rigidity in many cases when they are understood. Truck trains halted with proper intervals between sections would soon be filled up solidly by chauffeurs [staff cars] working their way forward. Then if a single vehicle of the column going in the opposite direction happened to have an accident, there would be a complete blocking of the traffic for a time.[17]

Clemenceau, stuck in his traffic jam, was appalled by the confusion. He later wrote, "They wanted an American army. They had it. Anyone who saw, as I saw, the hopeless congestion at Thiaucourt will bear witness that they may congratulate themselves on not having had it sooner."[18] Whatever the presenting symptoms, the situation was the inevitable result of trying to cram some half-million men with their equipment, transport, and supplies into a triangle roughly 20 miles on a side.

Many weaknesses in American training and staff work also emerged. Riflemen couldn't tell their own planes from the Germans'. They did not use cover when advancing against machine guns and, when retiring, remained upright. Rolling barrages advanced too slowly for the infantry, failed to use direct observation in favor of map direction, and wasted ammunition. Men on the march straggled, particularly when stopped. Mounted men, halted in traffic, remained in the saddle instead of dismounting to rest their horses and themselves. "Animals were misused, abused, or not used at all." Commanders failed to re-establish communication by horse relay once telephone lines were cut. French liaison officers reported that American commanders did not appreciate the value of armor and, believing in the irresistibility of an American assault, failed to soften up the German positions with artillery. They followed regulations to the letter and were incapable of improvisation when new situations arose. They neglected to establish fixed command posts, and those that they did set up were too far to the rear, making effective command and liaison impossible. Orders often were far too wordy, complex, and redundant to be understood or even read.[19] As a result of the road situation clothing and food were insufficient, and the tanks were held up by a lack of fuel for 32 hours.

The third area of deficiency was the artillery. Once the rolling barrage had ended, the artillery support on the first day was unsatisfactory. Batteries had great trouble moving forward over the torn-up ground, and those that did displace forward had trouble setting up their telephone lines. They were thus out of touch both with their regimental headquarters and with the infantry command posts that could tell them the positions of the troops in the front line. As a result, German artillery and machine guns were free to pound the US troops all afternoon. Although their French instructors had trained the American gunners in how to use their weapons, they did not train them in tactics. Not being skilled in rapid target acquisition and preparatory bombardments, the American gunners left many German batteries untouched and pounded many unoccupied positions to a pulp. The difficulty of moving artillery and ammunition forward, of communicating with the infantry, and of determining the position of the front line all indicated that a continuation of the St Mihiel offensive, had Foch allowed it, would have been possible only after prolonged planning and preparation or at the cost of greatly increased casualties.

These problems boded ill for the American participation in Foch's planned offensive. None were insurmountable, given time to train, reorganize, and re-equip; all armies had faced them at various points in the war. But between the end of the St Mihiel operation and the start of the Meuse–Argonne offensive, First Army had ten days.

Many of the American commanders whose troops flattened the St Mihiel salient thought that Metz was the great piece of unfinished business. The night after the operation ended Brigadier General Douglas MacArthur, a brigade commander in the 42nd Division, went through the German lines and observed the fortress of Metz from several miles away through binoculars, concluding that it was "practically defenseless." (How he could tell at that distance that the largely subterranean trenches and fortifications were undefended is a mystery.) He asked that his brigade be allowed to attack, promising he would be in possession of the town "by nightfall"; he was turned down.[20] Colonel George C. Marshall, on Pershing's planning staff, also thought the city could be taken in a day or two. But Major General Hunter Liggett, a veteran artilleryman who would soon take over command of First Army, disagreed; only a thoroughly experienced army could take the fortified town, and even so would most likely get bogged down on the Woëvre plain for the winter.[*21] In fact, the situation behind the former St Mihiel salient was very dangerous for the Germans. The fortress of Metz had been stripped of much of its artillery, leaving it exposed. The Germans were amazed that the Americans didn't take advantage of their initiative. But the issue was moot; Pershing, pressed by Foch, had already committed to redirect his troops northward for the Meuse–Argonne offensive.

Foch's overall plan was to give up hope of a breakthrough battle, which always ended in the attacker bogging down on the ruined battlefield and the defender using superior lateral transport to reinforce the threatened area. Instead, he designed a series of offensives all along the front to take advantage of the numerical superiority provided by the Americans, use up the Germans' reserves, and give them no time to regroup. In the words of Donald Smythe, "Unlike Ludendorff, Foch had the genius to finally see that a decisive, war-winning breakthrough was chimerical, for the defense could always move its reserves by rail and truck more quickly than the offense could move by foot, especially over devastated ground."[22] He therefore devised the following series of operations:

1. On September 26, the French Fourth Army and the American First Army would attack northward toward Mézières and Sedan. The Americans would operate between the Meuse River (to the east) and the Argonne Forest (to the west), the French west of the Argonne.

---

* In World War II it took Patton's XII Corps 14 days (November 8 through 22, 1944) to secure Metz, starting from positions less than ten miles to the west; the final assault itself took six days. Three days were required to take Fort St Julien, an old seventeenth-century fort defended by 362 Germans without heavy weapons. (Stephen E. Ambrose, *Citizen Soldiers: The U.S. Army from the Normandy Beaches to the Bulge to the Surrender of Germany* (New York: Simon & Schuster, 1997), pp. 161–65.)

2. A day later, the British would attack toward Cambrai with two armies comprising 27 divisions.
3. The day after that, the Belgians, French, and British in Flanders, at the extreme north of the German position, would stage a joint attack toward Ghent with a total of 28 divisions.
4. Finally, on September 29, the French and British would attack the center of the German line between Péronne and La Fère.[23]

Thus, all 200 miles of the enemy front would come under attack, although in staggered fashion so as to keep the Germans off balance. The first of these assaults was put under the command of Pétain, the French commander-in-chief, who would coordinate the actions of the French Fourth Army (under General Gouraud) and the American First Army (under Pershing).

Pétain issued his instructions on September 16. He called for a three-phased attack converging on Mézières: Operation B, the American attack between the Meuse River and the Argonne Forest; Operation C, the advance of the French Fourth Army in region Argonne Forest–Reims; and Operation D, the attack of the French Fifth Army between Reims and the lower Aisne River. (Operation A was the St Mihiel offensive.) B and C would take place on September 25, D on September 26. He described the goals of the American attack:

> An operation called B, carried out between the Meuse and the upper course of the Aisne, by the American First Army, designed to gain possession of the Hindenburg Line on the front Brieulles-sur-Meuse–Romagne-sous-Montfaucon–Grandpré, with subsequent exploitation in the direction of Buzancy-Mézières in order to outflank the enemy line Vouziers-Rethel from the east.[24]

Orders issued over the next few days specified the arrangements for supplying the Americans during the first phase of the campaign and prescribed measures to maintain security and surprise. Finally, on September 20, Pétain sent his ultimate order, reading in its entirety: "Operations B and C will take place on September 26."

Pershing's plan was embodied in Field Order No. 20, issued on September 20 by his Chief of Staff, Hugh Drum. First Army would attack on a 20-mile sector comprising some of the most challenging terrain on the Western Front. The right boundary was to be the Meuse River, overlooked to its east by the Heights of the Meuse. From the river the land rose westward in a series of undulating hills to the Barrois plateau, capped by the promontory of Montfaucon, approximately midway along the German position and four miles from the American front line. West of Montfaucon the surface dipped into the valley of the north-flowing Aire River, then rose sharply to a plateau on which rested the formidable Argonne Forest. Pershing's plan, developed under Drum's supervision by September 7, consisted of four phases:

1. A rapid ten-mile advance to a line level with the northern limit of the Argonne Forest, termed the "American Army Objective." This would cut off the defenders and allow a junction with the French at Grandpré.
2. Another quick ten-mile advance to a line Le Chesne–Stenay, called the "Army First Phase Line." This would force the Germans fighting the French on the left to withdraw.
3. An attack up the Heights of the Meuse to secure the right flank.
4. A concluding attack to cut the Sedan–Mézières rail line.

The key to the plan was rapid execution of the first phase. To accomplish this, Pershing allocated 12 divisions organized into three corps.[*] In each corps, three divisions were in the attack line and a fourth was in reserve. (Pershing's best divisions, of course, were still on the St Mihiel front and would not be able to participate in the opening assault on the Meuse–Argonne.) On the right was III Corps under Major General Bullard, with (from right to left) the 33rd, 80th, and 4th Divisions in the line. Its main job was to advance to the east of Montfaucon and secure the Americans' right flank along the Meuse River. The center was occupied by V Corps, commanded by Major General George H. Cameron and including the 79th, 37th, and 91st Divisions. It had the key role: to conquer Montfaucon— the "second German position," the *Etzel-Stellung*—and advance through Nantillois to Romagne-sous-Montfaucon a distance of about ten miles. To its left was I Corps under General Hunter Liggett, with the 35th, 28th, and 77th Divisions. It was to attack up the valley of the Aire to the east of the Argonne Forest, then with the French Fourth Army to its west cut off the forest at its north end, forcing the Germans to withdraw.

---

[*] Corps were groupings of (typically) two to four divisions.

ALIGNMENT OF US DIVISIONS FOR THE MEUSE–ARGONNE ATTACK,
SHOWING PLANNED ADVANCE, SEPTEMBER 26, 1918

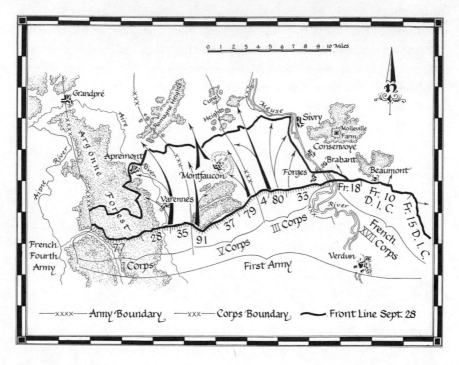

To accomplish this advance, Pershing established several intermediate objectives. The first was the "Corps Objective," to which the three corps were to advance independently. In the case of V Corps this line ran just north of Nantillois, about five miles from the starting point. No deadline for accomplishing this was given, but it was clear that it would have to be reached by mid-day. Once V Corps reached the Corps Objective, all three corps would attack in concert up to the line Aprémont–Romagne–Brieulles-sur-Meuse, roughly another five miles. This line, the "American Army Objective," was to be reached by the afternoon of the first day.[25] Subsequent attacks were to bring First Army to the "Combined Army First Objective," about 12 miles from the starting line, and eventually to the Meuse near Sedan.

The Germans had only five understrength divisions in the Meuse–Argonne sector and 15 more within three days' march. With nine divisions of 28,000 men each on a 20-mile front, Pershing had an initial 10-to-1 numerical advantage.[*][26] His divisions were not wholly without experience—seven had occupied front-line sectors and five had been in combat.[†] But none had served at the front for more than a few weeks, and many were populated largely by recent conscripts who were essentially untrained. It did not help that, just before the attack, staff officers of the five least-experienced divisions (35th, 37th, 79th, 80th, and 91st) were diverted to the General Staff College in Langres, virtually gutting the administrative capacity of the inexperienced divisions.

Most puzzling was (and still is) how the divisions were assigned to their places in the line. The 79th was placed opposite Montfaucon, the key German position. It had never served at the front and had never trained with its newly assigned artillery brigade (or, in fact, any artillery at all), yet it was to take the heights, four miles distant and towering some 400 feet above the division's jumpoff point, on the first day.[‡] At least the 79th was flanked by two more experienced divisions. On its left was the 37th; drawn from the Ohio National Guard, it had spent six weeks occupying a front-line (but quiet) sector in the Vosges Mountains. To its right was the 4th Division, a Regular Army unit (although much diluted with recent

---

[*] Other sources give the American superiority at 4-to-1 (Smythe, *Pershing*, p. 193) and 8-to-1 (Paul F. Braim, *The Test of Battle: The American Expeditionary Forces in the Meuse–Argonne Campaign* (Shippensburg, PA: White Mane Books, second revised edition, 1998), p. 85). The main differences seem to be in how one counts available reserves and nearby divisions.

[†] Braim puts these numbers at four and none, respectively. (Braim, *Test of Battle*, p. 85.) Smythe says that four divisions had seen action. (Smythe, *Pershing*, p. 192.) The numbers given above are taken from War Department reports. (Army War College, Historical Section, *Order of Battle of the United States Land Forces in the World War: Divisions*, Document 23a (Washington, DC: GPO, 1931), passim, Ayres, *Statistical Summary*, p. 33.)

[‡] The process by which divisions were assigned to places in the line is obscure. The first mention of the 79th in the plan for the Meuse–Argonne is in a memorandum titled, "Proposed Disposition of U.S. Divisions in Line," dated September 7. (G-3 Assistant Chief of Staff, AEF, "Proposed Disposition of U.S. Divisions in Line," September 7, 1918, RG 120, Entry 24, "AEF General Headquarters, 1st Army Reports, G-3," Box 3382, 114.0, NARA, p. 2.) It says that the 79th "is to take the left half of sector Meuse to Aire," in the general vicinity of where it ended up but covering what eventually was a three-division front. Three days later, Pershing dispatched a letter to Pétain containing a table showing all nine front-line divisions, with the 79th in the position it eventually occupied in the assault. (Historical Division, *USAWW*, vol. 8, p. 60.) But this was not a final arrangement, as several divisions switched places subsequently. It is possible that the divisions were allocated based on who was closest to their ultimate destination in the line, not with any tactical rationale in mind. In any event, as in so many cases, the archives contain only the results of decisions, not the deliberations that led up to them.

draftees) and veteran of the Aisne–Marne and St Mihiel campaigns. But the 4th Division was part of III Corps, not V Corps in which the 79th resided. This meant that any coordination between the two divisions during the battle—and coordination was critical to Pershing's plan, as we shall see— would have to go through First Army headquarters. In other words, if the right-most regiment of the 79th wanted help from its neighbor the left-most regiment of the 4th, the commanding officer's request would have to go up through the brigade, division, and corps headquarters to Pershing's staff, then the response would go back down the chain to the regimental commander in the 4th before any action could be taken.[*] This was not an arrangement for smooth cooperation.

First Army had at its disposal almost 4,000 guns of all calibers.[†] Of these about 600, mostly in French divisions, were assigned to neutralize the German artillery in the Heights of the Meuse and 640 remained on the St Mihiel front, leaving about 2,760 to support the nine attacking divisions directly. Divisional artillery brigades—each augmented by a regiment of nine batteries of 75mm field guns and other batteries—would provide 1,780 tubes to fire the rolling barrage. Corps artillery numbering 400 pieces would concentrate on German guns and strong points. The 542 guns of Army artillery would neutralize distant assembly areas and supply depots and interdict enemy movement behind the lines.[27] The firing plan was for one-quarter of the Army artillery to begin with a long-range bombardment at 11:30 p.m. on September 25—enough guns to disrupt the German rear areas but, it was hoped, not enough to alert them to a full-scale assault. At the same time, the French Fourth Army to the west would open its preparatory fire and the guns on the old St Mihiel front would lay down a diversionary bombardment toward Metz. At 2:30 a.m., all guns were to join the preparation.[28] At H-hour, divisional artillery was to begin the rolling barrage behind which the infantry would advance; the barrage would pound the German front-line trenches for 25 minutes, then advance at a rate of

---

[*] Adjacent units routinely swapped liaison officers, but their role appears to have been limited largely to communication, not tactical coordination.

[†] The divisions, the corps, and First Army itself all had their own artillery units. For the Meuse– Argonne campaign, the divisions (including those of attached French units) had a total of 2,568 guns; the corps had 870; and First Army had 542. (W.S. McNair, "Explanation and Execution of Plans for Artillery for St Mihiel Operation and Argonne–Meuse Operations to November 11, 1918," December 23, 1918, RG 120, Entry 22, Commander-in-Chief Reports, Box 30, NARA, p. 15.)

100 meters every four minutes. The men would follow at a distance of 300 meters.[29]

In some respects—brief preparatory fire to achieve surprise, the rolling barrage to neutralize the defenders—Pershing's artillery plan resembled Bruchmüller's innovative and successful use of his guns at Riga.* But key ingredients in the German general's success were missing: his attention to explaining the firing plan to the attacking troops; conducting drills that acclimated the men to the rolling barrage; and centralizing control of the artillery at the army level. Pershing's preparations included none of these; true to his infantry-first doctrine, artillery remained the poor cousin at the party. At the beginning of planning for the Meuse–Argonne, First Army artillery staff were not told anything about the date of the attack, its location, or the enemy forces, such information being deemed too secret for them to possess. They were simply told to prepare for an attack involving 12 divisions. They replied that they required more information to do any planning; it was given to them a day later.[30] Four of the divisions had had their artillery brigades stripped from them upon arrival in France; they now received, from other divisions, brigades with which they had never trained and whose officers they did not know. Complicating things further, the ultimate German defense line—the *Kriemhilde-Stellung*—was ten miles beyond the American starting point, well out of range of all but the very largest American guns. To support the advance, the guns would have to move forward behind the infantry over broken ground and torn-up roads in order to maintain fire superiority—a maneuver well beyond the capability of First Army. This was, in part, because all movement of divisional artillery was to be regulated by the corps commanders—an arrangement that erroneously assumed those commanders would have good communication with their subordinate divisions and with army headquarters.

Augmenting the artillery was a weapon new to American combat— tanks. Four French light tank battalions, two American battalions, and four groups of French heavy tanks were attached to First Army; almost all went to V Corps. The orders to the tank battalions were terse:

---

* See Chapter 4.

Tanks to assemble in the Forêt de Hesse.* On D day they will follow the infantry as soon as the way has been made passable for them, to their position of readiness in the Bois de Montfaucon and near Cheppy. Thence they will operate in the sectors Nantillois, Montfaucon, Gesnes, and Baulny-Exermont. On the Hindenburg Line being made passable for them, they should be in the best possible position for exercising their proper functions and will proceed to destroy machine-gun nests, strong points, and to exploit the success.[31]

No mention was made of cooperating with the infantry. Tank–infantry coordination was a difficult art. Tanks needed to precede the infantry in order to suppress machine guns and prevent casualties. Infantry, on the other hand, had to protect the tanks, which in combat had limited vision to the front and almost none to the sides or rear. This often made them prey to antitank guns and enemy soldiers armed with explosive charges. (Pétain had expressly urged this point on Pershing.[32]) If the infantry followed the barrage too closely, however, it could result in tank losses from one's own artillery. By now, the French and British had developed highly trained combined-arms units, as described in Chapter 4. But joint operations between tanks and infantry remained difficult even when the two arms had trained together. Of course the American infantry had never trained with tanks at all, let alone with the battalions furnished for this attack.†

Another innovation was air support. Eight hundred and forty aircraft were assigned to the offensive, a three-to-one superiority over the Germans. Three new American squadrons were included, one of which was the 166th Bombing Squadron flying two-seater DH-4s made in the United States.‡ During the artillery preparation, the objectives of the bombers included "troop concentrations, convoys, stations, command posts and dumps; to hinder his movement of troops and to destroy his aviation on the ground." During the

---

* Army orders printed locations and unit designations in all-capitals (they still do). These have been reduced to initial capitals herein to preserve readability.

† See Tim Travers, *How the War Was Won: Factors That Led to Victory in World War One* (Barnsley, UK: Routledge, 1992; repr., Pen & Sword, 2005), p. 115. Communication between infantrymen and tank crews, the latter sealed into reverberant steel boxes flooded with engine and machinery noises, was almost impossible in combat. The British tried putting bell-pulls on the outside of their tanks; it didn't work. French soldiers sometimes resorted to banging on the hulls with shovels to get the attention of those inside. (Ibid.; Philpott, *Three Armies*, p. 482.)

‡ But see Chapter 3 on the deficiencies of the DH-4.

attack itself, their additional missions were to prevent the arrival of reserves, break up counterattacks, and harass the enemy as he withdrew. Reconnaissance planes would photograph enemy positions and the results of bombing raids.[*] A pursuit group was assigned to accompany the attack; its instructions were to "protect our observation aviation at every altitude from the Meuse inclusive on the east to La Hazaree [*sic*] inclusive on the west; prevent enemy aviation from attacking through the Woëvre and ... attack concentrations of enemy troops, convoys, enemy aviation and balloons."[33] No instructions were issued for supporting the attacking infantry directly, nor were there any means for units engaged at the front to request air support.[†] No aviation units were assigned to individual corps or divisions.

The newest military innovation was also the one most feared and loathed, even by those who used it—gas. During the planning for the Meuse–Argonne, the First Army operations staff studied the intense and effective use the Germans made of gas during their Spring Offensives. These lessons were incorporated into Army orders for the attack. Sufficient gas was obtained from the French to neutralize German artillery and points of resistance, and to inflict casualties on personnel. Army field orders during the action pressed for its greater use. But in practice, First Army used little gas. The three battalions of the 1st Gas Regiment were distributed among the three attacking corps. During the artillery preparation, each was to fire non-persistent gas shells only after halts in the artillery shelling as ordered by the corps chief of artillery. (Persistent mustard gas was to be fired at the Heights of the Meuse to protect the attack's right flank.)[‡] During the

---

[*] Thirteen balloons were assigned to observe enemy activity and spot for the artillery. (Historical Division, *USAWW*, vol. 15, p. 235.) It is clear from the situation reports filed during the battle, however, that the balloons were generally grounded or blinded by bad weather, and those that got up suffered heavy casualties. (Ibid., vol. 9, pp. 160–209 passim.)

[†] Colored panels were issued for infantry units to spread on the ground so as to indicate their positions to friendly aircraft; but the men were not trained in their use and they were almost never deployed. (G. de la Chapelle, "Report with Regard to the Employment of the Squadron During the Battle from September 26th to 30th," *c.* October 1918, 17 N 128, SHD, p. 1.)

[‡] Gas came in several varieties. Non-persistent chemicals such as phosgene and diphosgene dispersed in 10–20 minutes; they were used to disable enemy positions that were about to be assaulted and occupied by friendly troops. Persistent types such as mustard gas could take several days to lose their effectiveness. These were used to make enemy positions—gun emplacements, command posts, transportation hubs—untenable for a relatively long period of time. By 1918 the threat from gas was no longer the infliction of mass deaths on the battlefield; effective gas masks and training had largely eliminated that possibility. Instead, by forcing the enemy to don masks, one greatly reduced his capability. The masks were difficult enough to wear on defense;

advance itself, only smoke and thermite (an incendiary) were to be fired. In the words of historian Rex Cochrane, "This was the final sop to Army's indecisive plans for the use of gas on the Montfaucon front, and even this was never carried out."[34] The reason was that Pershing's orders left the use of gas up to the discretion of the corps commanders, who were as inexperienced as their men with the new weapon and were reluctant to use it. As a result, many German positions that might have been neutralized by the preparatory bombardment were able to offer serious resistance.

In hindsight, perhaps the biggest flaw in Pershing's plan was a failure to address seriously the road problem. Supply and transportation had been the bane of every offensive in the war so far, even when the roads were good. In First Army's entire 20-mile sector only three roads led north, and all had been ruined by the previous four years' fighting. In the words of an after-action report by Pershing's logistics staff, "As a result, the map indications of roads leading north from Esnes, Avocourt, and Boureuilles actually represented the former locations of those roads. Instead, there was only shell-holed countryside, with wire entanglements, for a distance of 3 to 6 km in advance of the American lines."[35] Rainy weather would turn this moonscape of Jurassic clay into bottomless mud—the same mud that had almost immobilized Moltke's Prussians as he pursued Napoleon III northward almost 50 years earlier. Pershing's plan allocated repair of roads to the engineering companies and trains of the attacking units themselves; these were capable at most of assisting their own divisions, but not of coordinating road construction across the entire front. Truckloads of gravel and other materials would be stationed at convenient locations, but the major items of equipment were the pick and shovel. Although the Americans had invented the Holt caterpillar farm tractor, on which the tank was based, no one thought to create armored bulldozers, graders, and other earthmoving equipment that could follow the front-line troops and rapidly construct serviceable roads. (Of course, no other armies had hit upon this innovation, either.[*]) Further, the nine divisions would have to share the three roads that nominally existed, leading to conflicts of need and priority with no central

on the offense they were virtually impossible. Of course, gas casualties continued to occur, especially among inexperienced troops, and the victims suffered horribly. Unlike the other combatants the AEF never did develop an effective organization, doctrine, or training program for gas warfare.

[*] The bulldozer was not invented until 1923. The first US Army combat engineering battalions were established shortly before World War II.

authority to sort them out. They would have to advance against a tide of ambulances, prisoners, and empty supply wagons coming the other way. A circulation map was distributed on September 19, but it had no information on the roads that lay beyond the American lines of that date. On September 25 a map was distributed that had data on roads as far north as Cunel Heights but no further. Nonetheless, Field Order No. 20 optimistically assumed that roads would be available when needed. In its directive to the artillery, for example, it said, "Divisional artillery will follow the advance of our infantry to forward positions and this artillery will in turn be followed by corps artillery and then by army artillery. Corps commanders will prescribe roads available for these movements, and promptly inform the chief of artillery of arrangements made."[36] This was simply to ignore a reality that was manifest long before the attack itself.

Pershing's plan relied on surprise to keep the Germans from reinforcing the sector quickly. Thirteen of the Germans' 18 divisions were opposite St Mihiel. To encourage them to expect an attack toward Metz, First Army concealed its activities in the Meuse–Argonne by disguising its reconnaissance troops in French uniforms, relieving the French Second Army (then occupying the sector) only just before the attack, and moving only at night. Artillery registration fire and radio traffic were kept to a minimum. Groups of tanks in the St Mihiel salient moved as if preparing for an offensive against Metz. While long-range guns bombarded Metz, the Air Service bombed the railroad station and the supply depots there, and flew bombing and pursuit missions to the east up to Château Salins. The officers talked "confidentially" to the men about an upcoming attack on Metz; the men, of course, talked among themselves in the bars and cafés. Nevertheless, by the 25th the Germans got wind that something was up along the Meuse. They withdrew their forward troops back to the main line as a defense against artillery and started moving reinforcements toward the area.[*]

Field Order No. 20 was very detailed about the physical arrangements for the offensive—the divisions that would carry the assault; the artillery, tanks, planes, and other services that would support them; and the objectives

---

[*] A postwar German assessment published in an American journal noted, "When it is remembered that nine divisions were concentrated in the first line for this attack without the knowledge of the Germans, it must be realized that the efforts of the troops to camouflage their movements were most successful." (Hermann von Giehrl, "Battle of the Meuse–Argonne (Part 1 of 4)," *Infantry Journal* 19, August (1921), p. 132.)

to be reached by given dates. It did not make clear, however, exactly how the divisions were to achieve their objectives. V Corps was positioned so that Montfaucon was directly in the path of its right-most division, the 79th. Yet Drum's mission for V Corps was:

(a) With its corps and divisional artillery it will assist in the neutralization of hostile observation from Montfaucon.

(b) It will reduce the Bois de Montfaucon and the Bois de Cheppy by outflanking them from the east and the west, thereby cutting off hostile fire and hostile observation from these woods against the III and I Corps.

(c) Upon arrival of the III and I Corps at the corps objective ... it will continue the advance to the American Army objective ... and penetrate the hostile third position without waiting for the advance of the III and I Corps.[37]

The Bois de Montfaucon and the Bois de Cheppy were small, adjacent woods that lay immediately over the lines of V Corps; there was no mention of the corps capturing the town of Montfaucon itself. Nor would it be possible to "outflank" the two woods; they lay directly astride V Corps' path. More to the point was the mission assigned to III Corps, whose sector lay to the east of Montfaucon and did not include it:

(a) By promptly penetrating the hostile second position [an east–west line running through Montfaucon] *it will turn Montfaucon and the section of the hostile second position within the zone of action of the V Corps, thereby assisting the capture of the hostile second position west of Montfaucon* [emphasis added].

(b) With its corps and divisional artillery it will assist in neutralizing hostile observation and hostile fire from the heights east of the Meuse.

(c) Upon arrival of the V Corps at the corps objective ... it will advance in conjunction with the IV Corps to the American Army objective.[38]

Because it would become an issue later, one may ask what, exactly, was III Corps supposed to do at Montfaucon? Pershing's order was less than clear. Possibly it was for III Corps to bypass "Montfaucon and the section of the hostile second position within the zone of action of the V Corps," while staying within its own zone of operation. That might constitute "turning" the German position, as the defenders would believe themselves about to be cut off. Or it could attack westward behind Montfaucon into the zone of

V Corps, severing the German position from its lines of supply and reinforcement. The question hinges on the meaning of the term, to "turn" a position. It is resolved by examining the definition in a textbook written by a West Point professor and used there since 1889: "Turning movements, as distinguished from flank attacks, consist in detaching a force and sending it around the enemy's flank, with a view to an attack from that direction or to threatening his communications, etc."[39] Other popular texts had similar definitions. So First Army's intention—poorly stated—was that at least part of III Corps was to cross into V Corps' zone behind the hill of Montfaucon. It was a creative maneuver, well within the spirit of Pershing's open warfare doctrine. It would violate the corps zone boundaries laid out in Field Order No. 20; but as long as those boundaries were understood by everyone to be flexible and not to impede lateral movement for good tactical reasons, all would be well. In the event, all would not be well.

There are several yardsticks one can use to measure how realistic Pershing's plan for the Meuse–Argonne was. The first is the successful British attack at Amiens under General Rawlinson on August 8, which penetrated six to eight miles on the first day while capturing 400 guns and 27,000 prisoners. The assault was a masterpiece of combined-arms operations. Surprise and deception successfully concealed from the Germans the fact that the Australians and Canadians, the best assault troops in the British Army, would lead the attack. Artillery and machine guns provided more firepower than before. Ninety-five percent of the German guns had been located before the attack, and 2,000 artillery pieces were carefully preregistered to neutralize them. Air supremacy was provided by 1,900 planes, which were also used to mask the noise of the approaching tanks, which numbered 342 Mark Vs and 72 Mediums as well as troop carrier and supply tanks. Most important, the British had spent the previous year developing methods for mutual support among infantry, artillery, tanks, and aircraft, and had trained their troops in these methods.[40]

The British were helped by the fact that the Germans were caught in the middle of a front-line relief, their morale was low, and their defenses were thin. Indeed, the German positions in the summer of 1918 were of a considerably different nature than the ones the Allies had fruitlessly assaulted since late 1914. They were not designed as defensive positions at all; they were merely the furthest points the Germans had reached in their Spring Offensives, and were organized to support an attack. Rather than three zones of increasing toughness, they often comprised only a single, forward position with few wire defenses or shellproof dugouts. The troops themselves were exhausted and hungry; their offensive had petered out partly because they stopped to loot the abandoned food supplies of the retreating British.[41] Those were the advantages that allowed the British at Amiens to advance six to eight miles on the first day. The AEF had none of them.

The second comparison is with the 1916 German offensive at Verdun. As we have already seen, Falkenhayn's plan included a massive attack southward on the east bank of the Meuse. But, against the advice of his artillery advisers and of Crown Prince Rupprecht, he planned no action on the west bank, where there were large concentrations of French artillery.[42] The result was that the German troops were shot up by enfilading fire from the west. Falkenhayn had to regroup and divert troops to the Meuse–Argonne sector (Maas-West, to the Germans), resulting in the bloody battles for and around the Mort Homme and Hill 304.

Pershing's plan was, in this respect, identical to Falkenhayn's—indeed, on the identical battlefield, but rotated 180 degrees. Pershing ordered nine divisions to attack northward between the Argonne Forest and the Meuse River. East of the Meuse, where the Germans had heavy guns hidden in the hills, the French XVII Corps was only to lay down harassing bombardments and make local raids.[43] Like Falkenhayn, Pershing was attacking with the Meuse to his right while ignoring the strong enemy artillery across the river. The result could have been predicted, but was not.*

Finally, the history of the war showed that the problem of supply inevitably limited the most audacious penetrations. Rail transport flowed along static lines and could not follow a rapid advance. Roads capable of bearing heavy traffic, much of it from motorized vehicles, could not be built quickly. Construction methods, equipment, and training were all geared toward trenches and static emplacements, not rapid extension of roads and quick establishment of efficient logistical networks. As a result, supplies

---

* There were, of course, important differences between the two offensives. Falkenhayn wanted an artillery-heavy campaign of attrition. Pershing intended an infantry-led breakthrough.

could not reach the troops and artillery could not move forward to follow them. This problem had plagued almost all successful offensives in the war. The Russians' Brusilov offensive of 1916; the German counterattack against the British at Cambrai in July of 1917; the German–Austrian breakthrough at Caporetto three months later; all five of Ludendorff's attacks in the 1918 Spring Offensive; and the British advance at Amiens all ground to a halt because food and ammunition could not be moved forward fast enough over the churned-up ground. Even the Schlieffen Plan of 1914 faltered as much because the Germans outran their supply lines as because they ran into the French at the Marne.[44] The British, French, and German armies had four years' experience trying to move supplies forward across torn-up battlefields. The Americans had almost none.

In essence, then, First Army's plan for the initial Meuse–Argonne assault was a desperate gamble. The planners assumed the first two German lines would be lightly held, and that the enemy would be fooled as to the axis of the attack. They called for a ten-mile advance by nine divisions, followed by a breakthrough of the *Kriemhilde-Stellung*, on the first day, when no American division had yet advanced three miles in a single day, not even at St Mihiel, where the attacking troops were combat veterans and the Germans were already withdrawing. Only three roads would be available to support the advance, and those were roads in name only. If the Americans failed to break through on the first day, the Germans would be able to reinforce the sector with an additional 15 divisions within three days. Even though the German divisions were one-third the size of the Americans' and were disorganized and tired, Pershing's operations staff knew that they were still formidable defenders. Unless the Americans reached their first day's objectives, the breakthrough assault would turn into a protracted and bloody campaign. Hugh Drum and his staff convinced themselves that a first-day penetration was not only possible but likely. Pershing did not need to be convinced; he already believed it. Writing to his wife ten days before the attack, General Kuhn predicted Germany's imminent defeat:

> What a reversal of form since July 15 when everything seemed to be going the Kaiser's way. I don't see how there can be any come back now and Germany has surely hit the toboggan slide. Of course, things may not always go with perfect smoothness so we must be prepared for little setback now and then.[45]

He would find out what a "little setback" looked like.

CHAPTER 8

CONCENTRATION

Field Order No. 20 percolated downward to corps and division headquarters, each of which interpreted it for the use of their subordinate units. Brigadier General Wilson B. Burtt, chief of staff of V Corps, issued Major General Cameron's orders on September 21. The mission for the 79th Division was that:

> [by] maintaining close combat liaison with the 4th Division (IIIrd Corps) on its right and the 37th Division on its left, [it] will advance rapidly to the Corps Objective ... It will seize in succession Malancourt, Montfaucon, and Nantillois. The 37th Division and the 79th Division will mutually assist each other in the capture of Montfaucon.[1]

The 37th Division's assignment was:

> [to] maintain close contact with the 79th Division on its right and the 91st Division on its left, and, by proper echelonment in depth ... assist the 79th division in the runing [sic—should be "turning"] of Montfaucon ... It will seize Hill 261, and the village of Ivoiry, pressing forward without delay to the Corps Objective.[*][2]

Burtt informed everyone that "The 3rd Army Corps (US) on the right ... assists the advance of the 5th Army Corps by turning Montfaucon and later by turning

---

[*] The 91st Division, to the left of the 37th, was not involved in the capture of Montfaucon, although it sent patrols around its western edge before the 79th got there.

the section of the hostile 2nd Position within the zone of the 5th Army Corps."[3] Two days later he clarified his instructions for the advance: "The Divisions will push forward to the 'Corps Objective line' ... rendering mutual support, but not delaying their own advance by waiting for each other."[4]

Burtt's orders reflected the ambiguity surrounding Pershing's open warfare doctrine. The combination of independent advance of units and mutual assistance certainly sounded like open warfare, or at least as close as one could get with three divisions lined up cheek by jowl. The formula for artillery support, however, was quite different. Corps and divisional artillery, reinforced to more than twice their normal number of guns, would advance the rolling barrage at the rate of 100 meters every five minutes (about two miles per hour, a slow walk) until it had gotten through the Bois de Montfaucon, then speed up to 100 meters every four minutes. It would pause as the divisions reached each of their objectives to allow them time to capture and consolidate the enemy trenches, then resume until it reached a line one kilometer beyond Montfaucon; then it would end.[5] As the infantry had no reliable way of communicating its progress to the artillery, its own pace would be regulated by the firing schedule. This certainly was not open warfare.

In a separate memorandum Burtt specified, "Tanks are to assist the infantry in accomplishing their tasks. It is the infantry and infantry alone that take and hold positions ... The general principle may be enunciated that all specialties have but one end and aim, to aid the infantry in getting to that close contact where the 'will to use the bayonet' ... can find its expression."[6] This did not begin to address the proper use of tanks. As the British and French experience showed, tanks and infantry had trouble coordinating even when the two arms had trained together. The men of the 79th had hardly ever seen a tank, and Burtt's memorandum did nothing to help them.

General Kuhn based his orders (Field Order No. 6, September 25) on those of V Corps, adding details regarding the assembly points for tanks, tasks assigned to the engineering regiment, and liaison with neighboring divisions.[*] For the infantry and the artillery to communicate, "Telephone

---

[*] Two sentences in FO No. 6 reveal the army-wide ignorance of how tanks and infantry must cooperate. "If the tanks remain unemployed during the first stages of the infantry attack they will proceed to their second assembly position in the Bois Cunel, where they will arrive at H plus 12H ... Infantry brigade commanders are authorized to call upon the tank commander for assistance while the tanks are at the assembly points or enroute to the second assembly point." (Joseph E. Kuhn, "Field Orders No. 6," September 25, 1918, Hugh A. Drum Papers, Box 16; Folder: 79th Division, AHEC, p. 2.) In

lines will be maintained to infantry units and (should telephones fail) use made of projectors and visual signaling and couriers to maintain constant touch with the front."[7] Two features of his orders, however, had dangerous implications for coming events. For the infantry assault Kuhn placed the 157th Brigade in the front line, with its two regiments abreast. The 158th Brigade, also with its two regiments side by side, would follow at a distance of 1,000 meters and would constitute the divisional reserve. This formation was known as brigades in column, and was a workable arrangement for veteran divisions whose officers had served together and knew their jobs. But for inexperienced divisions that had never seen combat, it was guaranteed to cause problems. With each brigade spread out over a two-mile front, commanders would have a hard time communicating with their subordinate units. And while the trailing brigade was expected to support the leading one, the commander of the brigade up front would have no direct control over the rate of advance of the one behind him, the disposition of its regiments, or its mopping-up activities. Control of troops in action was always tenuous at best: telephone lines were quickly cut by shells and the passage of wagons and guns, and runners easily got lost or became casualties. Many officers had recently been detailed to Pershing's staff school at Langres; this would not help. Kuhn's dispositions compounded an already serious problem.

Second, Kuhn's order said that "The 4th Div (III Army Corps) is on our right and is to assist: in turning Montfaucon; and (later) by turning the sector of the hostile 2nd position in our divisional front."[8] Clearly Kuhn expected help from the 4th Division within his own zone of operation. Unfortunately, the same understanding did not hold in the 4th itself. General Bullard's orders described his III Corps' mission as follows:

> To penetrate promptly the hostile second position, in order to turn Montfaucon and the section of the hostile second position within the zone of action of the 5th Corps (center Corps) and thereby assisting in the capture of the hostile second position, west of Montfaucon.[9]

This mirrored the ambiguity in Pershing's original order—was III Corps supposed to enter the zone of V Corps or not? The question occurred to

---

other words, the tanks had no definite mission and were assigned to no particular infantry units. They would be on the battlefield; if infantry commanders wanted to use them, that would be fine.

Major General John L. Hines, commander of the 4th Division. He and his chief of staff, Lieutenant Colonel Christian Bach, went to Brigadier General Bjornstad, now III Corps chief of staff, and asked. According to Bach, Bjornstad agreed that it would be a proper tactical movement to attack westward into the V Corps zone. Hines and Bach returned to their PC, wrote a divisional order calling for Montfaucon to be encircled from the east and north, and sent it to III Corps for approval. This time, Bjornstad said to change the wording to read, "to provide for assisting the reduction of Montfaucon *but only within our own area* [emphasis in original]. We were not to go outside of our western boundary."*[10] Hines accordingly rewrote his order to say:

> The Division will assist (if necessary) the Division on its left, by turning Montfaucon; *not by an advance into the area of the Division on its left but by steady progression to the front* and energetic action by the left combat liaison group or by reserves, against hostile detachments on the left flank [emphasis added].[11]

Kuhn and Hines, intended by Pershing to cooperate in reducing Montfaucon, would be working at cross-purposes.

Having laid their plans, Pershing's staff had one more task: to assemble the men, guns, and equipment from their locations scattered over northeastern France. The job was assigned to a brilliant young officer on First Army's operations staff, Colonel George C. Marshall. The challenge facing him was immense. Two hundred and twenty thousand French troops and their equipment had to be removed from their trenches and 600,000 Americans (15 divisions plus corps and army headquarters, artillery, and supporting units) had to be moved in. Two-thirds of the American troops had to be extracted from the St Mihiel fighting while it was still in progress and sent as much as 50 miles northwest. Some divisions were brought from east of the Moselle River, another 60 miles to the southeast, crossing the rear of the St

---

* After the war, Bach and others searched for the original draft of the 4th Division order but never found it.

Mihiel fighting to get to their new positions. Three came from the Soissons area and one (the 79th) from training in the Haute-Marne region. Marshall had only three roads at his disposal. Two he dedicated to combined horse and foot traffic and one to motor transport. Moving only the men of a single division required 1,000 trucks in a line four miles long; adding artillery and supply trains increased the length to 20 miles. Four hundred and twenty-eight thousand men were sent by truck; the rest walked. Three thousand guns and 40,000 tons of ammunition (for the initial bombardment only) were hauled to the attack zone by 90,000 horses. To handle the load, the Army had to set up 19 railheads, 34 evacuation hospitals, and over 80 supply depots.[12]

In a report written shortly after the Armistice, Marshall described the difficulties. All movements had to be at night. Not all tractor-drawn artillery had motorized trains, so their baggage and supplies could not keep up with the guns and had to be sent on separate roads. To maintain solid columns on the roads, portions of different divisions and corps had to be mixed so that their travel speeds matched. Trucks arrived at loading points late, then had to be sent off immediately to maintain the maximum capacity of the system. Many horses were worn out and could not keep to the schedule. Artillery units engaged at St Mihiel had their withdrawal delayed by flare-ups in the fighting and by losses among their horses. The need to avoid having divisions and corps cross paths during the march made it necessary to send some far out of their way; even so, mix-ups in schedules caused marching columns to mingle on the road. Nonetheless, "Despite the haste with which all the movements had to be carried out, the inexperience of most of the commanders in movements of such density, the condition of the animals and the limitations as to roads, the entire movement was carried out without a single element failing to reach its place on the date scheduled; which was, I understand, one day earlier than Marshal Foch considered possible."[*][13]

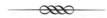

---

* A postwar report by the AEF General Staff's administration section credited the transfer from St Mihiel largely to a Captain Gorju of the French Commission Régulatrice Automobile, reducing Marshall's role to that of a liaison officer: ("General Staff First Section, A.E.F., "Report B-2: Account of the Argonne-Meuse Operation - 9th September to 11th November - Influence of G-1 Section and Part Taken in the Operation," 14 January, 1919, RG 120, Entry 24, "Report of Operation, G-1 Section, First Army, 10 Aug - 11 Nov '18," Boxes 3361, 3020, NARA, p. 5.)

On September 8 the 79th Division entrained for the journey to Robert-Espagne, south of the front in the sector of the French Second Army. The Second, commanded by General Auguste Hirschauer, held Sector 304, named for the ill-fated hill that lay just south of Montfaucon. Hirschauer would be responsible for placing the American divisions in the line, after which he would turn over the entire sector to the American First Army.

The scene in the 10th Training Area was controlled chaos. As described by the divisional historian:

> [I]n the small towns from Chalancey in the far west to Argillieres in the east, the Training Area was seething with activity, as Town Majors called for statements of claims and damages to settle their accounts; company clerks dismantled field orderly rooms; officers' trunks and boxes were pushed into far corners of billets to be stored; final instructions were given, packs rolled with care and properly adjusted, and farewells exchanged with the villagers.[14]

General Kuhn was everywhere, checking on his troops' readiness for the trip and hurrying along units that appeared to be slacking. In his diary he noted the names of subordinates who failed to stay with their commands, leaving them leaderless. He complained about the 66-pound packs the men carried, too heavy for a long march and impossible to fight in. "Movement as regards entraining points," he noted, "[is] made entirely for convenience of railroads and not for convenience of troops who had in many cases to march long distances on short notice."[*][15] When each train embarked, its commander was given the destination; the men were kept in the dark. As the trains of the 79th rolled southeast, the men noticed large volumes of traffic on the rails and on the roads:

---

* Once in France, Kuhn continued to impress his subordinates and fail to impress his superiors and colleagues. Samuel W. Fleming, Jr., an officer in the 315th Regiment, wrote of the division's training period in the summer of 1918: "We had battalion, regimental and brigade maneuvers. Gen. Kuhn, Division Commander, sometimes spoke at the Critiques and I was always impressed by his common sense, clarity and pleasant personality. He had been attached to the German Army as military observer prior to our entry in the War, and thus had the unique experience of serving on both sides in the fighting. Unfortunately he was not in the inner circle of the AEF High Command, why I do not know, but I suppose a carryover of army politics from prewar days. At any rate we looked on him as an excellent soldier and a gentleman, and it was too bad, we felt, that his qualities were not recognized by G.H.Q." (Samuel W. Fleming, Jr., "World War I Service," 1960, World War I Survey, Box: 79th Division, 157th and 158th Inf. Brig.; Folder: Fleming, Samuel W., Major, 315th Infantry, AHEC, p. 37.)

Great troop concentration was going on somewhere further east as the Division moved in. Just where and why intrigued the men. Those detraining at Révigny had passed columns of Italian infantry on the road, just coming out of the line, and all the troop trains had been delayed while specials, routed through and laden with Americans of other divisions, passed them bound eastward. On every side were preparations which indicated a big offensive somewhere near.[16]

It was the preparation for the St Mihiel campaign.

On September 12 orders arrived to leave Robert-Espagne and take over a section of the line. The men would travel by bus to their first stop, the towns of Récicourt, Dombasle, and Blercourt, all of them about five miles south of the front; from there they would walk. Strict measures were decreed to preserve secrecy. Unnecessary noises were to be avoided. Smoking at night was prohibited. "No member of the command will, pending arrival at debussing point, furnish any information as to his identity, the organization to which he belongs, his mission or destination, to any person other than an officer of the 79th Division or Military Police personnel."[17] As the men assembled their supplies and equipment for the move to the front line, they could hear the distant thunder of guns to the east. The reduction of the St Mihiel salient had begun.

Over the next few days the regiments and trains of the 79th boarded their buses, driven by French Annamite (Vietnamese) soldiers "who, bundled in great coats of goatskin and wearing French helmets, tam-o'-shanters, caps or turbans, presented odd spectacles to an American eye. The Anamites [sic] showed no expression on their faces, but soon proved that they could make their camions [trucks] go like the wind."[18] The convoys, unknown to the men, were traversing the Voie Sacrée that had saved Verdun in 1916. On September 16 the buses carrying the 304th Ammunition Train stopped at the edge of a wood and came under attack from a German plane. The few bombs dropped by the German missed, but if any of the men had been disinclined to observe the secrecy measures before, they weren't now. As the regiments disembarked at Récicourt, Dombasle, and Blercourt, the officers hurried the men into the woods and away from nosy German aircraft. "As they went, they eyed in awe the sight before them—villages in ruins, fields pitted with shell holes and showing only the rank vegetation which betokened neglect, and mud, mud everywhere, regular quagmires through which they sloshed."[19]

This was the residue of the German bombardments of 1916 that had attempted to destroy the supply lines to Verdun.*

At Récicourt the Machine Gun Company of the 314th Infantry got its first taste of fire. As Lieutenant John Kress recounted:

> A shell had crashed into a building in the village. It took only a moment for even the dullest to comprehend what had happened and act accordingly. It's debatable who took cover first. This shell was followed by about a dozen others—then silence. It was immediately decided to move the company out of the village and into one of the wood camps nearby.[20]

The 313th Infantry Regiment got to Dombasle on September 13. After spending the day in dugouts under occasional German artillery fire, they sent an advance party forward at night to inspect the trenches that would be their new home. These were held by a unit of the French 157th Division. The soldiers occupying the trenches wore the French Adriane helmet and carried the French Berthier rifle, but they were not French. They were American.

In partial fulfillment of its promise to the American black community the War Department formed two "colored" divisions, the 92nd and the 93rd. As we have seen, Pershing made a rare concession to the Allies' demands to "amalgamate" American units by parceling out the regiments of the 93rd to the French. (The 92nd served with the AEF as a complete division.) The 371st Infantry was one of them. On September 13 the regiment occupied the left-most part of Sector 304 as part of the French 157th Division. These were the Americans whom the 313th would be relieving.

---

* The accounts originating from the 79th and its component units make it appear as if the transfer from the 10th Training Area to the front went smoothly. The report of Major Paul Allegrini, a French observer attached to the division, reads differently. Loading of troop trucks was disorganized; the Americans did not want to divide up their units, so some trucks left partly empty. The supply system was highly defective—after leaving the Prauthoy departure area around September 8, some regiments did not receive new food supplies until the 15th. In between they ate their reserve rations. Although Allegrini rated the men's morale as generally excellent, he noted that about 50 men were absent without leave from the 313th Regiment as it went into the line; an officer had to be left at Bar-le-Duc to round them up. (Paul Allegrini, "Rapport Sur La 79e D.I.U.S.," September 21, 1918, 17 N 128, SHD, p. 1.)

Pershing's action in sending four black regiments to the French was not simply a manifestation of the Army racism typical of the time. While a first lieutenant he had commanded a troop of the 10th Cavalry, one of the Buffalo Soldier regiments that enforced Washington's rule over the Indian tribes.* He developed a sense of respect for his men and their military capabilities. In his memoirs he wrote that his "attitude toward the negro was that of one brought up among them. I had always felt kindly and sympathetic toward them and I knew that fairness and due consideration of their welfare would make the same appeal to them as to any other body of men. Most men, of whatever race, creed, or color, want to do the proper thing and they respect the man above them whose motive is the same."[21] Although patronizing, such sentiments were far in advance of the general Army attitude. In France, Pershing took every opportunity to get black troops into combat positions. When the War Department tried to divert colored regiments to stevedore duty Pershing cabled:

> [M]ust be some confusion Washington as to employment for Negro regiments referred to your cablegram. These regiments are not be used as labor troops but to be placed at disposition of French for combat service in French divisions. This utilization these regiments already approved by War Department.[22]

When the British rebuffed his offer to place black regiments in their service, he protested to General Haig:

> You will, of course, appreciate my position in this matter, which, in brief, is: These Negroes are American citizens. My Government, for reasons which concern itself alone, has decided to organize colored combat divisions and now desires the early dispatch of one of these divisions to France. Naturally I cannot and will not discriminate against these soldiers. I am informed that the 92d Division is in a good state of training and I have no reason to believe that its employment under your command would be accompanied by unusual difficulties.[†23]

---

* It was his association with the 10th Cavalry that won him his nickname. As a young tactical instructor at West Point Pershing, a strict disciplinarian, became known as "Nigger Jack" among the cadets. Reporters eventually softened this to "Black Jack." (Frank E. Vandiver, *Black Jack: The Life and Times of John J. Pershing*, 2 vols (College Station and London: Texas A&M UP, 1977), p. 171.)

† Pershing was proud of this letter, which he included in his World War I memoir. (Pershing, *My Experiences*, vol. 2, p. 45.) The leading book on the black experience in the war (Barbeau and Henri, *The Unknown Soldiers: African-American Troops in World War I*) does not mention it, although the authors cite Pershing's memoir in other contexts.

And when the War Department asked him for a statement about black soldiers he cabled:

> Exploit of 2 colored infantrymen some weeks ago in repelling much larger German patrol killing and wounding several Germans and winning croix de guerre by their gallantry has aroused fine spirit of emulation throughout colored troops all of whom are looking forward to more active service. Only regret expressed by colored troops is that they are not given more dangerous work to do.[24]

But Pershing's respect for black soldiers did not lead him to try to end their systematic mistreatment. The American Army was segregated and bigoted. Humiliation of black soldiers was routine, as witnessed by the crude "darky" jokes published in *Stars and Stripes*. The few white officers who objected were told not to be so sensitive, they "cannot expect to put the colored man above other Americans."[25]

Much different was the reception the black soldiers received in France. With a long tradition of Africans in the military and none of routine discrimination, France was to American blacks a virtual paradise. Captain Will Judy wrote in his diary of a group of black engineers that the 33rd Division passed on the march: "They sang, they laughed, they shouted, they enjoyed their work. All American negroes I have seen in France like their stay here. The French have accepted them almost with equality. I have seen them kissing French girls on the streets; French women everywhere have welcomed them warmly."[26]

The French attitude toward blacks astonished and outraged many white Americans, especially the Southerners, who insisted the French ran a serious risk in allowing them into their villages and who accused their hosts of encouraging American blacks to be "uppity" once they returned home. One incident was recounted by Captain de Metz-Noblat, a French liaison officer at Pershing's headquarters in Chaumont. The cover of the July 27 issue of *La Vie Parisienne* showed a bearded black soldier seated at table, fez and pipe on the ground, napkin around his neck, flirting with a white waitress. The caption read, "*L'enfant du dessert*"—the dessert kid. Arriving at mess the captain was accosted by an American officer. "I've been looking for you. Have you seen this picture? Your censors are crazy to publish a thing like that; our Negroes will buy it and send it home, and say, 'Here's how we're welcomed in France.'" In vain the captain explained that the soldier was a Senegalese, that the French did not discriminate among soldiers of different color, and that the censors didn't take account of the sensitivities of the Americans. But the officer continued to harangue him for quarter of an hour, with all of the staff listening.[*27] In August 1918 Colonel Linard, then head of the French mission to the AEF, prepared a memorandum to French units that attempted to accommodate the feelings of the white Americans toward their own black soldiers. He made it clear that the measures he proposed were in response to the whites' prejudices, particularly their fear that the race would degenerate physically and morally if it intermingled with blacks. The French were to refrain from addressing blacks familiarly, from praising black troops, from distributing sweets at their camps, and from all sexual relations between American blacks and French women. The memorandum, which was never circulated, nevertheless caused an uproar when, the day following the Armistice, the deputy from Senegal found out about it and protested to Clemenceau that it was a violation of the Declaration of the Rights of Man.[28]

The black units in France had varying experiences in combat. Undertrained and poorly equipped even by the standards of the badly prepared white divisions, officered largely by hostile and often incompetent whites, and subjected to systematic discrimination in the military hierarchy, the 92nd had a mixed performance. It repelled local German attacks in the Vosges Mountains in late August 1918, but its 368th Regiment failed to advance in the Meuse–Argonne (it had not been issued maps or wire cutters, among other reasons). This failure, which allowed the Germans to surround the "Lost Battalion" of the 77th Division, was ascribed to the entire 92nd, although most of its regiments had been in reserve during the battle.[29] General Bullard, an Alabaman and the commander of Second Army, to which the division was attached for the last weeks of the war, did his best to denigrate the performance of the 92nd. He exaggerated their failings, called the blacks "hopelessly inferior," and neglected to acknowledge that by the end of the war 1,700 of its men had become casualties and 21 had been awarded the Distinguished Service Cross. (More decorations would have been awarded but requests on behalf of black soldiers were often ignored.)[30]

---

* To a native French speaker, the humor would have revolved around a pun: *L'enfant du désert*, child of the desert, would refer to the African soldier. Adding the "s" makes ambiguous who is being referred to and adds a slightly off-color implication. (The American officer, of course, would not have had to understand French, let alone the play on words, to be outraged.) I am indebted to Ms Zehava Sheftel of Newton, Mass., for clarifying this point.

The four regiments of the 93rd Division suffered from the same deficiencies in training and equipment, favoritism to white officers, and discrimination as did the 92nd. But once assigned to French divisions, they were accepted by their new comrades in a fashion that caused great consternation among the white Americans. All of them ended the war with credit, although some got off to a slow start. The most accomplished among them, the 369th, formerly the 15th New York National Guard, fought well in the Aisne–Marne campaign and in the Meuse–Argonne, capturing a key German-held town. One of its sergeants became the first US soldier to be awarded the Croix de Guerre, for repelling a German trench raid. The 371st, mostly draftees from the Carolina farmlands, patrolled and raided in several "quiet" sectors, including Sector 304, before fighting with the French 157th Division in the Meuse–Argonne. It advanced rapidly and held off a major German counterattack that included gas. In all, the regiments collected three unit Croix de Guerre and 559 individual decorations, either Croix de Guerre or Distinguished Service Medals.[31]

The small advance party of the American 313th Infantry encountered the men of the 371st on the night of September 13. The newcomers "met and talked to the boys we were relieving—American negroes brigaded with the French wearing American uniforms but French equipped. They were closely questioned by the boys and each one agreed that it was a very quiet sector."[32] The next night the 79th relieved the 157th Division and the 313th Infantry moved into the trenches as the 371st filed out. Did the men whisper the usual front-line farewells of parting comrades-in-arms—"Good luck," "Keep your head down," and the like? Or did the boys from Baltimore only stare silently at the receding shadows of their black compatriots? No one seems to have recorded the scene.

The 79th began moving into Sector 304, now renamed the Avocourt Sector, on September 13. Private Schellberg of the 313th Infantry wrote to his brother, "Started for trenches 6 PM. Got in trenches 1am. Mud up to your knees. This is supposed to be a quiet sector. Germans were shelling the hell out of us. I was so tired and played out that I wish one of those shells would hit me."[33] By dawn of the 15th the relief was complete, and as the sun rose most of the men got their first look at the terrain they would be attacking: steep hills, matted with scrub and barbed wire, rising to the pinnacle of Montfaucon, "the white ruins of the village on its crest giving it a curious snow-capped appearance."[34] (Before the war, a large fifteenth-century church had dominated the town and its surroundings. Now its ruined walls were merely the tallest of the "snow-caps.") The French 157th Division held a two-brigade front stretching from the Bois de Cheppy on the left to the ruined village of Malancourt on the right. The front of each brigade sector was held by a single regiment. As the 79th relieved the French, it copied this arrangement. The 157th Brigade occupied the left sector, putting two battalions of the 313th Infantry side by side in the front line, each with a machine gun company in support. To the right, the 158th Brigade did the same with units of the 315th Infantry. A third battalion of each regiment was held in brigade reserve.

Everything the men saw was new and bizarre. In the words of the divisional historian:

> In the outpost lines, the battered, crumbling trenches, oftentimes only waist deep, which zig-zagged through the sea of shell holes, gave visible evidence of the titanic struggles of the past. This evidence was intensified by the unmistakable signs of the death and destruction which existed on every side. Scattered articles of French and German equipment, rusting helmets, broken rifles and bayonets, half-rotted bits of clothing, here and there a bleached bone protruding from the earth, in a word, the flotsam and jetsam of a battle field—all told their own gruesome tale of devastating conflict.[35]

Not all the novelties in the trenches were dead. Private Schellberg had some fun describing his new bunkmates to his family:

> The first time we went up in the trenches we had dugouts to sleep in and we had some unpleasant friends their [sic] to greet us, they were rats and coodies and let me tell you they were rats too they were so big that the first one I saw I thought it was a cat. While you were sleeping they would run over you. I had some reserve rations and I used them as a pillow and while I was asleep they ate part of my rations from under my head ... We had a can of corn beef their and they went as far as to eat through the can and eat that up too.[36]

Sergeant Ed Davies of the 315th had a more favorable reaction, confiding to his diary:

> The Trenches so far are not so bad. Plenty of mud and dirt, but we had good duck-boards to walk on, so we managed to keep dry. About 10 o'clock we reached an open space behind a big hill where our kitchens were located. They had the kitchens in a big dug-out right in the side of the hill. We rested here awhile and had some good hot stew.[37]

Life was bearable in other ways, too. The health of the men improved. The flu, which had afflicted the 79th in its training camps at Prauthoy and Champlitte, virtually vanished. Trench foot, caused by constant immersion of the soldiers' feet in stagnant water and a common ailment in the French and British armies, did not make an appearance. The chief danger was drinking sewage-contaminated water, and officers paid close attention to where their men filled their canteens. Mail, the soldiers' precious link to their loved ones and their former lives, arrived. Davies wrote:

> Mail, letters from home—Oh boy I am so happy I could weep. It was an eternity waiting for Sergeant Bowman to sort them out. Out at last, got mine, five of them think of it, the first since I left home. I am going to sneak off in a little corner and read them by myself ... Gone is the mud and slime of the trench, gone are the bursting shells and stinking gas. I am home for just a few minutes. I try to imagine myself home with Sis and the bunch, out with Billy and the boys. Oh, God, what a feeling of loneliness comes over me. Am I to see them again?[38]

Some soldiers tried to maintain a semblance of normality by observing old traditions. Corporal Oscar Lubchansky of the 313th wrote to his wife:

> Tomorrow is the Day of Atonement and I shall spend all my available time reading the bible. I have been doing this for a time now so you can see darling that I am trying my best to do right in every way. I am sorry I cannot fast, but we can never tell whether we can wait for our next meal or not, so you see it is unwise not to eat.[39]

For a few, however, the tension of awaiting combat was more than they could stand. A postwar roster of men who served with Company B of the 313th reported that Private Harry E. Dellinger:

... was evacuated on the 24th of September, 1918. At that time we had just returned from the sector #304, and were living in pup tents in the woods in the vicinity of Avocourt. He was taken sick immediately after dinner, suffering with vomiting and nervous spells. He was so nervous he could not stand still. They took him from his tent to the ambulance by aid of the Medical Detachment.[40]

Others appear to have taken matters into their own hands. One such was Sergeant Louis Rubin, who:

... accidentally shot himself through the foot on September 25th, the evening before we went over the top. Sgt. Rubin was in his tent when all at once I heard the report of a rifle, and heard him call out he had been shot. There were some first aid men near who bandaged his foot. The bullet passed through his heel. He was afterward evacuated to a Base Hospital.[41]

For two years Montfaucon had been a quiet sector to which both sides sent their depleted divisions to rest and recuperate. A live-and-let-live ethic had evolved in which neither side made life needlessly uncomfortable for the other by prolonged shelling, frequent sniping, or aggressive raiding. The outposts as a result were lightly held. To conceal the presence of newcomers, the 79th was commanded not to alter the situation. Raids were prohibited and only limited patrolling was allowed. Nevertheless, the Germans got wind that a relief had taken place. Apart from the differences between the French and American uniforms and the shapes of their helmets, the men behaved like the rookies they were, shooting at shadows and strange noises. It did not take long for German aircraft to react. On the night of September 15 a plane dropped a bomb on the regimental headquarters of the 315th Infantry on Hill 309, killing a corporal, the first combat death in the 79th since it arrived at the front. From then on air activity was common, especially at meal times when the men were assembled in the mess. The men watched German aircraft fly over the front, pursued by antiaircraft shells that exploded with a smudge of smoke and, moments later, a distant "pop." From the Bois de Brocourt behind Dombasle, the soldiers watched German planes shoot down French observation balloons and dove for shelter when shells landed on hillsides half a mile away—an event they would hardly notice two months later. At night they marveled at the light show, better than a hometown fireworks display, as flares and star shells illuminated the trenches to reveal any raiding parties that might have crossed No-Man's Land. Desultory shelling—about 50–70 rounds a day in the sector, from the front lines all the way back to Dombasle—kept the men on their toes. This routine was punctuated by an occasional deluge of high explosive and gas shells such as afflicted Company L of the 313th Infantry on the night of September 15, causing several casualties. To most of the men these were mere nuisances, and at times welcome diversions.

Despite the precautions taken by First Army, the Germans noticed the buildup in the Meuse–Argonne sector. Many breaches of the move-only-by-night orders occurred. A German flier spotted one battalion of the 79th getting out of their trucks after daybreak, and the French heavy artillery that moved up behind the division was impossible to miss. To determine who the new troops were on their front, the Germans on the night of September 19–20 made their first trench raid, falling upon Company E of the 313th Infantry, which held the extreme left of the division's sector. A half-hour melee ensued. In the words of the divisional historian, "The greatest battle ever fought at its very height never offered more terrifying thrills than is offered when twenty or so men, in the pitch dark, scramble around a group of trenches trying to kill and not be killed by twenty or so other men whom they cannot distinguish as friend or foe." The Germans were driven off but returned two hours later, trying unsuccessfully to recover the body of a comrade who had fallen in the first raid. His papers identified him as Lieutenant Frederick von Freideburg of the 1st Guards Division; he was between 19 and 20 years old. General Kuhn called the affair "a complete victory for the green Americans."[42]

On September 20 orders came from Pershing's headquarters assigning the 57th Field Artillery Brigade, commanded by Brigadier General George LeRoy Irwin, to the 79th. This was the first time the division had had an artillery brigade since it arrived in France. Of course there was no opportunity for the infantry and the gunners to train together, or even to establish communication procedures. The 57th barely had time to emplace its guns and prepare its firing tables; some of its regimental officers didn't even learn which division they would be supporting until shortly before the attack. At least the 57th had combat experience, having fought in a Franco-American offensive in the Vesle sector for most of August and early September. Other artillery assigned to the 79th included the 147th Field Artillery Regiment, usually part of the 41st Division; nine French batteries of 75mm guns and six of 155s; and two batteries of 9.2-inch guns from the Coast Artillery. All of these were under General Irwin's command. This assemblage, in principle, gave Kuhn's men the dedicated support of ninety-two 75s, forty 155s, twelve 6-inch trench mortars, and eight of the massive 9.2s.[43]

Other supporting units arrived. Two battalions of the French 505th Tank Regiment provided the 79th with approximately 75 light tanks each.* These were Renault FT-17s—small, lightly armed, and thinly armored but relatively fast (for their time) and maneuverable. (They were the first tanks ever to have fully rotating turrets.) Also assigned to the 79th was a *"groupe"* of 15 St Chamonds, 22-ton monsters each bearing a 75mm gun and four machine guns. They were slow and mechanically unreliable and tended to drive themselves into the mud instead of through it. Also joining were a company of the 1st Gas Regiment, a balloon company, and the French 214th Aero Squadron. The airmen received no plans or orders from the division until a few hours before the attack; one of the tank battalions never did.[44] The 79th had never trained in working with any of these supporting arms, except for theoretical classroom exercises. The only tanks most of the men had seen were in pictures. Sergeant Davies noted his first impression of them: "Sure were funny little things. Look like little steel houses all painted up."[45]

Early on Sunday, September 22, German raiders returned with a vengeance. Two attacks, preceded by heavy shelling, fell simultaneously on outposts of the unfortunate Company E of the 313th and of Company A at the other end of the regimental line. Four men were killed, two officers and nine men were wounded, and two were taken prisoner. A half-platoon of Company A used their Browning Automatic Rifles to drive off their attackers, who lost three killed and one taken prisoner. The bodies revealed the presence of the 117th Division in the opposing line. The captured German disclosed that the second raid was caused by the failure of its predecessor to come away with prisoners. This time they did better; the men from Company E were evidence that the 79th was in the line. Pershing visited Kuhn's PC on September 24 and told him that his plan was for the French to maintain the forward positions to prevent such an event as this. But the French, who had managed the transfer, apparently had not complied.[46]

---

* The nominal organization of a French tank battalion called for three companies, each with 25 tanks. In practice this count was rarely achieved due to breakdowns and combat losses. The Renault FT-17 weighed seven tons, had a crew of two, traveled at 4.8 miles per hour, and was armed with either a 37mm gun or an 8mm machine gun.

As the day of the attack neared, activity behind the lines of the 79th reached a crescendo. Every night brought convoys of guns to the front, which dispersed to their firing emplacements behind the trenches. Supplies and ammunition flowed into the depots on long columns of trucks. Tanks clattered over the roads to their assembly points. The infantrymen in the reserve units had to change locations constantly to accommodate the newly arrived guns and the mountains of supplies.

On the night of September 22–23 the 79th shortened its front by giving up the left half to the newly arrived 37th Division. This reduced its line from nearly three miles to one and three-quarters, room for a single brigade. Each regiment of the 158th Brigade put a battalion in the front line, but not in the outpost positions. To further confuse the enemy as to which units it was facing, the outposts were manned by a battalion of the 33rd Division, otherwise located at the far right of First Army along the Meuse River.[*]

On September 25 Kuhn moved his headquarters up from Dombasle to Hill 309, west of Montzéville and three miles behind the front line. General Pershing, inspecting the preparations for the assault, drove over and met with him. That afternoon Kuhn issued Field Order No. 6. Its key sentence read, "The 79th Division, maintaining close combat liaison with the 4th Division (III) Corps on its right, and with the 37th Division (V Corps) on its left, will advance rapidly to the Corps Objective, the line 05.5–77.5, 08.2–80.2, 11.5–81.0. It will seize in succession Mallancourt [*sic*], Montfaucon, and Nantillois."[47] The artillery would bombard the German front line for 25 minutes, then commence the rolling barrage. The barrage would "stand" on the enemy intermediate position—a line running through the "Redoute du Golfe" and north of Malancourt—for ten minutes and on the enemy second position—a line connecting Hill 233 and Fayel Farm, at the foot of the Montfaucon pinnacle—for 20 minutes. In between, it would advance at the rate of 100 meters every ten minutes.[†] As an officer in

---

[*] There is confusion in the records as to who was holding the outpost line at this point. The historian of the 79th says it was a battalion of the 33rd Division. Hirschauer's relief orders say it was units of the French Second Army. (Historical Division, *USAWW*, vol. 9, p. 60.) Yet the 79th lost men of its own in the German trench raid, who must have been in the forward positions.

[†] The documents give a confused picture of Kuhn's intentions for the rolling barrage. Pershing's original Field Order No. 20 specified a rate of advance of 100 meters every four minutes. Montfaucon was 6.5 kilometers from the front line, so including the "stands" this rate would have brought the 79th to Montfaucon in around five and a quarter hours. Other versions of FO 20, as well as V Corps

V Corps artillery wrote after the war, "According to the plan of attack only 5½ hours was allowed for the Infantry to cut through the first line of resistance, to reduce the Intermediate line, to advance six kilometres in the face of determined opposition, and finally to overcome the enemy on a difficult and well-defended objective."[48]

The attack was to be led by General William J. Nicholson's 157th Brigade, which would pass through the 158th to get to the starting line. Nicholson was 62 years old, a veteran of the Spanish-American War and Pershing's Mexican Expedition. He placed his two regiments side by side, the 313th, under Colonel Sweezey, on the left and the 314th, led by Colonel William H. Oury, on the right, each reinforced by one company of the brigade's machine gun battalion. Each regiment would have two of its battalions side by side, with the third assigned to brigade reserve. Each battalion would have its four companies in column (that is, one behind the other), the fourth being in regimental reserve.[49] Nicholson was uncertain about the support he would get from the artillery and the tanks. In a September 23 memorandum to Kuhn's headquarters he wrote, "It is understood that one battalion of field artillery will be placed at the disposal of each regimental commander," but he did not know whether additional artillery would be placed at the disposal of the brigade. Regarding tanks he wrote, "The detailed disposition of the forward infantry units will be affected by the number and plan of action of such tanks as may be assigned to this Division," about as vague a plan for infantry–armor cooperation as one can imagine.[50] There is no indication that his doubts were resolved before the attack.

In their encampments the men of the 79th prepared to go over the top. Quartermasters' assistants collected excess clothing and equipment for storage in the divisional dump. Wire-cutting instructions were issued to company commanders, along with admonitions to get their units to the jumpoff trenches on time. Men were issued extra ammunition and rations and were ordered to clean their rifles and bayonets for inspection. Sergeant Davies in the 314th recalled, "Lieut. Pollack called the platoon together about 4 P.M. and gave us quite a serious talk on what was expected of us when we get into action. I knew then that the time was very close ..."[51]

Commander Cameron's order, Kuhn's Field Order No. 6, and a memo by Tenney Ross, give different rates of advance. Which version of the firing plan reached General Irwin, Kuhn's artillery commander, is not clear. As events unfolded, it didn't much matter.

Organization of 79th Division until 4:53 a.m., September 27, 1918

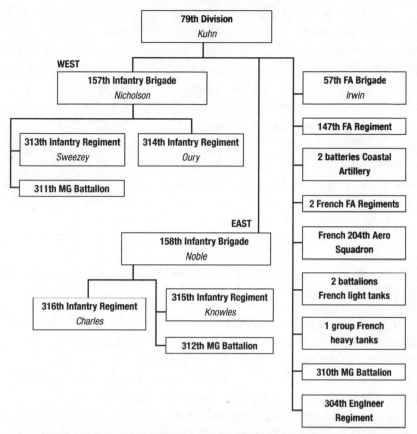

Private Kachik and other Catholics attended services in the field. The altar was a couple of big boxes with saplings bent over them to form an arch. He recalled that back home, people complained when their altars weren't fancy enough. This was the most beautiful altar he had ever seen.[52]

At nightfall the Avocourt–Malancourt road came alive with movement. Guns, motorized and horse-drawn, moved up to their advanced firing positions while trucks bore ammunition and supplies to the forward depots. Right of way was given to the heavy artillery brigades of the army and corps, which would deliver the opening bombardment. Patrols went forward into No-Man's Land to cut the German wire, followed by officers who marked the assault lanes with tape. The 313th departed its bivouac in the Bois de Lambechamp and marched five miles to its position in the front line; the last units did not reach their places until 4:10 a.m. The 314th did not receive the order until 7:10 p.m., when it was already on the move. The regiment left its camp in the Hesse Forest and headed for its assigned spot on Hill 304, getting into position only at 4:30 a.m. Not until then could the officers assemble to receive their maps and written orders. The two regiments of the 158th Brigade—those of their battalions not already holding the front lines—followed. Sergeant Davies recounted an incident on the march: "After many delays we entered the reserve trench. We hadn't gone very far when a poor old mule that had been on top of the trench fell in right in front of us. They couldn't get him out so they shot him and we had to climb over his body to go on."[53] (From the soldiers' diaries and memoirs it is apparent that every man who went down that trench remembered the mule to the end of his days.) Wet, cold, and tired, the men of the 79th reached their assault positions; no one got much sleep.

At precisely 11:30 p.m. on the 25th, one-quarter of the army artillery began firing at long-range targets. The 155mm howitzers and the huge 9.2s belched shells onto the main German defensive lines. Private Leo V. Jacks of the 119th Field Artillery described the scene lyrically:

> The deep muffled booming of the howitzers sounded like thunder coming out of a Cyclops' cave. Waves of sound seemed as material as waves of water. We were engulfed in them. They surged, and washed, and echoed from crest to crest in volcanic tones. The great forged-steel bolts passed with a rushing noise like a huge wind. Trees along the slopes of our hills bent heavily, with their branches waving and shaking, and their heads bowing as if a tornado were blowing above them, and little ripples ran along the grass tops as volley after volley raged past.[54]

By then the marching regiments of the 79th had come up level with the positions of the guns. Never having been so close to heavy artillery in action, the men were stunned by the noise, the smoke, and the flashes of light. The historian of the 316th Infantry wrote:

> It was the first time these men had been in front of the fire of their own guns. For a dazed moment there was a gasp of something like panic—scores dropped into the gutters beside the road—and then the true nature of all that cataclysm dawned on them, and somewhat sheepishly they rose to view in awe the spectacle unfolded. A thousand gorgeous sunsets—extinguished

in a second, recreated in a moment—unceasing rolls of thunder, a night indelibly written in memory.[55]

Three hours later, corps and divisional artillery and the remainder of the army guns opened up on targets within a few miles behind the German lines—artillery batteries, command posts, machine gun nests, crossroads, barracks, strong points. Almost 2,700 guns were firing at once, and their reports blended into a continuous roar. The sky glowed crimson, then a duller red as smoke filled the air. The landscape opposite First Army's lines lit up with the flashes of exploding shells. On his way before dawn to attack German observation balloons, Captain Eddie Rickenbacker flew over the front: "Through the darkness the whole western horizon was illumined with one mass of jagged flashes ... The picture made me think of a giant switchboard which emitted thousands of electric flashes as invisible hands manipulated the plugs."[56] The Germans' return fire was weak, but a few rounds dropped on the regiments of the 79th as they made their way forward through the communication trenches. One man was killed and several wounded. A corporal in Company B of the 313th remembered the fate of one of his comrades, Private David Rudolph: "His leg was torn by a shell fragment, face badly cut and bleeding freely. I saw him wave his helmet from a shell hole, calling for first aid." Private Rudolph later died of his wounds.[57]

The day dawned. A thick fog filled the valley between the 79th and the slopes ahead. At 20 seconds before 5:30 a.m., Company D of the 1st Gas Regiment used its 4-inch Stokes mortars to add a layer of smoke to the fog. Exactly on the half hour the divisional guns directed their aim to the German front line, on which they rained shells for 25 minutes. (In the preparatory fire and the rolling barrage, the 57th Field Artillery would fire a total of 40,000 75mm and 6,000 155mm shells.[58]) The order went out to fix bayonets. The scraping sound of blades clearing their sheaths filtered down the line—or would have, had it been audible over the roar of the guns. As the barrage began, commands rang out:

"F Company, over!"

"Third Platoon, advance! Combat groups about thirty paces. Scouts out."[59]

The men of the leading battalions climbed the parapet, threaded their way through the gaps in the wire, formed their lines, and stepped off into the smoke and fog.

CHAPTER 9

THE GERMANS

Major Albrecht Count von Stosch was worried about his machine guns. His regiment, the 11th Grenadiers, held the German line at the far left of its division, the 117th Infantry. The 11th Grenadiers' territory ran northward up the Barrois ridge all the way to Montfaucon. Stosch, newly appointed as regimental commander, was well aware that a defensive line is most vulnerable at the "seams" between units. It was his responsibility to make sure that the seam between the 117th and its neighbor to the east, the 7th Reserve Division, held firm if attacked. Earlier in the afternoon of September 25 the 7th had borrowed three of his heavy machine guns to support a large raid they were to make that night on the American lines. Stosch had been counting on those guns to cover the seam. Now there was a dangerous gap on the eastern end of his own line, made the more ominous because the major had no reserves left to plug the hole.

To calm his anxiety, Stosch paid a visit to the headquarters of his neighbor, Major Kuhr, commander of the 66th Infantry Regiment, which had borrowed the guns. No problem, Kuhr reassured him, he would have his machine guns back before dawn. Anyway, the raid would be against the enemy troops directly opposite the gap, so they could not possibly mount a surprise attack. Unconvinced, Stosch ordered Lieutenant Baum, the commander of the Liaison Company, to seal off the gap as best he could. He positioned a light *Minenwerfer* (trench mortar) platoon there and ordered his 1st Battalion a bit eastward into a ravine below Septsarges, except for a machine gun company, which he installed in a small hollow north of the

Bois de Montfaucon. Then, having done what he could, the major waited for events to unfold.[1][*]

One may reasonably wonder why Major Stosch was so concerned. On the map, the German position looked almost impregnable. The western end of the Meuse–Argonne sector was dominated by the high ridge of the Argonne Forest, crowned with dense, tangled woods, which overlooked the low ground to the south while providing excellent artillery cover against troops attacking up the Aire River valley to its east. On the extreme left (as seen by the Germans, who were facing south), the Meuse River protected their flank while, beyond, the Heights of the Meuse gave panoramic views of the American positions, which were laid bare to the heavy guns the Germans had hidden among the hills. In the center, the ridge leading south from Montfaucon, with its eroded spurs running east and west, was an ideal place for machine guns to fire on soldiers struggling up the slopes. Montfaucon itself, studded with concrete bunkers, offered superb views of the entire line.

The parallel spurs leading away from the Montfaucon ridge and the ravines that separated them were perhaps the most formidable natural defenses the Germans could hope for. Mostly unwooded, the slopes provided clear fields of fire for guns positioned on the ridges above them. As attackers advanced up a south-facing slope, they would be caught in the open by machine guns firing downward, parallel to the ground. Should the ridgeline be taken and the attacking infantry swarm over the top and down the opposite side, they would have no shelter from the guns on the next spur to the north, which could rain fire on them from above, seeking them out in the trenches and shell holes where they had taken cover. From the spine of the main ridge leading north up to Montfaucon, four such spurs ran to the east and four to the west.

Although much of the landscape had been cleared for farming, patches of woodland added to the defensive value of the terrain. The lower slopes of the sector held by the 117th Division, close to the American lines, were covered by a series of contiguous woods about four miles wide and two and a half miles deep in all. From west to east they were the Bois de Cheppy, the Bois de Béthincourt, the Bois de Montfaucon, and the Bois de Malancourt.

---

[*] Throughout, translations from German primary sources are by Julie Allen and Neil Berkowitz; I have edited these for military terminology and usage.

These woods were not the patches of bare sticks that protruded from the ground at Ypres and the Somme; many of the original trees remained standing, and enough time had passed since the Verdun battles for dense brush and brambles to cover the ground. In peacetime, these had been communal woodlots for the towns whose names they bore; in war, they were ideal defensive positions.

The Bois de Montfaucon, in particular, was a formidable obstacle. Two or three miles down the slope from the town of Montfaucon itself, this large expanse of woodland was divided laterally by a narrow valley with the obscure name of Ravin de Lai Fuon. An enemy coming up through the lower half of the wood would emerge from the shelter of trees and scrub into a wide but shallow clearing; from the far side, only a few tens of yards away, German machine guns and infantry would be able to fire on them while remaining concealed. At the Ravin's eastern end it opened to form the Golfe de Malancourt, a triangular field bordered on the south by the Bois de Malancourt and on the north by the Bois de Cuisy, an extension of the main Montfaucon wood. Guns positioned just inside the southern edge of the Bois de Cuisy would have an unobstructed field of fire one and a quarter miles wide and the same deep.

Other, smaller woodlots were scattered around the sector of the 117th. As one passed north and northwest from Montfaucon one came in succession upon the Bois de Beuge; a small wood known only by its elevation as Bois 268; another nameless wood designated Bois 250, to its east the Bois des Ogons; and north of them, and four miles north of the town, the twin woods of Bois de Cunel and Bois de Faye. None of these were larger than half a square mile. When the attacker was distant, they were good places in which to hide long-range artillery. As the enemy approached, they provided concealment for machine gun emplacements that commanded the open country around them.

Even the ground underfoot worked against the attacker. The 1916 battles for the Mort Homme and Hill 304 and the French counterattacks in 1917 had carved the landscape with trenches and pulverized it with shell fire. As an American intelligence officer described it, "The whole ground was pitted with shell craters; the half destroyed timber had sprouted up in a thick second growth; and across this tangled and broken ground ran elements of old trenches, wire entanglements and obstacles of every sort in almost inextricable confusion."[2] Here and there were ruined villages, their remains now practically obscured by grass and vines. When it rained, which was often, the ground melted into the gluey mud that had sucked at the boots and wagon wheels of Count von Moltke's army 58 years earlier. An editor of *Stars and Stripes* later wrote, "Whatever Prussian evolved the motto 'Gott mit uns' must have been thinking of the topography of the Meuse–Argonne."[3]

The Germans, of course, had not left the security of their defense solely to nature or to the detritus of past battles. But although their line in the Meuse–Argonne had been essentially stable since September of 1914, the defenses constructed in that sector, with some exceptions, were sketchy. In early 1917 Ludendorff had withdrawn his armies from the front between Arras and the Aisne to rest and reorganize in preparation for the great Spring Offensives of 1918. To cover the new position he had built a strong defensive zone from Lille in the north to Champagne, just west of the Argonne Forest. Later in 1917, almost as an afterthought, the construction was continued to the southeast, atop the old 1914 lines, as far as Metz. The various segments of this defensive zone were named after mythical Germanic heroes; the one in the Meuse–Argonne was called after Kriemhilde, the wife of Siegfried. The Allies named the whole complex the "Hindenburg Line."

As with the other parts of the Hindenburg Line, the name Kriemhilde denoted not only a specific set of obstacles and strong points but also a deep defensive complex consisting of at least four mutually supporting positions, or *Stellungen*. The first position in this sector was the *Wiesenschlenken-Stellung* and its eastward continuation, the *Haupt-Stellung*. This defensive belt was about three miles deep, from No-Man's Land to the northern edge of the Bois de Cuisy. It contained three lines of defensive positions. The first, only 30 or 40 yards from the American lines, consisted of little more than light machine gun nests in the swampy ground at the foot of the Bois de Montfaucon. About a hundred yards behind that, a parallel trench line supported the first line. The *Haupt-Widerstands Linie,* the "main line of resistance," was just over a mile further up the slope, on the north side of the Ravin de Lai Fuon, for as long as it remained within the Bois de Montfaucon. Once the line emerged to the east, however, it took a sharp left turn at a point the Germans called the Mount of Olives,[*] west of Malancourt, and climbed the hill northward for

---

[*] *Ölberg,* in the original. No such place appears on the German Army maps of the sector available to me, although they show the bend in the German line. Modern French maps show a roadside calvary just east of Malancourt; perhaps it was originally located to the west of the town, and was appropriately nicknamed by the German soldiers.

GERMAN DEFENSIVE LINES ("HINDENBURG LINE") IN THE MEUSE–ARGONNE

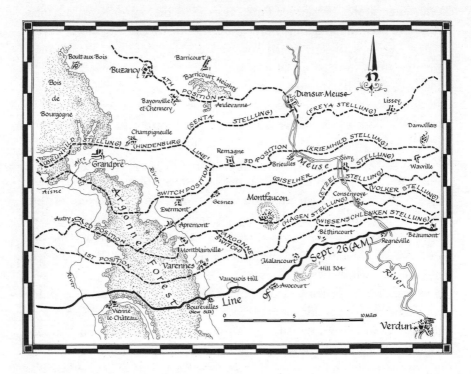

one and a quarter miles, turning east again once it got to the level of the Bois de Cuisy.[4] The western side of the sector was thus the most vulnerable, because the main line of resistance was relatively close to No-Man's Land, while the woods shielded advancing soldiers from view until the moment they emerged into the Ravin de Lai Fuon.

Behind the main line of resistance was the *Hagen-Stellung*, covering the southern slopes of Montfaucon; only partially completed, it contained a number of concrete shelters that were badly built and quickly became waterlogged when it rained. Otherwise, it was not much of a line at all. Still further north, running through and over Montfaucon itself, was the *Etzel-Stellung*. The barbed wire was in place here, but while the trench lines had been laid out and were well sited they had so far been dug only to a depth of a foot or two. The peak of Montfaucon, part of the *Etzel-Stellung*, was a daunting objective in itself, rising 360 feetabove the American lines. But although its crest was covered with concrete blockhouses (American engineers later counted 17 of them) and over a hundred dugouts, the hill itself was organized for observation and shelter, not defense.[5] Still, in the words of an officer of the American 37th Division, "Deep trenches and seemingly endless belts of barbed wire encircled the slopes rising to Montfaucon and gave notice of the difficulties to be encountered in storming the stronghold."[6]

Above Montfaucon, and extending northward from Nantillois and the Bois de Beuge, was the *Giselher-Stellung*. This was simply a string of natural positions that included various woods and ridgelines, but which offered many sites for machine gun nests and light artillery emplacements. Finally, the *Kriemhilde-Stellung* proper ran through the wooded heights of Cunel and Romagne roughly six miles north of the German front line. Begun in 1917 but never completed, it nonetheless sported a strong wire defense; its shallow trenches were made up for by the commanding positions on which they were sited. Behind that there were no more defensive lines; if the Germans had to retreat beyond the *Kriemhilde-Stellung*, they would be fighting in the open with their backs to the Meuse River. [*]

That the lines comprising the *Kriemhilde-Stellung* were only partially finished was, in itself, not much of a handicap. Since 1916 the Germans had abandoned a defense based on continuous trench lines, as had been used by both sides for much of the war. Instead, they adopted the defense in depth. Front lines were held thinly by small groups of men in fortified outposts. Artillery and machine guns were distributed throughout the defensive zone, placed so that their fields of fire overlapped and protected by emplacements such as pillboxes or blockhouses. This maximized the effect of defensive machine guns, which could sweep large areas. If one machine gun nest was attacked, the others could fire on its attackers. Concealed emplacements that were bypassed by the first line of infantry could chew up the second or third waves as they advanced, or fire into the flanks and rear of the formations that had passed them by. The attackers who were not killed or wounded would be forced to take cover in shell

---

[*] Each of these *Stellungen* was in turn subdivided and there were many switches and connections among them, so that their exact number and the meaning of the term itself were matters of confusion even at the time. See, e.g., G.M. Russell, "Summaries of Intelligence, 5th Army Corps, St Mihiel–Meuse Argonne," August–November 1919, C.E. Fogg Papers, World War I, USMA, entry for October 2, 1918, p. 1.

holes and old trenches, making them sitting targets for plunging shell fire from artillery situated behind the line. Scattering the machine gun and artillery positions over a broad area also diffused the effect of enemy artillery, which no longer had defined trenches to shell. It forced attacking formations to expose their flanks to machine guns located in the strong points and to lose cohesion. German infantry, held in reserve for the purpose, could then counterattack isolated groups of enemy soldiers. The counterattack came in two forms: the *Gegenstoss*, or immediate counterstroke, a quick strike on the attackers without extensive preparation, timed to catch the enemy when he was still disorganized from his recent advance; and the *Gegenangriff*, or deliberate assault, launched after a preparation lasting as long as several days against an enemy that had already consolidated itself in the captured positions.[7] If the counterattack failed to dislodge the enemy and the *Stellung* had to be abandoned, the remaining guns and men could quickly be withdrawn a few miles to the next defensive zone, where the process would begin again. In short, the German defenses no longer aimed to stop the enemy like a brick wall. They would absorb him like a sponge, then squeeze.

No terrain on the Western Front, save the nearby Heights of the Meuse, was as perfectly suited to these tactics as the Meuse–Argonne sector. Every ridge, rise, and hillock could be fortified as a strong point. Every large shell hole, fold in the ground, ruined house, or patch of brambles could conceal a machine gun and its crew. The climbing hills gave long fields of fire in all directions. A well-manned, well-trained, and well-equipped army could hold this line indefinitely.

But the German Army of September 1918 was not the efficient machine of 1914, or even of Ludendorff's huge offensives of the past spring. As long ago as the winter of 1917 the Germans had begun inducting undernourished youths, convalescents, and the elderly. Training was greatly cut back. Acts of rebellion began to appear. Men refused to board trains for the front. Almost 18,000 soldiers were under arrest for indiscipline; in the city of Cologne the Army counted nearly 30,000 deserters.[8] By the beginning of 1918 it was clear that most of the Army—particularly the older men, who made up a majority of the troops—had neither the physical nor mental capacity to serve as the "attack divisions" (*Angriffsdivisionen*) that Ludendorff required. Only about one-quarter of the infantry divisions were designated for that role; they were assigned the highest-quality replacements, supplies, and weapons and were trained in the new, sophisticated assault tactics. The others were classified as "positional divisions" (*Stellungsdivisionen*) and were assigned to defense. While the latter still possessed assault units, these were a minority, and did not compensate for the poor overall quality of the rank and file.[9]

It was with the attack divisions that Ludendorff gambled and lost in his five assaults against the western Allies between March and July 1918. Having suffered heavy casualties during the offensives, these units practically evaporated in the French and British counterattacks. In June, July, and August, the Germans lost 1.2 million men, of whom roughly half were prisoners or "missing," most of the latter being deserters. Since the end of May, divisional strength on the Western Front had fallen from about 200 to 125, of which only 47 were rated fit for combat.[*][10] Ludendorff had to break up some divisions to maintain the others at strength; to stretch manpower yet further, infantry battalions were reduced from four to three companies and some companies were reduced to 60 men. Additionally, soldiers had been taken from the front to work in industry and agriculture; the women, foreign workers, and prisoners of war who were sent to the farms and factories did not suffice to prevent severe shortages of industrial products and food. By the late summer of 1918, 2.4 million German soldiers had been diverted for this purpose.[11]

Morale had plummeted. Troops deserted or surrendered wholesale. Some formations had to be coaxed or bribed into an attack; others mutinied outright and killed their officers. Looting was a common occasion for rioting and violence against officers. Many new recruits jumped from troop trains. Few assault units remained, and those that did were rarely in shape to deliver the *Gegenstoss*. The infantry now consisted of static positional divisions and the tattered remnants of the assault divisions. The only dependable formations were the artillery and the machine gunners, who remained highly motivated and were able to conduct a mutually supporting defense in depth.[†]

---

* The number of available German divisions is often given as 185; see, e.g., Trask, *AEF and Coalition Warmaking*, p. 115. That figure is taken from the writings of British Major General Sir F. Maurice, who published only a year after the Armistice; see Sir F. Maurice, *The Last Four Months: The End of the War in the West* (Casswell and Co., 1919), p. 122. I have chosen to rely on the figure given by Herwig, who wrote in the 1990s and had superior access to German sources.

† It was widely reported in the AEF that German machine gunners had been found chained to their weapons to prevent them from fleeing. *Americans in Europe*, a German newspaper published in

Nevertheless, the Germans were confident enough in the defenses provided by the terrain and their own preparations, and (as we shall see) convinced enough that the Meuse–Argonne would remain a relatively quiet sector, to entrust the line to only four weak divisions with several more in reserve. The commander of this part of the front was General Max von Gallwitz, a veteran of the Franco-Prussian War and one of the few high-ranking German officers whose appointment resulted solely from his ability rather than from noble descent. An artilleryman, he had served on the German General Staff and had commanded the troops on the western flank of the Verdun offensive, including the bloody conquests of Hill 304 and the Mort Homme. For much of 1916 he was assigned to command the Second Army on the Somme; but now he was back to face the Americans on familiar ground. Army Group Gallwitz occupied the front from Grandpré in the Argonne Forest past Verdun to Metz, a distance of about 75 miles. It was the southernmost of Gallwitz's two armies, Composite Army C, that had failed to hold the line at St Mihiel, so he had seen the Americans fight. The other army, the Fifth, held the northern part of Gallwitz's sector, from the Argonne Forest to the Heights of the Meuse, almost exactly the sector designated by Pershing for his Operation B.

The four divisions that Gallwitz ordered into the line were a mixed bag.[*] The right-most position, in the Argonne Forest, was held by the 2nd Landwehr Division, a static unit that had been in Lorraine sector more or less continuously since September 1914.[†] To bring Ludendorff's assault

English for American POWs, excoriated *Stars and Stripes* magazine for publishing what it called "that four-year-old English lie," pointing out that cowardly soldiers do no better for having been chained to their guns than otherwise. An editor of *Stars and Stripes* later wrote, "I have forgotten (and neither tigers nor constitutional amendments would drag it from me if I had not) who was guilty of the chained-to-the-guns charge. Certainly we should have known better. The heavy German machine gun was equipped with chains so that its crew could haul it from position to position with readiest convenience, and some adroit intelligence [officer] in the early days of the war, perhaps discovering a dead crew with the chains in their hands, had jumped to the chained-to-the-guns conclusion." (John T. Winterich, ed., *Squads Write! A Selection of the Best Things in Prose, Verse and Cartoon from the Stars and Stripes* (New York and London: Harper & Brothers, 1931), p.79.)

[*] Unless noted otherwise, information on German divisions is from US War Office, *Histories of Two Hundred and Fifty-One Divisions of the German Army Which Participated in the War (1914–1918)* (London: London Stamp Exchange, Ltd., 1920, republished 1989).

[†] American intelligence reports put this division further east, in the Bois de Cheppy and the Bois de Malancourt. I rely instead on the German situation map for September 26 that is reproduced in Rexmond C. Cochrane, "The 79th Division at Montfaucon," in *U.S. Army Chemical Corps Historical*

divisions up to strength for the Spring Offensives, it had been stripped of most of its young men early in 1918. To its left, covering the valley of the Aire, the hill of Vauquois, and the Bois de Cheppy, was the 1st Guards Division. This was an elite shock formation, trained in open warfare, that had fought well in several of the spring battles both on the offensive and in retreat. By early September, however, it had been badly depleted. Gallwitz designated these two divisions the "Argonne Group."

Next in line to the east, covering the Montfaucon sector from the Bois de Malancourt to the ruined village of Haucourt (and almost exactly opposite the US 37th and 79th Divisions), was the German 117th Division. In May it had participated in Ludendorff's attack at the Lys River and taken heavy losses. One of its regiments was disbanded and the 11th Grenadier Regiment, recently arrived from Macedonia, was assigned to replace it. By August, the 117th had been assigned to Crown Prince Rupprecht's army group opposite Amiens. Just before Haig's August 8 counterattack in that sector, the German army commander rated it as one of only two divisions out of 13 available to him that was fully fit for combat.[12] But it had been in position less than a day when Haig struck; taken by surprise, it collapsed like the rest of the German line. So badly was it hit that, once it had been withdrawn to rest and refit, a second of its regiments was dissolved, its surviving men sent to fill out the rosters of other divisions. The 450th Regiment, itself a battered survivor of the same British attack, was brought in to bring the division up to something resembling full strength. But "full strength" was a dubious concept; by September 26, the companies of the 117th were down to between 55 and 80 men, with only one as high as 100.[13] Furthermore, with two of its three regiments new to the division, it was no longer a coordinated fighting organization.

Last in line in the Meuse–Argonne sector, holding the position from Malancourt clear to the Meuse, was the 7th Reserve Division. A static unit, the division had suffered heavily at Verdun in 1916. More recently, it had fought in several of Ludendorff's spring battles and in August defended against the French at Soissons; in all of these engagements it took many casualties. Having been in more or less continuous combat since March, it was withdrawn for training between September 8 and 17, then put into the

Studies: Gas Warfare in World War I (Washington, DC: US Army Chemical Corps Historical Office, 1960), p. 10.

left of Gallwitz's line. By this time its companies had fewer than 100 men. The 117th and 7th Reserve constituted Gallwitz's "Maas Group West." All told, the four German divisions between the Argonne Forest and the Meuse River could each muster about 4,300 men.*

The four front-line divisions were not the only ones Gallwitz had available. Four more were located within a few hours' march of the front and another eight within a day or two. Of the first group, two are worth examining because they played an important role in the events around Montfaucon on September 26–30. The 37th Division (not to be confused with the American division of the same number) was a first-class assault unit, trained in infiltration tactics and open warfare. It did very well in Ludendorff's spring battles at the Somme, the Aisne, and the Marne. Like all German divisions, however, it had lost many men in the course of 1918, and was badly depleted despite receiving large numbers of replacements. From August 13 until September 20 it was in Gallwitz's line south of Montfaucon, but was relieved by the 117th and moved back to a rest camp at Longuyon, about 25 miles northeast of Verdun. A mere five days later it was trucked to Dun on the Meuse River, assigned to army reserve, and told to be ready for action.[14]

The other division close to the Montfaucon sector was the 5th Bavarian Reserve Division, not an elite formation but one that had the great advantage of being fresh, having seen little heavy fighting so far in 1918. Nevertheless, it averaged only 60 men per company as the Meuse–Argonne campaign began. As they marched west to reinforce Fifth Army, they crossed the Meuse at Brieulles. There they were caught by the opening American bombardment and badly shot up; their artillery and support trains were heavily damaged and regiments, battalions, and companies were scattered over the countryside.[15]

The Germans were not simply negligent when they assigned only a few weak divisions to hold the front line in the Meuse–Argonne. Their troop

---

* The normal complement of a German infantry regiment was about 3,200 officers and men. (General Staff [UK], *German Army Handbook, April 1918* (London, Melbourne: Arms and Armour Press, 1977; reprint of 1918 edition).) A division had three infantry regiments and one artillery regiment as well as a heavy artillery battalion, a signal unit, pioneers, and trains, for a rough total of 13,000. By September 1918, however, most divisions were at one-third strength. (Trask, *AEF and Coalition Warmaking*, p. 120.) The divisions that faced the AEF therefore held on average about 4,300 men of all ranks.

dispositions were based on the knowledge that they could not mount a strong defense everywhere, and on their best guess as to where the next blow would fall. By August 9 Ludendorff knew that the Central Powers could not win the war; his job now was to keep from losing it. A month earlier, Foch's attack at Soissons, which had rolled up all the German gains since May and removed the threat to Paris, had come as a shock to OHL and to the government; never had the Army been forced into such a precipitous retreat. But Ludendorff, increasingly divorced from reality, refused to admit that the Army was morally beaten, blaming the setbacks on his commanders, his staff, and the poor quality of the reserve troops. Then, on August 8, Haig attacked at Amiens. The British tactics called for unprecedented coordination and mutual support among the infantry, artillery, tanks, and aircraft. They worked, as we have seen in Chapter 6; and the British advanced 12 miles before the assault was halted four days later. The Germans lost 228,000 men, half of them deserters. Ludendorff later called this the "black day of the German army."[16] At a meeting of the Crown Council at Spa on August 14, he joined the Austro-Hungarian Kaiser Charles in recommending immediate peace negotiations. Kaiser Wilhelm authorized Admiral Hintze, the Minister of Foreign Affairs, to begin negotiations through a neutral country; but before anything could come of this, Ludendorff calmed down and the initiative sputtered out.

The next blow came on September 12, when the Americans attacked the St Mihiel salient south of Verdun. As we saw in Chapter 7, the Germans were caught in the middle of a withdrawal; within two days almost all the salient was in American hands. The rapid overrunning of the salient accomplished two strategic objectives for the Americans, which they did not realize at the time. It further demoralized the German High Command, already rocked by the Allied successes at Soissons and Amiens. Gallwitz and Ludendorff were particularly disturbed that no meaningful resistance had been mounted and that large amounts of supplies were destroyed or captured. Ludendorff showed signs of coming unhinged: Admiral von Müller heard from another officer that the news of St Mihiel had rendered him "a completely broken man."[17] Another senior officer who saw Ludendorff on the first night of the attack considered him "so overcome by the events of the day as to be unable to carry on a clear and comprehensive discussion."[18] Hindenburg telegraphed Gallwitz, "The severe defeat of Composite Army C on September 12 has rendered the situation of the

Groups of Armies critical." Blaming the outcome on "faulty leadership," he continued, "I can only hope that the Group of Armies employing the forces which I am allotting to it will hold the position. The Group of Armies will bear the complete responsibility for this ... Wherever commanders and troops have been determined to hold their position and the artillery has been well organized, even weak German divisions have repulsed the mass attacks of American divisions and inflicted especially heavy losses on the enemy."[19]

On September 14 the Austro-Hungarian Kaiser Charles, following up his proposal (seconded by Ludendorff) of August 14, made a public appeal for the contending governments to "send delegates to a confidential and non-binding discussion on the basic principles for the conclusion of peace," to be held "in a neutral country and at an early date."[20] Over the next few days the offer was rejected in turn by the British, the Americans, and the French, who believed it was a tactic to divide the Allies. Puzzled German soldiers wondered why their side, which they had been told was doing so well, seemed to be offering an armistice; their officers explained that "it was not weakness but the desire to communicate that led to the offer. Every front-line soldier knows that an honorable peace can only then be achieved, when the Entente's desire for destruction is confronted by our unshakeable determination to defend ourselves."[21]

The second effect of the fall of the St Mihiel salient was to cement in the minds of the German High Command the idea that the Americans' true objective, whatever appearances might indicate, was the fortress of Metz. At first, the Germans were startled that the Americans did not continue their successful attack in that direction. On September 16, Gallwitz assessed the situation thus: "The enemy's delay is undoubtedly due to the fact that he has reconnoitered our outpost area, wishes to work his way forward over this terrain first and move his artillery up correspondingly. In addition, he must reconnoiter the possibilities of moving his numerous tanks before resuming his attack."[22] By that time, Pershing had already begun withdrawing his divisions and sending them on a 60-mile journey northwest to the Meuse–Argonne. Five days later Gallwitz's intelligence staff wrote, "[T]he attack will be directed principally against Composite Army C, and will probably be extended to the east bank of the Moselle." Composite Army C was, as we saw, the army now holding the line behind the former St Mihiel salient. Similar assessments emanated from various German headquarters every few days. On

September 27, as the Meuse–Argonne offensive was in its second day, the intelligence office of the German Crown Prince was writing, "[T]he possibility of an imminent, large scale, Franco-American attack in Lorraine has not been decreased by the Franco-American offensives which opened yesterday in eastern Champagne and between the Argonne and the Meuse ... The front between Verdun and Lunéville [i.e., opposite Metz] is still occupied by large numbers of fresh, trained troops."[23] As late as October 18 Gallwitz's intelligence section was warning, "The probable entrance into line of Americans in place of the French 69th Inf. Div. may have some connection with preparations for a large-scale American attack planned against Metz."[24]

The reduction of St Mihiel had a third, somewhat paradoxical, consequence. The Germans, although defeated, concluded that the Americans weren't very good fighters. An intelligence officer in Composite Army C headquarters wrote:

> Great clumsiness was shown in the movement over the terrain of the waves of riflemen which followed each other closely. The shock troops hesitated when met by the least resistance, and gave the impression of awkwardness and helplessness. Neither officers nor men knew how to make use of the terrain. When met by resistance, they did not look for cover but went back erect ... The command throughout was bad and clumsy. The enemy had obviously very many officers, but these officers lack all qualities of leadership. Unmistakable was the perplexity after the initial objective was reached. The enemy was helpless when confronted by a new situation and unable to exploit the success ... The entire lack of military skill was also evident in the pursuit. No advantage was taken of favorable opportunities for attacks on flanks and envelopments...
>
> ...
>
> Concluding Estimate: The American is too much of a dilettante, and therefore also in a major attack needs not to be feared. Until now, our men had a much higher opinion of Americans, due to the fact that in patrol undertakings they had shown themselves as dashing soldiers ... Our troops had expected much more of them in a major battle. In spite of some local reverses, their confidence of being able to deal with the Americans has been raised.[25]

Most of these criticisms were accurate, and were known to the Americans themselves. The flaw in the assessment lay in what it omitted: all of the shortcomings noted were to be expected in a newly formed army in its first battle; intelligent, highly motivated soldiers (which even the Germans knew the Americans to be) would quickly learn their jobs.

For all of these reasons—lack of clear thinking at OHL, fixation on Metz as the target, and disdain for the offensive abilities of the AEF—the Germans failed to credit that a massive assault on the Meuse–Argonne sector was imminent. They were aware of the American buildup there, but they did not see it as the main thrust. The Americans had decreed strict measures to disguise their concentration: no movement by day, no fires, and so forth. But they could not hide half a million men and their equipment completely. The German divisions holding the line knew that something was up, but not what it might be. On September 23, a Summary of Intelligence by a German division (most likely the 1st Guards) noted the presence of new American units near the front and concluded:

> All these identifications, particularly the circulation in hitherto quiet sectors, point to the possibility of an attack along the whole front from Reims to Verdun. During the day-time, only circulation far in the rear could be observed, but at night great activity reigned along our front. The noise of narrow gauge railways, motor trucks, the unloading of heavy material, loud cries, sirens and klaxons could be heard throughout the whole night.[26]

On the same day the 1st Guards Division's operations report stated, "Brown uniforms having been observed along our front on Sept. 23, it would appear, although not definitely, that the presence of American troops must be taken into consideration ... On the left of the neighboring group, in sectors previously held by the French, the presence of the 79th and 80th American infantry divisions has been confirmed." The same report noted that interrogation of a French prisoner revealed that "A vigorous attack for the purpose of creating a diversion from the American offensive in front of Verdun can be expected."[27] In other words, an attack was possible, but only as a diversion from a larger assault further east.

Only on September 25 did Gallwitz realize that the threat did not lie behind the old St Mihiel battlefield, it lay between the Argonne and the Meuse.[28] To meet it, he did what he could. The closest division to the front was the 5th Bavarian Reserve, camped at Fontaine only a few miles east of the Meuse; early on the morning of the 25th he ordered it to concentrate near Dun, preparatory to crossing the river westward. He also assigned to it a complement of aircraft for reconnaissance. Later in the day, as the American buildup continued, he released that division and the 602nd Field Artillery Regiment to Maas Group West, to be available for counterattacks. (The 5th Bavarians, as we have seen, were cut up by American shell fire at this time while crossing the Meuse to get to their assigned position.) Later in the day, Gallwitz ordered the 37th to move south by truck from its rest camp at Longuyon, up near the Luxembourg border, to Dun. To further bolster his line, he alerted the 28th Division, quartered six miles east of the river near Étain, to assemble and be ready to move.[29] Late in the evening Gallwitz had his corps commanders make their final dispositions.

At 2:00 a.m. on the 26th Gallwitz finally received the evidence he needed to confirm the imminence of a major attack. A raid yielded a prisoner from the American 4th Division, which he had previously seen at St Mihiel. The transfer of this veteran unit to west of the Meuse convinced Gallwitz that here was where the main American blow would fall. He did not have to wait long for further proof. At 2:30 a.m., as Pershing had ordered, all 2,700 American guns opened up at once, saturating the German defensive zone with shells. Locations that might harbor German artillery or observers were particular targets: the Heights of the Meuse, the eastern edge of the Argonne Forest, any woods that offered concealment, Montfaucon itself. Bivouac areas, headquarters, crossroads, and telephone exchanges received special attention.[30]

The concentration of fire against the Germans' strong points and communication centers left their front line largely untouched—for the moment. The 66th Infantry Regiment, the one that had borrowed Major Stosch's machine guns, sent its patrol out into the lines of the American 4th Division. It returned by 4:30 a.m. in a disorganized state.[31] The major would not get his guns back.

At exactly 5:30 a.m. American artillery, still following Pershing's plan, concentrated all of its fire on the German front line. In the words of an officer of the 66th Infantry, "All communications to the front line are immediately cut—telephone wires shot to pieces, too badly to be repaired by the crews that are sent out. Signal lights no longer work because of the thick fog and the smoke and dust of the shelling. Runners are sent forward but not heard from again. Brigade HQ is unreachable because it has moved, and the new location is unknown."[32] Next door, in the 11th Grenadiers, "The detonations followed each other without interruption and the air was torn by a constant droning sound. In the villages, the remaining ruins tumbled down; in the forested areas, the chaos of trees and roots became even more confused, and even the laboriously erected defenses could not hold out for long. A thick, dark cloud lay over the entire region, while a mix of dust and smoke, artificial and natural fog, and gas reduced visibility to 1 meter."[33]

Gradually the intensity of the bombardment on the front lines lessened as the rolling barrage moved northward. German machine gunners who had taken cover hastened back to their weapons and peered through the smoke and fog, trying to see movement. Shadows began to appear in the murk. Back through the woods and up the slopes sped the cry, "*Sie kommen! Sie kommen!*"[34]

CHAPTER 10

OVER THE TOP AND UP THE HILL, SEPTEMBER 26

Sergeant James Meehan of Company G, 313th Infantry Regiment, remembered the first moments of the attack:

> [O]rders came down the line to move out and in two minutes No Man's Land was full of men pushing ahead through barbed wire, jumping trenches, and across shell holes, there being a heavy fog or mist which made it very hard to see ahead. We had scarcely gone one hundred yards when our first man went down with a bullet in [his] leg, being Bernard Repp, an automatic gunner.[1]

As it happened, the Germans manning the forward outposts, following their doctrine of defense in depth, had withdrawn to the Main Line of Resistance once they had warned of the imminent attack. Except for a few bodies, the first trench line the Americans reached was empty. A corporal in the same company, Oscar Lubchansky, later wrote to his father:

> I have a hazy recollection of a hazy march, a cold night in a trench, an ear splitting artillery barrage. Our company was in reserve, our duties calling on us to mop up and clean out machine gun nests that our other waves had passed up. I can tell you it is some sensation. We had the whole of Malancourt Woods to traverse. Our artillery had torn everything to pieces, but the inevitable snipers and machine gun rats still remained. As I said it is some sensation to hear a rifle crack and bullet wiz [sic] past your ear and you not knowing where it comes from.[2]

The 313th, under Colonel Claude Sweezey, held the left half of the 79th Division's sector, with his 2nd Battalion on the left and his 3rd Battalion on the right.* Despite the almost zero visibility and the lack of resistance in the German front line, enemy artillery and machine guns further up the slope quickly began to take a toll. Corporal George Evans was ordered to go forward and locate the platoon leaders of Company B. "In doing so I stumbled across something which I thought was a sand bag on the edge of a little trench. Stooping down to rest my hand on it, I felt something soft and wet, and looking closer I saw it was the disfigured face of a doughboy. I was told later that it was [Private Frederic] Prettyman."[3] In the fog and smoke, men lost track of their units and of each other. The formations in which they had been so briefly trained—columns of half-platoons, companies in assault echelon—dissolved. The haze rendered the men largely invisible to their opponents, but neither could they see enemy positions until they practically tripped over them. It hardly mattered—to preserve secrecy, Pershing had banned raiding and had limited patrolling before the attack, so no one in First Army had current intelligence on the enemy's positions. The experience of Lieutenant Miller Johnson of Company K was typical of the confusion. His platoon did not get far into the woods when "suddenly what seemed like a million German machine guns opened on us." As he recalled soon afterward:

> Every time we would raise our head "Tut, tut, tut" would go the German Maxim ... I raised my head to see where we were, when lo and behold I was looking into the muzzle of a German gun two feet in front of me, manned by two Germans who had sickly grins; and one of them said "*In kommen*," which I readily understood. I did not stand up for fear of being hit by my own guns, because bullets were flying in all direction. I took a look around to see where my men were, and found that I was deserted.
>
> Just as I was about to enter the shell hole, which held two Huns and their machine gun, I heard, "Keep down, Lieutenant. There she comes," and bang, with a cloud of smoke, was the explosion of a grenade. When I recovered from the shock, I found that both Germans had been severely wounded and the machine gun knocked about five yards out of place. Immediately I decided that I was not deserted, as I had thought, but found

* In general, the action will be described from left to right across the battlefield.

later that the men had learned my predicament and had relieved me of an embarrassing position. The one German soon died and we left the other to his fate and pressed on.[4]

Johnson reorganized the platoon and discovered that, of the 50 men with whom he had started, ten remained. A few had been killed or wounded; most had simply lost contact in the fog and underbrush, some of them becoming caught up in their own small battles unknown to Johnson. Continuing forward, he encountered little resistance save a few snipers who, camouflaged and firing from the trees, brought down some more of his men.

Bigger problems were brewing. Heavily laden, the men of the 313th got tangled in the old wire, underbrush, and shell holes of the Bois de Malancourt. Gradually the rolling barrage, the moving line of shell fire that was supposed to neutralize their opponents, drew away from the advancing men. If the exploding line of shells got too far ahead of the infantry, the defenders would have time to emerge from their dugouts, set up their machine guns, and fire into the advancing ranks. This was not an immediate crisis because the Germans had largely abandoned the wood; but it would soon count for a lot. A similar problem plagued Company A of the 311th Machine Gun Battalion, assigned to support the advance of the 313th. The carts in which they carried their weapons and equipment quickly bogged down in the rough terrain. Abandoning the carts and carrying by hand their .30-caliber water-cooled machine guns, tripods, and ammunition, the gunners rapidly fell behind the infantry. Not for many hours would they catch up.

Trouble arose from yet a third source. Coming up in the rear of the 313th was the 316th Infantry Regiment. Its orders were to stay 1,000 yards behind, cleaning up bypassed German positions and standing ready to rush reinforcements forward if needed. Jumping off at 7:00 a.m., the 316th passed through the remains left by the regiment ahead of it. Captain Carl Glock, the regimental adjutant, recalled his journey up a communication trench that led through the Bois de Malancourt:

> At a turn in the [trench], as the head of the column approached, there lay a group of grotesquely huddled figures in American O.D. [olive drab]. The man in the lead putting his hand to the shoulder of one of these figures drew it away sharply in swift enlightenment—murmured a barely audible, "Dead!" and stumbled on. The column followed. It was the 316th's first sight of grim horror.[5]

The two lead battalions at first kept their proper distance. But, as with the regiment in front of them, officers quickly lost track of their units. Worse, neither the commanders nor the men seemed to understand their mission. In their inexperience and their eagerness to join the combat, the men of the 316th would not adhere to the slow pace set by the leading wave. Many rushed ahead, forgetting to mop up bypassed machine gun nests, which opened fire on their flanks and rear. This not only caused unnecessary casualties, it demoralized the men, who did not understand why the Germans were not put out of action once the front line had passed. Attached to the 316th was a French observer, the wonderfully named Captain Richard Feuardent. Frustrated by the regiment's dangerous lack of discipline, the captain decided to lead by example. Pulling his revolver, he plunged into a dugout and reappeared moments later with three Germans, their hands up and crying, "*Kamerad!*"[6] (His exploit so impressed the officers of the 316th that it was later recounted by the regimental and division historians as well as in the reports of the French liaison mission.) But the officers of the 316th fundamentally misunderstood their purpose. A field message sent by the leader of Company K to his battalion commander complained, "313th & Attached MG Co. holding us up. We cannot advance without blanketing their fire."[7] The idea that the regiment was to stay 1,000 yards behind the 313th, not advance on its own, had apparently made no impression.

Sometime between 8:00 and 9:00 a.m. the German 11th Grenadier Regiment, defending Montfaucon, detected a brief pause in the attack. They used it to evacuate the wounded, reposition their units, replenish their ammunition, and plug gaps with reserves or machine guns. But the quiet didn't last. The American artillery opened up again, trying to overwhelm the defenders and clear the road to Montfaucon. The fog, however, made it impossible for them to observe their fire, so it was ineffective, except for a few hits on the German artillery, whose positions were already known to the Americans.[8]

By 9:00 a.m. the 313th emerged from the Bois de Malancourt into the Golfe de Malancourt, the triangular clearing nearly a mile wide and somewhat less from bottom to top. Halfway up was the German *Haupt-Widerstands Linie*, the main line of resistance, a row of trenches looking down on the approaching Americans, heavily wired and studded with machine guns. More machine guns were sited in the Bois de Cuisy, which dominated the Golfe from the north. Of the 2,000 or so men with which the two lead battalions of the 313th had started that morning, only 300 remained in the front line; some had become casualties, but most of the rest were scattered in the foggy woods behind. Companies of the 313th repeatedly staged frontal attacks on the nearest machine gun nests, but the only result was to pile up their own dead and wounded. Among these were two battalion commanders, Major Benjamin Pepper of the 2nd Battalion, killed by machine gun fire, and Major Jesse Langley of the 3rd, wounded in both legs. A detachment was sent to the left, into the sector of the 37th Division, to circle the enemy positions; one platoon was able to overwhelm a machine gun nest and take 22 prisoners, but still no forward movement was possible. At 11:45 a.m. Colonel Sweezey sent an urgent request back to General Nicholson at 157th Brigade headquarters asking artillery to pound the German trenches and the woods beyond; shortly afterward he sent a telephone message: "Request that tanks be sent forward. I am suffering severe losses from M.G. fire apparently from south east of [Montfaucon]. We have no artillery barrage."[9] Nicholson relayed the message to Division headquarters, adding that he had no contact with the artillery, because he had moved forward from his PC of that morning and was out of communication with them.

By this time the 316th had caught up and mingled with the 313th, further disorganizing the front line. Sweezey did not have the authority to order the regiment behind him to slow down and keep its distance, nor could he ask Nicholson, his brigade commander and immediate superior, to do so, because the 316th belonged to General Robert H. Noble's 158th brigade. At some point Sweezey sent a message to Lieutenant Hurley on Nicholson's staff who, at 12:30 p.m., relayed it upward to Kuhn's headquarters: "Col. Sweezey is being held up ... He complains that he is being pushed by elements of Col. Charles command [the 316th]. In some places the companies are almost intermingled."[10] To reply, Kuhn had to order Hurley to get word to Noble to order Charles to disengage his men from the 313th. It is not clear from the records whether Charles ever got Kuhn's order or, if so, when. The convoluted chain of command, caused by Kuhn's column-of-brigades attack formation, was preventing officers from controlling the men they nominally led. In the words of Major Paul Allegrini, the French observer attached to Kuhn's headquarters, "At that moment the division was not a body of troops but a mob."[11]

Sweezey's request for tanks would not be easy to meet. A company of the 304th Engineers, part of the 79th Division, had been sent to build a road across No-Man's Land for the tanks, which could not negotiate the shell-cratered terrain. But as described by the commander of the French 14th Tank Battalion, assigned to support the 313th:

> By 9 a.m. the tanks were engaged in the Malancourt wood but the work on the trail was extremely slow; the laborers of the American engineering units, too scarce and having already undergone great exertion, made no headway … [A]s the work on the [trail] made no progress, the tanks remained, in fact, a very long time immobilized in the Malancourt wood.[12]

As for the guns, two battalions of the 147th Field Artillery Regiment, assigned to support the advance of the 157th Infantry Brigade, began to move forward once they had completed their barrage mission. At first they tried to use the road being built for the tanks, but got nowhere. Next they traveled west to Avocourt. From there the map showed a road angling northeast toward the village of Malancourt that could bring the regiment up behind the advancing 313th. But the road had been obliterated long before so the artillery was stalled, unable to fire a shot for the rest of the day. Not knowing this, Sweezey and the 313th waited.

In the right sector of the 79th, the 314th Infantry Regiment jumped off at 5:30 a.m. with its 3rd Battalion to the left and its 2nd Battalion to the right, each with one company in the lead and one company in support; they were accompanied by machine gun and trench mortar units. (The regiments' other infantry companies were allocated to brigade and regimental reserve.) From a height just behind the jumpoff line, Second Lieutenant John Kress of the regiment's Machine Gun Company got a clear view over the fog:

> The first sight of Montfaucon was appalling. From the top of the hill above Esnes, about five miles from Montfaucon, one could see the city itself standing out against the skyline. It was one great belching spout of dirt and dust as the heavy shells entered and burst among the buildings. This continued for hours, until the infantry had advanced so far it was necessary to stop the artillery fire.[13]

The infantry immediately ran into trouble. In some places the wire had not been properly cut, so it took more than the allotted 25 minutes to get past it. Then they had to cross Forges Brook, on the map an insignificant blue hairline but in reality a swampy morass with no banks or borders. Neither task was helped by the fog which, as with the 313th, concealed both the attackers and the positions they were attacking. At least they did not have to deal with trees and underbrush because this part of the sector, unlike that of the regiment to their left, faced mostly cleared farmland and small woodlots rather than continuous forest. The terrain, although badly shot up in four years of fighting, was less convoluted than that experienced by the 313th on their left—the 314th was attacking up the spine of the Barrois ridge, from which eroded valleys extended to the left as well as to the right, where the 4th Division was on their flank. Perhaps for these reasons, the companies of the 314th do not seem to have become disorganized as quickly or as badly as in their neighboring regiment. Nonetheless, the men gradually fell behind the rolling barrage, which proceeded up the hill at the inflexible rate of 100 meters every four minutes as Pershing had commanded in Field Order No. 20.

Once past the brook the men made good progress; here too the German outpost line had been abandoned. By 10:00 a.m. the leading companies had passed the ruins of the hamlet of Haucourt and were between Malancourt village on their right and Hill 277 on their left. But their progress was deceptive; many machine gun positions and sniper posts, undetected in the fog, remained in their rear as well as to their front and flanks. The situation became startlingly clear as, at about that hour, the fog lifted and gave way to a clear blue sky. The effect was like turning on a light in a dark and crowded room—much more of a problem for the Americans, who were in the open, than for the Germans, who were in concealed positions. In one incident related by Private Casper Swartz of Company C, his unit found itself pinned down inside a semicircle of German riflemen; every time one of the men looked up, bullets whizzed by. Private Swartz told the man next to him to keep down, but the man said, "I'll get them with this Brownie Automatic." He got to his knees and, as he was aiming his BAR, a bullet pierced his helmet and he fell backward, dead. Swartz never knew who he was.[14]

Machine gun fire poured into the American ranks from all directions, especially from the ruined village of Malancourt, where the German guns were dug in with overlapping and mutually supporting fields of fire. Fortunately, the men were well spread out. Colonel William Oury, commander of the regiment, wrote in his report, "In one case in particular our men found themselves right by a nest of machine guns, saw a machine gunner before he could traverse his gun, threw a bomb, and the gunner came out and surrendered with his whole crew. The lieutenant then took the man at the point of a gun, made him point out several other nests, and by this operation they were able to capture some 15 or 16 guns."[15] The regiment's own machine guns should have been there to suppress the opposition. But the torn-up ground was too much for the gunners, who were carrying their heavy weapons after abandoning their carts in the mud and could not keep up. One company was able to get far enough forward to silence several German machine gun nests. But the major commanding the battalion saw that the machine guns would not be able to negotiate the rugged terrain ahead and sent them back to the jumpoff point to await further assignment. The divisional artillery, still stuck on the road back at Avocourt, would be no help either.

The fight at Malancourt quickly became a struggle to preserve the advance of the 314th. As described by a participant, "The place was a village in name only. Years of bombardment had torn the tiny hamlet to fragments, until all that remained were some walls which had somehow escaped being struck by shells, a few trees with splintered trunks and dead limbs, and a great quantity of debris."[16] The battle quickly devolved into a series of local fights against machine gun positions. Typical was the experience of the automatic rifle squad of Company F, led by Sergeant John McCawley. Dispatched to work around a group of machine gun nests, it got within 50 yards and opened fire on three of them, wiping them out. But the action attracted the attention of other Germans, who commenced to fire on McCawley's squad. The sergeant was killed instantly, and almost every man in the patrol was killed or wounded. Wrote the divisional historian, with the sang-froid typical of divisional historians, "The sacrifice saved many, for it enabled the company to advance, while the patrol attracted the enemy fire."[17] Lieutenant Robert Christie of Company A led the scouts who reconnoitered ahead of the main body. He described the death of one of his men in a letter to the widow:

> We had passed through a difficult bit of woods under a heavy fire and were working out into the open to avoid snipers located in trees, when we were stopped by the fire of a large number of machine guns ... I ordered several scouts to move to my flank, over ground I had traversed, and Clarence P. Ferguson was the first to obey. I told him what he should do and he complied fearlessly and promptly. He passed beyond me, advancing deliberately. I was attracted by a faint gasp which indicated that he had been hit. He turned round, sat down and then lay flat for protection, as I thought. Not a word

was said and there was no indication that he desired assistance. One man was shot fatally just behind me, another scout was shot through the foot and another through the shoulder in quick succession. When I reached Ferguson he was dead, killed, I suspect, by a shot which was intended for me.[18]

Despite their losses and disorder, the men were slowly advancing. Soldiers who had separated from their units formed *ad hoc* combat groups.[19] Here and there parties of Germans began to surrender, more than willing to trade mud and machine gun fire for a warm meal and a safe cage behind the American lines. A private in the Machine Gun Company captured 22 of them in two groups, for which he was later awarded the Distinguished Service Cross. Sergeant Edward Davies was in Company B of the 315th Infantry, following behind the 314th. He wrote in his diary, "I shall never forget the first German prisoner I saw. He was a splendid big fellow with light curly hair and very good looking. His right arm had been torn off at the shoulder, but he was walking with a steady step with his captor. I couldn't help but admire his nerve."[20] But other Americans found their captives to be "middle-aged, dirty, miserably dressed, and apparently glad to be alive no matter what the cost."[21] For a few of the prisoners the cost was greater than they bargained for. Some of the Americans took the German resistance personally, especially if they had been shot at from behind. Second Lieutenant Arthur Joel of Company F in the 314th heard another lieutenant order a private to escort two captured men to the rear. The man returned almost immediately. "What did you do with the prisoners?" the lieutenant asked. "I tended to them, Sir," was the reply. In Joel's account, "His sheepish glance told better than words what had happened. Such occurrences were not uncommon on either side."[22]

Having reached Malancourt and Hill 277, the advance of the 314th began to bog down. The regiment had become disorganized. Companies mixed together; some were missing most of their men, others had extra. Soldiers found themselves with unfamiliar units. Two companies of the 315th Infantry, advancing too fast behind the 314th, barged into the front line. With bypassed enemy positions behind them, it was not always clear where the front line was; Colonel Oury's Headquarters Company, normally well in the rear, found itself attacking a machine gun nest, from which it captured five gunners.[23] An officer on the staff of the Inspector General, observing the field, later wrote:

At 10:00 o'clock there was considerable congestion of troops in Malancourt and on the south side of Hill 277. The movements of these troops resembled the actions of a reserve [i.e., staying put and awaiting orders] ... One company formed under cover of Malancourt, took the trench at the southeast edge of the Bois de Coude, northwest of Malancourt, and another trench in the Ravine de Fontenille, taking prisoners in both works. Arriving abreast [Hill] 269 this line came under heavy machine gun fire and fell back to cover. This was the only demonstration of aggressive leadership observed during a period of over five hours.[24]

Despite local successes against German positions, in Oury's words, "There still remained enough machine gun activity to more or less demoralize the command."[25] Not wanting to waste time, Oury ordered the advance to continue without pausing to reorganize; but it was hopeless. Around noon, barely half a mile north of Malancourt, the 314th ground to a halt. For several hours they traded fire with machine guns further up the hill, to little effect. By 4:00 p.m. the infantry was showing signs of panic, and a few men started to move back without orders. Oury, his staff officers, and Lieutenant Poulaine, the French observer with the regiment, stopped the movement and sent the men back to the lines; but no further advance would be possible that day.[26] The advance had cost Oury's regiment two officers and 52 men killed.[27]

Why were there no tanks to overrun the machine gun positions, no artillery to pulverize them from afar? One reason was that, throughout the division, communication was falling apart. Even before the attack began, Colonel Charles of the 316th had lost contact with his battalion commanders and with brigade headquarters. Kuhn received no word from the 314th as to whether they had reached their assigned jumpoff position; he had to send officers to find the regiment, which they did only after the attack had begun. V Corps immediately lost contact with the 79th because the division had been given the wrong kind of telephone wire—cotton-insulated, for indoor use, rather than rubber-insulated for the field—which soon short-circuited in the damp earth. V Corps operated all day with no reliable information on the whereabouts of the 79th Division.

Much had been expected of the 6th Balloon Company assigned to the 79th; their four balloons were to report the position of the front line and spot targets for the artillery. But when the fog lifted German planes attacked them; three balloons were shot down in flames, one of them burning the observer to death as he descended in his parachute. By 11:30 a.m. all contact with the Balloon Company had been lost and it remained out of communication the rest of the day.[28]

The 214th Aero Squadron, a French unit, was supposed to perform a function similar to that of the balloons. The plan was for infantry units to spread colored panels on the ground that would indicate their position to the airmen and convey messages such as requests for artillery fire or ammunition. The fliers would also look for German points of resistance and drop messages to the artillery telling them where to fire. The squadron got off to a bad start. Lieutenant de la Chapelle, the commander, received Kuhn's plan only three hours before the attack began and was never able to establish contact with division headquarters, remaining ignorant of Kuhn's intentions throughout the battle. According to de la Chapelle, the infantry almost never signaled its locations or its needs. Even divisional headquarters often failed to display their panels, so that pilots had to guess where to drop their messages.[29] Although the squadron took excellent aerial photos of the battlefield, these could not be developed and delivered until the next day, when they did no good. The little aerial intelligence that the division did receive was mostly inaccurate, such as the report of an American pilot who flew over Montfaucon on the morning of the attack taking low-altitude photographs. Upon landing, he described seeing no Germans in or around Montfaucon or within ten kilometers of it; only Americans were visible in the town. When the photos were examined long afterward, they showed German infantry south of the town and many targets nearby.[30]

Information from other sources was hard to come by. The 157th Brigade, the 314th Infantry, and the 316th Infantry were out of communication with the division's headquarters for most of the day. The 316th Infantry could not reach the 158th Brigade PC from the jumpoff until the morning of the 27th. The situation led to a flurry of increasingly worried messages, of which these were typical:

Kuhn to Nicholson, commander of the 157th Brigade, 7:10 A.M.:

Line to you reported out of order. Report not verified. Report situation at once by bearer and keep me informed by mounted messenger at frequent intervals.

157th Brigade Intelligence Staff to 157th Brigade Adjutant, 9:10 A.M.:

Signal men say tanks are destroying their wire. They are now working on wires forward from line. Pearson unable to locate Col. Oury—he will extend runner chain ... I will try from here to secure any information of his front line and flanks. Please advise by return runner.

Nicholson to Kuhn, 10:00 A.M.:

Following message dated 0725 from PC at 13.5–72.4 from Incite One (313th Regt) reports advance progressing without halt but cannot get any communication with Bn. Commanders.[31]

Throughout, General Kuhn was ignorant of his division's position. As he wrote late in the day in the midst of a long, angry message to General Nicholson (of which more later), "Have been without information all day regarding 313th Regiment and in the dark as to my front line."[*][32]

Lack of information was compounded by actual misinformation reaching the senior commanders, which grew as the day progressed. Around 10:15 a.m. V Corps reported to the operations staff of First Army, "79th Division reports they have reached their objective."[33] This vague message could have meant that Montfaucon had fallen, or that the division had reached the Corps Objective nearly two miles beyond. Whether it was taken seriously is not known, but other examples started piling up. At 2:15 p.m. the V Corps message center received a report, ostensibly from the 79th Division, stating that "our troops (79th Div.) advancing north of Montfaucon."[34] Late in the afternoon of the 26th and long into the evening—at 7:15, 7:30, and 10:15 p.m.—V Corps kept sending messages up the line saying that the 79th was north of Montfaucon. The division was, in fact, stuck just over a mile below the town until the next morning.[†]

The lack of reliable information led to a more insidious and far-reaching failure. The divisional artillery was, as we have seen, immobilized and unable to fire. But the corps and army artillery were still available

---

[*] In fact, the 313th sent several messages to brigade and division headquarters reporting its position; they appear in the files of V Corps and 79th Division headquarters in the National Archives. The problem may have lain less in neglect by Sweezey or in the communication link itself than in how Kuhn's inexperienced staff received and collated the information and presented it to him.

[†] The original source of these reports is not known. No such messages now appear in the archival files of the 79th Division or its subordinate units.

and although they were well behind the front, many of their large guns were within range of the German strong points. The problem was that corps headquarters were getting conflicting, optimistic, and unreliable information about their divisions' locations. Regiments tended to report where they ought to be, not where they actually were. At 12:30 p.m., for example, the 79th reported to V Corps that it had reached Fayel Farm, which was on the southeastern slope of Montfaucon hill.[35] In fact, it was stuck in the Bois de Malancourt, two and a half miles to the south. Not knowing where the divisions were, but believing them to be well north of their true positions, corps and army gunners feared to open fire lest they hit their own soldiers. In the early afternoon army artillery at the request of the two corps ordered: "All firing south of line 282.50 to cease."[36] That line was two and a half miles north of Montfaucon and a little more than half a mile north of Nantillois and included the territory the 79th was desperately trying to conquer. Until the divisional guns could free themselves from the muddy roads, neither the 79th nor any other division in V and III Corps could expect assistance from any artillery at all. Various versions of this order were renewed over the next four days, the stop line generally corresponding to the location that, in the words of the historian of the army artillery, "it was hoped the troops would reach."[37]

All of the problems recounted above—failing to keep up with the barrage, mixing of units, haphazard communication, poor aerial surveillance, faulty artillery support—could have been worked out during divisional training maneuvers. These were precisely the kinds of issues such exercises were intended to find and remedy. But there had been no maneuvers—there was no time. Nor had there been time to learn from the experience of the divisions involved in the St Mihiel offensive, who had faced the same obstacles. The 79th would learn on the job or not at all.

Maneuvers would not have helped overcome a huge difficulty faced by the 79th and all of the other divisions in the Meuse–Argonne: the roads. In the words of historian Rexmond C. Cochrane, "Ground plowed by some ten million shells during the previous four years could not be repaired in hours or days."[38] Furthermore, the 79th was constrained in its use of the roads that existed. On the 24th the divisional staff had requested authorization from III Corps to use the road from Esnes north to Malancourt; they were refused.[39] The road from Avocourt to Malancourt was, as we have seen, a road in name only.

The obvious need, as the chief engineer of the 79th reported to his superior at V Corps, was to rebuild the road from scratch. To this duty were assigned the companies of the 304th Engineering Regiment, reinforced by infantry, engineers, and pioneers from other regiments. By 11:15 a.m. it was clear that this force was insufficient and a company of the 310th Engineers and two companies of the 52nd Pioneers, all borrowed from V Corps, were added. German prisoners, some under their own NCOs, were thrown into the effort; they were happy to do physical labor if it kept them away from the worst of the fighting.[40] Despite the additional force, the work proceeded fitfully. Company A of the 304th was in the lead and was so far forward that it came under German machine gun fire, which forced it to drop its tools. Taking up combat formation, the company attacked and captured the position, coming away with the gun and eight prisoners. Supplies of paving material were insufficient. At first, stone could be taken from shell holes, but as the engineers advanced the topsoil got deeper and no stone was available.

By mid-morning the road situation was becoming critical. A seemingly permanent traffic jam developed at Avocourt that effectively throttled any transport to or from the front line.

The pioneer regiments provided the physical labor in an attempt to keep the traffic moving. Broken-down trucks were pushed into the ditch. "Many a French truck driver was compelled to move forward at the pistol's point."[41] Fortunately, the Germans concentrated their artillery on the American infantry rather than on the congested roads. Nevertheless, an impressive and increasing accumulation of bodies of men and horses and wreckage of trucks and wagons showed that the Germans were not wholly ignorant of the situation behind the American lines.

We left Colonel Sweezey and his 313th Infantry looking up at the Golfe de Malancourt and, beyond it, the Bois de Cuisy. The landscape was pitted with machine guns nests and swept by German artillery, which continued to exact casualties among the men huddled in the northern reaches of the Bois de Malancourt. For five hours they lay there. Company B of the 311th Machine Gun Battalion, ordered forward from brigade reserve, joined the regiment in the wood. Around 2:00 p.m., a company of tanks clattered up from the rear.[*]

---

[*] These were from the 13th (French) Tank Battalion, assigned to the 37th Division, which the 79th had asked for assistance. The division's own tank battalions, the 14th and 15th, were still stuck on the road

By then, Sweezey realized that no artillery would be coming to his aid; given the remaining daylight and the distance yet to go, he resolved to continue the attack without it. Halfway up the Golfe, the 313th was stopped by a previously undetected barbed wire obstacle and went to ground, waiting for pioneers to cut the wire. Many men fell dead or wounded. Worse from a strictly operational (certainly not a human) point of view, so did many officers. Captain Harry Ingersoll, commanding Company H, was hit in the throat and in the groin. Captain Effingham B. Morris, leader of Company K and Ingersoll's law partner before the war, crawled over and stayed with him until the wires were cut and the attack resumed. Ingersoll was evacuated to a field hospital but died of his wounds. Along with Ingersoll, Lieutenant William Fraley of the same company was mortally wounded. Even the division chaplain became a casualty. John Carroll Moore, a Catholic priest, was accompanying the attack, ministering to the wounded and dying. Following one group of men into a captured trench, Chaplain Moore saw a grenade land among them. He seized it and hurled it out of the trench; as it left his hand it exploded, wounding him severely. Chaplain Moore received the Distinguished Service Cross for his exploit.

At this point accounts of the capture of the Bois de Cuisy diverge. In the words of General Kuhn, written after the war (and consistent with other descriptions from within the division), "The light tanks having opportunely arrived, Colonel Sweezey organized another attack, using the tanks and a supporting machine gun barrage. This attack was launched about 2:00 p.m. and eventually drove the Germans from the wood."[42] A military artist witnessed the opening of the assault:

> A thrill went up my spine as I saw the tanks come out, strange lumbering creatures, crawling one after another, Indian file, rocking like ships in a heavy sea, but steadily creeping forward on their caterpillar feet toward the machine-gun nests hidden in the woods, that are their special prey. Shells with a lurid, saffron-colored smoke—the new antitank explosive—began to burst over them, and I could plainly see the hail of molten lead that shot directly downward from the ball of ruddy smoke.[43]

Lieutenant Colonel D.D. Pullen of the Corps of Engineers, who, along with Lieutenant H.J. Ellis of the Tank Corps, was accompanying the French

---

being built above Avocourt and did not catch up with the leading regiments until late in the evening. They took no part in the day's actions.

tanks, had a different version of events. I quote it here at length:

When we reached the point A [about half-way up the Golfe de Malancourt, at the wire obstacle] we found the leading Infantry Brigade was held up by a few snipers and one machine gun in the B. de Cuisy. The French refused to advance any further as they said that their orders were to proceed through the B. de Cuisy and not take part in any fighting until after the Infantry had taken B. de Cuisy. The Infantry apparently was very disorganized, as they made no attempt to go forward. After conferring with the French I requested them to fill their gas tanks and be ready to fight. They did this but refused to proceed further without written orders from the Brigade Commander. As the Brigade Commander could not be found I finally got hold of Captain Gaitan Liaras of the 13th Battalion. Upon being asked whether he would fight or not without written orders from the Brigade Commander his answer was, "I do not need any written orders; I will fight anybody at any time." Lieutenants Ellis and Sonstelie had gone ahead and located the resistance. Captain Liaras was given the information as to the direction of the resistance and he deployed his 5 tanks, the only ones he had available, personally took command of the 5, accompanied by Lieutenant Ellis and walked on foot and took his tanks up to the edge of the B. de Cuisy and drove the Germans out of the edge of the woods. He then entered the B. de Cuisy with his 5 tanks, lost 2 of them in large shell holes, proceeded with the other 3 with Lieutenant Ellis and a few engineers and surrounded 7 Germans who had been holding the edge of the woods. Captain Liaras killed 2 Germans, the tanks killed one and the others were taken prisoners by Lieutenant Ellis and the Captain. As soon as the Infantry saw the 5 tanks enter the woods the whole brigade came up out of the trenches and entered B. de Cuisy. No infantry commander could be found, so all the troops were gathered together and instructions were given to form skirmish lines on both sides of the road marked in red. After the Infantry were deployed and ready the 3 remaining tanks advanced straight up the road with the Infantry on either flank. The far edge of the woods was reached, point B on the map) and no further resistance was encountered until we started out of the woods. We halted at the edge of the woods sent back for more infantry, got them in the north edge of the woods in B. de Cuisy.[44]

The narrative as told by the divisional historian continues:

Once the southern edge of the Bois de Cuisy had been won, the Germans began to withdraw, but resisted stubbornly in rear-guard actions with the result that there was much hand to hand fighting. At the northern edge of the Bois de Cuisy, immediately opposite the heights of Montfaucon, the 313th was again checked by machine gun fire. Under its cover, the retreat of the enemy infantry was rapid to the comparative safety of Montfaucon. By now it was 16h and Colonel Sweezey paused to reorganize.[45]

Again, the account of Colonel Pullen differs:

We were nearly ready to advance from the north edge of the woods when 40 Germans came out of the woods about 100 yards to the right. The Infantry was ordered to open fire and the Tank Commander was asked if he would start after them. He replied he would and the Tanks and Infantry started after the Germans who were running for a trench northeast of the B. de Cuisy. We had advanced about 150 yards when we were met by severe machine gun fire from the northeast. The Tanks stopped to open fire and all of the Infantry laid down and made no attempt to advance. As soon as the tanks had stopped a 77[mm] gun using H.E. shell opened fire on us from Montfaucon. As soon as the 77 opened fire the Infantry all got up and fled into the woods to our rear. This left the Tanks in a very precarious position, so the Tank Captain was directed to get his Tanks to the edge of the woods while the Infantry were being rallied. Upon entering the wood all the Infantry was found in full retreat; most of the men were double-timing to the rear down the road. Lieutenant Sonstelie was sent to the rear with orders to stop the retreat and a guard was posted on the road with orders to shoot any man who went to the rear. The Infantry were brought up again, organized in the edge of the woods to resist possible counter attack and runners were sent out to try and find some Infantry Commanders. It was very difficult rounding up the Infantry in the woods as they were wholly disorganized and no one knew where any of their units were and what few Lieutenants could be found did not have the least control over any man. The whole situation can best be described by calling them a disorganized mob. After most of the Infantry in the woods had been located and brought forward Colonel Sweezey of the 313th Infantry arrived and took charge. At this time we had 2 Tanks ditched in the B. de Cuisy, 2 knocked out by shell fire in front of the B. de Cuisy and 5 ready for action. Colonel Sweezey was informed that the 5 Tanks would support him in any action he desired to take. After a great deal of delay in organizing for the attack an attempt was made to advance from B. de Cuisy, but this was repulsed again by the machine gun fire from the northeast.[*46]

The events are too distant for us to be able to disentangle the conflicting versions. No doubt the officers of the 79th understated the disorganization, verging on panic, of their troops. Pullen and Ellis, who could see only their small portion of the sector and who were under fire themselves, and who clearly in Pullen's report wanted to emphasize their point, may have exaggerated it.

By 4:00 p.m. the 313th had reached the northern edge of the Bois de Cuisy, facing the hill of Montfaucon. Many stragglers from the earlier fights had by now rejoined the regiment and Sweezey called a halt to reorganize. Captain George Burgwin of Company E was given command of the 2nd Battalion, replacing Major Pepper; Captain James Lloyd of Company L took over from Major Langley. But the men were so scattered and the units so intermingled that Sweezey was unable to restore cohesion.[47]

Earlier in the afternoon Pershing's staff noticed that the 79th was far behind schedule and concluded that Kuhn and his men weren't being aggressive enough. General Cameron at V Corps headquarters relayed to Colonel Ross, the divisional chief of staff, a peremptory message from Pershing: "The 79th Division is holding up the whole Army. The Army Commander desires that the 79th Division move forward at once." The same message gave the position of the 4th Division, to the right, as being two kilometers north and east of Montfaucon, or about four kilometers beyond Kuhn's front line.[48]

On the map, it certainly looked as if the 79th Division was the laggard. Virtually every other division had reached or approached the Corps Objective, which generally meant an advance of five to six miles. (It was a considerably shorter distance to the Corps Objective on the extreme left of the line, where the 77th and 28th Divisions were expected to run into heavy resistance in the

---

* Colonel Pullen's account is somewhat substantiated by an officer of the 37th Division, who witnessed what happened to the tanks: "The two tanks had hardly left the shelter of the woods when well directed shots fired at point-blank range by a battery of German seventy-sevens, reduced them to a pile of junk. The shells, striking the tanks squarely in front, smashed the steel armor like an egg-shell and converted the interiors into a shambles of machinery, control apparatus and human flesh." (Ralph D. Cole and W.C. Howells, *The 37th Division in the World War, 1917–1918*, 2 vols (Columbus, OH: The Thirty-Seventh Division Veterans Association, 1926), p. 208.)

Argonne Forest.) Even the 35th Division, which virtually collapsed a day later, had moved three miles forward. The 79th had managed only two and a half.[49] But what really held the army up was Pershing's instruction to his divisions to wait at the Corps Objective line until all of them had reached it before continuing the advance. This forced divisions that were perfectly capable of continuing the attack to stop in their tracks, allowing the Germans to reinforce their line unmolested, as we shall see. Here is where Pershing's open warfare dogma—"comparatively little regulation of space and time by the higher command ... variable distances and intervals between units and individuals ... and the greatest possible use of individual initiative"—would have paid large benefits.[50] Did the general himself order a halt at the Corps Objective or did someone on his staff, fearful of losing control of the advance, do it without his knowledge? Either way, it was a striking violation of Pershing's doctrine.*

Pershing's order for the divisions to wait at the Corps Objective line also exposed the fundamental illogic in Pershing's "holding up the whole army" message to the 79th. For the 4th Division to "turn Montfaucon," as prescribed in his Field Order No. 20, the 4th would, by simple geometry, have to be several miles beyond the town at a time when the 79th would still be in front of it. That is exactly what was happening. But Pershing either forgot his original intent or, more likely, did not follow the implications of his order to their logical conclusion.

At about 2:00 p.m. Ross forwarded Cameron's message on to Nicholson, who sent a runner to Sweezey with a direct order: "Corps directs that the attack be pushed to its fullest vigor that nothing must hold up army is dependent on action of the 79th Division. You will push attack and let

---

* Early the following morning Foch, as if to emphasize the folly of First Army's plan, sent Pershing a message that read, in part: "[A]ttacks must be incessantly sought to produce break-through, organizing for this purpose groups of infantry and artillery directed toward objectives, the possession of which will guarantee the crumbling of the enemy front. It is therefore necessary: in army corps—to select and assign distant and important objectives; in divisions—to select intermediate objectives; and, in small units (regiments or battalions)—to maneuver, rapidly and decisively, against machine gun posts which temporarily delay them. From now on, the fate of the battle rests on the decision of corps commanders, and on the initiative and energy of division commanders." (Conrad H. Lanza, "The End of the Battle of Montfaucon," *Infantry Journal* 23, July–August (1933), p. 351.)

This must have infuriated Pershing, who always maintained that he taught open warfare to the French, not the other way around. But not until October 4 did the Americans abandon the everyone-straight-ahead attack formation, after Pershing had promoted Hunter Liggett to command First Army; see Chapter 15 and Smythe, *Pershing*, p. 205.

nothing stop you."[51] This unhelpful message reached Sweezey just as the 313th was regrouping in the Bois de Cuisy. He was dismayed:

> I could not understand, as the regiment had been doing its utmost throughout the day. I deemed that an attack on Montfaucon without any artillery preparation and after dark when we could not see the barbed wire entanglements, against a position held by a large number of machine guns and heavy guns whose fire could be brought to bear on it, would be extremely inadvisable.[52]

But orders were orders. With the 1st Battalion—hitherto in support—in the front line and aided by two of the French tanks, the regiment advanced down into the valley that lay between the Bois de Cuisy and the hill of Montfaucon. All went well for about 200 yards; then the Germans opened up with machine guns and artillery from ahead and above. Major Israel Putnam, named for his famous Revolutionary War ancestor and commanding the 3rd Battalion, was immediately shot through the head. Sweezey had now lost all of his original battalion commanders. The advance became a series of short rushes. The tanks, no longer able to see targets in the dark, withdrew.* As night descended, the regiment had gotten to the bottom of the valley but no further.† Sweezey ordered his men back to the Bois de Cuisy, the nearest position that offered shelter.

A minor drama attended the withdrawal of Company K. It had advanced on the left end of the line, where a continuation of the Bois de Cuisy provided dense cover, and had immediately fallen out of contact with the rest of the regiment. Passing through the woods, the company came out on a rising slope and started up it. The German machine guns and artillery here were poorly directed and overshot the Americans, who got part way up the

---

* Of this part of the engagement Sweezey later wrote, "The tanks I expected much from, due to the extensive laudation of them which I had seen in the daily press. The tanks with this regiment, as used by the personnel with them, with one possible exception ... were of little use." (C.B. Sweezey, "Report of Operations of 313th Infantry from September 25, 1918 to November 11, 1918, Inclusive," November 18, 1918, RG 120, 79th Division, Box 16, 33.2, NARA, pp. 2–3.)

† The historian of the German 11th Grenadiers recorded Sweezey's attack thus: "A forceful infantry attack supported by tanks followed at around 5 pm, and was repeated continuously until dusk. There were moments where the front seemed to falter, but the brave grenadiers held their ground." ([no first name] von Prittwitz und Gaffron, [no first name] Peschek, H. Mende, H. von Schweinichen, and G. Gieraths, *Geschichte des Königlich Preußischen Grenadier-Regiments König Friedrich III. (2. Schles) Nr. 11 und seiner Grenzschutzformationen von 1914 bis 1920* (Berlin: Verlag Tradition Wilhelm Kolk, 1932), p. 239.)

FIRST ARMY FRONT LINE, EVENING OF SEPTEMBER 26

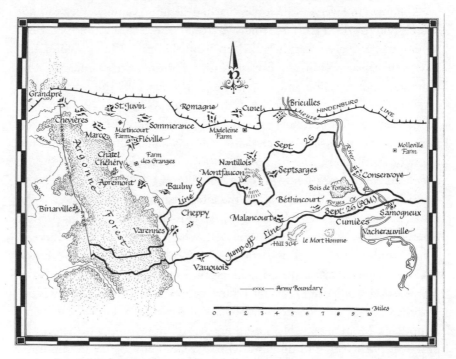

slope of Montfaucon itself, only to find themselves enfiladed by German fire. Darkness descended. Captain Morris, the company commander, told his men to dig in and they quickly fell asleep. But the captain was bothered by the lack of any indication that the rest of the regiment was advancing, so he sent a man back to find out what was going on. The runner returned with the news that Sweezey had called off the attack for the night. In the dark Captain Morris threaded his way back over the battlefield, found the regimental PC, and asked permission to bring his men back from their exposed position. Permission was granted, and the company withdrew without alerting the Germans. Had they remained on the exposed slope when the sun rose, they would have been slaughtered.

At 7:30 p.m. Sweezey conceded defeat for the day. Seven of his officers and 79 of his men were dead. By pigeon he sent a message to Nicholson: "Made an attack on Montfaucon but failed. Heavy machine gunfire, coordinates 11.0–77.4. Troops exhausted and have suffered heavy casualties. Am holding position edge of woods 11.4–77.3. Believe that Montfaucon cannot be taken by infantry fire alone."[53] There is no record of whether the message was received.

Unknown to Sweezey, the forces that repelled his evening attack did not belong only to the 11th Grenadiers. By 6:00 p.m. the position had been reinforced by reserves hastily called up from the rear. When Sweezey had started his advance from the Bois de Cuisy, Montfaucon was defended by only one weak battalion and a *Minenwerfer* company. By the time he quit, it was occupied by two full (albeit understrength) German regiments.[54]

Back in division headquarters, General Kuhn had problems of his own. His command had lost 13 officers and 211 men killed (although he did not know these numbers) and he was far short of his objective.* By 3:00 p.m. telephone communication with the division PC at Hill 309 had failed, so he moved nearly two miles forward to the advanced information center at PC Zouave, where the Esnes–Malancourt road crossed Hill 304, leaving Tenney Ross at the old location. It was about then that Cameron's "Move forward at once" order came in to Ross, who tried to forward the message to General Nicholson, whose 157th Brigade still led the division's advance. Also, Kuhn had received word from General Hines, commander of the 4th Division, that the latter would be sending a brigade into the sector of the 79th to try to outflank Montfaucon; Nicholson needed to know this. But there was a problem; Nicholson had disappeared. At some point in the afternoon he had moved his PC forward without informing the division staff. Private James M. Cain, an orderly (and, in civilian life, a reporter for the *Baltimore Sun*), was sent out with another soldier to find him. He did, and Cameron's order was delivered and relayed to Sweezey. When Cain found him Nicholson was about to move his PC forward again, so Cain followed in order to report the new location back to Kuhn. But it took Cain several hours to get back to 79th Division headquarters, and Kuhn remained out of touch.[55] By nighttime the general was desperately trying to learn the positions of his regiments. The phones were dead. The French 214th Aero Squadron, which was supposed to observe the situation on the ground, filed no reports. The balloon company assigned to the 79th tried to communicate by having its officers deliver messages by hand, but that was too slow to be

---

* There was no attempt at the time to count the wounded, many of whom were left unattended on the field, made it to aid stations on their own, or died of wounds later. In 1960 Rexmond Cochrane estimated from medical records that the division lost at least 222 wounded. (Cochrane, "79th Division," p. 21.) As a typical ratio of wounded to killed in battles of that time was three to one, Cochrane's number looks low.

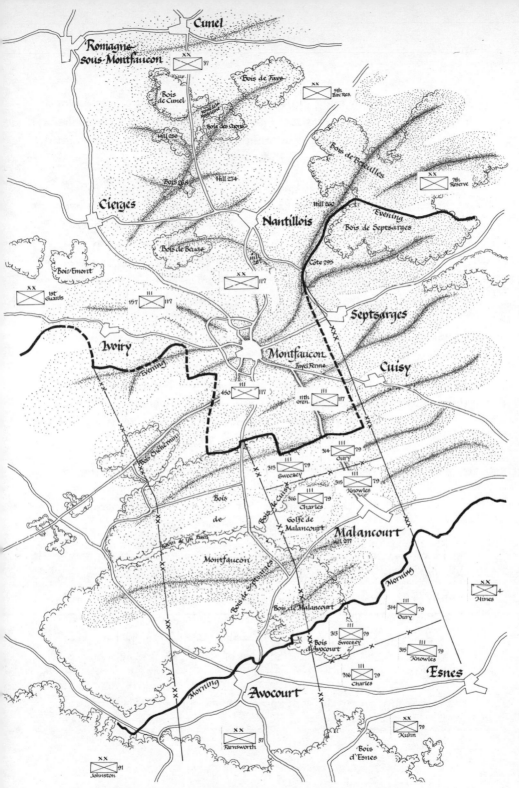

POSITIONS OF THE 79TH DIVISION'S REGIMENTS, MORNING AND
NIGHT OF SEPTEMBER 26

useful. The only remaining method was by runner or staff officer. Colonel Oury eventually sent a message reporting the front line position of the 314th; it arrived early the next morning. But no amount of effort seemed able to raise Colonel Nicholson. Kuhn was furious:

> Your advance from P.C. Gascogne to new P.C. has created a serious situation in that you did not provide for liaison with Div. Commander while making change. This is to advise you that CO 4th Divn. is sending forward a brigade in the direction of Cunel–Romagne to protect his left flank and to assist advance of 79th Divn. This movement may bring neighboring troops in front of our right and unless our troops are warned may result in casualties due to friendly troops being taken for enemy ... Have been without information all day regarding 313th Regiment and in the dark as to my front line ... You are directed hereafter not to move to a new P.C. until same is established and liaison maintained.[56]

Private Cain had found Nicholson's PC the previous night, so Kuhn handed the message to him hoping he could repeat the achievement. It didn't happen.

Kuhn's problem became an emergency at 6:27 p.m. when a message arrived at the division PC from Cameron at V Corps:

> 4th Division reports that they are N. of Nantillois ... They will halt for the night near Nantillois and their outposts will extend eastward [*sic*—should be westward] into the sector of the 79th Division. Notify your people to watch for these outposts after they pass Montfaucon. You must get by Montfaucon tonight.[57]

Ross promptly drafted an order to Nicholson:

> Itasca 1 [Kuhn] directs that you drive forward as fast as you can so that you will catch up with the divisions on our right and left and so that you will take Nantillois tonight ... It is believed that American troops have taken Montfaucon and therefore the advance of the 157th Brigade should be rapid.[58]

But he was shouting to the wind; no one knew where Nicholson was.

CHAPTER 11

LEFT, RIGHT AND STRAIGHT AHEAD, SEPTEMBER 26

To put the predicament of the 79th in perspective, we must visit events in the German lines and in the sectors of the American divisions flanking the 79th—the 37th to the left and the 4th to the right. All three divisions were opposed by Gallwitz's Maas Group West, comprising the 117th Division on the west, commanded by Major General Höfer, and the 7th Reserve Division on the east, led by Major General von Ribbentrop.* The right-most regiment of the 117th (from the German point of view, looking south) was the 157th Infantry, opposite the American 37th Division. Next to it was the 450th Infantry, covering the right-most sector of the 37th and the western half of the 79th. To its left was the 11th Grenadiers, directly in front of Montfaucon. East of the 11th Grenadiers was the 66th Reserve Infantry Regiment of the 7th Reserve Division, opposite the American 4th Division.[1] Each of these regiments numbered a little over a thousand men, or one-third of their normal strength.

The 37th Division was a greatly expanded reincarnation of the Ohio National Guard, in which many of its officers had served. Its commander, Major General Charles S. Farnsworth, graduated West Point in 1887 and served in the Spanish-American War and in Mexico with Pershing. Although he joined the division only in May 1918, he quickly exerted his influence

---

* The general's relationship to Hitler's Foreign Minister Joachim von Ribbentrop, if any, was distant.

over his brigade and regimental commanders, most of them officers of long Army service and many of them veterans of Cuba, the Philippine Insurrection, or Mexico. Before entering the line in the Meuse–Argonne, the 37th had trained in a supposedly quiet sector in the Vosges Mountains. It was quiet in the sense that no major offensives had taken place there, but it didn't seem quiet to the soldiers. Aerial bombing, shelling, and gas attacks were constant. The division learned to patrol in No-Man's Land, to conduct trench raids, and to take prisoners. Several times they had to repel large German raiding parties.

Like the 79th, the 37th lost its original artillery brigade when it moved to France. Support for the coming offensive would be provided by the 55th Field Artillery Brigade, borrowed from the 30th Division and commanded by Brigadier General James A. Shipton. Shipton graduated 15th in his West Point class of 1892, attended the Army War College, and for a year served as assistant commandant of Pershing's Army schools in Langres. Assigned to command the 55th in June 1918, he supervised the brigade's training in its French encampment. Most importantly, Shipton and the 55th gained invaluable combat experience in the St Mihiel campaign, in which they supported the 89th Division. Relative to the 79th, the 37th, including its attached field artillery, was an experienced and capable organization.

As we have seen, General Cameron's orders to the 37th specified that the division would "maintain close liaison with the 79th Division on its right ... and, by proper echelonment in depth, will assist the 79th Division in the runing [*sic*] of the Bois de Montfaucon and in the capture of Montfaucon."[2] No mention was made of "runing" Montfaucon itself; this was to be a straight-ahead attack to the Corps Objective, seven and a half miles away. To accomplish this, Farnsworth put his two brigades abreast, each with one regiment in the front line. Each front-line regiment—the 145th on the right, led by Colonel S.B. Stanbery, and the 147th on the left, commanded by Colonel Frederick W. Galbraith—had two battalions next to each other in the lead and one behind in support. The second regiment of each brigade was divided by battalions among the brigade and regimental reserves.[3] This columns-of-regiments formation was more efficient and flexible than the column-of-brigades arrangement Kuhn had adopted. Each brigade commander only had to worry about his own half of the division's sector, rather than the whole two-mile expanse. And by relegating two entire regiments to his reserves, Farnsworth avoided crowding all his troops into the front line while still having them available when needed.

The attack of the 37th got off on time. The initial resistance was light, mostly a few machine guns. The left-hand regiment, the 147th, met little opposition from the outset. It penetrated the Bois de Montfaucon and crossed the gully of the Ravin de Lai Fuon with little incident until, around noon, it ran into machine gun fire from the German 157th Infantry Regiment, which had retreated to the *Etzel-Stellung*. Overrunning the battalions of the 157th, the Americans continued north into the Bois Chehemin. Major Scherer, the German commander, sent a desperate plea for assistance; in response, the 450th Regiment to his left sent a company and a half to help stabilize the line. But before that could happen, Major Scherer and a battalion commander were killed.[4] The morale of German troops in the sector plummeted; when a cavalry captain tried to cut the roads and a narrow-gauge railroad track leading north, "[He] has great difficulty with the Pioneers, who do not want to leave their deep dugout and who no longer obey their commander's orders. He is able to drag the men from their dugout and assemble them only by means of threats, during which, however, individual men run away as soon as he turns his back."[5]

By nightfall Galbraith's regiment had reached the Tranchée du Crocodile, a line half a mile south of Ivoiry and nearly two miles due west of Montfaucon. There they spent the night. By then they had pushed the German 157th Regiment out of the *Etzel-Stellung*.[6] The German regiment to the east, the 450th, retreated almost as far as the Bois de Beuge on a false report that the line at Ivoiry had been broken. But realizing the mistake, the division commander ordered it back to the line in front of Montfaucon. Around 11:00 p.m. they were joined by the 151st Infantry Regiment, part of the newly arrived 37th (German) Division.[7]

On Farnsworth's right it was a different story. The 145th Infantry by mid-morning had entered the Bois de Montfaucon, crossed Ravin de Lai Fuon, and reached the northern edge of the wood. Major Ralph D. Cole described the scene:

> Only a few dugouts had escaped destruction; the balance were nothing but a sagging mass of splintered wood or concrete. Trees had been uprooted bodily and added to the already well-nigh unsurmountable tangle of barbed wire and underbrush ... Near the edge of the wood and alongside the road were the bodies of several Germans. One body was that of a comparatively elderly man. He lay with his head cushioned upon his arm, with wide open eyes staring glassily toward the road. As some of the men passed, they

imagined that the eyelids of the German slowly closed and opened, but a closer examination proved him to be quite dead.[8]

At about 11:00 a.m. the regiment sent one battalion plus two companies from the brigade reserve northward. They penetrated to within about half a mile of the southwestern outskirts of Montfaucon and sent patrols into the edge of the town. As it happened, the German 450th, seeing the 157th to its right retreating, pulled back into the *Etzel-Stellung*, opening a gaping hole between it and the right flank of the 11th Grenadiers defending Montfaucon. Into this hole pressed the reinforced battalion of Galbraith's 145th Infantry. But it didn't work; two German machine gun companies were able to close the gap. "Machine guns fired with glowing barrels, the cooling water long gone."[9]

Now Galbraith's own flank was exposed by the failure of the 79th on his right to advance beyond the Bois de Cuisy. The 147th continued to take heavy fire from machine guns dug in on the slopes of Montfaucon. Additionally, intermingling of the units was starting to make control difficult. At 3:00 p.m. the battalion was ordered back to the northern edge of the Bois de Montfaucon.

Around 5:00 p.m. General Farnsworth decided to have three of his reserve battalions take over the advance from the 145th. At 6:30 p.m. two battalions of the 146th Regiment, released from reserve, attacked through the 145th. By then, the German position was becoming untenable. As the war diary of the 450th Regiment recorded:

> All through the afternoon, the enemy could be seen exiting the edge of the forest of Chehemin in dense columns, moving north and entering the lower part of Ivoiry. The strength of these columns was estimated to be at least that of a combat-strength regiment (about 2000 men) ... As soon as the enemy was within reach of our machine guns, he was effectively shot off the hill east of Ivoiry. The regiment tried in vain to direct the artillery to the most productive targets, but no artillery liaison officer was present and only one firing gun could be found on the ground.[*][10]

The line of the 450th Infantry at Ivoiry had been broken and several companies were outflanked, causing them to retreat to a hill north of

---

[*] In fact, most of the German artillery had been ordered to retire and did not get into action until the following day. (Historical Division, *USAWW*, vol. 9, p. 141.)

Montfaucon. As we have seen, a report came through that the Americans had broken through the 21st Minenwerfer (heavy mortar) Company, directly in front of the town. The report was believed, as machine gun fire could clearly be heard below the hill, so the regiment was ordered to pull further back to the Bois de Beuge. The 21st Minenwerfer Company and 3rd Battalion did not get the order and stayed where they were; fortunately for them, it turned out that the report was in error. So the men of the 450th resumed their position in front of Montfaucon, where they remained for the night.[11]

But although the German defenses in the sector of the American 37th Division had crumbled, reinforcements were at hand. The morning before, Gallwitz had ordered the German 37th Division to leave its rest camp and proceed south. At first there was some confusion because Gallwitz still expected the American attack to fall east, not west, of the Meuse, and a shortage of trucks delayed the division's departure. But by late afternoon its three fresh infantry regiments—from left to right, the 150th, 151st, and 147th—began to arrive behind Montfaucon. At 4:00 p.m. the 150th was able to link up with the 7th Bavarian Reserve Infantry Regiment to its left, also newly arrived on the field, and counterattack toward the Bois Chehemin.[12]

The counterattack stopped the advance of Galbraith's three battalions. The 1st Battalion got to within 450 yards of Montfaucon hill; exposed and without support, it was ordered back to join the 145th Regiment at the top of the Bois de Montfaucon. The 2nd got to an old trench line called the Tranchée de Montfaucon, about half a mile from the southwest edge of the hill. Then it dug in. The 3rd Battalion of the 148th Regiment got as far as the Tranchée de l'Alligator, a defense line level with Montfaucon. It too dug in.

Throughout the attack the American 37th Division was hampered by the same problems that plagued the 79th. The road north from Avocourt was wrecked and unusable. Once the artillery had finished the rolling barrage it could not move forward, and by 8:25 a.m. the infantry was out of range of the 75s. (In his official report General Farnsworth recalled that one battery of the 55th Field Artillery Brigade had gotten forward, but he couldn't be sure about that.) Supplies could not get through; fortunately for the 145th, their left battalion happened upon an abandoned German kitchen with the coffee still hot on the stove and thousands of packages of crackers for the taking.[13]

At dusk the 37th found its battalions scattered over the battlefield. Its right-most regiment, the 145th, was still stuck at the northern edge of the Bois de Montfaucon, three miles from the starting line and about level with the 79th Division, which was still held up in the Bois de Cuisy. To the left of the 145th, two battalions of the reserve had dug in two miles further along and one battalion had made it yet another half a mile north. And in the far left of the division's sector, the 147th Regiment occupied a trench system abreast of Montfaucon and fully four miles from the jumpoff position. The division had shattered the original German line; but the time it took to do that allowed the enemy to bring up fresh divisions and re-establish their defense in strong positions.

This distribution of the units of the 37th at nightfall demonstrates several things. First, the closer one was to the hill of Montfaucon, the harder it was to capture ground. Second, this was as true for a relatively seasoned division like the 37th as for a rookie outfit like the 79th. Third, Pershing's objective of seven and a half miles for the first day of the attack was wholly unrealistic. The 37th—hardly the most veteran unit in First Army but not the least, either—had faced only moderate resistance in the left half of its sector. Even there, the regiment could advance only four miles before nightfall.

To the right of the 79th was the 4th, a Regular Army division and as experienced an outfit as the AEF could muster. Its commander, General Hines, had served before the war in Cuba, the Philippines, and the Mexican expedition; he would later rise to become Army Chief of Staff. Most of his brigade and regimental commanders were graduates of West Point, the Army War College, or the service schools, and had seen combat in America's various overseas campaigns. One, Colonel Fred Wise of the 59th Infantry, was a Marine who had fought in the Boxer Rebellion. After arriving in France in early May 1918, the division trained with the British and French, then fought at Soissons, on the Vesle River, and in the St Mihiel campaign. If any division in the AEF could call itself veteran, it was the 4th.

For the attack on the morning of the 26th Hines organized his division with the 7th Infantry Brigade, commanded by Brigadier General Benjamin A. Poore, in the front line with its two regiments abreast—the 39th on the left and the 47th on the right. This was the same column-of-brigades formation that Kuhn had adopted for the 79th Division, with two important differences. The staff of the 7th Brigade, with their extensive training and combat experience, would have no trouble controlling its two regiments across a two-mile front. And each regiment had only one battalion in the lead and one in support; all of the other battalions were in brigade reserve, and the entire 8th Brigade—half of the infantry—was in division reserve.[14] This infantry-light formation would avoid the congestion and intermingling of units that plagued the 79th. Also unlike the 79th and the 37th Divisions, Hines had the benefit of using his own field artillery brigade, the 4th, which had already trained and fought with the division's infantry. The guns of the 4th were augmented by two field artillery regiments borrowed from the 3rd Division and two more supplied by the French. Hines thus had at his command a total of 108 75mm guns and 60 of 155mm.[15]

The 39th Infantry was commanded by Colonel Frank C. Bolles and was adjacent to the 79th Division. Hines's plan for this regiment was for its 3rd Battalion, under Major Henry Terrell, Jr., to lead the way as far as the town of Cuisy, about two and a half miles from the starting line and just over a mile southeast of Montfaucon. Then it would stop as the barrage pounded the lines in front. This would allow the 1st Battalion under Major Roy Winton to leapfrog it and push to the Corps Objective, three miles further on. At that point the 4th would be well north of Montfaucon, but Hines's instructions made no provision for circling behind the town to help the 79th take it. Pershing's Field Order No. 20 had in fact given III Corps—of which the 4th Division was a part—the mission to "turn Montfaucon and the section ... within the zone of action of the V Corps." Such a maneuver would be tricky in any event but especially so at this time, because the 79th was in a different corps, answering to a different commander. This would make tactical coordination during the battle difficult to impossible. Knowing this, and fearing confusion if divisions operated outside their prescribed boundaries, the III Corps chief of staff, Brigadier General Alfred Bjornstad, had explicitly deleted a turning movement from Hines's initial attack order.[*] The 4th Division would therefore push straight ahead and hope for the best.

The initial assault of the 39th Infantry went off smoothly. Landmarks were invisible because of the fog, so engineers used compasses to navigate the

---

[*] See Chapter 7.

assault battalions through the gaps in the wire. The engineers also supplied ladders that the men used to cross the soggy expanse of Forges Brook. In this sector, the German outpost line was a mile and a quarter further up the slope than in the area of the 79th to the left (see Chapter 9), so at first resistance was light. In addition, the 4th was pushing against the seam between the 11th Grenadiers and Ribbentrop's 7th Reserve Infantry Division; Major Count Stosch had been right to worry about his missing machine guns. A desperate counterattack by the German Liaison Company yielded only the death of its commander, Lieutenant Baum, and loss of liaison with the neighboring 66th Infantry Regiment. The Grenadiers, however, managed to save their left flank from being turned when the vice-sergeant-major in charge of the left-most platoon of 5th Company, a former artilleryman, commandeered an antitank gun deserted by its crew and fired point-blank into the closely packed Americans.[16] Nevertheless, by 7:00 a.m. the right of the 66th Infantry—and therefore of the entire 7th Reserve Division—had been penetrated and there were no reserves available to plug the gap. Terrell's 3rd Battalion quickly overran the Main Line of Resistance and made it to Cuisy by 9:30 a.m., taking the town, 600 prisoners, many machine guns, and a field artillery battery. Then it stopped, waiting as ordered for 1st Battalion to take over the advance.[*]

At this point, all units of the German 7th Reserve Division were out of action and orders came to withdraw. The adjutant of the 66th Regiment burned whatever papers he couldn't carry and, with his orderly carrying the typewriter, tried to escape to the rear through heavy rifle and artillery fire. The adjutant made it; the orderly and the typewriter were captured. But just as the front of the 7th was collapsing, the 5th Bavarian Reserve Division arrived in the rear with three fresh regiments. One of them, the 10th Bavarian Reserve Infantry Regiment, was pushed forward to reinforce the line east of Nantillois.[17] At 10:15 a.m. Captain Hollidt, commanding a battery of the 5th Bavarian's artillery, arrived at the south end of Nantillois with orders to advance to Hill 287; but the Americans already held the hill. With no infantry support, Hollidt put two guns in open positions and poured fire at a range of 900 meters into the dense American formations attacking north, preventing them from advancing:

---

[*] Historian Allan Millett has characterized the rapid advance of the 4th Division as little more than a "dangerous hike." (Alan R. Millett, *The General: Robert L. Bullard and Officership in the United States Army, 1881–1925* (Westport, CT: Greenwood Press, 1975), p. 402.)

The enemy ... was advancing in dense columns, not skirmishing lines, from the direction of Septsarges and the forest of Septsarges, stretching over about two kilometers in width. [Artillery] fire was successful in turning back the entire enemy line, so that it came no further than Hill 287 and its eastern spurs. They had suffered extremely heavy losses, who could clearly be made out on the ground.[18]

Another problem now arose for the advance of the 4th Division. First Battalion had gotten disoriented in the fog and had gone too far to the left, passing 3rd Battalion undetected and bumping into the southeast slope of Montfaucon hill. Of Winton's two support companies, one had "melted away" under heavy fire from the left and the other was lost in the fog; his two attack companies were snarled in a tangle of trenches and wire at the foot of the hill. One of Winton's company commanders reported that his patrols showed the town to be unoccupied (in fact, it was not) and urged him to take it. Winton declined because he didn't want the 79th, advancing from the south, to shell his men; his six or seven platoons were a pretty slim force to take a fortified hill town in the event that it was not deserted; he could not contact his own regimental PC to tell them what he was doing; and he could not contact the brigade reserve for assistance. So he pulled his platoons back and rejoined the 3rd Battalion in the front line.[*][19] Meanwhile, Bolles had decided not to hold Terrell's battalion in check waiting for Winton, whose unit had apparently disappeared, so he directed them to continue the advance.[20] They arrived at the Corps Objective, just north of Septsarges, around 12:30 p.m.

On the division's right, the 47th Infantry led the advance with the 2nd Battalion, commanded by Major J.A. Stevens, in the lead. The regiment met

---

* Winton's account of his reception back in 3rd Battalion headquarters gives a more pungent flavor of events than do the dry operational reports. "When I arrived on the line of the assaulting battalion, I was met by Colonel Bolles who had a deal of righteous indignation as to what had happened to his support battalion, during the entire day. He said, 'Well, Winton, you have played hell. You have been on both sides of your objective all day, but never in front of it. What were you trying to celebrate [sic]?' I answered, 'I would have captured Montfaucon, a division objective [it wasn't—the author], if I had been able to put my hands on the G__ d__ Brigade Reserve.' I noticed Colonel Bolles's face change quickly and looked over his shoulder and saw General Poore seated behind the Colonel. General Poore peered up at me over his glasses and a wintry smile came to his face. Later in the United States, we both had a good laugh over the incident." (Roy W. Winton to Frank C. Mahin, February 9, 1931, Hugh A. Drum Papers, Box 9, "Personal Correspondence," File "F.C. Mahin", AHEC, p. 3.)

only minor opposition as it climbed the slope. At Cuisy it stopped to allow the 3rd Battalion to pass through the 2nd and take over the advance. Reaching Septsarges with minimal casualties, it now had to pause while the unit to its left (Terrell's battalion of the 39th) suppressed enemy machine gun positions.[*][21] Having reached the Corps Objective, the regiment, obedient to Pershing's Field Order No. 20, stopped to wait for the 79th to catch up, although Stevens's patrols reported the Bois de Brieulles ahead to be unoccupied. Bullard's staff sent the message to Pershing's headquarters: "III Corps objective reached at 13:45."[22] While they waited, the regiment took occasional casualties from German machine guns situated in Nantillois and on the slopes of Montfaucon. As he came up to the front line, Major Stevens was under the impression that the division's immediate front was empty of Germans. But as the hours passed, that impression changed:

> About mid-afternoon, the enemy began to pour in reinforcements around Nantillois. We could see their arriving infantry, and whole batteries of artillery. We reported their arrival to the artillery brigade commander; and our machine guns and one-pounders tried to reach them, but were just beyond range, and got severely punished for the effort by the enemy's counter fire.[23]

The "severe punishment" was administered by Captain Hollidt's gunners. He had used up all the ammunition for his field pieces, but there was an abandoned heavy howitzer battery 800 meters in front of his line. He and some volunteers went forward and were able to get one gun in working order. Firing 45 or so rounds at a range of 600 meters, they were able to force the Americans to retire back into the Bois de Septsarges.[24]

By 4:00 p.m., the Germans had strongly occupied Nantillois as well as the Bois de Brieulles to its east. And the 4th, like the 79th, was without artillery support. All three regiments of the 77th Field Artillery Brigade had tried to move forward behind the infantry. All three had gotten stuck

---

[*] Thus the historian of the American 47th Infantry. The history of the German 11th Grenadiers characterized the action south of Septsarges as a "desperate battle." Two German artillery battalions had to blow up their guns which, with losses to American shell fire, almost eliminated the artillery support. The situation was saved by the commander of the 1st Machine Gun Company, who put his four heavy weapons in the front line and fired directly into the close-packed American ranks, inflicting heavy losses and forcing them to retreat. (von Prittwitz und Gaffron, *Grenadier-Regiments Nr. 11*, p. 238.)

on the jammed, muddy roads and were unable to get into firing position.[*] At 5:30 p.m. General Poore ordered his 7th Brigade to advance to the Army Objective. Without artillery support and with darkness approaching, the attack got nowhere. The men, hungry and tired, dug in. Some of them found German rations in abandoned dugouts. Search parties went out to find warm clothing; they were able to bring back blankets, overcoats, sweaters, and other items, often full of lice, which were passed around to the men.[25]

The enemy buildup in front of the 4th Division boded ill for further progress, but Hines saw a new opportunity. The rapid advance had gained the 4th a battlefield position almost never seen on the Western Front: a commanding view of the open flank of a German division. An attack westward and a linkup with the American 37th Division would cut Montfaucon off from supplies and reinforcements and relieve the 79th from its predicament. It might even result in the capture of an entire German division, an unheard-of event on the battlefields of France. This would open a hole in the Hindenburg Line through which the Americans could pour into open country, rolling up the German defenses from the flanks and rear. Surely this was the embodiment of Pershing's open warfare doctrine. Surely this was what Pershing meant in his instructions to III Corps in Field Order No. 20, "By promptly penetrating the hostile second position it will turn Montfaucon and the section of the hostile second position within the zone of action of the V Corps, thereby assisting the capture of the hostile second position west of Montfaucon." Yes, III Corps had emasculated that part of the order by insisting that 4th Division stay within its own boundaries.[†] But the mandate and the opportunity were manifest; it was worth a try.[‡]

Hines put in a call around 2:00 p.m. to III Corps headquarters, hoping to reach General Bullard. He got General Bjornstad, the chief of staff.[26]

---

[*] After the war the chief of staff of the 4th Division described the congestion: "Light transportation was ruthlessly ditched. Trucks were started ahead under their own power or fitted with a tackle and pulled over and off the trail by straining men. Heavy howitzers, weighing, with their limbers, nearly five tons, which because of faulty driving in the darkness or crumbling of ground under their weight, had slid bodily into enormous shell craters, were lifted and pulled out by a hundred men, who with lever and rope reinforced the doubled teams." (Christian A. Bach, *The Fourth Division: Its Services and Achievements in the World War*, ed. Henry Noble Hall, vol. 368 (4th Division, 1920), pp. 170–71.)

[†] See Chapter 8.

[‡] Who first had the thought to attack westward is not revealed in the surviving records, but Hines was quick to jump on the idea.

This was the same General Bjornstad who had told Hines to change his order for the opening attack so as to forbid movement into the adjacent sector. Bjornstad was one of the AEF's most divisive characters. After winning the Distinguished Service Cross in the Philippines, he experienced a meteoric rise that saw him appointed chief of staff of the 30th Division despite being only 43 years old and having less than 20 years' service. But in that role he showed himself impatient with officers who lacked his intelligence, knowledge, and vigor, allowing his staff no independence or initiative and being "tyrannical, petty, and insulting" to almost everyone who worked with or for him.[27] Bullard had served in the same regiment as Bjornstad in the Philippines. While III Corps commander he found Bjornstad to be an excellent staff officer, drafting clear orders and solving complex logistical problems. But Bjornstad insisted on running the staff as a one-man show. All telephone messages for the commanding general had to go through him.[28] Major General George B. Duncan, commanding the 77th Division, on temporarily joining III Corps was dismayed to find that Bjornstad and his operations staff issued orders without the knowledge of the commanding general. (Bullard even told Duncan to ignore "damn fool" orders from III Corps until he had checked directly with Bullard.) [*][29]

In addition to his abrasiveness, the colonel was known for two attributes. The first was caution, and a habit of expressing it at inappropriate times. Twice, while III Corps was attached to the French Army—once at Soissons and once at Fismette—he had insisted that American units withdraw from their (to him) overly exposed positions. On both occasions he had gone over Bullard's head, and on both his request was abruptly dismissed by the French commanding general.[30] The second was a propensity to control personally everything that happened in his unit's headquarters—decisions, orders, communications—often to the exclusion of the commanding officer. That is why Hines reached him, not Bullard.

---

[*] On October 12 Hines would be promoted to command III Corps. According to his testimony after the war, Bjornstad continually failed to inform him of the division's activities, despite Hines's repeated insistence that he do so. He continued to act unilaterally, reassigning an officer intended for duty as a regimental commander to be a corps inspector instead, and signing the order "Hines" without telling his superior. Shortly thereafter he ordered an attack by III Corps without telling Hines, who bawled him out. Ten days after taking over III Corps, Hines relieved Bjornstad as his chief of staff. (US Senate Committee on Military Affairs, *Hearings on the Nomination of Col. Alfred W. Bjornstad, U.S. Army, for Promotion to Be a Brigadier General* (Washington, DC: GPO, 1925), pp. 16–19.)

While an instructor at the Leavenworth Schools in 1916, then-Captain Bjornstad had written a textbook called *Small Problems for Infantry*. As he listened to Hines explain his request, the general must have realized that he now had a large problem for infantry. The maneuver Hines was suggesting obviously made sense; it offered immediate tactical benefits and perhaps long-term strategic ones. But there were risks. Communication with the laterally attacking units might be lost, leading to a breakdown in command—potentially disastrous when operating behind enemy lines, which would essentially be the case. The 79th, the 37th, or the artillery attached to V Corps or First Army, not having up-to-the-minute information on where the fast-moving friendly units were located, might accidentally shell them. But the benefits appeared to outweigh the costs. After thinking it over, Bjornstad phoned Hines around 3:30 p.m. to deliver the following message:

> The division on your left is held up by Montfaucon. Therefore, in order to assist their progression you will send out strong patrols to the west to seize strong points in that division's area, and will outpost to-night not only your own front but also well over to your left. You will push up your reserve in order to do this, and to replace your supports, thus used.[*31]

By 4:00 p.m., Hines had issued his orders. His 8th Brigade, hitherto in reserve, would advance to the front line, attack westward, "take up a position on the American Army objective and establish a line of outposts along the general lines Cunel–Bantheville–Romagne, establishing liaison with the 7th Infantry Brigade on the right, the center [37th] division of the Vth Army Corps on the left and the 79th Division in its rear."[32] In other words, the 8th Brigade was to establish a line spanning the sector of the 79th Division but four miles beyond Montfaucon. This would cut the German division defending Montfaucon off from its communications and pinch the stalled 79th out of the American line. Hines sent word of his

---

* Postwar accounts differ as to exactly how the 4th Division was authorized to attack westward. General Hines remembered that it was in a phone conversation with Bjornstad, as did Bjornstad himself. (Hines to Booth, December 30, 1920, p. 1; A.W. Bjornstad to Christian A. Bach, December 24, 1924, RG 120, Historical Section Reports, Box 3, NARA, p. 3.) Lieutenant Colonel Hugh Parker, Hines's chief of operations, recalled that Bullard himself authorized the movement while visiting Hines's headquarters. (H.A. Parker to E.E. Booth, December 14, 1920, Hugh A. Drum Papers, Box 16, File 4th Division-Montfaucon, AHEC.) This narrative follows Hines's version, with which most of the officers of the 4th appear to have agreed after the war.

intentions to Kuhn, who at 7:30 p.m. acknowledged receipt and promised to alert his units "to the end that confusion may be avoided."[33] By 4:20 p.m. the 8th Brigade was already on the move and by 8:00 a.m. its units were reporting that they were in place to begin the westward attack. At about midnight Hines approved the arrangements that his chief of staff, Lieutenant Colonel Edwin Booth, had made for the assault, which would take place the next morning.[34]

Then things fell apart. Sometime between 1:00 and 3:00 a.m., a telephone call came to Hines's headquarters from III Corps ordering the movement of the 8th Brigade to be stopped and the brigade to be held within the boundaries of the 4th Division's sector.[35] For what reason and on whose authority the attack order was countermanded were either not stated or not recorded at the time. With regard to the reason, the officers of the 4th later attributed the cancellation to III Corps' over-eagerness to comply with an order received from First Army around 7:30 p.m.:

> The General directs that your Corps continue to advance to the army objective, and in pushing forward he wants the advance to be covered by strong covering detachments in advance and to your left flank. The 5th Corps has not advanced as far as you are and it has been directed to advance as soon as it can to the army objective.[36]

This order suggests that First Army was unaware that a westward move was being planned or even considered by III Corps. It certainly didn't prohibit such a move, at least not explicitly. At any event, III Corps could have protested the order and explained what the 4th Division was up to; but they didn't. The most likely reason for the cancellation, one that was believed at the time and later by many of the officers of the 4th, is that III Corps willingly seized on First Army's order as justification for abandoning the attack of the 8th Brigade, which had made them nervous from the beginning. The person most likely to have done this was the super-cautious, super-controlling chief of staff, Brigadier General Alfred W. Bjornstad.[*]

---

[*] William Walker makes a case that Bullard's ambitious and jealous personality led him deliberately to sabotage V Corps' advance on Montfaucon, thereby torpedoing Cameron's chance of becoming commander of Second Army. (William Walker, *Betrayal at Little Gibraltar; a German Fortress, a Treacherous American General, and the Battle to End World War I* (New York: Scribner, 2016), pp. 344–64.) If so, that could explain the deletion of the "turn Montfaucon" mission from III Corps'

With the leftward move of the 8th Brigade countermanded, the 4th Division would on the morning of the 27th plow straight ahead into the machine guns of the newly reinforced German line in the Bois de Brieulles.

By late afternoon the 11th Grenadiers had held on to their position on the slopes of Montfaucon, but they had been outflanked on both sides. Stosch ordered the main body of the regiment to withdraw to the southern slope of the hill; one company was sent forward to establish outposts behind the old main line of resistance. The left flank—exposed to the American 4th Division and therefore the one most endangered—was partly covered by the 7th Bavarians, posted on a hill north of Septsarges; Stosch therefore pulled two companies back from their unprotected position south of Septsarges and set them up in the Bois de la Tuilerie just east of the hill.[37] It was this partial withdrawal that allowed Sweezey and the 313th to enter the Bois de Cuisy, only to mount their futile attacks on the west slope.

Once night fell, Stosch realized that even his adjusted positions were too exposed. Apart from lack of cover from his retreating neighbors, his losses had been heavy and his line was thinly held. He ordered the establishment of a new main line of resistance in the *Etzel-Stellung*, running over and through Montfaucon itself. Three infantry companies were posted on the right flank; two plus a machine gun company were on the left facing east. Three other companies, one of them down to a single platoon, were distributed along the rest of the line, along with the remaining machine guns. The sole *Minenwerfer* was placed southwest of the hill.[38] Stosch sent an urgent message to brigade and division headquarters asking for at least one company to assist with counterattacks and to plug holes. No, they said, all division troops were already engaged; nor would it be possible to direct artillery fire against the dense American columns.[39]

The Grenadiers spent the night evacuating their wounded and bringing up supplies, which left the battle-weary men almost no time to rest. But the

---

September 21 orders to the 4th Division. But as to the identity of the person who canceled the 8th Brigade's westward attack on the night of September 26–27, the weight of evidence still falls on Bjornstad; see the Epilogue.

new supply officer, Reserve Lieutenant Knoll, was able to distribute warm food, lots of bread and spreads, tea, and even alcohol; morale greatly improved.[40]

Kuhn, back in his PC on Hill 304, still had to find Nicholson. Unless he did, the 157th Brigade would not advance and its commander would not know that the 4th Division intended to move into his sector ahead of him. Five minutes before midnight General Cameron, to make sure Kuhn understood his expectations, followed up on his earlier message: "Commander in Chief expects the 79th Division to advance tonight to position abreast of 4th Division in the vicinity of Nantillois."[*][41] For Kuhn, failure to achieve the objective might be forgiven once the circumstances were known. But failure to make the attempt would be inexcusable.

---

* To the copy of this order in the archives there is appended the plaintive note, "General Burt [Cameron's chief of staff] was informed that General Kuhn would make every effort to advance his troops, and is leaving no stone unturned to get in touch with his brigade commanders; that he would move any troops forward with which he could get in touch."

CHAPTER 12

"MONTFAUCON TAKEN," SEPTEMBER 27

General Kuhn's chain of command had collapsed, so he improvised. At around 1:00 a.m. a runner came in from Oury's 314th Regiment headquarters; Kuhn sent him back with an order to attack and, if possible, to transmit the same order to Sweezey of the 313th. When General Noble, commanding the 158th Brigade, showed up at his headquarters at 2:00 a.m., Kuhn ordered him to take his 315th Regiment forward to the line of the 314th, and see if they had followed his orders to attack:

> If, on arriving at the present location of the 314th Inf., you find that these instructions to its commanding officer have not been received or obeyed, you will take command of the 314th Infantry and will advance as rapidly as possible without regard to the progress made by the division on your right and left. Should you find that the 314th Infantry has moved forward, you will move forward in support of that regiment. You will take every possible measure to press the advance with the utmost vigor ... [1]

These actions had two effects. First, they cut the absent Nicholson out of the command loop and put Kuhn directly in contact with the 314th and (he hoped) the 313th. Second, they reorganized Kuhn's brigades without altering the positions of the regiments: instead of one brigade in front and one behind, there would now be two side by side, as there should have been in the first place. The right-hand brigade, the Provisional 158th, comprising the 314th Regiment in the lead and the 315th following, was the one just assigned to Noble. The one on the left, the Provisional 157th, with the 313th ahead and the 316th in support, would be commanded by Nicholson if he could ever be found. Just before 5:00 a.m. Kuhn followed up his message to Noble with a stiff order to Nicholson:

> Imperative orders from Commander-in-Chief require that the 79th Division advance at once to come in line with neighboring Division. Owing to your having broken liaison, it was necessary to place Gen' Noble in charge of the 315th and 314th Regiments to make an immediate advance. You are directed to take command of the 313th and 316th Regiments and to push on with all possible speed. Location of these Regiments not definitely known.[2]

By this time Private Cain and his companion had made it back to Kuhn's headquarters. Captain Edward Madeira, commander of the Headquarters Company, ran up to him. "General Nicholson has broken liaison, and we've got not a way on earth to reach him unless you fellows can do it." Cain had found Nicholson's PC once that night and figured he could do it again. Madeira dragged the private in to see Kuhn, who told him to deliver the order and report back to him in Malancourt. Cain vanished into the night in what he remembered to be the right direction.[3] General Noble, now in charge of the right-hand brigade, had received his command only after the 79th had reached France. Officers who knew him from prewar days out West remembered him mainly as a drinker and poker-player and someone who wasted time on unimportant details. "His appearance and actions did not inspire confidence."[4] Concerned whether Noble would carry out the advance he had ordered, Kuhn, accompanied by Ross and a couple of aides, went forward from Esnes to Haucourt, the location of Noble's PC, at 4:30 a.m. Fighting their way through the traffic jam, it took them an hour and a half to travel the two-mile distance. At Haucourt, Kuhn found to his dismay that Noble had not, in fact, attacked with the 315th as ordered. As Kuhn arrived, Major Samuel W. Fleming, Jr., adjutant of the 315th, was talking with Noble, who had just offered that it was a beautiful morning and that things were going well. Fleming described what happened next:

> It was not a beautiful morning and things were not going well. Just then we saw the Division Commander, General Kuhn, and Colonel Ross his

ORGANIZATION OF 79TH DIVISION AFTER 4:53 A.M., SEPTEMBER 27, 1918

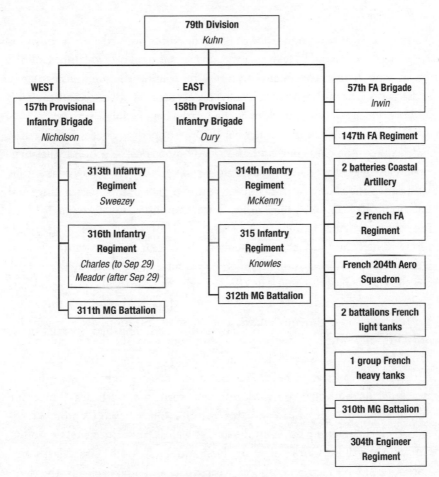

Chief of Staff striding, and I mean striding, down the trench apparently trailing Noble. As Kuhn reached us Noble put out his hand and greeted him with a cheerful, "Good Morning, General." Kuhn paid no attention to him and jumped to the top of the trench followed by Ross, and said sternly: "General Noble, by virtue of the office I hold, I hereby relieve you of command." That was all.

Noble's head dropped and he walked slowly to the rear with an aide. That was the last of him. He should never have been sent to France in the first place. We learned later that it was a question of Noble's scalp or Kuhn's, as the latter had been ridden for slowing down the offensive by his Corps Commander, who in turn was being ridden by GHQ which meant General Pershing.[5]

Turning to Colonel Knowles of the 315th, Kuhn ordered him to push his regiment forward and to take over the new provisional brigade until Colonel Oury, who would command it, could be found. Knowles immediately ordered his 2nd and 3rd Battalions to prepare for an advance and the tank and brigade artillery to join him at the north end of Malancourt.

Day did not break on September 27. It dripped, it oozed, it flowed. A sullen rain—not hard, but cold and steady—soaked the ground, the men, their clothing. The pale sky shed a dim light on the brown, scabrous landscape. The clayey earth deliquesced into a gray-orange paste, slimy and tenacious. To keep one's footing was an accomplishment, to make forward progress a struggle. Company F of the 314th occupied a winding trench formerly held by the German defenders. In addition to the rain, the men were sprayed with occasional bursts of machine gun fire from the nearby woods. The floor of the trench was littered with the bodies of German soldiers and a few Americans; to walk down it, one had to step on or over them.[6]

The two lead regiments, unaware of the reorganization, did not wait for orders from Kuhn or their brigade commanders to attack. Colonel Oury issued his instructions orally for an attack by the 314th at 4:00 a.m., the 3rd Battalion on the left and the 2nd Battalion on the right. The regiment, attacking up the Malancourt–Montfaucon road, met with heavy machine gun fire from straight ahead and also from the Ouvrage du Démon, a well-named German strong point on the left, as well as from the trenches around Cuisy on the right. Cries rang out: "First Aid! First Aid!" "Gas! Masks on!" "Break up! Deploy more, corporal! Keep apart and advance!"[7] In the dark, the enemy could not see well to aim, but neither could the men of the 314th see their tormentors. As a result, the lead companies of both battalions bypassed machine gun nests in the dark that then had to be taken by the support companies. The enemy positions were built with overlapping fields of fire, so that they were impossible to flank. On their own initiative and under fire, some of the men discovered the rudiments of fire-and-maneuver tactics, the proper procedure to counter a defense in depth. A platoon, a squad, or an informally organized combat group would send a few men crawling through the mud to the side or rear of a machine gun nest, there to fire at the defenders while the rest of the unit moved into grenade-throwing range. After that, a quick rush with rifle and bayonet would usually take the position. This was repeated many times on the field.[8]

To the left, Sweezey of the 313th wanted more light so he delayed his attack. At 7:00 a.m. the regiment moved north out of the Bois de Cuisy, the 1st Battalion on the right, the 2nd on the left, and the 3rd in support. A company of the 311th Machine Gun battalion provided overhead fire from north of the Bois de Montfaucon; six light tanks and one battalion of 75s from the 57th Field Artillery Brigade accompanied the attack. The 57th Field Artillery shelled Montfaucon with its huge 9.2-inch guns. As the men went down the slope they met no resistance; but as they started up the hill toward the town, it was another story. Machine gun fire raked the advancing troops from above; according to a prisoner, 32 machine guns were defending Montfaucon. But resistance was visibly weakening; the machine gun fire was not nearly as damaging as it had been the previous evening. With fire-and-maneuver tactics and the use of hand grenades, the machine gun posts were gradually overcome.[*]

Both regiments faced difficulties similar to those of the previous day. The road between Malancourt and Cuisy, a single-lane, unpaved track that the 79th Division shared with the 4th, remained jammed with vehicles. Things were slowly getting better, however. The 304th Engineers worked all of the night of the 26–27th on the Avocourt–Malancourt segment and by 2:45 a.m. Lieutenant Colonel J. Frank Barber, the regiment's chief of staff, reported that it was open for horse-drawn transport and that trucks would be able to use it at 8:00 a.m. Even the French liaison officers complimented the efforts of the engineers and their officers.[9] By 6:00 a.m. the divisional trains had reached Malancourt; but there they immediately bumped into the trains of the 4th Division and things again came to a halt. With road traffic frozen solid, the only reliable transport was pack animals; a shortage

---

[*] The French tank officers, as usual, told a different story. Major Guillot, commanding the 14th Light Tank Battalion, personally observed his 342nd Company support the attack of the 313th on the western slopes of Montfaucon. The tanks destroyed several machine guns, losing three of their number to German artillery. But although the tanks made progress, the Americans did not follow because of the German barrage. The tanks ended up circumnavigating Montfaucon clockwise, eventually meeting up with elements of the 314th Infantry Regiment coming north. ([no first name] Guillot, "Report Required by Note of October 2d 1918," October 30, 1918, 17 N 128, SHD, p. 2.) Neither the Americans nor the Germans report such a movement.

of these prevented enough ammunition from reaching the infantry and artillery. For the same reason, runners and mounted couriers were the only means of communication. The liaison staff of the 79th could send messages to the neighboring divisions because their orderlies were on horses. The reverse was not true because the flanking divisions used motorcycles and sidecars, which could not negotiate the impassable roads. Telephone lines, once cut, could be repaired only with difficulty. This, offered a French observer, was probably because the telephone repairmen were not integral members of the regiments. They refused to work on the lines during bombardments and disappeared for hours at a time.[10] Kuhn and his staff, in their inexperience, compounded the problem by operating their PC as if it were the location of the commanding officer himself, rather than the hub of his communication center. As Kuhn traveled all over his sector, messengers often could not find him. At one point on the afternoon of the 27th, according to the commander of the French liaison mission to the 79th, Kuhn and some of his staff, part of the intelligence staff, the chief of staff and the head of operations, and the chief of administration were in separate locations scattered over ten miles. He termed this "a new and unfortunate application of the principle of positioning in depth."[11]

Once again, the artillery advanced the barrage too fast for the infantry, giving sheltered Germans time to resume their positions in the trenches and machine-gun the advancing troops. The country in front of Montfaucon and the Bois de la Tuilerie, which bordered it to the right, was a rising slope over a mile in extent, unwooded and completely open to artillery and machine gun fire. As the highest point for miles around, it was fully visible to German guns as distant as seven miles to the east and west. The two regiments came under direct fire from heavy guns in the Argonne Forest to their left and on Hill 378 (the "Borne du Cornouiller") across the Meuse River to their right. Indirect fire came from woods to the north. The only artillery available to respond was a single battalion backing up the 313th Infantry that had finally made it through the traffic jam; their 75mm guns were no match in range or weight for those of the enemy. The results were visible from a distance: Leo V. Jacks, an enlisted man in the 119th Field Artillery, noticed that the bodies on the hillside ahead of him were arranged in small circles and he knew what that meant. The inexperienced infantrymen were bunching up, so that a single shell would disable eight or ten of them at once instead of one or two.

Artillery support remained a problem throughout the day. German shell fire inflicted many injuries. One of the American artillery's missions was to bombard the German batteries, and for once the regiments' lead battalions were able to spot good targets for them. But although General Irwin ordered his 147th and 121st Field Artillery Regiments to advance, "[t]he absolute impossibility of moving cross country on account of the great number of shell holes and mud, the great delay in securing permission to use roads, and the immobility of traffic after this permission was secured, delayed the forward movement of the batteries to such an extent as to be exasperating."[12] The regiments did not get into position until the afternoon. This left the work up to the heavies back at the 57th Artillery Brigade's position, which had the range to reach the battlefield. But the rapid advance and the slowness of communication to the rear made the risk of shelling their own men very high, so little help arrived from the 57th. What feeble artillery assistance there was came from the mobile 37mm guns carried by the Headquarters Companies. They had not kept up with the first day's attack, but came forward on the night of the 27th and were able to reinforce the infantry in the morning. Corps artillery and two French regiments attached to the 57th laid down "protective fire," according to Irwin, but they could have had no target designation or observation of fire.[13] Nor would army artillery be of any help. First Army's orders for the day gave no firing assignments to army batteries, and the previous day's order forbidding shelling below the Army Objective still stood.

Nonetheless, individual units of the army artillery attempted to support the infantry as best they could. Alden Brooks, an American officer serving with the French 81st Artillery Regiment assigned to the Aire grouping, tried to get target information from the 79th. Unable to reach Kuhn's headquarters by phone, he commandeered a motorcycle and went forward. Eventually the road became too cut up for the motorcycle, so he continued on foot. "One glance at telephone wires trampled deep in mud and slop told why communications everywhere had broken down." He finally reached Kuhn's PC at Malancourt:

> From their conversation, [Kuhn's staff] seemed for the moment to know little of what was happening, more than that there was urgent need up front for artillery support. I introduced myself as coming from the Aire grouping, mentioned our long-range guns standing idle, said I would return at once

with word of any objective that should be fired upon. Their reply was polite, and yet somewhat ambiguous ... To ask for artillery support is not sufficient; one must know on what objectives one wants it, and at what time.[14]

Kuhn, being out of touch with Nicholson at that time, had no idea where his front actually was or what targets were available.[*] The operations reports of the 57th Field Artillery told the story in numbers: on September 26, its massive 9.2-inch guns fired 695 shells, the heavy 155mm pieces 6,000, and the 75mm guns fired 39,102 rounds. On the 27th the 9.2s still managed 750 shells but the 75s achieved only 1,500 and the 155s fired a flat zero.[15]

Things were not much better to the left and right of the 79th. At 1:00 a.m. on the 27th, V Corps transmitted an order from First Army that the divisions were to advance independently to the combined First Army Phase Line, while keeping within their original zones of action.[16] This unshackled the 4th and the 37th Divisions from the lagging 79th, although it did not otherwise allow them much freedom of maneuver. At 7:00 a.m. the 4th, which had spent the afternoon and evening of the previous day watching the 5th Bavarian Reserve Division pour men and guns unimpeded into Nantillois and the Bois de Brieulles, gamely attempted to take the town. But 75mm guns were the heaviest available for support, and the morning attack failed.[†] The 39th Infantry Regiment, on the division's left, suffered the most. German resistance had greatly increased. The previous day one could walk upright; now one had to crawl or crouch. Because Montfaucon was still not taken, the regiment took heavy flanking fire from machine guns and artillery, which also came from the woods and defensive

---

[*] Elsewhere Brooks says that the heavy guns were unavailable because the Aire grouping, believing the false reports that Montfaucon had fallen on the 26th, had ordered them forward and they were still on the road. (Alden Brooks, *As I Saw It* (New York: Knopf, 1929), p. 258.)

[†] The sources are contradictory regarding the advance of the 4th Division on September 27. According to Lanza, the division first failed to capture Nantillois; later in the morning, with support from army and corps artillery, they took it, only to lose it to a German counterattack (Conrad H. Lanza, "The Army Artillery, First Army," unpublished manuscript in AHEC library, c. 1926, p. 225). Neither the operational summary by the ABMC, *4th Division: Summary of Operations in the World War*, nor the divisional history (Robert B. Cole and Barnard E. Eberlin, *The History of the 39th U.S. Infantry During the World War* (New York: Press of Joseph D. McGuire, 1919), makes any mention of capturing Nantillois on the 27th. The history of the 47th Infantry (James E. Pollard, *The Forty-Seventh Infantry, a History: 1917–1918–1919* (Saginaw, MI: Press of Seeman & Peters, 1919), p. 65) asserts that the regiment advanced all the way to the Bois de Fays (nearly two miles north of Nantillois) and spent the night there, although the ABMC puts the division no further north than the Bois de Septsarges, much to the south, on the same night.

General John J. Pershing, commander-in-chief of the American Expeditionary Forces. (AHEC)

Meeting of General Henri-Philippe Pétain, Field Marshal Sir Douglas Haig, Marshal Ferdinand Foch, and General John Joseph Pershing on the Western Front. (Photo by ullstein bild/ullstein bild via Getty Images)

Major General George H. Cameron, commander of V Corps during the Montfaucon battle. (NARA)

General Kuhn in conference with General Henri Claudel (in fur coat), commander of the French XVII Corps, and other French officers during the Heights of the Meuse battle. The 79th was part of Claudel's corps at that time. (AHEC)

Major General Joseph E. Kuhn, commander of the 79th Division. (AHEC)

Brigadier General William J. Nicholson, commander of the 157th Infantry Brigade. (NARA)

Brigadier General Robert H. Noble, relieved of command of the 158th Infantry Brigade by Kuhn on September 27. (NARA)

Brigadier General Evan M. Johnson, commander of the 158th Infantry Brigade in the Heights of the Meuse. (NARA)

Colonel Claude B. Sweezey, commander of the 313th Infantry Regiment. (AHEC)

Colonel Alden G. Knowles,
commander of the 315th Infantry
Regiment. (AHEC)

33083

Above: Private William Schellberg, Machine Gun Company, 313th Infantry Regiment. (AHEC)

Opposite: Colonel William H. Oury, commander of the 314th Infantry Regiment. Colonel Oury replaced General Noble as commander of the 158th Infantry Brigade during the Montfaucon attack. (NARA)

Brigadier General Alfred W. Bjornstad, chief of staff of III Corps. General Bjornstad countermanded the order for the 4th Division to attack behind Montfaucon, a maneuver that might have changed the outcome of the battle. (NARA)

Corporal Oscar Lubchansky, Company G, 313th Infantry Regiment. (Author's collection)

Camp Meade under construction. The barracks were being built even as the first draftees of the 79th were arriving. (AHEC)

Draftees on arrival at Camp Meade, 1918. (AHEC)

Street scene, Camp Meade, April 1919. (AHEC)

USS *Leviathan*, formerly the Hamburg–Amerika liner *Vaterland*, in "dazzle" camouflage. The *Leviathan* carried 96,804 American troops, among them the headquarters and one brigade of the 79th Division, to France. (US Naval Historical Center)

Troops on field maneuvers, Camp Meade. (AHEC)

Black troops being trained by a white officer at Camp Meade. In reality, most black soldiers were used as stevedores and laborers. (AHEC)

Second wave of the 79th going over the top at Montfaucon, September 26. (US Army Signal Corps)

Captured German pillbox at Haucourt. (AHEC)

PC of the 79th Division between Malancourt and Montfaucon. General Kuhn occupied the dugout on the right. (NARA)

Soldiers of the 79th Division marching past the "Crown Prince's Observatory." (AHEC)

Above: Soldiers of Company E, 314th Infantry Regiment, with captured German machine guns. (AHEC)

Below: American and French artillery observers on Montfaucon giving the range to the Bois des Ogons, September 28. (AHEC)

Oblique aerial view of Montfaucon after its capture. Note the foxholes and tank tracks. (AHEC)

View of Montfaucon from ground level one day after its capture. (AHEC)

Ruined church atop Montfaucon the day after the town's capture. (AHEC)

Wrecked limber and dead horse in a shell crater near Montfaucon. (AHEC)

Ruins of Montfaucon five days after its capture. (AHEC)

Wrecked Renault tank on top of a German machine gun post, Madeleine Farm. (AHEC)

Opposite: Crater left by a German mine that exploded on September 26 on the road north of Avocourt. (AHEC)

Dugout used as the PC of the 157th Brigade, Troyon sector. (AHEC)

Company G, 313th Infantry, on training maneuvers in the Troyon sector. (AHEC)

Above: Trenches occupied by the 79th at Vachereauville, General Kuhn's headquarters during the Heights of the Meuse operation. (AHEC)

Below: 304th Engineers build a ration dump near Samogneux. (AHEC)

Water tank trucks arrive in Brabant-sur-Meuse, November 3. The lack of water severely hampered the 79th at Montfaucon; in the Heights of the Meuse, they were much better supplied. (AHEC)

155mm howitzer of the 79th in action at Samogneux. (AHEC)

German machine gun nest at Molleville Farm near Etrayc. The body of an American soldier blocks one of the firing ports. (AHEC)

First-aid station in the Bois de Consenvoye, 315th Infantry Regiment. (AHEC)

Dead of the 79th Division near Molleville Farm. (NARA)

German billets at Etraye captured by the 79th Division. (AHEC)

The ruins of Ville Devant Chaumont, the 79th Division's furthest point of advance. (AHEC)

German guns captured by the 79th Division. (NARA)

Côte de Morimont, the position of the 79th Division at the Armistice. (AHEC)

Machine guns of the 79th on Hill 328 the day after the Armistice. Note the lack of trenches and barbed wire, as the Germans had been retreating rapidly. (AHEC)

The band of the 315th Infantry celebrates the Armistice. (AHEC)

Thanksgiving Day parade of the 315th Infantry Regiment, Damvillers. Note the German prisoners in the left distance. (AHEC)

A tired soldier will sleep anywhere. (AHEC)

The American cemetery at Romagne-sous-Montfaucon. Among its 14,000 graves lie many of the dead of the 79th Division. (Author)

The AEF monument atop Montfaucon. (Author)

Ruined German observation post atop Montfaucon. (Author)

Ruins of the church on Montfaucon. (Author)

positions in front. (Much of the fire came from the battery of Captain Hollidt, the artillerist from the 5th Bavarian Reserve Division, who had helped thwart the attack of the 4th Division the day before.) Two battalions of the 39th Infantry got as far as the east–west road from Nantillois, at which point they were stopped at Hill 266 by heavy machine gun fire. But their positions were fully exposed to the German artillery, which pounded them until they retired behind the hill with severe losses. In their refuge, a depression south of the Nantillois road, they were an even more compressed target for the German artillery. So, despite the efforts of their officers, they continued to withdraw about a mile to the southern slope of Hill 295, where they dug in.[17] The entire division spent the night in approximately the same positions from which they had started out that morning.

The 37th Division attacked at 5:30 a.m. Major Roy V. Myers, an officer of the 55th Field Artillery Regiment supporting the 37th, described the morning advance of the 148th Infantry on Ivoiry, in the left of the division's sector:

> We stood at the forward edge of the woods on top of a ridge. The un-wooded slope descended to our front to a near valley; thence a steeper slope to the top of the next ridge which was parallel to and about level with the one on which we stood. The distance to the skyline of ridge to our front was a little less than one kilometer. Silhouetted against the sky on that ridge was our Infantry ... Shells were bursting over and among them. Planes were flying overhead. Just what part in the battle they were taking was not evident. American troops were going forward in the narrow valley between my position and the battle line ridge. These reinforcement troops were in single file combat groups of approach formation. Shells were falling perilously close to some of them. Only then did they break their formation, as the men, never before under fire, would run a short distance from the fountain of smoke, earth and flying missiles of death. It reminded one of young partridges running instinctively from a danger suddenly thrust among them. Then the young soldiers would give the heavy packs on their backs a heave to adjust them from an uncomfortable angle which they assumed during the momentary excitement. The men were not scratched. They reformed their line and marched forward again apparently with a consciousness of experience under fire which veteranized them within the space of a few seconds of time.[18]

By 9:00 a.m. they had taken Ivoiry and gotten 500 yards beyond. There they were stopped by a German counterattack and got no further that day.

Southwest of Montfaucon, the 145th Infantry, the right-hand regiment of the 37th Division, attacked toward the town at dawn, but was immediately stopped. The 146th and 145th then renewed the attack using individual battalions. The 1st and 3rd Battalions of the 146th got the furthest, assaulting the ridge north of the Ivoiry–Montfaucon road; but it too was brought to a standstill by heavy machine gun and artillery fire. In the evening the leading regiments were withdrawn from what looked like an insecure salient. Like the 4th, the 37th ended the day in much the same position from which it had started.*

Army group commander Gallwitz had spent the night of September 26–27 strengthening the position of his Maas Group West. He reversed the previous day's withdrawal of his artillery, which had rendered it largely useless. The German 37th Division, which had arrived the previous evening, relieved the battered 117th of sector command. One battalion of its 151st Infantry Regiment was put north of the Bois de Beuge to hold the junction between the 37th's subsector and that of the 117th. Its 147th Regiment went into line in the Bois de Brieulles, reinforcing the 10th and 12th Bavarians who were facing the American 4th division.[19] What was left of the 117th was concentrated in Montfaucon facing Kuhn's 79th, and was augmented with several artillery battalions. Gallwitz ordered more reinforcements forward—the 115th and 236th Divisions, both rated by American intelligence as third class but both relatively fresh.[20] Expected to arrive on the afternoon of the 27th, they didn't reach the field until the next day. But although he had improved his line, Gallwitz still could not give up the idea that the entire attack west of the Meuse was a feint to cover a larger offensive against the Metz–Briey complex to the east. He therefore left considerable forces east of Verdun and out of the immediate action.[21]

At 5:00 a.m. the Germans took shelter as the Americans resumed their bombardment and at 6:30 a.m. they observed the infantry advancing, supported by tanks. They repulsed the first assault. To the surprise of the 11th Grenadiers the next attack, at 9:00 a.m., came from the west. (This was probably the battalion-level assault of the 145th and 146th Infantry

---

* In its divisional history and in affidavits and other statements after the war, officers of the 37th Division claimed to have sent at least ten patrols into or around Montfaucon on September 26 and 27, before the 79th Division took the town. The accounts vary in their detail and credibility and some contradict others.

Regiments mentioned above.) It was barely contained by a single company joined by the telephone technicians and regimental orderlies.[*] Major Stosch quickly transferred an infantry platoon and a heavy machine gun from his left flank to his right, all the while sending urgent requests to division and brigade headquarters for a reserve company.[22] But things were going badly in the adjacent sectors. Hard-pressed by the (American) 37th Division to his right, the 151st Regiment of the (German) 37th Division and the 450th Regiment of the 117th were forced to withdraw, leaving the 150th Regiment to extend its line eastward to fill the gap between it and the 11th Grenadiers.[23] To his left, the advance of the 4th Division forced the regiments in the Bois de Brieulles to pull back as well.[24]

General von Gallwitz looked at the map, saw the same indentation in the front line that Pershing had, but drew the opposite conclusion: Montfaucon and its defenders were about to be cut off. "I ordered that Montfaucon be relinquished and a new line established, running from Epinonville, by way of the heights to the north of Nantillois to Brieulles."[25] At 10:00 a.m. a motorcycle messenger reached Stosch's headquarters with an order from Major General Hoefer, commander of the 117th: the 11th Grenadiers were to withdraw to a line running south of the Bois de Beuge and through Nantillois and, with the other regiments, form a defensive position. In the words of the regimental historian:

> This order initially shocked the regiment to the core. Instead of ordering the other regiments [i.e., the 151st, 450th, and 147th] to resume their positions, the division ordered the 11th Grenadier Regiment to abandon the sector which they had defended with such great sacrifices and in such tenacious battles, when the allotment of a single strong reserve for the right flank would be enough to hold it. And to surrender in the middle of the day, when a new attack could be expected at any moment and a thrust into the retreating troops could lead to their utter destruction.[26]

On the other hand, it was clear that the thinness of the front line made it impossible to transfer troops to the regiment's right flank, which was too

---

[*] So says the regimental history of the 11th Grenadiers. The 117th Division's war diary credits the repulse to the combined efforts of its 450th Regiment and the neighboring 151st Regiment of the (German) 37th Division. ("117th Division (Subordinate Units): Diary and Annexes," September 25–30, 1918, RG 165, Army War College, Historical Section, Box 165, 117th Division, 22.3, NARA, p. 85.)

weak to withstand another assault. If the enemy broke through to Montfaucon now, only a fighting retreat would be possible. Stosch conferred with the artillery commanders attached to his regiment, then ordered the forward companies to withdraw from their positions quietly and assemble on the north slope of the hill. The 1st and 2nd Battalions were ordered to place their companies on both sides of Nantillois in line with the companies already there. The trickiest part of the withdrawal was the retreat of the 11th Company, holding the extreme western part of the line and in contact with American troops of the 37th Division; they were ordered to leave one by one using any available cover. The retreat was successful and, although it was noticed by American patrols, there was no attempt to interfere. "Doubtless the enemy himself did not believe that this entire area would be surrendered to him without a battle." One month later a messenger arrived at the regiment's headquarters. Major Count Stosch had been awarded the *Pour le Mérite*, the highest German military decoration, for his defense of Montfaucon.[27]

To the right of the 11th Grenadiers one battalion of the 450th Regiment retreated into the Bois de Beuge and, with the 150th Regiment to its right, formed a defensive line. The two other battalions of the 450th were too badly shattered to continue as separate commands; they were reorganized into provisional Battalion Wehber, named after the cavalry captain who took command. Assigned to cover the road out of Nantillois where it forked westward to Cierges and northward to Cunel, the battalion was forced to withdraw even further by American artillery fire. This left a gap between the Bois de Beuge and Nantillois, which was plugged by the emplacement of a group of heavy machine guns, joined by bits and pieces of two pioneer companies and a *Minenwerfer* company.[28]

All this was happening as Sweezey's 313th Infantry Regiment struggled up the hill toward the town and Oury's 314th, with the tanks of the French 340th Company, approached the Bois de la Tuilerie to its right. Those men not dodging machine gun bullets and hand grenades could admire the fireworks in the air above them:

> Six planes, some with black Prussian crosses, the others with allied circles, were maneuvering and shooting streams of machine gun bullets, each aviator striving for a position deadly to an enemy "bus." Like six big birds, some were climbing, others gliding in big curves, and others suddenly

diving. Red hot tracer bullets marked the path of each stream of steel-nosed peace notes—the gunner's guide to his mark. Suddenly an allied plane dropped, twisting and turning, apparently in a mad plunge to destruction. However, it didn't strike terra firma, but righted itself and climbed to a good position. It was the false dive of a dare-devil aviator.[29]

As the 314th advanced, the men had to step on or over the gray-green-clad bodies of German soldiers, and a few American ones as well. Lieutenant Joel in the 2nd Battalion noticed "the upturned face of a young German, about 16 years of age—an expression with something of the puzzle of Da Vinci's Mona Lisa. The innocent, child-like, questioning wonderment seemed to indicate that he had left this life puzzled as to what it was all about."[30] Despite the aid from their 37mm guns, the 314th suffered heavy casualties as they passed over the Fayel Farm ridge on their way to the Bois de la Tuilerie. One of them was Captain Clarence Patton Freeman, commander of Company M:

> The rattle of the rapid fire guns was the first warning the men received and the captain, badly wounded in the left thigh, went down headlong. Disregarding protection a number of his men ran to their captain, attempting to lift him up and carry him to safety. As they raised him to a sitting position, the Huns turned loose another blast of fire. Three bullets struck the already wounded officer, one passing through his head and effecting a mortal injury. Despite this hail of fire his men persisted and finally half-dragged, half-carried him to a shell hole where he lay until long after dark, when stretcher-bearers reached him and carried him back to the nearest field hospital. From there he was placed in an ambulance and taken to the mobile hospital, where he died early in the morning of September 30.[31]

Captain Freeman was a graduate of the University of Pennsylvania Law School and just before sailing for France had been admitted to the Pennsylvania bar. Other officers and men were killed by shell fragments. It was common for wounded men, ordered to the rear, to refuse to leave their comrades and to keep up with the advance as best they could. They reached the Bois around noon; entering the wood, they captured four 77mm guns.

For the 313th the withdrawal of the 11th Grenadiers made their going considerably easier than it had been at first light. Lieutenant Joel later described the scene as Sweezey's regiment climbed the hill:

With the buzz of tanks and aeroplane motors and the bursts of high explosive and shrapnel, the regiment started ahead in one of the most exciting fights of its history. It was an inspiring sight to see wave after wave of infantry following the advancing tanks, and the other troops in small groups coming behind and on the flanks; and to watch the shrapnel and high explosive shells bursting among the lines and over the heads of the khaki-clad files. Beyond the crest of the hill big things immediately began to happen. The storm of "H. E.'s" and "G. I. cans"—high explosive—increased in intensity, gas clouds became a great deal more concentrated, and the whining and snapping machine gun and sniper bullets added to the toll of casualties.[32]

By 11:00 a.m. Sweezey's lead battalion had reached the outskirts of the town; by 11:55 a.m. they had occupied it fully. The colonel wrote out the following message:

> Took town of Montfaucon 11h 55 after considerable fighting in town. Many snipers left behind. Town shelled to slight extent after our occupation. Am moving on to Corps objective and hope to reach it by 16h.[*][33]

The phone lines were dead, so Sweezey sent the message by a runner, who got to Kuhn's PC at 1:30 p.m. Shortly thereafter, a wounded pigeon, dispatched at the same time as the runner, fluttered into Kuhn's PC at Haucourt.

As it happened, Kuhn had already heard the news. Sometime after 11:00 a.m. Private Cain finally showed up in Malancourt. Kuhn was standing by the side of the road, "all smeared up and looking like hell." Cain saluted and confessed that he had gotten lost and had not delivered the attack order to General Nicholson. But Kuhn did not have a chance to react because at that moment Nicholson himself suddenly appeared. He started to speak, but Kuhn cut him off.

"What do you mean by breaking liaison with me? And where have you been anyway?"

"Where have I been?" demanded Nicholson, "I've been taking that position, that's where I've been. And I did not break liaison with you!" It

---

* Colonel E.E. Haskell of the Inspector General's staff commented, "It was reported that the town was stubbornly defended and that there were many casualties. This latter report was not borne out by personal observation." (Army War College, Historical Section, "The Seventy-Ninth Division, 1917–1918," (1924), p. 38.)

turned out that Nicholson's runners had stayed with his old PC. In their inexperience, they did not understand that their job was to follow him north and establish a link to his new position. Cain reported that a good deal of swearing ensued, "and the generals can outcuss the privates, I'll say that for them."* As Cain went off, he was approached by Captain Madeira.

"What's the matter?" Madeira asked.

"Nothing much," Cain replied.

"You didn't make it, hey?"

"No. Didn't make it."

"Don't worry about it. You did the best you could."

"Yeah, I done the best I could."

"You're not the only one. It's been a hell of a night and a hell of a day."

"Yeah, it sure has."

"Well—don't worry about it."

"Thanks."[34]

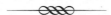

Having taken the town, the Americans now had a chance to examine their prize. They found an amazing array of defensive works, some of them German-built and some adapted from pre-existing structures. Many of the hilltop homes had deep wine cellars with arched stone roofs; the Germans had connected these with galleries and used them as observation posts and machine gun positions. More than a hundred dugouts were eventually found in and around the town, as well as in the Bois de la Tuilerie. On the northern slope was a camp of about 30 buildings including barracks, storerooms, and officers' quarters. Especially impressive were 17 concrete shafts, inserted into ruined buildings, the tops of which housed observation rooms. The most spectacular of these was a massive tower inside a three-story house on the western side of the hill, inside which was a telescopic

---

* The following April, Kuhn sent his wife two newspaper articles written by Cain describing this incident. "Strange to say," he wrote, "they are unusually accurate but what I am wondering at is how Private Cain got the dope. When I climbed Montfaucon on Sept 27, I went alone, leaving orderly and horses under shelter at foot of hill which was under heavy shell fire. No one saw me save Col. Sweezey and his surgeon Major Jackson and some of the 313th moving forward to the attack on some woods." (Joseph E. Kuhn to Helen Kuhn, April 8, 1919, Kuhn Papers, Box 5, USMA.)

periscope mounted on the ground floor and protruding through the roof, from where the entire countryside could be observed. At the moment of capture the periscope was intact; but shortly afterward someone stole the eyepiece for a souvenir, making it useless.[*][35]

Now that the Americans occupied the heights, they could turn the tables on the Germans. They were aided by a break in the weather. Private Jacks of the 119th Field Artillery described a scene worthy of a painting by Turner or Constable:

> About four o'clock a gold flood of sunlight broke through the clouds and we saw the plain ahead dotted by thin lines of doughboys straggling forward ...
> The sky was serried with towering tiers of cloud, and the fields and plains were just feeling the first strokes of frost. The horizon was a violet mist, and distant clumps of trees seemed covered with a blue canopy.[36]

Apart from its aesthetic merits, this meant that the division had good observation to the north. Three companies of the 311th Machine Gun Battalion emplaced their pieces on the hillside and shot up the retreating German columns. A squad from the division's Headquarters Company was detailed to set up an observation post in the periscope tower. (A sergeant and two privates operated the post for three days while the Germans shelled the building; they were eventually awarded the Distinguished Service Cross.[37]) In the process of securing the town, the 313th found several Germans who had been left behind to operate an artillery spotting post. With their capture, the enemy artillery quickly became less intense and less accurate. Kuhn made sure to secure the hill against a rumored German counterattack. The 311th Machine Guns and a battalion of the 316th Infantry formed a defensive line on the northern slope. To their right, the 310th Machine Gun Battalion and two battalions of the 147th Field Artillery were able to come forward through the traffic jam to reinforce the 314th Infantry, which was now holding the Bois de la Tuilerie. As it happened, the counterattack never materialized.

But the day was not over for the 79th; they were still short of the Corps Objective, which they were supposed to have reached the previous evening.

---

[*] Many of the concrete shafts with their observation decks can still be explored on top of the hill of Montfaucon (the town itself was rebuilt at the southwestern foot of the slope). The large house containing the periscope has disappeared, although a commemorative plaque remains.

This line ran along the north edge of the Bois de Beuge—over a mile away from the 313th in the left of the sector—and just behind Nantillois, a mile and a half beyond the position of the 314th on the right.

Sweezey's message reporting the capture of Montfaucon had included a request for artillery fire on the Bois de Beuge, beginning at 2:30 p.m. and ending an hour and a half later. But the barrage lasted only half an hour and few shells were actually fired because, back at army artillery headquarters, no one knew exactly where the 313th was. "The Army Artillery has not sufficient information in regard to the location of friendly troops to open fire at that range. The Army Artillery Commander will be glad to open fire if he can get necessary information and instructions," was the message sent back to V Corps.[38] Most of the division's own guns were still stuck on the road.

Why was there so little support from army artillery, not just for the 79th but for the entire offensive? As we saw, the previous day First Army had forbidden its gunners to fire below an east–west line running about half a mile north of Nantillois. On the 27th they even extended the no-fire zone to a range of six miles beyond Montfaucon.[39] But it is clear that individual army artillery commanders were perfectly willing to support the infantry if they had current information on enemy strong points and batteries. That was the problem: most of the time, no one could give target coordinates to the gunners. The observation posts manned by the attacking divisions provided no data, balloons very little. Liaison officers gave some information but by the time it got to the artillery it was too late and conditions had changed. But had the guns been available, other problems would have interfered. According to Colonel Lanza, First Army artillery's chief of operations, even such shelling as the army guns were able to provide at this time was generally ineffective. The artillery had not adjusted to the Germans' defense in depth with its dispersed strong points; instead they assumed that the enemy was in continuous trenches and they bombarded the places the Germans should have been—such as the leading edges of woods—according to the prewar manuals.[40] In any event, firing on woods and hilltops was no replacement for counterbattery fire. The best way to protect the infantry was to neutralize the German guns, many of which were in the open; this was not done.[41]

Failing artillery support, the 79th should have been able to rely on assistance from the French tank battalions, which had finally caught up with the lead regiments after being stuck on the Malancourt road the previous day. Kuhn's reorganization of the brigades, however, threw the French tank commanders into confusion. Major Guillot's 14th Light Tanks had been assigned to the original 157th Brigade; he put his 340th and 341st companies on the right with the 314th Infantry. But as the tanks rolled forward with Oury's regiment into the Bois de la Tuilerie, an officer from the 15th Light Tank Battalion arrived with an order announcing that the brigades had been reorganized and the 14th was now to support the 157th Provisional on the left, the 15th to take over with the 158th Provisional on the right. Having been dismissed from their sector, Guillot's 340th and 341st companies tried to get orders from the headquarters of the 157th; but they found that Nicholson's staff were ignorant of the reorganization. They spent the rest of the day trying to find someone to report to.[42] In the meantime, the three companies of the newly arrived 15th Light Tank Battalion did not reach their assigned regiments, the 314th and 315th, until mid-afternoon.[43]

Nonetheless, at 3:30 p.m. the 313th with several tanks of the French 342nd Company (which had not been affected by the reorganization) and two companies of the 311th Machine Guns started north. Kuhn watched from the north slope of Montfaucon: "Wave after wave of khaki clad infantry was pouring over the hill and down its northern slope in full view of the enemy while over their heads German shells were bursting, fortunately too high to inflict serious casualties."[44] Kuhn was wrong about the casualties; the attack did not get far before it was stopped by machine gun and mortar fire from the Bois de Beuge, accompanied by heavy artillery from the Heights of the Meuse. Once again, Captain Hollidt of the 5th Bavarians was on the spot with his battery, firing at 500 meters range: three of the French tanks were destroyed and the rest retired. (Sweezey later credited the tanks with suppressing German machine gun nests and helping his regiment get as far as it did.[45] Hollidt and three of his NCOs were decorated for their actions on the 26th and 27th.[46]) Officers and men fell dead and wounded. The losses among battalion commanders continued. Captain Effingham Morris of Company K took over command of 3rd Battalion from Captain Lloyd, who had commanded it only since the previous day and who was now wounded. Morris himself had already been hit in the leg, but insisted on remaining with his battalion. The medical officers of the 313th attended to the casualties on the field, even acting as stretcher-bearers to take men to safety in the rear.

At 6:00 p.m. Sweezey called a halt to the advance and ordered the men to bivouac for the night.* But rest was not to be had; other divisions' artillery fire fell on the front line of the 313th, and an officer had to be sent to the rear with an order for them to cease. Most of the regiment spent the night of September 27–28 on a line about half a mile north of Montfaucon; some units got as far north as the south edge of the Bois de Beuge. Despite not having reached their objective, largely because of the lack of artillery, the 313th had some accomplishments to show for the day. It had taken Montfaucon and advanced two-thirds of a mile beyond, in the face of heavy opposition. Sweezey later estimated that the regiment had captured about 75 machine guns and 11 field guns and had taken 300 prisoners.[47] These had come at the cost of 21 dead, including those of the 311th Machine Gun Battalion; as usual, no one counted up the wounded.[48]

Early in the afternoon, as Sweezey and the 313th were reorganizing for their push toward the Bois de Beuge, Lieutenant Colonel H.J. McKenney took over the 314th from the promoted Colonel Oury and prepared for an attack on Nantillois. He called up one battalion from the 315th, formerly in support, to fill out his line. His orders for the advance read:

> Invade One [the 315th Infantry] will advance on Nantillois, enveloping West and South of that town. Invading [3rd Battalion] will advance to Nantillois attacking South edge of town. It is imperative that all troops cross shelled area south of Nantillois without further delay. Artillery will shell Bois de Beuge southwest of Nantillois. Invaded [2nd Battalion] will follow in support. Make every effort to get N. of Nantillois. This is an imperative order to Bn Commdrs. Request Instruct One [314th Infantry] to give close support. You are covered by our artillery firing on Nantillois.[49]

---

* The war diary of the German 117th Division reports a further attempt on the Bois de Beuge by tank-supported infantry at 6:00 p.m. that was broken up by artillery fire. ("117th Division (Subordinate Units): Diary and Annexes," p. 86.) The histories and combat reports of the 79th and 37th Divisions, the only American divisions in the vicinity, do not attest to such an attack. The history of the 7th Bavarian Reserve Infantry Regiment describes repelling, sometime after 7:00 p.m., a large attack northward from Montfaucon toward Nantillois, supported by eight tanks. (Otto Schaidler, *Das K.B. Reserve-Infanterie-Regiment 7*, Erinnerungsblätter Deutscher Regimenter (Munich: Verlag Max Schick, 1934), p. 212.) This is hard to credit. No American accounts mention such an attack and it would have been dark at the time; sunset was at 5:38 p.m.

The details of the attack out of the Bois de la Tuilerie are obscure. It is clear from the American accounts that it was immediately met by ferocious German artillery fire. According to Major Richard, the French tank battalion commander, his 343rd Company led the advance into Nantillois but the infantry failed to follow any closer than 1,500 meters. The tanks even passed through Nantillois without meeting any Germans (who at that time had retired just north of the town). His 344th Company then advanced from the southeast corner of Fayel Farm and mopped up the ground south of Nantillois as well as the area to its east and southeast. The infantry still did not move from its position 1,500 meters to the south.* After losing several of their number and without infantry support, the tanks had to withdraw. Had the infantry followed the tanks and occupied the captured positions, Richard wrote, they could have advanced three kilometers on a two and a half kilometer front.[50] The American and German reports essentially confirm the French version. Once again, the Hollidt Battery contributed to the repulse of the attack.[51]

Exhausted, unsupplied with food or water since the initial attack the previous day, and unsupported by artillery, the 314th made little progress by nightfall. Colonel Oury called off the attack and the men dug in, a third of a mile north of a line Montfaucon–Bois de la Tuilerie, a mile and a half south of Nantillois. To its right, the 310th Machine Gun Battalion emplaced its guns in former German trenches north of the Montfaucon–Septsarges road.† They found no shelter from the German artillery. A battalion commander in the 315th sent a message to Oury, "Under terrific bombardment and should have counter-artillery ... Heavy machine gun fire on both flanks."[52] Sergeant Davies of the 315th described what it felt like:

> About 8:30 the Germans started to shell us. My God, it was awful, we lost men right and left. Poor Pritchard got his tonight, had his head blown off. Just a kid too. The cries of the wounded and dying was awful and I can never forget them. Everywhere you could hear them crying for "First Aid." The

---

* The American soldiers did not know much about working with armor, but they did know that tanks were magnets for artillery and machine gun fire. In the absence of training in joint operations, they reasonably declined to be in their vicinity. Given the heavy German bombardment and the general lack of progress of the 158th that day, the French report appears to be accurate.

† Thus the divisional history. The American Battle Monuments Commission puts the bivouac position of the 314th at least half a mile further north, after a withdrawal of a third of a mile. (ABMC, *79th Division: Summary of Operations in the World War* (Washington, DC: GPO, 1944), p. 17.)

hospital men did their best, but every time a shell landed we lost men ... I am wondering if any of us will be alive by morning.[53]

Together the 314th Infantry and the 310th Machine Guns ended the day with 22 dead, three of them officers.[54] The toll for the division as a whole was three officers and 59 men, many fewer than the previous day because the Germans spent much of the time withdrawing from their forward positions, including Montfaucon.[*]

The traffic jam behind them was beginning to take its toll on the men. No supplies of any description had reached the regiments of the 79th since they had left their trenches the previous morning and the front-line troops had long exhausted their food and water. At 3:50 p.m. Tenney Ross sent an officer with a message to the division's chief of administration in the rear, "Push ammunition forward with all speed together with water & food. Ammunition to lead."[55] That officer was trying his best; he replied:

> Procured 130 donkeys from the French, sent them forward with limited amount of supplies to Malancourt at 17 h. under command of Major Miller and Lt. Clark, 304th Ammunition Train ... The horse drawn ammunition section, 107th Ammunition Train of 57th Brig. attached to the 79th Div. cleared Avocourt with remainder of trains. 13 truck loads of small arms ammunition at this time still blocked in Avocourt.[56]

The little food those donkeys carried was welcome, but even that small amount could not be distributed efficiently because the regimental supply companies were under constant artillery fire. (Behind the lines, a well was found that sustained the troops in Montfaucon and was a great solace to the wounded.[57]) Nor were the roads going to be clear any time soon. South of Malancourt, where the engineers had had time to do their work, the roads were hard-packed, well drained, and gravel-surfaced. But north of there the rain had turned the ruined tracks into a sticky soup. Even beyond Montfaucon, where the bombardment had not been as severe, the situation was dire. The Germans, it became clear, had relied on narrow-gauge railroads for supply and had neglected repair of the roads. They had, however, seeded them generously with mines, some of which exploded, leaving large craters. The ground was

---

[*] Cochrane later counted in the records 142 men brought to hospitals, likely a severe underestimate of the wounded. (Cochrane, "79th Division," p. 29.)

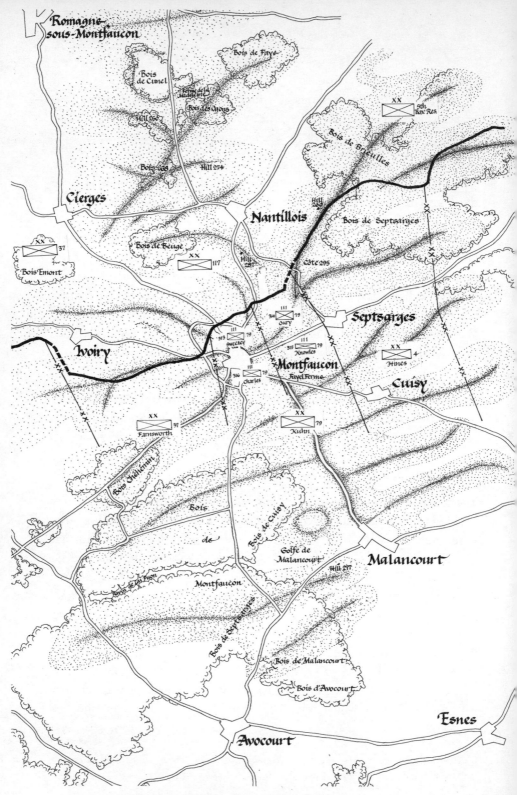

POSITIONS OF THE 79TH DIVISION'S REGIMENTS,
night of SEPTEMBER 27

soft, and rock was hard to come by; it was carried in on wagons and pack mules, even on stretchers.[58] A few hours after Montfaucon fell, the Avocourt–Malancourt road segment was declared one-way going south. Northbound traffic for both the 79th and the 4th Divisions was now to use the Esnes–Malancourt road. This meant that the trains of the 79th, stuck south of Malancourt, had to turn around, retrace their steps to Avocourt, find their way east to Esnes, and then proceed north. Colonel Billy Mitchell, flying over the front, looked down and was horrified, realizing that a concentrated air attack—or artillery attack directed by air observers—on the mass of vehicles below could crush the offensive. As air commander in the zone of advance, he ordered his bombers to concentrate on the enemy airfields, drawing the observation planes away and keeping them in the German rear.[59] And indeed, with notable exceptions, there are few reports of German air attacks on ground units in general or on the roads in particular.

Those who suffered most from the ruined roads were the wounded. As the 119th Field Artillery made its slow way forward, Lieutenant Jacks noticed the columns of ambulances facing the other way, pulled over to the side of the road to let the artillery (which had priority) pass:

> From time to time our men would glance curiously into the ambulances, at the shattered and bleeding forms, many of them blackened, disfigured, and torn beyond recognition, as if trying to decide what they themselves would look like shortly. Their own mothers could never have recognized most of the bloody wrecks that lay in the ambulances.[60]

William L. Hanson, an Illinois physician with past service in the Royal Army Medical Corps, was adjutant of the 304th Sanitary Train. His responsibility was to evacuate the wounded of the 79th to a field hospital about 25 miles to the rear. But he had 200 men to transport and few ambulances, and the road blockages meant that ammunition trucks came first. So Hanson commandeered all the empty ammunition and supply trucks around, loaded up his wounded, and shipped them south.* Hanson's

---

* Long after the war Hanson wrote, "I was, frankly, rather pleased at the efficiency of that maneuver if I say so myself. It wasn't until a half-century later that I learned it almost backfired on me. When those truck-ambulances arrived at the field hospital, the commanding officer was most unhappy and critical of my move. He let that be known to several other physicians within earshot. My old friend, Dr. O.C. Snyder, happened to be one of them. He immediately advised the commanding officer that he (Dr. Snyder) had served a year with me at the Dartford War Hospital, that I was an efficient and level-

urgent requests for help resulted in a full field hospital being sent to the 79th the next day. As soon as their tents were set up, they were filled with patients still awaiting evacuation. Soon more physicians and ambulances arrived, and the situation came under control.

Back on Montfaucon things were getting warm for Kuhn, too. Soon after the hill had fallen he had moved his PC to its southern side, below the crest; but the German guns found the range. At 5:18 p.m. he asked V Corps for counterbattery fire. "I wish Army and Corps artillery would begin to fire as soon as possible because the enemy is shelling Montfaucon very heavily and our people are in that vicinity and beyond."[61] As the evening wore on his tone grew more urgent: "They have been pounding Montfaucon for the last three hours. A battery is reported by Balloon just south of Nantillois. I suggest that the Bois de Burge [sic] and the known battery positions on the road therefrom to Nantillois be bombarded by army and corps artillery as soon as possible. Our troops are not, I think, close enough to be in danger from such artillery fire."[62] Of course, "just south of Nantillois" was hardly precise enough for accurate aiming. V Corps later reported, "Orders were given the Corps Artillery Commander to fire on the above points as requested, intermittently until 12 o'clock, and then again early in the morning. This fire was later called off upon request of 79th Division."[63] This bombardment was probably the one that discomfited the German 11th Grenadiers, who were in their new position just north of Nantillois.

That night the supporting regiments came forward to take the lead, Charles's 316th relieving the battered 313th and Knowles's 315th replacing the 314th. As the men of Company F of the 314th marched to the rear, they welcomed the prospect of a hot meal, the first since they had left their bivouac two days earlier. They arrived in the Bois de Montfaucon around dawn and found that:

> ... our mess Sergeant Vought had been killed the night previous. Faithful to duty he had slept under the kitchen to see that all would be well with the horses. But when the cooks tried to wake him in the morning, the mangled animals and the wound on the sergeant's head showed what had happened.

headed physician, and that if I had deemed using the trucks an expedient and necessary procedure, then it damn well was. Dr. Snyder was so effective in his presentation that there was no further comment." (William L. Hanson, MD, *World War I: I Was There* (Gerald, MO: The Parice Press, 1982), p. 79.)

A piece of an exploding shell had added one more to the total of millions already claimed by the war. Had the soldier worn his helmet the piece would almost undoubtedly have glanced off. As it was the man whom soldiers figure had a safe job was among the first killed.[64]

Company F never got its hot meal; orders soon arrived to advance again, this time in support of the 315th. Loaves of bread were quickly torn apart and distributed as once more the men got to their feet and picked up their weapons.

CHAPTER 13

BOIS DE BEUGE AND NANTILLOIS, SEPTEMBER 28

The problems of the 79th were not unique; no one in First Army had gotten very far against the German lines. Things had started out well early on the first day, September 26, when most of the divisions were able to advance several miles against little opposition. But as the morning progressed, divisional and brigade staffs lost contact with their units, which began to go astray, bog down, or simply break up as they got deeper into the German defenses. All of the problems that had plagued the attackers at St Mihiel reappeared. In their inexperience, the men bunched up in the advance, failed to dig in when halted, and neglected to mop up bypassed machine gun nests. Much of the infantry had never trained with artillery and none had trained with tanks, so they failed to use those weapons to reduce German strong points. The rolling barrage almost always ran away from the infantry, so that German machine gunners were free to emerge from their shelters, resume their posts, and pour bullets into the advancing ranks. In the absence of effective counterbattery fire, German artillery, especially the big guns east of the Meuse, made life a constant hell. The American artillery itself was virtually blind, having no communication with the front lines except for runners; in fact, almost all communication between rear elements and the front lines was agonizingly slow when not entirely absent. The roads had been poorly reconnoitered and the preparations for their repair were inadequate so guns, ammunition, food, supplies, and ambulances were immobilized for days. Military police were ignorant of road discipline and of the locations of important command posts.

Progress was worst on the far left, where I Corps had to attack up the heavily wooded hogback of the Argonne Forest, thickly sown with German obstacles and strong points, and along the Aire valley to its east. Its 77th and 28th Divisions made only a little over a mile the first day and hardly that the second. The 35th Division to their right advanced further but at the cost of an almost complete breakdown in cohesion and command that would cost it dearly in the next few days. In V Corps, in the center of the line, the 91st Division got five to six miles from its starting point on the first day, then stalled. We have already seen the fortunes of the 37th and 79th Divisions. Only on the right were the divisions of III Corps—the 4th, 80th, and 33rd—able to reach the Corps Objective on schedule. The 4th got stuck a day later; the other two reached the Meuse River where, according to plan, they sat tight.

Elsewhere on the Western Front, however, Foch's offensive against the Hindenburg Line was proceeding apace. On September 26 the French Fourth Army attacked north toward Mézières on a 24-mile front. They didn't get much further than the Americans to their right (calling into question the belief of the French advisers with the AEF that their army knew what it was doing while the Americans did not). The next day the British First and Third Armies, comprising 27 divisions led by the Canadian Corps, attacked eastward from the old Somme battlefield, crossing the Canal du Nord and gaining more than four miles. A day later, they broke through the Hindenburg Line and reached the outskirts of Cambrai. The same day, September 28, a combined force of Belgians, French, and British totaling 28 divisions assaulted the German line at Passchendaele, of bloody memory.[*] Unlike in 1917, they overran four German defensive lines, captured the town, and advanced five miles. More was to come.

None of this was apparent to the officers and men of the 79th, still sheltering on the hillsides north of Montfaucon. At 20 minutes past midnight on the 28th, Kuhn received Pershing's orders: The enemy was expected to withdraw. First Army was to continue its advance to the Combined Army First Objective (a line about six to nine miles ahead of its

---

[*] Fighting with the British Fourth Army were two American divisions, the 27th and 30th. Their story is told in Mitchell Yockelson's book, *Borrowed Soldiers: Americans under British Command, 1918* (Norman, OK: University of Oklahoma Press, 2008).

current position and thus impossible to achieve in one day). The attack would resume at 7:00 a.m. The missions of corps, divisions, and auxiliary units would remain the same as the previous day—a sign that Pershing's operations staff was out of touch with events. Once again no mission was assigned to army artillery.[1] Nevertheless, V Corps added the injunction, "Divisions will advance independently of each other pushing the attack with the utmost vigor and regardless of cost."[2] By now Kuhn was in close contact with his brigades' PCs and, knowing what to expect, he had anticipated V Corps by issuing his own Field Order No. 8: The 157th Brigade would advance on the left, the 316th Infantry Regiment leading and the 313th following 1,000 meters to its rear. On the right, the 158th would attack in parallel, with the 315th Infantry in front and the 314th the same distance behind. The 57th Field Artillery Brigade would shell the ground ahead for "not less than one hour's duration," to end at H-hour. Accompanying batteries were to advance with the regiments and provide supporting fire, but there would be no rolling barrage; by now, Kuhn had no unrealistic expectations of the artillery.[3] His order specified no objectives or axes of attack, but everyone knew what they were. Nearly a mile ahead of the 157th Brigade, straddling the dividing line between the 79th and the 37th Division to its west, loomed the Bois de Beuge; to its right, at the same distance from the 158th, sat Nantillois. Other wooded hills lay behind those immediate targets—Bois 268 on the left, Bois 250 behind it, the Bois des Ogons on the right—before each of which lay a treeless valley, easily observed by the German machine guns, which the men would have to cross. Tenney Ross ordered Irwin's artillery to shell the woods in the hope of disrupting the German machine guns, but it was too early for the infantry to worry about those somewhat distant objectives.

At 2:30 a.m. an officer came to the headquarters of the 316th with verbal orders to relieve the 313th and lead the attack. Colonel Charles and his staff immediately went forward to the top of Montfaucon hill, where amid the ruins of the church he gave his instructions to his battalion commanders. German artillery fell on the American lines, sending Charles's staff scampering back down the hill; but at 7:00 a.m. sharp the regiment attacked in line with the 315th to its right, 1st and 3rd Battalions in the lead. Across their path lay an unwooded valley that dipped and rose to the Bois de Beuge. As they crossed, the regiment was shredded by fire from machine guns, trench mortars, and Austrian 88mm guns from the Bois de Beuge and

Bois 268. Captain L.E. Knowlton, commanding the Machine Gun Company, described the regiment's first taste of front-line combat: "Just as the battalions had deployed the Boche came to life. Then for the first time our men saw comrades fall; for a space of perhaps twenty minutes the greater part lay crouched in shell holes, terrified and dazed, uncertain whether to go forward or back."[4] Cries for first aid filled the air from those wounded who could do more than moan. Major John Baird Atwood, commander of the 3rd Battalion, sent a runner to regimental headquarters with the message: "Being fired at point blank by field pieces. For God's sake get artillery or we'll be annihilated." But the phone lines were dead—no one could get through to the artillery for two critical hours.[5] Atwood halted the attack to await machine guns or artillery that could destroy the obstacles; but he was peremptorily ordered to advance without waiting.[6]

Despite their losses, the 316th continued to crawl forward, assisted by three one-pounder mobile guns that disposed of several machine gun positions. At a critical moment, a corporal in Company C led a badly depleted platoon around the flank of a machine gun post and took it from the rear. At 8:20 a.m. the artillery that Major Atwood had requested landed in the Bois de Beuge, inflicting heavy losses on the Germans and forcing them to abandon many of their guns and much of their ammunition. This cleared the way for the advance into the Bois de Beuge. At 8:51 a.m. Atwood sent a message, "Our troops now entering southern edge of Bois de Beuge"; nine minutes later he was dead.[7] Captain John Somers took command and sent a message to Charles that 3rd Battalion was badly disorganized. Virtually every company in the two lead battalions had officers killed or wounded. Company L lost all its officers; three others lost their company commanders. At 10:15 a.m. Charles reported to the Division PC that he had lost 17 officers and 250 men "so far."[8] In reply, Kuhn informed him that he was sending a company of large tanks to help capture the Bois de Beuge. But by the time Charles got the message the Bois was in American hands and the 316th was beyond it, crossing yet another open vale on its way to Bois 268.

It was obvious by now that the enemy had received major reinforcements. New German regiments appeared in the line, and the volume of artillery fire greatly increased. The Germans had placed their artillery under central control, allowing them quickly to concentrate large volumes of fire on any part of the front. Visibility improved to the point that German aircraft and balloons could observe the American positions. More than 60 batteries were firing at First Army, mainly from the high ground to the north of Montfaucon and from the Heights of the Meuse, which enfiladed the American lines from the east. Heavy shells fell on the attacking divisions' flanks and rear, on occupied towns, woods, and camps, and on traffic stuck on the roads. At noon Kuhn sent a plea to V Corps:

> Hostile artillery fire upon our troops seems to be increased. Believed to come from positions in Bois de Cunel, Bois des Ogons, and Bois de Fays, which are also infested with machine guns. If heavy gun fire can be regulated by balloon or airplane so as not to fire on advancing troops, request heaviest artillery concentration possible be placed on known artillery positions, but generally on above named three woods ... Our observation balloon at Malancourt shot down about one hour ago ... My people are straining every effort to put good wire through to you. Deem it essential that Corps co-operate in every possible way.[9]

For once, the 79th could provide good artillery direction; the post in the "château" atop Montfaucon was able to keep continuous observation to the north, despite German shelling. This was fortunate, because the sole tethered balloon belonging to the 6th Balloon Company was shot down at 9:45 that morning. Aerial observation was no help; apart from the weather, the air over the battlefield was dominated by the Germans, who had as many as 20 planes at a time in the sky, strafing the infantry, bombing trucks on the roads, shooting down balloons, and spotting for their own artillery. (By now the soldiers had learned that enemy planes overhead meant that accurate shell fire would quickly follow.) But although the 79th had an unobstructed view for many miles to the north, and although the artillery of the 79th had been reinforced that morning by two French and three American batteries, the requested bombardment apparently never materialized. The division's operations report for September 28 does not mention artillery support, except for the opening barrage, and field messages make it clear that enemy fire was not neutralized all day.[*]

The new direction of German fire caused many Americans to believe they were being shelled by their own artillery. At 2:00 p.m. a garbled radio

---

[*] Army and corps artillery did fire intense barrages on the line Fléville–Romagne-sous-Montfaucon. But that line was nearly two miles beyond the front and several miles south of the German artillery positions, so little damage was done. (Lanza, "The End of the Battle of Montfaucon," p. 356.)

message arrived at Kuhn's headquarters from an unknown source begging the American guns to stop shelling their own troops in the Bois de Beuge.[*] In fact, it was enemy fire that was landing on the 316th, directed by a distant balloon. Nevertheless, at 2:30 p.m. Ross sent a message to V Corps, "Stop all artillery fire south of horizontal line 83.0. Our troops approaching that line. Have aeroplane observe and report to you the positions of our troops."[10] The designated line ran east–west north of Bois 268 but south of the Bois de Cunel. The men of the 79th were actually more than a mile south of it. They would sorely miss the guns of V Corps.

One of the first units to advance against Bois 268 was the 1st Platoon of Company G. When it was about halfway across the valley several machine guns opened up with heavy fire and some of the men volunteered to take them out. One of these, Private Harry Wagner, crawled for about 20 yards carrying a pistol and two hand grenades. Creeping up on one of the nests, he saw three Germans; he threw a grenade, killing two of them. The third threw up his hands and called "*Kamerad.*" Wagner made the survivor carry the machine gun and drove him to the rear. A French officer, an adviser with the 316th, saw the action and reported it. A few days later, recovering from a gas attack, Wagner was awarded the Croix de Guerre.[11]

As the infantry of the 316th approached Bois 268, its supporting machine guns finally caught up with them for the first time since the initial attack three days earlier. Now the rolling character of the countryside favored the Americans, who from their hilltop positions in the Bois de Beuge had a clear view of the German lines. Captain L.E. Knowlton, commanding the 316th's Machine Gun Company, wrote after the war:

Then came my machine-gunners' turn. For three days they had carried their heavy burdens, striving to keep up with the fast-travelling and more lightly-burdened riflemen with never a chance to get back at the Boches, who were picking them off in ever increasing numbers. Suddenly about one thousand yards away along the foot of the hills about Romagne a battalion of Germans appeared in the open, and moved toward us in rather close lines—the heaven-sent machine-gun target! We opened up on them until they began

---

[*] The body of the message, as transcribed by Kuhn's radio operator, read, "Heavy – (F – R – I E N D L Y) – Artillery – on our – right – are – shelling – BOIS – (null) They E – B – E Tru G – E – Have – it – stopped – we – do not need – it." One can almost hear the shells landing in the background. ("79th Division Field Messages," 1918, RG 120, 79th Division, Boxes 4–5, 32.16, NARA, sent 2:00 p.m.)

to scatter and seek cover and then ceased firing, hoarding our scanty supply of ammunition.[12]

They were joined by Company C of the 312th Machine Gun Battalion, which by 1:30 p.m. had emplaced its three platoons facing Bois 268. The 2nd Platoon opened fire on machine gun positions behind a railroad line ahead of them; this attracted return fire that killed the battalion sergeant major and two privates and wounded a lieutenant. But one of the men repaired a shrapnel-damaged German machine gun under fire and sprayed the German gunners, who withdrew, leaving one heavy and three light machine guns plus assorted rifles and equipment. The 2nd Platoon and the Machine Gun Company of the 316th continued to fire on groups of Germans at a range of about one kilometer, inflicting casualties, scattering the survivors, and preventing them from establishing a defensive line. By dark they had run out of ammunition and dug in.

Still not knowing to which of the reorganized brigades they were now assigned, the three companies of the French 14th Light Tank Battalion spent most of the day immobile. Finally, Captain Toutain, commander of one of the tank companies, unable to find Colonel Charles and not wanting to waste any more time, moved his platoons toward and beyond the Bois de Beuge. Linking up with the forward elements of the 316th, two of his platoons attacked Bois 268 from the east while the third attacked it from the west. At first, reported Major Guillot, the battalion commander, the American infantry followed; but it soon lost contact with the tanks. Twice the tank platoon leaders tried to get the infantry to advance. Toutain's company lost two tanks in the action.[13] By nightfall, the tanks were back at their assembly point in the Bois de Beuge.

In the late morning General Kuhn, having received no reports from Colonel Charles, was becoming concerned about the 316th and asked Colonel Oury to send an officer from 158th Brigade headquarters to locate the regiment and report back. Oury assigned the task to Lieutenant Clifton Lisle, who found Charles's PC just north of Montfaucon hill. He sent a message to Kuhn, "Found Col. Charles at 11H15. He was then moving forward. He was at point 11.4–78.8. At that time they were under heavy shrapnel fire."[14] Lisle remained with Charles as the 316th advanced; about 3:15 p.m. he informed Oury that the front companies of the 316th had reached the southern edge of Bois 268 and that three of the large

St Chamond tanks had entered the wood. He added, "Artillery support throughout the day entirely inadequate. Lack of phone wire has reduced communication to runners. Troops now without food or water."[15] (For his exploit in crossing the battlefield under fire, finding the 316th, and reporting back, Lisle was later awarded the Silver Star.) In fact, elements of the regiment had advanced even further than Lisle knew. Captain Somers's 3rd Battalion had made it to the north edge of Bois 268 and one platoon of Company G had passed through that wood entirely, crossed the slope beyond, and entered Bois 250, where it dug in. By mid-afternoon most of the 316th was in Bois 268 and Charles took the opportunity to reorganize. It was clear that German artillery fire would allow no further advance that day, so the colonel ordered the 316th to bivouac. He sent a runner forward to the platoon that had reached Bois 250, telling them to fall back to join the regiment after dark. Efforts were made to get food up to the men, but the only result was the death of a lieutenant in the supply train. Charles's advance on the 28th had left four officers and 43 men dead.[16]

At least the dead had no more worries; the ordeal of the wounded continued. A historian of the 79th described their plight:

> The entire back area was so thoroughly shelled, behind the 313th, 316th and 315th regiments that even the proper medical attention could not be given the men. The nearest field hospitals were unable to advance within several miles of the fighting line and stretcher-bearers carried the more desperately hurt through shell fire which frequently further injured the original sufferer and struck the carriers as well. Other men, less severely wounded, hobbled or crawled back, yard after yard, kilometer after kilometer, until they came at last to the dressing stations.[17]

Private Schellberg of the 313th Infantry's Machine Gun Company wrote to his brother:

> Every place you went you heard the wounded calling for firstaid, it was awful. A Frenchman told some of us that as long as he was at war thats the worst he has seen. We lost two Leuts and a hole lot of other men in this battle. We lost three carts and mules and one driver was killed and two wounded. One of the drivers had his horse shot and he kept on going with the rope he was leading him with thinking he still had his horse. He was wounded in the leg.[18]

Nor were doctors immune to losses from enemy fire. Dr Hanson wrote in his memoirs:

> After a trip up to the battalion dressing station and an ambulance dressing station in Montfaucon I returned to the hospital to get some grub. Shortly afterwards two of my doctor friends came limping in gassed, clothes torn and scared, saying that the Boche had shelled the battalion station I had just left and killed two of my friends, a doctor and a dentist, and a number of patients. I had barely made them a little more comfortable when I got word that the ambulance station in Montfaucon was shelled too. Here I lost several friends, enlisted men in the ambulance company.[19]

During the day the rain had been intermittent but at night the skies opened up, washing the field in torrents, turning the ground into a muddy morass, and inflicting further suffering on the men. They continued to be hampered by their gas masks, which they were afraid to take off. At least the shelling stopped, so stretcher-bearers were able to evacuate more of the wounded to field hospitals. By the end of the day, the advanced dressing stations had passed over 2,000 casualties to the rear—sick, wounded, and gassed. The round trip from the hospital just over a mile west of Avocourt was 42 hours. Frequently light, horse-drawn ambulances, less road-bound than the motorized ones, would be used to relieve the pressure.

As ever, the roads were a bottleneck not only for the wounded but for artillery, supplies, and ammunition needed at the front. The 304th Engineers reported that it spent the 28th maintaining the section from Avocourt through Malancourt, which was "passable," and by 9:00 p.m. the stretch from Malancourt to Montfaucon was in "fair condition."[20] Colonel W.T. Hannum, an officer on the AEF General Staff returning from a visit to the 4th Division, saw things differently:

> The road from Malancourt to Avocourt was exceptionally poor. It was there that most of the delay in troop movement and traffic was experienced. The ground was very much disturbed by previous shell fire. The old road was, in spaces, completely destroyed. Foundation of new road was very poor. The troops engaged in preparing the road were apparently very poorly handled and were not accomplishing much of a permanent or even semi-permanent value.[21]

It took him six and a half hours to travel 13 miles. It did not help that French troops using the V Corps roads had not been informed of the direction of travel and frequently blocked traffic by going the wrong way.[22] By the end of the day the 304th Supply Train was able to get one truck convoy past Malancourt to the supply trains of the regiments and machine gun battalions, but the latter were still mired below Montfaucon, and even carrying parties couldn't get food through to the front lines. The motorized ammunition convoy was similarly stuck, but the horse-drawn section was able to deliver 900,000 rounds of .30-caliber ammunition despite being shelled. This was the first ammunition resupply received by the regiments since the jumpoff on the 26th. But neither food nor ambulances could reach the front.

While Nicholson and his 157th Brigade assaulted on the left, Oury's 158th was to go into action on the right. But by 2:00 a.m. on the morning of the attack, Oury had received no orders from Kuhn, so he sent his adjutant to division headquarters to pick up Field Order No. 8. It said that the 315th Infantry under Colonel Knowles, hitherto in support, was to lead the attack on Nantillois with the 314th following at 1,000 meters. H-hour was set for 7:00 a.m. At 5:30 a.m. Knowles sent a message to the headquarters of the 157th Brigade next door, asking for tanks to assist his 1st Battalion, as they had none to counter the machine gun nests in front of him. At 7:00 a.m. he dispatched a runner to Kuhn's PC with the request:

> Have artillery pound 10.2–80.2, 13.1–80.5, 12.6–81.5 and line 10.0–82.3 to 11.0–82.6. These hostile positions form a cup into which we cannot advance without ruinous losses. Some guns to be directed on Nantillois. The artillery must get busy fast if they are to assist infantry ... Please rush artillery fire.[23]

The German positions formed a rough semicircle centered on Nantillois with a radius of half a mile to a mile—easy range for their guns. The 158th Brigade had been ordered to attack into a heavily defended cul-de-sac. The runner did not reach Kuhn's PC until nine hours later.

By H-hour the tanks had not arrived, and only four batteries of 75s were in position to fire. The opening bombardment was, in the words of Kuhn himself, "feeble"—so feeble that the 315th Infantry didn't know it was happening because they couldn't hear it above the din of the German shells.[24] Knowles sent an urgent message back to Kuhn asking for more artillery on the German lines and on Nantillois. But by 7:30 a.m. he realized that no support would be coming, so he ordered the 315th forward.

The 1st Battalion was to encircle the town from the west while the 3rd Battalion was to attack from the south. Things went well for the first couple of hundred yards, despite strafing from German aircraft and enfilading artillery fire. But as the leading companies climbed to the top of a rise below the town, machine guns and riflemen opened up from the Bois de Beuge to the west and the Bois de Septsarges to the east, accompanied by heavy artillery. Major Fred Patterson, commanding the 1st Battalion, sent a desperate message to Colonel Oury:

> We cannot get out of this pocket. Any cut we take covered by MG. We find no troops on left. They should be there to skirt Bois du Boyce [sic—may mean "Beuge"]. Tanks are not with us. First Aid badly needed. Must have artillery.[25]

A coordinated advance was now impossible; progress could be made only by small groups making brief rushes, then taking cover. Once again, officers and men fell dead and wounded. Patterson himself was badly wounded in the leg, but refused to give up command until that night. Despite everything, the leading companies reached what was left of Nantillois by 10:50 a.m., capturing six 77mm guns. Each of the three companies that took the town had lost one-third of its men, and the other companies suffered almost as much. The support companies were left to mop up the machine guns and snipers that had been bypassed in the rush while the main body continued on, reaching Hill 274 about half a mile to the north at 1:00 p.m. Sergeant Davies of Company B wrote in his diary:

> We are getting some artillery support now. The German artillery is very active guided by their planes which are constantly over us, and they seem to be able to place their shells wherever we happen to be. We move up the road to our left and then up the hill. The Germans seem to have machine guns all over this hill. With D Co. on our right and L Co. of the 3rd battalion on our left we work our way to the top of the hill. We lost quite a few men there.[26]

At the top of the hill, Knowles called a halt to reorganize. He had already sent a message to Oury, who at 11:25 a.m. dispatched a runner to Kuhn announcing the fall of Nantillois. Half a mile ahead of them loomed the Bois des Ogons.

The 1st and 3rd Battalions were now joined on Hill 274 by the French tanks, which had come up behind the attacking infantry. The single artillery battery accompanying the 315th was ordered to lay down a half-hour bombardment on the Bois des Ogons and the Madeleine Farm, a fortified position to its west. But before the attack could get properly going, German field pieces in the Bois des Ogons and heavier guns east of the Meuse plastered the landscape with high explosive shells. Sergeant Davies continued in his diary:

> Just ahead of us about 700 yards is another hill crowned by a dense wood. The Germans seem to be preparing for a counter attack here. They are pouring a heavy machine gun and rifle fire on us from there. Major Patterson ordered our company to form in line of skirmishers and go over after them. We formed our line 1st and 2nd platoon in front and the 4th platoon in support. A shell landed just in front of where I was laying killing Buckwald and wounding Lieut. Conahan and another officer. I was thrown about 10 feet but fortunately was not injured. Lieut. Bagans jumped out in front of the company and led us on the run for the woods. How any of us got there is more than I can tell. Bullets just pelted around us like hail. The bottom of my rain slicker was cut to ribbons. With L and D Companies we managed to get to the edge of the woods. We had to fight for every inch of ground now.[27]

Two of the huge St Chamond tanks and two of the Renaults were almost immediately destroyed. The rest of the tanks went ahead of the two attacking battalions, getting as far as the southern edge of the wood. At that point, the machine gun and artillery fire became too much to withstand and the battalions withdrew back to Hill 274. Sergeant Davies described the retreat:

> The woods were full of machine guns and snipers and several of our men got hit. We were making good progress when we were ordered out of the woods. Word had been received that the Germans were going to set the woods on fire, so we had to give it up. Lieut. Bagans actually cried when we had to evacuate, he said it had cost so much to take the woods, it seemed a crime to give them up now.[28]

Major Richard, the French tank battalion commander, had a somewhat different view of the action. As he wrote in his report, one platoon of his 344th Company destroyed centers of resistance in the Bois des Ogons while another demolished Madeleine Farm along with a large number of machine guns and field pieces. Nevertheless, because the infantry failed to follow, his tanks had to retire. Tired of taking positions and then not having the infantry occupy them (as he saw it), he sent the following order to his company commanders with translated copies to the commanders of the 314th and 315th Infantry Regiments:

> The encounters of September 27th distinctly show that the American Infantry follows the tanks only at a great distance, and does not join them, when the latter have reached the objective. Thus, Nantillois, carried off by the 343d Co, has not been occupied by the American troops, which remained 1500 ms. behind. The Company Commanders will cause explanations to be made to the Regimental commanders to whom they are attached that the help should be a reciprocal one and that the regulations applying to the Artillery of Assault [i.e., tanks] prescribes that the Infantry should take as honor to go where the tanks go. Forgetting of this rule may have unfortunate consequences for tank platoons working isolately [sic]. Consequently, the Battalion Commander orders formally not to get ahead of the American Infantry more than of 200 ms., and if it does not follow any further, to take positions behind the infantry lines. [Translation in the original].[29]

It helped, up to a point; in his report Major Richard acknowledged that the infantry kept within 200 meters of his tanks. But they still failed to hold the positions the tanks had overrun, forcing the armor to withdraw.

At 2:36 p.m. Oury sent a message to Kuhn's PC reporting his situation:

> Have been stopped by heavy H.E. fire & MGs due to greenness of troops rather than the danger involved ... Due to casualties & exhaustion 314, my Cos are much reduced in strength. All stragglers collected this A.M. & returned to commands. I am moving with the 314th Inf. well around Montfaucon to come in on the flank of our sector across the ridge, hoping to get in rear of MGs & Inf. 15 tanks cover our next advance. I'm waiting for them to get in position, hence delay. Request all possible Artillery support on objectives already indicated to Artillery liaison officers. Men are suffering due to lack of water none having been gotten since start of advance.[30]

A little over an hour later Colonel Knowles sent Kuhn a second message giving sobering details. Men were deserting their positions in search of food and water. Soldiers from the other regiments had mixed in with his own, disorganizing his command. Many officers were dead or wounded; the medical officers were wholly exhausted. The supply train could not get through because of the shelling. The machine guns were low on ammunition.

"Wounded with practically no help but 1st Aid and many who could be saved are dying because of lack of attention and exposure."[31]

By now the 2nd Battalion had reached Hill 274; with Knowles's entire regiment in one place, Oury had no choice but to try again. He sent the 315th against the Madeleine Farm, a fortified German position just west of the Bois des Ogons whose heavy defenses—still effective, despite Major Richard's claim—belied its charming name. The attack was supported by four small and two large French tanks, a single battery of artillery, and one company of the 312th Machine Gun Battalion, which fired a barrage overhead. At 4:00 p.m. the 315th moved forward but once again ran into the fire of field guns from the Madeleine Farm, machine guns from the Bois des Ogons, and heavy artillery from the Heights of the Meuse, the last being accurately directed by a tethered balloon over Cote Lemont three miles to the east. As Kuhn watched from the summit of Montfaucon, the two St Chamonds blew up and three of the light Renaults, aflame and with their drivers wounded, went to the rear.[32] Others were disabled even though not set afire; their crews abandoned the inert hulks and hurried rearwards. Lieutenant Miller Johnson of Company K stopped a fleeing French soldier. "What's the matter with the tanks?" he demanded. "Too much Boche artillery," answered the Frenchman, barely stopping in his retreat. "American no good, damn fool. American no give damn for artillery. Big damn fool."[33]

Eventually, amid heavy losses, the 1st and 3rd Battalions reached the Bois des Ogons; but it was obvious that they could not hold it under the heavy German bombardment, especially since no counterbattery fire was forthcoming from the American guns despite Oury's request. As Kuhn later wrote, "Again the leading elements reached the edge of the woods and again they melted away under the whirlwind of fire."[34] For a second time the men withdrew to the southern slope of Hill 274 to reorganize for another advance.[*] Knowles sent a plea to Kuhn's PC: "Men of 315th Inf. must have food. Too weak for further advance without food."[35] But the supply trains were still stuck in the traffic jam below Montfaucon.

---

[*] The historian of the German 147th Infantry Regiment wrote that the withdrawal of the Americans from the Bois des Ogons resulted from a counterattack that caught the Americans in the flank and inflicted great loss, including four tanks that were left behind. (Heinrich Siebert, *Geschichte des Infanterie-Regiments Generalfeldmarschall von Hindenburg (2. Masurisches) Nr. 147*, Erinnerungsblätter Deutscher Regimenter (Berlin: Gerhard Stalling, 1927), p. 281.)

Once again Knowles reorganized his regiment and at 6:00 p.m., still without artillery support, the 315th lunged for a third time into the valley separating it from the Madeleine Farm and the Bois des Ogons. This time Sergeant Davies's 1st Battalion penetrated several hundred yards into the wood, using their grenades to capture a collection of wooden shacks. Upon exploration, these proved to be a command post including an artillery plotting room, where the 315th found maps and other papers. One hundred yards further into the wood was a building with a Red Cross flag, which the men took to be a hospital. Lieutenant Bagans, who was leading the advance of Davies's Company B, wanted to explore the building, but changed his mind. That was a good thing; the flag was a disguise, and the building was a fortified German machine gun position.[36] Word came that the Germans were about to launch a counterattack, and a heavy bombardment emphasized the point. Yet again the 315th was ordered back to Hill 274. At some point during the day General Hoefer of the 117th Infantry Division ordered the 5th Storm Battalion, then attached to his command, to take Hill 274. The 5th was Captain Willy Rohr's outfit, the original assault battalion—and now one of the only remaining ones—trained and experienced in infiltration and combined-arms tactics.[*] Fortunately for the men of the 315th, Hoefer canceled the order and held the 5th in the Bois de Cunel to serve as local support.[37]

In the words of the division historian, "The night of September 28–29, on the front lines, was one of horror."[38] The steady rain turned the earth to bottomless mud; the shell holes were viscous ponds. Everyone was soaked to the skin. The blackness was complete. German machine guns raked the ground and heavy artillery blanketed the area with shrapnel and high explosive. For the 315th, a small bit of refuge could be found on the reverse slope of Hill 274, which the men had taken to calling "Suicide Hill"; to their west, the 316th sheltered behind the stumps of Bois 268. But these offered no relief from the plunging howitzer shells or from the groans of the wounded, many of whom still lay exposed on the field in front. Still no food was forthcoming. Sergeant Davies of the 315th somehow found the will power to write in his diary:

---

[*] See Chapter 4.

We got back to the hill [274] again under heavy shell fire and was ordered to dig in for the night. Our dead all over the hill. We have lost pretty heavy in this scrap. Saw Baimbridge carried off wounded. Heard Charlie Lynn was killed. I hope to God it is not true. It would be a great loss to me. As darkness comes on it starts to rain. I'm all in. Hungry and thirsty, I haven't eaten since yesterday morning. About 10 P.M. the Germans started to shell our position, God it was awful. Saw a man blown to pieces just below where Monty and I were lying. We decided to move off the hill. Monty and I and a few others got down near the base of the hill when a shell landed right among us killing Cook and taking Richardson's leg off at the knee I was stunned for a few minutes and Monty dragged me over to a big shell hole, where he and Mike Campbell and I spent the rest of the night. We were in mud up to our waists, but it looked like the safest place around here. I am sick and disgusted with this life. It seems to me that the men who are killed are better off. This is simply a living death, Hell can hold no terrors for me after this. We are not men any more, just savage beasts.[39]

The men spent the night under a cold, steady rain in shell holes filled with mud, sheltered only by raincoats and overcoats. Exhausted as they were, sleep overcame discomfort and hunger. "But in the morning one felt far worse than after a night of intoxication. Deadened nerves, stiff muscles and rheumatism produce a state of mind dangerous to a soldier—the attitude of caring little what happens to him next."[40] The officers of the 147th Field Artillery, which by now had come up about half a mile behind the infantry, were aware of the exhausted state of the attacking regiments and figured they were incapable of defending against a nighttime counterattack. So they ordered their machine guns forward and had the gunners stand guard all night with their pistols.[*]

---

[*] The night was dangerous not only at the front. The frequent failure of the support companies to mop up after the attackers left many Germans behind the American lines. Leroy Haile, an enlisted man in the 304th Engineers, gave this account of his attempt to find a place to sleep that night: "I found a dugout and as usual I called down in French and in German to see if anyone was there. I got no answer and started down. It was quite dark and as my candle was very short, I wanted to save it for the exploration of the interior. I got to the bottom of the steps and suddenly had the sensation of a bee sting in my left leg. I suddenly realized there was a person immediately in front of me and automatically started to shoot; I had an automatic ready in my hand. I shot four times and as the case with the automatic, it tends to rear up. I heard no sound from the man in front of me, the concussion was terrific in the small room and I felt something running down my left side of my face. I later found

The divisions on either side of the 79th did not do much better that day. Farnsworth's 37th Division, to the west, had its 74th Brigade on the left and its 73rd Brigade on the right. The 74th began the day's attack starting from a line a bit more than half a mile south of the Bois Emont; the 73rd, to its right, was about the same distance south of the Bois de Beuge. At 7:00 a.m. or a little after, each brigade attacked the wood in front of it. By then the accompanying artillery had reached the front line but their ammunition had not, so they were unable to lay down a preparatory barrage. The two brigades entered the Bois Emont and the Bois de Beuge respectively at 7:35 a.m. Three hours later the 74th had taken Cierges and sent a company 500 yards further to the northwest; the 73rd had passed through the Bois de Beuge to just south of the Cierges–Nantillois road. At this point the two brigades fell under heavy German fire from the three woods that the 79th had failed so far to take: the Bois de Fays, Bois des Ogons, and Bois de Cunel. The division, having only its accompanying guns, was unable to respond effectively. Once again the support elements crowded the advancing units and caused congestion at the front, increasing casualties and making the men yet more exhausted and harder to supply. Compounding their misery, infantry of the German 150th Regiment counterattacked, supported by machine guns and artillery firing high explosive and gas. On the right, the 73rd Brigade held the attackers; on the left, however, the 74th was pushed back through the Bois Emont and another 500 yards south, erasing their gains for the day. But the Germans failed to occupy the Bois in strength, and at 5:25 p.m. the 74th was able to advance back into the wood, occupying its southern two-thirds. By nightfall the division's line ran through the top of the Bois Emont, skirted Cierges half a mile to its south and southeast, then ran northeast to link up with the front of the 79th Division at the northern edge of Bois 268. Altogether it had advanced one and a half miles for the day.[41] At 7:20 p.m. General Farnsworth sent a message to his brigade commanders: "Have notified Corps Commander that we cannot advance and am insisting that the division be relieved

it to be blood as I had ruptured my eardrum. I fished out my candle and when I saw what I had done it was awful. The German had lunged at me, trying for the stomach but sticking my left leg with his bayonet. When I shot him, the bayonet came out and fortunately it had gone in my leg only a short distance. My shots had almost cut the man in half." (LeRoy Yellott Haile, "A Civilian Goes to War," n.d., World War I Survey, Box: 79th Division-Trains; Folder: Haile, Leroy Y, 304th Engineer, 79th Division, AHEC, pp. 54–55.)

immediately. It will probably be impracticable to expect the relief before tomorrow morning."[42]

To the right of the 79th the 4th Division under General Hines also attacked at 7:00 a.m. This time they had good artillery support which, by 10:00 a.m., was able to suppress the fire from the German guns enough to allow the infantry to advance relatively unhindered. In the division's left sector the 39th Infantry Regiment attacked from its line on Hill 295 past Hill 266 toward the Bois des Ogons, about one and a half miles away. Reaching the railroad line south of Nantillois around noon, it made contact with the 315th Infantry Regiment. Now, unlike two days earlier, there were no qualms in the 4th about violating divisional boundaries. A company from the 39th moved into the sector of the 79th and joined up with a company of the 315th Regiment. This impromptu battalion attacked the town, pushing the enemy out and forcing them to withdraw as far as the Bois de Fays. The two companies then advanced together through Nantillois to Hill 274 where the battalions of the 39th reorganized and moved back into their own sector. Resuming its advance, the regiment got as far as the Bois de Fays a mile further on before it was stopped by machine gun fire; among the wounded was Colonel Bolles, the regimental commander. But the 79th had gotten stuck on Hill 274; this uncovered the left flank of the 4th, which came under heavy machine gun fire from the west as well as bombardment from the Heights of the Meuse. At 5:00 p.m. General Bullard, commanding the III Corps to which the 4th belonged, sent a stiff message to Kuhn:

> Your message received stating that your 79th Division front troops were entering Organ [sic] Woods and Bois de Fay N. of Nantillois. Since that time the left flank of the 4th div. was at Cunel; was counter attacked and driven into the Bois de Fay to the S. edge; so reported. I think that the counter attack was not against my left flank of the advance line, but against the left flank of my reserve.[43]

In fact, the 4th had gotten nowhere close to Cunel, which was over half a mile beyond the Bois de Fays. Nor do the records of the division mention a counterattack against its left flank at that time. But the intent was clear. Bullard was telling Kuhn, your delay in advancing is uncovering the flank not only of my front line but also of my reserve line. Eventually the 39th Infantry was ordered to withdraw to a ridge below the Nantillois–Brieulles road, where it spent the night. To its right, the 47th Infantry quickly penetrated the Bois de Brieulles, stopping at its northern edge. Capturing an ordnance dump, the regiment turned the munitions against the retreating Germans. That night the 7th Brigade, to which the 39th and 47th Regiments both belonged, was relieved by the 8th. It had advanced 11 miles, losing over 100 dead and over 500 wounded. It captured almost 2,000 prisoners, 30 guns, and many machine guns, *Minenwerfer*, and trench mortars.[44]

The advance up the Barrois plateau by the American 79th, 37th, and 4th Divisions might have been thwarted for the day, but the Germans were feeling the pressure. By noon on the 28th the Germans were in retreat. The battered 117th Infantry Division had withdrawn from Nantillois to the Bois des Ogons; the 5th Bavarian Reserve Division and the left flank of the 7th Reserve Division drew back to the south edge of the Bois de Brieulles. Orders came down from Fifth Army to withdraw entirely the 117th and the 7th Reserve Division, which had held the line since the 26th, "[a]s soon as the situation permits."[45] But there was to be no general retreat; on the contrary, Fifth Army decided to put up a stiff resistance based on artillery:

> The situation requires that the artillery on both banks of the Meuse River be under one control. Effective 28 September, General M[arwitz] will assume command of all this artillery under direct orders of the Army ... The period, while the enemy has little artillery and munitions available in face of our Meuse West Group (SSI Corps), is to be profitably employed by our artillery. Hostile batteries will be counter-batteried; hostile camps and dug-outs will be gassed. Interdiction fire will be laid on Bois d'Avocourt–Malancourt–Montfaucon roads; Bethincourt; Cuisy and Septsarges."[46]

Artillery was especially to be used to stop infantry attacks. To replace the withdrawn units, the 115th Infantry Division moved up to the Bois des Ogons, joining the (German) 37th, which was already there. The 115th was rated third class by American intelligence and had taken heavy losses in the Aisne–Marne campaign back in July; but it had had two months' rest and was the best formation available. Coming up behind them were elements of the 236th Division and the 45th Reserve Division. There was no time to maintain divisional integrity; as fast as individual regiments and even battalions reached the battlefield, they were thrown into the line wherever it needed reinforcement or wherever a gap had appeared.[47]

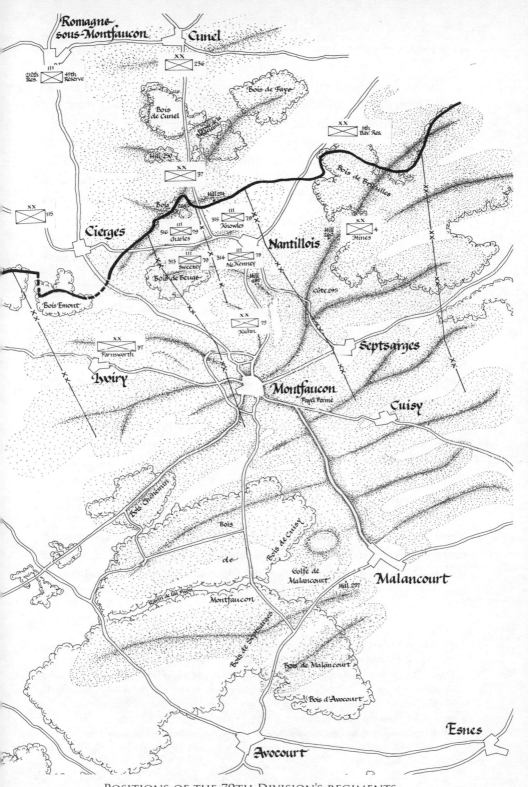

POSITIONS OF THE 79TH DIVISION'S REGIMENTS,
NIGHT OF SEPTEMBER 28

The 117th, although slated for withdrawal, was literally not yet out of the woods. With the 151st Infantry Regiment (of the German 37th Division) on its right, the division held the southeast edge of the Bois de Beuge on the morning of the 28th. A massive American attack at 10:00 a.m. caused the men of the 151st to break and run. (This is almost certainly the attack of the 316th Infantry Regiment in which Major Atwood was killed.) In the words of the historian of the 117th, "The men of the 151st Regiment fled in groups and could not be restrained by the staff of the neighboring 450th Regiment. The men made it clear that their officers were no longer there, so they would not remain either."[*48] The 1st Battalion of the 450th was thus exposed to its right and had to withdraw eastward. The battalion commander, Captain Kühne, was evacuated with wounds that later proved fatal; Reserve Lieutenant Hartmann, who took over the battalion, tried to establish a defensive line facing west. But the battalion was almost completely surrounded; those who escaped joined the fighting in the sector of the 5th Bavarian Reserve Division behind Nantillois. Lieutenant Hartmann was seen no more.[49]

The Americans continued to advance.[†] Battalion Wehber withdrew to the eastern portion of the Bois des Ogons north of Nantillois. The 151st Regiment having disappeared, the battalion had no one on their right flank, so they placed two machine guns facing westward just as the Americans emerged from a small wood. The combined fire of Battalion Wehber and the machine guns, with help from the four guns of a light artillery battery that showed up at the right moment, pushed them back. The 450th continued to retreat, however, having no one on their right and only tenuous contact with the 11th Grenadiers on their left. The commander of the 450th ordered Wehber to move laterally to his right in order to cover the entire southern edge of the Bois des Ogons, but it quickly became clear that this was impossible; the Americans were too close to risk a flank

---

[*] According to the history of the 151st Infantry Regiment, it was the 450th that retreated first, exposing the 151st to flanking machine gun fire. The situation was saved by two battalions from the 115th Division which ran up and repelled the American advance. (Heinrich Plickert, *Das 2. Ermländischen Infanterie-Regiment Nr. 151 im Weltkriege*, Truppenteile des ehemaligen Preussischen Kontingents (Berlin: Gerhard Stalling, 1929), p. 304.) The two accounts differ even as to which regiment was on the left and which was on the right.

[†] The German historian does not identify the American units; but based on locations and times, they were the 79th Division's 316th Infantry Regiment on the east and the 145th Infantry Regiment of the 37th Division on the west.

movement. With the 11th Grenadiers retreating and the Bois des Ogons under German artillery fire, Wehber decided to pull back half a mile to the southern edge of the Bois de Cunel. There his battalion renewed contact with the Grenadiers on the left, now at the Madeleine Farm, and the 157th Infantry Regiment on the right. The retreat was finally stopped by the newly arrived 115th Division, which counterattacked against the American 37th, pushing it out of Cierges and back to the Bois Emont, where it spent the night.[50]

The Germans hardly had a monopoly on confusion. On the night of September 28 Pershing's First Army had only a hazy idea of where the enemy actually was. The day's Summary of Intelligence for V Corps read, "Enemy Front Line: For the most part, undetermined at the end of the day by any of our sources of information."[51] Clemenceau's Chief of Staff, General Jean-Henri Mordacq, visited Pershing that morning and later wrote:

> I could read clearly in his eyes that, at that moment, he realized his mistake. His soldiers were dying bravely, but they were not advancing, or very little, and their losses were heavy. All that great body of men which the American Army represented was literally struck with paralysis because 'the brain' didn't exist, because the generals and their staffs lacked experience. With enemies like the Germans, this kind of war couldn't be improvised.[52]

(General Mordacq's ability to read people's thoughts in their eyes was apparently remarkable.) None of this affected the orders Pershing issued for the next morning:

> 1. (a) The enemy is resisting on the heights of the Bois de Romagne and east of Romagne-sous-Montfaucon. This resistance consists mainly of artillery and machine-gun fire. Movements of convoys indicate a retirement to the north
>
> . . .
>
> 3. (A) The III, V and I Corps will advance within their zones of action as specified in Field Orders No. 20. without regard to objectives. The hour of attack will be designated by corps commanders but will not be later than 7 a.m., September 29.[53]

Although the advance was to proceed "without regard for objectives," V Corps' stated goal was to drive the Germans from the Bois de Gesnes on the Romagne Heights, two and a half miles north of the corps' line.[*] (As things turned out, the Bois de Gesnes would not be reached until October 10.) Once again the army artillery would not fire below a line roughly three miles ahead of the American troops. Colonel Lanza, chief of operations for First Army Artillery, was in the artillery's PC at 1:30 a.m. when two officers from the First Army Operations Section came in. The attacking divisions had lost over 5,000 men the day before from hostile shell fire alone, they said, and it was essential to give them more artillery support. "It was explained to these officers that the fighting was way south of the line within which the mass of the artillery was prohibited from firing by formal written orders, and that there were no targets beyond this line." Corps were authorized to request fire from the army guns, they were told, but they rarely did so.[54] As we have seen, of course, army gunners cheerfully disobeyed their no-fire orders whenever they got target information from the infantry. But even then, miscommunication prevented much of the army artillery from participating in the fight. Alden Brooks, the American officer assigned to the French 81st Heavy Artillery Regiment, found his unit unable to obtain information, unable to get into communication either with the divisions at the front or with First Army headquarters, and unable to convince the French general in command to fire without orders from above. Although assigned to support V Corps, the 16 high-powered 155mm guns of the 81st were silent for the entire five days of the first assault.[55]

The men of the 79th had more immediate concerns. Already lying in muddy shell holes to avoid German artillery, they were made even more miserable by the steady rain that resumed during the night. Divisional and corps artillery laid down fire on the next day's objectives, Bois des Ogons,

---

[*] Pershing maintained after the war that the French eventually adopted open warfare from the Americans; General Bach, who was a brigade commander in the 4th Division and, after the war, in close correspondence with Pershing, cites this "without regard to objectives" order as proof of American priority. (Pershing, *My Experiences*, vol. 2, p. 357; Bach, *Fourth Division*, vol. 368, pp. 166–67.) But three months earlier Pétain, in Directive No. 5 to his commanders, had specified, "To go far, it is necessary to aim from the start at distant objectives, without limiting, in advance and deliberately, the chances of success. One can also envision the possibility of advancing beyond the initial objectives that one has set, and, as a result, giving to large units general marching orders and extended zones of action far beyond those objectives." (Ministère de la Guerre, Service Historique, *AFGG*, Tome Vi, 2e Volume, Annexes – 3e Volume, pp. 451–54.)

the Madeleine Farm, the Bois de Cunel, and Cunel itself, but no target information was forthcoming either from the French 214th Aero Squadron or the 6th Balloon Company. As the locations of the German batteries were therefore unknown, the fire was ineffective and the enemy guns continued to plague the prostrate, sodden infantrymen. As daylight started to seep over the landscape, the volume of German fire increased. Not only did it pound the front line, it saturated the reserve regiments' positions and the road back to Malancourt. A tethered balloon gave the Germans almost continuous observation; Allied planes were rarely in sight. High explosive mixed with gas poured in from the Bois de Cunel, La Mamelle Trench to its rear, Cunel itself, the Madeleine Farm, and the Ville aux Bois Farm. As always, the worst of all were the heavy shells from Hill 378 to the east of the Meuse.

By the morning of the 29th the men were starving. On the previous day the supply train of the 314th had advanced too far and been shelled to its destruction; the soldiers would get only one meal in the five days of the Montfaucon attack. Horses, mindless of the falling shells, wandered about searching for any edible vegetation. Men rifled German bodies looking for any rations they might carry; many became casualties as they exposed themselves to search for food. The only water was in the shell holes, dangerous to drink because of dissolved gas. Sergeant Davies of the 315th described his hunger to his diary:

> I am so weak that I can hardly stand. None of us have had any food or water for days now. My throat and tongue feel like sandpaper. I have discarded my pack. I haven't the strength to carry it any further ... There are a number of hospital men here caring for our wounded and we beg some food. They divide what they have with us, its not much, just a small piece of canned beef, and some soggy crackers but it tastes like the finest food in the world.[56]

Faint from lack of sleep and food, chilled through from the incessant rainfall, their guns and equipment coated with rust, the men braced themselves for another advance against the hardening German opposition.

CHAPTER 14

Bois 250 and Madeleine Farm, September 29–30

Kuhn's Field Order No. 9 spelled out his arrangements for the advance on September 29. The infantry would attack at 7:00 a.m. On the left, the 316th Infantry under Colonel Charles would lead as before, its 1st Battalion (Major Parkin) to the west and its 3rd Battalion (Captain Somers) to the east; the 2nd Battalion (Captain Lukens) and the Machine Gun Company would follow in support. The immediate objective would be Bois 250, half a mile ahead. On the right, Charles's 315th would be in front, with its 2nd Battalion (Major Borden) to the west and its 3rd Battalion (Major Lloyd) to the east, supported by the 1st Battalion (Captain Noonan) and its own machine gun company supporting from behind. Facing it at a distance of half a mile were the Bois des Ogons and Madeleine Farm, filled with German artillery and machine guns. Between the two regiments would be Company C of the 312th Machine Gun Battalion. Four French tanks would accompany the 315th, which had tried and failed three times the previous day to advance past Hill 274; none were allocated to the 316th. The support regiments would follow, Sweezey's 313th on the left, the 314th under Colonel Oury (who was also commanding the 158th Brigade) on the right.

That looked fine on paper, but Kuhn was getting unwelcome news. Half an hour before the attack, Major Pleasonton, an officer in his headquarters, passed on a message from Sweezey "to the effect that his regiment was much depleted due to straggling, was low in ammunition owing to the failure to connect with combat train which was under shell fire, and represented a generally bad state of affairs."* Kuhn told Pleasonton to ignore the report, "which was probably largely exaggerated, and that no attention could be paid to such tales."[1] An hour later Knowles sent Kuhn a message that was even more blunt:

> We have been under artillery fire all night which has given us losses amounting to 50%. We have not been able to get our rations up because the train was shelled on the whole road. The men are getting so weak on account of getting no food there is not much driving power left. We are going to do the best we can but I am afraid the losses will be very heavy.[2]

Kuhn's response is not recorded, but it cannot have been much different than what he told Pleasonton. At least one of his brigade commanders, he could tell himself, was following orders instead of complaining. As the attack began, Oury sent a message to Kuhn describing his dispositions and adding, "All formed in depth according to orders. I am in liaison with the division on our right ... Reports will be rendered as advance progresses."[3] In return Oury received at a message at 8:07 a.m. from Colonel Ross informing him that sound-ranging equipment, used to locate enemy guns, had arrived and "consequently our counter-battery work should become more effective." Ross also betrayed divisional headquarters' frustration with the general lack of information regarding its regiments' progress when he added, "The 316th Infantry is practically on line with you according to last reports. Have heard nothing from them since the hour of attack. Itasca [79th Division] appreciates the tone of your message and wishes you every success."[4] Here was one brigade commander, Ross must have thought, who knew his job.

An artillery bombardment was ordered between 6:00 and 7:00 a.m.; but the division's guns, scattered across an area nearly four miles deep by two and a half miles wide, were either in transit or out of communication, so

---

* Sweezey's actual report read, "Your message just received ordering attack. I fear the most dire results on account of condition of men. Invent [i.e., the 316th Infantry] I do not believe has half his strength in our front due to straggling. My men have had no sleep for 3 nights, only cold food, have been out in cold rain all night without any protection whatever and many without overcoats. I of course will comply with orders and do my best under conditions but due to heavy casualties among officers I cannot guarantee results. Request 2 combat wagons be sent immediately with ammunition." ("Field Messages of the 157th Infantry Brigade," 1918, RG 120, 79th Division, Box 16, 32.16, NARA, September 29, 1918, time sent not given.)

almost nothing happened."[5] Despite the lack of either a barrage or counterbattery fire, at 7:00 a.m. the two lead regiments crested Hill 274 and advanced down its north slope. The result was a repetition of the previous day. Within five minutes they ran into heavy machine gun fire from the Bois des Ogons, the Madeleine Farm, and seemingly every bush and ditch on the landscape. As the two battalions of the 316th emerged from Bois 268 on their way to the wood ahead, the left of the line was particularly hard hit. Machine gun fire from three directions cut down one company commander and two battalion officers; four other officers were wounded, one mortally. In the 1st Battalion, Company C had one officer remaining, Company D had none; in the 3rd, Companies I and L, having lost all of their officers, were led by sergeants.[6] The 1st Battalion got 300 yards from Bois 268, then stopped in its tracks. At 10:10 a.m. Colonel Charles reported his situation to Nicholson in 157th Brigade headquarters: "300 yards ahead of North Western edge 268. Troops being cut to pieces by artillery and machine gun fire. 2nd Battalion, 119th Field Artillery now here." He quickly followed that up with, "Retrograde movement very difficult to check. Field back of our P.C. now under constant shell fire."[7] Nicholson relayed the information to V Corps as well as to Kuhn and Oury, adding, "Hostile artillery fire practically unopposed by our artillery."[8] Pleas continued to come in from Charles:

> Request 155's for counter battery on Bois de Cunel guns and draw at 09.0–82.3. Tanks south of Bois de Bigors [sic] refuse to operate without artillery support. Our lines on right and left this regiment have fallen back exposing both our flanks. My men too are retiring. Am reorganizing in woods No. 268 to advance as soon as flanks are covered.[9]

For once, Charles's pleas were answered. The artillery liaison officer in Nicholson's headquarters got the message to General Irwin, who ordered his 121st and 454th Artillery Regiments to deliver the fire. That, plus whatever the 119th Artillery was able to do, had the desired effect. A few minutes later Charles sent a runner back to Sweezey with the message, "Enemy retreating rapidly under our fire. Please throw in full support at once to

---

* The eight 9.2-inch guns of the 65th Coastal Artillery Corps, assigned to the 57th Field Artillery Brigade, were stuck in traffic many miles to the south. Some of the French heavy artillery regiments could be located no more precisely than "on road."

drive him before he reorganizes."[10] Sweezey pressed his regiment forward; but on their own Charles's men continued to withdraw into Bois 268, mingling with the advancing soldiers of the 313th; only with difficulty could the regiment's officers stop them from retreating further.

The right side of Charles's line did better than the left, at least to first appearances. The 3rd Battalion got all the way into Bois 250 and cleared it of machine guns, but it was unsupported and badly disorganized. Many small groups, thinking they were isolated and perhaps left behind, withdrew back to their starting point. Remaining in the wood, at its northern edge, were three officers and about 50 men from Companies I, K, and M and the 312th Machine Gun Battalion, all under Captain Somers, the acting battalion commander. Around noon, as the rest of the regiment drew back into Bois 268, Somers's detachment became isolated half a mile ahead of the nearest American troops. It threatened to turn into, if not a Lost Battalion, then perhaps a Lost Platoon.

At about the same time General Nicholson came forward to the position of the 316th on horseback, fully visible to the Germans and oblivious to their fire. His intent was to gauge the situation and order Colonel Charles to make a further assault on Bois 268, but he quickly realized that the 316th had nothing left to give. Locating Colonel Sweezey, he ordered him to pass his regiment through the 316th, take over the front line, and attack. Charles organized what was left of the 316th, amounting to 500 men (out of a full complement of 3,800), into a single battalion commanded by Major Parkin, so it could follow the 313th in support. Kuhn, not knowing of Nicholson's attack order, sent at 12:55 p.m. a message to Charles:

> Message stating your troops falling back received. Do all you can to restore order and confidence as there is no cause for alarm—organize holding line north edge Bois de Beuge with machine guns, reorganize troops and omit [sic—?] orders—am arranging for protection artillery barrage in case of need.[11]

The Bois de Beuge was half a mile south of the current position of the 316th; this order shows that Kuhn had accepted the impossibility of further advance and was now only interested in stabilizing his front, even if it meant giving up hard-won ground. Kuhn informed V Corps:

> Line enfiladed by artillery fire from right and left, principally right and forced to fall back because of this fire, machine gun fire, and total exhaustion

of troops. I consider them incapable of further driving power. Am organizing and holding line N. edge Bois de Beuge–Nantillois to re-organize and to meet possible hostile counter attack ...[12]

But Kuhn's communication was premature. His order to Charles did not arrive at the regimental headquarters until two hours later, after Charles's attack had jumped off.

While this exchange was going on, Captain Somers's impromptu force was still holding its isolated position in Bois 250. The captain sent five runners back to get in touch with the rest of the 316th. All five were shot down; three ultimately died of their wounds. Fortunately, Somers's little band was joined a few hours later by a platoon from the 312th Machine Gun Battalion, which had followed in support. Spotting a group of German machine gunners coming toward them from the northwest, the new arrivals opened fire; the Germans dropped their weapons and fled. From their vantage point Somers and his men could see the German flank to their left, along with an artillery observation post and several machine gun nests. On these they turned their own machine guns and automatic rifles, but were rewarded with a deluge of artillery shells and machine gun bullets. At this point their own machine gun platoon ran out of ammunition, but the German fire had slackened enough to allow them to return to the lines of the 316th and get more. The rest of Somers's group stayed put, awaiting either relief or further orders.[13]

At 2:30 p.m. the 313th attacked out of Bois 268, followed by Major Parkin's battalion of the 316th in support; there was no time to organize an artillery barrage. The 313th suffered heavy casualties right away. Companies G, B, and A had their commanders killed or mortally wounded. Lieutenant James Towsen was wounded eight times before he would consent to being sent to the rear. Moreover, the regiment veered too far to the east, taking it as far as the Bois de Cunel and within a hundred yards of Madeleine Farm, but out of its own sector. Behind them Parkin's battalion, attacking straight ahead, quickly found itself back in Bois 250, with the 313th nowhere in evidence. As it got to the northern edge of the wood, there were Somers and his band. Parkin set up a defensive line and advanced into the open field to survey the area. To the northeast was a hospital; to the northwest the town of Romagne; and in between large German troop concentrations. To his right in the sector of the 158th Brigade was the Bois des Ogons, which he was now in a position to outflank. Parkin sent Lieutenant Mowry Goetz back to the Brigade PC to report this fact and to ask for reinforcements so he could pull off the maneuver. But Goetz could not find Colonel Nicholson and no one else in the PC would authorize an attack, given that Kuhn had ordered the brigade to assume the defensive. At any rate, Parkin's battalion was under heavy fire and taking many casualties. Even though it now included Captain Somers's scratch platoon it was down to 250 men.[14]

Back at the PC of the 316th there had been a change of command. As Colonel Charles was dictating a message to his signals sergeant a shell exploded nearby, wounding him in the leg and killing the sergeant; Lieutenant Colonel Robert Meador, the second-in-command, took over the regiment. It was Meador who finally received Kuhn's order to withdraw to the Bois de Beuge. By carrier pigeon he replied:

> Order to organize Beuge received 15 H 25, but 313th Inf. has relieved us for assault, & is held up with ruinous losses on northern edge wood 268.[*] Am calling in scattered troops, & trying to communicate with Sweezey.[†] Charles slightly wounded. This Regt's effectives about 400. 313th also fast melting away.[15]

Among the "scattered troops" was Parkin's battalion. Bowing to circumstances, Meador ordered Parkin to retire and at the same time sent a messenger to the 57th Field Artillery to cancel a bombardment that was to open up on the Bois de Cunel. Once again Lieutenant Goetz volunteered to deliver the message. He and a private went forward at great risk to Bois 250 to convey Meador's order. With the order in hand, Major Parkin withdrew his men, now numbering 160, from Bois 250 at 9:00 p.m. By the time he reached the Bois de Beuge the defensive line Kuhn had ordered was in place and strongly held. The position Somers and Parkin had reached in Bois 250 was the furthest forward, not only of the 79th, but of all the other divisions in the Meuse–Argonne that day.[16] Sweezey, also under orders, withdrew his

---

[*] The accounts by members of the 316th uniformly express the belief that the 2:30 p.m. attack of the 313th never got far from Bois 268 before being pinned down. It is clear from the records of the 313th itself, however, that they made it to the southeast edge of the Bois de Cunel, almost a mile further on. The confusion probably arises from the fact that the 313th, having wandered out of its sector, became for a while invisible to officers of the 316th.

[†] Thus the handwritten original. The typed transcript, in place of "calling in scattered troops," reads, "falling in scattered groups."

313th Infantry from the Bois de Cunel and joined the 316th in the Bois de Beuge a mile and a half to the rear. Retiring was as expensive as advancing; two more companies, C and D, had their commanding officers killed and the regimental operations officer dropped with a bad leg wound. As before, sergeants and corporals led companies and platoons when their officers fell.[*] At 7:00 p.m., Meador reported his situation to Kuhn; he was not encouraging:

> Have divided defensive sector North edge Bois de Beuge with 313th. Even so, line untenable. This Reg't has 3 M.G.s and 150 infantry to hold a front of one kilometer. Ammun. 7000 rounds; food none; water, little.[17]

To the right of the 316th, the attack of the 158th Brigade was led by Knowles's 315th Infantry. Their orders said that the 4th Division, to their right, was half a mile further along than the 79th, so their flank would be covered as they attacked from Hill 274. They would be accompanied by four Renaults of the French 345th Tank Company.[†] A request for artillery support was denied; no guns were available other than those already accompanying the regiment.[18] The attack went off on time. Company I of 3rd Battalion made it to the Bois des Ogons with light casualties but then things got difficult as they came under fire from front and flanks. Captain Albert Friedlander, the company commander, had been evacuated for shell shock the previous day; the two surviving lieutenants, although both

---

[*] Colonel Sweezey remained bitter about having been ordered to withdraw, believing that he would have been in a position to outflank the Bois des Ogons had he been supported by the adjacent units. In his operations report after the Armistice he wrote, "I give it, however, as my unqualified opinion, that had we received expected support by the troops on our left, the combined Army Objective ... could have been reached that evening by 18h, with the consequent capture of a great many field pieces which were seen in operation just beyond the woods not more than 400 to 500 meters distant. This belief is confirmed by the statements of both battalion commanders of the attacking line who reached the position referred to." (Sweezey, "Report of Operations, September 25–November 11," p. 4.) As noted above, Parkin of the 316th also thought he could have turned the Bois des Ogons given reinforcements. In fact, there was no realistic prospect of such a maneuver by either unit. Both were depleted in manpower, ammunition, and provisions, and both would have been turning their flanks toward the enemy, who was well supplied with precisely aimed artillery. As the 313th and 316th at this point were unaware of each other's presence at the wood, they likely would have ended up shooting at each other.

[†] The Army War College account says 15 tanks. This is yet another illustration of the frequent disagreements among the sources. (Army War College, Historical Section, "The Seventy-Ninth Division, 1917–1918," p. 45.)

wounded, continued to lead the unit. Companies L and K ran into fire coming from the Bois de Brieulles on their right flank. Company L quickly lost its commander, Captain Francis Awl, and was down to a single lieutenant. Sergeants took over its two platoons. Getting into the woods, Company K bumped up against a machine gun nest. The commander, Captain William Carroll, and a sergeant worked around the flank of the nest, shot one gunner, and captured two others. The experience of 2nd Battalion was similar. Company F immediately lost two of its lieutenants, one killed and one fatally wounded. As Company G tried to take Madeleine Farm its commander, Captain Earl Offinger, was wounded, leaving one officer in the company. The Headquarters Company's 37mm gun, the last in the regiment for which there was ammunition, ran out while shelling a machine gun nest and had to retire. Thereupon the 2nd Battalion ran into the same flood of machine gun bullets that had stopped the 3rd Battalion and took to ground.[*]

It was apparent from the flanking fire that the 4th Division, far from being ahead of the 79th, was nowhere nearby, and by 9:00 a.m. the advance of the 315th had come to a full stop. Colonel Knowles telephoned General Kuhn: "We have no recent information as to the location of front line, 4th Div. It was abreast of us yesterday afternoon. 4th Division must go forward before I can. Hostile artillery in location 11.8–83.4 is enfilading my front line."[19] At that point the connection went dead. The coordinates Knowles gave corresponded to the southern edge of the Bois de Fays, where the 4th Division would have been, had it, in fact, been half a mile ahead of the 79th. Kuhn immediately contacted General Hines, commander of the 4th Division: "Cannot advance unless your left brigade also advances at the same time. Request present location of your front line and your intentions."[20] This must have been a novel experience for Kuhn: the 4th Division was holding him up, instead of the reverse. There is no record of a reply in the archives of the 79th.

---

[*] Once again, the report of French tank commander Richard tells a different story. According to it, the 345th Tank Company cleaned out the left side of Bois de Cunel; but the infantry, taking fire from the hills near Romagne, were stopped. The same happened when the tank company turned to attack the Bois des Ogons; the infantry failed to follow and the tanks had to withdraw. ([no first name] Richard, "Report of the Battalion Commander Richard, Commanding the 15 Light Tank Battalion to the Commanding Officer of the 505th Regiment of Artillery of Assault," October 2, 1918, 17 N 128, SHD, p. 2.)

At 11:15 a.m. Colonel Oury sent a runner to Kuhn summarizing his brigade's situation:

> Since writing last message have had a definite report from the front ... The advance has been stopped. It appears to be held up on right and left divisions who are still behind us. The enemy fortification at Madelaine Swamps consists of anti-tank guns, machine guns, renders imperative further artillery preparation before advance can be resumed. Bois de Cunel is also strongly held. Request that heavy artillery be again laid on Farm de la Madeleine and that the 37th Div. be requested to push up guns to prevent enfilading machine gun fire from nests in their fronts.[21]

The message got to Kuhn more than three hours later. Around noon, Oury followed up with a more realistic assessment:

> The situation has again changed. The 315 Inf is retreating from its position. It is now passing my P.C. I have given orders to Maj. Borden to reorganize and proceed back to the front. I have given the same orders to Col. Knowles. This to be accomplished by 13H00. 314th Inf is in place but are making no attempt to move forward with it. Our position in front is strongly held and must be reduced by artillery before infantry can take it. Request that preparation start at once with strongest artillery preparation that can be given us.[22]

This did not reach the general until 8:47 p.m, by which time events had passed it by. By 1:00 p.m. the 315th was back on Hill 274.

Although positioned 800 yards to the rear in support of the 315th Infantry, the 314th suffered as well. At 9:20 a.m. Lieutenant C.A. Webb, the 79th Division liaison officer to the artillery, reported that two battalions had made in into Bois des Ogons—how far he didn't know—but that several companies were held up back on Hill 274 by a single machine gun that had not been suppressed. Any further advance was blocked by artillery fire, high explosive mixed with gas. The Germans had not dropped gas shells on the front line for fear of hitting their own troops, so they concentrated on the rear area where the 314th was positioned. The men had to advance with their gas masks on.* As it happened, almost all of the losses of the

---

* In general, gas was a minor factor in the Montfaucon battle. Captain Clark, the division gas officer, reported on September 29 that the 79th suffered no gas attacks until after noon on the 27th. This was

314th were from shell fire rather than machine guns. One of the dead was Major Alfred R. Allen, who had just a few hours earlier taken over command of 1st Battalion. Hit in the head, he died in the hospital a few days later. He had been a prominent neurologist and faculty member at the University of Pennsylvania Medical School. Another was the regiment's French adviser, Lieutenant Poulaine, a veteran of the elite Chasseurs Alpins, nicknamed the "Blue Devils." As he was meeting with two officers of 2nd Battalion on how to conduct the attack, a machine gun bullet hit him in the head. One of the officers reported his words: "Ah! Captain, I was a fool—I was careless. After four years I let them get me that easy! Kiss mother for me." Some personal details and a final "Goodbye" were the last words the officer heard. A stretcher was fashioned from rifles and overcoats and the lieutenant was carried to the rear; but he died soon after reaching the first aid station.[33] By evening, the 314th had withdrawn to where they had started that morning, dug in on a line a third of a mile northwest of Nantillois.

Not only the infantry regiments of the 79th suffered that day. In the morning the 119th Field Artillery Regiment moved up through Montfaucon in thick fog and took the road toward Nantillois. About 9:00 a.m., as the tail of the column was coming down the hill, the fog lifted and German artillery opened up on the regiment with great accuracy. Private Jacks of the regiment's Machine Gun Company believed ever afterward that the 119th had somehow gotten past the American infantry and bumped headlong into the German gun positions. Several enemy batteries, in Jacks's telling, blazed away at the 119th at virtually point-blank range. The men of his company could clearly see the enemy's muzzle flashes and quickly unlimbered their machine guns to fire on their tormentors. The scene was chaotic:

> The orchards and gardens by the highway in an instant were dotted with dead men and horses, and the dim atmosphere became sticky and choking with the poisonous fumes of gas and the sickening odor of high explosives. Gassed and wounded horses staggered screaming and plunging through this bedlam, there was yelling and yelping on every hand, the flaming

presumably because the Germans were pulling their guns back in anticipation of the September 26 attack. The 79th first ran into gas as it attacked north of Montfaucon and in the Bois de la Tuilerie to its east, but only about 50 shells fell up until mid-day on the 28th, causing 45 gassing cases, of which Clark suspected that three-quarters were malingerers. Clark was unaware of the over 400 cases that were arriving at the gas hospitals in the 79th's sector. (Cochrane, "79th Division," p. 45.)

machine-guns set up their clattering yammer in every direction, and all around rose the drumming roar of heavy guns and the crash of incoming shells ... The naked slopes were covered with mournful relics, including many fragments of the 79th Division infantry, who came up irregularly and were shot down on the exposed open. I saw one man who fell over on his back and was clutching a blood-soaked letter in his hand. I walked over to him with another machine-gunner, thinking he might have some ammunition we could use. He was dead when we reached him, and a shot carried away part of the letter, but we picked up the red fragment remaining and read all that was left, the last couple of lines scrawled in a small feminine hand, "—come back to me and I will never fool you any more. Lovingly, Betty." He had been shot through the throat and had bled to death and had evidently dragged out her letter, to read it again before he died.[24]

The episode Jacks describes undoubtedly happened, but there are problems with his account. On the 29th, the enemy lines were just over a mile north of Nantillois; the 119th could not possibly have run into the hostile artillery, which was positioned several miles yet further to the German rear, mostly around the towns of Romagne and Cunel.[25] There was also no possibility that an American artillery column could pass through several regiments of friendly and hostile infantry without noticing. A much more likely explanation is offered by the version of Charles M. Engel, a private in Battery A of the 119th. According to him, the regiment was put under the command of the infantry, whose colonels ignorantly deployed the guns in broad daylight, without an opportunity for concealment or camouflage. "We were in direct sight of the enemy observation balloons and before our guns were in firing position the enemy opened fire on the second battalion and men were flying in the air before they knew what was happening and we lost more men right there than in any other action in our five steady months in action."[26] And indeed, the presence of German balloons is attested by many other American accounts. Thus is the same event interpreted differently by different eyewitnesses.

For the attack of the 79th to move forward at all, artillery support was crucial, especially counterbattery fire. At 11:15 a.m., the 158th Brigade's artillery liaison officer sent to General Irwin asking for fire on Madeleine Farm at 11:30 a.m., to last for half an hour. Irwin ordered the 121st and 330th (French) Artillery Regiments to begin firing at the requested time. At the same time he sent a message to Kuhn saying that the firing could not begin at exactly 11:30 a.m., but it would stop at 12:00 noon in any event. "It will be heavy fire while fired. Tell Colonel to use his own batteries." By the last sentence he meant the colonel commanding the 120th Artillery, which had been detailed to support the brigade. Kuhn, figuring that even with Irwin's caveat the firing schedule was optimistic, commanded the 75s instead to start firing on the southern edge of the Bois de Cunel at 1:00 p.m. and end an hour later. The 155s would fire on "la Mamelle trench, upon Cunel village, and upon le Ville aux Bois farm until further orders." At 12:45 p.m. Kuhn ordered Knowles, "Reorganize your command. We are having strong artillery fire in Bois de Cunel. Hold at all costs your position well in front of Nantillois–Bois de Beuge line." But it is not clear that any bombardment actually materialized; six years later, researchers at the Army War College could find no evidence that it did.[27]

Lack of artillery was not the only impediment to progress; the men of the 315th were drifting to the rear. Around 2:00 p.m. Oury saw the flood of stragglers passing his PC and took action. "This retrograde movement was stopped by myself and Staff Officers as they passed my P.C. The Commanding Officer of the 315th Infantry was directed to reorganize his regiment and put it back in line. This was accomplished later in the afternoon."[28] Oury may have been an optimist but Knowles, the commanding officer in question, was a realist. At 3:00 p.m. he sent an assessment of his situation to Oury and Kuhn. Yes, stragglers were being collected, but most of them were merely searching for food and water. Machine gun ammunition was low. Men from the 314th, 316th, and 313th Infantry Regiments were mixed in with his own. His effective strength was down to 50 percent. Most tellingly:

> Men are of good moral [sic], but badly exhausted, because of lack of food, water and sleep. Officers getting scarce, Med. officers left all in. Wounded with practically no help but 1st aid and many who could be saved are dying because of lack of attention and exposure. Supply train near my P.C., but unable to go further on account of shelling.[29]

An hour and a half later, Oury repeated his situation report but, apparently fearing that he had been too subtle, came to the point:

> It is my opinion that now is the occasion for fresh troops to be sent in right away. The men are tired and against the evident resistance on our front will

not get far under any circumstances. They will if ordered, of course, attempt to advance but this may develop the possibility of a stampede somewhere along the line.[30]

And, a little later:

Find that the casualties have been growing worse. Major Allen just killed by shell fire. We are lying in the open accomplishing nothing in our present positions, but getting men destroyed. Request that I be permitted to withdraw. The 2d and 3d Battalions, 315th Infantry, are falling back without orders.[31]

Oury's terse summary of the plight of his casualties did not, of course, capture the despair of the afflicted men. Private Casper Swartz and another man of the 314th came across a wounded soldier who begged to be put out of his misery. Swartz was unwilling to shoot him; but as he stood there two stretcher-bearers came up. Swartz asked them to evacuate the wounded man but they refused, saying he was from a different outfit. Swartz said to his buddy, "Take aim on the one guy and I will take the other." That stopped the stretcher-bearers in their tracks. Swartz said, "If you fellows start moving toward the rear without taking this wounded man along, we will kill both of you." Without further objection, the former recalcitrants placed the casualty gently on their stretcher and took him to the rear.[32] An intelligence specialist from First Army headquarters who had trained with the 313th Infantry watched as the wounded of the 79th—those lucky enough not to be left lying on the field—came in to the field hospital:

After dark, truck after truck arrived piled crisscross with wounded on stretchers, one row lengthwise on the bottom, another crosswise with ends on the body sides of the trucks. The drivers said that they had been forty-eight hours on the way in a drizzle. The distance is not so great but the roads are jammed and often impassible [sic] and they had to go carefully over the rough spots for fear of shaking these human wrecks to pieces. Many of them, when lifted out, certainly looked more dead than alive. One man's face was covered with blood and his uniform stiff with clots. I thought he was dead, but it turned out to be blood that had dripped on him from the man above ... Minor wounds had to wait as the surgeons worked feverishly hour after hour trying to keep up with the incoming tide. Mud-caked, rain-soaked and blood-stained men lay silently row on row, patiently waiting their turn.[33]

Not all the wounds were physical. As the intelligence man looked for his former buddies among the casualties of the 313th:

> I came across the most dejected kid I have ever seen. Pale as a ghost, smeared with grime, he sat against a wall and stared before himself as though in a trance; 313 "D" was on his collar button and he nursed a bandaged hand.
>
> "What's the matter, buddy, downhearted?" I asked. "'D' is my old company. I was with them for two months at Camp Meade. How is everybody?"
>
> He looked up a moment gloomily and then continued to stare at the wall. "They're all dead," he said listlessly, "gassed and shelled—nobody left."
>
> "Aw, cheer up," I said, "probably not that bad. You'll find nine-tenths of them in hospital. Men don't die that easily."
>
> He shook his head and looked as if he were about to burst into tears ... I could not shake him out of his dejection and so left him wrapped in gloom, convinced that all his comrades were no more and not comforted at all in that he had escaped with a minor hurt.[34]

Getting to a hospital was no guarantee of safety. At 2:00 p.m. a triage center opened at Fayel Farm, consisting of the 315th and 316th Field Hospitals. In the words of an intelligence officer on General Irwin's staff, one hour later:

> ... a German plane circled slowly over the hospital which was plainly marked by large red crosses on top of the tents. Then, following each other at intervals of thirty seconds, ten German shells fell among the tents, eight being direct hits. Patients, litters and tents were scattered in all directions and numbers of men laying there helpless, but only slightly wounded, were killed outright or received mortal wounds. There was no hesitation on the part of the men near enough to help, and dozens rushed into the bursting shells and carried out the helpless to places of safety, cursing the maliciousness that could have instigated such inhuman fire.[35]

Twenty-one men died, several of them wounded German prisoners. Officers and men helped evacuate the wounded under fire; walking wounded gave their places in ambulances to those more seriously hurt. The patients were transferred to the former first aid station on the Avocourt–Malancourt road, but continued shelling forced the 315th and 316th Field Hospitals all the way back to Clair Chêne, where they had started out. Nine men of the

304th Sanitary Train were killed, some while attempting to retrieve the wounded from the field.[*][36]

Most soldiers were neither dead nor wounded, but all were desperately hungry. The supply situation, which depended on the roads, had not abated. On September 29 Premier Clemenceau decided to visit Montfaucon, the greatest prize of the American offensive so far. He got within five miles, then became stuck in the enormous traffic jam that was starving First Army of guns, ammunition, and food. Angrily abandoning his car, he strode forward far enough to overlook the road north packed solid with vehicles, horses, and guns. He finally gave up in disgust, returned to his car (which took some effort to turn around) and went off to visit the more hospitable French sector nearby. It was perhaps fortunate for Pershing that Clemenceau got no further; he could not see the full extent of American disorganization. (In addition to Clemenceau, André Tardieu, the high commissioner for Franco-American cooperation, also wanted to visit Montfaucon, but Pershing dissuaded him. President Poincaré tried, but could get no further than Esnes.) The traffic jam behind the American front, Pétain's observers reported to him, was "unimaginable." Lieutenant Colonel Nodé-Langlois saw two regiments camped in the middle of the road. Some vehicles were stalled in place for up to 30 hours; when they moved, the average speed was two kilometers per hour. The road between Clermont and Baulny was blocked by two huge craters, and although alternate tracks had been cut into the neighboring fields, the going was so poor that many trucks broke down. The few military police were ineffective in enforcing road discipline—drivers simply ignored them. The only way to get obedience was with a drawn pistol.

---

[*] The episode achieved notoriety in First Army as a typical German atrocity. A common reaction was that of Gerald F. Gilbert, an enlisted man in the 304th Sanitary Train: "Damn the Germans for such a dirty deed. I am in favor of killing every one of them ... They are the meanest, dirtiest, low-down people on earth and should be exterminated." (Gerald F. Gilbert, Jr., untitled diary, n.d., World War I Survey, WWI-158, 304th Sanitary Train, AHEC, p. 67.) But the reality was likely different. Dr Hanson, now serving as assistant to the hospital's commanding officer, noticed earlier in the day that the 1st Division, newly arrived at the Meuse–Argonne front, had camped across the road from the hospital. He immediately became upset, knowing that if the presence of the division was detected by the Germans, it would come under attack with inevitable damage to the hospital. Hanson got his chief to talk to the commander of the 1st Division, but the latter merely replied that they had been ordered up to help the infantry. (Hanson, *I Was There*, p.81.)

A Colonel Bourgerie exclaimed, "And our policemen go to New York to learn traffic control!" Repair work on the badly damaged roads was poorly done; although plenty of laborers were available, they were poorly organized and equipped, and worked at cross-purposes. The Americans to whom the French protested, realizing the criticality of the situation, blamed the mud, the exhaustion of the troops, and the cross-traffic caused by the relief of the front-line units.[37] But officers could also be a problem. Captain W.R. Eastman, a V Corps surgeon trying desperately to get forward to Montfaucon, found the direct route barred by the MPs. Instead, he was shunted to the one-way road going east to Avocourt:

> Along came a big staff car in the opposite direction, pushed my little old Dodge off the plank road into the mud and went on. The next M.P. I asked why he had let that car go through. He replied that he had signalled for him to stop, that the officer had yelled to him that he had the right of way to Hell and pushed along. I hope he reached his destination. Have been looking for him ever since, but I have never run across him.[38]

Responding to the barrage of bad news from his brigade commanders, Kuhn sent a stiff order to Oury telling him to establish a defensive line near Nantillois, "if possible in the North thereof,"—over half a mile behind his present position on Hill 274. With regard to artillery support, Kuhn could offer little reassurance: "Corps has been informed of our situation and of the direction from whence the fire is coming and it is believed that some measure will be taken in the very near future by Corps or Army to afford relief." He ended with a warning: "Rumors have been prevalent that the 79th Division is to be relieved. This rumor has no foundation in fact and must be suppressed."[39]

The rumor was more accurate than Kuhn knew. At 12:45 p.m. the general had sent a message to Cameron at V Corps requesting that the 79th be relieved:

> My whole line falling after advance on Ogons woods and troops on my right also reported retiring in some disorder due to concentration artillery crossfire and exhaustion of troops. Am reorganizing retiring units and am preparing to hold line in front of Nantillois against possible counter-attack. Request fresh divisions rushed forward at once.[40]

V Corps staff had forwarded the message on to Pershing's headquarters with the note, "General Cameron does not recommend relief." But First Army decided otherwise. At 4:30 p.m. Colonel Drum, Pershing's Chief of Staff, issued Field Order No. 31 directing that the 3rd Division relieve the 79th in the line that night. The order was sent to V Corps. Kuhn, not knowing this, kept sending messages to Cameron indicating that he was still game as long as he got help:

> It is my opinion that no advance by infantry is possible until effective counter battery work has been instituted. It has been impossible for the divisional artillery to cope with the situation. I deem it my duty to bring these matters to you attention in order that proper action may be taken in the premises ...[41]

And at 10:20 that night he told Oury not to expect relief any time soon:

> Your message describing the conditions of your troops received. It is impossible to provide for any relieve [sic] this morning and I must impress upon you the necessity of exerting all your influence to maintain discipline and uphold the morale of the men. Every effort will be made to supply the men with rations. I hope to avoid calling on the men for any exertion beyond the requirements of security and protection of their line. The men have done well and it would be a pity should they fail to maintain discipline.[42]

Finally, at 3:30 a.m. on the morning of the 30th, Kuhn received V Corps' order commanding the 3rd Division to relieve the 79th—all but the 304th Engineers, who would be attached to the 3rd for another week. He quickly sent notes to Nicholson and Oury telling them that the 5th Brigade of the 3rd Division was "marching to your relief" and ordering them to set up liaison arrangements.[43] Three hours later he made this formal in his Field Order No. 10. The ordeal of the 79th—at least the September part of it—would soon be over.

The concern at First Army headquarters was much broader than the plight of the 79th. Pershing had been receiving reports of stagnation all along his line. From I Corps on the left he heard:

> Infantry advancing from the corps objective met with determined resistance. The 77th Division on the left was unable to advance any distance through

the forest. The 28th Div. was held approximately on the line it occupied yesterday. The 35th Div. attempted to move forward from Montrebeau [Woods] but was driven back by machine-gun and artillery fire.[*][44]

III Corps on the right reported:

All along our front the infantry met considerably more resistance. Very heavy M.G. and artillery fire prevented further advance during the day. At the closing of this report our line remains approximately the same.[45]

V Corps sent the hardly reassuring message, "Troops advancing slowly"; the details of its report dwelt on difficulties and delays.[46] At 8:30 p.m. Colonel Willey Howell, Drum's chief of intelligence, issued a situation estimate that began, "All day long on the 29th, the enemy has maintained himself by means of machine gun fire, artillery and counter attacks ... It is becoming quite obvious that his intention is to hold this ridge (Aprémont–Exermont–Cierges–Brieulles line) as long as he can do so." After recapitulating the fruitless American attacks and repulses of the previous two days he concluded:

I believe that the Germans were overwhelmed by our original advance, but that the advance has been so mismanaged and has been so dilatory as to enable them to recover from their first surprise, to readjust and establish themselves in a defensive position, to bring up several reserve divisions and to commence a very much stronger defense than they were able to conduct at the start. We can expect, I think, no further withdrawal under present conditions. The great success of the French Fourth Army (on our left) will possibly attract some of the troops in our front to the front of that army, unless we continue to hammer at the enemy. However, on the other side, it seems that our proper action would be to cease this hammering, to reorganize our advance, and to renew our attack in an orderly manner with fresh troops.[47]

In reality, the German position on the 29th was not nearly as secure as Howell believed. In the sector of the 151st Infantry Regiment, confusion reigned. Regiments, battalions, and individual soldiers from three divisions were mixed

---

[*] This was generous. The 35th Division had virtually disintegrated; its fate has been described in detail by Robert Ferrell. (Robert H. Ferrell, *Collapse at Meuse–Argonne: The Failure of the Missouri-Kansas Division* (Columbia, MO and London: University of Missouri Press, 2004).)

randomly, and officers could not locate their commands. "At a few locations, groups of staff officers gathered to ask each other despairingly for news of their troops."[48] A massive attack by the American 37th Division forced the 212th Infantry to retreat before it itself was stopped. Gallwitz's diary recorded a series of violent artillery bombardments and continuing infantry attacks by the Americans, requiring Fifth Army to commit its own reserves to restore the line.[49] But it was clear to the German troops that they would not be overrun any time soon and morale, if not high, was sufficient in most units to ensure a vigorous defense. In particular, they had lost their fear of the tanks. Lieutenant Berger in the 150th Infantry wrote home about how his battalion stopped the tank attack of the American 37th Division in front of Cierges:

> The tanks ... drove into our trench and one hit the dug-out entry with his gun. The situation became awkward. I drew my pistol and came close to one of the tanks in the road. Just as I stuck my pistol into the observation loophole, the crew noticed me and shut the loophole a moment before the shot. I felt rather stupid, but continued on next to the tank in case the loophole opened again. This did not happen, however. After a while several other people arrived with hand grenades and we brought the thing to a halt. I threw several grenades, which I had tied together with my handkerchief, beneath the caterpillar tracks of a second tank. It continued on about 50 paces, then the crew gave up. When the men saw that nothing happened to someone who was right up against the tanks—although one still had to watch out for the other tanks' machine guns—it became a sport to take care of the tanks. Of 10 tanks, the battalion disposed of 7. The men even climbed on top and cried, 'Give it to him! Give it to him!' and so on. One man fell, unfortunately, and was run over. The American infantry, accompanied by our machine-gun and now also infantry fire, pulled back.[50]

By the end of the day, the regimental histories report, infantry attacks had ceased; the Americans contented themselves with periodic artillery bombardments.

Bowing to reality, Drum on Pershing's instruction issued an order canceling further offensive action—although it did not read that way. First, it recited the good news. "The Allied attack has been successful all along the front ... Our left has completely repulsed the counterattack of a fresh hostile division and gained many prisoners." Then came the important information:

2. The American First Army will continue the attack *on further orders.*

. . .

3. (B) The III Corps, the V Corps and the I Corps:

 (1) These corps will *organize for further attack.*

 (2) They will organize for defense the line—Bois de Forges–Gercourt-et-Drillancourt–Bois-Jure–Dannevoux–Bois de Dannevoux–Bois de la Cote-Lemont–Bois de Brieulles–Nantillois–Bois de Beuge–etc. [Emphasis added.][51]

In the parlance of First Army, "organize for further attack" meant dig in, relieve depleted units, resupply, and wait for orders. Four exhausted divisions—from west to east the 35th, 91st, 37th, and 79th—were taken out of the line. For all of them, this had been their first battle; their replacements were veterans. The 1st Division under Major General Charles P. Summerall took over from the 35th; it had been in France since July 1917, and had fought in every major American action including St Mihiel. The 32nd Division, commanded by Major General William G. Haan, had fought with the French in the Aisne–Marne and Oise–Aisne campaigns; it replaced the 37th and, a few days later, the 91st. The 3rd Division, the "Rock of the Marne," had stopped the German advance at Château Thierry and then attacked beside the French at Aisne–Marne; commanded by Beaumont Buck, it assumed the sector of the 79th. Pershing's lineup for the next phase of the offensive would be a much more capable, experienced army.

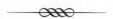

Accounts began immediately of why the 79th Division failed to take Montfaucon on the first day or to advance further than seven miles in all. Two days after the relief, Colonel S.F. Dallam, the V Corps inspector, wrote to the AEF Inspector General saying that three things had stopped the attack: exhaustion and hunger; the strong defensive positions in the Bois des Ogons and the Madeleine Farm; and the heavy artillery fire from the flanks, which could not be countered because the faulty telephone network prevented the 79th from giving coordinates to their own artillery for counterbattery fire.[52] Memoranda and reports by the division's own officers

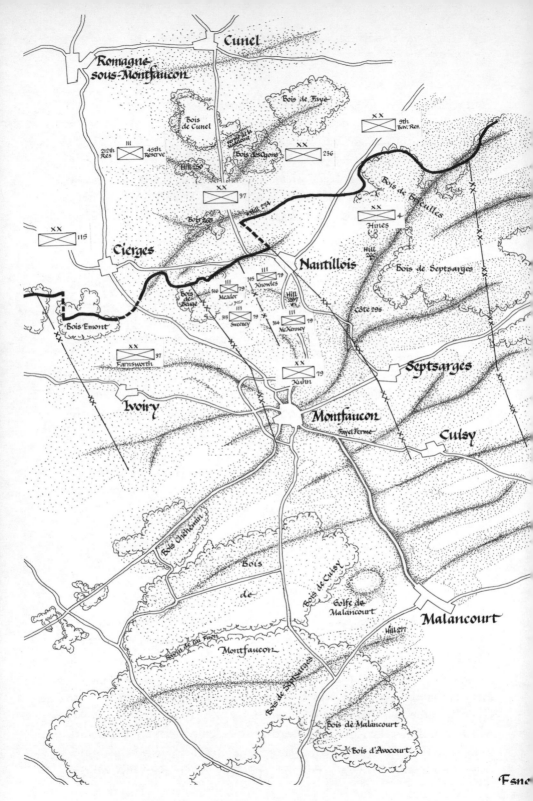

POSITIONS OF THE 79TH DIVISION'S REGIMENTS, NIGHTS OF
SEPTEMBER 29 AND 30

told essentially the same story. Subsequent analyses added lack of training and lack of combat experience as major factors; the Assistant Inspector General wrote:

> The 79th Division came under fire for the first time since its organization. More than half of its strength was made up of draftees of not more than 4 months service and considerable less of actual training due to time lost in transport from the US and in moving about while in France. As is the case with all green troops there was lacking the experience which comes only from thorough training or actual contact with the enemy.[53]

Another inspector's report, commenting on the performance of the 79th and 37th Divisions, concluded:

> There was confusion, there was lack of resolution. At times there were conditions bordering on panic. But the fact remains that these two green divisions, entering battle for the first time, crossed three highly organized enemy positions and captured a good many hundred prisoners each. Their maiden efforts were, under all the circumstances, all that could be expected.[54]

In May 1919, the Historical Section of the AEF General Staff assigned officers to walk the American battlefields and report their findings. Colonel C.F. Crain surveyed the Montfaucon sector and noticed that there were few shell holes in the southern edges of the woods in which German machine guns had been emplaced. He wrote in his report's conclusion:

> Considering this fact it seems to me, proven that the Infantry of the 79th division attacked the strong German machine gun positions with very little artillery support, and to this fact is due its disorganization and failure to take its objectives ... To recapitulate, the infantry of the 79th division attempted to capture the German positions with their bare hands.[55]

Crain's criticism of the artillery was seconded by Colonel Lanza, who after the war wrote extensively on the subject. Narrow divisional zones limited firing essentially to straight ahead; batteries could not support adjacent divisions.[*] Deep no-fire zones allowed the enemy to operate unmolested

---

[*] Captain Harry S. Truman, commanding a battery in the 35th Division, was threatened with court martial for destroying one German battery and disabling two others—they had been in the zone of the next-door 28th Division, and therefore off limits. The threat was not made good, and the veterans

and to arrange artillery fire in advance for their own counterattacks. Divided command of the artillery among the division, corps, and army made coordination difficult to impossible. The divisions themselves had insufficient artillery; this was especially a problem when facing counterattacks, because poor communications often rendered them unable to request assistance from corps or army guns. Most important, according to Lanza, was the failure to open each day with a preparatory bombardment, on the assumption that the Germans were retreating and if the Americans fired it would just slow down their infantry.[56] Problems Lanza could have listed, but did not, included the failure of the infantry to give target coordinates to the artillery and the long delays in communication, which quickly made information obsolete.

The French advisers, always fecund sources of criticism, went into great detail on the failings of the 79th. Major Paul Allegrini, the commander of the French Military Mission to the 79th, began his report with faint praise and progressed downward from there:

> The infantry, whose morale is good, attacks with zeal; but it can't be denied that it has not fulfilled its task; it has made progress but it has neither fought nor maneuvered: starting in effect from the moment the enemy stiffens its resistance, or the bombardment becomes more intense, the men are surprised, as if astonished to be shelled, whereas the bombardment is most frequently caused by their inexperience, which leads them to show their profile and to walk along crests, to bring the mobile kitchens close to the lines, and finally, to neglect to dig in; the pick and shovel were not handled by anyone.[57]

Whenever resistance developed, it was overcome "solely thanks to the assistance of the French tanks." The infantry had not been trained in working with tanks, so when the tanks advanced, the infantry rarely followed, leading to the loss of ground. The top officers didn't know their jobs—commanders got separated from their staffs, plans and orders were delivered late if at all. Not having worked with artillery or aircraft before the battle, the commanders did not know how to use them. The artillery, led by French officers, did fairly well, but on their own initiative and without target

of the 28th remembered the favor when Truman ran for President in 1948. (Martin Gilbert, *The First World War: A Complete History* (New York: Henry Holt, 1994), p. 467.)

information from the infantry.[*] The support units knew nothing about mopping up, so the reserve regiments suffered losses after the assault troops had passed. Worst of all, no provision seemed to have been made for resupplying the men, who went for three days without food or water. Probably for this reason there were far too many stragglers, who greatly reduced the regiments' front-line strength. But even Allegrini had to concede:

> Despite all of the notable failings, despite the inadequate command, if one remembers that 60% of the men of the division had at most three months of service, that all of them had heard their first shell eight days before the attack, that they went from the impression of a very quiet sector, without a transition, to one of attack; one must admit that the attitude of the men of the division suited the occasion; that the attack succeeded; and that the division advanced as far as, if not further, than, the US divisions that surrounded it.

In one or two months, he predicted, the men of the 79th would be capable of doing quite well.[†58]

The Germans, not knowing of the difficulties behind the American lines, certainly knew they had been in a fight, and not a winning one. In their war diaries, combat reports, and regimental histories they wrote of a highly motivated if inexperienced enemy who, despite repeated setbacks and outright failures, just kept coming. No word here of American infantry cowering in trenches while French tanks did all the work; the tales told by officers and regimental historians are ones of unremitting and violent pressure from the enemy and constant, although stubborn, retreat by the Germans. An after-action report by the Operations Section of the 117th Division observed:

> The division has very little combat value at the present time. After the arrival of replacements and a training period of 8 days, beginning then the division

---

[*] The V Corps artillery was largely composed of French regiments and its commander, General René Alexandre, was French, as were several of the artillery battalions assigned to the 79th.

[†] Major Allegrini was not around to see his prediction come true. Tired of his carping, Kuhn wrote to the Adjutant General of the AEF in October asking that the major be assigned elsewhere. He was. (Joseph E. Kuhn, "Major Paul Allegrini, French Mission," October 15, 1918, RG 120, Entry 6, Adjutant General File, General Correspondence, Box 1017, 20087, NARA, pp. 1–2.)

will be fit to be put in line or on a quiet front, after a training period of 5 weeks, on any front at all.[59]

The battalions in all three regiments were at about half-strength; trained crews were on hand for fewer than half of the machine guns. Although 1,300 recruits were available in the recruit depot, many of these were only 18 years old. Of the remainder, more than a hundred were to face courts-martial for mutiny.[60] General Hoefer, the division commander, commended his troops:

> Days of heavy fighting lie behind us. To all troops of the division who have fought valiantly during these days I express my highest commendation for their attainments. The units of the 11th Grenadiers and the 450th Infantry are to be praised especially, because, although enveloped on both sides, as a deep wedge they tenaciously held their positions south of Montfaucon for a long time and did not withdraw until so ordered.

But this was no triumph, as Hoefer continued:

> If each one in his turn had fought as courageously as these brave men, the enemy assault would have been broken sooner. The voluntary surrender of positions, because the enemy has forced his way into the flank, is a blunder prompted by weakness and unsoldierly conduct toward those elements who bravely defended themselves ...[61]

Kuhn, also, had reason to be proud of his division. It had advanced six miles against heavy opposition, conquered the most heavily fortified portion of the German line, and taken over 900 prisoners.[62] A few days after the relief he published the following message:

> During the recent fighting the 79th Division received its first baptism of fire in the Montfaucon sector. The commanding general takes this means of expressing to his command his satisfaction and gratification for the courage, fortitude and tenacity displayed by all the troops, especially the infantry, which, though frequently subjected to heavy machine gun and artillery fire, not only held all the ground conquered but gallantly strove to advance whenever called upon to do so ... He feels confident that the 79th division will not fail to maintain its excellent record and that the experience gained in the recent fighting will be turned to profit when again confronting the enemy.[63]

Privately, however, the general was near despair. To his diary he confided:

> More inspectors and I guess they are after me, OK. Looks like Blois or States with fewer stars. I have nothing for which to reproach myself and think division did well and showed grit and nerve.[64]

Blois was the reclassification center for American officers who had been relieved of duty. Being sent to Blois was a visible sign of failure.* To his wife he wrote:

> The division did well in my opinion although it failed to fully accomplish the task set to it. God knows I did all I could to make things go but it would not quite connect. Four nights without sleep and a bad cold on top left me pretty well down & out but a good night's rest last night has restored me greatly and I shall be OK shortly. Casualties were moderate but, as is always the case, some of the best and bravest are gone.[65]

In fact, the 79th did no worse than most other divisions of First Army and better than some. The Meuse–Argonne offensive as a whole failed to achieve Pershing's objectives. The plan for the initial advance had been for the three corps to reach the Army Objective—an advance of ten miles—on the afternoon of the first day, September 26. Instead, his divisions stalled nearly four miles short of their goal and would not reach it until mid-October. Many blamed V Corps—and the 79th in particular—for failing to capture Montfaucon and penetrate the German line that first day, thus allowing the enemy time to reinforce. Others were not sure it would have made a difference. The fall of Montfaucon would not have alleviated the traffic

---

* Pershing relieved many generals during the war, but Kuhn was not among them. In June 1917 he dismissed General William Sibert, an elderly engineering officer, from command of the 1st Division. In October 1918 he removed Beaumont Buck from command of the 3rd Division, Cameron from command of V Corps (sending him to lead the 4th Division upon the promotion of Hines to III Corps commander), and John McMahon of the 5th Division, all of them for displaying lack of spirit in their troops and themselves. Clarence Edwards, a politically appointed officer of the Massachusetts National Guard, was removed from command of the 26th for maintaining poor discipline, disloyalty, and generally being a nuisance. (Smythe, *Pershing*, p. 214.) Kuhn escaped their fate. Perhaps Pershing remembered the brilliant upperclassman of his Academy days. Perhaps Kuhn had earned the goodwill of the officer corps when, as president of the Army War College, he had recommended 120 colonels for promotion to general. (Millett, *The General*, p. 307; Joseph E. Kuhn to Col. Frederick Palmer, July 10, 1930, Kuhn Papers, Box 5, USMA, p. 1.) Or perhaps Pershing and his staff realized that they had ordered him to take an inexperienced, largely untrained, poorly supplied division and work wonders.

jams, which throttled supply lines and prevented the artillery from moving forward. Lieutenant Colonel Frederick Palmer, a war correspondent in Pershing's headquarters, wrote:

> There are those who say that if we had taken Montfaucon on the first day, we might have reached the crest of the whale-back [i.e, the Barrois plateau] itself on the second or third day and looked down on the apron sweeping toward the Lille–Metz railway ... They forget the lack of road repairs; the lack of shields [?] to continue the advance; and the interdictory shell-fire which the enemy laid down on the ruins of the town and on the arterial roads which center there. If we had taken Montfaucon on the first day, I think there would still have been a number of other 'ifs' between us and the crest.[66]

Indeed, apart from the 79th Division's lack of training and experience, it suffered from the same ills that plagued the other divisions: ignorance of combined-arms operations, poor communications leading to defective artillery support, and, above all, failure to maintain the roads. As we have seen, all offensives in World War I—even the apparently successful ones, from Moltke's advance to the Marne in 1914 to Ludendorff's Spring Offensives—were limited by their supply lines.[*] Sooner or later, generally after an advance of no more than ten miles, the men would run out of food and ammunition. Moreover, the disorganization that resulted from an attack would have to be sorted out before the operation could continue much further; even the victorious British and French offensives north of the Meuse–Argonne ground to a halt in the first week of October. Had the 79th taken Montfaucon on the first day, First Army would have stopped shortly thereafter anyway, strangled by its own lack of supplies. A balanced judgment has been offered by the historian Martin Gilbert: "By former Western Front standards the Americans were successful. Montfaucon, which Pétain had believed could hold out until the winter, was taken on September 27, and advances were made of up to six miles. But the plan had been far more ambitious, making the set-back all the more galling."[†][67]

---

* See Chapter 7, p. 169.

† The idea that Pétain thought Montfaucon could hold out until winter is often repeated in American World War I histories; see, e.g., Edward M. Coffman, *The War to End All Wars: The American Military Experience in World War I* (New York: Oxford UP, 1968), p. 301. It appears to be a slight distortion of a sentence in Pershing's memoirs: "In the event that we should attack between the Meuse and the Argonne, Pétain thought all that could be done before winter would be to take Montfaucon." (Pershing, *My Experiences*, vol. 2, p. 253.) No one seems to offer an original source for Pétain's opinion.

The failure of the 4th Division to "turn Montfaucon" by attacking into the zone of V Corps, as Pershing's Field Order No. 20 had prescribed, was debated within the AEF at the time but was ultimately smoothed over in the official record. It will be recalled that General Alfred Bjornstad, chief of staff of III Corps, canceled the movement because he did not want to violate corps boundaries (see Chapter 11). Drum and Pershing therefore blamed III Corps for not making the attack. General Bullard, the III Corps commander, replied that First Army had, in effect, canceled the attack by insisting that all corps advance straight to the Army Objective. In the words of historian Alan Millett, "General Drum's ingenuous defense of Army headquarters was that the III Corps should have understood that it had the freedom to cross corps boundaries without Army approval. Such a response from Drum was self-serving, for he had insisted in practice on a high degree of Army control over the corps' movements. It was not the first or last time he and Pershing disassociated themselves from schemes of maneuver that had turned sour."[68]

R.T. Ward, the colonel in Pershing's Operations Section who had written the attack plan for the Meuse–Argonne, was diplomatic in his final report: "Corps boundaries were given on the operation map and also division lines. Possibly there was a misunderstanding at times as to what these division lines meant. These lines were intended to show the army conception of the maneuver and were not intended to act as barriers between corps and division and thus limit their operations and prevent lateral maneuver."[69] Pershing picked up the "misunderstanding" theme in his memoirs. Of the 4th Division he wrote, "It was abreast of Nantillois and its left was more than a mile beyond Montfaucon, but through some misinterpretation of the orders by the III Corps the opportunity to capture Montfaucon that day was lost."[70] In fact, the lost opportunity was due to Pershing's own failure and that of his staff to communicate his intentions clearly to his three corps commanders and to make sure that the corps' own orders reflected those intentions. But the whole issue was a red herring. As Edward M. Coffman has pointed out, had the attack of the 4th Division gone forward, Nantillois would have fallen a day earlier, but the offensive would have bogged down anyway.[71]

Oblivious to the challenges faced by First Army and the fact that their own offensives had stalled, the Allied leaders redoubled their criticisms of Pershing after the Meuse–Argonne offensive bogged down. Haig blamed "inexperience and ignorance on the part of the Belgian and American Staffs of the needs of a modern attacking force."[72] Clemenceau, who still resented Pershing's resistance to amalgamation, wrote to Foch:

> The French Army and the British Army, without a moment's respite, have been daily fighting, for the last three months ... but our worthy American allies, who thirst to get into action and who are unanimously acknowledged to be great soldiers, have been marking time ever since their forward jump on the first day; and in spite of heavy losses, they have failed to conquer the ground assigned them as their objective. Nobody can maintain that these fine troops are unusable; they are merely unused.[73]

But those closer to the action were more generous. On November 1, General Edmond Buat, Pétain's chief of staff, said to Major Paul H. Clark, Pershing's liaison officer:

> When I learned that your army were to undertake the operations you assumed last September, I said it is prodigious ... You made mistakes and had difficulties certainly, but why not? Are you supermen? Are you Americans Gods that you can do the miraculous? If you had not had the difficulties that you did have I would certainly have said you were miracle workers ... given the conditions that existed—enemy—terrain—degree of training there are no other troops in the world who would have given one half the result that the US army did give.[74]

A modern French historian renders a favorable decision on the performance of the AEF in the Meuse–Argonne. André Kaspi points out that attacking in the Argonne was Foch's idea, not Pershing's. All of the AEF's previous preparations were aimed at continuing its offensive eastward toward Metz and Briey. To oblige Foch, Pershing turned his army into the right wing of a combined Allied offensive and successfully shifted half a million men westward in two weeks. "No one has ever denied them this glory." Furthermore, the Americans achieved substantial results, even if those did not amount to the spectacular victory that they later claimed. They learned as they went and passed through the crises that all improvised armies encounter. As Pétain grudgingly admitted to Foch on October 12, "Some organizational improvements have been made. They would have been more perceptible and faster if an inordinate national pride had not impeded the influence that the French officers assigned to the American staffs should legitimately have exercised."[75]

The American offensive had gotten stuck, but Ludendorff could take no comfort from the fact. Already on September 16, the German army group commander in Macedonia had warned of an imminent collapse in the face of a Franco-Serbian offensive; but at the time Ludendorff and Hindenburg could not be distracted from trying to figure out what Foch's plans for a September offensive were about.[76] On September 28, as the two of them assessed the military balance in their headquarters at Spa, things looked bleaker than ever. The French, British, and Americans were continuing their advances against the Germans' main line of defense in the West. In his memoirs, Ludendorff wrote:

> In Champagne and on the western bank of the Meuse a big battle had begun on the 26th of September, French and American troops attacking with far-reaching objectives. West of the Argonne we remained masters of the situation, and fought a fine defensive battle. Between the Argonne and the Meuse the Americans had broken into our positions. They had assembled a powerful army in this region, and their part in the campaign became more and more important.[77]

In the south and east, an Italian offensive against a weakened Austria-Hungary was imminent. The Turks had abandoned Amman (in present-day Jordan) on the 25th and the next day Bulgaria had asked for an armistice, increasing the despair of the civilian populace. This was shown by the collapse of the Berlin Stock Exchange, which had held steady in the face of German military reverses since early August. The worst worry, however, was the naked vulnerability of the Balkan front, where an unhindered Allied advance to the Danube from Greece seemed a real possibility.*[78] As

---

* Brook-Shepherd and others cite Ludendorff's memoirs as proof that only the disasters on the Eastern Fronts caused his decision to seek negotiations. (Gordon Brook-Shepherd, *November 1918* (Boston, Toronto: Little, Brown, 1981), p. 201.) It is true that Ludendorff cites the threat to Serbia, Hungary, and Turkey, to Rumanian neutrality, and Austro-Hungarian weakness as his immediate reasons. But his recital of the situation in France a couple of pages later makes it clear that fear of a breakthrough by the western Allies was a large part of his motivation as well. Colonel Albrecht von Thaer, Ludendorff's chief of staff, met with him on October 1; his diary shows Ludendorff to have been

Ludendorff studied the situation with his staff his agitation increased until he fell to the floor, convulsing and foaming at the mouth. That evening he had recovered just enough to conclude that he must ask for an armistice. This was Ludendorff's second "black day," and unlike the first he never recovered.

Having ordered his regiments to await relief, Kuhn decided to make no further attacks on the 30th. This was not easy; German shells, unimpeded by American counterbattery fire, continued to fall on the hastily constructed defensive line, which was held by the 311th and 312th Machine Gun Battalions and two platoons of the 310th Machine Guns— normally assigned in support, not as the main defensive units. Fortunately, no counterattack materialized. Food finally arrived and the men ate their first good meal since the jumpoff four days earlier.

Throughout the afternoon the troops of the 3rd Division replaced Kuhn's worn-out regiments. Shelling and bad roads had prevented the 3rd from arriving in time to effect the relief at night, so it was done in broad daylight. To the amazement of Kuhn's men, the columns of the 3rd marched up the roads under shell fire, then deployed in combat formation as they approached the trenches. In the words of a lieutenant in the Machine Gun Company of the 314th, "It was an inspiring sight to see those long thin waves billowing forward without hesitation, pressing onward with guns slung as if on a casual promenade. But, however spectacular, it was an entirely uncalled-for procedure to carry out a relief in this manner in the light of day while subject to enemy fire."[79] Men of the 3rd died uselessly as a result.

By 6:00 p.m. all four infantry regiments had left the line and started their march to the rear. Only two companies of the 311th Machine Gun Battalion remained, not to be relieved until the morning of October 1. Lieutenant Joel of the 314th described the procession:

desperately worried about the imminent collapse of the Western Front, partly as a result of the fresh American troops. (Albrecht von Thaer, "Diary Notes of Oberst Von Thaer, 1 October 1918," www.lib.byu.edu/~rdh/wwi/1918/thaereng.html, accessed December 2, 1998.)

Hoboes could hardly look more uncouth than the columns of soldiers trailing over the ruins of Montfaucon on the evening of September 30th. With seven-day beards, clothing ripped and shredded by barbed wire, and a thick coating of Argonne mud cemented to the hide with perspiration, the men hardly looked human. Everyone was emaciated and hollow-eyed, most of them suffering from bad colds and related ills. Swollen feet and stiffened muscles were the common lot of all. Guns and bayonets were covered with thick layers of rust. Even the ordinarily well-dressed officers were hardly presentable to a self-respecting hobo.[80]

The 304th Engineers made it as far as Malancourt when the order came through from V Corps reassigning them temporarily to the 3rd Division; worn out by five days of heavy manual labor as well as combat, they had to retrace their steps to the front.

Those who could stagger to the rear were, of course, the lucky ones. The division lost many men in its five days of action, but the actual numbers are unclear. Immediately after being relieved, the 79th reported its losses as 149 officers and 4,966 men killed, wounded, or missing, but there was little basis for these figures.[81] Certainly Kuhn's September 30 estimate of a 50 percent reduction in strength included several thousand stragglers and those wounded who had reached first aid stations or hospitals without being counted. After the war the US Army Medical Department reported that the division lost 597 killed, 2,375 wounded, and 473 gassed between September 26 and 30, including those who subsequently died of wounds.[82]

As the men of the 314th Infantry trudged back through Montfaucon, the battle offered up a final, bizarre event for their contemplation. A solitary enemy airplane had been flying over the German lines for some time, unmolested by Allied fighters or antiaircraft fire. Suddenly it crumpled, burst into flames, and "spun like a pinwheel to earth—a mass of fire."[83] Perhaps it was hit by one of the Germans' own high explosive shells, or perhaps the gasoline tank caught fire. To the hungry, exhausted soldiers it was just one more apparently pointless event at which to wonder.

CHAPTER 15

INTERLUDE—TROYON SECTOR, OCTOBER 1–28

The battered 79th wended its way back through the familiar towns of Malancourt, Avocourt, and Esnes. By October 2 the division, except for its engineers and field hospitals, had entered bivouac at Jouy-en-Argonne, 12 miles south of the Meuse–Argonne line. Trailing the procession were the MPs and the 304th Supply Train, which had the job of cleaning up the roads behind them. It wasn't easy, as the 79th was going south on the same roads that the 3rd was using to come north. Although 18 of the division's trucks had been wrecked by overturns or shell fire, all were retrieved—the division didn't lose a truck.[1] They rested for a day; then Kuhn issued Field Order No. 11, ordering the 79th to hit the road that night. For a destination he gave only the sector of the "II Colonial Corps," a French organization unknown to the men, who assumed that they were going to a rest area. A little later a supplement to the order specified that three columns would march respectively to Ancemont, Senoncourt, and les Monthairons— villages on the west bank of the Meuse, about six miles south of Verdun. The men had never heard of these places, certainly not in connection with any military action. But it was clear they would be moving south, which to them meant away from the front. Buoyed by the prospect, the 79th made good time in its march on the night of October 3–4. In the morning they rested, concealed by woods from German planes. On the afternoon of the 4th they left for a two-day march southward, glad still to be headed away from the line. En route, they received Field Order No. 12: they were to "relieve the 26th Division in the Troyon Sector during the night of October 7–8, 1918. The relief of the infantry and of the machine guns will be completed by the morning of 8th October." The meaning was clear: the 26th, whose sector the 79th would be taking over, had held the north part of the line on the old St Mihiel battlefield since activity there had ended on September 16. This was no rest area.[2]

And they needed rest. Captain Antoine Brondelle, a French observer with the 313th Infantry, wrote in his report, "The men are very tired as a result of their loss of initiative and also because their leaders appear uninterested in the physical and moral condition of their troops."[3] General A.W. Brewster, Inspector General of the Army, rated the division's morale as good but its physical condition as poor.[4] Lieutenant Colonel Harvey Cushing, a neurosurgeon in Field Hospital No. 6, had a private conversation with Brewster and wrote in his diary, "We have unquestionably been severely handled ... The 79th came out much bedraggled, and General Brewster says it will probably be broken up or have its number changed, as there's no use trying to build up an esprit from a unit with a bad name."[*5] General Kuhn himself was feeling the effects of the past week. In his diary he wrote, "Paid a visit to the troops and did what I could to cheer them up ... Many stragglers which is the most discouraging feature of the affair ... Troops arriving painfully and much used up."[6] To make matters worse, he came down with the flu that was now ravaging the AEF.[†] For almost two weeks the burden of running the division fell on Tenney Ross and a few others of his staff. By October 8 Kuhn was starting to recover and wrote to his wife:

> I am up for the first time after 10 days of wretched sickness, following immediately on the heels of the big fight. The Division has been withdrawn to another part of the line to reorganize and prepare for further fighting. We are getting into shape rapidly and will no doubt be called upon to try it again. The division did very well in my opinion although it failed to

---

[*] After the war Dr Cushing became famous as a pioneer of modern neurosurgery.

[†] The War Department estimated that as many as 100,000 soldiers were stragglers, lurking behind the lines and not participating in combat. In an October 21 memorandum it recommended that repeat offenders be tried by court martial and sentenced to death. It is highly likely, however, that many of those presumed skulkers and cowards were in fact flu victims prostrated by the onset of their illness. (Byerly, *Fever of War*, p. 171.)

accomplish the full task set to it at the beginning of operations. For that matter so did others. The behavior of both officers and men under fire was excellent and they are a brave lot; but they lack experience. They will do better next time, and I have no fear but what they will make a fine fighting division.[7]

On October 14 he could write, "Feeling much better and occupied my real office for the first time, but doctor still forbids my going out. Am eating with a good appetite which is a good sign."[8] By the next day he was running the division again.*

The sector to be occupied by the 79th was named Troyon, after a nearby nineteeth-century fortress that had withstood the German advance in 1914. In the words of the division's historian, the sector was "of a peculiar nature." The Main Line of Resistance ran along the eastern edge of the Heights of the Meuse, looking northeast over the Woëvre plain 300 feet below. Because the Heights were heavily cut with gullies, the line followed a wavy course along the cliffs. It was rare in this war for the Americans to occupy a commanding height so to avoid being overlooked, the Germans had retreated a further four miles from the base of the cliffs. The 26th had followed them, establishing a line consisting of lightly held outposts on the plain. This region below the cliffs was termed the "zone of observation." The historian of the 315th Infantry described the view:

> By day, the low-lying expanse of the Woëvre lay in solemn stillness, no life or movement visible on its broad surface, but at night came a miraculous change. The hills to the east became lit with the flash of Austrian guns, star shells rose and threw their weird light over the plain below, while overhead the German planes droned ceaselessly throughout the night.[9]

---

* Although statistics for the 79th are not readily available, the division does not appear to have suffered greatly from influenza once they left their training areas at Prouthoy and Champlitte. The divisional historian attributes this to headquarters' orders to company commanders to inspect their men daily, to make sure living quarters, food, and clothing were kept clean and sanitary, and to report the onset of colds immediately to a medical officer. (J. Frank Barber, *History of the Seventy-Ninth Division A.E.F. During the World War: 1917–1919* (Lancaster, PA: Steinman & Steinman, n.d.), p. 196.) But as the flu infection was airborne, that seems unlikely. Possibly it was because the 79th had been exposed to the weaker outbreak of July and August, which is believed to have conferred partial immunity to the much more virulent wave of September through December. ("Summer Flu Outbreak of 1918 May Have Provided Partial Protection against Lethal Fall Pandemic," National Institutes of Health, Fogarty International Center, http://www.fic.nih.gov/News/GlobalHealthMatters/Pages/Flu-1918.aspx, accessed January 14, 2015.)

Although the division was assigned once again to the front line, two provisions of Field Order No. 12 were a pleasant surprise. The 157th Brigade, which was to hold the main line of resistance on the Heights, would have in front of it two French battalions that would occupy the zone of observation. The 158th Brigade would stay in a rear area to train, re-equip, and compile its reports. In the dark of October 6, the French battalions entered the observation zone. The following night, in a cold rain, the two regiments of the 157th Brigade relieved the 26th Division, the 316th taking the right-hand subsector, called "Massachusetts," with the 313th on their left, occupying "Connecticut" (the 26th was the Yankee Division, after all).

Exploring their new home, the men of the 157th Brigade found huge piles of equipment, weapons, and supplies left by the Germans. They also found very comfortable quarters, especially for the officers: "Elaborately furnished officers' clubrooms, billiard rooms, dance halls, recreation huts, baths and vegetable gardens had been left behind." Even in the rear areas of the sector, which the German offensive had never reached, the dugouts formerly occupied by the French sported electric lights, showers, and comfortable beds.[10] But investigating old battlefields had its risks. Looking for a place to put their first aid station, a medical officer and a dental officer entered a mine gallery abandoned by the Germans. The enemy had not taken all of their explosives with them. The medical officer accidentally dropped a match; both men were fatally burned.[11]

As they recuperated from their ordeal at Montfaucon the men had a chance to write letters home and the officers, acting as military censors, to read them. Lieutenant Joel of the 316th described what he read:

> One cook apparently spent about all his spare time writing to "Dear, sweet wonderful little honey bunch" – ten sheet editions delivered about every other day. Another fellow simply couldn't stay with one idea, writing about as follows: "And we had nothin' to eet for five days and its raining hard all day today and meals is better now and if you send that swetter put some plugg and tobacco in. I hope this war stops soon and I got cooties now so good bye and rite when you get this." The common topics of discussion were the "grub", rumors, cooties, and reports of the end of the war or the capture of the Kaiser.[12]

Troyon was a "quiet" sector, meaning that there was no current or anticipated offensive activity by either side. But it was quiet only in the formal sense; the

Germans kept up a steady bombardment of high explosive and gas all the time the 79th was there. A continual stream of casualties resulted, although not nearly as many as in the Meuse–Argonne operation. The German artillery paid particular attention to the points at which the roads from the Heights crested the ridge on their way down to the Woëvre plain. By zeroing in their guns on those locations during the day, they could keep up an effective bombardment even at night. Supply trucks could not reach the troops in the observation zone; they had to be unloaded at the top and their cargoes carried by hand down the footpaths that led to the bottom of the cliffs.

The division spent the next few days reorganizing and consolidating its position. On the night of October 8–9, the 313th Infantry went forward and took over the left half of the observation zone from the French battalions. The next night the 316th did the same on the right. The artillery brigade of the 26th, which had stayed behind to support the 79th, rejoined its division; it was replaced by the 55th Artillery Brigade, borrowed from the 30th Division. On October 10 the 304th Engineers arrived, so by now the 79th had regained all of its original units except for the artillery. Also on the 10th, Kuhn reorganized his infantry brigades and by the 26th he had replaced most of his commanders. The new 157th, under Nicholson, had the 313th Regiment in line and the 314th in reserve. Colonel Sweezey had fallen ill and had been evacuated, so command of the 313th would devolve for the rest of the war on Colonel William C. Rogers, formerly commander of the Division Trains. Colonel Oury resumed leadership of the 314th while command of the 158th Brigade was given to Colonel George Williams, a newly arrived former cavalryman, who had previously replaced Meador at the 316th. The re-formed 158th Brigade had the 316th (also commanded by Williams) in front and the 315th (Knowles) behind. The regiments were thus restored to the organizations to which they had belonged before the Montfaucon attack. But now the brigades were side by side, avoiding the column-of-brigades formation that had given so much trouble on September 26. On October 12 the 79th Division became part of the French II Colonial Army Corps; this in turn was assigned to the newly created American Second Army, led by General Robert L. Bullard, promoted from command of III Corps. Second Army occupied the American sector from Fresnes-en-Woëvre (south of Verdun) to its southern extremity east of the Moselle. The 79th thus held the northernmost sector of Second Army.

But before the men could get properly situated, the Germans dealt them a surprise. In the Meuse–Argonne, the 79th had benefited from the infrequent use of gas by the German artillery. The penalty was a lack of experience with gas attacks, and now they would pay the price. The German line opposite Second Army was held by German Army Detachment C. All of its good units had been transferred to the Meuse–Argonne front. Those that were left were depleted and worn out. Expecting an American attack eastward on the Longwy–Briey industrial region, their only effective means of defense, they believed, was to saturate the Allied sectors with gas to break up assault formations and prevent an offensive from getting organized. The principal weapon was mustard gas, known as yellow cross, a highly persistent blistering agent. The Germans immediately across from Kuhn's division also had a more personal reason for using gas. Unknown to the men of the 79th, a few days before they took over the sector the 75mm guns of the 26th Division had fired a thousand gas shells into the German lines opposite them.[13]

On the night of October 9–10 the artillery of the 26th was still in place and the Germans took their revenge. As the 157th Brigade was replacing the French battalions in the zone of observation, the German guns opened up with a massive bombardment of yellow cross. At 11:30 p.m. on the 9th the villages of Hannonville and Saulx came under heavy fire from a new kind of shell that combined yellow cross with high explosive. Because it burst like an HE shell (that is, with a blast, not a dull "thump"), the gas could not be detected except by odor, by which time it was often too late. The gas officer of the 79th, Captain A.B. Clark, estimated that 9,500 shells of mustard gas, diphosgene, and blue cross (diphenlychloroarsene, a non-persistent respiratory irritant) were fired. The 316th, occupying the ground around Hannonville, was worst hit, taking almost 1,000 shells. Three platoons in particular were caught in the open while going to relieve the French troops in the observation zone. Although they donned their masks and took shelter in the town, they removed the masks too soon on the advice of an NCO who had not had gas training. Over a period of two days all became casualties; the town had to be evacuated entirely. The battalion headquarters of the 316th and 313th Regiments were gassed and had to be abandoned. The gas officer of the 26th Artillery estimated that 7,500 shells, mostly yellow cross, fell on his batteries. The gunners, having faced heretofore only minor attacks with few casualties, were overconfident; they wore only parts of their masks and took them off too soon. More than 25 percent of the gunners became casualties (by Captain Clark's estimate, more than half). In the rest of the 79th, 750 men were exposed to gas and 192 became casualties. (The HE component of the shells caused little damage.) Ninety percent of the affected troops developed eye and skin burns; 40 percent developed lung complications.[*] For several days after the bombardment, gas victims continued to stumble into the treatment stations—men blinded and gasping, not yet suffering from the inflamed skin that would develop days later. Some casualties were due to the continuing, low-level shelling carried out by the Germans, but many occurred because men were passing through areas previously saturated with mustard gas without wearing their masks.[†14]

Captain Clark, the gas officer, attributed the division's casualties to the troops' inexperience compounded by a shortage of trained gas specialists, both commissioned and non-commissioned.[15] Training had largely neglected gas operations, either offensive or defensive. The weapon was too new and officers begrudged the time taken away from traditional subjects such as drill and marksmanship. The situation was aggravated by the utter lack of an Army doctrine regarding use of and defense against gas. Clark was eventually able to persuade the divisional staff to take some correctional measures, such as placing fewer troops in the zone of observation and tightening gas discipline. Gas officers were relieved of all other duties, and rules requiring the carrying of gas masks were strictly enforced. These measures had limited effect at first because the men's morale still had not recovered from the trauma of the Montfaucon fight and the onset of flu and diarrhea. (The division surgeon put the physical efficiency of the men at a maximum of 40 percent.) Clark found that most men carried their masks improperly, and many had no masks at all. Officers showed little interest and continued to assign gas specialists to other duties. Although the division

---

[*] One such casualty was Colonel Ross, Kuhn's chief of staff. At some point he had to remove his mask to issue orders over the phone. He coughed heavily for the rest of his life. (Betsy Ross, *I Fly the Flag* (Champaign, IL: Graphix Group, Inc., 1984), p. 40.)

[†] Oddly, the divisional historian does not record this gas attack, which is well attested in the unit's archives. Instead, he writes about a gas bombardment on October 14 that concentrated on the dressing station and quarters of the 315th Ambulance Company. (Barber, *79th Division*, pp. 189–90.) The history of the 316th Infantry mentions no gas attacks at all. (Carl E. Glock, *History of the 316th Regiment of Infantry in the World War, 1918* (Philadelphia, PA: Biddle-Deemer Printing Co., 1930, second printing).)

staff had apparently awakened to the problem, the morale of the men was still too low for them to respond energetically.[16]

Within a few weeks both morale and attention to gas defense had improved. On the night of October 21–22 the Germans sent yellow cross shells into woods occupied by two companies. The men evacuated the woods promptly and only one casualty resulted. Two days later the area in front of the trenches around Fresnes was heavily shelled with blue cross; there were no immediate casualties, although three men were sent to the treatment station a day later. By the time the division left the Troyon sector Captain Clark was able to report, "[C]ooperation with Staff Departments is very good, indeed. An active interest is manifested in gas work, necessary orders are published, and support is given in every way ... to assist the Division Gas Officer in maintaining gas discipline and protective measures."[17]

In this "quiet" sector the 79th sent out nightly patrols to reconnoiter enemy positions and take prisoners; the Germans raided the American lines for the same purposes. But the men of the division had learned the virtues of stealth and patience. No longer did they give away their positions by firing at noises and shadows. On one occasion a German patrol tried to get through the line of Company K, 313th Infantry, to see whether Fresnes-en-Woëvre was occupied. It was detected by a private who waited until it had passed and then opened up on it from behind with his automatic rifle. This attracted fire from the rest of the company. The patrol leader was killed, the rest scattered, one man surrendered.[18] Excitement picked up on the night of October 20 when a heavy bombardment hit the 313th's positions on the left of the sector. The next morning a German deserter told of at least one reserve division being brought into the line, and observation balloons appeared over the enemy's front. Kuhn rushed his reserve battalions forward to help resist an attack, but it was a false alarm. Apparently, this kind of activity simply meant that one German division was relieving another. The reserves were ordered back to the rear.[19]

The men kept improving their combat technique. Before dawn on October 23 a platoon of the 316th Infantry, stationed at Doncourt in the zone of observation, reported that the wire in front of its position had been cut. Suspecting an impending raid, the lieutenant in charge of the platoon sent a patrol forward to set up an ambush and withdrew the rest of the unit behind the town. The German attack fell upon vacant trenches. The ambush patrol then hit the raiders in the flank with automatic rifle fire killing four, wounding more, and sending the enemy back in disarray. A simultaneous raid against the division's line at Wadonville, to the south, surprised the defenders, who nevertheless repelled the Germans after a sharp fight. After that, enemy raids and patrols ceased for as long as the 79th held the sector.[20]

That would not be long. The same morning, the 79th received orders saying that the 33rd Division would relieve it that night. Sure enough, the first units of the 33rd started arriving in the zone of the 79th in the evening. For the next two nights the components of the 79th marched rearward to the Dieue zone, on the Meuse River, for reorganization. At this time 2,200 replacements arrived, bringing the division close to full strength. They would have arrived sooner but they had been quarantined for flu and spinal meningitis. They were replacements in numbers, but not in quality. Hailing mostly from the American west and south, they were almost entirely untrained; many had never fired their rifles.[21]

By October 27 all the troops of the 79th had left the Troyon sector and headed north. They had lost 42 dead in the 19 days they had been there, almost all in the infantry regiments and almost all from shell fire. The next day all of the division's elements were at their destinations in or around Verdun: the 314th six miles to the southeast, the 315th three miles to the west, the two regiments of the 157th Brigade and the two machine guns battalions in the city itself. The adjutant of the 316th described the march of his regiment through the ruined streets:

> Hushed—save for the clattering of hobnails on ringing cobbles, the boom of a vagrant cannon, the crash of an occasional shell, and the solemn striking of the hour in the battered cathedral, invisible in the dark. Slowly the column wound its way between gaping houses, and all the usual grimness of a ruined city, past the still upright Hotel de Ville, and on into the massive citadel whose sheltered galleries and sturdy walls gave an unaccustomed sense of security to men inured to shell-holes and deceptive dugouts.[22]

William Schellberg of the 313th—who had been promoted to corporal—reacted less lyrically to Verdun and its citadel:

> Well we had to leave our cozy little dugouts which I referred to in my last letter, and are now billeting in a French jail, "thats going some aint it." I had to come all the way to France to have this experience; well when I get back I can say I was in jail anyway. We have had some good times since being here

in this place it seems funny to see one another in a cell, and we are having a good time the reason for this is they have not got us locked up if they would have us locked up I don't think we would be having such a pleasant time.[23]

In its bivouacs around Verdun, the 79th received orders to rejoin First Army as part of the French XVII Corps commanded by General Henri Claudel. The left-most division of XVII Corps was the American 29th Division. The 79th would relieve the 29th in the Grande Montagne sector, an extension of the Meuse–Argonne battlefield to the east of the river. The relief would take place on the nights of October 28 and 29; shortly thereafter, the division would take over part of the line held by the 26th Division as well. No "quiet" sector now; this meant combat.

By the time Pershing's offensive stalled on September 30, the French command had concluded from its observations of First Army that there was a serious risk that the Germans would mount a strong counterattack. This would force the Americans into a fighting retreat. They also believed that, although the US divisions were formidable combat organizations when well led, their staffs did not yet know their jobs; the solution would be for the experienced French to take over the coordination of American movements. Third, they found that things could not be left as they were. Pétain proposed that the American Army go on the defensive, while its divisions were to be rotated into French corps where they would get offensive experience. Once the US divisions and their staffs were properly seasoned, the AEF could resume the offensive.[24] And indeed, the American situation was ripe for disaster, presenting to the Germans the best circumstance an attacker can face: an immobile and disorganized enemy backed by inadequate roads— the same state of affairs that had allowed the British and French to crush Ludendorff's stalled offensives in July and August. Fortunately, the Germans did not realize the American predicament, and were unable at any rate to mount more than local counterattacks.

The French perception of First Army's failure was magnified by the success of the British Fourth Army in the north—especially its spectacular breakthrough on September 29 across the St Quentin Canal—and of the

French themselves in the center. The British feat occurred even before any German reserves could be moved south to meet the Americans. Foch sent a message to Pershing on September 30 suggesting that Liggett's I Corps be placed under the command of the French Fourth Army to its west, so that the Fourth would then completely surround the Argonne Forest.[25] The next day General Maxime Weygand, Foch's chief of staff and a close confidante of Clemenceau, met with Pershing to announce Foch's plan to divide First Army. Pershing agreed with many of Foch's points, but rejected completely the idea of splitting up the American forces. Foch was forced to accede to Pershing's terms, but with a stipulation:

> Amending what I wrote you September 30, I agree to maintaining the present organization of command, as you propose, under the condition that your attacks start without delay and that, once begun, they be continued without any interruptions such as those which have just arisen.[26]

Pershing had halted his army to replace depleted divisions and repair the roads; now he was under pressure to resume the offensive.[*] He had swapped four badly mauled, novice divisions for three veteran ones, but in other ways his situation had deteriorated. The lethal second wave of the flu had ravaged the training camps in the States and forced a curtailment of the draft.[†] As a result, troop shipments were not sufficient to make up for losses, forcing him to break up two newly arrived divisions for replacements and to reduce

---

[*] One division—the 77th, enmeshed in the Argonne Forest on First Army's extreme left—apparently did not get the word to stop offensive action on September 30. Sent on October 1 to capture the German position at the Moulin de Charlevaux, the division was to be protected on its left by a regiment of the French Fourth Army. But the "French" regiment was actually the 368th Regiment of the American 92nd Division, a black division that Pershing had lent to Pétain. Poorly led by incompetent and hostile white officers, the 368th failed to advance (see Chapter 8), uncovering the flank of the 77th. When the latter's attack stalled on October 2, the Germans were able to surround the leading elements of the division, consisting of seven infantry companies from two regiments and parts of one machine gun battalion. Dubbed by the press the "Lost Battalion," these men endured, isolated and under heavy fire, until rescued on October 7. (Robert H. Ferrell, *America's Deadliest Battle: Meuse–Argonne, 1918*, ed. Theodore A. Wilson, Modern War Studies (Lawrence, KS: UP of Kansas, 2007), pp.74–78.)

[†] The flu was a worldwide epidemic. In Great Britain, about 225,000 civilians died. In the British Expeditionary Force, 313,000 cases were reported, probably a low count. In France, 135,000 civilians and 30,000 soldiers lost their lives. The Germans lost 225,000 civilians; over 700,000 soldiers fell ill, with 80 percent occurrence in some units. In the United States as many as 675,000 died. (Byerly, *Fever of War*, p. 99.)

the size of an infantry company from 250 to 175 men.[27] The Germans, in the meantime, had reinforced their line from four divisions on September 25 to nine on October 2 with more on the way. Pershing determined to renew the attack on October 4. His aim was to eliminate the strong enemy positions facing First Army, especially the artillery concentrations. III Corps under Bullard would capture the heights northeast of Cunel; V Corps under Cameron would take the Romagne Heights; and I Corps under Liggett would take the hills north of Exermont and clear out the eastern edge of the Argonne Forest at Châtel-Chéhéry and Cornay. Corps were now to advance independently regardless of progress on their flanks. There would be no advance artillery preparation that might alert the Germans to the impending attack. The Germans, however, had figured out what was coming and had stiffened their defense. By October 7 Pershing's three corps had regained most of the ground given up on September 28 and 29 and gotten a bit beyond. The 1st Division recaptured the Bois de Montrebeau, which the 35th had abandoned, and got past Exermont. The 32nd Division, replacing the 91st and the 37th, got through the Bois Emont and took Gesnes. The 3rd Division, in the old sector of the 79th, got past Bois 250 and the Bois des Ogons but still could not capture the Madeleine Farm. And the 4th Division took the Bois de Fays.

But the October 4 attack suffered again from inexperience. American artillery plastered the hilltops and tree lines, where they expected the enemy machine guns to be. But the German reinforcements had dug in on the forward slopes of the hills or in the middle of the woods, which were untouched by the bombardment. Americans continued to charge recklessly into machine gun fire, evoking the admiration and pity of the Germans. The Army's official statistical summary reported over 6,500 deaths in the first week of October, eclipsing the 1,600 fatalities of the previous week.[*28] One event only allowed the AEF to claim a triumph. Hunter Liggett, commanding I Corps, brought a brigade of the 82nd Division up from reserve and put it between the 77th and the 28th Divisions. Then he had it attack westward into the flank of the Argonne Forest, behind the Germans who were holding up the advance of his corps. This forced the Germans to withdraw, relieving the Lost Battalion and clearing the forest by October 10.

---

* It is possible that many of the deaths reported in early October were from wounds suffered in September, which would tend to even out the distribution over time.

In this attack Sergeant Alvin York single-handedly killed 28 Germans and captured 132, as well as 35 machine guns. But overall the second phase of the offensive so far was disappointing; Pershing needed to raise his sights.

Giving up half his command was not the only thing Foch had suggested to Pershing in his September 30 memo. Throughout the campaign, the American infantry had been hammered by German heavy guns firing unopposed from east of the Meuse. It was time to end this harassment. Like Falkenhayn in 1916, Pershing would have to extend his offensive across the river to protect his right flank. Foch wrote:

> The action to be launched on the right bank of the Meuse should be designed to seize the heights of the Meuse between Damvillers and Dun-sur-Meuse. This result would secure the flank of our general offensive toward the north and afford greater liberty of movement to our armies through the possession of the roads and of the railroad in the valley of the Meuse.[29]

On October 5 Pétain ordered First Army to attack on the right bank of the Meuse, the attack to be led by the French XVII Corps, reinforced by whatever American divisions were available. The XVII Corps had defended First Army's line on the right bank of the Meuse ever since Pershing's nine divisions had attacked northward on September 26. Now it was time for it to join the fray. Pershing ordered it to advance straight north while the 33rd Division pushed eastward from the left bank of the Meuse. On October 8 they attacked, taking Consenvoye in a day but failing to make it to the top of the Heights. Even so, the pressure on the German defenders had the effect of reducing the volume of flanking fire on III and V Corps.[30]

Meanwhile, the attacks west of the Meuse continued with little better success than before. Pétain continued to press for results; Pershing promised him a major renewal of the offensive on October 14. The general had changed all three of his corps commanders. Major General Joseph T. Dickman replaced the promoted Liggett at I Corps; General Summerall, an aggressive artilleryman, supplanted Cameron at V Corps; and General Hines took over I Corps to replace Bullard, who had been promoted to command the new Second Army. Two first-rate divisions had been added to the lineup, the 42nd and the 5th, both veterans of St Mihiel. But the October 14 attack didn't go any better than the earlier ones, for much the same reasons. German counterattacks forced the Americans to take and retake positions many times over. The 5th Division put too many troops into the front line while holding none in reserve, causing it to become disorganized. German artillery and gas gave accurate support to the defenders, who fought until completely surrounded. Pershing had no choice but to urge his commanders to keep on pushing; according to historian Allen Millett, to do otherwise would have been to admit that his opposition to amalgamation had been wrongheaded and "that his dream of an independent American army playing a decisive role in the defeat of Germany was nothing more than another delusion of the Great War."[31] By the 19th, casualties— almost 18,000 killed since October 1—forced Pershing to give up attacking on a broad front.[32] By then the 32nd Division had cracked the *Kriemhilde-Stellung* at the Côte Dame Marie and the 42nd at the Côte de Châtillon.[*] Pershing had finally achieved his goal for September 26.

Although firm in his commitment to a unified American army, Pershing must have understood that his forces were exceeding his span of control. After refusing Foch's September 30 demand that he turn over part of his army to French command, he had consulted Pétain, whom he considered a supporter. Pétain suggested that Pershing create and lead an American army group under the direct command of Foch, on an equal footing with the French and British armies.[33] With Foch's agreement, on October 10 Pershing activated Second Army to take over the American line from the old St Mihiel sector southward. Two days later he appointed Bullard as its commander, moving himself up to army group commander and thereby removing himself from day-to-day control of operations. To lead First Army he promoted General Hunter Liggett from I Corps.

Liggett, an Academy graduate, had served in the American West and the Philippines and had attended the Army War College, where he preceded Kuhn as president. He was respected throughout the Army as an upright and reliable officer. His only failing was his excessive weight; to his critics he retorted that none of the fat was above the collar.[34] In January 1918 Pershing gave him command of I Corps, which he led at Château-Thierry and in the Aisne–Marne and St Mihiel offensives. In the Meuse–Argonne his three divisions, on the western end of the line, came to a halt on September 30 like the rest of them; but as V Corps took most of the blame, Liggett's reputation was unharmed. Taking command of First Army on October 16, he immediately spent several days visiting his units to build cohesion and morale. This was critical; food and shelter were still lacking, and Liggett

---

[*] *Côte* as used here means hill.

estimated that 100,000 men had become stragglers. He also resisted pressure from Pershing to mount an attack before the army was rested, resupplied, and retrained. In particular, they needed instruction in fire-and-maneuver tactics, how to attack fortified positions, and how to use artillery support.

For the two weeks after October 19, First Army made only local attacks to improve the line. One such action, however, would dictate the terms of the 79th Division's next engagement. The French XVII Corps held First Army's right flank across the river in the Heights of the Meuse. This range of hills was another of the north-trending ridges, like the Argonne and Barrois plateaus to its west, that in earlier centuries had defended Paris from invasion from the east. Like those plateaus, its north-trending whaleback was cut on both sides by eroded valleys. Unlike those formations, however, the ridges that formed the west-facing valleys terminated in sharp bluffs that overlooked the Meuse River. As we have seen, the contorted, wooded landscape of the Heights offered concealment for the big German guns; the promontories gave their artillery observers a perfect view as far as Montfaucon, 12 miles to the west. It was clear that further success west of the Meuse would depend on silencing the German artillery.

From October 8 through 10, XVII Corps had advanced about three miles northward while the American 33rd Division to its west had crossed the Meuse and gained a further two and a half miles. On October 15 Pershing ordered the XVII Corps to continue its attack. By the 23rd it had taken the strategic position of Molleville Farm and had established positions in the Bois d'Etraye and atop a peak almost level with the highest ridge on that side of the river, the Grand Montagne. The right-hand peak of this massif was at an elevation of 370 meters, 28 meters higher than Montfaucon. Its northwesterly extension, the Borne de Cornouiller (also called Hill 378 by the Americans) reached to the flats along the river and allowed the Germans to survey all of First Army. In English, the name of this ridge would have been the deceptively placid "Dogwood's End." Once the 79th joined XVII Corps, the Borne would be its first objective.

As the 79th marched from Troyon to its bivouacs around Verdun, the warring nations moved erratically toward peace. On September 28, the same day as Ludendorff's collapse, Foreign Minister Paul von Hintze convinced Reichstag leaders that President Wilson's Fourteen Points represented the best deal for Germany; but that to approach Wilson to negotiate an armistice and peace would first require democratization of the German government. The next day Kaiser Wilhelm, Hintze, Ludendorff, and Chancellor Count Hertling met at Spa. That is when Wilhelm first learned of Ludendorff's determination to ask for peace terms not, Ludendorff said, because defeat was imminent but to "avoid further loss of life." The Kaiser made no protest and asked no questions, docilely approving an approach to Wilson that would bypass France and Britain. Separately, he proposed a parliamentary government to Hertling and Hintze but did not inform the High Command. Hertling, who for the past year had consistently failed to impose government control over Ludendorff, resigned. This made way for Prince Maximilian von Baden, a monarchist, a Centrist, and a decent man but otherwise a nonentity, to become Chancellor.[35]

Hintze had promised to send a peace offer to Wilson by October 1 but Prince Max had not yet formed a government, so there was no chancellor in place to sign it. Ludendorff insisted hysterically that the offer be sent anyway, as his lines were about to crumble. The representative of the Foreign Office at Spa was so shaken that he sent a message to Berlin pressing them to contact Wilson right away because everyone in OHL appeared "to have completely lost their nerve here." Max delayed, convinced that to ask for armistice terms on such a precipitate basis would be to admit defeat and invite political and social upheaval. He also realized that he had been set up as what later generations would call the fall guy.[36] Finally, under increasing pressure from the High Command, the Kaiser, and his own cabinet, he dispatched the note asking for an immediate armistice to be followed by peace negotiations on the basis of the Fourteen Points.

The note reached Wilson on October 6. After requesting clarification as to what Prince Max was offering and receiving a vague response, Wilson responded on October 14 insisting that the Allies, not the Germans, would set terms for evacuation of occupied territories and would accept an armistice only if it precluded further hostilities. He also demanded the dismantling of the German government as an "arbitrary power" and its replacement with one that represented "the action of the German people themselves."[37] Six days later the Chancellor acceded to Wilson's conditions, agreeing to abandon submarine warfare and outlining a program of voting reform.

Wilson replied that he was now in a position to present these developments to his allies and ask them to prepare their terms. But he objected to dealing with the Imperial government, demanding to negotiate with "veritable representatives of the German people who have been assured of a genuine constitutional standing as the real rulers of Germany."[38]

If Wilson thought he and the new German government were making progress, he was premature. As the Allied advance bogged down in mid-October and the German line did not collapse, the mercurial Ludendorff recovered some of his nerve. Asked by the Kaiser for advice on how to reply to Wilson, he insisted that the German Army was capable of continued resistance. He discounted the likelihood of an Allied penetration, and maintained that a withdrawal to a position holding Antwerp and the Meuse would shorten and stabilize the line and give the Germans time and resources to plan a spring offensive for 1919. He had lost all credibility with the government, especially after renewed attacks by one French and three British armies on October 17 through 20 crossed the Selle and Sambre Rivers and the Oise Canal, demolishing the last German position before the Antwerp–Meuse line.[39] Nevertheless, he and Hindenburg refused to meet Wilson's demand for their armistice proposals and sent a telegram to all army group commanders ordering them to "fight to the finish." One commander objected, so the telegram was canceled; but a radio operator who was a member of the Independent Socialist Party sent the text to the party's Reichstag members. On October 25, Ludendorff's canceled telegram was published in the newspapers. Prince Max insisted that the Kaiser demand Ludendorff's resignation or the government would quit. Ludendorff, in turn, went to Berlin to see the Kaiser and to insist that he reject Wilson's most recent note, blaming the crisis on the lack of support for the Army among the German people. But the Kaiser, himself no rock of stability, had finally had enough of his insubordinate Quartermaster General. Outraged that Ludendorff had sent such a telegram directly to the army commanders, Wilhelm barked, "Excellency, I must remind you that you are in the presence of your Emperor." Seeing that he had lost Wilhelm's trust, Ludendorff resigned the next day. General Wilhelm Groener, commander of the German occupation of the Ukraine and a man in touch with reality, took his place. Groener's job was to buy the government time to negotiate favorable terms from the Allies but not so much time as would lead to internal collapse. The question now was not whether the killing would end but how long it would take.

CHAPTER 16

BORNE DE CORNOUILLER AND THE HEIGHTS OF THE MEUSE, OCTOBER 29– NOVEMBER 10

By November 1 Liggett believed that First Army was rested and ready to resume the offensive. Foch, the commander in chief, concentrated on severing German rail communications along the Western Front, particularly at Sedan and Mézières, in the sectors of First Army and the neighboring French Fourth Army respectively. He wanted Liggett to attack westward from the Romagne Heights into the Bois de Bourgogne, a wooded plateau that formed a northward extension of the Argonne Forest and that dominated both the left flank of First Army and the right flank of the French Fourth. Liggett, not wanting to get bogged down in another forest battle, decided instead to attack northward across Barricourt Heights, leaving the Bois de Bourgogne to be occupied after the bypassed German defenders had withdrawn. Unlike many of the divisions used in the initial attack on September 26, his troops now were experienced veterans, adept in artillery coordination and sophisticated tactics such as infiltration and night attacks. V Corps in the center, now commanded by Summerall, would deliver the main attack northward while I Corps on the left pinned the Germans to the Bois de Bourgogne and III Corps on the right drove the enemy back to and across the Meuse. Ever the artillerist, Summerall developed a firing plan for the November 1 assault that included several days of gas, shrapnel, and high explosive on "all enemy organizations, batteries, and routes of communication." Sudden, intense firing several times a day would keep the Germans guessing as to when the next phase of the attack would open and would shield the registration of the American guns. A complex pattern of standing and rolling barrages was devised. Liggett's order for the operation prescribed that "fire superiority, rather than sheer man power, be the driving force of the attack."[1] Liggett's army had come a long way from Pershing's infantry-first doctrine.

But since the first week of the Meuse–Argonne offensive it had been obvious that sustained forward progress would depend on silencing the formidable German artillery east of the river. Of the 77 heavy batteries facing First Army early in October, 28—almost 40 percent—were hidden in the defiles of the Heights of the Meuse, directed from observation posts on the Borne de Cornouiller and other promontories overlooking the Meuse valley and the countryside to its west.[2] Numbers alone do not reveal the problem they posed for the Americans. Not only were the German guns unthreatened by enemy infantry, they were firing in enfilade, making aiming particularly easy. Precision in elevation was not critical; as long as they got the azimuth right, they were pretty certain to hit something. Conversely, the trenches and reverse hillsides on which the Americans relied for shelter ran the wrong way—parallel to the German line of fire rather than across it. The attacks of the American 29th and 33rd Divisions and the French XVII Corps in October had made progress on the east bank of the river, and the volume of fire had diminished somewhat; but the attacks stalled short of the Borne de Cornouiller itself, and the Germans continued to pummel the divisions to the west.

There was a strategic element to the Borne position as well. By the last week of October Ludendorff was withdrawing his forces all along the line, hoping to maintain a continuous defense that would keep the Allies out of Germany. His plan was to retire to a holding position along the Meuse north of Verdun. But doing so required that the supply lines through the Carignan–Sedan–Mézières railroad, which lay in the path of the American advance, be kept open, so retreating from the *Kriemhilde-Stellung* in front of First Army was impossible; it would have to be defended.[3] Ludendorff's line resembled a door swinging northeastward, its hinge the hilly terrain around the Borne de Cornouiller. If the door could be removed from its hinge, it might fall flat.

On the night of October 27–28 the men of the 79th marched from Verdun to the Bois des Forges, on the west side of the Meuse. There they halted for the day to avoid observation by the ever-present German reconnaissance planes. But the woods had been so wrecked by shell fire that little cover was available; soon enough, shells started to land, killing several engineers. At least the men left with one fond memory of the Bois: a meal of bacon, bread, jam, and coffee, a rare treat.[4] The following night the division crossed the Meuse to take up its new position in the line of the French XVII Corps, Major General Henri Claudel commanding.

The line held by XVII Corps on October 27 was an arc with its left end anchored on the Meuse and then reaching to the east, southeast, and south. The French 15th Colonial Infantry Division held the left-most sector, a two and a half-mile stretch running eastward south of the riverside town of Sivry-sur-Meuse. To its right was the American 29th Division, now to be relieved by the 79th, holding a front that faced north where it met the 15th D.I.C. but east at its lower extremity. The next division to the right was the American 26th, also facing east and scheduled to shift southward; the 79th would take up the vacancy left by its northernmost brigade. Two more French divisions and the American 81st Division to the south completed the front of XVII Corps and First Army.

The sector assigned to the 79th was a difficult one. To the north and nearly a mile away towered the Borne de Cornouiller, fronted by Molleville Farm, a fortified agricultural compound nestled in a depression at the foot of the hill. The hill itself was bald and offered no cover to attackers. To its right was the forested slope of the Grande Montagne, rising to a peak of 388 meters; its dense woods would let the well-sited German machine guns fire into the flank of any unit attempting to take the Borne. Proceeding clockwise around the arc one encountered a series of small, interlinked woods: the Bois d'Etraye, Bois de Wavrille, Belleu Bois, Bois des Chênes, and Bois d'Ormont, which bordered the position of the neighboring 26th Division. All of them were sited on small hills or the slopes of larger hills, and most were at least partially occupied by the enemy, whose trenches were often only a hundred yards away. As in September, the Germans overlooked the Americans at almost all points along the line. Having been in the sector a long time, their artillery was very familiar with the positions to be taken up by the 79th and would be able to drop shells accurately among them from the moment the division moved in.[5]

But the division had several advantages it had not enjoyed in its previous fight. Its total frontage was a little less than five miles—three times the breadth of its original attack at Montfaucon.[6] Someone had figured out that jamming 27,000 men into a sector a mile and a half wide had served only to prevent maneuvering and make supply almost hopeless. Second, the division was well served by roads. Two—from Consenvoye to Etraye and from Brabant to Etraye—converged immediately behind the left subsector of the division's line. The road to Etraye continued parallel to and behind the front, where it was joined by a road coming up from Samogneux to the south. A spur of the latter branched northeastward near the village of Ormont, passing through the Bois des Chênes on the division's right. Supplying the troops, while always difficult in battle, would not be impossible. As the regiments of the 79th went into the line, the 304th Supply Train set up a station in the rear to distribute supplies, hot food, spare parts, and first aid. The 304th Sanitary Train set up a gas hospital and dressing stations along the roads leading from the front. The 304th Ammunition Train set up dumps at locations convenient for truck transport. Traffic control and road discipline worked well.[7] Third, mindful of the poor support the artillery had provided in the opening days of the offensive, Liggett had First Army reorganize the army and corps artillery and change the target acquisition system. An operations section was assigned to each army and corps artillery headquarters to assist the staffs in coordinating fire against important targets. Because of their long range and wide field of fire, the heavy guns could now support many divisions on a single day without moving. Also, several heavy artillery brigades could combine their fire on a single objective. This allowed the artillery to adapt its fire to different conditions across the battlefield. And instead of liaison officers assigned solely to units, they were assigned to areas as well. Anything they observed within their assigned area was reported to the artillery, whether it involved an American unit or not. Observers attached to units were responsible for reporting the unit commander's plans in advance so that artillery support could be arranged.[8] Most important, Liggett removed the restriction on artillery bombardments close ahead of the attacking infantry. This permitted the guns to assist the attackers all the way to the objective.[9] Moreover, Kuhn and his staff had learned how to call on corps artillery for support and how

79TH DIVISION OPERATIONS, OCTOBER 30–NOVEMBER 11, 1918

to use their own guns to advance the attack and to aid in defense. The machine gun battalions in particular had become skilled at beating off counterattacks.[10] The men now knew to spread out and to dig in quickly in anticipation of artillery fire. Officers had learned to avoid frontal attacks in favor of flank assaults and small-unit strikes on individual strong points.[11]

One may reasonably ask how the division acquired its newfound proficiency. Some of it came from above: on October 14, Drum, now a brigadier general, ordered all divisions not serving in the front lines to resume their training. "Special emphasis must be placed on the training of recruits and the correction of tactical deficiencies noted in recent engagements."[12] Accompanying this order was a flood of directives and memoranda on tactics: how to use combined arms—infantry, artillery, smoke, tanks—to silence German machine gun nests; how to coordinate artillery with infantry to avoid shelling one's own troops; and others.[13] Even the French got into the act, despite Pershing's aversion to taking advice from foreigners. Their liaison mission issued a note on how to organize captured positions against counterattacks.[14] General Claudel, commanding XVII Corps, sent the 79th a memorandum on methods for attacking in wooded and rugged terrain.[15] These directives did not merely rest on paper. As we have seen, when the 79th occupied the Troyon sector Kuhn held the 158th Brigade back for training. He augmented this with exercises for cadres, drawn from each regiment and battalion, who would return to their units to impart the lessons they had learned.[16] But while helpful, such measures could not by themselves instill in the officers and men the battlefield instincts they would need to dominate the enemy. The answer can only be that, in the words of historian Andrew Wiest, the AEF had "learned to fight by fighting." American field- and company-grade officers, learning from their mistakes, taught themselves on the spot the rudiments of staff work, logistics, and tactics.[17]

Kuhn assigned his 158th Brigade, now under Brigadier General Evan Johnson, to the left half of the division's sector and the 157th, under Nicholson, to the right. Johnson, in turn, would place the 316th Infantry Regiment on his left, facing north to the Borne and northeast to the Grande Montagne, and the 315th to its right in the Bois d'Etrayes. Each regiment was to be reinforced by a company or two of the 312th Machine Gun Battalion. Nicholson's subsector would have the 314th Infantry Regiment (Oury) on the left, spread across the Bois Belleu and the Bois d'Ormont, facing northeast to east, and the 313th (under Colonel Rogers, replacing Sweezey, who was ill) in the Bois d'Ormont on the right facing due eastward. Between them the 311th Machine Gun Battalion would hold the Bois des Chênes. For artillery support the 79th took over the 52nd Field Artillery Brigade from the departing 33rd Division. Commanded by Brigadier General George Albert Wingate, the brigade had been in the area for over a month, so it knew the terrain and the enemy positions.

As the division crossed the Meuse the 158th Brigade turned north. In his diary, Sergeant Davies of the 315th described the march to his platoon's front-line position:

> As we go up thru the dense woods we stumble over many bodies both American and German. The stench from the decaying flesh is terrible and I am almost sick. I think, as we pick our way over these poor bruised bodies, how little the value of life is here ... I can picture the sorrow of the loved ones

when they get the word "Killed in Action," but I wonder if they can realize the living death their boys experienced before the long sleep came to them.[18]

The Germans had only recently abandoned these positions, and the countryside showed the detritus of October's attacks by the French XVII Corps:

> The open land across the road, sloping into the ravine of Molleville Farm, was pock-marked with enemy fire, and the farm at the bottom was a crumbled heap of stone. On the far side of the ravine, both to the east and the north, the Germans held the woods, and had the P. C. and the road leading northward to the crossroad under perfect observation. This deathdealing road was lined with broken water carts, dead horses, ammunition boxes, empty marmite cans, and every description of equipment left by men killed while carrying supplies up to the lines.[19]

To the south, the regiments of the 157th Brigade had to get to their new lines by hiking up a ravine shown on the map as the Fond de Walonsevaux but called by the men "Death Valley," a name bestowed by the French former occupants of the sector. As the darkness receded, Lieutenant Kress of the 314th's machine gun company observed the scene before him:

> Here lay a German, his arm drawn back and in his hand a grenade, caught at the critical moment by the messenger of death. There lay another with a flare pistol in his hand, crouched as if he were about to fire, even as a final bullet pierced his brain ... All about lay the shattered bodies of American and German dead, torn and retorn by the constant fall of shells and mortars. Investigation of the bodies showed them to belong to three divisions, the 26th, 29th, and 33rd. Some of them must have been lying there for weeks.[20]

Nonetheless, many in the division were eager to take the Heights, nursing a grudge as they did over the rough handling they had received from the German guns back in September.

General Claudel's first task for the 79th was to attack northward, taking the Borne de Cornouiller. Kuhn assigned this mission to the 158th Brigade, while the 157th held its east-facing line until further orders. The Borne not only overlooked the Meuse valley to its west, it also commanded the roads leading east through the Heights to the Woëvre plain where, in addition to their large guns, the Germans had concentrated their railheads, supply depots, and major troop encampments at Etraye, Réville, and Ecurey. Claudel's orders were phrased in terms of a pursuit eastward, assuming that the Borne would fall easily. This was quickly revealed to be optimistic; patrols reported that the hill was strongly held by German troops who showed no inclination to leave. In fact, German intelligence had identified the 79th Division as soon as it appeared east of the Meuse and predicted that an attack in that sector was imminent. Ludendorff himself, looking on the offensive as a threat to the vital railroad through Mézières, forbade withdrawal from the Heights and sent reinforcements, eventually committing 27 of his reserve divisions to this sector.[21]

Opposing the 158th Brigade would be two German divisions, the 228th and the 192nd, entrenched in the *Giselher-Stellung*, which ran across the Borne. The 192nd, to the east, was a veteran of the Verdun battles of 1916 and the British counterattack at Amiens in August 1918. In September it had been put into the tip of the salient at St Mihiel, almost immediately retreating as part of the general German withdrawal. Reaching the Borne de Cornouiller on October 24, it had come under heavy bombardment; its 192nd Infantry Regiment had lost four officers and many men in three days and morale was low. American intelligence rated the 192nd as third class.[22] The 228th, to its west, had been formed only in May 1917 from regiments scavenged from other divisions; it had suffered many casualties in the French attacks west of the Meuse in August of that year. Reorganized and sent to rest in the Heights of the Meuse, it had then participated in Ludendorff's Operation *Michael* in April 1918; all three of its regiments lost heavily. In early October it had been sent to the Meuse–Argonne front, where it fought at Cunel, and was then switched to the east bank of the Meuse. Its regiments reported morale to be high, which its officers ascribed to a policy of shipping "questionable revolutionary forces" to the rear. It too was rated third class by the Americans.[23] But the Germans held the high ground, they were fighting in defense, and they knew the terrain well.

The brigades of the 79th were in position by the morning of November 1 but no movements were ordered for two more days, except for short-range patrols. At first the men thought their accommodations looked pretty good, but they soon found out the hard way that the Germans knew they were there. Captain Glock of the 316th Infantry later wrote of his new regimental PC:

Four of the staff were in an end room working on maps, and two, who had been lying in the middle room resting from a dose of gas, had just gone out for fresh air when a "250" landed a square hit, clove through rock and logs, split the rails, and dropped the roof in the middle room. The officers in the end room were trapped and had to dig out through a little aperture.[24]

Running short of high explosive ammunition, the German guns soon switched to gas as their primary weapon. On the night of October 31 they shelled the brigade with yellow cross while laying down blue cross and HE on the roads and gullies in the area. Two similar bombardments took place over the next two days. (The 79th would suffer 159 wounded and 80 gassed in its first six days in the Grande Montagne sector.)[25] The brigade had started out with two battalions in the front line of each of its two regiments and one in support. But enemy shell fire was so heavy that General Johnson had them each pull one battalion back to minimize casualties. So each regiment had one battalion in front with three companies in the front line and one in support; a second battalion in support; and one company assigned to brigade reserve in the rear. But the shelling continued, heavy and unrelenting, causing many casualties especially among the ration and ammunition carriers, runners, and telephone linemen, all of whom had to cross exposed terrain to accomplish their missions. Several were later awarded the Distinguished Service Cross—the second-highest decoration— for their daring.[26]

As the 79th got acclimated to its new sector, Liggett's November 1 attack west of the Meuse got off to a roaring start. First Army artillery fired one-quarter of a million shells, over twice the number used on September 26.[27] Summerall's V Corps drove five and a half miles northward and by evening had seized the Barricourt Heights; III Corps to its right made half the distance but took the strategic towns of Andevanne and Aincreville. A day later the Germans withdrew from the outflanked Bois de Bourgogne, as Liggett had predicted; north of the wood, at Boult aux Bois, men of I Corps and the French Fourth Army met and shook hands. The war diary of Army Group Gallwitz reported, "Lieut. Col. Wetzell [Chief of Operations at OHL] ... states that all of the front line commanders report that the Americans are attacking in mass formations in the general direction of Stenay, that the [German] troops are fighting courageously but just cannot do anything. 'Therefore it has become imperative that the Army be withdrawn in rear of the Meuse and that said withdrawal be effected immediately.'"[28] On November 4, Groener ordered a withdrawal to the Antwerp–Meuse line. The entire German line west of the river was in full retreat, and the American attack there turned from an advance into a pursuit. Foch and Pétain were impressed; the latter summarized the reports of the French observers:

> These officers inform me that a very remarkable improvement has taken place, that there has been a conspicuous absence of difficulties which occur[r]ed in the advance of September 26th; road movements occur in order, orders in all the units are given well and timely, and ... that the already splendid advance can yet be continued because of the excellent manner in which the whole affair has been managed.[29]

On November 2, XVII Corps ordered a strong reconnaissance northward for the next day to determine whether the Germans were withdrawing east of the Meuse as well, as First Army airplane reports had led them to believe. The 79th was directed to send patrols against the Borne de Cornouiller; General Johnson gave the mission to the 316th Infantry. Three patrols would advance, each consisting of a forward platoon and one in support plus a section of machine guns and a 37mm mobile gun. Even as they moved into attack position, the three patrols were heavily shelled with HE and gas. Lieutenant Ira Lady of Company E sent a message to Colonel Williams at the PC of the 316th, "Caught in box barrage by H.E. and Phosgene at corner of trail to Headquarters from 1st Battalion P.C. and public roads. Half men gassed. Am waiting orders. Thirty men from E Company gassed. Two wounded."[30] An officer went forward to reorganize the patrols and lead them to the jumpoff point. As shells burst around them, the NCOs distributed ammunition and automatic rifle magazines. Fortunately, no shells fell among the tightly clustered men.

At 5:30 a.m. on November 3 the guns of the 52nd Field Artillery opened up on the German lines; 30 minutes later the three patrols moved forward. The right-most group, heading northeast into the Bois de la Grande Montagne, immediately ran into impenetrable underbrush and got nowhere. The left group, under Captain Francis Johnson and Lieutenant Lady, went straight for the Borne; but machine guns from the trenches above quickly stopped them cold, killing Captain Johnson and wounding Lieutenant Lady. Lieutenant Harold Allston, leading the machine gun section, took command and fought in place until noon, taking prisoners and destroying several machine gun nests. In the center, the patrol under Lieutenants Harry Gabriel and Rudolph Peterson moved slightly northeast, heading for the wooded rise on the eastern flank of the Borne, designated Hill 370. They had gotten about 1,200 yards when they ran into strong machine gun fire. Dropping back to reorganize, they made another 300 yards but then, almost surrounded by German machine guns, withdrew again down the slopes of Hill 370. Unable to maintain his position and with German troops, familiar with the woods and trails, infiltrating around him, Gabriel moved his command to the left to support Allston's group. After some anxious moments Captain Louis C. Knack brought up his Company B to reinforce the two groups. This was sufficient for the 316th to hold the ground gained; although the Germans continued to shell the position, the regiment spent the night consolidating its new territory and running telephone lines to the rear.[31]

The dead of the 316th for the day were three officers and 20 men.[32] There was no count of the wounded; but at least now they were being well cared for. An inspector found that in the 79th:

> All wounded questioned stated they had received good care and water and had reached the triage within from one to three hours after having been wounded. As the triage is situated by the side of Evacuation hospital #15 it is only a question of a few minutes in getting the wounded from the triage to the hospital.[33]

Sergeant Davies, wounded that day, described his experiences to his diary:

> I am now laid in a row with about forty other stretcher cases in another room. The poor chap on my left died before I was taken into the operating room. Finally two huskies came in and grabbed my stretcher and started off with it. I asked one of them where we are bound for and he tells me I am very lucky as I was to be operated on by the famous Major Graves ... I was placed on a table, and I suppose it was the famous Graves, started to poke around my leg. I heard him say something about infection and hemorrhage in the wound then he turned to a chap, who was standing over me with a bottle and a cloth and said, "smother him." This guy dropped the cloth over my face and started to feed me ether ... Can I believe my eyes, I am in a real honest to God bed, and its got a white sheet on it. I sure don't know how to act. This is the first time since I left the States that I have been in a real bed.[34]

Although the cost was excessive, the reconnaissance-in-force had real results. It gained a foothold on the Borne from which an attack could be mounted on the crest and on Hill 370 nearby. It made the Germans reveal their strength, positions, and tactics, particularly their way of rapidly changing positions and moving back into unoccupied territory once the Americans had passed. It demonstrated the enemy's system for coordinating artillery and infantry, allowing them to drop a barrage wherever it was needed. Still, the operation took its toll on morale. At 2:30 the next morning the commander of Company K reported:

> Effectives – 2 officers, 115 men ... Connection with both flanks. Line solid. Estimate killed of old K. Co. here, Lt. Peterson & 5 men, of new Co. K 1 man. Wounded. Lt. Sayres and 10 men of old K Co., of new Co. 14 men. Self inflicted wounds 2, Deserted posts 4, left 8. Morale low. Rations none. Last rations received night before last. Men from both Cos – no packs or equipment. Automatics out of order from lack of automatic [illegible] and oil. Under heavy shelling and rifle grenade fire. Intermittent sniping. No water or means of chlorination. Think I can hold out tho. Might have to shoot some men for example. If this can not be done let me know.[*] Get us rations & ammunition. Am sending Peterson's wallet for your safe keeping. [Emphasis in the original.][35]

Still on the theory that only rear guards opposed the French 15th Division and the 158th Brigade, General Claudel ordered another attack on the Borne for the next morning, November 4. Johnson assigned the 315th to make a supporting attack into the Bois de la Grande Montagne on the east while the 316th's 1st Battalion would attack the Borne on the left and the 3rd Battalion would attack its east slope as well as Hill 370 to its right. The artillery would lay down preparatory fire at 5:45 a.m. and the infantry would attack 15 minutes later.

The supporting attack of the 315th got off on time. The terrain in front of them was the same that had confronted the patrol of the 316th the previous day: a tangle of woods and underbrush heavily defended by

---

[*] The reference to shooting men as an example, which occurs in other messages from company commanders, was certainly an expression of frustration, not of intent. Eleven soldiers were executed in the AEF, all for murder or rape. No one was executed for desertion or cowardice. (Subcommittee on Military Affairs United States Senate, "Establishment of Military Justice–Proposed Amendment of the Articles of War," (Washington, DC, September 25, 1919), p. 566.

machine guns. The leading battalion used infiltration tactics, sending small parties of men forward between the defending positions, which allowed them to capture some of the machine guns. Nonetheless, they suffered heavy losses and had to halt after a few hundred yards. One platoon of C Company, 1st Battalion, got too far ahead of its neighbors and lost contact, fighting for 27 hours before it could be brought back. By 11:00 a.m. the advance had halted and 1st Battalion dug in to defend its position.[36]

The main attack was carried out by two battalions of the 316th. Covered by morning fog, the 1st on the left, under Major Parkin, went straight up the hill while the 3rd, under Major Manning, covered their right flank by moving into the woods on the eastern shoulder of the Borne. By 7:13 a.m. Manning was able to telephone back to Colonel Williams, "Everything going well. We have captured 7 machine guns and 39 prisoners," and 20 minutes later, "Things are going along as reported before. Ten more prisoners, one machine gun. Enemy artillery has not increased in its fire. Hill 370 practically in our hands as far as the 365 contour."[37]

The attack of the 1st Battalion, however, did not go well. Progress up the bare slope of the Borne was slow, the Germans contesting every foot, and hand-to-hand combat was common. By 7:55 a.m. Major Parkin sent a runner back to regimental headquarters saying that his right had reached the crest of the hill and his left was not far behind, but that he expected to be shelled once the fog lifted and would need counterbattery fire.[38] In the words of the divisional historian, "What happened in the ensuing hour or two is vague." Parkin was with Company B on the left of his battalion. Company C on the right was down to 25 men and, although it gained the crest, could not hold its position; it withdrew to the shelter of the Bois de la Grande Montagne. Company B should have been protected on its left by the French 15th Division, which was to have attacked simultaneously; but it found itself taking heavy fire from that direction, with the French nowhere to be found. Parkin sent a runner back at 12:10 p.m. describing his position. Shortly thereafter he was seriously wounded and his successor, Captain Knack, was killed. As the fog lifted, two companies of German infantry rushed Company B. Badly outnumbered, three officers (including Major Parkin) and 21 men surrendered and were taken prisoner.[39]

When no further word came from Parkin after 7:55 a.m. but the noise of the battle continued, Colonel Williams became concerned and ordered the 1st Battalion reserve, Company D, forward; soon thereafter he sent

Captain Carl Glock up the hill with a machine gun detachment to help out. Then Parkin's runner arrived, too exhausted to give a coherent account of the situation; all he could remember of the message was, "Am being outflanked."[40] Surmising that the crest had been lost, Williams ordered a company of the 312th Machine Gun Battalion to fire on the position. This they did for 20 minutes. Then, knowing to expect retaliatory fire, they dismounted their guns and sought shelter. The German response demolished their now-empty positions. Company D, meanwhile, was able to locate Company C but found no trace of Company B or the French. Its commander, Lieutenant Maxwell McKeen, was mortally wounded. The company traded fire with German machine guns, capturing four of them with their gunners; but it was obvious the position could not be held without protection on their left, so Company D fell back to the southern slope of the Borne. Glock's detachment of about 60 men, coming up behind, found a badly depleted force on top of the hill. Glock himself described their advance:

> As the men crept up the lower slopes of the hill an enemy plane swooped close over their heads, opening its machine gun on them. After a brief concealment in a patch of underbrush, they resumed their slow advance, and in the trenches on the hill found the dead left by the morning attack. But there remained not a living soul, not one man of the battalion that had swept up the hill in the morning ... There were not enough men in the reinforcement to fill the whole gap between I Company and the French far to the left, and the line merely zigzagged east and west in shell-hole groups of two and three just back of the open crest of the hill, ignorant of the fate of the 1st Battalion that morning, and awaiting into the night the fortunes of war.[41]

Glock and his men joined Company C on the southern slope where they spent the night, withstanding heavy shelling and several enemy patrols that attempted unsuccessfully to make them abandon the position. The 316th had taken and lost the crest twice in the same day. It had suffered three officers and 34 men killed, 22 taken prisoner, and an unknown number wounded.[42]

That night word came from XVII Corps that the Germans on the west bank of the Meuse were retiring in disorganized fashion and had exhausted all their reserves, and it was possible that the Heights of the Meuse were now being held with reduced forces. III Corps was planning to cross the Meuse at Dun-sur-Meuse to drive the Germans to the northeast. The 79th Division was ordered to continue its attacks on the Borne de Cornouiller to support III Corps. The supposed weakening of the German defenses in front of him must have been news to Kuhn; First Army's own operations report said that in his sector, "... not only was there violent resistance to any attack, but also repeated counterattacks to regain the lost positions."[43] Nevertheless, Kuhn ordered Johnson to send one battalion northward as the assaulting force with another battalion in support. The attack would start at 9:00 a.m. on the 5th, accompanied by a preparatory bombardment by two corps batteries of 240mm howitzers from 8:30 to 10:15 a.m.; interdiction would be laid down by the division's 155mm guns and its 75mms would furnish a barrage.

The problem was that the battalions of the 315th and 316th were badly depleted by the actions of the previous two days, with their companies scattered south and east of the crest of the Borne and some of them down to one platoon's strength. Eventually Colonel Williams put together a provisional battalion with three companies from the 316th and one from the 315th that had not been as badly used up; Major Manning was to lead it. But two of the companies could not be found in time, so Manning decided to attack with the remaining two. Supported by the 310th Machine Gun Battalion and part of the 312th, the detachment took off at 8:30 a.m. and joined Glock's detachment below the ridge at 9:00 a.m. The combined force advanced into heavy machine gun fire, Major Manning in front swinging his cane in the fashion of a British battalion leader on the Somme. They were able to sweep the Germans off the top by 9:30 a.m., but as he cleared the crest the major was killed by machine gun fire. As they proceeded slowly down the northern slope, two more officers and two NCOs were quickly killed, along with many men. Glock's narrative continued:

> The fragments of the command, now joined on the right by the men who had spent the night on the hill, filtered over the crest and down the bare northern slope. From the left, at Sillon Fontaine Farm, from the nests along the Sivry–Réville Road, at the very base of the slope, from Solferino Farm, a cluster of stone houses on the opposite slope of the valley, and from the woods to the east, the Bois de la Grande Montagne, a hail of machine-gun fire broke out. From the Bois d'Ecurey and the Réville Valley the enemy poured high explosive upon the scattered troops, who were gradually

dwindling to nothing. German aeroplanes were now overhead, observing the effect of the German fire. Soon there would be no one left to protect the right flank beyond I Company against attack from the woods.[44]

On the left of the line a sergeant, the only NCO remaining, took five men to attack a machine gun nest; all became casualties. Although wounded, the sergeant picked up the BAR of one of his comrades, finished off the machine gunners, and took command of that part of the line.

Coming up 300 yards behind Manning's provisional battalion was the 2nd Battalion of the 316th, led by Captain Paul Strong. With Manning's death, Strong went ahead and took over command. Lieutenant Colonel George Haedicke, accompanying Glock's small force on the right, saw the losses being taken by the companies on the left that had pushed over the crest and ordered Strong to pull back to the south slope. In the meantime Colonel Williams, gassed and exhausted, had collapsed, so Haedicke was called back to take over command of the regiment. The men on the crest had spotted German forces massing in the Tranchée du Canif, a major fortified line about two miles to the north of the Borne. Suspecting a counterattack, they sent their last carrier pigeon to division headquarters, requesting an artillery concentration on the trench. Half an hour later the three artillery regiments of the division plus two assigned batteries of 240mm howitzers dropped their shells on the German assembly area. General Johnson himself climbed a tree to see the terrible result.[45]

By the afternoon of the November 5 the remnants of nine companies of the 158th Brigade held the crest of the Borne—barely—but could advance no further. General Johnson telephoned Tenney Ross at 4:30 p.m. to summarize the situation:

316th Regiment of this brigade has been engaged for three days in what may be called a minor operation, but the task assigned to it has been one of extreme difficulty owing to the objectives being dominating points and the whole area in which the objective was situated being covered by machine gun and artillery fire of the enemy. The objective was gained but at a very heavy loss. The Lieut. Colonel now in command of the regiment, who has been on the objective for two days and over every part of the line, estimates that the present effective strength of the regiment is about 600 ... Every company with one exception, is now on the line and even under those conditions is holding it but thinly. The one company mentioned is in reserve. The position is organized and will be held, but I believe that the regiment should be relieved and re-organized before it can be effective for any further work.[46]

The day's attack had cost the 315th 53 men and the 316th three officers and 19 men killed.[47] Most of the men had received no food for two days and the only water was from gas-contaminated shell holes. Only on the left, where reinforcements for Company K had brought up rations, could the men have a meal. The attack of November 5 left the Americans technically in possession of the hill, but German artillery and machine gun fire from the north kept them from advancing further. While the divisional artillery planted a barrage on the far slope to prevent a counterattack, the provisional battalion took cover for the night below the crest. Army Group Gallwitz's war diary reported, "The fighting for Höher Eichenberg [Borne de Cornouiller] was particularly violent. The enemy did not succeed in holding it."[48]

That night, XVII Corps informed the 79th that III Corps had crossed the Meuse eastward and must be supported by a renewed attack on the Borne de Cornouiller the next day, November 6. But the companies of the 316th, scattered over the hillside, were down to around 100 hungry, exhausted men each, low on ammunition and able to do no more than hold on. Kuhn ordered the 2nd Battalion of the 313th Infantry, hitherto in division reserve near Samogneux, to pass through the line held by the provisional battalion of the 316th and lead the attack at 8:00 a.m. One battalion of the 315th was to follow in support. It didn't happen; continued heavy German shelling from north of the Borne cut up the companies of the 313th with high explosive, shrapnel, and gas as they approached the jumpoff line. Even divisional headquarters, far to the rear, was shelled with mustard gas; despite all precautions, gas seeped into the dugouts, disrupting operations and sending 35 officers and men to the hospital with gas burns.[49] German aircraft emerged to direct artillery fire and strafe the American lines. Captain George Burgwin commanded the 2nd Battalion; a major in the 315th called him a "tough-looking officer ... usually on the smartly dressed side," although at the moment he was pretty dirty.[50] Burgwin reorganized for an attack at 2:00 p.m., but another German bombardment scattered the battalion. Eventually American planes arrived and drove off the Germans; but by the time Burgwin could reorganize again it was too late to attack. So General Johnson ordered the battalion to take over the left of the line, held by the two provisional battalions, that night. The right of the line would continue to be held by the 3rd Battalion of the 316th. In the meantime, the French 15th Colonial Division to the left of the 79th captured Vilosnes, then attacked northeast toward Brandeville, outflanking the German line from Sivry to the Borne de Cornouiller. That night, Maas Group East ordered a general retirement to the line Mouzay–Bois de Remoiville–Vittarville, roughly six miles to the northeast. The German line, although not broken, was now pulling back across the entire front.

On the night of November 6–7, the 79th was assigned to the French II Corps, which took over the sector east of the Meuse. Major General Claudel was still in command. Late in the evening, an order went to the 79th saying that the enemy was disorganized and retreating, and the assault would continue on the morning of the 7th. The 79th was to secure the Borne and continue attacking north. Kuhn told his artillery to begin its preparation at 7:45 a.m., the infantry to advance at 8:10 a.m. using the same formations as the previous day; these would now be commanded by Lieutenant Colonel Franklin Burt. The objective would be the road from Sivry-sur-Meuse to Réville, half a mile north of the Borne. Further advance would be only at the order of the division commander. As per schedule, the artillery bombarded the hills north of the Borne while the heavy machine guns shot up its north summit. At 8:00 a.m. the 2nd Battalion of the 313th Infantry and the 3rd Battalion of the 315th followed a rolling barrage down the north slope of the Borne. The men, burdened by having to wear their gas masks, bunched up; a single shell killed six and wounded 15 others.[51] But the German fire was relatively light—apparently they were moving their guns north. By 11:00 a.m. the improvised regiment had reached the Sivry–Réville road, taking prisoners along the way. Three of them, from the 35th Regiment of the 228th Division, told their captors that orders had been given to withdraw to Hill 373, three miles north of the Borne, where trenches had been prepared. The historian of the 35th Regiment gave the view from the German side:

> The incoming artillery fire increases starting at 9:00 a.m. At 11:00 a.m., the 6th [battalion] of the 35th must retreat because of the threat to its left flank, while the 12th of the 35th must retreat at 4:00 p.m. The enemy presses hard and large numbers of enemy soldiers come down Eichenberg Hill. The

Kriemhild [*sic*] line is heavily bombarded, the enemy penetrates the line's forwardmost positions.[*][52]

The American artillery was doing a good job of suppressing the German machine guns so General Johnson, commanding the 158th Brigade, ordered a further advance of 600 meters to the trenches at Claires Chênes on Hill 329 at 1:30 p.m. But the barrage fell short by 200–300 yards, endangering the attackers and making it impossible to jump off. Lieutenant Colonel Burt, not knowing this, angrily got Major Francis Lloyd, now leading the two attacking battalions, on the phone. The major explained the situation; the artillery barrage was quickly lifted and the attack got off at 3:00 p.m. It made progress against increasing resistance, mostly from machine guns. An artillery barrage preceded the assault, but by 4:10 p.m. the men had caught up with it and were again in danger of being hit. At that point, having no clear targets, the guns stopped firing and the men continued on. They met more machine guns in the trenches at Claires Chênes, but the 312th Machine Gun Battalion brought up two of its heavy weapons and silenced several of them. By now it was dark and the 313th's 2nd Battalion was exhausted so Company I of the 315th picked up the attack. Two volunteers crept forward and found the German wire and the trench behind it. At that the combined battalions rushed over Hill 329, captured the trenches, and dug in in the Ravine de Vaux. Ahead and above them the German defenders continued to pepper them with fire but the two battalions, now down to a remnant of their original force, maintained their position.

The 79th had taken the Borne de Cornouiller and had passed over a mile beyond. Gallwitz's war diary, after a week of reporting courageous repulses and valiant counterattacks, conveyed the news in a low key: "The right flank of the 228th Division was forced back a few hundred meters and [Höher-] Eichen-Berg was evacuated by us after some fighting."[53] The historian of the German 183rd Infantry Regiment added telling detail:

> Due to further enemy advances in the area of Brandeville–Breheville, the high command orders a retreat from the Côte, to begin on November 8th.

---

[*] By November, German clock time was one hour ahead of French clock time. (Army War College, Historical Section, Order of Battle of the United States Land Forces in the World War: General Headquarters, Armies, Army Corps, Services of Supply, Separate Forces (Washington, DC: Center of Military History, reprinted 1988, orig. pub. 1931), p. 405.)

> One battalion of each regiment in the division's sector will remain to conceal the withdrawal of all the other troops. These three battalions are placed under the command of the 183rd Infantry Regiment's commander. Displacement of materiel is to begin immediately.[54]

With the capture of the Borne de Cornouiller and the hills beyond, the 79th held a six-mile front, from Hill 329 and Claires Chênes trench in the north, southward through the Bois de la Grande Montagne and then eastward to the Bois d'Etrayes; then southeast through the Bois de Wavrille to Belleu Bois, south again through the Bois des Chênes and across the Samogneux–Crépion road, over the Bois d'Ormont and a bit beyond to the sector of the 26th Division. On November 7 those units not consolidating the position north of the Borne de Cornouiller spent the day strengthening the line by relieving tired battalions and bringing up others to reinforce the positions. The division surgeon reported that the troops were "now in very poor physical condition, due to long continued loss of sleep, and lack of sufficient nourishment combined with a high degree of mental strain."[55] But the 79th would not be relieved; it would only change the direction of its attack. West of the Meuse the American divisions had reached the river by the night of the 7th; from First Army came the order for them to halt while operations in the plain of the Woëvre, east of the Heights, continued.[56] The brunt of the division's advance would now be borne by the east-facing 157th Brigade, which hitherto had been holding a defensive line.

The 157th had reached its sector on the night of October 30–November 1, taking over from the 26th Division, which side-stepped southward. Its left, bordering the 158th Brigade, was held by two battalions of the 314th Infantry in the Bois de Wavrille and the Belleu Bois. To its right the Machine Gun Company of the 314th held the area straddling the Samogneux–Crépion road, overlooked by the Germans on the crest of Hill 360. From the Bois d'Ormont south, the line was held by the 1st Battalion of the 313th with two battalions in support.

Facing the 79th was the German 1st Landwehr Division, a territorial unit (similar to the American National Guard) that had spent most of the war on the Eastern Front and had arrived in France only the previous February, in time to take part in Ludendorff's second Spring Offensive, the battle on the Lys River. In October, east of the Meuse, it had lost heavily at the hands of the 29th Division and the French 15th Colonials. American intelligence rated it third class, "a mediocre division composed of old men and of others that have little military value."[57] Their own officers were worried about their effectiveness. "These last few weeks with inadequate food and little rest, and constantly being wet, had worn down the troops. The unit was decaying more and more as its soldiers were killed, wounded, or became ill, and no replacements came from home. The old fighting spirit that was so necessary was harder and harder to come by." In addition to exhaustion, morale was sapped by rumors that socialist political elements in Germany were spreading leaflets calling on soldiers to disobey orders and possibly to kill their officers.[*][58] But although depleted in numbers and sagging in morale, the "old men" knew their business.

Upon reaching their new lines at 2:00 a.m., the 79th let the Germans know they had arrived; within an hour its 52nd Artillery Brigade opened an intense bombardment of the enemy positions. The retaliatory fire was beyond what they expected, saturating the entire Samogneux–Crépion road and the back areas. Many men fell wounded in the 314th and some in the 313th. The Machine Gun Company of the 314th, which had gone down the wrong road, failed to reach the front until the next day. Depot and carrier details, wire stringers, all the rear-area elements were disrupted. One detachment establishing a forward ammunition dump for the 314th was almost wiped out; a sergeant major reorganized the scattered survivors and continued the work. A shell hit an ambulance, killing a wounded man in the front seat. The driver, a private, tried to repair the vehicle but found it wrecked beyond use. Instead, he hiked back to the ambulance park, got another one, went back, retrieved his patients, and evacuated them to an aid station.[59]

The artillery fire continued all day and into the evening as the 314th and 313th were trying to establish their entrenchments. The bombardment included gas, which ruined the hot meals that the cooks were trying to serve. Most feared by the men were the *Minenwerfer*, large-caliber mortars whose shells, unlike those of the guns, were inaudible as they fell.[60] As night

---

*   The historian of the 31st Landwehr Infantry Regiment, one of the units of the 1st Landwehr Division, was quick to add, "No such written appeal is ever shown to me, and in any case, if such a leaflet exists, this meaning is not ascribed to it. In our regiment, the officers and men are comrades, and have stuck together as comrades in good times and bad, and they will share their joys and sorrows to the bitter end. If I mention these rumors, I do so only to show how the constant flow of them made everyone so tense." (Wilhelm Suhrmann, *Geschichte Des Landwehr-Infanterie-Regiments Nr. 31 im Weltkriege* (Flensburg/Oldenburg/Berlin: Gerhard Stalling, 1928), p. 384.)

descended, a large German raiding party attacked an outpost at the left end of the line of the 313th. The outpost was manned by two squads totaling 11 men. Spotting the raiders in the dark, the men of the 313th fired on them with rifles and automatic weapons. Although two of the defenders were killed and one wounded 22 times, they drove the raiders off with heavy losses. Other parts of the line saw similar acts of resistance. By the end of the day the 313th had lost nine men killed; the 314th had lost 29.[61]

The next day, as the liaison group of Company C, 313th Infantry, tried to make contact with the 26th Division to its right, the German bombardment caught it in the open. The Liaison Company of the 26th drew back and suggested the corporal in charge of the platoon of the 313th do the same. But the corporal wasn't taking orders from some other division; he had to hear it from his own officers. He stayed put, and for two days the regiment was unable to reach his detachment. When found, he "had his detail well in hand, all equipment intact, although the men were completely exhausted."[62]

The food situation improved. After losing five men of the carrying detail killed and eight wounded on the night of November 2–3, Colonel Oury of the 314th ordered that no more than one party from each battalion should be on the road at a time and that food should be brought up in daylight so carriers could find shelter from the bombardment. The 313th cooked all their food in their rear area near the Meuse. The Supply Company wagons carried it at night to a point behind the lines from which carrying parties took it forward. In this fight, at least the men would not starve.

By November 4, having consolidated its position, the 157th sent out a series of night patrols. Although they lost no men, they found the German positions heavily defended so that it was impossible to take prisoners. Over the next few nights the front-line battalions of the brigade sent out more patrols, locating German machine gun positions and strong points but not engaging the enemy. By then Kuhn had ordered his regiments to maintain contact with the enemy so that they should not slip away unmolested. On the afternoon of November 7 Major Theodore Schoge, commanding the 2nd Battalion of the 314th, led three combat groups of three squads each on a reconnaissance in force. They immediately ran into heavy machine gun fire followed within ten minutes by intense shelling. After holding their position for 45 minutes Schoge ordered them to withdraw. As they did so, eight shells fell among them, "each shell throwing blue flame and sparks around it for a radius of 30 yards, the flame burning for five minutes and giving the impression that the enemy was resorting to liquid fire."[63] Seven men were killed and no prisoners taken. Schoge's raid established, however, that the German position was too strongly held to be taken by infantry alone and that artillery would be needed.

Kuhn's efforts on the 7th to relieve tired units and reinforce his line left no battalions in division reserve, so he asked II Corps to lend him two battalions from the 26th Division. This would let him relieve the 3rd Battalion of the 313th, then in line in the Bois d'Ormont, and put it in reserve. Claudel agreed. The relief was done under heavy shell fire that caused several casualties, not least among a supply detail carrying food to the 3rd Battalion. Although the line of the 79th was not shortened it freed up a battalion for use as a mobile reserve.

Until the night of November 7–8 the German 31st Landwehr Infantry Regiment, part of the 1st Landwehr Division, had occupied the Bois d'Haumont and the Bois des Caures opposite the American 26th Division. But on the 7th the American 90th Division crossed the Meuse and broke through at Stenay, threatening the northern flank of the German forces east of the river. The 31st was ordered to withdraw eastward and set up defensive positions on the Côte Morimont and the adjoining Hills 328 and 319, which the Germans called Wettin Hill. Four companies were left behind as a rear guard; their comrades expected never to see them again. This movement brought them opposite the 79th. The regimental historian described the retreat:

> The companies' march to Morimont Hill in the limited light of early morning is very hard on the soldiers, particularly since they take as much equipment and ammunition with them as they can ... The companies wade on through thick mud to Morimont Hill, to occupy the Kriemhild [sic] fortifications there. Regrettably, these positions consist mainly of a single trench, which has begun to fill up with water due to the rain. It does not offer much protection and is not a great place to sleep; there are some tunnels on the northern slope of Morimont Hill, which can accommodate a good number of people ... While this was going on, Second Battalion occupied positions in front of and on Wettin Hill during the night of the 7th and 8th."[64]

Around 3:00 p.m., to the amazement of the regiment—"We don't believe our eyes"—the four rear-guard companies appeared on Côte Morimont.

Having received the withdrawal order at 1:00 p.m., "They departed while there was still daylight, somehow without an unpleasant encounter with the Americans, who stayed in their bunkers and watched the four companies' withdrawal, waving at the departing German soldiers. The Americans seem to have no interest in fighting anymore."[65]

On November 7 Claudel gave Kuhn his orders for a renewed offensive. First, the 158th Brigade would disengage from its northward advance and attack east toward Etraye, Réville and Ecurey. The 315th Infantry on the right was to pass through the lines of the 3rd Battalion, 316th Infantry, in the woods to the east of the Borne de Cornouiller. On the left Burt's provisional regiment would advance on Réville. That would allow the brigade to catch up with the 157th, already facing east, to form a solid north–south line. The night of November 7–8 was spent preparing for the attack. Heavy artillery was repositioned to fire eastward. Light artillery and companies of the 312th Machine Gun Battalion moved up behind the assault units. Signal corps men laid telephone wire across freshly captured ground to the advance PCs and all the way up to the outposts.

At 6:00 a.m. that morning the 312th Machine Guns let loose their preparatory fire on time; but the infantry had not yet reached the jumpoff line, so it was wasted. The 1st and 2nd Battalions of the 313th, each leading one of the provisional regiments, did not get to the front line until 11:00 a.m. and did not attack until noon. To their south, the 2nd Battalion of the 315th, which had not been relieved from its former position in the Bois d'Etraye–Bois de Wavrille line until 7:00 a.m., did not reach its starting line until 2:15 p.m. This time, however, the late start hardly mattered. As they advanced, the leading companies quickly discovered that the Germans had abandoned their positions during the night. From time to time German machine guns would fire long, sustained bursts; but when American patrols went forward to scout their positions, they found the guns and the gunners gone.[66] A newspaper reporter who happened to be in brigade headquarters described General Johnson's reaction as the telephone reports came in: "We've lost contact with 'em! We're going ahead and can't find any Boche!" he yelled into the phone. "Keep at 'em! Keep at 'em! Don't let 'em get away!" To the officers around him he moaned, "If only we had some cavalry!"[67] At 2:05 p.m. Johnson sent a message to Kuhn who relayed it to Claudel at II Corps:

Lieut. Col Burt went up and took command himself of the left ... and since that time he has been going so fast that I cannot keep in touch with him. He sent back message two or three times that he was going forward without resistance, but has not given definite coordinates. No doubt but that he will gain the objective. In the south area the same way; the troops are pushing right along without resistance.[68]

As the 158th advanced eastward it was quickly obvious that its right would lose touch with the left of the 157th, which had been ordered to stay put and send out patrols. So Kuhn ordered Nicholson to telephone Oury in the 314th ordering him to advance his left wing in conformity with the 158th. They too found that the Germans had withdrawn, so in the mid-afternoon Oury ordered all his battalions to advance on the ridges previously defended by German machine guns. Nicholson ordered the battalion of the 26th Division that had taken over from the 313th Infantry to capture the crest of Hill 360.

By mid-afternoon the entire 79th Division was moving eastward on a more-or-less straight north–south front four and a half miles wide. As the afternoon progressed, the rain, which had been falling all day, turned heavy. The only resistance was German harassing fire and enemy airplanes that flew below the clouds to strafe the advancing columns. A few machine gunners willingly gave themselves up as prisoners. At dusk the 2nd Battalion of the 313th Infantry entered Réville and the 1st Battalion took over Etraye. To their south, the 314th Infantry also found the country ahead of them deserted. By 6:00 p.m. its 3rd Battalion had cleared the Bois d'Etraye and the Bois de Wavrille as far as the bluff south of Etraye. The 1st Battalion had gotten through the Ravin la Hazelle along the Samogneux–Crépion road. The battalion of the 26th Division completed the capture of Hill 360 and passed through the Bois d'Ormont. By 9:45 p.m., all objectives were reached. Units of the 304th Engineers followed closely behind the infantry to clear roads for the supply trains. Both brigades of the 79th had reached the eastern extremity of the Heights of the Meuse and now overlooked the plains of the Woëvre. As they rested, the men could hear the Germans destroying their ammunition. Little shell fire came their way; the front was unusually quiet. Patrols sent out into the Woëvre plain returned with the news that the Germans had withdrawn at least as far as the Thinte River one to two miles beyond the front line. Writing home that night, Kuhn was ebullient:

We have been in a hard push in what the communique has been reporting as a warm corner and a warm one it was. I cannot tell you details but I am proud of my men who stood a very heavy pounding from shells and gas during this time, while desperately endeavoring to gain ground. We inched forward little by little and drew upon ourselves the activity of many Germans. Yesterday we made a fine bulge in their line and today, well, we pretty well shoved them off the map.[69]

On the night of the 8th, II Corps informed Kuhn that his front had changed yet again. The 79th was to turn over the northern half of its sector—that occupied by the 158th Brigade—to the French 15th Colonial Infantry Division and concentrate both of its brigades in the southern half, bounded by Etraye on the north and Moirey on the south. This would require the two provisional regiments of the 158th Brigade to sideslip two and a half miles south, into the sector occupied by the 314th Infantry. The 314th with its two battalions would remain in the front of the division's narrowed sector, leading the attack. The 315th would fall in to their left as it arrived in the sector, and the 314th would move to its right to make room. The 313th and 316th would come up behind them in support. The machine gun battalions, artillery, and engineers would follow.[70] The new zone of advance extended eastward to an arc-shaped line of hills in the plain of the Woëvre. From north to south, these hills were the Côte d'Orne, the Côte de Morimont, the Côte de Romagne, and Hills 328 and 319. They formed an amphitheater into which the division would be attacking.

The key to this complicated maneuver was for the 314th to shield the crabwise move of the 158th Brigade by attacking Hill 328, the closest part of the German defensive line. The attack began at 6:00 a.m., preceded by a bombardment of 75s from the 104th Field Artillery Regiment on the assumed position of the German line, as heavy guns shelled important points to their rear and the weapons of the 311th Machine Gun Battalion fired overhead to protect the flanks. As the men left their trenches, they found that the enemy had vanished.[71] Nevertheless, as the regiment moved down from the heights, the 1st Battalion ran into trouble, entering the Bois de Crépion and losing touch with the regimental PC. The 2nd Battalion on its right, meeting no resistance, reached the village of Crépion, an advance of half a mile, at 8:20 a.m. Despite heavy shelling it continued forward; at about 10:15 a.m. it reached the edge of Moirey just as the 26th Division to its right took over the town. Then it lengthened its line to the north, trying to make contact with the 3rd Battalion so the 1st Battalion could retire according to plan. The 3rd Battalion attacked east and south from near Etraye, capturing Wavrille and continuing on to the road and rail line behind the town, where it stopped and made contact with the 2nd Battalion to its right, just as the 1st Battalion took Gibercy.

Although the Germans were in retreat, they professed to be unintimidated by the American advance:

> They [the German soldiers] slowly work their way up to the new line, moving as individuals, in groups, and in skirmish lines. We see that we are facing a unit which does not have much combat experience. Individual detachments sometimes appear in the open, not taking cover, and of course this is a gift to our artillery, which takes the advancing enemy under fire. The Second Battalion's machine guns on Wettin Hill also weigh in substantially from time to time. The Americans' main objective is Gibercy. They attack in that direction from all sides, and our artillery also directs a heavy volume of fire at Gibercy.[72]

By 11:00 a.m. the 79th had advanced from one to one and a half miles. But as the 2nd Battalion passed through Moirey and approached Hill 328, it ran into machine gun fire from the slopes; it had finally found the Germans. The regiment's Machine Gun Company sent out a detachment to drive the enemy off, an action that quickly developed into a full-scale assault with infantry in support. As the infantry advanced past the machine guns, someone cried out that the Germans had gotten behind them and were attacking. Firing broke out in the rear, then stopped—it had been a false alarm. But a few of the machine gunners had been watching the affair, and saw a figure on the hillside behind them fall. They investigated and found it was the body of their commanding officer, Captain Frank Battles, apparently killed by the fire of the American infantry.[*][73] One platoon of Company G got too far ahead and threatened to be wiped out by the machine gun and rifle fire. Its sergeant carefully showed each man how to maintain cover

---

[*] The company's historian wrote after the war, "To this day, it is a mystery why the infantry fired on Captain Battles. It is thought that the long green slicker he wore for protection from the rain made him resemble a German soldier and caused someone to open fire on him." (John W. Kress, *One of the Last 'Rugged Individualists'* (privately printed, n.d.), p. 61.) Barber has Captain Battles being killed on November 10 in the attack on Hill 319. (Barber, *79th Division*, p. 302.)

while getting back to the battalion safely; just as the last man departed, the sergeant was fatally shot. Nevertheless, the 2nd Battalion was able to take the lower slopes of Hill 328, an advance of one and a half miles, before getting stuck and digging in.[74]

By now the Germans were having a hard time of it. Repeated assaults depleted their front-line companies and reinforcements had to be brought forward:

> The Americans make further progress. The force on Wettin Hill is not large, and the Americans are able to take ground by exploiting dead spaces. Company 3, which had been attached to Third Battalion, must also be transferred to Second Battalion, and, around 10:00 PM, Machine Gun Company 1, which had also been attached to Third Battalion, must be transferred, as well. The commander on Morimont gives up these forces only reluctantly, since Morimont is supposed to be the main line of resistance, and according to the orders is to be held to the last man, while Wettin Hill, a forward position, is supposed to be evacuated soon.[75]

As the 314th attacked eastward, the 158th Brigade executed its flank march to the southeast, a difficult maneuver in any conditions and especially at night, under fire, and in a hurry. The two battalions of the 313th Infantry got an early start and reached Wavrille just after the 314th captured it. They were then sent further south to bivouac in the Bois de Brabant. The 315th Infantry did not get started until 9:00 a.m., but by 11:00 a.m. its 1st Battalion had reached the railroad line between Wavrille and just south of Damvillers, north of their intended destination, where it and the 2nd Battalion, coming up behind, were hit by heavy shelling that kept it from advancing further. As he surveyed the situation the battalion commander, Major Ward W. Pierson, was killed by a shell. At 7:30 p.m. the 3rd Battalion, 314th Infantry, passed through the 315th on its way to the rear and the position of the 315th became the front line. After dark, both brigades got into position for a morning attack.

Intelligence reports for the day described an enemy in full retreat. "Wounded Prussian prisoner 31st Division reports no prepared line between Crépion and Metz. His unit was ordered to retreat as far as possible. He says there is a stronghold 4 km. from Crépion, where there are 10 batteries of field artillery," read one message.[76] II Corps' Intelligence section reported, "Airplane at 15H reported to Corps that road East and North of Bois

Dombras and Bois du Merles were jammed with enemy convoys. 15 kilometers further east, roads were also crowded. These convoys were all going eastward."[77] None of this, however, was of immediate help to the two brigades of the 79th, which were once again facing enemy machine guns well entrenched on the arc of hills overlooking their positions. That evening Kuhn sent a message to Claudel at II Corps:

> These hills are strongly defended by wire, machine guns, some 77 guns, and the equivalent of 37mm. cannon. Probably defended by comparatively few men. Unless enemy withdraws tonight I do not believe these hills can be taken by frontal attack. Possibly a concentric attack from the North, West, and South might succeed. I recommend that in case an energetic forward movement is contemplated for Nov. 10th, that as much Corps artillery as is available, and such divisional 155's as can range thereto, concentrate on the following centers of impact from 2H to 6H November 10th [coordinates follow].[78]

But Claudel, in his order for the next day's operations, said that the resistance his divisions were meeting was likely only a rear guard, citing the reports of roads choked with retreating German columns; he urged the attacking units to overcome local strong points by maneuver and infiltration.[79] There is no record of a reply to Kuhn's plea for corps artillery.

Notwithstanding, next morning's attack by the 157th Brigade started off well. The 52nd Field Artillery smothered Hill 328 with shells from 4:00 to 6:00 a.m., causing many secondary explosions. Then the 2nd Battalion of the 314th charged up the slope. Twenty-five minutes later Major Schoge, the battalion commander, sent a message to Kuhn: He had occupied Hill 328 and was a third of a mile past the crest, on the leading edge of Hill 319. But they could get no farther; machine guns on Hill 319, artillery from further ahead, and airplanes strafing the troops unmolested prevented an advance. Many officers were wounded; as they fell, NCOs took over their platoons and continued the attack. The fight became a series of small-unit contests. A Stokes mortar team from the Headquarters Company advanced under fire a hundred yards ahead of the infantry and destroyed a heavily defended strong point. Enlisted men risked their lives to recover wounded comrades; several were later decorated. But without continual artillery support, Hill 319 could not be taken. By noon the attack of the 157th had bogged down.

While the 157th Brigade attacked Hills 328 and 319, the 158th was to make a demonstration against Côtes d'Orne and Morimont.[*] Although the Côte d'Orne was actually in the sector of the French division to the north, the French had bypassed the hill, so it still threatened any advance by the 79th and had to be taken. Direct fire from artillery and two companies of the 312th Machine Gun Battalion shelled the hills until 7:30 a.m. Fog in the valley of the Thinte prevented accurate German fire, but machine guns and artillery still struck the leading elements of the 1st and 2nd Battalions of the 315th and the 2nd Battalion of the 316th as they advanced at 7:30 a.m. Wading across the Thinte, they reached the lower slopes of the Côte d'Orne but could get no further. They withdrew to the east bank of the river and took shelter, trying again an hour later. The second attack by the 315th stopped in the same place. But the 2nd Battalion of the 316th had got as far as half a mile east of Gibercy when the fog lifted, exposing it to machine gun fire from the front and both sides. Captain Strong, the battalion commander, decided that retiring was as dangerous as advancing so he ordered the men to dig in. Only the Machine Gun Company got back to the railroad line.[80]

By the afternoon of the 10th, Colonel Oury completed his artillery plan that would allow the 314th, in the vanguard of the 157th Brigade, to resume its attack. Shot-up wires hampered coordination with brigade headquarters, so Oury sent a messenger to Nicholson with his plan. At that moment, a runner came from Nicholson saying that the 158th Brigade could not take their objectives until Oury took Hill 319, and please hurry up about it. In the meantime, Kuhn had come forward to Nicholson's PC to supervise the artillery preparation personally. He approved Oury's plan, which directed the heavy guns to pound German positions beyond the hill while the 75s hit the hill itself. The opening salvoes fell short but communication to the artillery was good, so the sights were raised 200 yards and the shells hit effectively. As the bombardment ended, six companies of the 314th hurried forward. Lieutenant Joel described the attack:

"Second Battalion, over!" came the command at 4:20, and there followed the most exciting charge the outfit ever made. The first thin wave passed

---

[*] A demonstration is an attack intended to pin down or deceive the defenders but not necessarily to drive them off or capture their position.

through the machine gun barrage, which was cutting a belt of underbrush half way down the hill. Then right at the heels of the barrage, the thin line crossed the bottom land and charged up 319. Lieutenant Cabla on the right flank was yelling like a crazy Mexican, waving his pistol as they do in the sixteen-reel serials. The men quickly picked up the spirit and rushed the hill, yelling and shooting their rifles, automatics and rifle grenades as they advanced.[81]

The German troops in the front lines were starting to hear how their army was collapsing. "The vehicle drivers who come up from the rear tell stories about stores being looted by hordes of rear echelon troops who have suddenly grown bold thanks to the bad example provided at home." Of course, wrote the historian of the 31st Landwehr, "It must also be noted that none of our drivers, receivers of orders, scribes, or supply handlers are seduced by this awful example, but rather do their duty under the command of their commanders, the logistics officers and sergeants, and in doing so make it possible for the men on the front lines to hold on and not fall apart."[82] Nonetheless, the men prepared frantically to meet the assault. "For us, everything depends on getting ammunition to Wettin Hill. Ammunition, ammunition! The constantly firing machine guns consume every resupply as soon as it comes in. Everyone takes part in belting rounds of ammunition for the machine guns."[83] Captain Frohm, commanding the 2nd Battalion on the crest of Hill 328, described the attack:

> From our commanding position, our observation posts saw, as on an earlier maneuver field, the approach march of the enemy unit in larger and smaller sections, and as they came closer they sometimes advanced more spread out. We couldn't believe our eyes when we watched one detachment, with their weapons shouldered, march directly into our machine guns positioned above Gibercy between Wettin Hill and the Morimont road. Soon after they were in range, there wasn't much left of them ... Despite heavy losses, the enemy kept replenishing their front lines and slowly took ground. They even managed to ascend to the summit of Wettin Hill. Their attempt to bring up a light machine gun to the summit was initially broken up when its whole crew was shot down by one of our light machine guns. One gallant enemy soldier, who managed to advance 40 paces towards the trenches of our blocking position and take cover in a shell hole, discomfited us quite a bit. From the cover of the shell hole, he was able to shoot three of our men

in the head, without getting scratched himself, because he immediately disappeared into his hole after each shot. The hand grenades that were thrown at him fell short of the hole where he'd taken cover. As I made my way through the trenches, fairly exposed, he fired an aimed shot at me, as well, but this time he missed. He was finally suppressed by our grenades, when a sergeant, whose name escapes me, sprang at him and threw a grenade into his hole. The sergeant's comrades killed at the hand of this enemy were finally avenged.[84]

But the hill could not be held. Around 5:00 p.m., as American machine gun fire became stronger, the 2nd Battalion started to give way. Its men drifted rearward to the Côte Morimont, where they were immediately put into the line. Captain Frohm and his headquarters section remained on Hill 319, loading the ammunition onto a truck; Frohm was the last man to leave the hill.[85]

Reaching the crest, the men of the 157th Brigade discovered that the positions on Hill 319 had been destroyed. General Kuhn allocated some of the credit to himself; in his diary he wrote, "[F]inally took hill 328 and 319 after exerting my personal influence with General Nicholson."[86] Pressing up and over the hill, the 314th dug in on the eastern slope for the night—the last night of the war.

CHAPTER 17

ARMISTICE TO HOME,
NOVEMBER 11,
1918–JUNE 5, 1919

Although Ludendorff was gone, the German military establishment refused to admit defeat. General Heinrich Scheüch, the new Prussian War Minister, grasping at straws, had told Ludendorff that the call-up of men born in 1900 would add 637,000 soldiers to the ranks. General Groener, Ludendorff's replacement since October 29, now pointed out that only 300,000 of them would make serviceable soldiers. Instead, he told his staff, the Army was falling apart. Between 200,000 and 1.5 million soldiers were missing or had deserted; two Austro-Hungarian divisions were about to be sent home in the wake of the Empire's surrender; and thousands of soldiers were disobeying orders to fight. Shortly afterward OHL estimated that the number of combat-ready divisions from the Channel to the Rhine was no more than a dozen.[1] Early in November Groener inspected the troops on the Western Front and concluded that they could not resist another resolute offensive. Unrest in the navy added to the pressure. Sailors in the ships at Kiel, led by left-wing agitators, rebelled against orders to sail out and engage the British Grand Fleet in a climactic battle. The rebellion spread, protesters marched, dockworkers joined them; within a few days Hamburg and Bremen were ruled by Workers' and Soldiers' Councils and revolutionary agitation mushroomed throughout Germany. On November 6 Groener went to Berlin to tell Prince Max of Baden that suing for an armistice within a few days was necessary and inevitable.[2]

As the political situation in Germany deteriorated, the Allies accelerated their advance. On November 1 a single Canadian brigade, backed by one of the most concentrated artillery bombardments of the war, pulverized the German defenses at Valenciennes on the Scheldt River, taking 1,300 prisoners with only 60 fatalities. On the 4th, three British armies attacked the German line on a 20-mile front along the Sambre–Oise Canal, crossing countryside laced with woods, streams, and canals, and approaching Mons. South of them the French First Army also attacked on a 20-mile front, toward the town of La Capelle. The German defenses were nothing more than scrapes in the ground; both attacks achieved their objectives on schedule, throwing the defenders into further retreat. Estimates of German losses from July 18, the British counterattack at Amiens, to the end of the war are as high as 420,000 dead and wounded and 385,000 lost as prisoners. Added to the possible million lost in the Spring Offensives, it was clear that the German Army was dying.

While Groener was trying to talk sense to Prince Max in Berlin, a message arrived from President Wilson announcing that Foch would parley with any German armistice mission that might appear. On November 8 Foch, leading the French contingent, met a German delegation headed by Matthias Erzberger, a Catholic Centrist, in an isolated railroad carriage in the Forest of Compiègne. Foch presented the Allied terms as non-negotiable: the evacuation of occupied lands, repatriation of deportees, compensation for the destruction in France and Belgium, and the surrender of a long list of weapons, supplies, and ships. The victors would occupy all of Germany west of the Rhine and three bridgeheads across it, the cost to be borne by Germany. Erzberger forwarded the terms to Berlin.[3]

By that time, Kaiser Wilhelm and Prince Max were more anxious about Bolshevist revolution than about the armistice terms. Max insisted to the Kaiser that he should abdicate to avoid civil war. Wilhelm, as usual divorced from reality, wanted to turn his army around and lead it against the traitors; but a poll of field officers by Hindenburg made it clear that there was no support for such a move. Max now faced the imminent prospect of a takeover by the radical mob in the capital itself. On November 9, without consulting Wilhelm, he issued a proclamation: "The Kaiser and King has decided to renounce the throne." A constituent assembly would be called to erect a new form of German government. Wilhelm at first raged against his betrayers; but by evening Hindenburg and Admiral Scheer prevailed on him to abdicate as Kaiser (he insisted on remaining King of Prussia). At 5:00 a.m. the next day he boarded a train for Holland.[4]

Back in the Forest of Compiègne, after waiting for more than two days, Matthias Erzberger finally received word from Berlin accepting the armistice terms and authorizing him to sign them. Several hours of haggling over details of the text ensued; but after a formal statement of protest by Erzberger, the document was signed at 5:10 a.m. on the morning of November 11. Foch ordered all his commanders, "Hostilities will cease at 11 a.m. today."[5]

On the afternoon of November 10, First Army issued an order: "The 1st American Army will continue to press the enemy along the entire front and will rapidly follow up any hostile withdrawal."[6] In the sector of II Corps, the objectives given lay about seven and a half miles to the northeast and east. That night, as the men of the 79th dug in on the slopes of Hill 319, Kuhn received a message from Claudel commanding the 79th to continue its advance the next morning and be ready to move on Azannes, on the southern edge of its sector and nearly two miles away, to follow up an attack to be carried out by the 26th Division around Ornes. Kuhn in turn ordered the 158th to continue its demonstration on the two Côtes. At the same time, in the 157th Infantry Brigade, one battalion of the 313th with supporting artillery would demonstrate toward Côte de Romagne while detaching troops to capture Azannes. The northern flank facing Ville-devant-Chaumont would have to be protected in case it was occupied by the Germans. If resistance weakened, the troops were to take advantage and press ahead. The 52nd Artillery Brigade would fire at the direction of the infantry. The attack would jump off at 9:30 a.m.[7] Before he gave his orders, Kuhn sent a request to Claudel at II Corps:

> In connection with tomorrow's operation, of which I have just received some advanced information and based on today's operations, I am of the opinion that progress tomorrow would be facilitated if all available corps

artillery concentrated for four hours before the attack tomorrow on Cote Romagne, Cote du Chateau, Cote d'Orne, and Cote Morimont ... Request early information as to whether these concentrations will be ordered, so that I may coordinate the fire of the Divisional Artillery therewith.[8]

Two hours later Claudel called back to say that no corps artillery would be available to support the 79th. Furthermore, he said, Kuhn's request was based on a misconception; a demonstration was not an attack. The staff officer who took Claudel's call reported the corps commander's reasons and conveyed a hint of his frustration:

Itasca 1 [i.e., Kuhn] is to understand that of course some Corps artillery will fire upon the Cote Romagne, this being a part of the program that is assigned to Corps artillery in cooperation with the exploitation of the attack to be made by the 26th Division. He [Claudel] does not expect the Itasca division [i.e., the 79th] to take the heights named in Itasca One's message but merely to exercise pressure. They are not making the sacrifice of more men needlessly in attacking these heights.[9]

This was an opportunity for Kuhn to tell his commanders to take it easy and conserve lives; he didn't take it.

On November 8 First Army, at Foch's order, had sent a telegram to all corps commanders notifying them that hostilities would cease "at a date and hour not yet determined." The notice continued, "The fact must be emphasized that the proposed arrangement is an Armistice only and not a peace, and that there must be no relaxation of vigilance on the part of all concerned. Troops must be prepared at any time for further operations." Lest the prospect of a cease-fire sap the troops' motivation, Pershing quickly followed up with a second telegram: "You will not act upon former message until orders are received from these headquarters to do so. You will continue and push to the limit any operations you had in prospect."[10]

Shortly before 9:00 a.m. on the 11th, Kuhn's signals staff picked up a radio transmission: Marshal Foch was ordering all army and corps commanders to cease hostilities at 11:00 a.m. Then came an order from First Army, which Kuhn quickly telephoned to his brigade commanders:

Hostilities will cease on the whole front at 11h, today, French time. Until that hour the operations previously ordered will be pressed with vigor. At 11h our lines will halt in place and no man will move one step backward or forward. All men will cease firing and dig in. In case the enemy does not likewise suspend fire, firing will be resumed but no further advance be permitted. No fraternization will be allowed. Brigade and other commanders concerned are charged with the important duty of transmitting these orders to the troops and securing their strict enforcement ...[11]

Runners—at the risk of their lives—hurried forward to bring the news to the assaulting formations, some of which received it only minutes before the deadline.

Armistice or not, the morning attack had to go on as ordered. The guns of First Army fired off 66,900 shells, more than in the previous six days combined.[12] At 9:30 a.m. the 315th and 314th Infantry began their advance, accompanied by an overhead barrage from the 311th and 312th Machine Gun Battalions The men of the 79th were already aware that a cease-fire was in the offing. But because the attacking regiments got the actual order late that morning, the troops do not appear to have exhibited the same dismay as men in other divisions who knew even as they left their trenches that the fighting would end at 11:00 a.m.[*]

Fog prevented accurate fire by the Germans, who made up for it in volume. An intense concentration of shells landed in an open area between the 1st and 2nd Battalions of the 315th; two enlisted men serving as runners and a third who was laying telephone wire were killed. The 315th moved forward cautiously on either side of the road northeast out of Gibercy toward the Côte d'Orne, the lead company capturing a German gun. By then the regiment was fully aware of the impending Armistice but it continued up the lower slopes of the Côte de Morimont nonetheless. Two battalions of the 314th attacked due east from Hill 319. Sheltered by the fog, they got as far as the foot of the Côte de Romagne. The 1st Battalion of the 313th Infantry advanced southeast toward Azannes in the face of strong artillery fire, which did little damage because the sogginess of the ground absorbed much of the blast. They did not receive the armistice order until 10:44 a.m. The Germans had got the order an hour earlier.[13]

---

[*] Lieutenant Judy of the 33rd Division, then in the Troyon sector, wrote, "Some of our men cried as they went over the top, fearing that having gone thru the bloody strife thus far, they would be slaughtered at the last moment, and remembering that already for two days the announcement that peace had come was expected." (Judy, *A Soldier's Diary*, p. 159.)

At ten minutes to 11:00 a.m., Private Henry Gunther of Company A, 313th Infantry, spotted a German machine gun. His good friend and sergeant, Ernie Powell, who lay next to him opposite the Côte de Romagne, wondered for the rest of his life why Gunther rose to attack the gun. Earlier in the war Gunther had been broken from sergeant for writing a letter home that criticized the army; perhaps he wished to redeem himself in front of his comrades. As the private approached the German position the gunners, who knew of the Armistice, tried to wave him off; but he kept coming and they were compelled to fire a five-round burst. Hit in the head, Gunther died instantly, one minute before the war ended. The Americans claimed him as the last Allied soldier to die on the Western Front.[14]

Precisely at 11:00 o'clock the guns fell silent. Lieutenant Kress of the 314th described the scene:

> One moment, it was an inferno along the line! The next, the line was silent as the grave. It was too unreal; it must surely be a dream. A second of silence ... then, up out of the fog around us rose voices full of heartfelt emotion. Cries came from the German lines; cries of "Gott sei dank," and other expressions of thanks and rejoicing.[15]

Sergeant Fleming of the 315th recorded a similar experience:

> In a minute tin hats were discarded and we were in overseas caps, singing and cheering. Instructions came forbidding fraternizing with the enemy but it went on for several hours between the lines ... In a few hours everyone disappeared. A few must have stayed on the hills until nightfall as we were treated after dark to a remarkable display of rockets, flares and lights of every description, as far as one could see along the line to both horizons. It was better than a Fourth of July show.[16]

Colonel J. Frank Barber, commanding officer of the 304th Engineers and the division's historian, wrote:

> Perhaps the greatest relief was the knowledge that an exposed head would not draw rifle fire, that a man could stand erect without being sprayed by machine gun bullets, that shell holes no longer were necessary as protections against enemy fire, and that real hot food was coming up from the rear ... No night ration parties, no dangerous reliefs, no panting runners, no detailed field orders, no bursting high explosive or shrapnel, no raiding

airmen on the open roads, no stifling powder smoke in the air, no litter bearers on the trails, no moaning wounded at the first aid stations, no turmoil, no tragedy—only peace.[17]

A few German soldiers came forward but they were rebuffed; the Americans were still too upset by the loss of their comrades to fraternize.[*]

The attitude of the Allied leaders was mixed. For some time Foch, Clemenceau, and Haig had wanted an armistice as soon as possible to avoid sacrificing lives for nothing and to forestall something going wrong. In addition, as the American contribution would inexorably exceed their own if the war extended into 1919, the French and British wished to prevent President Wilson from being able to dictate peace terms.[18] But as early as mid-October, at an unofficial meeting of British war leaders, Lloyd George, the British Prime Minister, had worried about the problems of a peace short of victory. If democracy did not take root in Germany, militarists could tell the public that the "miserable democrats had taken charge and had become panic stricken, and the military party would get to power again ... and that by better preparation and organization they would be able to bring about victory next time."[19] He was seconded by Pershing, who believed that "[I]f civilization is to receive the full benefit of this terrible war it must end only with the unconditional surrender of Germany. The military situation is such that in his judgment there can be no excuse for not obtaining unconditional surrender."[20]

In reality, the Allies' hands were forced. By early November the British and French armies were almost completely exhausted and had come close to outrunning their supplies, being as far as 50 miles beyond their railheads. Depleted units had not been reinforced and the men were starting to resent the continual pressure to advance. Even the Americans were starting to reach their limits. Whereas the AEF had received 53 pounds of supplies per man per day from the States in February, by October the figure had dropped to 22 pounds. In some divisions horses were nonexistent and men had to pull wagons themselves. Medical staff were overworked to exhaustion. Locomotives, railroad cars, and transport workers were in alarmingly short supply; after the war, Harbord wrote that the Armistice was all that prevented

---

[*] According to the historian of the 31st Landwehr Regiment, however, the Americans were eager to buy medals and weapons from the Germans they met, who sold them uniform buttons instead. (Suhrmann, *Des Landwehr-Infanterie-Regiments Nr. 31*, p. 397.)

the AEF from being unable to fight. Given the Allies' exhaustion, it is likely that if hostilities had continued many units of the German Army would have escaped behind the Rhine. While an offensive in 1919 might have finished them off, it would have been a major undertaking that would have been highly unpopular in Britain and France.[21]

Pershing and his subordinate commanders have been bitterly criticized— at the time and since—for pressing their attacks up to the last moment before the Armistice. Foch had not ordered a continuation of the offensive to the very end, and although fighting went on to the last minute at some points along the British and French lines these were local situations only.[*][22] But the Americans, who were not nearly as exhausted morally and physically as their allies, were not wholly wrong to persist in their offensive. The war was emphatically not over. An armistice was not a peace, much less a surrender. It was an agreement to suspend hostilities for a stated period of time, in this case 36 days subject to renewal (not until February 12, 1919, was it extended indefinitely).[23] Unless renewed by both sides, firing would resume. Precedent was not encouraging. In 1912, in the First Balkan War, a two-month armistice between the Balkan League (Bulgaria, Greece, Montenegro, and Serbia) and the Ottoman Empire broke down and bloody fighting went on for another three months.[24] On the Eastern Front, the new Bolshevik government of Russia obtained an armistice on November 21, 1917. But it balked at Berlin's draconian territorial demands, so, on February 18, 52 German divisions crossed the cease-fire line to continue the fight.[25] Even after the Armistice the German commanders, once they saw the terms handed them at the Versailles Peace Conference, considered resuming the war. A meeting of senior general and staff officers, led by Groener and Minister of War Noske, advocated rejecting the peace terms, establishing a military dictatorship, and renewing the fighting (they were overruled).[26] To

---

* Nevertheless, Hunter Liggett was eager to assign Foch the responsibility. In his memoirs he wrote, "Certain persons have criticized the action of the Armies in keeping up the offensive to the last moment. This criticism is unwarranted. The Allied Generalissimo, from long and bitter experience, knew his foe well, and realized fully that our shifty enemy would quickly take advantage of any let-up on our part." (Hunter Liggett, *Commanding an American Army: Recollections of the World War* (Boston and New York: Houghton Mifflin, 1925), p. 125.) But the November 9 message from Foch that Liggett cited in support was a general exhortation to his commanders to show "*énergie et initiative*" and did not even mention the possibility of an armistice. (Ministère de la Guerre, Service Historique, *AFGG*, Tome Vii, 2e Volume, Annexes (Paris: Imprimerie Nationale, 1920–1938), p. 837.)

anticipate such eventualities by improving First Army's field position as much as possible was the only responsible course for Pershing and his staff. If there is a criticism to be made, it is that the November 10 order for an unremitting offensive applied everywhere along the line, regardless of the tactical value of the local objectives. But to maintain that Pershing stupidly and needlessly wasted the lives of his men just as the war was ending is to view in hindsight what was not at all apparent at the time.

In its actions east of the Meuse since October 29 the 79th Division had lost 52 officers and 1,724 men wounded and gassed; ten officers and 453 men were killed, 36 of them on the last day of the war.[27] No accounting was made of those who had died of the flu. The division was still not a wholly efficient fighting force; it never made up fully for its lack of training. But the officers and men had learned a lot since the September attack. Kuhn and his subordinates were now able to coordinate their activities on the spot and assign and reassign units as the battle unfolded, even creating provisional regiments out of available battalions as the moment required. Infantry commanders had learned how to ask for artillery support, which often arrived within 20 minutes of the request. Their men now followed the rolling barrage closely. Machine gun companies could keep up with the infantry and provide indirect fire to support the attack. (Prisoners captured on the Borne de Cornouiller reported that the American machine guns had often broken up their counterattacks.[28]) Tactics had improved; small units now reconnoitered machine gun nests and strong points in advance and encircled them rather than attacking frontally. Brigades were able to maneuver in complex terrain, the sideways march of the 158th on the night of November 8–9 being a particularly impressive example. There were no reports of traffic jams, major supply interruptions, or failures to evacuate the wounded.[*] Much of the improvement was made possible by the careful attention the signalmen gave to maintaining the telephone network. In his report of November 20 Kuhn summarized the progress his command had made:

---

[*] One inspector assigned to the 79th reported three days after the Armistice that traffic control in the division's sector was "woefully lacking." But it turned out that the problems were caused by the 26th Division, which was moving out. "This Division apparently had not taken proper precautions in regard to traffic control and numerous blocks were occasioned." (J.G. McIlroy, "Daily Report on Certain Divisions," November 14, 1918, RG 200, Pershing Papers, Box 29, Miscellaneous Records and Reports, NARA, p. 2.)

The Division fought with much more skill, as a result of their first experience at Montfaucon. The energies of combat units were husbanded and not dissipated so rapidly as on the first offensive. Troops were kept well in hand, and straggling was kept at a gratifyingly low limit. After 8 days of severe combats, the 158th Brigade, although somewhat depleted, was still capable of further effort while the 157th brigade, after 3 days offensive was still relatively fresh and the Division as a whole could have maintained considerable driving power for a number of days.[29]

By the morning of November 12 the German fireworks had burned themselves out and quiet returned to the front. Across from the 314th, around noon, 24 Germans approached the lines, soon followed by another 250. A major went out to find out what was happening. It developed, according to the historian of the 79th, that the men's officers had deserted them two days earlier, the NCOs a day later, and they wanted to know if the war had really ended. The major put them into column, pointed them toward Germany, and ordered them to march. German officers were amused when the 79th posted sentries to prevent further fraternizing. "The Americans are apparently afraid that their soldiers could be incited by Bolsheviks among our troops; this is a serious misjudgment of the feelings of our soldiers at the front, who are anything but happy about the disturbances in the homeland."[30]

A month's heavy fighting had prevented proper care of the dead so the bodies of four American divisions, in addition to those of the French and Germans, lay heavy on the ground. Burial details, under the supervision of chaplains, collected the scattered remains. They were taken to four provisional cemeteries, one on the Borne de Cournouiller, one outside Etraye, and two near Molleville Farm:

It was a heart-rending task. The bodies were in all stages of decomposition and many were shot to pieces. The ground was broken and shattered into uneven sections with shell holes almost overlapping each other. The woods were a confused tangle almost impassable. Every foot of ground must be carefully searched and the dead gathered into groups. This frequently involved a carry of a half mile on stretchers. The bodies must be searched for valuables and personal effects to be forwarded back to the relatives at home. The bodies must be searched also for identification. Occasionally tags had been shot away or removed and identification must be secured through letters or marks on clothing or equipment. The graves must be dug in a soil so sticky and heavy with clay that it clung tenaciously to the shovels and wearied the muscles of the toiling men without much progress being made. But for one long week the work went on until the area was cleared of dead bodies.[31]

Across the old battlefield streamed lines of people—French, Italian, Russian, and American prisoners returning from German captivity and refugees returning to find their homes, which were often in ruins. The men of the 79th welcomed and assisted them as best they could. Kuhn reported that nearly 800 former POWs crossed his front on November 15 alone. "It is a regular migration of races." As he met French soldiers, he was often greeted with sentiments such as, "*La guerre est finie; grace aux Américains; nous sommes très reconnaissants* [grateful]." "I guess they are," he wrote.[32]

As the Germans evacuated their lines in front of the 79th, they kept the division informed of their movements. Kuhn's officers sent out daily patrols to explore the empty positions, prevent looting and destruction, round up any unauthorized intruders, and send returning civilians and POWs to reception centers. Small groups of returning POWs were taken to the division PC; those of more than 150 men were held at the outpost positions while instructions were sought from higher authority. The men were set to work at the immense task of cleaning up the battlefield. Unexploded and abandoned shells were piled and then blown up. Usable equipment was salvaged and coated with protective grease. Roads were rebuilt. The countryside behind the old German lines was littered with masses of camp equipment—beds, fuel, stoves, timbers, and other paraphernalia, once so vital to the *Frontsoldaten* but now wholly abandoned. On November 13, German officers showed up at the headquarters of the 157th Brigade to deliver maps of minefields and other obstacles, as stipulated in the Armistice agreement. The 304th Engineers kept busy destroying mines and booby-traps; after a while German prisoners were used.[33]

To the intense disappointment of its officers and men, from the commander on down, the 79th was left at the Armistice line while other divisions were withdrawn or sent to Germany with the occupying army. It ended up holding a position from Stenay and Montmédy in the north to Les Eparges in the south, an arc of over 40 miles. Living conditions were no better than they had been during the fighting. Huddled in old German dugouts, the men continued to put up with mud, cold, and the fumes of mustard gas seeping out of the ground. Rats were a plague; General Kuhn could hear them making hideous noises at night behind the tar paper lining of his 6-by-7-foot dugout. But rank had its privileges, even among rats. "Annoying as these pests were," he wrote, "they had the good grace to keep on their side of the tar paper and never ventured into my room."[34]

The dead lay not far under the surface of the men's emotions. Corporal Lubchansky wrote to his family:

> I have never seen such a collection of dead men in my life as I saw on those hills, trenches, ditches, in open fields, they lay. Somehow or other one would think that looking at so many dead would at least cause some pity or sympathy, but seeing our own boys lying near rather brings on a spirit of hate and revenge. This is no place for a minister's son as the saying goes; although I personally do not profess to be a hard guy.[35]

Colonel Sweezey performed the saddest of a commander's duties, writing to the families of the dead. To the father of one of his men the colonel wrote:

> I regret to inform you that the official report which you received from the Adjutant General of the Army notifying you of the death of your son who was a member of Company "C", this regiment is correct. He was killed by high explosive shell fire during the afternoon of September 30th in the advance north of Montfaucon. He was with his company and battalion and doing his duty at the time of his death. We had a very heavy shell fire on us during that afternoon in which your son was killed and the regiment advanced under great difficulty. I regret to say that we lost a good many men, both killed and wounded, but as you say you can have the satisfaction of knowing that he gave all he had and we must all take consolation from such facts that we can. I extend to you our sympathy in your grief on his death.[36]

Others, like Corporal Schellberg, wrote more intimately to their dead comrades' relatives:

> You stated in your last letter that Tony's sister would like to know how he was killed, well I am not allowed to tell but some might slip through so I will write some of it. Tony was killed by a sniper the first day out while we were mounting our gun. He was a little in back of the gun and nobody knew he was dead until he was blue and cold. We don't know where he was shot but

think through the heart, he did not say a word and the only place you could [see?] blood was on one of his fingers. I got a first aid man and he said he was dead.[37]

Other correspondence showed the soldiers' anxieties for their families back home, largely because of the flu epidemic. "Received your letter today Sis and was glad to hear that all at home were well. Looks like the "Flu" has come out again and all of you must take care. What you wrote about poor Norma Leeser and Rose Meyers nearly took me off my feet. I have not gotten over it yet. It surely was sorrowful. Be sure you take good care of yourselves," wrote Corporal Lubchansky.[38] Another of his letters betrayed reluctance to disturb his family with the truth about his experiences: "I surely do hope they forget war by the time we come home. It may seem odd to you mother but the less is said about it the better it will be, and the sooner forgotten the better for all. Things such as we have seen and gone through are better untold."[39] But not all letters were grim. Colonel Sweezey replied to a Philadelphia lad whose dog had gone missing shortly after a troop train of the 313th had stopped near his home, and who wondered if a soldier had taken it to France:

Dear John:—

... If he came over to France you can rest assured he has been doing his duty as all other Americans have been over here, but you can take consolation in the fact that he got into the war in his old age which is old for a dog, and he was over the draft age if he was eleven years old. I am very sorry indeed that I can not find your dog for you as I would take pleasure in doing my best to see that he was returned to you, could I do so ... Hoping you find your dog, I am

Yours very truly,

C.B. Sweezey,

Colonel, 313th U.S. Infantry[40]

Much of the men's time was taken up with the two preoccupations of peacetime soldiers: food and rumors. Schellberg wrote to his sister, "Received your letter and also the bar of chocolate and was glad to receive same. This chocolate went pretty good and all the boys mouths watered when I pulled it out."[41] And he was looking forward to Christmas:

We expect to have turkey for Christmas and my mouth is watering allready. All we get now is beans hash & stew and only two meals a day ... We eat at four o'clock in the afternoon and at five o'clock the Salvation Army sells crullers and hot chocalate and the machine gun company is well represented their every night ... This organization is the best one of them all, they do more for us than any of the others, and when I get back this is the one I am going to help.[42]

The men's second preoccupation was guessing when they would be going home. In an interview with *Stars and Stripes*, General Harbord tried gently to deflate the soldiers' expectations of a speedy return. Although 300,000 men per month had been brought to Europe in wartime, he said, only about 175,000 embarkations per month could be predicted until the spring. The reason was that during the war the Allies had sacrificed their food imports to free up shipping for bringing Americans over. Now Britain, especially, had to build up its food stocks and transport its colonies' troops back to India, Australia, New Zealand, Canada, and South Africa. When that had been done, more transports would be available for the AEF.[43] This did not stop the soldiers from interpreting every movement order and every unit detached for some remote assignment as an indication that the division was headed either for Germany or for the States. (In fact, the 79th would remain in France until May.) Schellberg wrote in his diary, "Some new rumors around again we are to go back 200 miles to some training area and then to a seaport then home. I hope its some truth in this. We were supposed to be homeward bound once before but orders changed and we thought we were going to the german border we even turned in our mules and horses but we got them back again."[44] The rumors subsided on February 22, 1919, when Kuhn issued an order telling his men that they would depart in June. At least they now had something definite to look forward to.

They needed it because, as they endured the rain, snow, mud, and cold, the men were subjected to an endless series of field maneuvers which, given the absence of an enemy, did not generate much enthusiasm. The misery was enough for the surgeon of the 313th, Captain Frank Wheelock, to point out to Sweezey that most men had only one uniform and one pair of shoes, and that if the drill schedule of five hours per day, regardless of weather, continued, it would cause much illness. He requested that the schedule be adjusted so that the health of the troops would not suffer.[45] Sweezey forwarded the request to the division's operations officer who replied on behalf of General Kuhn, "Until possible ill effects of the present system become decidedly apparent in the health of the command, the division commander does not desire to submit the matter to higher authority. The policy is to continue training regardless of weather."[46] In other words, get sick first; then we'll worry about it. Immediately, the flu made its third appearance in the ranks of the AEF, sending 31,000 to the hospital. Although the death rate was lower than it had been in the fall, many men suffered the cruel fate of having survived the war only to die in the epidemic.[47]

After the Armistice a lack of recreation and educational activities, poor living conditions, and resentment at the apparently pointless training caused morale throughout the army to plummet. The problem was acute in the 79th, which had been left on the November 11 lines while other divisions were withdrawn to barracks or sent to Germany. An inspector assigned to the 79th, Major Edward C. Sammons, wrote to the commander of the YMCA describing living conditions: drill in the cold and wet until dark, no light or heat in barracks after dinner, and so on. The YMCA responded with candles, reading material, and table games. "In retrospect, it is remarkable that an informal IG action was needed to obtain this kind of support, and even more surprising that the request did not originate in command channels."[48] General Kuhn insisted later that, "In spite of all handicaps the troops maintained a cheerful attitude. There was always plenty of work to be done but as for recreation and diversion, the men were entirely dependent on their own resources. They never lost their sense of humor and always made the best of every situation." Still, when General Bullard, commanding the Second Army, came by on an inspection tour, he said, "Kuhn, your Division must get out of here or else its morale will break." Kuhn said he had no worries over the men's morale, but would indeed appreciate being sent to a more civilized location.[49] Eventually the Army provided diversions from the grim life in the field. Schools, furloughs to the south of France, and amusements such as athletic competitions, horse shows, and dramatics distracted the men somewhat from their homesickness. Particularly appreciated were the welfare workers—many of them women—of the YMCA and the Salvation Army who distributed games, athletic equipment, good food, and other small luxuries.[50]

The divisional history records that the officers went all out to give the men a memorable Christmas. Each battalion held services, many units put on plays, parties, and other amusements, and copious amounts of fruit, nuts, and well-cooked food were supplied. As electricity was lacking, candles were passed out to illuminate the festivities; the men found that salvaged German pyrotechnics worked better. The men made particular efforts to provide toys and candy to the children of returning refugees, many of whom were homeless.[51] Corporal Schellberg wrote to his sister in anticipation: "We are all looking forth to our great dinner which will be turkey pot pie. Look out for the second and third [helping] lines." But it was not to be: "Christmas. Had bacon & prunes for breakfast. Went to church. Snowing, again. Dinner Turkey pot pie it was rotten they must of busted the bowl. Rice was burnt. Biscuits & coffee. Only two meals. Received some candies and cakes. 1 keg of beer on tap at 3.30 P.m Price 14 franks. Everybody sick." He consoled himself on New Year's Day by going AWOL into Bar-le-Duc and gorging on steak, eggs, beer, and cake. "Wandered all around the town went in a cafe and had some party." Given a summary court martial, he pleaded guilty and was reduced to private at two-thirds pay.[*52]

By then the division had moved to Souilly, the town that had been Pershing's headquarters during the Meuse–Argonne campaign. Although it meant a 60-mile march through the frozen countryside the men welcomed the hike, because it meant they were leaving at last the trenches, the wire, the shell holes, and the wreckage for warm, decently appointed quarters on a way station home.[53] Once there, attention turned in earnest to training. The AEF set up a number of schools at the corps and division levels and officers and NCOs were sent to study infantry weapons and to hold field exercises. Danger was not absent; Schellberg described one accident:

> About 220 P.M had an accident on the stokes mortar. Five men were killed instantly and 37 wounded. Two more died after we got them to the first aid … The man was told to pull a pin out and instead he pulled it harder than he was supposed to & tape started to unroll and he got excited, the instructor told him not to throw it but it was to late he had thrown it allready. He threw it right in a crowd and as soon as it hit something it went off. It was

---

* The Army's vengeance had its limits. Schellberg's discharge papers did not mention his reduction in rank, described his character as "excellent," and under "Remarks" it said, "No unauthorized absences, services honest and faithful." (Jerry Harlowe, ed., *Your Brother Will: The Great War Letters and Diary of William Schellberg, Machine Gun Company, 313th Infantry, "Baltimore's Own"* (Ellicott City, MC: Patapsco Falls Press, 1992), p. 97.)

about a 100 men in the crowd and 42 were hurt. After I heard the cry I went up and it looked even worse than a battle field. We started to carry them in to the camp or first aid it was 7 PM before any ambulances came, and the last men left 10 that night. They do not expect several more to live.[54]

At Souilly, inspectors descended on the division. According to the divisional historian, these resulted in "a flood of commendations for the various units," and the archives support his assertion.[55] General Bullard himself complimented the 2nd Battalion of the 316th:

> The condition of the town of Issoncourt in general, order and sanitation in billets, mess halls established in billeting space set aside for the purpose, improvised bathing facilities, features of entertainment, and the variety of athletic activities in progress at the time, denote a keen appreciation on the part of its command of the welfare and comfort of the men as well as the maintenance of interest on the part of the men in their work.[56]

Life continued to improve. In addition to the ministrations of the Red Cross, YMCA, Jewish Welfare Board, and other welfare organizations, the men organized athletic events—boxing, baseball, volleyball, and football competitions from companies on up, all the way to division, corps, and army championships. Men formed amateur theatrical troupes. One, the "Kellam Four," a Vaudeville group organized by an enlisted man of the 316th Infantry, became so popular that it toured the entire AEF, giving 450 performances in nine months.[57] Opportunities for study and travel multiplied. Some officers and men were given leave to take classes at British and French universities. Every two weeks or so, a group of 1,200 men went to southern France to enjoy themselves. With the absences, many of the division's units were down to half strength. Leave, which had begun a few weeks after the Armistice, became common. Oscar Lubchansky, who had been promoted to sergeant, wrote home from Aix-les-Bains:

> Just think of it. Go to sleep whenever you so desire and get up whenever you are ready. Live in hotels where millionaires resided before the war and eat the best of food. As they say nothing is too good for the doughboy ... Am writing this in the big Casino where Harry Thaw spent most of his time and money.[*][58]

---

* Harry Kendall Thaw, a wealthy playboy, in 1906 shot the society architect Stanford White. White had had an affair with the showgirl Evelyn Nesbit, who was Thaw's wife and the model for the Gibson

Even Private Schellberg, the congenital malcontent, admitted grudgingly to enjoying himself:

> This place called Vals-Les-Bains is a good place for some one thats had lots of fun and excitement but us soldiers after being in a dead place for so long want to see lots of people and plenty of amusements which was very scarce down their. One thing they did have that all of us like and that was a real bed with white sheets on it, and fairly good eats. We were boarding at Hotel Lyon and beleave me we were some sports or at least thought we were. We had a maid to make our beds and clean our room and come in or get up when ever we felt like, several times I thought I had my discharge from the army but looked down and saw my O.D. clothes and knew I made a mistake and a big one at that.[59]

Kuhn himself wrote to his wife from the Riviera, "Many beautiful 'villas,' in reality palaces with beautiful gardens of semi-tropical character abound ... It is an impressive aggregation of wealth and splendor well calculated to arouse the Bolshevism in the proletariat." No doubt the proletariat would have appreciated the "[m]any French and Italian girls present, the younger ones gowned in very short shifts tied around the middle with a string, so it looked to me. The general impression of the dance floor was a sea of silk stockinged legs, very bad for a man's soul."[60]

On March 24 came an order that the 79th had been waiting for—but it was not quite what they expected. Kuhn wrote in his diary, "A telegram this morning announces that 79th goes to 4th training area north of Chaumont with Headqrs at Miraumont. What a useless move when we are so near going into the debarkation area! To make a week's march in mud and rain for only a few weeks stay at the new area."[61] Four days later the 79th began a 60-mile hike to Rimocourt. The march started in a blizzard, but the snow yielded to good weather in a few days. Although the direction was south, not west, it was the way home, so morale was good and straggling minimal. As they entered the valley of the Marne, the men marveled at the scenic countryside, its trim cottages and well-tended fields untouched by war. At Rimocourt the division underwent its final review by Pershing. The men worked for days to groom every horse, clean every gun, paint every truck,

Girl. The trial, at which Thaw was found not guilty of murder by reason of insanity, caused a national sensation.

polish every buckle, and shine every piece of leather; but the day before the event the skies opened up. The 20,000 men of the division marched the four miles to the reviewing ground through mud and rain, so that their hard work went for naught. Nevertheless, the commanding general was ecstatic:

> Nothing daunted, the troops swept by their Commander-in-Chief in serried ranks to the stirring music of seven massed bands, first the infantry and the Engineers, then the horse-drawn trains and the artillery. With faces aglow with the pink of health and a cascade of raindrops dripping from their steel helmets they strode past with resolute and elastic step. Line after line emerged from the rain and mist on the left to disappear again in the rain and mist on the right. I have witnessed many parades and reviews in many places, but none so wonderful and inspiring as the review of the 22,000 men of the 79th Division in a downpour of rain on that April morning in France.[62]

Pershing took the occasion to award Distinguished Service Crosses to 44 of the men. Visiting generals from other corps and divisions crowded round to congratulate Kuhn. Kuhn wrote to his wife that as he and Pershing drove away together, "The General simply remarked, 'It is the best I have yet seen,' and he has seen many divisions. So I am very proud of my men."[63]

The review over, the 79th got busy turning their equipment, guns, vehicles, and animals over to the Services of Supply at the railheads. On April 18, orders came to leave the next day to Nantes, on the way to the embarkation port at St Nazaire. (The 304th Engineers, as always, were left behind to police the area; it left for St Nazaire on May 10.) The trip, in the same creaky trains and 40/8 boxcars that had borne them eastward, took 40–48 hours; most of the division did not reach Nantes until April 27. Once there, the men found to their dismay that part, at least, of their ordeal was not over. A flurry of inspections kept officers, NCOs, and clerks jumping, at the same time that they were immersed in the paperwork attending the movement of any large force. The division historian described the interminable lists that were required in order to account for seemingly every paper clip ever issued to the 79th: "Squading [sic] lists, company rosters, clothing and equipment lists, arms and ammunition lists, property lists, passenger lists, individual records, audits of company funds, audits of vouchers for pay, baggage certificates, examination of identification tags, of wound chevrons, and so on, indefinitely."[64] At least the weather was good and the countryside beautiful.

Finally the division entrained for St Nazaire, where it embarked on 12 transports between May 13 and May 19. For the troops it was a very different experience from their previous voyage. "No zigzagging in the war zone, no running with lights out, no watchful guard to check the chap who wanted to light a match on deck. Band concerts and entertainments, games and amusements with enough drill to enable the men to man the boats in case of accident."[65] The ships were generally war-weary tubs that rolled and pitched, causing the men constant seasickness. But as Kuhn wrote, "Poor accommodations but who cares."[66]

Even as the last ships left St Nazaire, the first to depart were arriving in the United States. Three docked in Hoboken, four in Philadelphia, one in Brooklyn, three in Newport News, and one in Charleston. They were met by ferry boats, pleasure boats, excursion boats, all filled with cheering relatives, friends, and local citizens. The reception continued as the ships approached the docks, where crowds lined the piers and rooftops, bands played, and flags flew. The men, casting off military discipline, returned the cheers.[67]

Most of the division reassembled in Camp Dix, New Jersey. A triumphal parade was planned for Philadelphia, but three of the regiments would have none of it; they wanted to go home. As quickly as possible, therefore, they were sent to the demobilization centers closest to their homes; there they received their pay, changed their clothes, and became civilians.[68] The 313th, however, wanted its parade. As the transport *Essex* docked at Pratt Street in Baltimore harbor, the men filed off and formed ranks. To cheering crowds the regiment marched from the pier north to City Hall Plaza, west a few blocks on Baltimore Street and right on St Paul for the two-mile stretch to Mount Royal Avenue, then west to the gray granite pile that was (and still is) the Fifth Regiment Armory. Halfway up St Paul Street rose the Washington Monument where General Kuhn stood on the main reviewing stand, receiving the salutes of his men. But the star of the parade along its entire route was Colonel Sweezey, on horseback as befitted an old cavalryman. Wrote the *Baltimore Sun*, "As the Colonel swung into Holiday Street from the City Hall Plaza at the head of the parade, the crowd on the reviewing stands there rose as one person and, as one person, shouted one word: 'Sweezey!' This was followed by deafening cheers, cheers that made faint the strains of 'Maryland, My Maryland,' which the Three Thirteenth Band was playing as lustily as it knew how."[69] The rest was anticlimax. The regiment proceeded to Camp Meade where between June 9 and 10 it was demobilized. Kuhn wrote of his command, "A few days of paper work sufficed to wipe out the splendid fighting machine, built up after months of patient training, exhausting marches and gruelling battles."[70] The 79th Division now existed only in the memories of its veterans.

EPILOGUE

What was America's contribution to the Allied victory? General Pershing had no doubts: at the review in Rimaucourt he told the men of the 79th Division, "America won the war; it was the arrival of you and your comrades at a time when Allied leaders were beginning to doubt their ability to crush Germany that turned the scales and sealed the doom of autocracy."[*][1] His only regret was that the war had stopped before the German Army was beaten in the field. He later said, "If they had given us another ten days we would have rounded up the entire German army, captured it, humiliated it ... The German troops today are marching back into Germany announcing that they have never been defeated ... What I dread is that Germany doesn't know that she was licked. Had they given us another week, we'd have *taught* them."[2] Pershing's views on the victory were seconded by many of his commanders. Liggett, for example, wrote:

> The results achieved by the First Army in the Meuse–Argonne operation are so evident that little discussion is required ... The retreat of the enemy on his whole Front pivoted on the sector attacked by the First Army, and the holding of these positions was essential to the orderly withdrawal of his forces. For that reason the operations of the First Army were of prime importance in the general strategical plan of attack. The penetration of the enemy's position by the First Army on November 1st was a signal for a general withdrawal on the part of the enemy, all along the line West, and North to the junction of the Mons Canal with the Scheldt.[3]

In other words, after November 1 the advances of the French and almost all

---

[*] Pershing stressed this theme in his talks to most of the divisions he reviewed. In his *Final Report* and in his memoirs, however, Pershing was careful not to overshadow the efforts of the other Allies.

of the British armies were made possible only by the American success. Nor did Pershing ever reconsider his insistence that the rifleman trained in open warfare was the primary instrument of combat; as far as he was concerned, American doctrine and training were appropriate to the occasion and superior to those of its Allies.* Such perceptions quickly became the standard American view of the war.

Pershing, in fact, had reason to be proud, if not quite as proud as he was. In the Meuse–Argonne the AEF fought continuously for 47 days. Twenty-two of its 29 divisions—1.2 million soldiers—engaged at one time or another one-quarter of all German divisions on the Western Front. Almost 2,500 guns fired more tonnage of shells than the entire Union Army in the Civil War. On the other hand First Army advanced only 34 miles, lost 120,000 men of whom 24,000 were killed, and took only 16,000 prisoners— about the same as were taken in four days at St Mihiel. The offensive did succeed in pulling precious German reserves from the British and French sectors to the American, which probably was a factor in the British Expeditionary Force's rapid advance at the end of the war. "The result was a less spectacular American military contribution to the Allied victory than Wilson and Pershing had sought."[4]

Until the early 1980s American historians, while not subscribing to Pershing's triumphalism, implicitly or explicitly accepted his pronouncements.† Then there started to appear works that overturned the standard interpretation of the United States' military role in World War I. They documented in detail the deficiencies of Pershing's open warfare doctrine; the faulty (or absent) training of the troops; the naïveté regarding the roles of artillery, tanks, and machine guns; the consequent lack of practice in combined-arms operations; and the confusion and needless casualties that often resulted on the battlefield.[5] No longer could historians

---

* Pershing wrote, in a cover memorandum to a 1920 report by the AEF's Superior Board on Organization and Tactics, "The true principle is that the necessity for maneuver always exists and that the only proper limitation on maneuver during the break-through is that imposed by the amount of available terrain." The top-down direction and trench warfare tactics used in the Meuse–Argonne, he wrote, were aberrations caused by assigning many divisions to a narrow front, the unpreparedness of divisional staffs, and the "conceptions which we inherited from our Allies of limited objectives, intermediate objectives, lines of maneuver and similar artificial limitations and lapses from fundamental principles." (John J. Pershing, "Wrapper Endorsement, Report of Superior Board on Organization and Tactics," June 16, 1920, Army War College Curricular Files, file 52-15, AHEC, p. 4.)

† See the footnote on page 142.

credit Pershing's claim, "Ultimately, we had the satisfaction of hearing the French admit that we were right, both in emphasizing training for open warfare and insisting upon proficiency in the use of the rifle."[6]

In fact, America's contribution strictly in terms of combat operations was marginal. Yes, the timely arrival of the 2nd and 3rd Divisions (and others) in the Allied lines in early June 1918 was critical in stemming the tide of Ludendorff's Spring Offensives and buoying the morale of the French. But on the attack, the Americans accomplished much less than did their allies. In 1918 the French and British combined took 327,000 German prisoners and 4,720 guns, far overshadowing the American totals of each.[7] In the final offensive the French and British each progressed 40 miles on a 75-mile front, a total of 14 times the area conquered by First Army. But wars are won on the margin, and historian Andrew Wiest has offered what seems like a fair assessment of the purely military aspects of the AEF's performance:

> [T]he American combat experience of the Great War lasted for a total of six months. Is it any wonder, then, that the AEF, regardless of the advantages to be gained by learning from the experience of its allies, had difficulties? Contrary to accepted opinion, the American military experience in the Great War can be seen as a leading example of lightning-fast military innovation. Although the process arguably was hampered by stubbornness, from a standing start, the AEF in six months went from an untested military to being able to best the vaunted Germans in battle.[8]

The chief American contribution to victory was not its battlefield performance, although that was far from negligible. It was to make clear to the exhausted Germans that they could no longer hope to win a war of attrition. No matter how many Americans became casualties, there would always be millions more.

One group did not wait for the historians to tell them what had really happened: the professional soldiers of the Regular Army. All of the Chiefs of Staff from 1921 to the outbreak of World War II—Pershing, Hines, Summerall, Douglas MacArthur, Malin Craig, George Marshall—had seen the travails of the AEF up close. They understood that what had almost worked in 1918 would not work at all in future conflicts. Popular and Congressional isolationism after the war meant that not much could be done immediately. But by the late 1930s the rise of Nazi Germany and Imperial Japan impelled Army planners to acknowledge that the depleted armed forces could not give even minimal protection to the United States. From 1937 to 1938 Malin Craig, the Army Chief of Staff (and formerly Hunter Liggett's chief of staff in I Corps) developed a Protective Mobilization Plan, aimed at creating a force of 1.2 million men in eight months. It was never implemented, but it set a precedent. Mobilization actually began on September 8, 1939, when President Roosevelt proclaimed a "limited national emergency ... for the purpose of strengthening our national defense." George Marshall, appointed Chief of Staff the week before, immediately took measures to revive the stagnant army.[9]

One of Marshall's first actions was to replace the ponderous square division of 28,000 men with the triangular division of 15,000. The former was designed for attrition warfare (see Chapter 3); the latter was optimized for mobile combat. Each division had three infantry regiments. One would attack an enemy formation from the front, one would maneuver to the side and rear, and the third would stand in reserve. An artillery regiment provided fire support for all. This triangular organization was repeated at lower echelons, down to the battalion level.[10] With the example of the Wehrmacht's *Blitzkrieg* before him, Marshall concentrated the tanks into two armored brigades—soon to become the 1st and 2nd Armored Divisions—that would serve as autonomous strike forces rather than infantry support.[11] In the summer of 1941, Congress overthrew the rigid principle of strict seniority and gave Marshall the authority to promote officers according to ability.[12] The former policy had forced Marshall himself to languish as a colonel for 16 years after the war. The new one allowed him to promote Eisenhower from colonel to brigadier and then major general in ten weeks, jumping over 228 general officers who had greater seniority.[13]

Changes in equipment and doctrine also sprang directly from the World War I experience. Between 1929 and 1941 much attention was paid to providing artillery support to the infantry. Radio—more mobile but also more vulnerable to jamming and eavesdropping—replaced the telephone at the front line. Map-based fire adjustment methods and integrated fire-direction centers allowed a sole observer to lay and adjust the fire of as many guns as necessary, from a single battery to many battalions' worth, on a target.[14] Heavy weapons—machine guns, mortars, light antitank guns—were integrated into all levels of the infantry organization: each rifle company had a heavy weapons platoon, each battalion had a heavy weapons company, and so on. By early 1941 new, efficient 105mm howitzers and modern support aircraft became available to combat units, with the capable M4 Sherman tank on the way.[15] Transportation was revolutionized; anticipating an amphibious war, the Army designed new landing craft, especially the DUKW, which could serve as a boat at sea and a truck on land.[16] Almost all infantry divisions were assigned their own trucks, enough to carry at least a regiment without shuttling back and forth. Mechanized infantry traveled in armored half-tracks.

Strangely, the problem of getting supplies to the attacking forces while under fire, which had throttled the first phase of the Meuse–Argonne offensive, did not receive early attention. General Craig, still thinking of engineers as builders of ports, fortifications, and roads in the rear of the combat zone, wanted to eliminate them from the divisional structure. The idea that they were critical to maintain the supply network immediately behind the front did not catch on right away. It was the German use of engineers in blitzkrieg tactics that caused the Army to preserve the divisional engineering battalion.[17] The engineers' role was publicized by Captain Paul W. Thompson, who had been a military observer in Germany before the war. In 1940 he published several articles describing in detail the Wehrmacht's use of engineers in combat. He was much impressed with their role in demolishing the fortifications of the Belgian fortress of Eben Emael. He concluded his article saying, "[T]he campaigns have demonstrated that the engineers are now an elite member of the team." When in 1940 the Army created the two armored divisions, it assigned a combat engineering battalion to each.[18]

As early as 1930, it had become obvious that the engineers' reliance on hand and horse power was inadequate for the fast pace of modern military operations. By 1937 light tractors, air compressors, power shovels, road graders, and dump trucks were being issued to engineering units. In the following year was added the heavy 7.5-ton bulldozer. In the words of several historians of the Corps of Engineers, "Pearl Harbor found the Corps possessed of the basic engineering tools of mobile warfare. The bulldozer had replaced the pick and shovel as the symbol of the engineer soldier."[19]

To furnish the weapons and equipment needed for a modern army, Congress in June 1940 streamlined military procurement and production and passed an initial appropriation of $4 billion for rearmament. Contracting procedures were revolutionized; the old cost-plus-percentage-fee arrangements were replaced with cost-plus-fixed-fee contracts, which reimbursed private manufacturers for their often unpredictable expenses while limiting the opportunities for profiteering.[20] In the earlier war, the United States had to beg the French and British for weapons and equipment; in the coming one, America would send to its allies tanks and planes by the tens of thousands and trucks by the hundreds of thousands.

Rather than waiting for a declaration of war in order to introduce conscription, as Wilson had done, Congress on September 16, 1940, put in place the first peacetime draft. By mid-1941, 16 million men were registered and 1.4 million were in uniform.[21] To avoid the training debacles of World War I (see Chapter 5), a system was set up in which draftees first arrived at reception centers where they were screened and assigned to occupational specialties, then sent to Replacement Training Centers (RTCs) at which they underwent basic training and some instruction in their specialties. ("Replacements" referred to virtually all enlisted men, not just those making up for combat losses.) They were then sent to their combat arm or supporting service for unit training. The organization broke down in late 1944 because the demand for riflemen in Europe overwhelmed the capacity of the RTCs. But until then it was a great improvement over the methods of 1918, and formed the basis for the "boot camp" system that obtains to this day.[22]

Even the Army's new headquarters symbolized the determination to rearm before the next war had started rather than after. Construction of the Pentagon—still the world's largest office building—began three months before Pearl Harbor; it was completed 16 months later.[23]

The memory of the bitter political and military schisms among the World War I leaders spurred Allied planners to integrate their command structures. At the Arcadia conference from late December 1941 to early January 1942, Churchill and Roosevelt established the Combined Chiefs of Staff, comprising the top Army, Navy, and Air Force officers of each country. It set new levels of collaboration in coalition warfare. Marshall then got the British and the Americans to agree that in each theater there should be a single supreme commander. This meant not only that one nation's armed forces would subordinate themselves to a leader from another nation, but within each country's armed forces one service would be supreme over the others. Given national pride and inter-service jealousies, this was a greater accomplishment even than the creation of the Combined Chiefs. Thus did the Allies' war in Western Europe come to be commanded by Dwight D. Eisenhower.[24]

It is reasonable to propose that the outstanding legacy of America's participation in World War I was the experience that enabled the government and the military to mobilize for World War II and to fight its battles effectively. American political and military leaders made many mistakes in the latter conflict but most of them were new ones. Not least among the lessons they learned was how to transport, operate, and sustain a modern army of several million men across an ocean several thousands of miles wide. No country had done that before 1917; no country has done it since, save for the United States in World War II.

The search for the identity of the person who canceled the September 26 order for the 8th Brigade to attack westward behind Montfaucon was pursued in a 20-year correspondence involving many of the officers of the 4th Division. Colonel Bach, the division's chief of staff, was particularly assiduous in canvassing the officers of the division and of III Corps on this question.[25] Most professed no knowledge; General Bjornstad, the corps' chief of staff, replied, "This cannot be answered by me. I remember nothing concerning it ... [I]f you ask who directly ordered the cancellation of F.O. 56, I can't tell you."[26] But Bach and a few of his correspondents believed all along that it was Bjornstad. As Bach wrote in a handwritten note to General Booth, the former brigade commander, "We are still on the trail of the Montfaucon affair. Attached is a copy of a statement from Bjornstad ... I suppose it is too much to expect of any man to ask him to admit to posterity—that he made a mistake."[27] The controversy simmered fitfully through the years. Finally in 1940 General Pershing himself wrote to Booth: "Some time after the event I was speaking to the chief of staff of the III Corps regarding the failure of the units on the left of that Corps to give assistance in the capture of Montfaucon. He told me that an inquiry came from whoever was in command of those troops nearest as to whether they should give assistance to the troops attacking from the front. His reply was, 'No, keep in your own sector.' This is my recollection of what happened. General Bjornstad, the chief of staff in question, regretted very much that he had not given instructions to those troops to turn and assist in the capture, and attributed it to his rather ironclad adherence to the principle of boundary lines."[28]

Of the two million men who had gone to France, 205,000 returned having been wounded; almost 72,000 returned not at all.[29] Most came back proud of their service and convinced of their accomplishments. There was no Lost Generation except in novels and poems, many by the writers who gathered around Gertrude Stein in Paris.* Yet the country to which they returned was very different from the one they had left. Immigration, urbanization, industrialization, and war had shaken society to the point of backlash. The election of 1918 gave both houses of Congress to the Republicans for the first time since 1910; the next election gave them the Presidency as well. The Republicans would control national politics until the Depression and the advent of Roosevelt. The Progressive ideal—that government should intervene to improve the social, economic, and moral well-being of the citizenry—was now dead, or at least comatose. Internationalism died, too, when in November of 1919 the Senate rejected the Versailles Treaty and

---

* The American writers most closely associated with the Lost Generation idea—Faulkner, Dos Passos, Cummings, Hemingway, Fitzgerald—had all been in uniform, but had not fought at the front (Hemingway was wounded as an ambulance driver in Italy). The only prominent antiwar author who fought was Laurence Stallings, a lieutenant in the Marine Brigade who lost a leg to wounds suffered at Belleau Wood. In 1924 he wrote the play *What Price Glory?* with Maxwell Anderson. Forty years later, however, he published a history of the AEF that can only be described as celebratory. (Laurence Stallings, *The Doughboys: The Story of the AEF, 1917–1918* (New York: Harper & Row, Publishers, 1963).) After analyzing over 30,000 responses to a questionnaire administered to returning veterans in 1919, historian Edward Gutiérrez wrote of the Lost Generation idea, "It continues to misguide our understanding of the conflict. The war shocked them, but it did not shatter them. Duty- and honor-bound, the doughboys were young and eager to fight on the Western front. Only when they returned home did they have a full understanding of the brutality of war. Even though the doughboys experienced the horrors of modern warfare, it ennobled them. They were honored to make the sacrifice." (Edward A. Gutiérrez, *Doughboys on the Great War: How American Soldiers Viewed Their Military Service* (Lawrence, KS: UP of Kansas, 2014), p. 15.)

with it the League of Nations, the founding instruments of the new world order that Wilson had intended as the redeeming outcome of the war. Unions, which had gained members, benefits, and power during the conflict, were turned on by industry, which had a large labor pool of returning soldiers on which to draw. The federal government, preoccupied with demobilization and economic conversion, did not intervene. Wage gains were rolled back, efforts to organize and bargain collectively were suppressed. Strikes, often accompanied by violence, broke out in the steel, lumber, railroad, and mining industries. Radical agitation—including some bombings—let industry blame the labor troubles on Bolsheviks and anarchists. A. Mitchell Palmer, Wilson's Attorney General, exploited public alarm by instigating a campaign, headed by the young J. Edgar Hoover, to flush out radicals. The campaign went beyond the wartime antisedition efforts, conducting illegal break-ins and arrests and concentrating on aliens who, unlike citizens, could be deported for mere membership in a suspect organization; had no right to inspect the warrants against them; and could be deported without trial.[30] Labor unrest, the glut of workers, and a decline in crop prices among other factors led to a brief but sharp depression in which prices dropped, stocks fell, and unemployment soared. But for people who weren't industrial workers or radicals, the change that affected them most directly was Prohibition. Before the war, Progressives—who viewed alcohol as a social ill—and rural Protestants—who regarded it as sinful and as fuel for mobs of urban, largely Catholic, immigrants—had united to agitate for a ban on intoxicating drink. In 1919 their efforts bore fruit in the Eighteenth Amendment and the Volstead Act, which effectively banned the production, importation, distribution, and sale of alcoholic beverages. The returning veterans could not (legally) buy themselves a beer.

For one group of veterans, even this was not the most immediate problem. Many African-Americans thought their service, both military and civilian, would entitle them to civil rights. Having fought for democracy, bought war bonds, donated to relief organizations, and volunteered for charities, they believed that equality in law and fact was their fair compensation. Officials of the federal government understood that American blacks would expect better treatment after the war. But, facing what they considered to be unalterable social realities and fearing bloodshed, they urged top military officers to work with state governments and black community leaders to tamp down black hopes. Discharged black soldiers were given a pamphlet entitled, "A Greeting to our Colored Soldiers," which advised patience and faith in America. "Then—not all at once, perhaps, but slowly and surely—a better day will dawn for you and your children."[31] Racial tensions, in fact, increased. Over 100,000 whites, by no means all of them Southern, joined a reinvigorated Ku Klux Klan; many embarked on campaigns of terror against blacks who asserted civil or social rights. Lynchings increased to 77 in 1919, among them ten black veterans in uniform. Race riots erupted in many cities. The legacy of the 92nd and 93rd Colored Divisions would wait 40 years to become manifest.

As Pershing sailed home on the storm-tossed *Leviathan*, he received word that Congress had appointed him General of the Armies—the highest rank possible. Only George Washington had held such a rank, and then only posthumously. He arrived to a hero's welcome in New York Harbor, complete with a parade down Fifth Avenue.[32] After a brief vacation, the general immersed himself in Army work, writing reports, visiting military posts, and testifying against an Army Reorganization Bill that would have expanded the peacetime force to half a million (it was defeated).[33] In July 1921, he was appointed Chief of Staff; but with no war to plan and Congress in a stingy humor, there was not much to do in Washington. So Pershing took to the road, promoting an army based on the citizenry as the best protector of America's liberties. His speeches and articles probably saved the Army from effective extinction.[34] In 1923 he was made head of the American Battle Monuments Commission, created by Congress to oversee the proper burial of American dead and to commemorate the efforts of the AEF. After his Army retirement in September 1924 he continued to serve the country, heading a diplomatic mission to South America for President Coolidge.[35]

During the 1920s, Pershing wrote his memoir of the war, assisted by Major Dwight D. Eisenhower among others. Marshall read the draft and was appalled—instead of the measured judgment and understated diplomacy the general had so often exhibited in France, it was full of vituperation against allies and countrymen alike—Clemenceau, Lloyd George, Foch, Haig, the War Department in general, and Peyton March in particular. Marshall beseeched Pershing to moderate his language and the general accommodated him a bit, but much of the resentment remained. (March later wrote his own memoir, much of which was a stinging rebuttal of Pershing.) To the surprise of many, *My Experiences in the Great War* won the 1932 Pulitzer Prize for history.[36]

Pershing spent the 1930s deeply involved in the activities of the American Battle Monuments Commision, planning and supervising the creation of cemeteries and monuments. His most satisfying moment came in August of 1937 with the dedication of a 180-foot-high shaft, topped with a statue representing Liberty, on the crest of Montfaucon. On July 15, 1948, after a long period of failing health, he died.[37]

Pershing's funeral procession assembled at noon on July 19 at the Capitol. Fourteen lieutenant generals—much of the top command of World War II—and two major generals followed the casket; 24 more generals were honorary pallbearers. As they marched down Constitution Avenue the heavens opened and torrents drenched the mourners; but by the time they reached Arlington Cemetery the sun had reappeared. Greeting the procession were President Truman, Secretary of Defense Marshall, Chief Justice Vinson, General Eisenhower (then president of Columbia University), Chief of Staff General Omar Bradley, hundreds of general officers, and thousands of lesser ranks and civilians.[38] Pershing was laid to rest in the World War I section among the men he had led. The stone placed later by his son was regulation Army issue, the same as provided to any veteran or their spouse.[39]

Pershing's reputation has changed with time. His allies thought him ignorant of the realities of modern warfare and pig-headed in his refusal to amalgamate American soldiers into their armies. In reality, his "ignorance" of trench tactics was a sincere if badly realized belief that open warfare offered the only path to victory.* He was not wrong, only premature; the war ended, after all, in a pursuit of the rapidly retreating Germans. His stubbornness regarding the independence of the American Army was consistent with President Wilson's desire and his orders from the War Department, even if it did coincide with his own prejudices about the

---

* It has been suggested that Pershing understood the need for trench tactics well enough, but insisted on open warfare as the only doctrine suitable for the AEF in order to establish his case for an independent American army. (James W. Rainey, "The Questionable Training of the AEF in World War I," *Parameters*, 22, Winter (1992–93), p. 92.) That is hard to credit, as it implies that he was willing to condemn his untrained divisions to heavy losses as they struggled through the German defenses. There is no evidence that Pershing was endowed with such ruthlessness.

inherent superiority of the American rifleman. And indeed, a separate army was the only form in which the American public would have supported their country's military participation. As a commander, Pershing showed a greater ability to adapt in a shorter amount of time than did the Allied leaders; within eight weeks of the formation of First Army he replaced himself with Liggett as its commander, going a long way toward solving his tactical problems. In the States he was idolized after the war, the adulation softening over the years to admiration for his military leadership and diplomatic skills. Today he is criticized by American historians for ignoring the need for trench tactics and for failing to convert "open warfare" from a vague concept to a concrete, trainable doctrine. But, especially given the officer corps of 1917, it is hard to imagine an American who would have made a better Commander-in-Chief.

Returning to the States, General Kuhn was assigned to command Camp Kearney in San Diego, then Schofield Barracks at Pearl Harbor, and finally Fort Vancouver in the State of Washington. In 1925 he retired with the full-time rank of major general (like most officers, his wartime rank had been for the duration only). He had enjoyed San Diego so he settled there and became active in community causes, among them the local Red Cross chapter, which he served as chairman.[40] He wrote his memoirs, which were published in installments in the *Washington Post* in March 1926. He remained intensely proud of the 79th; neither in his memoirs nor anywhere else did he complain that the 4th Division had failed to "turn" Montfaucon. He died in 1935.

The veterans of the 313th remembered Colonel Sweezey with pride and fondness. Even the curmudgeonly Will Schellberg wrote, in his down-to-earth prose, "Col. Sweezy is the only man he is the bravest man that ever walk in a pair of shoes. On the Monfaucon drive he was up front all the time directing his regiment and this aint no bull because you can ask anyone in the regiment that was their ..."[41] In 1920 the colonel resigned from the Army and came back to Baltimore as warden of the state penitentiary. Sweezey, who opposed capital punishment, made changes in accordance with his idea that prison was a place to rehabilitate inmates to society, not merely to punish them. But after a series of escapes the Board rescinded many of the privileges Sweezey had granted the prisoners. Despite hundreds of letters from civic clubs, veterans' organizations, and prisoners themselves urging him to stay, in 1925 he resigned, always maintaining that there was no laxity in his administration.[42] He remained in Baltimore, serving as State Commander of the American Legion and showing special attention to Baltimore's Montfaucon Post. In 1932 he ran for Congress as a Republican but was defeated in the Roosevelt landslide. Two years later he moved to Berkeley, California, where, in 1939, at the age of 71, he died .[43]

Private James M. Cain returned to his job at the *Baltimore Sun* but, frustrated by the limits of local journalism, quit to report on the burgeoning violence in the labor movement. He contributed 12 articles to the *American Mercury*, whose guiding light, H.L. Mencken, became his close friend; wrote editorials for the *New York World* under Walter Lippmann; and hung around New York speakeasies with the likes of Sinclair Lewis, Franklin P. Adams, and Heywood Broun. For 17 years he worked as a scriptwriter for Hollywood studios but rarely for more than a few weeks at a time. None of his scripts was produced. On the side he wrote novels—*The Postman Always Rings Twice* in 1934, *Double Indemnity* in 1936, and *Mildred Pierce* in 1941, all of which appeared on the screen and became monuments of American film noir. Eventually he wrote 17 books, nine of which were made into movies. Yet always he identified himself as "a newspaper man" and, before his death in 1977, told his biographer that he felt no sense of accomplishment in his life.[44]

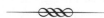

Corporal Will Schellberg resumed his quiet life in Baltimore, working as a bookbinder at the Government Printing Office and commuting to

Washington daily, eventually moving to Silver Spring, Maryland. In 1927 he married a young woman of Irish descent whom his mother described as "being a good wife in spite of her ancestry." His main social activity was the Rexton Athletic Club, a bicycling society he had helped found before the war. Among the club's rules were "that ladies are not permitted in the club except on special occasions sanctioned at the regular meeting," and "that gambling of any kind is not permitted on the club premises." As time passed, both rules were gradually relaxed. In 1979 he died, aged 85.[45]

Sergeant Oscar Lubchansky returned to Baltimore, shortened his name to Lobe, and resumed his prewar job as a plumbing supply salesman, a career he pursued until his death in 1958. Upon the advent of World War II he descended on the local recruiting office and demanded to enlist, if not as a combat soldier then as an MP. He had beaten the Germans once, he figured, and now he intended to finish the job. The recruiting sergeant told him he was too old for service, whereupon Lobe invited the sergeant outside to settle just who was too old for what. Apparently, cooler heads prevailed. He never talked about his wartime experiences to his daughter or son; but late in life he enjoyed telling his daughter's two little boys old-soldier stories, some of them no doubt true. Portraying the Germans he met on the slopes of Montfaucon he would throw his arms aloft, open his eyes wide, and mournfully intone, "*Kamera-a-ad, Kamera-a-ad!*" Once the older boy asked artlessly, "Did you kill any Germans, Grandpa?" Lobe was silent for a moment, his eyes taking in some faraway scene. Then, almost to himself, he said, "God, I hope not." The grandson did not understand then what the old man meant, but he does now.

Appendix A
Divisional Table of Organization (Abbreviated)
American Expeditionary Forces

Unit	Commander	Major Subordinate Units	Approx. Full Strength
Division	Major general	2 infantry brigades 1 field artillery brigade 1 engineer regiment 1 machine gun battalion Trains—sanitary, ammunition, supply, engineers	28,000
Infantry brigade	Brigadier general	2 infantry regiments 1 machine gun battalion	8,500
Field artillery brigade	Brigadier general	2 75mm field artillery regiments 1 155mm field artillery regiment 1 trench mortar battery	5,100
Infantry regiment	Colonel	3 infantry battalions 1 machine gun company 1 supply company	3,800
Field artillery regiment	Colonel	6 batteries (4 guns each) 1 supply company	1,600
Infantry battalion	Major	4 rifle companies	1,025
Rifle company	Captain	4 platoons	250
Platoon	First lieutenant	1 section hand grenadiers 1 section rifle grenadiers 1 section riflemen 1 section automatic riflemen	45

APPENDIX B
*The Periscope of Montfaucon**

On September 27, as the men of the 313th Infantry Regiment consolidated their position atop newly captured Montfaucon, they discovered many dugouts, observation posts, and defensive positions dug into the sides of the hill— eventually more than a hundred, some constructed from old wine cellars and the basements of ancient ruins. One of the observation posts was exceptional: inside a large, three-story building on the west slope stood a tower with thick, reinforced-concrete walls extending from the basement to the roof. On the first floor was a carriage-mounted periscope, the telescoping pole of which was extended to the roof, a height of 35 feet (the full height of the pole was 85 feet). Under the roof was a chart room with a map of the surrounding countryside and a scale marked off in mils of deflection so that the periscope could quickly be aimed at any desired point. Observers could view a target from the ground floor through eyepieces or from other floors using a system of mirrors and prisms. The equipment was in working order except that, in the words of the historian of the 79th Division, "Before it could be brought to bear on the enemy lines, some thoughtless souvenir hunter stole the eyepieces, rendering it useless."

The first phase of the offensive was still under way so the 79th quickly advanced beyond the town, chasing the retreating Germans. But it left behind a squad from the Headquarters Company to operate the observation post. For three days a sergeant and two privates manned the position— although not the periscope—under heavy fire; for this they were later awarded the Distinguished Service Cross.

---

* A version of this Appendix appeared on War History Online at ww.warhistoryonline.com/ guest-bloggers/german-periscope-montfaucon.html.

On September 30 the exhausted 79th was relieved and the veteran 3rd Division, the Rock of the Marne, moved in. They found the periscope in place, dismounted it—it took four-and-a half days—and sent it to III Corps on October 30. They reported that it was "in excellent condition except that some of the hoisting cables were broken, the telescopic eye-pieces smashed, and one section of the elevating pole dented by shrapnel." In February 1919 the periscope was shipped from the French port of St Nazaire directly to the United States Military Academy at West Point.

The periscope and the building in which it had stood quickly became known as the "Crown Prince's Observatory" from which he was said to have directed the battle of Verdun in 1916. Who among the Americans first made this attribution is not known. It is unlikely that the Crown Prince "directed" the battle from that position, or that the periscope was intended for such a purpose, as it was more than 12 miles west of the main action and the building in which it was housed was on the far slope of Montfaucon and below the crest. The observatory's purpose was clearly to survey the south and southwest to guard against a French attack from those directions. It is certain that German Crown Prince Wilhelm, who commanded that portion of the German line from 1914 to the end of the war, used it for that purpose. As he wrote in his memoirs, "On December 29th [1915, before the attack on Verdun] I was inspecting the front of the 6th Reserve Corps from the observatory of Montfaucon, and from this magnificent view-point my eyes first sought out, *not the Argonne forest at my feet, as they had been wont to do hitherto*, but the eastern bank of the Meuse, where, behind the hills of Horgne, Morimont and Komagne [*sic*], such fateful matters were in preparation [emphasis added]."[1]

Soon after its arrival at West Point the periscope became the subject of a minor controversy. In his transmittal letter Major General Robert Howze, commander of the 3rd Division, requested that it be labeled, "Captured by the units of the Third Division." Brigadier General Douglas MacArthur, then superintendent of the Academy, sensed trouble and forwarded Howze's letter to Major General Joseph Kuhn, former commander of the 79th, requesting that he work out the matter with Howze so that a properly worded plaque could be affixed to the object. In the meantime, other former officers of the 79th got wind of the proposed attribution, which they regarded as "clearly an injustice to our dead who helped take the town." The upshot was that the plaque was worded to read, "Montfaucon captured by

313th Regiment, 79th Division, September 27, 1918. Periscope dismounted by 3rd Division and presented by it to the Military Academy."

The periscope quickly became a prominent and celebrated trophy at West Point. Graduates and their families were photographed in front of it. Newspapers and magazines printed its image. But with the advent of World War II, the previous war and its memorabilia fell into the shadows; the periscope was relegated to the West Point Museum and in 1967 it was transferred to the National Armed Forces Museum Advisory Board. But NAFMAB disbanded soon thereafter without cataloging all of its acquisitions, so the location of the periscope became a mystery. Inquiries to the Army Historical Foundation, the Center of Military History, and the Smithsonian Institution yielded the suggestion that it might be in the US Army Field Artillery Museum at Fort Sill, Oklahoma. In 1999 the museum's director, Towana Spivey, wrote that the item had been in the collection for many years "and yours is the first inquiry I have received about it." It was not clear, however, that the museum staff understood the history of the piece; it was identified only as a German fire-control periscope. But in a recent exchange the current curator of the Artillery Museum, Gordon Blaker, confirmed that the item is now exhibited in the main gallery and, after reading the documentation, acknowledged that it is the periscope captured on Montfaucon. One hopes that the object will be properly identified on its label, so that visitors may appreciate what was once the very embodiment of the American achievement in World War I.

NOTES

The following abbreviations are used in the references:

ABMC	American Battle Monuments Commission
AEF	American Expeditionary Forces
AFGG	*Les armées françaises dans la grande guerre*
AHEC	US Army Heritage and Education Center, Carlisle, PA (formerly the Military History Institute)
GPO	Government Printing Office
NARA	National Archives and Records Administration, College Park, MD
RG	Record Group
RG 120	Record Group 120, Records of the AEF
SHD	Service historique de la défense, Château de Vincennes, Paris (formerly Service historique de l'Armée de terre)
USAWW	*The United States Army in the World War, 1917–1919*
USMA	Archives of the United States Military Academy at West Point

Notes from the Author

1. Army War College, Historical Section, Order of Battle of the United States Land Forces in the World War: General Headquarters, Armies, Army Corps, Services of Supply, Separate Forces (Washington, DC: Center of Military History, orig. pub. 1931, reprinted 1988), p. 405.

Prologue

1. "79th Division Field Messages," 1918, RG 120, 79th Division, Boxes 4–5, 32.16, NARA, September 27, 1918, sent 4:53 a.m.
2. "Gen. Kuhn Reviews Division; Expects to Get to Berlin," *Philadelphia Press*, October 12, 1917, pp. 1, 4.

Introduction

1. Garry Ryan, "Disposition of AEF Records of World War I," *Military Affairs* 30, Winter (1966–67), p. 212.

2.   "79th Division Field Messages," September 29, 1918, sent 7:30 a.m.

Chapter 1: Setting the Stage

1.   John Keegan, *Fields of Battle: The Wars for North America* (New York: Knopf, 1996), p. 8.
2.   Eugen Weber, *Peasants into Frenchmen: The Modernization of Rural France, 1870–1914* (Stanford: Stanford UP, 1976), pp. 197–200.
3.   D.W. Johnson, *Battlefields of the World War: Western and Southern Fronts: A Study in Military Geography* (New York: Oxford UP, 1921), p. 325.
4.   Richard Holmes, *Fatal Avenue: A Traveller's History of Northern France and Flanders, 1346–1945* (London, Melbourne, Sydney, Auckland, Johannesburg: Pimlico, 1992), p. 198.
5.   Michael Howard, *The Franco-Prussian War: The German Invasion of France, 1870–1871* (London and New York: Routledge, 1961, reprinted 1999), p. 194.
6.   Alistair Horne, *The Price of Glory: Verdun 1916* (London: Penguin, 1962, republished 1993), pp. 161–2.

Chapter 2: War Comes to Baltimore

1.   US Department of State, "Venezuela Boundary Dispute, 1895–1899," https://history.state.gov/milestoncs/1866-1898/venezuela, accessed May 30, 2016.
2.   Albert Bernhardt Faust, *The German Element in the United States, with Special Reference to Its Political, Moral, Social, and Educational Influence*, 2 vols (Boston, New York: Houghton Mifflin, 1909), p. 581.
3.   David M. Kennedy, *Over Here: The First World War in American Society* (Oxford, New York, Toronto, Melbourne: Oxford UP, 1980), p. 24.
4.   Gerald Sorin, *A Time for Building: The Third Migration*, ed. Henry L. Feingold, vol. III, The Jewish People in America (Baltimore and London: Johns Hopkins UP, 1992), p. 58.
5.   Barbara W. Tuchman, *Practicing History. Selected Essays* (New York: Ballantine, 1981), p. 162.
6.   Martin Gilbert, *The First World War: A Complete History* (New York: Henry Holt, 1994), p. 308.
7.   Ibid., p. 306.
8.   Robert H. Ferrell, *Woodrow Wilson and World War I, 1917–1921* (New York: Harper & Row, 1985), p. 9; Marc Ferro, *The Great War, 1914–1918* (London: Routledge & Keegan Paul, 1969; trans. pub. 1973), p. 114.
9.   Maurice Matloff, ed., *American Military History* (Washington, DC: GPO, 1973, revised edition), pp. 365–66.
10.   Kennedy, *Over Here*, p. 24.
11.   Alan Palmer, *Victory 1918* (London: Weidenfeld & Nicholson, 1998), p. 94.

12. Thomas Fleming, *The Illusion of Victory: America in World War I* (New York: Basic Books, 2003), p. 94.
13. Kennedy, *Over Here*, p. 68.
14. Ibid., p. 74.
15. Ibid., pp. 25, 35.
16. "Colored Citizens Show Patriotism," *Afro-American Ledger*, April 28, 1917, p. 1.
17. Minnesota Population Center, "National Historical Geographic Information System: Pre-Release Version 0.1," University of Minnesota, http://www.nhgis.org, accessed 7 August 2011.
18. "Zion Church and World War I," http://www.zionbaltimore.org/vthistory_1900s_sons_of_zion_ww1.htm, accessed August 30, 2011.
19. "Irish Arraign England," *Baltimore Sun*, June 12, 1916, p. 12.
20. "Says Irish Will Fight for U.S.," *Baltimore Sun*, February 2, 1916, p. 14.
21. Harvey A. DeWeerd, *President Wilson Fights His War*, ed. Louis Morton, The Wars of the United States (New York, London: Macmillan, 1968), p. 7.
22. "The Blessing of War," *Baltimore Sun*, January 13, 1916, p. 6.
23. "Our Preparedness Parades," *Baltimore Sun*, May 15, 1916, p. 8.
24. "Called Outlaw's Work," *Baltimore Sun*, May 8, 1915, p. 2.
25. "Wilson Gave Notice to Neutral Nations of Proposed Action," *The Morning Herald*, February 5, 1917, p. 1.
26. Cited in Jerry Harlowe, ed., *Your Brother Will: The Great War Letters and Diary of William Schellberg, Machine Gun Company, 313th Infantry, "Baltimore's Own"* (Ellicott City, MC: Patapsco Falls Press, 1992), pp. 6–8.
27. "The Call to Action," *Baltimore Sun*, April 3, 1917, p. 8.
28. "Wipe German out of Public Schools," *Baltimore Sun*, July 7, 1918, p. 1.
29. "What Is a Pro-German? You Ask. Your Question Is Answered Here," *Baltimore Sun*, March 7, 1918., p. 2B
30. "Cheers for Maryland All Along the Line," *Baltimore Sun*, March 6, 1917, p. 16.
31. "Foreign Born Pledge Fealty," *Baltimore Sun*, July 5, 1918, p. 12.
32. "Glimpses of the Side Lines," *Baltimore Sun*, September 6, 1917, p. 6
33. "Hebrew Orphans Patriotic," *Baltimore Sun*, June 23, 1918, p. 14.
34. "Zionism a War Issue," *Baltimore Sun*, January 14, 1918, p. 6.
35. "Colored Troops Called to Arms," *Afro-American Ledger*, March 31, 1917, p. 1.
36. "Dean Pickens for Training Camp," *Afro-American Ledger*, March 10, 1917, p. 1.
37. "57,000 Men Enrolled in City with No Mark of Disorder; Patriotism Shown All Day," *Baltimore Sun*, June 6, 1917, p. 5.
38. Ibid., p. 14.

Chapter 3: Creating an Army

1. Matloff, *History*, p. 328.
2. Gary Mead, *The Doughboys: America and the First World War* (Woodstock and New York: Overlook Press, 2000), p. 69.
3. Ferrell, *Wilson*, p. 15.
4. John Ellis, *The Social History of the Machine Gun* (Baltimore: Johns Hopkins UP, 1986, paperback edition), p. 74.
5. War Department, *Field Service Regulations, United States Army, 1914; Corrected to April 15, 1917*, Document No. 475 (Washington, DC: GPO, 1917), p. 74.
6. Boyd Dastrup, *King of Battle: A Branch History of the U.S. Army's Field Artillery*, ed. Henry O. Malone and John L. Romjue, TRADOC Branch History Series (Fort Monroe, VA and Washington, DC: Center of Military History, 1992), p. 149.
7. Robert H. Ferrell, *Collapse at Meuse–Argonne: The Failure of the Missouri–Kansas Division* (Columbia, MO and London: University of Missouri Press, 2004), p. 4.
8. Dastrup, *King of Battle*, pp. 152–54.
9. Conrad H. Lanza, "Counterbattery in the AEF," *Field Artillery Journal* 28, September–October (1936), p. 454.
10. Charles E. Heller, *Chemical Warfare in World War I: The American Experience, 1917–1918*, Leavenworth Papers No. 10 (Fort Leavenworth, KS: Combat Studies Institute, US Army Command and General Staff College, 1984), p. 37.
11. Major General William J. Snow, "Extracts from the Report of the Chief of Field Artillery for the Fiscal Year 1919," *Field Artillery Journal* 9, no. 5 (1919), pp. 575–76.
12. Matloff, *History*, pp. 25, 265, 350.
13. John H. Morrow, Jr., *The Great War in the Air: Military Aviation from 1909 to 1921* (Washington, DC: Smithsonian Institution Press, 1993), p. 338.
14. Matloff, *History*, pp. 345, 372.
15. Edward Coffman, "The AEF Leaders' Education for War," in *The Great War, 1914-18: Essays on the Military, Political and Social History of the First World War*, ed. R.Q. Adams (College Station: Texas A&M UP, 1990), p. 151.
16. Kennedy, *Over Here*, p. 158.
17. Edward M. Coffman, *The War to End All Wars: The American Military Experience in World War I* (New York: Oxford UP, 1968), p. 8.
18. John J. Pershing, *My Experiences in the World War*, 2 vols (New York: Frederick A. Stokes Co., 1931), vol. 1, p. 43.
19. John Whiteclay Chambers, II, *To Raise an Army: The Draft Comes to Modern America* (New York: Free Press, 1987), p. 186.
20. Alan Lomax, *The Folk Songs of North America in the English Language* (Garden City, NY: Doubleday & Company, 1960), p. 341.

21. Donald Smythe, *Pershing: General of the Armies* (Bloomington: Indiana UP, 1986), p. 9.
22. Kennedy, *Over Here*, p. 13.
23. Coffman, *War to End All Wars*, pp. 27–29.
24. Ibid., pp. 25–29.
25. Kennedy, *Over Here*, p. 152.
26. "Go in Service at Once," *Baltimore Sun*, July 31, 1917, p. 12.
27. "Many Slackers Register," *Baltimore Sun*, June 30, 1917, p. 12.
28. Ibid.
29. Kennedy, *Over Here*, p. 166.
30. Nancy Gentile Ford, *Americans All! Foreign-Born Soldiers in World War I* (College Station, TX: Texas A&M UP, 2001), p. 3.
31. Ford, *Americans All*, pp. 68–75 passim.
32. William and Dixon Wecter Matthews, *Our Soldiers Speak: 1775–1918* (Boston: Little, Brown, 1943), p. 270.
33. Matloff, *History*, p. 377.
34. Alan R. Millett, *The General: Robert L. Bullard and Officership in the United States Army, 1881–1925* (Westport, CT: Greenwood Press, 1975), pp. 32, 40.
35. Ferrell, *Wilson*, p. 14.
36. Coffman, "Education", p. 154.
37. Joseph E. Kuhn, "Two Years with the German Army During the World War: Address before the Association of the Army of the United States at San Francisco, Cal.," September 30, 1923, Kuhn Papers, Box 3, USMA, p. 1.
38. Ibid., pp. 6–7.
39. "Tribute to General Kuhn," *Army Navy Journal*, August 25, 1917, pages unnumbered.
40. Joseph E. Kuhn to Helen Kuhn, Kuhn Papers, Box 5, USMA, September 20, 1917.
41. Millett, *The General*, p. 307; Joseph E. Kuhn to Col. Frederick Palmer, July 10, 1930, Kuhn Papers, Box 5, USMA.
42. Memorandum of LTC W.S. Graves, secretary to CofS, to Adj. Gen., March 23, 1917, cited in Chambers, *To Raise an Army*, p. 133.
43. War Department, "Reports of Military Observers Attached to the Armies in Manchuria During the Russo-Japanese War, Part III: Report of Major Joseph E. Kuhn, Corps of Engineers," (Washington, DC: GPO, 1906), p. 228.
44. Coffman, "Education," p. 153.
45. AEF Office of the Chief of Staff, "Confidential Memorandum for the Commander-in-Chief," February 22, 1918, RG 200, Pershing Papers, Box 26, Miscellaneous Records and Studies, NARA, p. 4.
46. William E. Matsen, "The Battle of Sugar Point: A Re-Examination." *Minnesota History Magazine* 50, Fall (1987); Betsy Ross, *I Fly the Flag* (Champaign, IL: Graphix Group, Inc., 1984), pp. 8–9.

47. Samuel W. Fleming, Jr., "World War I Service," 1960, World War I Survey, Box: 79th Division, 157th and 158th Inf. Brig.; Folder: Fleming, Samuel W., Major, 315th Infantry, AHEC, p. 17.

48. J. Frank Barber, *History of the Seventy-Ninth Division A.E.F. During the World War: 1917–1919* (Lancaster, PA: Steinman & Steinman, n.d.), p. 21.

49. Joseph E. Kuhn to Helen Kuhn, September 20, 1917, Kuhn Papers, Box 5, USMA.

50. Barber, *79th Division*, p. 24.

51. Fleming, "World War I Service," p. 8.

52. Ibid., p. 15.

53. Ibid., p. 12.

54. Joseph E. Kuhn, "D.C. Boys at Camp Meade: Intimate Reminiscences of Commander of Camp Meade, Md., Consisting of Drafted Men from District of Columbia, Maryland and Pennsylvania, Who Afterward Constituted the Famous Seventy-Ninth Division in France, Still Led by Man Who Trained Them," *Washington Post*, March 14, 1926, p. MS10.

55. William L. Hanson, MD, *World War I: I Was There* (Gerald, MO: The Parice Press, 1982), p. 51.

56. Edward A. Davies, "War Diary of Sergeant Edward A. Davies, Company B, 315th Infantry, 79th Division," n.d., World War I Survey, AHEC, p. 4.

57. Barber, *79th Division*, p. 26.

58. "Great Welcome at Camp Meade," *Baltimore Sun*, September 30, 1917, p. 16.

59. John W. Kress, *One of the Last "Rugged Individualists"* (privately printed, n.d.), p. 15.

60. "South Opposes Negro Soldiers," *Afro-American Ledger*, April 14, 1917, p. 6.

61. Arthur E. Barbeau and Florette Henri, *The Unknown Soldiers: African-American Troops in World War I* (Philadelphia: Temple University Press, 1974), pp. 38–43.

62. Ibid., pp. 50, 63, 97, 100.

Chapter 4: What Pershing Should Have Known

1. War Department, *Infantry Drill Regulations, United States Army, 1911, with Text Corrections to February 12, 1917* (New York: Military Publishing Co., 1917), pp. 108, 114.

2. Ibid., p. 123.

3. Ibid., p. 114.

4. Cable 228-S, October 19, 1917, Department of the Army Historical Division, *USAWW*, 17 vols (Washington, DC: GPO, 1948), vol. 14, p. 306.

5. Ibid., vol. 2, p. 491.

6. Ibid., vol. 3, p. 122.

7. Pascal Marie Henri Lucas, *The Evolution of Tactical Ideas in France and Germany During the War of 1914–1918*, (Paris: Berger-Levrault, 1923),

unpublished US Army translation by P.V. Kieffer, 1925 in library of AHEC, p. 248 of original.

8. Ibid.

9. Russell F. Weigley, "Strategy and Total War in the United States: Pershing and the American Military Tradition," in *Great War, Total War: Combat and Mobilization on the Western Front, 1914–1918*, ed. Roger Chickering and Stig Förster (Washington DC and Cambridge, UK: Cambridge UP, 2000), p. 341.

10. Richard M. Watt, *Dare Call It Treason* (New York: Simon and Schuster, 1963), p. 29.

11. Ibid., p. 61.

12. Robert A. Doughty, *Pyrrhic Victory: French Strategy and Operations in the Great War* (Cambridge, MA and London: Belknap Press, 2005), pp. 121, 171, 253.

13. Ministère de la Guerre, Service Historique, *AFGG*, Tome V, 1er Volume, Annexes – 1er Volume (Paris: Imprimerie Nationale, 1920–38), p. 998.

14. Watt, *Treason*, pp. 171–72.

15. Hubert C. Johnson, *Breakthrough! Tactics, Technology, and the Search for Victory on the Western Front in World War I* (Novato, CA: Presidio Press, 1994), pp. 230–31. Anthony Clayton, *Paths of Glory: The French Army 1914–18* (London: Cassell, 2003), pp. 136–37.

16. Doughty, *Pyrrhic Victory*, p. 464.

17. Ibid.

18. Tim Travers, "The Allied Victories, 1918," in *World War I: A History*, ed. Hew Strachan (Oxford, New York: Oxford UP, 1998), p. 280.

19. Martin Samuels, *Command or Control? Command, Training and Tactics in the British and German Armies, 1888–1918* (London: Frank Cass, 1995), pp. 83, 85.

20. War Office (Great Britain), *Statistics of the Military Effort of the British Empire During the Great War, 1914–1920* (London: His Majesty's Stationery Office, 1922), pp. 252–57.

21. Pershing, *My Experiences*, vol. 1, p.114.

22. David F. Trask, *The AEF and Coalition Warmaking, 1917–1918* (Lawrence, KS: University Press of Kansas, 1993), p. 95.

23. Quoted at ibid.

24. Tim Travers, "The Evolution of British Strategy and Tactics on the Western Front in 1918: GHQ, Manpower, and Technology," *Journal of Military History*, 54, April (1990): pp. 194–95; Tim Travers, *How the War Was Won: Factors That Led to Victory in World War One* (Barnsley, UK: Routledge, 1992; repr., Pen & Sword, 2005), p. 145.

25. Historical Division, *USAWW*, vol. 3, pp. 330–31.

26. Martin Samuels, *Doctrine and Dogma: German and British Infantry Tactics in the First World War* (Westport, CT: Greenwood Press, 1992), p. 19.

27. Bruce I. Gudmundsson, *Stormtroop Tactics: Innovation in the German Army, 1914–1918* (New York, Westport, CT, London: Praeger, 1989), pp. 85, 65.

28. David Stevenson, *Cataclysm: The First World War as Political Tragedy* (New York: Basic Books, 2004), p. 307; David T. Zabecki, *Steel Wind: Colonel Georg Bruchmuller and the Birth of Modern Artillery*, ed. Bruce I. Gudmundsson, The Military Profession (Westport, CT; London: Praeger, 1994), pp. 28–29.

29. Bruce I. Gudmundsson, *On Artillery* (Westport, CT, London: Praeger, 1993), p. 94.

30. Ibid., pp. 88–89.

31. Gudmundsson, *Stormtroop Tactics*, pp. 147, 149.

32. Travers, "British Strategy and Tactics," p. 189. Palmer, *Victory 1918*, p. 174.

33. Travers, "The Allied Victories, 1918," p. 280.

34. Historical Division, *USAWW*, vol. 2, p. 521.

35. Millett, *The General*, p. 315; Douglas Valentine Johnson, II, "A Few 'Squads Left' and Off to France: Training the American Army in the United States for World War I" (Ph.D. thesis, Temple University, 1992), p. 168.

Chapter 5: Training—The Army at War With Itself

1. Peyton C. March, *The Nation at War* (Westport, CT: Greenwood, 1970), pp. 246–48.

2. Historical Division, *USAWW*, vol. 14, p. 312.

3. Cable 952-S, April 18, 1918, Ibid., p. 320.

4. War Department, *Infantry Drill Regulations, United States Army, 1911, with Text Corrections to July 31, 1918*, Document No. 394 (Washington, DC: GPO, 1918), pp. 112, 127; War Department, *Field Service Regulations, United States Army, 1914; Corrected to July 31, 1918*, Document No. 475 (Washington, DC: GPO, 1918), pp. 74, 79.

5. Army War College, *Infantry Training*, Document No. 656 (Washington, DC: GPO, 1917), pp. 5, 14.

6. Ibid.

7. Historical Division, *USAWW*, vol. 2, p. 296.

8. Ibid., vol. 14, p. 317.

9. Ibid.

10. War Department, *Instructions on the Offensive Conduct of Small Units*, Document No. 583 (Washington, DC: GPO, 1917), pp. 5, 6.

11. HBF [Harold B. Fiske], "Program of Training for Divisions in the United States," unpublished document in AHEC library, p. 12.

12. James W. Rainey, "The Questionable Training of the AEF in World War I," *Parameters*, 22, Winter (1992–93), p. 45.

13. Johnson, "Squads Left," p. 198.

14. Ernest L. Loomis, *History of the 304th Ammunition Train* (Boston: Gorham Press, 1920), pp. 20, 22.

15. Harlowe, *Your Brother Will*, p. 23.

16. Loomis, *304th Ammunition Train*, p. 22.

17. Andrew J. Kachik, untitled memoir, n.d., World War I Survey, Box: 79th Division; 157th and 158th Inf. Brigades; File: Kachik, Andrew, 314th Inf., AHEC, p. 9.

18. F.M. Caldwell, "Report of Inspection of 79th Division and Other Troops, Camp Meade, Maryland," January 24, 1918, RG 120, 79th Division, Boxes 7, 9, 11, file 56.2, NARA, pp. 1–2.

19. Ibid., p. 3.

20. Barber, *79th Division*, p. 28.

21. "These Russians Loyal," *Baltimore Sun*, February 13, 1918, p. 5.

22. Loomis, *304th Ammunition Train*, p. 28.

23. Kress, *Rugged Individualists*, p. 22.

24. Lonnie J. White, *The 90th Division in World War I: The Texas–Oklahoma Draft Division in the Great War* (Manhattan, KS: Sunflower UP, 1996), p. 3.

25. Vincent De P. Fitzpatrick, "Kuhn as Poster Censor," *Baltimore Sun*, November 25, 1917, p. 14.

26. Barber, *79th Division*, p. 34.

27. Kachik, untitled memoir, p. 9.

28. Kress, *Rugged Individualists*, pp. 22–23.

29. Joseph E. Kuhn, "Division Carried by Great Armada across Atlantic," *Washington Post*, March 17, 1926, p. 5.

30. Barber, *79th Division*, p. 35.

31. "Annal of Mobilization," 1918, RG 120, 79th Division, Box 2, NARA, p. 2.

32. Barber, *79th Division*, p. 37.

33. E.A. Helmick, E.G. Beuret, D. Lewis, A.J. Niles, "Inspection of 79th Division, Camp Meade, Md., June 19–27, 1918," n.d.; c. June 1918, RG 120, 79th Division, Box 11, 56.2, NARA, p. 2.

34. Ibid., p. 1.

35. Loomis, *304th Ammunition Train*, p. 29.

36. Stephen Harding, *Great Liners at War: The Military Adventures of the World's Largest, Fastest and Most Famous Passenger Steamships* (Osceola, WI: Motorbooks International, 1997), p. 68.

37. Ibid., p. 76.

38. Kachik, untitled memoir, p. 9.

39. Gerald F. Gilbert, Jr., untitled diary, n.d., World War I Survey, WWI-158, 304th Sanitary Train, AHEC, p. 25.

40. Fleming, "World War I Service," p. 27.

41. Barber, *79th Division*, p. 42.

42. Loomis, *304th Ammunition Train*, pp. 31, 34.

43. Kress, *Rugged Individualists*, p. 29.

44. LeRoy Yellott Haile, "A Civilian Goes to War," n.d., World War I Survey, Box: 79th Division-Trains; Folder: Haile, Leroy Y, 304th Engineer, 79th

Division, AHEC, p. 38.

45. Oscar Lubchansky to author, *c.* 1954, personal communication.
46. Kuhn to Kuhn, July 26, 1917, p. 1.
47. Fleming, "World War I Service," pp. 35–6.
48. Davies, "War Diary," p. 17.
49. Cable 990-S, April 24, 1918, Historical Division, *USAWW,* vol. 2, p. 344
50. Army War College, Historical Section, "The Seventy-Ninth Division, 1917–1918" (unpublished, 1924), p. 16.
51. Cable 952-S, April 18, 1918, Historical Division, *USAWW,* vol. 14, p. 320.
52. Timothy K. Nenninger, "Tactical Dysfunction in the AEF, 1917–1918," *Military Affairs,* October (1987), p. 178.
53. Ibid., p. 149.
54. Mark E. Grotelueschen, *Doctrine under Trial: American Artillery Employment in World War I,* Contributions in Military Studies (Westport, CT, and London: Greenwood, 2001), pp. 20, 23.
55. James J. Cooke, *Pershing and His Generals: Command and Staff in the AEF* (Westport, CT; London: Praeger, 1997), p. 141.
56. Ibid., p. 43; Timothy K. Nenninger, "American Military Effectiveness in the First World War," in *Military Effectiveness, Vol 1: The First World War,* ed. Allan R. Millett and Williamson Murray, Series on Defense and Foreign Policy (Boston, London, Sydney, Wellington: Allen & Unwin, 1988), p. 147.
57. Cooke, *Pershing and His Generals,* pp. 43, 81.
58. James B. Gowen, "Report of G-5: Appendix No. 31, Divisional Training," n.d., *c.* 1919, Timberman-Fiske Family Papers, Box 11, AHEC, p. 56.
59. James W. Rainey, "The Training of the American Expeditionary Forces in World War I" (Master's thesis, Temple University, 1981), p. 160.
60. Historical Division, *USAWW,* vol. 3, p. 330–31.
61. Cited in Rainey, "Training of the AEF," p. 162.
62. Nenninger, "Tactical Dysfunction," p. 178.
63. Historical Division, *USAWW,* vol. 2, p. 554.
64. Kuhn, "Armada," p. 5.
65. Davies, "War Diary," p. 15.
66. Army War College, Historical Section, "The Seventy-Ninth Division, 1917–1918," p. 17.
67. Joseph E. Kuhn, "Memorandum No. 32," August 22, 1918, Kuhn Papers, Box 3, USMA, p. 2.
68. Joseph E. Kuhn, "Combat Instructions for Troops of 79th Division," September 4, 1918, Kuhn Papers, Box 3, USMA.
69. Historical Division, *USAWW,* vol. 3, p. 350.
70. H.A. Drum, "Combat Instructions for Troops of First Army," August 29, 1918, RG 120, Fifth Corps, Box 17, Fifth Corps Field Orders, 32.14, NARA, p. 1.

71. Harold E. Craig, untitled diary, 1918, World War I Survey, Box: 79th Division HQ-Craig, AHEC., entry for August 28, 1918.

72. Raymond S. Tompkins, *Maryland Fighters in the Great War* (Baltimore: Thomas & Evans Printing Co., 1919), p. 90.

73. Mrs. J. Talbott Kelley to C.B. Sweezey, August 1918, Records of US Army Mobile Units RG 391, 313th Infantry, Box 3163, NARA.

74. C.B. Sweezey to Mrs. J. Talbott Kelley, September 5, 1918, ibid.

75. Mrs. Lillian Meyers to C.B. Sweezey, August (?), 1918, ibid.

76. *History of Company F, 316th Infantry, 79th Division, A.E.F. In the World War, 1917–18–19* (Philadelphia: Company F Association of the 316th Infantry, 1930), p. 45.

77. Historical Division, *USAWW*, vol. 3, p. 722.

Chapter 6: Americans Reach the Battlefield

1. Trask, *AEF and Coalition Warmaking*, pp. 22–24.

2. Smythe, *Pershing*, p. 63.

3. Historical Division, *USAWW*, vol. 2, pp. 232–33.

4. Ibid., p. 234.

5. William J. Wilgus, *Transporting the A.E.F. In Western Europe, 1917–1919* (New York: Columbia UP, 1931), p. 15.

6. James A. Huston, *The Sinews of War: Army Logistics, 1775–1953* (Washington, DC: Office of the Chief of Military History, United States Army, 1966), pp. 368, 376.

7. Wilgus, *Transporting the A.E.F.*, pp. 32–34.

8. Douglas V. Johnson, II, and Rolfe L. Hillman, Jr., *Soissons 1918* (College Station, TX: Texas A&M UP, 1999), p. 25.

9. André Kaspi, *le temps des américains: le concours américain à la France en 1917–1918*, Publications de la Sorbonne, Série Internationale (Paris: Université de Paris, 1976), pp. 294–95.

10. John Toland, *No Man's Land: 1918, the Last Year of the Great War* (Garden City, NY: Doubleday, 1980), p. 103.

11. Trask, *AEF and Coalition Warmaking*, p. 59.

12. Ibid., p. 61; Smythe, *Pershing*, pp. 108–09, 113–15, 133.

13. Smythe, *Pershing*, pp 125–29.

14. Historical Division, *USAWW*, vol. 2, p. 434.

15. Trask, *AEF and Coalition Warmaking*, p. 77.

16. Smythe, *Pershing*, pp. 129–31.

17. Toland, *No Man's Land*, pp. 261–62.

18. Gilbert, *First World War*, p. 429.

19. James G. Harbord, *The American Army in France, 1917–1919* (Boston: Little, Brown, 1936), p. 272.

20. Ibid., p. 283.

21. Grotelueschen, *Doctrine under Trial*, p. 39.

22. Ibid., pp. 40–44.
23. Smythe, *Pershing*, p. 140, citing a "German intelligence officer on June 17, 1918."
24. Toland, *No Man's Land*, p. 322.
25. Kaspi, *Le temps des américains*, p. 238.
26. Travers, *How the War Was Won*, p. 108.
27. Leonard P. Ayres, *The War with Germany: A Statistical Summary* (Washington, DC: GPO, 1919), p. 110.
28. Johnson and Hillman, *Soissons 1918*, pp. 74, 77, 147–48, 151, 154.
29. Trask, *AEF and Coalition Warmaking*, p. 92.
30. Kaspi, *Le temps des américains*, pp. 276–77.
31. Coffman, *War to End All Wars*, p. 246.
32. Cited in Grotelueschen, *Doctrine under Trial*, p. 72.
33. Rainey, "Training of the AEF," pp. 192–94.
34. Gilbert, *First World War*, p. 444.

Chapter 7: First Army Takes the Field

1. Ministère de la Guerre, Service Historique, *AFGG*, Tome Vi, 2e Volume, Annexes – 3e Volume (Paris: Imprimerie Nationale, 1920–1938), pp. 451–54; Ralph Haswell Lutz, ed., *The Causes of the German Collapse in 1918* (Stanford, CA: Board of Trustees of the Leland Stanford Junior University, 1934, reprinted in Hamden, CT: Archon, 1969).
2. Historical Division, *USAWW*, vol. 2, p. 519.
3. Trask, *AEF and Coalition Warmaking*, p. 20; Smythe, *Pershing*, p. 27.
4. Historical Division, *USAWW*, vol. 2, pp. 528–29.
5. Ibid., p. 530.
6. Cited at Smythe, *Pershing*, p. 175.
7. Historical Division, *USAWW*, vol. 8, p. 39.
8. Smythe, *Pershing*, p. 177.
9. Trask, *AEF and Coalition Warmaking*, p. 106.
10. Smythe, *Pershing*, p. 181.
11. Kuhn, "Armada," p. 5.
12. Cited at Grotelueschen, *Doctrine under Trial*, p. 86.
13. Smythe, *Pershing*, pp. 184–85.
14. Ibid., p. 187; Toland, *No Man's Land*, p. 424.
15. Cited at Trask, *AEF and Coalition Warmaking*, p. 113.
16. Kaspi, *Le temps des américains*, p. 289.
17. Ernest Hinds, "Memorandum for the Chief of Staff," September 25, 1918, RG 200, Pershing Papers, Box 29, Miscellaneous Records and Reports, NARA, p. 1.
18. Gilbert, *First World War*, p. 459.
19. Smythe, *Pershing*, p. 188. Kaspi, *Le temps des américains*, p. 292.
20. Smythe, *Pershing*, p. 188.

21. Trask, *AEF and Coalition Warmaking*, pp. 112–13.
22. Smythe, *Pershing*, p. 202.
23. Trask, *AEF and Coalition Warmaking*, p. 119.
24. Historical Division, *USAWW*, vol. 8, p. 68, translation from the cited source.
25. Ibid., vol. 9, p. 87.
26. Toland, *No Man's Land*, p. 430.
27. W.S. McNair, "Explanation and Execution of Plans for Artillery for St Mihiel Operation and Argonne-Meuse Operations to November 11, 1918," December 23, 1918, RG 120, Entry 22, Commander-in-Chief Reports, Box 30, NARA, p. 15; Conrad H. Lanza, "The Battle of Montfaucon," *Infantry Journal* 23, May–June (1933), p. 226.
28. Historical Division, *USAWW*, vol. 9, pp. 126–27.
29. "Alsace," in *The Encyclopedia Britannica* (New York: Encyclopedia Britannica, Inc., 1911), p. 87.
30. Conrad H. Lanza, "The Start of the Meuse–Argonne Campaign," *Field Artillery Journal* 23, January–February (1933), p. 62.
31. Historical Division, *USAWW*, vol. 9, p. 97.
32. Ministère de la Guerre, Service Historique, *AFGG*, Tome Vii, 1er Volume, Annexes – 2e Volume (Paris: Imprimerie Nationale, 1920–1938), pp. 471, 613.
33. Historical Division, *USAWW*, vol. 9, pp. 100–02.
34. Rexmond C. Cochrane, "The 79th Division at Montfaucon," in *U.S. Army Chemical Corps Historical Studies: Gas Warfare in World War I*, Study no.19 (Washington, DC: US Army Chemical Corps Historical Office, 1960), pp. 13–14.
35. AEF, General Staff First Section, "Report B-2: Account of the Argonne–Meuse Operation – 9th September to 11th November – Influence of G-1 Section and Part Taken in the Operation," January 14, 1919, RG 120, Entry 24, "Report of Operation, G-1 Section, First Army, 10 Aug–11 Nov '18," Boxes 3361, 3020, NARA, p. 6.
36. Historical Division, *USAWW*, vol. 9, p. 97.
37. Historical Division, *USAWW*, vol. 9, p. 84.
38. Ibid.
39. James Mercur, *The Art of War: Prepared for the Use of the Cadets of the United States Military Academy*, First ed. (West Point: United States Military Academic Press, 1889), p. 147.
40. Johnson, *Breakthrough!*, pp. 248–52; Smythe, *Pershing*, p. 170; Travers, "The Allied Victories, 1918," p. 281.
41. Correlli Barnett, *The Swordbearers: Supreme Command in the First World War* (New York: William Morrow and Company, 1964), p. 318; Holger H. Herwig, *The First World War: Germany and Austria-Hungary, 1914–1918* (London: Arnold, 1997), p. 405; J.H. Johnson, *1918: The Unexpected Victory* (London: Arms and Armour Press, 1997), p. 90.

42. Christina Holstein, *Verdun – the Left Bank*, ed. Nigel Cave, Battleground Europe (Barnsley, S. Yorkshire: Pen & Sword, 2016), p. 24.

43. Historical Division, *USAWW*, vol. 9, p. 83.

44. Barnett, *The Swordbearers*, p. 324; Jack Snyder, *The Ideology of the Offensive: Military Decision Making and the Disasters of 1914*, ed. Robert J. Art, Robert Jervis, and Stephen M. Walt, Cornell Studies in Security Affairs (Ithaca and London: Cornell UP, 1984), p. 120.

45. Kuhn to Kuhn, September 16, 1918, p. 2.

Chapter 8: Concentration

1. W.B. Burtt, "Field Orders No. 31, Fifth Army Corps, A.E.F.," September 21, 1918, RG 120, Entry 1118, Fifth Corps Historical File, Box 14, 32.1, NARA, p. 2.

2. Ibid.

3. Ibid., p. 1.

4. W.B. Burtt, "Field Orders No. 31, Part II, Fifth Army Corps, A.E.F.," September 23, 1918, RG 120, Entry 1118, Fifth Corps Historical File, Box 14, 32.1, NARA, p. 1.

5. Ibid.

6. W.B. Burtt, "Memorandum for Employment of Tanks," August 23, 1918, RG 120, Entry 1118, Fifth Corps Historical File, Box 17, 50.4, NARA, p. 2.

7. Joseph E. Kuhn, "Field Orders No. 6, Annex A: Plan of Liaison," September 25, 1918, Kuhn Papers, Box 3, USMA, p. 2.

8. Kuhn, "Field Orders No. 6," p. 1.

9. Robert L. Bullard, "Field Order No. 18," September 21, 1918, RG 120, Entry 1043, III Corps Historical File, 32.1, NARA, p. 1.

10. Christian A. Bach to C.L. Bolte, June 25, 1922, RG 120, Historical Section Reports, Box 3, NARA, p. 1.

11. John L. Hines, "Field Orders No. 54," September 24, 1918, RG 120, Entry 1241, 4th Division Historical File, Box 16, 32.1, NARA, p. 1.

12. Gordon Brook-Shepherd, *November 1918* (Boston, Toronto: Little, Brown, 1981), p. 195; Smythe, *Pershing*, pp. 192–93.

13. G.C. Marshall, Jr., "Movement of Troops from St Mihiel Operation to Argonne–Meuse Operation," November 19, 1918, RG 120, Entry 24, "AEF General Headquarters, 1st Army Reports, G-3," Box 3382, 114.01, NARA, p. 2.

14. Barber, *79th Division*, p. 52.

15. Joseph E. Kuhn, "General Kuhn's Diary," July 13, 1918–May 25, 1919, Kuhn Papers, Box 5, USMA, p. 19.

16. Barber, *79th Division*, p. 54.

17. Ibid., p. 55.

18. Ibid.

19. Ibid., p. 56.

20. Kress, *Rugged Individualists*, p. 23.
21. Cited in Frank E. Vandiver, *Black Jack: The Life and Times of John J. Pershing* (College Station and London: Texas A&M UP, 1977), p. 150.
22. Historical Division, *USAWW*, vol. 3, p. 271.
23. Ibid., vol. 3, p. 95.
24. Ibid., vol. 2, p. 479.
25. Guy Visknikki, editor of *Stars and Stripes*, quoted in Mead, *Doughboys*, pp. 76–77.
26. Will Judy, *A Soldier's Diary: A Day-to-Day Record in the World War* (Chicago: Judy Publishing Co., 1930), p. 163.
27. Kaspi, *Le temps des américains*, p. 303; translation by the present author.
28. Ibid., pp. 303–04.
29. Barbeau and Henri, *The Unknown Soldiers*, pp. 145–52 passim.
30. Ibid., pp. 138, 160–63.
31. Ibid., pp. 116–35 passim.
32. Sgt James E. Meehan, Co. G, 313th Infantry, "My Diary," World War I Survey, WWI-380, AHEC, p. 5.
33. Harlowe, *Your Brother Will*, p. 42.
34. Barber, *79th Division*, p. 59.
35. Ibid., p. 61.
36. Harlowe, *Your Brother Will*, p. 42.
37. Davies, "War Diary," p. 19.
38. Ibid., p. 21.
39. Oscar Lubchansky to Lillian S. Lubchansky, September 14, 1918, author's personal collection, p. 2.
40. James R.L. Gibbons, "Complete Roster of Officers and Men of Company "B," 313th US Infantry, from July 15th, 1918 to April 15th, 1919, and Their Status," July 3, 1930, RG 120, 79th Division, Box 16, NARA, p. 12.
41. Ibid.
42. Barber, *79th Division*, p. 65; Kuhn, "General Kuhn's Diary," p. 25.
43. Army War College, Historical Section, "The Seventy-Ninth Division, 1917–1918," p. 24.
44. G. de la Chapelle, "Report with Regard to the Employment of the Squadron During the Battle from September 26th to 30th," *c.* October 1918, 17 N 128, SHD, p. 1; [no first name] Guillot, "Report Required by Note of October 2d 1918," October 30, 1918, 17 N 128, SHD, p. 1.
45. Davies, "War Diary," p. 22.
46. Kuhn, "Armada," p. 5.
47. Kuhn, "Field Orders No. 6," p. 1.
48. Brooke Payne, "Observations Upon the Conditions Affecting the Artillery Support During the First Day of Attack—79th Division," May 25, 1919, RG 120, V Corps, Box 4, NARA, p. 2.
49. Army War College, Historical Section, "The Seventy-Ninth Division,

1917–1918," pp. 22–23.

50. W.J. Nicholson, untitled memorandum, September 23, 1918, RG 120, Entry 1241, 79th Division, Box 6, NARA, p. 1.

51. Davies, "War Diary," p. 22.

52. Kachik, untitled memoir, p. 15.

53. Davies, "War Diary," p. 22.

54. L.V. Jacks, *Service Record by an Artilleryman* (New York, London: Scribner's, 1928), p. 181.

55. Carl E. Glock, *History of the 316th Regiment of Infantry in the World War, 1918* (Philadelphia, PA: Biddle-Deemer Printing Co., 1930, second printing), p. 36.

56. Toland, *No Man's Land*, pp. 431–33.

57. Gibbons, "Roster of Company B," p. 16.

58. Cochrane, "79th Division," p. 15.

59. Arthur H. Joel, *Under the Lorraine Cross: An Account of the Experiences of Infantrymen Who Fought under Captain Theodore Schoge and of Their Buddies of the Lorraine Cross Division, While Serving in France During the World War* (privately printed, 1921), p. 26.

Chapter 9: The Germans

1. [no first name] von Prittwitz und Gaffron, [no first name] Peschek, H. Mende, H. von Schweinichen, and G. Gieraths, *Geschichte des Königlich Preußischen Grenadier-Regiments König Friedrich III. (2. Schles) Nr. 11 und seiner Grenzschutzformationen von 1914 bis 1920* (Berlin: Verlag Tradition Wilhelm Kolk, 1932), p. 241.

2. "Intelligence Section, 5th Corps, in Meuse–Argonne Operations," January 27, 1919, RG 120, V Corps, Box 9, NARA, p. 4.

3. John T. Winterich, ed., *Squads Write! A Selection of the Best Things in Prose, Verse and Cartoon from the Stars and Stripes* (New York and London: Harper & Brothers, 1931), p. 185.

4. Bayerische Vermessungs-Abteilung 15, "Stand Am 9.9.18," in RG 165, Army War College Historical Section Box 165, 117th Division, NARA; von Prittwitz und Gaffron, *Grenadier-Regiments Nr. 11*, p. 233.

5. J. Frank Barber, *Official History of the 304th Engineer Regiment, 79th Division, U.S.A., During the World War* (Lancaster, PA: Steinman & Foltz, 1920), pp. 292–94.

6. Ralph D. Cole and W.C. Howells, *The 37th Division in the World War, 1917–1918*, 2 vols (Columbus, OH: The Thirty-Seventh Division Veterans Association, 1926), p. 204.

7. Samuels, *Doctrine and Dogma*, p. 70.

8. Herwig, *First World War*, p. 325.

9. Gudmundsson, *Stormtroop Tactics*, p. 151.

10. Herwig, *First World War*, pp. 416, 419, 424.

11. David Englander, "Soldiering and Identity: Reflections on the Great War," *War in History* 1, 3 (1994), p. 373.

12. Brook-Shepherd, *November 1918*, pp. 49–50.

13. Louis M. Stacy, "Books Furnished by the War Department to Troops before Leaving U.S.," September 28, 1918, RG 120, Entry 332, General Headquarters G-5, "Correspondence Relating to Publications," Box 1805, 23m, NARA, unpaginated.

14. Vereinigung der Offiziere, ed., *Geschichte des 1. Ermländischen Infanterie-Regiments Nr. 150*, ehemals Preussische Truppenteile (Zeulenroda (Thüringen): Bernhard Sporn, 1935), p. 192.

15. Otto Schaidler, *Das K.B. Reserve-Infanterie-Regiment 7*, Erinnerungsblätter Deutscher Regimenter (Munich: Verlag Max Schick, 1934), p. 206; Hans Etzel, *Das K.B. Reserve-Infanterie-Regiment 10,* ibid., p. 129; Ernst Demmler, Karl Ritter von Bucher, Ludwig Leupold, *Das K.B. Reserve-Infanterie-Regiment 12,* ibid., p. 272.

16. Barnett, *The Swordbearers*, p. 351.

17. Ibid.

18. Quoted in Smythe, *Pershing*, p. 187.

19. Historical Division, *USAWW*, vol. 8, p. 312.

20. Quoted in Palmer, *Victory 1918*, p. 210.

21. Schaidler, *Reserve-Infanterie-Regiment 7*, Erinnerungsblätter Deutscher Regimenter, p. 736.

22. Historical Division, *USAWW*, vol. 8, p. 311.

23. Ibid., p. 515.

24. Ibid., vol. 9, p. 559.

25. Ibid., vol. 11, pp. 413–14.

26. Quoted in "Intelligence Section, 5th Corps, in Meuse–Argonne Operations," p. 11.

27. Russell, "Summaries of Intelligence, 5th Army Corps, St Mihiel–Meuse Argonne," Annex to Summary of Intelligence #7, September 27, 1918, p. 1.

28. Max von Gallwitz, *Erleben im Westen, 1916–1918* (Berlin: Verlag von E.S. Mittler & Sohn, 1932), p. 390.

29. Ibid., pp. 390–91.

30. Historical Division, *USAWW*, vol. 9, p. 96.

31. Curt Wunderlich, *Fünfzig Monate Wehr im Westen: Geschichte Des Reserve-Infanterie-Regiments Nr. 66* (Eisleben (Lutherstadt): Winkler, 1935), p. 774.

32. Ibid.

33. von Prittwitz und Gaffron, *Grenadier-Regiments Nr. 11*, p. 236.

34. Ibid.

Chapter 10: Over the Top and up the Hill, September 26

1. Meehan, "My Diary," p. 7.

2. Oscar Lubchansky to Dr J.W. Lubchansky, November 24, 1918, author's

personal collection.

3. Gibbons, "Roster of Company B," p. 25.

4. William Bell Clark, *War History of the 79th Division, National Army* (Williamsport, PA: privately published, 1918), p. 9.

5. Glock, *316th Regiment*, p. 37.

6. Paul Allegrini, "Compte Rendu (21 Septembre–3 Octobre)," *c.* October 1918, 17 N 128, SHD, p. 4.

7. "Messages of the 316th Infantry," 1918, RG 120, 79th Division, Box 20, 32.16, NARA, September 26, 1918, sent 9:15 a.m.

8. von Prittwitz und Gaffron, *Grenadier-Regiments Nr. 11*, pp. 237–38.

9. "79th Division Field Messages," September 28, 1918, sent 10:30 a.m.

10. "Field Messages of the 157th Infantry Brigade," 1918, RG 120, 79th Division, Box 16, 32.16, NARA, September 26, 1918, sent 12:30 p.m.

11. Allegrini, "Compte Rendu (21 Septembre–3 Octobre)," p. 2.

12. Guillot, "Report Required by Note of October 2d 1918," pp. 1–2.

13. Kress, *Rugged Individualists*, p. 39.

14. Casper Wilt Swartz, Co. C, 314th Infantry Regiment, "Some Things That Happened between May 1916 and June 1, 1919," n.d., World War I Survey, AHEC, p. 30.

15. W.H. Oury, "Report of Operations for the 314th Infantry and 158th Infantry Brigade for the Period September 25–26, 1918 to September 30, 1918," 1918, RG 120, 79th Division, Box 18, 33.2, NARA, p. 2.

16. Clark, *79th Division*, p. 11.

17. Barber, *79th Division*, p. 92.

18. Clark, *79th Division*, p. 11.

19. Army War College, Historical Section, "The Seventy-Ninth Division, 1917–1918," p. 26.

20. Davies, "War Diary," p. 23.

21. Joel, *Lorraine Cross*, p. 27.

22. Ibid.

23. Barber, *79th Division*, p. 88.

24. Army War College, Historical Section, "The Seventy-Ninth Division, 1917–1918," p. 30.

25. Oury, "Report of Operations for the 314th Infantry and 158th Infantry Brigade," p. 2.

26. Ibid.

27. Barber, *79th Division*, p. 103.

28. James F. Lawrence, "History of the 57th Field Artillery Brigade: The Iron Brigade," April 10, 1919, RG 120, 32nd Division, Box 26: 57th Field Artillery Brigade, NARA, p. 43.

29. de la Chapelle, "Report with Regard to the Employment of the Squadron During the Battle from September 26th to 30th," p. 1.

30. Lanza, "Counterbattery in the AEF," p. 461.

31. "79th Division Field Messages," September 26, 1918, sent at 7:10 a.m., 9:10 a.m., and 10:00 a.m.

32. Ibid., time sent not given but late in the day from internal evidence.

33. "Fifth Corps Field Messages," September 26–30, 1918, RG 120, V Corps, Box 19, 32.16, NARA, September 26, 1918, sent 10:15 a.m.

34. "79th Division Field Messages," September 26, 1918, sent 10:35 a.m.

35. "Telephone Messages Sept.–Oct. 1918 Received and Sent," September–October 1918, RG 120, V Corps, Box 30, G-2 Telephone Messages, 32.16, NARA, September 26, 1918, sent 12:30 p.m.

36. Conrad Lanza, "The Army Artillery, First Army," unpublished manuscript in AHEC library, c. 1926, p. 168.

37. Ibid., p. 203.

38. Cochrane, "79th Division," p. 20.

39. Army War College, Historical Section, "The Seventy-Ninth Division, 1917–1918," p. 28.

40. Haile, "Civilian Goes to War," p. 52.

41. Moses N. Thisted, *Pershing's Pioneer Infantry of World War I* (Hemet, CA: Alphabet Printers, 1981–1982), p. 298.

42. Joseph E. Kuhn, "Two Regiments of Seventy-Ninth Go into Battle," *Washington Post*, March 18, 1926, p. 5.

43. Ernest Peixotto, *The American Front* (New York: Charles Scribner's Sons, 1919), p. 167.

44. D.D. Pullen, "Report of Operation of French Tanks," September 28, 1918, RG 120, First Army Reports, Inspector General, Box 3411; unnumbered enclosure in G.E. Thorne, Report of Inspector General, 1st Army, A.E.F.; File Number 1616, NARA, pp. 1–2.

45. Barber, *79th Division*, p. 95.

46. Pullen, "Report of Operation of French Tanks," p. 2.

47. Barber, *79th Division*, p. 95.

48. "Fifth Corps Field Messages," September 26–29, 1918, RG 120, V Corps, Box 20, 32.16, NARA, September 26, 1918, sent 2:00 p.m.

49. ABMC, *American Armies and Battlefields in Europe: A History, Guide, and Reference Book* (Washington, DC: GPO, 1938), inserted map, "The Meuse–Argonne Offensive of the American First Army, September 26–November 11, 1918."

50. Historical Division, *USAWW*, vol. 2, p. 491.

51. "Field Messages of the 157th Infantry Brigade," September 26, 1918, sent 1:45 p.m.

52. C.B. Sweezey, "Report of Operations of Regiment, Sept. 26 to Oct. 1, 1918," October 3, 1918, RG 120, 79th Division, Box 16, 33.2, NARA, p. 2.

53. George Leroy Irwin, "Disposition of Artillery," September 26, 1918, RG 120, 32nd Division, Box 27, Historical 57th Field Artillery Brigade, 32.16, NARA.

54. "117th Division (Subordinate Units): Diary and Annexes," September 25–30, 1918, RG 165, Army War College Historical Section, Box 165, 117th Division, 22.3, NARA, p. 83.

55. James M. Cain, III, "The Taking of Montfaucon," in *Americans vs. Germans: The First AEF in Action*, ed. Editors of The Infantry Journal (Washington, DC: Penguin Books and The Infantry Journal, Inc., 1942), pp. 69–71.

56. "79th Division Field Messages," September 26, 1918, time sent not given but late in the day from internal evidence.

57. Ibid., September 26, 1918, sent 6:27 p.m.

58. Ibid., September 26, 1918, sent 5:35 p.m.

Chapter 11: Left, Right, and Straight Ahead, September 26

1. Wunderlich, *Fünfzig Monate*, p. 774.

2. Burtt, "Field Orders No. 31, Fifth Army Corps, A.E.F.," p. 2.

3. ABMC, *37th Division: Summary of Operations in the World War* (Washington, DC: GPO, 1944), p. 11.

4. [no first name] Tiede, [no first name] Himer, and [no first name] Röhricht, *Das 4. Schlesische Infanterie-Regiment Nr. 157*, Erinnerungsblätter Deutscher Regimenter (Berlin: Gerhard Stalling, 1922), pp. 62–63; "117th Division (Subordinate Units): Diary and Annexes", p.83.

5. Ibid.

6. von Prittwitz und Gaffron, *Grenadier-Regiments Nr. 11*, p. 239.

7. "117th Division (Subordinate Units): Diary and Annexes," p. 84.

8. Cole and Howells, *37th Division*, p. 206.

9. von Prittwitz und Gaffron, *Grenadier-Regiments Nr. 11*, p. 239.

10. "117th Division (Subordinate Units): Diary and Annexes," p. 84.

11. Ibid.

12. Vereinigung der Offiziere, *Infanterie-Regiments Nr. 150*, p. 192.

13. Cole and Howells, *37th Division*, p. 212.

14. ABMC, *4th Division: Summary of Operations in the World War* (Washington, DC: GPO, 1944), p. 51.

15. Army War College, Historical Section, *Order of Battle*, Document 23a, p. 60.

16. von Prittwitz und Gaffron, *Grenadier-Regiments Nr. 11*, p. 237.

17. Wunderlich, *Fünfzig Monate*, p. 776.

18. Erich Baron von Guttenberg and Georg Meyer-Ehrlach, *Das K.B. Reserve-Feldartillerie-Regiment Nr. 5*, vol. 89, Erinnerungsblätter Deutscher Regimenter (Munich: Verlag Max Schick, 1938), p. 169.

19. Roy W. Winton to Frank C. Mahin, February 9, 1931, Hugh A. Drum Papers, Box 9, "Personal Correspondence," File "F.C. Mahin," AHEC, pp. 1–3.

20. Robert B. Cole and Barnard E. Eberlin, *The History of the 39th U.S. Infantry During the World War* (New York: Press of Joseph D. McGuire, 1919), pp. 58–61.

21. James E. Pollard, *The Forty-Seventh Infantry, a History: 1917–1918–1919* (Saginaw, MI: Press of Seeman & Peters, 1919), p. 64.
22. "III Corps, Report No. 909," September 26, 1918, RG 120, Historical Section Reports, Box 3, 15.45, NARA.
23. J.A. Stevens to H.A. Drum, December 23, 1920, Hugh A. Drum Papers, Box 16, File: 4th Division–Montfaucon, AHEC, p. 1.
24. Guttenberg, *Reserve-Feldartillerie-Regiment Nr. 5*, vol. 89, Erinnerungsblätter Deutscher Regimenter.
25. Bach, *Fourth Division*, vol. 368, p. 171.
26. John L. Hines to E.E. Booth, December 30, 1920, Hugh A. Drum Papers, Box 16, File: 4th Division-Montfaucon, AHEC, p. 1.
27. Millett, *The General*, p. 379; US Senate Committee on Military Affairs, *Hearings on the Nomination of Col. Alfred W. Bjornstad, U.S. Army, for Promotion to Be a Brigadier General* (Washington, DC: GPO, 1925), p. 3.
28. US Senate Committee on Military Affairs, *Bjornstad Hearings*, pp. 81–83, 222.
29. Millett, *The General*, p. 387.
30. Johnson and Hillman, *Soissons 1918*, p. 76; Millett, *The General*, p. 387.
31. Oliver L. Spaulding, Jr., to E.E. Booth, February 18, 1921, Hugh A. Drum Papers, Box 16, File: 4th Division–Montfaucon, AHEC, p. 2.
32. Christian A. Bach to C.L. Bolte, November 18, 1922, RG 120, Historical Section Reports, Box 3, NARA.
33. J.E. Kuhn, September 26, 1918, RG 120, ibid.
34. Christian A. Bach to C.L. Bolte, November 18, 1922, RG 120, ibid., p. 4.
35. E.E. Booth to Oliver L. Spaulding Jr., February 1, 1921, Hugh A. Drum Papers, Box 16, File: 4th Division–Montfaucon, AHEC, p. 1; E.E. Booth to H.A. Drum, 25 March 1921, Hugh A. Drum Papers, Box 16, File: 4th Division–Montfaucon, AHEC, p. 2.
36. Chief of Staff First Army, "Report No. 964," September 26, 1918, RG 120, Historical Section Reports, Box 3, NARA.
37. von Prittwitz und Gaffron, *Grenadier-Regiments Nr. 11*, p. 238.
38. Ibid., p. 239.
39. Ibid., p. 240.
40. Ibid.
41. "Fifth Corps Field Messages," September 26, 1918, sent 1:55 p.m.

Chapter 12: "Montfaucon Taken," September 27

1. "79th Division Field Messages," September 27, 1918, sent 1:15 a.m.
2. "79th Division Field Messages," September 27, 1918, sent 4:53 a.m.
3. Cain, "The Taking of Montfaucon," pp. 72–73.
4. Fleming, "World War I Service," pp. 37, 39.
5. Ibid., p. 70.
6. Joel, *Lorraine Cross*, p. 29.

7.   Ibid.

8.   Barber, *79th Division*, pp. 108–09.

9.   Allegrini, "Compte Rendu (21 Septembre–3 Octobre)," p. 4.

10. "Resumé d'observations faites pendant les opérations de la 79ème D.I.U.S. du 26 au 30 Septembre," October 3, 1918, 17 N 128, SHD.

11. Allegrini, "Compte Rendu (21 Septembre–3 Octobre)," p. 2.

12. George Leroy Irwin, "Report on the Operations of the 57th F.A. Brigade in Supporting the 79th Divisional Infantry, Sept. 22nd–30th 1918," n.d., RG 120, 32nd Division, Box 27: 57th Field Artillery Brigade, 33.2, NARA, p. 2.

13. Ibid.

14. Alden Brooks, *As I Saw It* (New York: Knopf, 1929), p. 260.

15. Army War College, Historical Section, "The Seventy-Ninth Division, 1917–1918," p. 54.

16. Cole and Howells, *37th Division*, p. 226.

17. Cole and Eberlin, *39th Infantry*, p. 63.

18. Roy V. Myers, "Notes on the World's War," n.d., World War I Survey, The Roy V. Myers Papers, AHEC, p. 54.

19. Heinrich Siebert, *Geschichte des Infanterie-Regiments Generalfeldmarschall von Hindenburg (2. Masurisches) Nr. 147*, Erinnerungsblätter Deutscher Regimenter (Berlin: Gerhard Stalling, 1927), p. 280.

20. US War Office, *Histories of Two Hundred and Fifty-One Divisions of the German Army Which Participated in the War (1914–1918)* (London: London Stamp Exchange, Ltd., 1920, republished 1989), pp. 608, 728.

21. Max von Gallwitz, "The Meuse–Argonne Battles in the Fall of 1918," in *As They Saw Us: Foch, Ludendorff, and Other Leaders Write Our War History*, ed. George Sylvester Viereck (Garden City, NY: Doubleday, Doran, 1929), p. 244.

22. von Prittwitz und Gaffron, *Grenadier-Regiments Nr. 11*, p. 240.

23. Vereinigung der Offiziere, *Infanterie-Regiments Nr. 150*, p. 196.

24. Siebert, *Infanterie-Regiments Nr. 147*, Erinnerungsblätter Deutscher Regimenter, p. 289.

25. Gallwitz, "The Meuse–Argonne Battles in the Fall of 1918," p. 243.

26. von Prittwitz und Gaffron, *Grenadier-Regiments Nr. 11*, p. 240.

27. Ibid., pp. 240–41, 244.

28. "117th Division (Subordinate Units): Diary and Annexes," p. 83.

29. Joel, *Lorraine Cross*, p. 30.

30. Ibid., p. 29.

31. Clark, *79th Division*, p. 14.

32. Joel, *Lorraine Cross*, p. 30.

33. "79th Division Field Messages," September 27, 1918, sent 1:55 p.m.

34. Cain, "The Taking of Montfaucon," p. 80.

35. Barber, *79th Division*, p. 122.

36. Jacks, *Service Record*, p. 184.

37. Philadelphia War History Committee, *Philadelphia in the World War, 1914–1919* (New York: Wynkoop Hallenbeck Crawford, 1922), p. 145.
38. "Telephone Messages Sept.–Oct. 1918 Received and Sent," September 27, 1918, sent 5:50 a.m.
39. Lanza, "Army Artillery," p. 230.
40. Lanza, "The End of the Battle of Montfaucon," p. 349.
41. Lanza, "Army Artillery," p. 228.
42. Guillot, "Report Required by Note of October 2d 1918," pp. 1–2.
43. [no first name] Richard, "Report of the Battalion Commander Richard, Commanding the 15 Light Tank Battalion to the Commanding Officer of the 505th Regiment of Artillery of Assault," October 2, 1918, 17 N 128, SHD, p. 1.
44. Joseph E. Kuhn, "Recollections of a Division Commander," March 14, 1926, Kuhn papers, Box 3, USMA, p. 38.
45. Sweezey, "Report of Operations, September 25–November 11," p. 3.
46. Guttenberg, *Reserve-Feldartillerie-Regiment Nr. 5*, vol. 89, Erinnerungsblätter Deutscher Regimenter, p. 171.
47. Sweezey, "Report of Operations, September 25–November 11," pp. 1–2.
48. Barber, *79th Division*, p. 125.
49. "315th Infantry Field Messages," 1918, RG 120, 79th Division, Box 22, 32.16, NARA, September 27, 1918, sent 2:00 p.m.
50. Richard, "Report of Battalion Commander," pp. 1–2.
51. Schaidler, *Reserve-Infanterie-Regiment 7*, Erinnerungsblätter Deutscher Regimenter, p. 211.
52. "79th Division Field Messages," September 27, 1918, sent 7:10 p.m.
53. Davies, "War Diary," p. 24.
54. Barber, *79th Division*, pp. 135–37.
55. "79th Division Field Messages," September 27, 1918, sent 3:50 p.m.
56. Ibid., September 27, 1918, sent 10:00 p.m.
57. Barber, *79th Division*, p. 120.
58. John H. Ruckman, ed., *Technology's War Record* (Cambridge, MA: Alumni Association of the Massachusetts Institute of Technology, 1920), p. 185.
59. James J. Hudson, *Hostile Skies: A Combat History of the American Air Service in World War I* (Syracuse, NY: Syracuse UP, 1968), p. 271.
60. Jacks, *Service Record*, p. 184.
61. "Telephone Messages Sept.–Oct. 1918 Received and Sent," September 27, 1918, sent 5:18 p.m.
62. "79th Division Field Messages," September 27, 1918, sent 8:00 p.m.
63. Russell, "Summaries of Intelligence, 5th Army Corps, St Mihiel–Meuse Argonne," p. 3.
64. Joel, *Lorraine Cross*, p. 30.

Chapter 13: Bois de Beuge and Nantillois, September 28

1. Historical Division, *USAWW*, vol. 9, p. 140.
2. W.B. Burtt, "Field Orders No. 46, Fifth Army Corps, A.E.F.," September 28, 1918, RG 120, Fifth Corps Historical File, Box 14, 32.1, NARA.
3. Joseph E. Kuhn, "Field Order No. 8," September 27, 1918, RG 120, 79th Division, Box 3, 32.1, NARA, pp. 1–2.
4. Ruckman, *Technology's War Record*, p. 185.
5. Barber, *79th Division*, p. 134.
6. Philadelphia War History Committee, *Philadelphia in the World War, 1914–1919*, p. 145.
7. Barber, *79th Division*, p. 134.
8. Ibid., p. 135
9. "79th Division Field Messages," September 28, 1918, sent 12:00 noon.
10. "Telephone Messages Sept.–Oct. 1918 Received and Sent," September 28, 1918, sent 2:30 p.m.
11. Clark, *79th Division*, p. 17.
12. Ruckman, *Technology's War Record*, p. 186.
13. Guillot, "Report Required by Note of October 2d 1918," p. 3.
14. "Field Messages of the 157th Infantry Brigade," September 28, 1918, sent 12:15 p.m.
15. Clifton Lisle, "U.S. Army Field Message[s]," September 28, 1918 through early November 1918, World War I Survey, Clifton Lisle Papers, AHEC, September 28, 1918, sent 3:15 p.m.
16. Barber, *79th Division*, pp. 137–38.
17. Clark, *79th Division*, p. 20.
18. Harlowe, *Your Brother Will*, p. 45.
19. Hanson, *I Was There*, p. 103.
20. Army War College, Historical Section, "The Seventy-Ninth Division, 1917–1918," p. 43.
21. W.T. Hannum, "Report on Operations, 4th Division, September 26 to 28th, 1918," 1918, RG 165, Army War College, Historical Section Records, Box 3, 33.1, NARA, p. 8.
22. Army War College, Historical Section, "The Seventy-Ninth Division, 1917–1918," pp. 43–44.
23. "315th Infantry Field Messages," September 28, 1918, sent 7:00 a.m.
24. Joseph E. Kuhn, "Untried Troops March Forward under Hot Fire," *Washington Post*, March 20, 1926, p. 4.
25. "79th Division Field Messages," September 28, 1918, sent 7:42 a.m.
26. Davies, "War Diary," p. 25.
27. Ibid.
28. Ibid.
29. Richard, "Report of Battalion Commander," p. 4.

30. "79th Division Field Messages," September 28, 1918, sent 2:36 p.m.

31. "315th Infantry Field Messages," September 28, 1918, sent 3:00 p.m.

32. Kuhn, "Untried Troops March Forward under Hot Fire," p. 4.

33. Clark, *79th Division*, p. 17.

34. Kuhn, "Untried Troops March Forward under Hot Fire," p. 4.

35. "79th Division Field Messages," September 28, 1918, sent 4:40 p.m.

36. Barber, *79th Division*, p. 141.

37. "Translations: German 117th Inf. Div., Sept. 26–Nov. 11, 1918, Folder I, Meuse–Argonne," Operations Section No. 4835, p. 1.

38. Barber, *79th Division*, p. 149.

39. Davies, "War Diary," p. 25.

40. Joel, *Lorraine Cross*, p. 31.

41. ABMC, *37th Division: Summary of Operations in the World War*, map insert.

42. Cole and Howells, *37th Division*, p. 305.

43. "79th Division Field Messages," September 28, 1918, sent 5:00 p.m.

44. Cole and Eberlin, *39th Infantry*, p. 65.

45. Historical Division, *USAWW*, vol. 9, pp. 519, 521.

46. Lanza, "The End of the Battle of Montfaucon," p. 354; Staff of the Commander-in-Chief of the Allied Armies, "German Mode of Attack," RG 120, Entry 335, "General Headquarters, General Staff, G-5, "English Translations of French Technical Studies, 1917–19," Box 1837, 1986–1999, NARA.

47. Historical Division, *USAWW*, vol. 9, pp. 134, 189; Russell, "Summaries of Intelligence, 5th Army Corps, St. Mihiel–Meuse Argonne," p. 1.

48. "117th Division (Subordinate Units): Diary and Annexes," p. 87.

49. Ibid.

50. Cole and Howells, *37th Division*, p. 294; Heinrich Plickert, *Das 2. Ermländischen Infanterie-Regiment Nr. 151 im Weltkriege*, Truppenteile des ehemaligen Preussischen Kontingents (Berlin: Gerhard Stalling, 1929), p. 304.

51. Russell, "Summaries of Intelligence, 5th Army Corps, St. Mihiel–Meuse Argonne," p. 1.

52. Cited in Smythe, *Pershing*, p. 200.

53. Historical Division, *USAWW*, vol. 9, p. 144.

54. Lanza, "The End of the Battle of Montfaucon," p. 359.

55. Brooks, *As I Saw It*, p. 262.

56. Davies, "War Diary," p. 26.

Chapter 14: Bois 250 and Madeleine Farm, September 29–30

1. "79th Division Field Messages," September 29, 1918, sent 6:30 a.m.

2. Ibid., September 29, 1918, sent 7:30 a.m.

3. Army War College, Historical Section, "The Seventy-Ninth Division, 1917–1918," p. 35.

4. Barber, *79th Division*, p. 151.

5. J.W. Snyder, "Memorandum: 5th Corps Artillery," September 29, 1918, RG 120, 32nd Division, Box 27: Historical – 57th Field Artillery Brigade, 32.16, NARA, p. 1.
6. Barber, *79th Division*, p. 154.
7. "Messages of the 316th Infantry," September 29, 1918, sent 10:10 a.m; Ibid., time sent not given but immediately follows preceding message.
8. "79th Division Field Messages," September 29, 1918, sent 10:53 a.m.
9. Ibid., time sent not given.
10. "Messages of the 316th Infantry," September 29, 1918, sent 11:20 a.m.
11. "79th Division Field Messages," September 29, 1918, sent 12:55 p.m.
12. Ibid., September 29, 1918, sent 2:12 p.m.
13. Barber, *79th Division*, p. 159; 1st Lt George L. Bliss, Co. I, 316th Infantry, "Report of Actions of Company," October 2, 1918, World War I Survey, WWI-8172, AHEC, p. 2.
14. Glock, *316th Regiment*, p. 42.
15. "Messages of the 316th Infantry," September 29, 1918, sent 3:40 p.m.
16. Barber, *79th Division*, p. 161.
17. "79th Division Field Messages," September 29, 1918, sent 7:00 p.m.
18. Historical Board of the 315th Infantry, *The Official History of the 315th Infantry, U.S.A.* (Philadelphia: Historical Board of the 315th Infantry, 1920), p. 71.
19. "315th Infantry Field Messages," September 29, 1918, sent 9:00 a.m.
20. Ibid., September 29, 1918, sent 9:15 a.m.
21. Quoted at Barber, *79th Division*, p. 157.
22. "79th Division Field Messages," September 29, 1918, time sent not given.
23. Joel, *Lorraine Cross*, p. 31.
24. Jacks, *Service Record*, pp. 195, 202.
25. Lanza, "The Army Artillery, First Army," unpublished manuscript in AHEC library, c. 1926, p. 240.
26. Charles M. Engel, "Army Service Experiences Questionnaire," 1988, World War I Survey, Box: 57th FA Brigade, Divisional Troops; Folder: Engel, Charles M., 119th FA, AHEC, p. 3.
27. Barber, *79th Division*, pp. 157–58; Army War College, Historical Section, "The Seventy-Ninth Division, 1917–1918," p. 46.
28. W.H. Oury, "Operations Report," November 16, 1918, RG 120, 79th Division, Box 18, 314th Infantry Regiment, 33.2, NARA, p. 3.
29. "315th Infantry Field Messages," September 29, 1918, sent 3:00 p.m.
30. "Messages of the 158th Brigade," 1918, RG 120, 79th Division, Box 18, 32.16, NARA, September 29, 1918, sent 4:25 p.m.
31. Ibid., September 29, 1918, sent 5:52 p.m.
32. Swartz, "Some Things That Happened," p. 37.
33. Ernest H. Hinrichs, Jr., ed., *Listening In: Intercepting German Trench Communications in World War I* (Shippensburg, PA: White Mane Books, 1996), p. 78.

34. Ibid., p. 79.
35. Lawrence, "57th Field Artillery," p. 44.
36. Barber, *79th Division*, p. 165.
37. Kaspi, *Le temps des américains*, p. 317.
38. W.R. Eastman, "Evacuation of Sick and Wounded During the Meuse–Argonne Operation," January 27, 1919, RG 120, Entry 22, Commander-in-Chief Reports, Box 29, NARA, p. 1.
39. "79th Division Field Messages," September 29, 1918, sent 7:05 p.m.
40. "Fifth Corps Field Messages," September 29, 1918, quoted in message from V Corps to First Army sent 9:20 p.m.
41. "79th Division Field Messages," September 29, 1918, sent 7:30 p.m.
42. Ibid., September 29, 1918, sent 10:20 p.m.
43. Ibid., September 30, 1918, sent 4:35 a.m.
44. Historical Division, *USAWW*, vol. 9, p. 177.
45. Ibid., p. 180.
46. Ibid., p. 184.
47. Lanza, "The End of the Battle of Montfaucon," p. 362.
48. Plickert, *Infanterie-Regiment Nr. 151*, Truppenteile des ehemaligen Preussischen Kontingents, p. 304.
49. Historical Division, *USAWW*, vol. 9, p. 524.
50. Vereinigung der Offiziere, *Infanterie-Regiments Nr. 150*, p. 202.
51. Historical Division, *USAWW*, vol. 9, p. 157.
52. S. Field Dallam, "Preliminary Report on 79th Division," October 2, 1918, RG 200, Pershing Papers, Box 29, Miscellaneous Records and Reports, NARA, p. 1.
53. George E. Thorne, "Report of Inspector General, 1st Army, A.E.F.; File Number 1616," December 11, 1918, RG 120, First Army Reports, Inspector General, Box 3411, NARA, p. 14.
54. Quoted in Elbridge Colby, "The Taking of Montfaucon," *Infantry Journal* 47, March–April (1940), p. 13.
55. C.F. Crain, "79th Division – Field Notes – Argonne–Meuse Offensive (Sept. 26–Nov. 11/18)," May 16, 1919, RG 120, 79th Division, Box 2, 18.8, NARA, pp. 2–3.
56. Lanza, "Army Artillery," p. 250.
57. Allegrini, "Compte Rendu (21 Septembre–3 Octobre)," p. 3.
58. Ibid., pp. 3–5 passim.
59. "Translations: German 117th Inf. Div., Sept. 26–Nov. 11, 1918, Folder I, Meuse–Argonne," Operations Section No. 4909, p. 1.
60. Cochrane, "79th Division," pp. 43–44.
61. "Translations: German 117th Inf. Div., Sept. 26–Nov. 11, 1918, Folder I, Meuse–Argonne," Order 4866, October 1, 1918.
62. Army War College, Historical Section, "The Seventy-Ninth Division, 1917–1918," p. 54.

63. Clark, *79th Division*, p. 28.
64. Kuhn, "General Kuhn's Diary," p. 31.
65. Kuhn to Kuhn, undated, but probably October 2, 1918.
66. Quoted in Cole and Howells, *37th Division*, p. 230.
67. Gilbert, *First World War*, p. 466.
68. Millett, *The General*, p. 405.
69. R.T. Ward, "Explanation and Execution of Plans of Operation, 1st American Army for Argonne–Meuse Operation to November 11, 1918," December 18, 1918, RG 120, Entry 22, Commander-in-Chief Reports, Box 30, NARA, p. 11.
70. Pershing, *My Experiences*, vol. 2, p. 295.
71. Coffman, *War to End All Wars*, p. 310.
72. Quoted in Trask, *AEF and Coalition Warmaking*, p. 130.
73. Quoted in Coffman, *War to End All Wars*, p. 340.
74. Quoted in ibid., p. 339.
75. Quoted in Kaspi, *Le temps des américains*, p. 325.
76. Palmer, *Victory 1918*, p. 218.
77. Erich Ludendorff, *My War Memories, 1914–1918*, vol. 2 (London: Hutchinson & Co., 1920), p. 719.
78. Brook-Shepherd, *November 1918*, pp. 149, 200.
79. Kress, *Rugged Individualists*, p. 43.
80. Joel, *Lorraine Cross*, p. 32.
81. 79th Division Commanding General, "Report of Operations, October 2," 1918, RG 120, 79th Division, Box 6, 33.1, NARA, p. 3.
82. J.C. Johnson, "Observations 79th Division Sept. 28–30, 18," September 30, 1918, RG 120, Entry 24, "AEF General Headquarters, 1st Army Reports, G-3," Box 3384, 120.02, NARA, p. 2; Cochrane, "79th Division," pp. 44, 84–85.
83. Joel, *Lorraine Cross*, p. 32.

Chapter 15: Interlude—Troyon Sector, October 1–28

1. Barber, *79th Division*, pp. 172–73.
2. Ibid., pp. 179–82.
3. Antoine Brondelle, "Compte Rendu; Mission Francaise 79e D.I.U.S.," October 10, 1918, 17 N 128, SHD, p. 1.
4. A.W. Brewster, "Daily Report on Certain Divisions, 15 Oct., 18," October 15, 1918, RG 200, Pershing Papers, Box 29, Miscellaneous Records and Reports, NARA.
5. Harvey Cushing, *From a Surgeon's Journal* (Boston: Little, Brown, 1936), p. 462.
6. Kuhn, "General Kuhn's Diary," pp. 31–32.
7. Kuhn to Kuhn, October 8, 1918, p. 1.
8. Joseph. E. Kuhn, "General Kuhn's Diary," p. 36.

9. Historical Board of the 315th Infantry, *315th Infantry*, p. 79.
10. Barber, *79th Division*, p. 184.
11. Ibid., p. 186.
12. Joel, *Lorraine Cross*, p. 37.
13. Cochrane, "79th Division," p. 54.
14. Ibid., pp. 50–57 passim.
15. A.B. Clark, Division Gas Officer, "Report Gas Bombardment Night 9/10 October," October 12, 1918, RG 120, 79th Division, Box 11, NARA, p. 2.
16. Cochrane, "79th Division," pp. 58–59.
17. Ibid., p. 61.
18. Barber, *79th Division*, p. 190.
19. Ibid., p. 193.
20. Ibid., p. 195.
21. Ibid., p. 197.
22. Glock, *316th Regiment*, p. 55.
23. Harlowe, *Your Brother Will*, pp. 59, 67.
24. Historical Division, *USAWW*, vol. 8, p. 82; Kaspi, *Le temps des américains*, p. 318.
25. Historical Division, *USAWW*, vol. 8, p. 81.
26. Ibid., p. 85.
27. Smythe, *Pershing*, p. 207.
28. Ayres, *Statistical Summary*, p. 120.
29. Historical Division, *USAWW*, vol. 8, p. 81.
30. Paul F. Braim, *The Test of Battle: The American Expeditionary Forces in the Meuse–Argonne Campaign* (Shippensburg, PA: White Mane Books, second revised edition, 1998), p. 115.
31. Millett, *The General*, p. 411.
32. Ayres, *Statistical Summary*, p. 120.
33. Kaspi, *Le temps des américains*, p. 328.
34. Holger H. and Neil M. Heyman Herwig, *Biographical Dictionary of World War I* (Westport, CT and London: Greenwood, 1982), p. 256.
35. Brook-Shepherd, *November 1918*, p. 207.
36. Toland, *No Man's Land*, p. 452.
37. Woodrow Wilson, "Correspondence between the United States and Germany Regarding an Armistice," *American Journal of International Law* 13, 2, Supplement: Official Documents (April 1919), pp. 88–89.
38. Brook-Shepherd, *November 1918*, p. 253.
39. Trask, *AEF and Coalition Warmaking*, pp. 146, 148.

Chapter 16: Borne de Cornouiller and the Heights of the Meuse, October 29–November 10

1. Grotelueschen, *Doctrine under Trial*, pp. 117–20.
2. Conrad H. Lanza, "The First Battle of Romagne," *Field Artillery Journal* 23, November–December (1933), p. 505.
3. Matloff, *History*, p. 401.
4. Glock, *316th Regiment*, p. 56.
5. Joseph E. Kuhn, "Seventy-Ninth Serves until the Armistice," *Washington Post*, March 21, 1926, p. MS1.
6. 79th Division Commanding General, "Report of Operations, November 20, 1918," RG 120, 79th Division, Box 7, Reports of Operations, 33.1, NARA, p. 43.
7. Barber, *79th Division*, p. 212.
8. Conrad H. Lanza, "The Artillery Support of the Infantry in the A.E.F.," *Field Artillery Journal* 26, January–February (1936), pp. 69, 75.
9. Grotelueschen, *Doctrine under Trial*, p. 117.
10. 79th Division Commanding General, "Report, December 15, 1918," RG 120, 79th Division, Box 8, Report to Army Chief of Staff, 33.6, NARA, p. 13.
11. Fleming, "World War I Service," pp. 76, 79.
12. Hugh A. Drum, "Memorandum for Division Commanders: Reorganization of Divisions and Perfection of Their Tactical Training," October 14, 1918, RG 120, 1st Army Historical, Box 74, 50.4, NARA, p. 1.
13. G.A. Wildrick, "G-3 Memorandum No. 7: Information from Infantry to Artillery," October 20, 1918, RG 120, 79th Division, Box 4, 32.15, NARA, p. 1.
14. French liaison mission [signature illegible], "Note for the Infantry Divisions," October 26, 1918, RG 120, 79th Division, Box 7, 32.7, NARA.
15. General Commanding 17th Army Corps, "Note for the Division," October 27, 1918, ibid.
16. Tenney Ross, "Divisional Terrain Exercise #6: Liaison between Infantry and Air Service," October 17, 1918, RG 120, 79th Division, Box 12, 56.3, NARA.
17. Andrew Wiest, "Preferring to Learn from Experience: The American Expeditionary Force in 1917," in *1917 – Tactics, Training and Technology; the Chief of [Australian] Army's Military History Conference 2007*, ed. Peter Dennis and Jeffrey Grey (Australian Military History Publications, 2007), p. 153.
18. Davies, "War Diary," p. 35.
19. Glock, *316th Regiment*, p. 59.
20. Kress, *Rugged Individualists*, p. 52.
21. Matloff, *History*, p. 401.

22. Paul Henckell, *Das 18. Koeniglich Sächsiche Infanterie-Regiment Nr. 192* (Dresden: Verlag der Buchdruckerei der Wilhelm un Bertha v. Baensch Stiftung, 1925), p. 154; US War Office, *251 Divisions*, pp. 633–35.

23. Hans Taeglichsbeck, *Das Füsilier Regiment Prinz Heinrich Von Preussen (Brandenburgisches) Nr. 35* (Berlin: Gerhard Stalling, 1921), p. 66; US War Office, *251 Divisions*, pp. 715–16.

24. Glock, *316th Regiment*, p. 62.

25. Cochrane, "79th Division," p. 67.

26. Commanding General, "Report of Operations, November 20, 1918" p. 28; Barber, *79th Division*, p. 221.

27. Army General Staff College, "Staff Ride: The Meuse–Argonne Operations, Part I, Chapter II," January 1919, Kuhn Papers, Box 9, USMA, p. 18.

28. Historical Division, *USAWW*, vol. 9, p. 576.

29. Coffman, *War to End All Wars*, p. 347.

30. "Messages of the 316th Infantry," November 3, 1918, sent 2:10 a.m.

31. Barber, *79th Division*, p. 228; Glock, *316th Regiment*, pp. 65–66.

32. Barber, *79th Division*, p. 224.

33. A.W. Brewster, "Daily Report on Certain Divisions," November 3, 1918, RG 200, Pershing Papers, Box 29, Miscellaneous Records and Reports, NARA, p. 3.

34. Davies, "War Diary," p. 44.

35. "Messages of the 316th Infantry," November 4, 1918, sent 2:30 a.m.

36. Kuhn, "Seventy-Ninth Serves until the Armistice," p. MS7.

37. Glock, *316th Regiment*, p. 69.

38. Ibid., p. 70.

39. Barber, *79th Division.*, pp. 234–36.

40. Glock, *316th Regiment*, p. 71.

41. Ibid., p. 72.

42. Barber, *79th Division*, p. 238.

43. Historical Division, *USAWW*, vol. 9, p. 385.

44. Glock, *316th Regiment*, pp. 75–76.

45. Barber, *79th Division*, p. 242.

46. "79th Division Field Messages," November 5, 1918, time sent not given.

47. Barber, *79th Division*, p. 247.

48. Historical Division, *USAWW*, vol. 9, p. 588.

49. Kuhn, "Seventy-Ninth Serves until the Armistice," p. MS7.

50. Fleming, "World War I Service," p. 75.

51. Sweezey, "Report of Operations, September 25–November 11," p. 6.

52. Taeglichsbeck, *Füsilier Regiment Nr. 35*, p. 70.

53. Historical Division, *USAWW*, vol. 9, p. 593.

54. Armin Hase, *Das 17. Koeniglich Sächsische Infanterie-Regiment Nr. 183* (Dresden: Verlag der Buchdruckerei der Wilhelm un Bertha v. Baensch Stiftung, 1922), p. 109.

55. Cochrane, "79th Division," p. 78.
56. Historical Division, *USAWW*, vol. 9, p. 395.
57. US War Office, *251 Divisions*, pp. 36–38.
58. Wilhelm Suhrmann, *Geschichte Des Landwehr-Infanterie-Regiments Nr. 31 im Weltkriege* (Flensburg/Oldenburg/Berlin: Gerhard Stalling, 1928), pp. 384, 392.
59. Barber, *79th Division*, pp. 262–63.
60. Kress, *Rugged Individualists*, p. 54.
61. Barber, *79th Division*, p. 263.
62. Ibid., p. 266.
63. Barber, *79th Division*, p. 269.
64. Suhrmann, *Des Landwehr-Infanterie-Regiments Nr. 31*, p. 388.
65. Ibid., p. 389.
66. Kress, *Rugged Individualists*, p. 60.
67. Tompkins, *Maryland Fighters*, pp. 100–01.
68. "79th Division Field Messages," November 8, 1918, sent 2:30 p.m.
69. Kuhn to Kuhn, November 8, 1918.
70. Cochrane, "79th Division," p. 80; "79th Division Field Messages," November 8, 1918, sent 8:10 p.m.
71. "Field Messages of the 157th Infantry Brigade," November 9, 1918, sent 9:45 a.m.
72. Suhrmann, *Des Landwehr-Infanterie-Regiments Nr. 31*, p. 389.
73. Kress, *Rugged Individualists*, p. 61.
74. Barber, *79th Division*, p. 291–92.
75. Suhrmann, *Des Landwehr-Infanterie-Regiments Nr. 31*, p. 391.
76. "Field Messages of the 157th Infantry Brigade," November 9, 1918, sent 2:25 p.m.
77. "79th Division Field Messages," November 9, 1918, sent 5:40 p.m.
78. Ibid., November 9, 1918, sent 8:30 p.m.
79. General Commanding II CAC (Claudel). "Order of Operations No. 41," November 9, 1918, RG 120, 79th Division, Box 7, 32.7, NARA.
80. Barber, *79th Division*, pp. 303–05.
81. Joel, *Lorraine Cross*, p. 44.
82. Suhrmann, *Des Landwehr-Infanterie-Regiments Nr. 31*, p. 396.
83. Ibid., p. 397.
84. Ibid., pp. 393–94.
85. Ibid., pp. 391–92.
86. Kuhn, "General Kuhn's Diary," p. 50.

Chapter 17: Armistice to Home, November 11, 1918–June 5, 1919

1. Herwig, *First World War*, p. 442.
2. Palmer, *Victory 1918*, pp. 278–79.
3. Ibid., p. 279.
4. Ibid., p. 282–83.
5. Ibid., pp. 284–85.
6. Hugh Drum, "First Army Field Orders No. 111," November 10, 1918, RG 120, First Army Reports – Miscellaneous Papers – Box 3454, NARA.
7. Barber, *79th Division*, pp. 309–10.
8. "79th Division Field Messages.", November 10, 1918, sent 8:10 p.m.
9. Ibid., November 10, 1918, sent 10:10 p.m.
10. Historical Division, *USAWW*, vol. 9, p. 400.
11. Barber, *79th Division*, p. 314.
12. College, "Staff Ride: The Meuse–Argonne Operations, Part I, Chapter II," p. 18.
13. Barber, *79th Division*, p. 315; Suhrmann, *Des Landwehr-Infanterie-Regiments Nr. 31*, p. 397.
14. Joseph E. Persico, *11th Month, 11th Day, 11th Hour: Armistice Day, 1918: World War I and Its Violent Climax* (New York: Random House, 2004), p. 351.
15. Kress, *Rugged Individualists*, p. 65.
16. Fleming, "World War I Service," p. 82.
17. Barber, *79th Division*, pp. 318–20.
18. Ferro, *The Great War, 1914–1918*, p. 220; Kaspi, *Le temps des américains*, pp. 320, 343; Palmer, *Victory 1918*, p. 257.
19. Palmer, *Victory 1918*, p. 256.
20. Diary of Charles G. Dawes, quoted in Coffman, *War to End All Wars*, p. 342.
21. Nick Lloyd, *Hundred Days: The Campaign That Ended World War I* (United Kingdom: Basic Books, 2014), p. 277; Smythe, *Pershing*, p. 230.
22. Ministère de la Guerre, Service Historique, *AFGG*, Tome Vii, 2e Volume, Annexes, p. 876; Lloyd, *Hundred Days: The Campaign That Ended World War I*, pp. 267–68; Palmer, *Victory 1918*, p. 285.
23. Historical Division, *USAWW*, vol. 10, p. 56.
24. Richard C. Hall, *The Balkan Wars, 1912–1913: Prelude to the First World War* (London and New York: Routledge, 2000), p. 1.
25. Gilbert, *First World War*, pp. 384, 398.
26. Palmer, *Victory 1918*, p. 303.
27. Commanding General, "Report of Operations, November 20, 1918" p. 41.
28. Ibid.
29. Ibid., p. 43.
30. Barber, *79th Division*, p. 328; Suhrmann, *Des Landwehr-Infanterie-Regiments Nr. 31*, p. 397.

31. Loomis, *304th Ammunition Train*, p. 59.
32. Kuhn to Kuhn, November 12 and November 16, 1918.
33. Barber, *79th Division*, p. 330.
34. Joseph E. Kuhn, "Burial of Dead 79th's Sad Task after Armistice," *Washington Post*, March 22, 1926, p. 4.
35. Oscar Lubchansky to his family, December 5, 1918, author's personal collection, p. 1.
36. C.B. Sweezey to Mr. John W. Campbell, November 30, 1918, Records of U.S. Army Mobile Units RG 391, 313th Infantry, Box 3163, NARA.
37. Harlowe, *Your Brother Will*, p. 99.
38. Oscar Lubchansky to Sadie Lubchansky, February 7, 1919, author's personal collection, p. 1.
39. Oscar Lubchansky to his parents, December 21, 1918, author's personal collection, p. 2.
40. C.B. Sweezey to Master John Hamilton, November 30, 1918, Records of U.S. Army Mobile Units RG 391, 313th Infantry, Box 3163, NARA.
41. Harlowe, *Your Brother Will*, p. 109.
42. Ibid., p. 82.
43. Winterich, *Squads Write*, p. 234.
44. Harlowe, *Your Brother Will*, p. 78.
45. Frank R. Wheelock, "Memorandum Re Exposure of Men," December 19, 1918, RG 120, 79th Division, Box 17, NARA.
46. G.A. Wildrick, "Response to Wheelock, Memorandum Re Exposure of Men," December 24, 1918, RG 120, 79th Division, Box 16, NARA.
47. Carol R. Byerly, *Fever of War: The Influenza Epidemic in the U.S. Army During World War I* (New York and London: NY UP, 2005), p. 146.
48. Joseph W.A. Whitehorne, *The Inspectors General of the United States Army, 1903–1939* (Washington, DC: Center of Military History, Department of the Army, 1998), p. 243.
49. Kuhn, "Burial of Dead 79th's Sad Task after Armistice," p. 4.
50. Ibid.
51. Barber, *79th Division*, p. 337.
52. Harlowe, *Your Brother Will*, pp. 87–91.
53. Barber, *79th Division*, p. 337.
54. Harlowe, *Your Brother Will*, p. 107.
55. Col. Albert T. Rich, "Military Courtesy," March 11, 1919, Kuhn Papers, Box 3, USMA; E.S. Pleasonton, "Memorandum to Col. Brewer," April 7, 1919, Kuhn Papers, Box 3, USMA, p. 2.
56. Barber, *79th Division*, p. 350.
57. Ibid., p. 351.
58. Oscar Lubchansky to his family, January 6, 1919, author's personal collection.
59. Harlowe, *Your Brother Will*, p. 124.

60. Kuhn to Kuhn, March 21, 1919.
61. Joseph E. Kuhn, "General Kuhn's Diary," p. 102.
62. Joseph E. Kuhn, "The 79th Marches in Driving Rain in Final Review," *Washington Post*, March 23, 1926, p. 5.
63. Kuhn to Kuhn, April 13, 1919.
64. Barber, *79th Division*, p. 365.
65. Ibid., p. 367.
66. Kuhn, "General Kuhn's Diary," p. 116.
67. Barber, *79th Division*, p. 367.
68. Ibid., p. 372.
69. "Baltimore Received Her Boys of the 313th with Wide-Open Arms," *Baltimore Sun*, June 5, 1919, p. 8.
70. Kuhn, "The 79th Marches in Driving Rain in Final Review," p. 5.

Epilogue

1. Barber, *79th Division*, p. 361.
2. Cited in Smythe, *Pershing*, p. 232.
3. Hunter Liggett, *Commanding an American Army: Recollections of the World War* (Boston and New York: Houghton Mifflin), p. 121.
4. Allan R. Millett, "Over Where? The AEF and the American Strategy for Victory, 1917–1918," in *Against All Enemies: Interpretations of American Military History from Colonial Times to the Present*, ed. Kenneth Hagan and William R. Roberts, Contributions in Military Studies (New York, Westport, CT, and London: Greenwood, 1986), pp. 246, 249.
5. Rainey, "Ambivalent Warfare," passim; Smythe, *Pershing*, especially p. 237; Millett, "Over Where?," pp. 247–51; Rod Paschall, *The Defeat of Imperial Germany, 1917–1918* (Chapel Hill: Algonquin Books, 1989), pp. 167–69; Nenninger, "Tactical Dysfunction," passim; Trask, *AEF and Coalition Warmaking*, passim; Grotelueschen, *Doctrine under Trial*, passim.
6. Pershing, *My Experiences*, vol. 1, p. 153.
7. Travers, "The Allied Victories, 1918," p. 290.
8. Wiest, "Preferring to Learn from Experience: The American Expeditionary Force in 1917," p. 141.
9. Christopher R. Gabel, *The U.S. Army GHQ Maneuvers of 1941* (Washington, DC: Center of Military History, 1992), p. 9.
10. Ibid., pp. 9–11.
11. Ibid., p. 24.
12. Jean Edward Smith, *Eisenhower in War and Peace* (New York: Random House, 2012), p. 159.
13. Ibid., p. 200.
14. Jonathan M. House, *Combined Arms Warfare in the Twentieth Century*, ed. Theodore A. Wilson, Modern War Studies (Lawrence, KS: UP of Kansas, 2001), p. 101.

15. Gabel, *Maneuvers*, p. 49.
16. Robert B. Patterson, *Arming the Nation for War: Mobilization, Supply, and the American War Effort in World War II*, ed. G. Kurt Piehler, Legacies of War (Knoxville: University of Tennessee, 2014), p. 165.
17. House, *Combined Arms*, Modern War Studies, p. 99.
18. Blanche D. Coll, Jean E. Keith and Herbert H. Rosenthal, *The Corps of Engineers: Troops and Equipment*, United States Army in World War II (Washington, DC: Center of Military History, United States Army, 1988), pp. 19, 23.
19. Ibid., pp. 31–32, 62.
20. Patterson, *Arming the Nation*, Legacies of War, pp. 22–23.
21. Smith, *Eisenhower*, p. 152.
22. Robert R. Palmer, Bell I. Wiley, and William R. Keast, *The Army Ground Forces: The Procurement and Training of Ground Combat Forces*, United States Army in World War II (Washington, DC: Center of Military History, 1991), pp. 170–72.
23. Smith, *Eisenhower*, p. 329.
24. Ibid., p. 184.
25. Bach to Bolte, November 18, 1922; Bach to J. Hines, November 19, 1922, RG 120, Historical Section Reports, Box 3, NARA; Bach to Edwin E. Booth, n.d., RG 120, Historical Section Reports, Box 3, NARA.
26. A.W. Bjornstad to Christian A. Bach, December 24, 1924, ibid., p. 5.
27. Christian A. Bach to Edwin E. Booth, n.d., ibid.
28. J.J. Pershing to E.E. Booth, June 17, 1940, Hugh A. Drum Papers, Box 20, File "Booth, Gen. E.E.", AHEC, p. 1.
29. Ayres, *Statistical Summary*, pp. 123–24.
30. Kennedy, *Over Here*, p. 290.
31. Nina Mjagkij, *Loyalty in Time of Trial: The African American Experience During World War I* (Lanham, MD: Rowman & Littlefield, 2011), pp. 141–43.
32. Vandiver, *Black Jack*, pp. 1,035–42.
33. Smythe, *Pershing*, p. 262.
34. Vandiver, *Black Jack*, p. 1,058.
35. Smythe, *Pershing*, p. 284.
36. Vandiver, *Black Jack*, p. 1,085.
37. Ibid., pp. 1,087, 1,093.
38. "Pershing Laid to Rest with Military Splendor," *Baltimore Sun*, July 20, 1948, p. 1; "General Pershing's Funeral," *Army and Navy Journal*, July 24, 1948, pp. 1,287, 1,319.
39. Smythe, *Pershing*, p. 309.
40. Leo J. Daugherty, "Kuhn, Joseph Ernest," in *American National Biography*, ed. John A. Garraty and Mark C. Carnes (New York, Oxford: Oxford UP, 1999), p. 945.
41. Harlowe, *Your Brother Will*, p. 103.

42. "Colonel Sweezey Goes Down Fighting for His Principles," *Baltimore Sun*, March 10, 1925, p. 26.

43. "Col. Sweezey, Former Head of Pen, Dies," *Baltimore Sun*, September 23, 1939, p. 22.

44. Roy Hoopes, *Cain: The Biography of James M. Cain* (New York: Holt, Rinehart and Winston, 1982), passim.

45. Harlowe, *Your Brother Will*, pp. 151, 155.

Appendices

1. Crown Prince William, *My War Experiences* (London: Hurst and Blackett, 1922), p. 169

BIBLIOGRAPHY

"III Corps, Report No. 909," September 26, 1918. RG 120, Historical Section Reports, Box 3, 15.45, NARA.

79th Division Commanding General [Joseph E. Kuhn]. "Report, December 15, 1918." RG 120, 79th Division, Box 8, Report to Army Chief of Staff, 33.6, NARA.

79th Division Commanding General [Joseph E. Kuhn]. "Report of Operations, November 20, 1918." RG 120, 79th Division, Box 7, Reports of Operations, 33.1, NARA.

79th Division Commanding General [Joseph E. Kuhn]. "Report of Operations, October 2, 1918." RG 120, 79th Division, Box 6, 33.1, NARA.

"79th Division Field Messages," 1918. RG 120, 79th Division, Boxes 4–5, 32.16, NARA.

"117th Division (Subordinate Units): Diary and Annexes," September 25–30, 1918. RG 165, Army War College Historical Section, Box 165, 117th Division, 22.3, NARA.

"315th Infantry Field Messages," 1918. RG 120, 79th Division, Box 22, 32.16, NARA.

ABMC. *79th Division: Summary of Operations in the World War*. Washington, DC: GPO, 1944.

ABMC. *American Armies and Battlefields in Europe: A History, Guide, and Reference Book*. Washington, DC: GPO, 1938.

ABMC. *37th Division: Summary of Operations in the World War*. Washington, DC: GPO, 1944.

ABMC. *4th Division: Summary of Operations in the World War*. Washington, DC: GPO, 1944.

"Alsace." In *The Encyclopedia Britannica*. New York: Encyclopedia Britannica, Inc., 1911.

Allegrini, "Compte Rendu (21 Septembre–3 Octobre)," *c.* October 1918, 17 N 128, SHD.

Ambrose, Stephen E. *Citizen Soldiers: The U.S. Army from the Normandy Beaches to the Bulge to the Surrender of Germany*. New York: Simon & Schuster, 1997.

American Expeditionary Forces. *The German and American Combined Daily Order of Battle: 25 September to 11 November 1918, Including the Meuse–Argonne Offensive*. Chaumont, France, 1919.

American Expeditionary Forces. *Supplement to Instructions for the Offensive Combat of Small Units*. Vol. no. 160-A, April 1918.

American Expeditionary Forces, General Headquarters. *Memorandum for Corps and Division Commanders. Subject: Training*. Document No. 1325: Adjutant General Printing Department, 1918.

American Expeditionary Forces, General Headquarters. *Tanks: Organization and Tactics*. Document No. 1432: American Expeditionary Forces, December 1918.

American Expeditionary Forces, General Staff. *Order of Battle of the American Expeditionary Forces*. General HQ, AEF, n.d.

American Expeditionary Forces, First Section General Staff, "Report B-2: Account of the Argonne–Meuse Operation – 9th September to 11th November – Influence of G-1 Section and Part Taken in the Operation," January 14, 1919. RG 120, Entry 24, "Report of Operation, G-1 Section, First Army, 10 Aug–11 Nov '18," Boxes 3361, 3020, NARA.

American Expeditionary Forces, Fifth Section General Staff. *Problems in Minor Tactics: Infantry Patrol, Open Warfare*. Document No. 1009. Adjutant General Printing Office, GHQAEF, 1918.

American Expeditionary Forces, General Staff, War Plans Division. *Training Circular No. 8: Provisional Infantry Training Manual*. Document No. 844. Washington, DC: GPO, August 1918.

American Expeditionary Forces, General Staff, War Plans Division, Historical Branch. *A Study in Troop Frontage*. Monograph No. 4. Washington, DC: GPO, 1919.

American Expeditionary Forces, Office of the Chief of Staff. "Confidential Memorandum for the Commander-in-Chief," February 22, 1918. RG 200, Pershing Papers, Box 26, Miscellaneous Records and Studies, NARA.

American Expeditionary Forces, Training Section. *Provisional Trench Orders for the American Troops in France*. Document No. 738: Headquarters, American Expeditionary Forces, n.d. (before 30 April 1918).

Army General Staff College, "Staff Ride: The Meuse–Argonne Operations, Part I, Chapter II," January 1919. Kuhn Papers, Box 9, USMA.

Army War College. *Infantry Training.* Document No. 656. Washington, DC: GPO, 1917.

Army War College, Historical Section. *Order of Battle of the United States Land Forces in the World War: Divisions.* Document No. 23a. Washington, DC: GPO, 1931.

Army War College, Historical Section. *Order of Battle of the United States Land Forces in the World War: General Headquarters, Armies, Army Corps, Services of Supply, Separate Forces.* Washington, DC: Center of Military History, originally published 1931, reprinted 1988.

Army War College, Historical Section. "The Seventy-Ninth Division, 1917–1918." Unpublished,1924.

Army War College, War Plans Division. *Training Circular No. 5: Infantry Training.* Document No. 849. Washington, DC: War Department, August 1918.

"Annal of Mobilization," 1918. RG 120, 79th Division, Box 2, NARA.

Asprey, Robert B. *The German High Command at War: Hindenburg and Ludendorff Conduct World War I.* New York: William Morrow, 1991.

Association of Graduates, US Military Academy. *Annual Report.* West Point, 1937.

Atwood, John H. *What I Saw of the War.* Privately printed, 1919.

Ayres, Leonard P. *The War with Germany: A Statistical Summary.* Washington, DC: GPO, 1919.

Bach, Christian A. and Henry Noble Hall, *The Fourth Division: Its Services and Achievements in the World War.* 4th Division, 1920.

Bairnsfather, Bruce. *From Mud to Mufti: With Old Bill on All Fronts.* London: G.P. Putnam's Sons, 1919.

Banks, Arthur. *A Military Atlas of the First World War.* Barnsley, S. Yorks.: Leo Cooper, 1975, reprinted 1997.

Barbeau, Arthur E. and Florette Henri. *The Unknown Soldiers: African-American Troops in World War I.* Philadelphia: Temple University Press, 1974.

Barber, J. Frank. *Official History of the 304th Engineer Regiment, 79th Division, U.S.A., During the World War.* Lancaster, PA: Steinman & Foltz, 1920.

Barber, J. Frank. *History of the Seventy-Ninth Division A.E.F. During the World War: 1917–1919.* Lancaster, PA: Steinman & Steinman, n.d.

Barnett, Correlli. *The Swordbearers: Supreme Command in the First World War.* New York: William Morrow and Company, 1964.

Barr, Niall J.A. "The Elusive Victory: The BEF and the Operational Level of War, September 1918." In *War in the Age of Technology: Myriad Faces of Modern Armed Conflict,* edited by Geoffrey and Andrew Wiest Jensen. The World of War. New York and London: New York UP, 2001.

Bayerische Vermessungs-Abteilung 15, "Stand Am 9.9.18." RG 165, Army War College Historical Section, Box 165, 117th Division, NARA, 1918.

Beaver, Daniel R. *Modernizing the American War Department: Change and Continuity in a Turbulent Era, 1885–1920*. Kent, OH: Kent State University Press, 2006.

Bendersky, Joseph W. *The "Jewish Threat": Anti-Semitic Politics of the U.S. Army*. New York: Basic Books, 2000.

Bidwell, Sheldon and Dominick Graham. *Fire-Power: British Army Weapons and Theories of War, 1904–1945*. London: Allen & Unwin, 1982.

Bland, Larry I., and Sharon R. Ritenour, eds. *The Papers of George Catlett Marshall, Volume 1: "The Soldierly Spirit," December 1880–June 1939*. Baltimore: Johns Hopkins University Press, 1981.

Bliss, 1st Lt George L, Co. I, 316th Infantry. "Report of Actions of Company," October 2, 1918. World War I Survey, WWI-8172, AHEC.

Braim, Paul F. *The Test of Battle: The American Expeditionary Forces in the Meuse–Argonne Campaign*. Shippensburg, PA: White Mane Books, second revised edition, 1998.

Braynard, Frank O. *World's Greatest Ship: The Story of the Leviathan*. New York: South Street Seaport Museum, 1972.

Brewster, A.W. "Daily Report on Certain Divisions," RG 200, Pershing Papers, Box 29, Miscellaneous Records and Reports, NARA.

Brondelle, Antoine. "Compte Rendu; Mission Francaise 79e D.I.U.S.," October 10, 1918. 17 N 128, SHD.

Brook-Shepherd, Gordon. *November 1918*. Boston and Toronto: Little, Brown, 1981.

Brooks, Alden. *As I Saw It*. New York: Knopf, 1929.

Bryan, Kirk. "The Role of Physiography in Military Operations." *The Scientific Monthly* 11, November (1920).

Bugnet, Charles. *Foch Speaks*. New York: Dial Press, 1929.

Bullard, Robert L. "Field Order No. 18," September 21, 1918. RG 120, Entry 1043, III Corps Historical File, 32.1, NARA.

Burg, David F. and L. Edward Purcell. *Almanac of World War I*. Lexington, KY: University Press of Kentucky, 1998.

Burtt, W.B. "Field Orders No. 46, Fifth Army Corps, A.E.F.," September 28, 1918. RG 120, Fifth Corps Historical File, Box 14, 32.1, NARA.

Burtt, W.B. "Field Orders No. 31, Part II, Fifth Army Corps, A.E.F.," September 23, 1918. RG 120, Entry 1118, Fifth Corps Historical File, Box 14, 32.1, NARA.

Burtt, W.B. "Field Orders No. 31, Fifth Army Corps, A.E.F.," September 21, 1918. RG 120, Entry 1118, Fifth Corps Historical File, Box 14, 32.1, NARA.

Burtt, W.B. "Memorandum for Employment of Tanks," August 23, 1918. RG 120, Entry 1118, Fifth Corps Historical File, Box 17, 50.4, NARA.

Byerly, Carol R. *Fever of War: The Influenza Epidemic in the U.S. Army During World War I.* New York and London: NY UP, 2005.

Cain, James M., III. "The Taking of Montfaucon." In *Americans vs. Germans: The First AEF in Action*, edited by Editors of The Infantry Journal. Washington, DC: Penguin Books and The Infantry Journal, Inc., 1942.

Caldwell, F.M. "Report of Inspection of 79th Division and Other Troops, Camp Meade, Maryland," January 24,1918. RG 120, 79th Division, Boxes 7, 9, 11, file 56.2, NARA.

Capozzola, Christopher. *Uncle Sam Wants You: World War I and the Making of the Modern American Citizen.* Oxford and New York: Oxford UP, 2008.

Chambers, John Whiteclay, II. *To Raise an Army: The Draft Comes to Modern America.* New York: Free Press, 1987.

Chapelle, G. de la. "Report with Regard to the Employment of the Squadron During the Battle from September 26th to 30th," *c.* October 1918. 17 N 128, SHD.

Chief of Staff, First Army, "Report No. 964," September 26, 1918. RG 120, Historical Section Reports, Box 3, NARA.

Clark, A.B. Division Gas Officer, "Report Gas Bombardment Night 9/10 October," October 12, 1918. RG 120, 79th Division, Box 11, NARA.

Clark, William Bell. *War History of the 79th Division, National Army.* Williamsport, PA: privately published, 1918.

Clayton, Anthony. *Paths of Glory: The French Army 1914–18.* London: Cassell, 2003.

Cochrane, Rexmond C. "The 79th Division at Montfaucon, October 1918." In *U.S. Army Chemical Corps Historical Studies: Gas Warfare in World War I* Study no. 19. Washington, DC: US Army Chemical Corps Historical Office, 1960.

Cochrane, Rexmond C. "The Use of Gas in the Meuse–Argonne Campaign, September–November 1918." In *U.S. Army Chemical Corps Historical Studies: Gas Warfare in World War I* Study no.10. Washington, DC: US Army Chemical Corps Historical Office, 1958.

Coffman, Edward M. "The AEF Leaders' Education for War." In *The Great War, 1914–18: Essays on the Military, Political and Social History of the First World War*, edited by R.Q. Adams. College Station: Texas A&M UP, 1990.

Coffman, Edward M. "American Command and Commanders in World War I." In *New Dimensions in Military History*, edited by Russell F. Weigley. San Rafael, CA: Presidio Press, 1975.

Coffman, Edward M. *The War to End All Wars: The American Military Experience in World War I*. New York: Oxford UP, 1968.

Coffman, Edward M. "Conflicts in American Planning: An Aspect of World War I Strategy." *Military Review* 43 (June 1963).

Cohen, Eliot A. *Supreme Command: Soldiers, Statesmen, and Leadership in Wartime*. New York: Simon & Schuster, 2002.

Cohen, Eliot A. and John Gooch. *Military Misfortunes: The Anatomy of Failure in War*. New York: Free Press, 1990.

Colby, Elbridge. "The Taking of Montfaucon," *Infantry Journal* 47, March–April (1940).

Cole, Ralph D. and W.C. Howells. *The 37th Division in the World War, 1917–1918* (2 vols). Columbus, OH: The Thirty-Seventh Division Veterans Association, 1926.

Cole, Robert B. and Barnard E. Eberlin, *The History of the 39th U.S. Infantry During the World War*. New York: Press of Joseph D. McGuire, 1919.

Coll, Blanche D., Jean E. Keith and Herbert H. Rosenthal. *The Corps of Engineers: Troops and Equipment*. United States Army in World War II. Washington, DC: Center of Military History, United States Army, 1988.

Cooke, James J. *Pershing and His Generals: Command and Staff in the AEF*. Westport, CT, and London: Praeger, 1997.

Cooke, James J. and Mark E. Grotelueschen. "American Tactics: Was General Pershing's Emphasis on Open Warfare Appropriate for the Western Front?" In *History in Dispute*, Vol. 9, Second Series, edited by Dennis Showalter. Detroit, New York, et al.: St. James Press, 2002.

Craig, Harold E. Untitled diary, 1918, World War I Survey, Box: 79th Division HQ-Craig, AHEC.

Crain, C.F. "79th Division – Field Notes – Argonne–Meuse Offensive (Sept. 26–Nov. 11/18)," May 16, 1919. RG 120, 79th Division, Box 2, 18.8, NARA.

Crampton, R.J. "The Balkans, 1914–1918." In *World War I: A History*, edited by Hew Strachan. Oxford and New York: Oxford UP, 1998.

Creveld, Martin L. Van. *Supplying War: Logistics from Wallenstein to Patton*. London, New York, and Melbourne: Cambridge UP, 1977.

Crocker, H.W., III. *The Yanks Are Coming: A Military History of the United States in World War I*. Washington, DC: Regnery History, 2014.

Cron, Hermann. *Imperial German Army, 1914–1918: Organisation, Structure, Orders-of-Battle.* Translation of *Geschichte des Deutschen Heeres im Weltkriege 1914–1918,* Berlin, 1937 edition. Solihull, UK: Helion, 2002.

Cullum, George W., and ed. Wirt Robinson. *Biographical Register of the Officers and Graduates of the U.S. Military Academy at West Point, New York, Since its Establishment in 1802. Volume VI-A, 1910–1920.* Saginaw, MI: Sherman & Peters, 1920.

Cushing, Harvey. *From a Surgeon's Journal.* Boston: Little, Brown, 1936.

Dallam, S. Field. "Preliminary Report on 79th Division," October 2, 1918. RG 200, Pershing Papers, Box 29, Miscellaneous Records and Reports, NARA.

Dastrup, Boyd. *King of Battle: A Branch History of the U.S. Army's Field Artillery.* TRADOC Branch History Series. Fort Monroe, VA and Washington, DC: Center of Military History, 1992.

Daugherty, Leo J. "Kuhn, Joseph Ernest." In *American National Biography*, edited by John A. Garraty and Mark C. Carnes. New York and Oxford: Oxford UP, 1999.

Davies, Edward A. "War Diary of Sergeant Edward A. Davies, Company B, 315th Infantry, 79th Division." n.d. World War I Survey, AHEC.

Demmler, Ernst, Karl Ritter von Bucher, Ludwig Leupold. *Das K.B. Reserve-Infanterie-Regiment 12.* Erinnerungsblätter Deutscher Regimenter. Munich: Verlag Max Schick, 1934.

Department of the Army Historical Division. *The United States Army in the World War, 1917–1919* (17 vols). Washington, DC: GPO, 1948.

Dickson, Thomas J. "War Fables Taught in American Schools." *Current History 7, August* (1927).

Doughty, Robert A. *Pyrrhic Victory: French Strategy and Operations in the Great War.* Cambridge, MA and London: Belknap Press, 2005.

Doughty, Robert Allan. *The Seeds of Disaster: The Development of French Army Doctrine, 1919–1939.* Hamden, Conn.: Archon Books, 1985.

Drum, Hugh A. "First Army Field Orders No. 111," November 10, 1918. RG 120, First Army Reports – Miscellaneous Papers – Box 3454, NARA.

Drum, Hugh A. "Memorandum for Division Commanders: Reorganization of Divisions and Perfection of Their Tactical Training," October 14, 1918. RG 120, 1st Army Historical, Box 74, 50.4, NARA.

Drum, Hugh A. "Combat Instructions for Troops of First Army," August 29, 1918. RG 120, Fifth Corps, Box 17, Fifth Corps Field Orders, 32.14, NARA.

Eastman, W.R. "Evacuation of Sick and Wounded During the Meuse–Argonne

Operation," January 27, 1919. RG 120, Entry 22, Commander-in-Chief Reports, Box 29, NARA.

Ellis, John. *The Social History of the Machine Gun.* Paperback edition. Baltimore: Johns Hopkins UP, 1986.

"Enemy Order of Battle, Midnight – Sept. 25/26, 1918." Hugh A. Drum Papers, Box 13, Folder: F.A.A.E.F., AHEC, n.d.

Engel, Charles M. "Army Service Experiences Questionnaire," 1988. World War I Survey, Box: 57th FA Brigade, Divisional Troops; Folder: Engel, Charles M., 119th FA, AHEC.

Englander, David. "Soldiering and Identity: Reflections on the Great War." *War in History* 1 (1994).

Eisenhower, John S.D. *Yanks: The Epic Story of the American Army in World War I.* New York, London, Toronto, Sydney, and Singapore: The Free Press, 2001.

Esposito, Vincent J., ed. *The West Point Atlas of American Wars, Volume II: 1900–1918.* New York: Henry Holt, 1959, reprinted 1997.

Etzel, Hans. *Das K.B. Reserve-Infanterie-Regiment Nr.10*, Erinnerungsblätter Deutscher Regimenter. Munich: Verlag Max Schick, 1934.

Farwell, Byron. *Over There: The United States in the Great War, 1917–1918.* New York and London: W.W. Norton, 1999.

Faust, Albert Bernhardt. *The German Element in the United States, with Special Reference to Its Political, Moral, Social, and Educational Influence* (2 vols). Boston and New York: Houghton Mifflin, 1909.

Fein, Isaac M. *The Making of an American Jewish Community: The History of Baltimore Jewry from 1773 to 1920.* Philadelphia: Jewish Publication Society, 1971.

Ferrell, Robert H. *America's Deadliest Battle: Meuse–Argonne, 1918.* Lawrence, KS: UP of Kansas, 2007.

Ferrell, Robert H. *Collapse at Meuse–Argonne: The Failure of the Missouri-Kansas Division.* Columbia, MO and London: University of Missouri Press, 2004.

Ferrell, Robert H. *Woodrow Wilson and World War I, 1917–1921.* New York: Harper & Row, 1985.

Ferro, Marc. *The Great War, 1914–1918.* London: Routledge & Keegan Paul, 1969; translation published 1973.

"Field Messages of the 157th Infantry Brigade," 1918. RG 120, 79th Division, Box 16, 32.16, NARA.

"Fifth Corps Field Messages," September 26–30, 1918. RG 120, V Corps, Box 19, 32.16, NARA.

Fischer, Fritz. *Germany's Aims in the First World War*. New York: Norton, 1961.

Fiske, Harold B., "Program of Training for Divisions in the United States," n.d., *c.* 1918, unpublished document in AHEC library.

Fitzsimmons, Bernard, ed. *The Illustrated Encyclopedia of 20th Century Weapons and Warfare* (24 vols). New York: Purnell & Sons, Phoebus Publishing, 1967/1969.

Fleming, Samuel W., Jr.. "World War I Service." 1960, World War I Survey, Box: 79th Division, 157th and 158th Inf. Brig.; Folder: Fleming, Samuel W., Major, 315th Infantry, AHEC.

Fleming, Thomas. *The Illusion of Victory: America in World War I*. New York: Basic Books, 2003.

Foch, Ferdinand. *The Memoirs of Marshal Foch*. Translated by T. Bentley Mott. Garden City, NY: Doubleday, Doran, 1931.

Foley, Robert T. "The Other Side of the Wire: The German Army in 1917." In *1917 – Tactics, Training and Technology; the Chief of [Australian] Army's Military History Conference 2007*, edited by Peter Dennis and Jeffrey Grey. Australian Military History Publications, 2007.

Fontaine, de la [no first name]. "Report Concerning the French-American Attack between the Argonne and Lorraine Flank from 25/9–15/10, 1918." 5th [German] Army High Command, Hugh A. Drum Papers, Box 17, Folder: German 5th Army Report, AHEC, October 28, 1918.

Ford, Nancy Gentile. *Americans All! Foreign-Born Soldiers in World War I*. College Station, TX: Texas A&M UP, 2001.

Ford, Nancy Gentile. ""Mindful of the Traditions of His Race": Dual Identity and Foreign-Born Soldiers in the First World War American Army." *Journal of American Ethnic History* 16, (Winter 1997).

Fosten, D.S.V, R.J. Marrion, and G.A. Embleton. *The German Army, 1914–1918*. Edited by Martin Windrow. Men-at-Arms Series. London: Reed International Books Ltd., 1978.

French liaison mission [signature illegible]. "Note for the Infantry Divisions," October 26, 1918. RG 120, 79th Division, Box 7, 32.7, NARA.

Gabel, Christopher R. *The U.S. Army GHQ Maneuvers of 1941*. Washington, DC: Center of Military History, 1992.

Gallwitz, Max von. *Erleben im Westen, 1916–1918*. Berlin: Verlag von E.S. Mittler & Sohn, 1932.

Gallwitz, Max von. "The Meuse–Argonne Battles in the Fall of 1918." In *As They Saw Us: Foch, Ludendorff, and Other Leaders Write Our War History*, edited by George Sylvester Viereck. Garden City, NY: Doubleday, Doran, 1929.

G-3 Assistant Chief of Staff, AEF. "Proposed Disposition of U.S. Divisions in Line," September 7, 1918. RG 120, Entry 24, "AEF General Headquarters, 1st Army Reports, G-3," Box 3382, 114.0, NARA.

General Commanding 17th Army Corps. "Note for the Division," October 27, 1918. RG 120, 79th Division, Box 7, 32.7, NARA.

General Commanding II C.A.C. (Claudel). "Order of Operations No. 41," November 9, 1918. RG 120, 79th Division, Box 7, 32.7, NARA.

General Staff [UK]. *German Army Handbook, April 1918*. London, Melbourne: Arms and Armour Press, 1977, reprint of 1918 edition.

General Staff [UK]. *Vocabulary of German Military Terms and Abbreviations*. London and Nashville: Imperial War Museum and Battery Press, 1918, reprinted 1995.

Gibbons, James R.L. "Complete Roster of Officers and Men of Company "B," 313th US Infantry, from July 15th, 1918 to April 15th, 1919, and Their Status," July 3, 1930. RG 120, 79th Division, Box 16, NARA.

Giehrl, Hermann, von. "Battle of the Meuse–Argonne (Part 1 of 4)," *Infantry Journal* 19, August (1921).

Gilbert, Gerald F., Jr. untitled diary, n.d., World War I Survey, WWI-158, 304th Sanitary Train, AHEC.

Gilbert, Martin. *The First World War: A Complete History*. New York: Henry Holt, 1994.

Glock, Carl E. *History of the 316th Regiment of Infantry in the World War, 1918*. Philadelphia, PA: Biddle-Deemer Printing Co., 1930, second printing.

Gowen, James B. "Report of G-5: Appendix No. 31, Divisional Training," n.d., *c.* 1919. Timberman-Fiske Family Papers, Box 11, AHEC.

Griffith, Paddy. "Infantry Armament and the Perception of Tactical Need, 1789–1918." In *War in the Age of Technology: Myriad Faces of Modern Armed Conflict*, edited by Geoffrey and Andrew Wiest Jensen. The World of War. New York and London: New York UP, 2001.

Griffith, Paddy, ed. *British Fighting Methods in the Great War*. Ilford, Essex: Frank Cass & Co. Ltd., 1996.

Griffith, Paddy. *Battle Tactics of the Western Front: The British Army's Art of Attack*. New Haven: Yale UP, 1994.

Grotelueschen, Mark E. *Doctrine under Trial: American Artillery Employment in World War I*. Contributions in Military Studies. Westport, CT, and London: Greenwood, 2001.

Gudmundsson, Bruce I. *On Artillery*. Westport, CT, and London: Praeger, 1993.

Gudmundsson, Bruce I. *Stormtroop Tactics: Innovation in the German Army, 1914–1918*. New York, Westport, CT, London: Praeger, 1989.

Guillot, [no first name]. "Report Required by Note of October 2d 1918," October 30, 1918. 17 N 128, SHD.

Gutiérrez, Edward A. *Doughboys on the Great War: How American Soldiers Viewed Their Military Service*. Lawrence, KS: UP of Kansas, 2014.

Guttenberg, Erich Baron von and Georg Meyer-Ehrlach. *Das K.B. Reserve-Feldartillerie-Regiment Nr. 5*. Erinnerungsblätter Deutscher Regimenter. Munich: Verlag Max Schick, 1938.

Hagood, Johnson. *The Services of Supply: A Memoir of the Great War*. Boston and New York: Houghton Mifflin, 1927.

Haile, LeRoy Yellott. "A Civilian Goes to War," n.d., World War I Survey, Box: 79th Division-Trains; Folder: Haile, Leroy Y., 304th Engineer, 79th Division, AHEC.

Hall, Richard C. *The Balkan Wars, 1912–1913: Prelude to the First World War*. London and New York: Routledge, 2000.

Hallas, James H., ed. *Doughboy War: The American Expeditionary Force in World War I*. Boulder, CO, and London: Lynne Rienner, 2000.

Hallas, James H. *Squandered Victory: The American First Army at St. Mihiel*. Westport, CT, and London: Praeger, 1995.

Hannum, W.T. "Report on Operations, 4th Division, September 26 to 28th, 1918," 1918. RG 165, Army War College, Historical Section Records, Box 3, 33.1, NARA.

Hanson, William L., MD. *World War I: I Was There*. Gerald, MO: The Parice Press, 1982.

Harbord, James G. *The American Army in France, 1917–1919*. Boston: Little, Brown, 1936.

Harbord, James G. *Leaves from a War Diary*. New York: Dodd, Mead & Company, 1925.

Harlowe, Jerry, ed. *Your Brother Will: The Great War Letters and Diary of William Schellberg, Machine Gun Company, 313th Infantry, "Baltimore's Own."* Ellicott City, MC: Patapsco Falls Press, 1992.

Harding, Stephen. *Great Liners at War: The Military Adventures of the World's Largest, Fastest and Most Famous Passenger Steamships*. Osceola, WI: Motorbooks International, 1997.

Harries, Meirion and Susan Harries. *The Last Days of Innocence: America at War, 1917–1918*. New York: Random House, 1997.

Hase, Armin. *Das 17. Koeniglich Sächsische Infanterie-Regiment Nr. 183*. Dresden: Verlag der Buchdruckerei der Wilhelm un Bertha v. Baensch Stiftung, 1922.

Haythornthwaite, Philip J. *World War One Source Book*. London: Arms and Armour, 1992.

Heller, Charles E. *Chemical Warfare in World War I: The American Experience, 1917–1918*. Leavenworth Papers No. 10. Fort Leavenworth, KS: Combat Studies Institute, US Army Command and General Staff College, 1984.

Helmick, E.A., E.G. Beuret, D. Lewis, and A.J. Niles, "Inspection of 79th Division, Camp Meade, Md., June 19–27, 1918," n.d.; *c*. June 1918. RG 120, 79th Division, Box 11, 56.2, NARA.

Henckell, Paul. *Das 18. Koeniglich Sächsische Infanterie-Regiment Nr. 192*. Dresden: Verlag der Buchdruckerei der Wilhelm und Bertha v. Baensch Stiftung, 1925.

Herrmann, David G. *The Arming of Europe and the Making of the First World War*. Princeton NJ: Princeton UP, 1996.

Herwig, Holger H. *The First World War: Germany and Austria-Hungary, 1914–1918*. London: Arnold, 1997.

Herwig, Holger H. and Neil M. Heyman. *Biographical Dictionary of World War I*. Westport, CT, and London: Greenwood, 1982.

Hines, John L. "Field Orders No. 54," September 24, 1918. RG 120, Entry 1241, 4th Division Historical File, Box 16, 32.1, NARA.

Hinds, Ernest. "Memorandum for the Chief of Staff," September 25, 1918. RG 200, Pershing Papers, Box 29, Miscellaneous Records and Reports, NARA.

Hinrichs, Ernest H., Jr., ed. *Listening In: Intercepting German Trench Communications in World War I*. Shippensburg, PA: White Mane Books, 1996.

Historical Board of the 315th Infantry. *The Official History of the 315th Infantry, U.S.A.* Philadelphia: Historical Board of the 315th Infantry, 1920.

History of Company F, 316th Infantry, 79th Division, A.E.F. In the World War, 1917–18–19. Philadelphia: Company F Association of the 316th Infantry, 1930.

Hogg, Ian V. *Allied Artillery of World War One*. Ramsbury, Wilts.: Crowood Press, 1998.

Holmes, Richard. *Fatal Avenue: A Traveller's History of Northern France and Flanders, 1346–1945*. London, Melbourne, Sydney, Auckland, and Johannesburg: Pimlico, 1992.

Holstein, Christina. *Verdun – the Left Bank*. Edited by Nigel Cave. Battleground Europe. Barnsley, S. Yorkshire: Pen & Sword, 2016.

Horne, Alistair. *The Price of Glory: Verdun 1916*. London: Penguin, 1962, republished 1993.

Horne, Alistair. *The French Army and Politics, 1870–1970*. New York: Peter Bedrick Books, 1984.

Horne, Charles F., ed. *Source Records of the Great War* (7 vols). National Alumni, 1923.

Hoopes, Roy. *Cain*. New York: Holt, Rinehart and Winston, 1982.

House, Jonathan M. *Combined Arms Warfare in the Twentieth Century*. Lawrence, KS: UP of Kansas, 2001.

Howard, Michael. *The Franco-Prussian War: The German Invasion of France, 1870–1871*. London and New York: Routledge, 1961, reprinted 1999.

Howard, Michael. *The Lessons of History*. New Haven and London: Yale UP, 1991.

Hudson, James J. *Hostile Skies: A Combat History of the American Air Service in World War I*. Syracuse, NY: Syracuse UP, 1968.

Hussey, John. "The Movement of German Divisions to the Western Front, Winter 1917–1918." *War in History* 4 (1997).

Huston, James A. *The Sinews of War: Army Logistics, 1775–1953*. Washington, DC: Office of the Chief of Military History, United States Army, 1966.

"Intelligence Section, 5th Corps, in Meuse–Argonne Operations," January 27, 1919. RG 120, V Corps, Box 9, NARA.

Irwin, George Leroy, "Disposition of Artillery," September 26, 1918. RG 120, 32nd Division, Box 27, Historical 57th Field Artillery Brigade, 32.16, NARA.

Irwin, George Leroy. "Report on the Operations of the 57th F.A. Brigade in Supporting the 79th Divisional Infantry, Sept. 22nd–30th 1918," n.d. RG 120, 32nd Division, Box 27: 57th Field Artillery Brigade, 33.2, NARA.

Jacks, L.V. *Service Record by an Artilleryman*. New York and London: Scribner's, 1928.

Joel, Arthur H. *Under the Lorraine Cross: An Account of the Experiences of Infantrymen Who Fought under Captain Theodore Schoge and of Their Buddies of the Lorraine Cross Division, While Serving in France During the World War*. Privately printed, 1921.

Johnson, Douglas V., II. "A Few 'Squads Left' and Off to France: Training the American Army in the United States for World War I." Ph.D. thesis, Temple University, 1992.

Johnson, Douglas V., II, and Rolfe L. Hillman, Jr. *Soissons 1918*. College Station, TX: Texas A&M UP, 1999.

Johnson, Douglas Wilson. *Battlefields of the World War: Western and Southern Fronts: A Study in Military Geography*. New York: Oxford UP, 1921.

Johnson, Douglas Wilson. *Topography and Strategy in the War*. New York: Henry Holt, 1917.

Johnson, Hubert C. *Breakthrough! Tactics, Technology, and the Search for Victory on the Western Front in World War I.* Novato, CA: Presidio Press, 1994.

Johnson, J.C. "Observations 79th Division Sept. 28–30, 18," September 30, 1918. RG 120, Entry 24, "AEF General Headquarters, 1st Army Reports, G-3," Box 3384, 120.02, NARA.

Johnson, J.H. *1918: The Unexpected Victory.* London: Arms and Armour Press, 1997.

Judy, Will. *A Soldier's Diary: A Day-to-Day Record in the World War.* Chicago: Judy Publishing Co., 1930.

Kachik, Andrew J. Untitled memoir, n.d., World War I Survey, Box: 79th Division; 157th and 158th Inf. Brigades; File: Kachik, Andrew, 314th Inf., AHEC.

Kahn, Philip Jr. *Uncommon Threads: Threads That Wove the Fabric of Baltimore Jewish Life.* Baltimore: Pecan Publications, 1996.

Kaspi, André. *Le temps des américains: le concours américain à la France en 1917– 1918.* Publications de la Sorbonne, Série Internationale. Paris: Université de Paris, 1976.

Keegan, John. *The First World War.* New York: Knopf, 1998.

Keegan, John. *Fields of Battle: The Wars for North America.* New York: Knopf, 1996.

Keegan, John. *A History of Warfare.* New York: Knopf, 1993.

Keene, Jennifer D. *Doughboys, the Great War, and the Remaking of America.* Baltimore: Johns Hopkins UP, 2001.

Kennedy, David M. *Over Here: The First World War in American Society.* Oxford, New York, Toronto, and Melbourne: Oxford UP, 1980.

Kennedy, Paul. "Military Effectiveness in the First World War." In *Military Effectiveness, Volume 1: The First World War.* Series on Defense and Foreign Policy. Boston, London, Sydney, and Wellington: Allen & Unwin, 1988.

Kiesling, Eugenia C. "'If It Ain't Broke, Don't Fix It': French Military Doctrine Between the World Wars." *War in History* 3 (1996).

Kress, John W. *One of the Last "Rugged Individualists."* (Privately printed, n.d.).

Kuhn, Joseph E. "Recollections of a Division Commander," March 14, 1926. Kuhn Papers, Box 3, USMA.

Kuhn, Joseph E. "Two Years with the German Army During the World War: Address before the Association of the Army of the United States at San Francisco, Cal.," September 30, 1923. Kuhn Papers, Box 3, USMA.

Kuhn, Joseph E. "General Kuhn's Diary," July 13, 1918–May 25, 1919. Kuhn Papers, Box 5, USMA.

Kuhn, Joseph E. "Field Order No. 8," September 27, 1918. RG 120, 79th Division, Box 3, 32.1, NARA.

Kuhn, Joseph E. "Field Orders No. 6," September 25, 1918. Hugh A. Drum Papers, Box 16, Folder: 79th Division, AHEC.

Kuhn, Joseph E. "Field Orders No. 6, Annex A: Plan of Liaison," September 25, 1918. Kuhn Papers, Box 3, USMA.

Kuhn, Joseph E. "Major Paul Allegrini, French Mission," October 15, 1918. RG 120, Entry 6, Adjutant General File, General Correspondence, Box 1017, File 20087, NARA.

Kuhn, Joseph E. "Memorandum No. 32," August 22, 1918. Kuhn Papers, Box 3, USMA.

Kuhn, Joseph E. "Combat Instructions for Troops of 79th Division," September 4, 1918. Kuhn Papers, Box 3, USMA.

Kuhn, Joseph E. "Report on Russo-Japanese War." In *Reports of Military Observers Attached to the Armies in Manchuria During the Russo-Japanese War*, Office of the Chief of Staff, War Department. Washington, DC: GPO, 1906.

Kuhn, Joseph E. "From Port Arthur to Mukden with Nogi." *Infantry Journal* 2, April (1906).

Lanza, Conrad H. "The Army Artillery, First Army," unpublished manuscript in AHEC library, *c.* 1926.

Lanza, Conrad H. "Counterbattery in the AEF." *Field Artillery Journal* 28, September–October (1936).

Lanza, Conrad H. "The Artillery Support of the Infantry in the A.E.F." *Field Artillery Journal* 26, January–February (1936).

Lanza, Conrad H. "Three Battles in One." *Field Artillery Journal* 24, March–April (1934).

Lanza, Conrad H. "The First Battle of Romagne." *Field Artillery Journal* 23, November–December (1933).

Lanza, Conrad H. "The End of the Battle of Montfaucon." *Infantry Journal* 23, July–August (1933).

Lanza, Conrad H. "The Battle of Montfaucon," *Infantry Journal* 23, May–June (1933).

Lanza, Conrad H. "The Start of the Meuse–Argonne Campaign," *Field Artillery Journal* 23, January–February (1933).

Lawrence, James F. "History of the 57th Field Artillery Brigade: The Iron Brigade," April 10, 1919. RG 120, 32nd Division, Box 26: 57th Field Artillery Brigade, NARA.

Lengel, Edward G., ed. *A Companion to the Meuse–Argonne Campaign*. Wiley Blackwell Companions to American History. Malden, MA, and Oxford: Wiley, 2014.

Liggett, Hunter. *Commanding an American Army: Recollections of the World War.* Boston and New York: Houghton Mifflin, 1925.

Linn, Brian M. "The American Way of War Revisited." *Journal of Military History* 66, April (2002).

Linn, Brian McAllister. *The Echo of Battle: The Army's Way of War.* Cambridge, MA and London: Harvard UP, 2007.

Lisle, Clifton. "U.S. Army Field Message[s]," September 28, 1918 through early November 1918. World War I Survey, Clifton Lisle Papers, AHEC.

Livesey, Anthony. *The Historical Atlas of World War I.* New York: Henry Holt and Company, Inc., 1994.

Lloyd, Nick. *Hundred Days: The Campaign That Ended World War I.* United Kingdom: Basic Books, 2014.

Lomax, Alan. *The Folk Songs of North America in the English Language.* Garden City, NY: Doubleday & Company, 1960.

Loomis, Ernest L. *History of the 304th Ammunition Train.* Boston: Gorham Press, 1920.

Lucas, Pascal Marie Henri. *The Evolution of Tactical Ideas in France and Germany During the War of 1914–1918.* Translated by P.V. Kieffer, 1925. Unpublished US Army translation in AHEC library. Paris: Berger-Levrault, 1923.

Ludendorff, Erich. *My War Memories, 1914–1918.* London: Hutchinson & Co., 1920.

Lupfer, Timothy T. *The Dynamics of Doctrine: The Changes in German Tactical Doctrine During the First World War.* Leavenworth Papers No. 4. Fort Leavenworth, KS: Combat Studies Institute, US Army Command and General Staff College, 1981.

Lutz, Ralph Haswell, ed. *The Causes of the German Collapse in 1918.* Stanford, CA: Board of Trustees of the Leland Stanford Junior University, 1934, reprinted in Hamden, CT: Archon, 1969.

Luvaas, Jay. *The Military Legacy of the Civil War: The European Inheritance.* Lawrence, KS: UP of Kansas, 1988.

MacMillan, Margaret. *Paris 1919: Six Months That Changed the World.* New York: Random House, 2003.

MacQuarrie, Hector. *How to Live at the Front.* Philadelphia and London: J.B. Lippincott, 1917.

March, Peyton C. *The Nation at War.* Westport, CT: Greenwood, 1970.

Marcus, James Rader. *United States Jewry, 1776–1985.* Detroit: Wayne State UP, 1993.

Marshall, George C. *Memoirs of My Services in the World War, 1917–1918*. Boston: Houghton Mifflin, 1976.

Marshall, G.C., Jr. "Movement of Troops from St Mihiel Operation to Argonne–Meuse Operation," November 19, 1918. RG 120, Entry 24, "AEF General Headquarters, 1st Army Reports, G-3," Box 3382, 114.01, NARA.

Massie, Robert K. *Dreadnought: Britain, Germany, and the Coming of the Great War*. New York: Random House, 1991.

Matthews, William and Dixon Wecter. *Our Soldiers Speak: 1775–1918*. Boston: Little, Brown, 1943.

Matloff, Maurice, ed. *American Military History*. Washington, DC: GPO, 1973, revised edition.

Matsen, William E., "The Battle of Sugar Point: A Re-Examination." *Minnesota History Magazine* 50, Fall (1987).

Maurer, Maurer, ed. *The U.S. Air Service in World War I* (5 vols). Washington, DC: Office of Air Force History, Headquarters USAF, 1978.

Maurice, Sir F. *The Last Four Months: The End of the War in the West*. Casswell and Co., 1919.

McIlroy, J.G. "Daily Report on Certain Divisions," November 14, 1918. RG 200, Pershing Papers, Box 29, Miscellaneous Records and Reports, NARA.

McNair, W.S. "Explanation and Execution of Plans for Artillery for St Mihiel Operation and Argonne–Meuse Operations to November 11, 1918," December 23, 1918. RG 120, Entry 22, Commander-in-Chief Reports, Box 30, NARA.

Mead, Gary. *The Doughboys: America and the First World War*. Woodstock and New York: Overlook Press, 2000.

Meehan, Sgt James E. Co. G, 313th Infantry, "My Diary," World War I Survey, WWI-380, AHEC.

Mercur, James. *The Art of War: Prepared for the Use of the Cadets of the United States Military Academy*. First edition. West Point: United States Military Academic Press, 1889.

"Messages of the 158th Brigade," 1918. RG 120, 79th Division, Box 18, 32.16, NARA.

"Messages of the 316th Infantry," 1918. RG 120, 79th Division, Box 24, 32.16, NARA.

Millett, Allan R. "Over Where? The AEF and the American Strategy for Victory, 1917–1918." In *Against All Enemies: Interpretations of American Military History from Colonial Times to the Present*, edited by Kenneth Hagan and William R. Roberts. Contributions in Military Studies. New York, Westport, CT, and London: Greenwood, 1986.

Millett, Alan R. *The General: Robert L. Bullard and Officership in the United States Army, 1881–1925*. Westport, CT: Greenwood Press, 1975.

Ministère de la Guerre, Service Historique, *Les armées françaises dans la grande guerre*. Tomes II, V, VI, VII. Paris: Imprimerie Nationale, 1920–38.

Minnesota Population Center, "National Historical Geographic Information System: Pre-Release Version 0.1," University of Minnesota, http://www.nhgis.org, accessed 7 August 2011.

Mitchell, William. *Memoirs of World War I*. New York: Random House, 1960.

Mitchell, William. "The Air Service at the Argonne–Meuse." *World's Work*, September (1919).

Mjagkij, Nina. *Loyalty in Time of Trial: The African American Experience During World War I*. Lanham, MD: Rowman & Littlefield, 2011.

Morrow, John, Jr. "The War in the Air." In *World War I: A History*, edited by Hew Strachan. Oxford, New York: Oxford UP, 1998.

Morrow, John H., Jr. *The Great War in the Air: Military Aviation from 1909 to 1921*. Washington, DC: Smithsonian Institution Press, 1993.

Muller, E. Lester. *The 313th of the 79th in the World War*. Baltimore: Meyer and Thalheimer, 1919.

Myers, Roy V. "Notes on the World's War," n.d., World War I Survey, The Roy V. Myers Papers, AHEC.

Nenninger, Timothy K. "American Military Effectiveness in the First World War." In *Military Effectiveness, Volume 1: The First World War*, edited by Allan R. Millett and Williamson Murray. Series on Defense and Foreign Policy. Boston, London, Sydney, and Wellington: Allen & Unwin, 1988.

Nenninger, Timothy K. "Tactical Dysfunction in the AEF, 1917–1918." *Military Affairs* 51, October (1987).

Nenninger, Timothy K. "The Army Enters the Twentieth Century, 1904–1917." In *Against All Enemies: Interpretations of American Military History from Colonial Times to the Present*, edited by Kenneth J. Hagan and William R. Roberts. Contributions in Military Studies. New York, Westport, CT, and London: Greenwood, 1986.

Nenninger, Timothy K. *The Leavenworth Schools and the Old Army: Education, Professionalism, and the Officer Corps of the United States Army, 1881–1918*. Contributions in Military History. Westport, CT, and London, England: Greenwood Press, 1978.

Nenninger, Timothy K. ""Unsystematic as a Mode of Command": Commanders and the Process of Command in the American Expeditionary Forces, 1917–1918." *Journal of Military History* 64, July (2000).

Nicholson, W.J. Untitled memorandum, September 23, 1918. RG 120, Entry 1241, 79th Division, Box 6, NARA.

Oury, W.H. "Operations Report," November 16, 1918. RG 120, 79th Division, Box 18, 314th Infantry Regiment, 33.2, NARA.

Oury, W.H. "Report of Operations for the 314th Infantry and 158th Infantry Brigade for the Period September 25–26, 1918 to September 30, 1918," 1918. RG 120, 79th Division, Box 18, 33.2, NARA.

Page, Arthur W. "The Truth About Our 110 Days' Fighting, III: The Campaign in the Argonne-Meuse." *World's Work* 38, June (1919).

Palmer, Alan. *Victory 1918.* London: Weidenfeld & Nicholson, 1998.

Palmer, Robert R., Bell I. Wiley, and William R. Keast. *The Army Ground Forces: The Procurement and Training of Ground Combat Forces.* United States Army in World War II. Washington, DC: Center of Military History, 1991.

Paret, Peter, ed. *Makers of Modern Strategy from Machiavelli to the Nuclear Age.* Princeton, NJ: Princeton UP, 1986.

Payne, Brooke. "Observations Upon the Conditions Affecting the Artillery Support During the First Day of Attack—79th Division," May 25, 1919. RG 120, V Corps, Box 4, NARA.

Paschall, Rod, *The Defeat of Imperial Germany, 1917–1918.* Chapel Hill: Algonquin Books, 1989.

Patterson, Robert B. *Arming the Nation for War: Mobilization, Supply, and the American War Effort in World War II.* Edited by G. Kurt Piehler. Legacies of War. Knoxville: University of Tennessee, 2014.

Peixotto, Ernest. *The American Front.* New York: Charles Scribner's Sons, 1919.

Pershing, John J. *My Experiences in the World War* (2 vols). New York: Frederick A. Stokes Co., 1931.

Pershing, John J. *Final Report of John J. Pershing, Commander in Chief, AEF.* Washington, DC: GPO, 1920.

Pershing, John J. "Wrapper Endorsement, Report of Superior Board on Organization and Tactics," June 16, 1920. Army War College Curricular Files, file 52-15, AHEC.

Persico, Joseph E. *11th Month, 11th Day, 11th Hour: Armistice Day, 1918: World War I and Its Violent Climax.* New York: Random House, 2004.

Philadelphia War History Committee. *Philadelphia in the World War, 1914–1919.* New York: Wynkoop Hallenbeck Crawford, 1922.

Philpott, William. *Three Armies on the Somme: The First Battle of the Twentieth Century.* Knopf paperback edition of Little, Brown hardcover edition. New York: Knopf, 2009.

Pitt, Barrie. *1918: The Last Act*. New York: W.W. Norton, 1962.

Pleasonton, E.S. "Memorandum to Col. Brewer," April 7, 1919. Kuhn Papers, Box 3, USMA.

Plickert, Heinrich. *Das 2. Ermländischen Infanterie-Regiment Nr. 151 im Weltkriege*. Truppenteile des ehemaligen Preussischen Kontingents. Berlin: Gerhard Stalling, 1929.

Pollard, James E. *The Forty-Seventh Infantry, a History: 1917–1918–1919*. Saginaw, MI: Press of Seeman & Peters, 1919.

Porch, Douglas. "The French Army in the First World War." In *Military Effectiveness, Volume 1: The First World War*, edited by Alan Millett. Series on Defense and Foreign Policy. Boston, London, Sydney, and Wellington: Allen & Unwin, 1988.

Pratt, Fletcher. "Then Came Summerall." *American Legion Magazine* 26, March (1939).

Prittwitz und Gaffron, [no first name] von, [no first name] Peschek, H. Mende, H. von Schweinichen, and G. Gieraths. *Geschichte des Königlich Preußischen Grenadier-Regiments König Friedrich III. (2. Schles) Nr. 11 und seiner Grenzschutzformationen von 1914 bis 1920*. Berlin: Verlag Tradition Wilhelm Kolk, 1932.

Pullen, D.D. "Report of Operation of French Tanks," September 28, 1918. RG 120, First Army Reports, Inspector General, Box 3411; unnumbered enclosure in G.E. Thorne, Report of Inspector General, 1st Army, A.E.F.; File Number 1616, NARA.

Du Quenoy, Paul and Phil Giltner. "American Impact: Was American Participation in the Great War Decisive?" In *History in Dispute*, edited by Dennis Showalter. Detroit, New York, et al.: St. James Press, 2002.

Rainey, James W. "The Questionable Training of the AEF in World War I," *Parameters* 22, Winter (1992–93).

Rainey, James W. "Ambivalent Warfare: The Tactical Doctrine of the AEF in World War I," *Parameters* 13, September (1983).

Rainey, James W. "The Training of the American Expeditionary Forces in World War I." Master's thesis, Temple University, 1981.

Raymond, Senius J. "Operations of the 5th Corps in the 2nd Phase of the Meuse-Argonne." In *Monographs of the World War*, Infantry School, US Army. Ft. Benning, GA, 1923.

Records of US Army Mobile Units. RG 391, 313th Infantry, Box 3163, NARA.

Reardon, Carol. *Soldiers and Scholars: The U.S. Army and the Uses of Military History,*

1865–1920. Lawrence, KS: UP of Kansas, 1990.

"Resumé d'observations faites pendant le opérations de la 79ème D.I.U.S. du 26 au 30 Septembre," October 3, 1918. 17 N 128, SHD.

Ribadeau Dumas, François. *Histoire Secrète De La Lorraine*. Albin Michel, 1980.

Rich, Col. Albert T. "Military Courtesy," March 11, 1919. Kuhn Papers, Box 3, USMA.

Richard, [no first name]. "Report of the Battalion Commander Richard, Commanding the 15 Light Tank Battalion to the Commanding Officer of the 505th Regiment of Artillery of Assault," October 2, 1918. 17 N 128, SHD.

Ross, Betsy. *I Fly the Flag*. Champaign, IL: Graphix Group, Inc., 1984.

Ross, Tenney. "Divisional Terrain Exercise #6: Liaison between Infantry and Air Service," October 17, 1918. RG 120, 79th Division, Box 12, 56.3, NARA.

Ruckman, John H., ed. *Technology's War Record*. Cambridge, MA: Alumni Association of the Massachusetts Institute of Technology, 1920.

Russell, G.M. "Summaries of Intelligence, 5th Army Corps, St Mihiel–Meuse Argonne," August–November 1919. C.E. Fogg Papers, World War I, USMA.

Ryan, Garry. "Disposition of AEF Records of World War I." *Military Affairs* 30, Winter (1966–67).

Samuels, Martin. *Command or Control? Command, Training and Tactics in the British and German Armies, 1888–1918*. London: Frank Cass, 1995.

Samuels, Martin. *Doctrine and Dogma: German and British Infantry Tactics in the First World War*. Westport, CT: Greenwood Press, 1992.

Schaffer, Ronald. *America in the Great War: The Rise of the War Welfare State*. New York and Oxford: Oxford UP, 1991.

Schaidler, Otto. *Das K.B. Reserve-Infanterie-Regiment Nr. 7*. Erinnerungsblätter Deutscher Regimenter. Munich: Verlag Max Schick, 1934.

Sheffield, G.D. "The Morale of the British Army on the Western Front, 1914–18: A Case Study in the Importance of the 'Human Factor' in Twentieth-Century Total War." In *War in the Age of Technology: Myriad Faces of Modern Armed Conflict*, edited by Geoffrey and Andrew Wiest Jensen. The World of War. New York and London: New York UP, 2001.

Showalter, Dennis E. *German Military History, 1648–1982: A Critical Biography*. Edited by Robert and Jacob Kipp Higham. Military History Bibliographies. New York and London: Garland, 1984.

Shrader, Charles Reginald, ed. *Reference Guide to United States Military History, 1865–1919*. New York: Facts on File, Inc., 1993.

Siebert, Heinrich, *Geschichte Des Infanterie-Regiments Generalfeldmarschall Von*

Hindenburg (2. Masurisches) Nr. 147. Erinnerungsblätter Deutscher Regimenter. Berlin: Gerhard Stalling, 1927.

Smith, Jean Edward. *Eisenhower in War and Peace.* New York: Random House, 2012.

Smythe, Donald. *Pershing: General of the Armies.* Bloomington: Indiana UP, 1986.

Smythe, Donald. "The Ruse at Belfort." *Army* 22, June (1972).

Snow, Major General William J. "Extracts from the Report of the Chief of Field Artillery for the Fiscal Year 1919," *Field Artillery Journal* 9, (1919).

Snyder, Jack. *The Ideology of the Offensive: Military Decision Making and the Disasters of 1914.* Edited by Robert J. Art, Robert Jervis, and Stephen M. Walt. Cornell Studies in Security Affairs. Ithaca and London: Cornell UP, 1984.

Snyder, J.W. "Memorandum: 5th Corps Artillery," September 29, 1918, RG 120, 32nd Division, Box 27: Historical – 57th Field Artillery Brigade, 32.16, NARA.

Sorin, Gerald. *A Time for Building: The Third Migration.* (Baltimore and London: Johns Hopkins UP, 1992).

Spears, Edward L. *Prelude to Victory.* London: Jonathan Cape, 1930.

Stacy, Louis M. "Books Furnished by the War Department to Troops before Leaving U.S.," September 28, 1918. RG 120, Entry 332, General Headquarters G-5, "Correspondence Relating to Publications," Box 1805, 23m, NARA.

Staff of the Commander-in-Chief of the Allied Armies. "German Mode of Attack." RG 120, Entry 335, "General Headquarters, General Staff, G-5, "English Translations of French Technical Studies, 1917–19," Box 1837, 1986–1999, NARA.

Stallings, Laurence. *The Doughboys: The Story of the AEF, 1917–1918.* New York: Harper & Row, Publishers, 1963.

Steiner, Zara. "The Peace Settlement." In *World War I: A History*, edited by Hew Strachan. Oxford, New York: Oxford UP, 1998.

Sterba, Christopher M. "The Melting Pot Goes to War: Italian and Jewish Immigrants in America's Great Crusade, 1917–1919." Ph.D. thesis, Brandeis University, 1999.

Stevenson, David. *Cataclysm: The First World War as Political Tragedy.* New York: Basic Books, 2004.

Suhrmann, Wilhelm. *Geschichte Des Landwehr-Infanterie-Regiments Nr. 31 im Weltkriege.* Flensburg, Oldenburg, and Berlin: Gerhard Stalling, 1928.

Summers, Owen. "The Fourth Division (U.S.) in the First Phase of the Meuse–Argonne." In *Monographs of the World War*, Infantry School, US Army.

Ft. Benning, GA, 1923.

Sumner, Ian, and Embleton, Gerry. *The French Army, 1914–18*. Edited by Lee Johnson. Men-at-Arms Series. London, Auckland, Melbourne, Singapore, and Toronto: Osprey, 1995.

Swartz, Casper Wilt, Co. C, 314th Infantry Regiment. "Some Things That Happened between May 1916 and June 1, 1919," n.d. World War I Survey, AHEC.

Sweezey, C.B. "Report of Operations of Regiment, Sept. 26 to Oct. 1, 1918," October 3, 1918. RG 120, 79th Division, Box 16, 33.2, NARA.

Sweezey, C.B. "Report of Operations of 313th Infantry from September 25, 1918 to November 11, 1918, Inclusive," November 18, 1918. RG 120, 79th Division, Box 16, 33.2, NARA.

Swift, Eben. *Course in Tactics: Orders*. Fort Leavenworth, Kansas: Staff College Press, 1905.

Taeglichsbeck, Hans. *Das Füsilier Regiment Prinz Heinrich Von Preussen (Brandenburgisches) Nr. 35*. Berlin: Gerhard Stalling, 1921.

"Telephone Messages Sept.–Oct. 1918 Received and Sent," September–October 1918. RG 120, V Corps, Box 30, G-2 Telephone Messages, 32.16, NARA.

Terraine, John. *White Heat: The New Warfare, 1914–1918*. London: Leo Cooper, 1982, reprinted 1992.

Terraine, John. *To Win a War: 1918, the Year of Victory*. Garden City, NY: Doubleday, 1981.

Thaer, Albrecht, von. "Diary Notes of Oberst Von Thaer, 1 October 1918." www.lib.byu.edu/~rdh/wwi/1918/thaereng.html , accessed December 2, 1998.

Thisted, Moses N. *Pershing's Pioneer Infantry of World War I*. Hemet, CA: Alphabet Printers, 1981–82.

Thomas, Nigel. *The German Army in World War I (3), 1917 1918*. Martin Windrow (ed.) Men-at-Arms Series. Oxford: Osprey, 2004.

Thomas, Shipley. *History of the A.E.F.* New York: George H. Doran, 1920.

Thorn, Henry C., Jr. *History of the 313th Infantry, "Baltimore's Own."* New York: Wynkoop Hallenbeck Crawford Company, 1920.

Thorne, George E. "Report of Inspector General, 1st Army, A.E.F.; File Number 1616," December 11, 1918. RG 120, First Army Reports, Inspector General, Box 3411, NARA.

Tiede, [no first name], [no first name] Himer, and [no first name] Röhricht. *Das 4. Schlesische Infanterie-Regiment Nr. 157*. Erinnerungsblätter Deutscher Regimenter. Berlin: Gerhard Stalling, 1922.

Toland, John. *No Man's Land: 1918, the Last Year of the Great War.* Garden City, NY: Doubleday, 1980.

Tompkins, Raymond S. *Maryland Fighters in the Great War.* Baltimore: Thomas & Evans Printing Co., 1919.

Tolzmann, Don Heinrich. *The German-American Experience.* Amherst, NY: Humanity Books, 2000.

"Translations: German 117th Inf. Div., Sept. 26–Nov. 11, 1918, Folder I, Meuse–Argonne," September 27, 1918. RG 165, 117th Division Translations, Box 164, German Military Records Relating to the World War, 1917–19, 117th Infantry, 33.5, NARA.

Trask, David. "The Entry of the USA into the War and Its Effects." In *World War I: A History*, edited by Hew Strachan. Oxford, New York: Oxford UP, 1998.

Trask, David F. *The AEF and Coalition Warmaking, 1917–1918.* Lawrence, KS: University Press of Kansas, 1993.

Travers, Tim. *How the War Was Won: Factors That Led to Victory in World War One.* Barnsley, UK: Routledge, 1992, reprinted Pen & Sword, 2005.

Travers, Tim. "The Allied Victories, 1918." In *World War I: A History*, edited by Hew Strachan. Oxford, New York: Oxford UP, 1998.

Travers, Tim. "Reply to John Hussey: The Movement of German Divisions to the Western Front, 1917–1918." *War in History* 5, Fall (1998).

Travers, Tim. "Could the Tanks of 1918 Have Been War-Winners for the British Expeditionary Force?" *Journal of Contemporary History* 27 (1992).

Travers, Tim. "The Evolution of British Strategy and Tactics on the Western Front in 1918: GHQ, Manpower, and Technology." *Journal of Military History* 54, April (1990).

Tuchman, Barbara W. *Practicing History: Selected Essays.* New York: Ballantine, 1981.

US Department of State, "Venezuela Boundary Dispute, 1895–1899." https://history.state.gov/milestones/1866-1898/venezuela , accessed May 30, 2016.

"U.S. Merchant Ships, Sailing Vessels, and Fishing Craft Lost from All Causes During World War I." American Merchant Marine at War, www.usmm.org/ww1merchant.htm, accessed August 15, 2011.

US Senate Committee on Military Affairs. *Hearings on the Nomination of Col. Alfred W. Bjornstad, U.S. Army, for Promotion to Be a Brigadier General.* Washington, DC: GPO, 1925.

US Senate Subcommittee on Military Affairs. *Establishment of Military Justice–Proposed Amendment of the Articles of War.* GPO: Washington, DC, September

25, 1919.

US War Office, *Histories of Two Hundred and Fifty-One Divisions of the German Army Which Participated in the War (1914–1918)*. London: London Stamp Exchange, Ltd., 1920, republished 1989.

Vandiver, Frank E. *Black Jack: The Life and Times of John J. Pershing* (2 vols). College Station and London: Texas A&M UP, 1977.

Venzon, Anne Cipriano, ed. *The United States in the First World War: An Encyclopedia*. Military History of the United States. New York: Garland Publishing, Inc., 1995.

Vereinigung der Offiziere, ed. *Geschichte Des 1. Ermländischen Infanterie-Regiments Nr. 150*. Ehemals Preussische Truppenteile. Zeulenroda (Thüringen): Bernhard Sporn, 1935.

Wagner, Arthur L. *Organization and Tactics*. New York, London, Leipzig, Paris: B. Westermann, 1895.

Walker, William. *Betrayal at Little Gibraltar; a German Fortress, a Treacherous American General, and the Battle to End World War I*. New York: Scribner, 2016.

War Department. *Battle Participation of Organizations of the American Expeditionary Forces in France, Belgium and Italy, 1917–1918*. Washington, DC: GPO, 1920.

War Department. *Field Service Regulations, United States Army, 1914; Corrected to April 15, 1917*, Document No. 475. Washington, DC: GPO, 1917.

War Department, *Field Service Regulations, United States Army, 1914; Corrected to July 31, 1918*. Document No. 475. Washington, DC: GPO, 1918.

War Department. *Historical Report of the Chief Engineer, American Expeditionary Forces, 1917–1919*. Washington, DC: GPO, 1919.

War Department. *Infantry Drill Regulations, United States Army, 1911, with Text Corrections to February 12, 1917*. New York: Military Publishing Co., 1917.

War Department. *Infantry Drill Regulations, United States Army, 1911, with Text Corrections to July 31, 1918*. Document No. 394. Washington, DC: GPO, 1918.

War Department. *Instructions on the Offensive Conduct of Small Units*. Document No. 583. Washington, DC: GPO, 1917.

War Department, *Provisional Drill and Service Regulation for Field Artillery (Horse and Light), 1916, Corrected to April 15, 1917* (3 vols). Document No. 538. Washington, DC: GPO, 1917.

War Department, "Reports of Military Observers Attached to the Armies in Manchuria During the Russo-Japanese War, Part I: Reports of Lieutenant-Colonel W.S. Schuyler, General Staff, Captain J.F. Morrison, 20th Infantry,

Captain Carl Reichmann, 17th Infantry, Captain Peyton C. March, General Staff." Washington, DC: GPO, 1906.

War Department, "Reports of Military Observers Attached to the Armies in Manchuria During the Russo-Japanese War, Part III: Report of Major Joseph E. Kuhn, Corps of Engineers." Washington, DC: GPO, 1906.

War Department. *Tables of Organization, United States Army*. Washington, DC: GPO, 1917.

War Department, Adjutant General's Office. *Official Army Register*. Washington, DC: GPO, 1947.

War Office [Great Britain]. *Statistics of the Military Effort of the British Empire During the Great War, 1914–1920*. London: His Majesty's Stationery Office, 1922.

Ward, R.T. "Explanation and Execution of Plans of Operation, 1st American Army for Argonne–Meuse Operation to November 11, 1918," December 18, 1918. RG 120, Entry 22, Commander-in-Chief Reports, Box 30, NARA.

Watt, Richard M. *Dare Call It Treason*. New York: Simon and Schuster, 1963.

Weber, Eugen. *Peasants into Frenchmen: The Modernization of Rural France, 1870–1914*. Stanford: Stanford UP, 1976.

DeWeerd, Harvey A. *President Wilson Fights His War*. New York, London: Macmillan, 1968.

DeWeerd, H.A. "American Adoption of French Artillery 1917–1918." *Journal of the American Military Institute* 3 (1939).

Russell F. Weigley, "Strategy and Total War in the United States: Pershing and the American Military Tradition." In *Great War, Total War: Combat and Mobilization on the Western Front, 1914–1918*, edited by Roger Chickering and Stig Förster. Washington DC and Cambridge, UK: Cambridge UP, 2000.

Weigley, Russell F. *The American Way of War: A History of United States Military Strategy and Policy*. Bloomington, IN: Indiana UP, 1973.

Weigley, Russell F. *History of the United States Army*. The Wars of the United States. New York, London: Macmillan, 1967.

Weigley, Russell F. *Towards an American Army: Military Thought from Washington to Marshall*. New York and London: Columbia UP, 1962.

Werner, Bert. *Uniforms, Equipment, and Weapons of the American Expeditionary Forces in World War I*. Atglen, PA: Schiffer Publishing Ltd., 2006.

Wheeler, J[unius] B[rutus]. *A Course of Instruction in the Elements of the Art and Science of War for the Use of the Cadets of the United States Military Academy*. New York: D. Van Nostrand, 1879.

Wheelock, Frank R. "Memorandum re Exposure of Men," December 19, 1918. RG 120, 79th Division, Box 17, NARA.

White, Lonnie J. *The 90th Division in World War I: The Texas–Oklahoma Draft Division in the Great War*. Manhattan, KS: Sunflower UP, 1996.

Whitehorne, Joseph W.A. *The Inspectors General of the United States Army, 1903–1939*. Washington, DC: Center of Military History, Department of the Army, 1998.

Who Was Who in American History – the Military. Chicago: Marquis Who's Who, 1975.

Wiest, Andrew. "Preferring to Learn from Experience: The American Expeditionary Force in 1917." In *1917 – Tactics, Training and Technology; the Chief of [Australian] Army's Military History Conference 2007*, edited by Peter Dennis and Jeffrey Grey. Australian Military History Publications, 2007.

Wildrick, G.A. "Response to Wheelock, Memorandum re Exposure of Men," December 24, 1918. RG 120, 79th Division, Box 16, NARA.

Wildrick, G.A. "G-3 Memorandum No. 7: Information from Infantry to Artillery," October 20, 1918. RG 120, 79th Division, Box 4, 32.15, NARA.

Wilgus, William J. *Transporting the A.E.F. In Western Europe, 1917–1919*. New York: Columbia UP, 1931.

Willcox, Cornelis De Witt. *A French-English Dictionary with a Supplement Containing Recent Military and Technical Terms*. New York, London: Harper & Brothers, 1917.

William, Crown Prince. *My War Experiences*. London: Hurst and Blackett, 1922.

Wilson, Woodrow. "Correspondence between the United States and Germany Regarding an Armistice." *American Journal of International Law* 13, Supplement: Official Documents (April 1919).

Winterich, John T., ed. *Squads Write! A Selection of the Best Things in Prose, Verse and Cartoon from the Stars and Stripes*. New York and London: Harper & Brothers, 1931.

Wunderlich, Curt. *Fünfzig Monate Wehr im Westen: Geschichte des Reserve-Infanterie-Regiments Nr. 66*. Eisleben (Lutherstadt): Winkler, 1935.

Yockelson, Mitchell. *Borrowed Soldiers: Americans under British Command, 1918*. Norman, OK: University of Oklahoma Press, 2008.

Zabecki, David T. *Steel Wind: Colonel Georg Bruchmuller and the Birth of Modern Artillery*. Edited by Bruce I. Gudmundsson. The Military Profession. Westport, CT, and London: Praeger, 1994.

Zaloga, Steven and Tony Bryan. *French Tanks of World War I*. Oxford: Osprey, 2010.

"Zion Church and World War I," http://www.zionbaltimore.org/vthistory_1900s_sons_of_zion_ww1.htm, accessed August 30, 2011.

Newspaper Archives

Philadelphia Press
Baltimore Sun
Afro-American Ledger
Army and Navy Journal
Washington Post

Letters

Kuhn to Kuhn letters
Joseph E. Kuhn to Helen Kuhn, March 21, 1919, Kuhn Papers, Box 5, USMA.
Other letters
Joseph E. Kuhn to Col. Frederick Palmer, July 10, 1930, Kuhn Papers, Box 5, USMA.
Mrs. J. Talbott Kelley to C.W. Sweezey, August 1918, Records of U.S. Army Mobile Units RG 391, 313th Infantry, Box 3163, NARA.
C.B. Sweezey to Mrs. J. Talbott Kelley, September 5, 1918, ibid.
Mrs. Lillian Meyers to C.W. Sweezey, August (?), 1918, ibid.
C.B. Sweezey to Mr. John W. Campbell, November 30, 1918, ibid.
C.B. Sweezey to Master John Hamilton, November 30, 1918, ibid.
From NARA (same box)
Christian A. Bach to C.L. Bolte, June 25, 1922. RG 120, Historical Section Reports, Box 3, NARA, p. 1.
Christian A. Bach to C.L. Bolte, November 18, 1922. RG 120, Historical Section Reports, Box 3, NARA.
J.E. Kuhn, September 26, 1918. RG 120, ibid.
Christian A. Bach to C.L. Bolte, November 18, 1922. RG 120, ibid., p. 4.
Bach to Bolte, November 18, 1922; Bach to J. Hines, November 19, 1922. RG 120, Historical Section Reports, Box 3, NARA; Bach to Edwin E. Booth, n.d. RG 120, Historical Section Reports, Box 3, NARA.
From Hugh A. Drum Papers
John L. Hines to E.E. Booth, December 30, 1920. Hugh A. Drum Papers, Box 16, File: 4th Division-Montfaucon, AHEC, p. 1.
A.W. Bjornstad to Christian A. Bach, December 24, 1924. Ibid., p. 5.

Christian A. Bach to Edwin E. Booth, n.d. Ibid.

J.J. Pershing to E.E. Booth, June 17, 1940. Hugh A. Drum Papers, Box 20, File "Booth, Gen. E.E.", AHEC, p. 1.

Roy W. Winton to Frank C. Mahin, February 9, 1931. Hugh A. Drum Papers, Box 9, "Personal Correspondence," File "F.C. Mahin", AHEC, pp. 1–3.

J.A. Stevens to H.A. Drum, December 23, 1920. Hugh A. Drum Papers, Box 16, File: 4th Division-Montfaucon, AHEC, p. 1.

Oliver L. Spaulding, Jr., to E.E. Booth, February 18, 1921. Hugh A. Drum Papers, Box 16, File: 4th Division-Montfaucon, AHEC, p. 2.

E.E. Booth to Oliver L. Spaulding, Jr., February 1, 1921. Hugh A. Drum Papers, Box 16, File: 4th Division-Montfaucon, AHEC, p. 1; E.E. Booth to H.A. Drum, 25 March 1921, Hugh A. Drum Papers, Box 16, File: 4th Division-Montfaucon, AHEC, p. 2.

Oscar Lubchansky letters

Oscar Lubchansky to author, *c.* 1954, personal communication.

Oscar Lubchansky to his family, December 5, 1918, author's personal collection, p. 1.

Oscar Lubchansky to Sadie Lubchansky, February 7, 1919, author's personal collection, p. 1.

Oscar Lubchansky to his parents, December 21, 1918, author's personal collection, p. 2.

Oscar Lubchansky to Lillian S. Lubchansky, September 14, 1918, author's personal collection, p. 2.

Oscar Lubchansky to his family, January 6, 1919, author's personal collection.

Oscar Lubchansky to Dr J.W. Lubchansky, November 24, 1918, author's personal collection.

Oscar Lubchansky to Dr J.W. Lubchansky, November 24, 1918, author's personal collection.

INDEX

References to footnotes are indicated by fn; references to maps and tables are in **bold**.

K

L

זה הספר תם ונשלם
שבח לאל אלהי עולם
והודות ———— להודי
למודי ולאשר ———— י
אני אליקים געצל
בן דוד צבי